Forbes

TRAVEL GUIDE

Formerly Mobil Travel Guide

SOUTHWEST

ACKNOWLEDGMENTS

We gratefully acknowledge the help of our representatives for their efficient and perceptive inspections of the lodgings listed. Forbes Travel Guide is also grateful to the talented writers who contributed to this book.

Some of the information contained herein is derived from a variety of third-party sources. Although every effort has been made to verify the information obtained from such sources, the publisher assumes no responsibility for inconsistencies or inaccuracies in the data or liability for any damages of any type arising from errors or omissions.

Neither the editors nor the publisher assume responsibility for the services provided by any business listed in this guide or for any loss, damage or disruption in your travel for any reason.

ISBN: 9-780841-61428-4   Manufactured in the USA

10 9 8 7 6 5 4 3 2 1

TABLE OF CONTENTS

SOUTHWEST ★★★★★★

STAR ATTRACTIONS

If you've been a reader of Mobil Travel Guide, you will have heard that this historic brand partnered with another storied media name, Forbes, in 2009 to create a new entity, Forbes Travel Guide. For more than 50 years, Mobil Travel Guide assisted travelers in making smart decisions about where to stay and dine when traveling. With this new partnership, our mission has not changed: We're committed to the same rigorous inspections of hotels, restaurants and spas—the most comprehensive in the industry with more than 500 standards tested at each property we visit—to help you cut through the clutter and make easy and informed decisions on where to spend your time and travel budget. Our team of anonymous inspectors are constantly on the road, sleeping in hotels, eating in restaurants and making spa appointments, evaluating those exacting standards to determine a property's rating.

What kind of standards are we looking for when we visit a proprety? We're looking for more than just high-thread count sheets, pristine spa treatment rooms and white linen-topped tables. We look for service that's attentive, individualized and unforgettable. We note how long it takes to be greeted when you sit down at your table, or to be served when you order room service, or whether the hotel staff can confidently help you when you've forgotten that one essential item that will make or break your trip. Unlike other travel ratings entities, we visit the places we rate, testing hundreds of attributes to compile our ratings, and our ratings cannot be bought or influenced. The Forbes Five Star rating is the most prestigious achievement in hospitality—while we rate more than 8,000 properties in the U.S., Canada, Hong Kong, Macau and Beijing, for 2010, we have awarded Five Star designations to only 53 hotels, 21 restaurants and 18 spas. When you travel with Forbes, you can travel with confidence, knowing that you'll get the very best experience, no matter who you are.

We understand the importance of making the most of your time. That's why the most trusted name in travel is now Forbes Travel Guide.

STAR RATED HOTELS

Whether you're looking for the ultimate in luxury or the best value for your travel budget, we have a hotel recommendation for you. To help you pinpoint properties that meet your needs, Forbes Travel Guide classifies each lodging by type according to the following characteristics:

★★★★★These exceptional properties provide a memorable experience through virtually flawless service and the finest of amenities. Staff are intuitive, engaging and passionate, and eagerly deliver service above and beyond the guests' expectations. The hotel was designed with the guest's comfort in mind, with particular attention paid to craftsmanship and quality of product. A Five Star property is a destination unto itself.

★★★★These properties provide a distinctive setting, and a guest will find many interesting and inviting elements to enjoy throughout the property. Attention to detail is prominent throughout the property, from design concept to quality of products provided. Staff are accommodating and take pride in catering to the guest's specific needs throughout their stay.

★★★These well-appointed establishments have enhanced amenities that provide travelers with a strong sense of location, whether for style or function. They may have a distinguishing style and ambience in both the public spaces and guest rooms; or they may be more focused on functionality, providing guests with easy access to local events, meetings or tourism highlights.

★★The Two Star hotel is considered a clean, comfortable and reliable establishment that has expanded amenities, such as a full-service restaurant.

★The One Star lodging is a limited-service hotel or inn that is considered a clean, comfortable and reliable establishment.

For every property, we also provide pricing information. All prices quoted are accurate at the time of publication; however, prices cannot be guaranteed.

$=Up to $150
$$=$151-$250
$$$=251-$350
$$$$=$351 and up

STAR RATED RESTAURANTS

Every restaurant in this book comes highly recommended as an outstanding dining experience.

★★★★★Forbes Five Star restaurants deliver a truly unique and distinctive dining experience. A Five Star restaurant consistently provides exceptional food, superlative service and elegant décor. An emphasis is placed on originality and personalized, attentive and discreet service. Every detail that surrounds the experience is attended to by a warm and gracious dining room team.

★★★★These are exciting restaurants with often well-known chefs that feature creative and complex foods and emphasize various culinary techniques and a focus on seasonality. A highly-trained dining room staff provides refined personal service and attention.

★★★Three Star restaurants offer skillfully-prepared food with a focus on a specific style or cuisine. The dining room staff provides warm and professional service in a comfortable atmosphere. The décor is well-coordinated with quality fixtures and decorative items, and promotes a comfortable ambience.

★★The Two Star restaurant serves fresh food in a clean setting with efficient service. Value is considered in this category, as is family friendliness.

★The One Star restaurant provides a distinctive experience through culinary specialty, local flair or individual atmosphere.

Because menu prices can fluctuate, we list a pricing range rather than specific prices. The pricing ranges are per diner, and assume that you order an appetizer or dessert, an entrée and one drink.

STAR RATED SPAS

Forbes Travel Guide's spa ratings are based on objective evaluations of more than 450 attributes. About half of these criteria assess basic expectations, such as staff courtesy, the technical proficiency and skill of the employees and whether the facility is clean and maintained properly. Several standards address issues that impact a guest's physical comfort and convenience, as well as the staff's ability to impart a sense of personalized service. Additional criteria measure the spa's ability to create a completely calming ambience.

★★★★★Stepping foot in a Five Star spa will result in an exceptional experience with no detail overlooked. These properties wow their guests with extraordinary design and facilities, and uncompromising service. Expert staff cater to your every whim and pamper you with the most advanced treatments and skin care lines available. These spas often offer exclusive treatments and may emphasize local elements.

★★★★Four Star spas provide a wonderful experience in an inviting and serene environment. A sense of personalized service is evident from the moment you check in and receive your robe and slippers. The guest's comfort is always of utmost concern to the well-trained staff.

★★★These spas offer well-appointed facilities with a full complement of staff to ensure that guests' needs are met. The spa facilities include clean and appealing treatment rooms, changing areas and a welcoming reception desk.

ARIZONA

HIKE THE GRAND CANYON. RELAX AT A SPA. HIT THE LINKS. THIS RAPIDLY GROWING STATE—
its population has more than tripled since 1940—offers all of this and more.

Arizona is known for its hot summers, mild winters and desert landscape.
But the northern mountains, cool forests, spectacular canyons and lakes offer
a variety of vacation activities, including fishing, white-water rafting, hiking
and camping. The northern, central part of the state is on a plateau at higher
altitudes than the desert in the southern region of the state and has a cooler
climate.

There are also meadows filled with wildflowers, ghost and mining towns,
dude ranches and intriguing ancient American Indian villages. The state has
23 reservations and one of the largest Native American populations in the
United States. More than half of that population is Navajo. Visitors can scoop
up craft specialties including basketry, pottery, weaving, jewelry and kachina
dolls.

Arizona has scores of water parks, interesting museums, zoos and wildlife
exhibits. And who says it doesn't snow in Arizona? There are several places
for downhill skiing, including the Arizona Snowball in northern Arizona, Mt.
Lemmon Ski Valley near Tucson and Sunrise Ski Resort in the east.

Of course, there is also plenty of what people have come to expect here.
There are more than 300 golf courses across the state, making it home to
several stops on the PGA Tour, most notably the Phoenix Open. You'll also
find some of the best spas in the country. All of these add up to make Arizona
one of the nation's favorite spots for recreation and relaxation.

.AJO

See also Tucson

Once a copper-mining hub, Ajo is located about 40 miles from the Mexico
border. It's a prime spot to stop while visiting nearby Organ Pipe Cactus
National Monument.

WHAT TO SEE
ORGAN PIPE CACTUS NATIONAL MONUMENT

10 Organ Pipe Drive, Ajo, 520-387-6849; www.nps.gov/orpi

This 516-square-mile Sonoran desert area on the Mexican border is Arizona's largest national monument. The organ pipe cactus grows as high as
20 feet and has 30 or more arms, which resemble organ pipes. The plant
blooms in May and June, and the blossoms are white with pink or lavender flowers. During February and March, depending on rainfall, parts of the
area may be covered with Mexican gold poppy, magenta owl clover, blue
lupine and bright orange mallow. Many desert plants thrive here, including
mesquite, saguaro, several species of cholla, barrel cacti, paloverde trees,
creosote bush and ocotillo. You can take two scenic drives, both self-guided:
the 53-mile Puerto Blanco and the 21-mile Ajo Mountain drives. There is
a 208-site campground near headquarters May-mid-January, 30-day limit;
mid-January-April, 14-day limit.

CAREFREE

See also Chandler, Mesa, Phoenix, Scottsdale, Tempe

The immense Tonto National Forest stretches to the north and east. In the center of town is the largest and most accurate sundial in the Western Hemisphere.

SPECIAL EVENTS

CAREFREE FINE ART AND WINE FESTIVALS

15648 N. Eagles Nest Drive, Fountain Hills, 480-837-5637;
www.thunderbirdartists.com

At each of these pleasant outdoor festivals, more than 150 booths feature the work of nationally recognized artists. You'll find a wide range of mediums from paintings and pottery to sculptures and stained glass, in all price ranges. In the wine pavilion, host to Arizona's largest wine-tasting event, visitors can sample vintages from around the world. These popular festivals draw more than 180,000 art lovers each year.

Late October, early November, mid-January, early March: Friday-Sunday 10 a.m.-5 p.m.

FIESTA DAYS

28th Street and New River Road, Memorial Arena, Carefree, 480-488-3381

This three-day event features a rodeo, family entertainment and a parade. Usually the second weekend in April.

WHERE TO STAY

THE BOULDERS RESORT & GOLDEN DOOR SPA

34631 N. Tom Darlington Drive, Carefree, 480-488-9009, 888-579-2631;
www.theboulders.com

Located in the foothills of the Sonoran Desert just north of Scottsdale, the Boulders Resort and Golden Door Spa blends perfectly with the surrounding rock outcroppings, ancient boulders and saguaro cactus plants. The adobe casitas are distinguished by overstuffed leather chairs, exposed beams and Mexican tiles, while one-, two- and three-bedroom Pueblo Villas are ideal for families. The resort boasts a first-rate tennis facility and an 18-hole championship golf course. There's also rock climbing, hiking and tours of Native American cave dwellings and ruins. Guided night hikes using night vision equipment are especially fun.

215 rooms. Pets accepted. Restaurant, bar. Fitness center. Spa. Pool. Golf. Tennis. Business center. $$$$

WHERE TO EAT

★★★LATILLA

34631 N. Tom Darlington Drive, Carefree, 480-488-7316, 888-579-2631;
www.theboulders.com

The cuisine at this glass-enclosed restaurant in the Boulders Resort and Spa focuses on fresh, organic produce, free-range meats and poultry and responsibly caught seafood from clean waters. The restaurant also features an organic wine list. The rustic, cozy dining room is decorated with Ocotillo branches (called latillas, which means "little sticks" in Spanish). The outdoor patio, warmed by a blazing fire, is an ideal spot to have a drink after dinner.

American. Dinner. Bar. Reservations recommended. Outdoor seating. $$$

SPAS
★★★GOLDEN DOOR SPA AT THE BOULDERS
34631 N. Tom Darlington Drive, Carefree, 480-595-3500, 888-579-2631; www.theboulders.com

This branch of the original California spa is the jewel in the crown of the Boulders Resort. Many treatments are a nod to the region's Native American history. Ancient Ayurvedic principles are revived in the mystical treatments of bindi balancing, where crushed herbs exfoliate and light oils moisturize your skin, and shirodhara, which begins with massaging warm oil into your scalp and concludes with a mini facial massage and a heated hand and foot treatment. The 33,000-square-foot spa also includes a meditation labyrinth inspired by Hopi medicine wheels and a movement studio, which offers yoga, tai chi, Pilates, kickboxing and more.

CHANDLER
See also Phoenix, Scottsdale, Tempe

Chandler is one of the major suburbs of Phoenix. A growing number of high-technology companies have facilities here, including Intel, Motorola and MicrochipTechnologies.

WHAT TO SEE
CASA PALOMA
7131 W. Ray Road, Chandler, 480-777-2272; www.shopcasapaloma.com

It's worth stopping at this upscale strip mall with 35 shops. After shopping, pamper yourself at Rolf's Salon at the Foothills or dine at one of five restaurants. Daily.

CHANDLER CENTER FOR THE ARTS
250 N. Arizona Ave., Chandler, 480-782-2680; www.chandlercenter.org

This 64,000-square-foot performance center is known for its superb acoustics. The London City Opera, Jay Leno, Anne Murray, Rita Moreno, Bob Newhart and the Phoenix Boys Choir are among the performers who have helped the center earn its reputation for staging shows that bring audiences to their feet. The main auditorium seats 1,550 but can be subdivided into three separate halls holding 1,000, 350 and 250 people, respectively.

WILD HORSE PASS CASINO
5550 W. Wild Horse Pass, Chandler, 800-946-4452; www.wingilariver.com

With nearly 170,000 square feet of gaming action, this casino offers lots of options. The card room is decked out with 19 poker tables, while the bingo hall has 1,200 seats. There's also a 24-hour live keno section, more than 500 slot machines, a hotel and plenty of restaurants and entertainment options to choose from.

SPECIAL EVENTS
CHANDLER JAZZ FESTIVAL
Chandler, 480-782-2735; www.chandleraz.gov
More than 20 bands perform mostly swing music. The two-day event attracts about 6,000 jazz lovers.
Late April.

CHANDLER OSTRICH FESTIVAL & PARADE
Tumbleweed Park, 2250 S. McQueen Road, Chandler, 480-963-4571;
www.ostrichfestival.com
This festival features ostrich racing, food, entertainment, arts and crafts, carnival with rides and other amusements such as a petting zoo and pony rides.
Early March.

WHERE TO STAY
★★★CROWNE PLAZA SAN MARCOS GOLF RESORT
1 San Marcos Place, Chandler, 480-812-0900, 800-528-8071;
www.sanmarcosresort.com
Built in 1912, this property was the first golf course in Arizona. Located just a few miles from companies such as Motorola and Intel, it's a great choice for business travelers. Families can enjoy tennis and horseback riding. Updated guest rooms include eye pillows, ear plugs, lavender spray and sleep CDs. 295 rooms. Restaurant, bar. Pets accepted. Pool. Golf. Tennis. Business center. $

★FAIRFIELD INN PHOENIX CHANDLER
7425 W. Chandler Blvd., Chandler, 480-940-0099; www.marriott.com
66 rooms. Complimentary breakfast. Pool. $

★★RADISSON HOTEL PHOENIX-CHANDLER
7475 W. Chandler Blvd., Chandler, 480-961-4444, 800-395-7046;
www.radisson.com/chandleraz
159 rooms. Restaurant, bar. Pets accepted. Pool. Business center. Fitness center. $

★★★SHERATON WILD HORSE PASS RESORT & SPA
5594 W. Wild Horse Pass Blvd., Chandler, 602-225-0100, 800-325-3535;
www.wildhorsepassresort.com
This unique resort on Gila River tribal land blends the look and feel of the area with the amenities and service of a contemporary hotel. Each detail of the interior has been included for its significance to Native American traditions, including the petroglyph-engraved furniture. The destination resort also features two 18-hole golf courses, the 17,500-square-foot Aji spa, an equestrian center for riding lessons and trail rides, jogging paths and tennis courts. Be sure to plan on dinner at Kai Restaurant, where chef Michael O'Dowd creates contemporary American cuisine inspired by local ingredients. A two-mile replica of the Gila River runs through the property and offers boat rides to the Wild Horse Pass Casino or the Whirlwind Golf Club. 500 rooms. Restaurant, bar. Spa. Pets accepted. Golf. Tennis. Pool. $$$

WHERE TO EAT

★★C-FU GOURMET

2051 W. Warner Road, Chandler, 480-899-3888; www.cfugourmet.com

Chinese. Lunch, dinner. Bar. Reservations recommended. $$

★★★★★KAI

*Sheraton Wild Horse Pass Resort & Spa, 5594 W. Wild Horse Pass Blvd., Chandler,
602-385-5726; www.whpdining.com*

Located in the Sheraton Wild Horse Pass Resort, this sophisticated restaurant, under the helm of chef Michael O'Dowd, showcases locally grown produce and a surprisingly rich Arizona-made olive oil in recipes that merge contemporary tastes and time-honored Native American techniques. (Kai means "seed" in Pima.) The results include lobster tail, corn and avocado atop fry bread, and rack of lamb sauced with a mole made from American Indian seeds. The staff guides diners through the experience with a laidback but confident manner, and can aptly describe any of the hundreds of fine bottles of wine on the list.

Southwestern. Dinner. Closed Sunday-Monday. Bar. Outdoor seating. $$$

SPA

★★★★AJI SPA

*Sheraton Wild Horse Pass Resort & Spa, 5594 W. Wild Horse Pass Blvd., Chandler,
602-225-0100; www.wildhorsepassresort.com*

This resort spa will transport you a million miles away. Traditional Native American healing therapies are the backbone of Aji Spa, such as the Ho'dai Massage, which uses hot rocks to soothe muscles. You'll get a dose of culture along with your comfort, too—meditation sessions, medicinal massages and a one-of-a-kind healing treatment that combines massage and ancient Pima techniques are among the treatments that honor Native American traditions.

12 FLAGSTAFF

See also Sedona, Williams, Winslow

In 1876 the Boston Party, a group of pioneers, made camp in a mountain valley on the Fourth of July. They stripped a pine tree of its branches and hung a flag at its top. Afterward, the tree was used as a marker for travelers who referred to the place as the spring by the flag staff. In 1882, Flagstaff became a railroad town when the Atlantic and Pacific Railroad (now the Santa Fe) was built.

Today, Flagstaff, home of Northern Arizona University, is an educational and cultural center. Tourism is the main industry—the city is a good place to see the Navajo country, Oak Creek Canyon, the Grand Canyon and Humphreys Peak (12,670 feet), the tallest mountain in Arizona. Tall pine forests fill the surrounding area.

WHAT TO SEE

ARIZONA HISTORICAL SOCIETY PIONEER MUSEUM

2340 N. Fort Valley Road, Flagstaff, 928-774-6272; www.arizonahistoricalsociety.org

This museum highlights the history of Flagstaff and northern Arizona. There are changing exhibits throughout the year.

Monday-Saturday.

ARIZONA SNOWBOWL SKI & SUMMER RESORT

6355 Highway 180, Flagstaff, 928-779-1951; www.arizonasnowbowl.com

The 50-acre resort has two triple, two double chairlifts; patrol, school, rentals; restaurants, bars, lounge; lodges. Thirty-two trails, longest run more than two miles; vertical drop 2,300 feet.

Mid-December-mid-April, daily. Skyride (Memorial Day-Labor Day) takes riders to 11,500 feet.

COCONINO NATIONAL FOREST

1824 S. Thompson St., Flagstaff, 928-527-3600; www.fs.fed.us/r3/coconino

This national forest surrounds the city of Flagstaff and the community of Sedona. Outstanding scenic areas include Humphreys Peak—Arizona's highest point—as well as parts of the Mogollon Rim and the Verde River Valley, the red rock country of Sedona; Oak Creek Canyon (where Zane Grey wrote Call of the Canyon) and the San Francisco Peaks. Includes extinct volcanoes and high country lakes.

Fishing, hunting, winter sports, camping.

LOWELL OBSERVATORY

1400 Mars Hill Road, Flagstaff, 928-774-3358; www.lowell.edu

The dwarf planet Pluto was discovered from this observatory in 1930. Guided tours, slide presentations, telescope viewing. Telescope domes are unheated so appropriate clothing is advised.

Daytime hours: November-February, daily noon-5 p.m.; March-October, daily 9 a.m.-5 p.m. Evening hours: September-May, Wednesday, Friday, Saturday 5:30-9:30 p.m.; June-August, Monday-Saturday 5:30-10:00 p.m.

MORMON LAKE SKI CENTER

5075 N. Highway 89, Flagstaff, 928-354-2240

The terrain includes snowy meadows, huge stands of pine, oak and aspen, old logging roads and turn-of-the-century railroad grades. There are also more than 20 miles of marked, groomed trails. School, rentals, ski shop. Guided tours (including moonlight tours on full moon weekends).

Restaurant, bar. Daily 8 a.m.-5 p.m.

SUNSET CRATER VOLCANO NATIONAL MONUMENT

7133 N. US 89, Flagstaff, 928-526-0502; www.nps.gov/sucr

Between the growing seasons of 1064 and 1065, violent volcanic eruptions built a large cone-shaped mountain of cinders and ash called a cinder cone volcano. Around the base of the cinder cone, lava flowed from cracks, creating the Bonito Lava Flow on the west side of the cone and the Kana'a Lava Flow on the east side. The approximate date of the initial eruption was determined by examining tree rings of timber found in the remains of American Indian pueblos at Wupatki National Monument. This cinder cone, now called Sunset Crater, stands about 1,000 feet above the surrounding terrain. Mineral deposits around the rim stained the cinders, giving the summit a perpetual sunset hue. Park rangers are on duty all year. Do not attempt to drive off the roads; the cinders are soft and the surrounding landscape is very fragile. The U.S. Forest Service maintains a campground (May-mid-September) opposite the visitor center. Guided tours and naturalist activities are offered during the summer. Visitor center daily. A 20-mile paved road leads to Wupatki National Monument.

MUSEUM OF NORTHERN ARIZONA

3101 N. Fort Valley Road, Flagstaff, 928-774-5213; www.musnaz.org
Exhibits on the archaeology, geology, biology, paleontology and fine arts of the Colorado Plateau.
Daily 8 a.m.-5 p.m.

OAK CREEK CANYON

Slide Rock State Park, 6871 N. Highway 89A, Sedona, 928-282-3034; www.fs.fed.us/r3/coconino/
This spectacular gorge may look familiar to you—it's a favorite location for Western movies. The northern end of the road starts with a lookout point atop the walls and descends nearly 2,000 feet to the stream bed. The creek has excellent trout fishing. At the southern mouth of the canyon is Sedona.

RIORDAN MANSION STATE HISTORIC PARK

409 Riordan Road, Flagstaff, 928-779-4395; azstateparks.com/parks/rima/index.html
This six-acre park features an Arts and Crafts-style mansion built in 1904 by Michael and Timothy Riordan, two brothers who played a significant role in the development of Flagstaff and northern Arizona. Original artifacts, hand-crafted furniture, mementos. There are picnic areas and guided tours available (reservations are recommended).
Admission: adults $6, children $2.50, children under 7 free. May-October, daily 8:30 a.m.-5 p.m.; November-April, daily 10:30 a.m.-5 p.m.

WALNUT CANYON NATIONAL MONUMENT

Walnut Canyon Road, Flagstaff, 928-526-3367; www.nps.gov/waca
The monument is a spectacular, rugged 400-foot-deep canyon with 300 small cliff dwellings dating back to around A.D. 1100. The dwellings are well preserved because they are under protective ledges in the canyon's limestone walls. There are two self-guided trails and an educational museum in the visitor center. Picnic grounds. Daily.

WUPATKI NATIONAL MONUMENT

6400 N. Highway 89, Flagstaff, 928-679-2365; www.nps.gov/wupa
The nearly 2,600 archeological sites of the Sinagua and Anasazi cultures were occupied between A.D. 1100 and 1250. The largest of them, Wupatki Pueblo, was three stories high, with about 100 rooms. The eruption of nearby Sunset Crater spread volcanic ash over an 800-square-mile area and for a time, made this an active farming center. The half-mile ruins trail is self-guided. Books are available at its starting point. The visitor center and main ruin are open daily. Wupatki National Monument and Sunset Crater Volcano National Monument are located on a 35-mile paved loop off of Highway 89. The nearest camping is at Bonito Campground (May-October; 520-526-0866).

SPECIAL EVENTS
COCONINO COUNTY FAIR
Flagstaff, 928-774-5139; www.coconino.az.gov/parks.aspx
This annual fair in Coconino County features livestock auctions, contests, entertainment, fine arts and food.
Labor Day weekend.

HOPI ARTISTS' EXHIBITION
Museum of Northern Arizona, 3101 N. Fort Valley Road, Flagstaff, 928-774-5213; www.musnaz.org
Exhibition and sale of Hopi artwork.
Late June-early July.

NAVAJO ARTISTS' EXHIBITION
Museum of Northern Arizona, 3101 N. Fort Valley Road, Flagstaff, 928-774-5213; www.musnaz.org
Last weekend in July-first weekend in August.

WINTERFEST
Flagstaff, 928-774-4505; www.flagstaffchamber.com
Features theater performances, sled dog and other races, games, entertainment and more. February.

WHERE TO STAY
★★EMBASSY SUITES
706 S. Milton Road, Flagstaff, 928-774-4333; www.embassysuites.com
119 rooms. Complimentary breakfast. Bar. Pool. Business center. fitness center. $

★FAIRFIELD INN FLAGSTAFF
2005 S. Milton Road, Flagstaff, 928-773-1300, 800-574-6395; www.fairfieldinn.com
131 rooms. Complimentary breakfast. Pool. Spa. Fitness center. $

★HAMPTON INN & SUITES FLAGSTAFF
2400 S. Beulah Blvd., Flagstaff, 928-913-0900, 800-426-7866; www.hampton.com
87 rooms. Complimentary breakfast. Pool. Fitness center. $

★★★INN AT 410 BED & BREAKFAST
410 N. Leroux St., Flagstaff, 928-774-0088, 800-774-2008; www.inn410.com
This charming bed and breakfast, located in a 1894 Craftsman house, offers fresh-baked cookies in the evenings. Each room has its own individual theme and is decorated with antiques.
10 rooms. No children under five. Complimentary breakfast. $$

★★★LITTLE AMERICA HOTEL
2515 E. Butler Ave., Flagstaff, 928-779-2741, 800-865-1401; www.littleamerica.com/flagstaff
Located on 500 acres of pine forest, this hotel has its own private hiking trails. The outdoor pool offers views of the mountains. The spacious guest

rooms include floor-to-ceiling windows and flat-screen TVs. Guest can enjoy complimentary hors d'oeuvres which are served nightly.

247 rooms. Restaurant, bar. Business center. $

WHERE TO EAT
★KACHINA DOWNTOWN
522 E. Route 66, Flagstaff, 928-779-1944, 877-397-2743; www.kachinarestaurant.com
Mexican. Lunch, dinner. Bar. Children's menu. $$

FOUNTAIN HILLS
See also Scottsdale
An affluent community located close to Scottsdale in the Valley of the Sun, Fountain Hills offers distinct beauty and lots of opportunities for outdoor recreation.

WHAT TO SEE
FORT MCDOWELL CASINO
Fort McDowell Road and Beeline Highway, Fountain Hills, 800-843-3678;
www.fortmcdowellcasino.com
This casino boasts the state's largest card room, a 1,400-seat bingo hall with jackpots as high as $50,000, a keno lounge with million-dollar payouts and 475 slot machines that keep the decibel level high night and day. Spend some of your winnings in one of four restaurants or at the lounge, which offers live entertainment daily. Only those 21 and older can play.

WHERE TO STAY
★★★INN AT EAGLE MOUNTAIN
9800 N. Summer Hill Blvd., Fountain Hills, 480-816-3000, 800-992-8083;
www.innateaglemountain.com
This small boutique hotel is located on the 18th fairway with views of Red Mountain, overlooking Scottsdale and Arizona. The suites have kiva fireplaces, sitting areas and whirlpool tubs. Six of the rooms have a theme, ranging from the Frank Lloyd Wright inspired décor in the Prairie suite to the cowboy items in the Wild West suite.

42 rooms. Restaurant, bar. Pool. $$

GRAND CANYON NATIONAL PARK
See also Flagstaff, Williams
Look out over the great expanse of the Grand Canyon (www.nps.gov/grca) and the awe-inspiring vistas reveal a spectacular desert landscape. Rocks in this great chasm change colors from sunrise to sunset and hide an ecosystem of wildlife. It's no wonder millions of visitors pay a visit to this world wonder every year.

Visitors come here to hike the trails, travel down by mule, camp at the base, or simply stare in awe from the rim. The entire park is 1,904 square miles in size, with 277 miles of the Colorado River running through it. At its widest point, the north and south rims are 18 miles across, with average elevations of 8,000 feet and 7,000 feet, respectively. The canyon averages a depth of one mile. At its base, 2-billion-year-old rocks are exposed.

The South Rim, open all year, has the greater number of services, including day and overnight mule trips through Xanterra Parks & Resorts, horseback riding through Apache Stables (928-638-2891) and air tours (both fixed-wing and helicopter) through several local companies.

In addition to these tours, there are a variety of museums and facilities on the South Rim. The Kolb Studio in the Village Historic District at the Bright Angel Trailhead features art displays and a bookstore. It was once the home and business of the Kolb brothers, who were pioneering photographers here. The Yavapai Observation Station, one mile east of Market Plaza, contains temporary exhibits about the fossil record at Grand Canyon.

The North Rim, blocked by heavy snows in winter, is open from mid-May to mid-October. Due to the higher elevation, mule trips from the North Rim do not go to the river. Trips range in length from one hour to a full day. For more information, contact Grand Canyon Trail Rides at 435-679-8665.

Fall and spring are the best times for to trek into the canyon, when it's less crowded. Don't plan to hike to the base and back up in one day—changing elevations and temperatures can exhaust hikers quickly. It's best to camp in the canyon overnight (plan on an additional night if hiking from the North Rim). Fifteen main trails provide access to the inner canyon. Make reservations for camping or lodging facilities early.

Rafting the Colorado River through Grand Canyon National Park also requires reservations far in advance of your intended visit. Trips vary in length from 3 to 21 days and can be made through a commercial outfitter, a private river trip or a one-day trip (which may or may not be in Grand Canyon National Park). For one-day whitewater raft trips, contact Hualapai River Runners, 928-769-2119. Half-day smooth-water raft trips are provided by Wilderness River Adventures, 800-992-8022.

WHAT TO SEE
DRIVE TO CAPE ROYAL
North Rim (Grand Canyon National Park), about 23 miles from Bright Angel Point over paved road; www.nps.gov/grca

You'll encounter several good viewpoints along the way—many visitors say the view from here is better than from the South Rim. Archaeology and geology talks are given in summer and fall.

WHERE TO STAY
★★GRAND CANYON LODGE
Highway 67, Grand Canyon, 928-638-2611; www.grandcanyonlodgenorth.com/
214 rooms. Closed mid-October-mid-May. Restaurant, bar. $

WHERE TO EAT
★★ARIZONA ROOM
South Rim, Grand Canyon Village, 928-638-2631; www.grandcanyonlodges.com
American. Lunch, dinner. $$

★★GRAND CANYON LODGE DINING ROOM
AZ 67, Grand Canyon, 928-638-2611; www.grandcanyonnorthrim.com
American. Breakfast, lunch, dinner. Reservations required for dinner. Closed November-April. $

★JACOB LAKE INN
Highway 89A and AZ 67, Jacob Lake, 928-643-7232; www.jacoblake.com
American. Breakfast, lunch, dinner. $

GOLD CANYON
See also Tucson
At the foot of the Superstition Mountains, Gold Canyon is a tiny town with golf courses, cacti and craggy rocks. The community is a popular area for second homes.

WHERE TO STAY
★★★GOLD CANYON GOLF RESORT
6100 S. Kings Ranch Road, Gold Canyon, 480-982-9090, 800-827-5281;
www.gcgr.com
Located on 3,300 acres in the foothills of the Superstition Mountains, this resort is a good choice for golfers who want a value-focused retreat. The resort features a golf school and many scenic holes. The accommodations include suites and private casitas, some with fireplaces or whirlpools.
101 rooms. Restaurant, bar. Spa. Pets accepted. Golf. Fitness center. $

GRAND CANYON NATIONAL PARK (SOUTH RIM)
WHAT TO SEE
DRIVES TO VIEWPOINTS
1 Main St., South Rim (Grand Canyon National Park); www.nps.gov/grca
The West Rim and East Rim drives out from Grand Canyon Village are both rewarding. Grandview Point and Desert View on the East Rim Drive are especially magnificent. West Rim Drive is closed to private vehicles from early April to early October. Free shuttle buses serve the West Rim and Village area during this period.

GRAND CANYON IMAX THEATRE
Highways 64 and 180, Tusayan, 928-638-2468; www.explorethecanyon.com
Large screen film (35 minutes) highlighting features of the Grand Canyon. March-October, 8:30 a.m.-8:30 p.m.; November-February, 10:30 a.m.-6:30 p.m.; movie is shown hourly on the half hour.

KAIBAB NATIONAL FOREST
800 Sixth St., Williams, 928-638-2443; www.fs.fed.us/r3/kai
More than 1.6 million acres; one area surrounds Williams and includes Sycamore Canyon and Kendrick Mountain wilderness areas and part of National Historic Route 66. A second area is 42 miles north on Highway 180 (Highway 64) near the South Rim of the Grand Canyon; a third area lies north of the Grand Canyon (outstanding views of the canyon from seldom-visited vista points in this area) and includes Kanab Creek and Saddle Mountain wilderness areas, the Kaibab Plateau and the North Rim Parkway National Scenic Byway.

BEYOND THE GRAND CANYON

This loop drive, a side trip for visitors to the South Rim of Grand Canyon National Park, combines scenic beauty with archeological, historical, geologic and scientific sites. It can be done in one full day or divided into a day and a half with an overnight stop in Flagstaff.

From Grand Canyon Village, head south on Highway 64/Highway 180, turning southeast on Highway 180 at Valle for a drive through the San Francisco Mountains. Those interested in the history of the area, including prehistoric peoples and more recent Native Americans, will want to stop at the Museum of Northern Arizona (3101 N. Fort Valley Road, Flagstaff). Continue along Highway 180 to the turnoff to Lowell Observatory (1400 W. Mars Hill Road, Flagstaff), which has been the site of many important astronomical discoveries since its founding in 1894. Guided tours of the facilities are offered, and there's a public observatory.

You are now on the north edge of Flagstaff. From the city, go east on Interstate 40 (I-40), and take the turnoff to Walnut Canyon National Monument to see dozens of small cliff dwellings built by the Sinagua people some 700 years ago. The monument can be explored via two trails. One is a fairly easy walk along a mesa top; the other is a bit more strenuous but provides a much closer look at the cliff dwellings as it drops about 185 feet into Walnut Canyon.

Leaving the monument, head back toward Flagstaff on I-40 and go north on Highway 89 to the Sunset Crater Volcano/Wupatki national monuments loop road, where there is an extinct volcano, fields of lava rock and ruins of prehistoric stone pueblos. Wupatki National Monument's main attraction is Wupatki Pueblo, a 100-room dwelling built in the 12th century by the Sinagua. This handsome apartment house was constructed of red sandstone slabs, blocks of pale beige limestone and chunks of brown basalt and cemented together with clay. Nearby, Sunset Crater Volcano National Monument offers an intimate look at a dormant volcano, with its rugged landscape of jet-black basalt, twisted into myriad shapes. Sunset Crater's primary eruption was in the winter of 1065.

After rejoining U.S. 89, continue north into the Navajo Reservation and the community of Cameron, with the historic but still operating Cameron Trading Post, which sells museum-quality items as well as more affordable rugs, baskets, jewelry and other American Indian crafts. From Cameron, head west on Highway 64 back into the national park. Approximately 215 miles.

★★★★★ ARIZONA

MULE TRIPS INTO THE CANYON

South Rim (Grand Canyon National Park), 928-638-3283; www.nps.gov/grca/
A number of trips are scheduled, all with guides. Trips take one, two or three days. Reservations should be made several months in advance.

TUSAYAN MUSEUM

Desert View Road, South Rim (Grand Canyon National Park); www.nps.gov/grca
Exhibits on prehistoric man in the Southwest. Excavated pueblo ruin (circa 1185) nearby.
Daily 9 a.m.-5 p.m., weather permitting. Tours: daily 11 a.m.-1:30 p.m.

YAVAPAI OBSERVATION STATION

South Rim (Grand Canyon National Park); www.nps.gov/grca
The station features a small museum, scenic views, geological exhibits and a bookstore.
Daily 8 a.m.-8 p.m.

WHERE TO STAY
★★BEST WESTERN GRAND CANYON SQUIRE INN
100 Highway 64, Grand Canyon, 928-638-2681, 800-622-6966;
www.grandcanyonsquire.com
250 rooms. Complimentary breakfast. Restaurant, bar. Pool. Tennis. $

★★BRIGHT ANGEL LODGE
Highway 64, Grand Canyon, 928-638-2631, 888-297-2757;
www.grandcanyonlodges.com
89 rooms. Restaurant, bar. $

★★★EL TOVAR
On the Canyon rim, 928-638-2631, 888-297-2757; www.grandcanyonlodges.com
The premier lodging facility at the Grand Canyon, El Tovar Hotel—named in honor of the Spanish explorer Don Pedro de Tovar, who reported the existence of the Grand Canyon to fellow explorers—opened its doors in 1905 and was said to be the most expensive log house in America. Just 20 feet from the edge of the Canyon's South Rim, the building is charming and rustic. The hotel features a fine dining room, lounge and a gift shop highlighting Native American artists. With so much to do right at your doorstep—hiking, mule rides, train excursions, interpretive walks, cultural activities—El Tovar offers the best of the Grand Canyon, combining turn-of-the-century lodge ambience with the highest standard of service. Advance reservations are recommended, especially for the summer season, which is usually booked up a year in advance.
78 rooms. Restaurant, bar. $

★★THE GRAND HOTEL
149 State Highway 64, Grand Canyon, 928-638-3333, 888-634-7263;
www.grandcanyongrandhotel.com
121 rooms. Restaurant, bar. Pool. $

★THUNDERBIRD LODGE
On the Canyon rim, 928-638-2631, 888-297-2757; www.grandcanyonlodges.com
55 rooms. $

★★YAVAPAI LODGE
Half-mile from the Canyon Rim, 928-638-2631, 888-297-2757;
www.grandcanyonlodges.com
358 rooms. Closed two weeks in mid-November, three weeks in early December, also January-February. Restaurant. $

WHERE TO EAT
★★★EL TOVAR DINING ROOM AND LOUNGE
1 Main St., South Rim, 928-638-2631; www.grandcanyonlodges.com
Considered the premier dining establishment at the Grand Canyon, this restaurant provides a memorable experience, thanks to the spicy regional cuisine and spectacular Canyon views. The atmosphere is casually elegant with native stone fireplaces, Oregon pine-vaulted ceilings, American Indian

artwork and Mission-style accents. Diners can select from a well-rounded menu that blends regional flavors and contemporary techniques and offers many vegetarian options. The wine list is extensive.

Southwestern. Breakfast, lunch, dinner. Children's menu. Reservations recommended. $$

HOLBROOK

See also Winslow

This small town has a lot to offer, especially when it comes to the histories of the Navajo, Hopi, Zuni and White Mountain Apache Indian tribes. Stop here on your way to the Petrified Forest National Park to learn about these unique tribes.

WHAT TO SEE

NAVAJO COUNTY HISTORICAL MUSEUM

100 E. Arizona, Holbrook, 928-524-6558; www.ci.holbrook.az.us

Exhibits on Navajo, Apache, Hopi and Hispanic cultures. Includes petrified forest and dinosaur exhibits.

Monday-Friday 8 a.m.-5 p.m., Saturday-Sunday 8 a.m.-4 p.m.

PETRIFIED FOREST NATIONAL PARK

1 Park Road, Holbrook, 928-524-6228; www.nps.gov/pefo

These 93,532 acres include one of the most spectacular displays of petrified wood in the world. The trees of the original forest may have grown in upland areas and then been washed down onto a floodplain by rivers. Subsequently, the trees were buried under sediment and volcanic ash, causing the organic wood to be filled gradually with mineral compounds, especially quartz. The grain, now multicolored by the compounds, is still visible in some specimens.

The visitor center is located at the entrance off Interstate 40 (I-40). The Rainbow Forest Museum (off US 180) depicts the paleontology and geology of the Triassic Era. Service stations and cafeteria are located at the north entrance. Prehistoric Pueblo inhabitants left countless petroglyphs of animals, figures and symbols carved on sandstone throughout the park.

The park contains a portion of the Painted Desert, a colorful area extend-

HOPI INDIAN RESERVATION

Inside the Navajo Indian Reservation is the 1.5-million-acre Hopi Indian Reservation. The Hopi are pueblo people of Shoshonean ancestry who have lived here for more than 2,000 years in some of the continent's most intriguing towns.

Excellent farmers, the Hopi also herd sheep, as well as craft pottery, silver jewelry, kachina dolls and baskets. Both the Navajo and Hopi are singers and dancers—each in their own style. The Hopi are most famous for their Snake Dance, which may not be viewed by visitors, but there are dozens of other beautiful ceremonies that visitors are allowed to watch. (The photographing, recording or sketching of any events on the reservation is prohibited.)

The Hopi towns are located, for the most part, on three mesas. On the first mesa is Walpi, founded around 1680, one of the most beautiful Hopi pueblos. It is built on the tip of a narrow, steep-walled mesa, along with its companion villages, Sichomovi and Hano, which are inhabited by the Tewa and the Hano. Hanoans speak a Tewa language as well as Hopi. You can drive to Sichomovi and walk along a narrow connecting mesa to Walpi. Only passenger cars are allowed on the mesa; no RVs or trailers. Individuals of Walpi and First Mesa Villages offer Hopi pottery and kachina dolls for sale; inquire locally.

The second mesa has three towns: Mishongnovi, Sipaulovi and Shungopavi, each fascinating in its own way. The Hopi Cultural Center, located on the second mesa, includes a museum and craft shops, a restaurant serving both Hopi and American food and a motel. Reservations (928-734-2401) for May through August should be made at least three months in advance. Near the Cultural Center is a primitive campground.

The third mesa has Oraibi, the oldest Hopi town, and its three offshoots, Bacavi, Kyakotsmovi and Hotevilla, a town of considerable interest. A restaurant, a small motel and tent and trailer sites can be found at Keams Canyon. There are not many places to stay, so plan your trip carefully. All major roads leading into and across the Navajo and Hopi Reservations are paved.

Information: 928-734-3283; www.hopi.nsn.us

ing 200 miles along the north bank of the Little Colorado River. This highly eroded area of mesas, pinnacles, washes and canyons is part of the Chinle formation, a soft shale, clay and sandstone stratum of the Triassic. The sunlight and clouds passing over this spectacular scenery create an effect of constant, kaleidoscopic change. There are very good viewpoints along the park road.

Picnicking facilities at Rainbow Forest and at Chinle Point on the rim of the Painted Desert; no campgrounds. It is forbidden to take even the smallest piece of petrified wood or any other object from the park. Nearby curio shops sell wood taken from areas outside the park.

Daily.

SPECIAL EVENTS
NAVAJO COUNTY FAIR AND RODEO

Navajo County Fairgrounds, 404 E. Hopi Drive, Holbrook, 928-524-4757; www.navajocountyfair.org

Includes livestock judging, a 4-H competition and exhibitors.

Mid-September.

OLD WEST CELEBRATION

Navajo County Historic Courthouse, 100 E. Arizona St., Holbrook, 928-524-6558;
www.ci.holbrook.az.us

This celebration includes running, swimming and biking races, a quilt auction, arts and crafts and more.
Mid-September.

WHERE TO STAY
★★BEST WESTERN ARIZONIAN INN

2508 Navajo Blvd., Holbrook, 928-524-2611, 877-280-7300; www.bestwestern.com

70 rooms. Complimentary breakfast. Restaurant. Pets accepted. Pool. $

★HOLIDAY INN EXPRESS HOLBROOK-NAVAJO BLVD.

1308 E. Navajo Blvd., Holbrook, 928-524-1466, 877-863-4780; www.holiday-inn.com

59 rooms. Complimentary breakfast. Pets accepted. Pool. $

WHERE TO EAT
★★MESA ITALIANA

2318 N. Navajo Blvd., Holbrook, 928-524-6696

Italian. Lunch, dinner. Bar. Children's menu. $$

KAYENTA

Located in the spectacular Monument Valley, Kayenta's surrounding area offers some of the most memorable sightseeing in the state, including the great tinted monoliths.

WHAT TO SEE
CRAWLEY'S MONUMENT VALLEY TOURS

Kayenta, 928-697-3463; www.crawleytours.com

Guided tours in backcountry vehicles to Monument Valley, Mystery Valley and Hunt's Mesa. Half- and full-day rates. Sunset tours are also available. Daily.

NAVAJO NATIONAL MONUMENT

19 miles southwest of Kayenta on Highway 163, then nine miles north on paved road
Highway 564 to visitor center, 928-672-2700; www.nps.gov/nava

This monument comprises three scattered areas totaling 600 acres and is surrounded by the Navajo Nation. Each area is the location of a large and remarkable prehistoric cliff dwelling. Two of the ruins are accessible by guided tour. Headquarters for the monument and the visitor center are near Betatakin, the most accessible of the three cliff dwellings. Guided tours, limited to 25 people (Betatakin tour), are arranged on a first-come, first-served basis (May-September; phone for schedule). The hiking distance is five miles round-trip, including a steep 700-foot trail, and takes five to six hours. Betatakin may also be viewed from the Sandal Trail overlook—a 1/2-mile, one-way, self-guided trail. Daily.

The largest and best-preserved ruin, Keet Seel (Memorial Day-Labor Day, phone for schedule), is 8½ miles one-way by foot or horseback from headquarters. A permit is required either way, and reservations can be made up to two months in advance. A primitive campground is available for overnight hikers. The horseback trip takes all day. Horses should be reserved when making reservations (no children under 12 without previous riding experience). The visitor center has a museum and film program.

NAVAJO INDIAN RESERVATION
www.explorenavajo.com

The Navajo Nation is the largest Native American tribe and reservation in the United States. The reservation covers more than 25,000 square miles within three states—with the largest portion in northeastern Arizona and the rest in New Mexico and Utah.

More than 400 years ago, the Navajo people (the Dineh) moved into the arid southwestern region of the United States and carved out a way of life that was in harmony with the natural beauty of Arizona, New Mexico and Utah. In the 1800s, westward-moving settlers interrupted this harmonious life. For the Navajo, this conflict resulted in their forced removal from their ancestral land and the "Long Walk" to Fort Sumner, New Mexico. The plan was judged a failure and in 1868, they were allowed to return to their homeland. Coal, oil and uranium have been discovered on the reservation. The income from these resources, which is handled democratically by the tribe, has helped improve the economic and educational situation of its people.

The Navajo continue to practice many of their ancient ceremonies, including the Navajo Fire Dance and the Yei-bi-chei (winter) and Enemy Way Dances (summer). Many ceremonies are associated with curing the sick and are primarily religious in nature. Visitors must obtain permission to view these events—photography, recording and sketching are prohibited.

There are a number of paved roads across the Navajo and Hopi Reservations, as well as some unpaved gravel and dirt roads. During the rainy season (mostly August to September), the unpaved roads are difficult or impassable.

Some of the most spectacular areas in Navajoland are Canyon de Chelly National Monument, Navajo National Monument, Monument Valley Navajo Tribal Park (north of Kayenta) and Four Corners Monument. Accommodations on the reservation are limited; reservations are recommended months in advance.

WHERE TO STAY
★★GOULDING'S LODGE
1000 Main St., Monument Valley, 435-727-3231; www.gouldings.com
62 rooms. Restaurant. Pets accepted. Pool. $$

★★HOLIDAY INN
Highways 160 and 163, Kayenta, 928-697-3221, 888-465-4329;
www.holidayinnkayenta.com
164 rooms. Restaurant. Pool. $

KINGMAN

See also Lake Havasu City

The heart of Kingman lies on historic Route 66, and is a convenient stop on the way to the Grand Canyon. Several lakes are nearby with year-round swimming, waterskiing, fishing and boating. To the south are the beautiful Hualapai Mountains. Kingman was once a rich silver and gold mining area and several ghost towns are nearby.

WHAT TO SEE
BONELLI HOUSE

430 E. Spring St., Kingman, 928-753-3175; www.kingmantourism.org
One of the earliest permanent structures in the city, this restored home is furnished with many original pieces.
Monday-Friday 11 a.m.-3 p.m.

MOHAVE MUSEUM OF HISTORY AND ART

400 W. Beale St., Kingman, 928-753-3195; www.mohavemuseum.org
See a portrait collection of U.S. presidents and first ladies at this museum that traces local and state history. Also featured is a turquoise display, a rebuilt 1926 pipe organ, a local artists' gallery and more.
Monday-Friday 9 a.m.-5 p.m., Saturday-Sunday 1-5 p.m.

OATMAN

Highway 66, Oatman, 928-768-6222; www.oatmangoldroad.org
In the 1930s, this was the last stop in Arizona before entering the Mojave Desert in California. Created in 1906 as a tent camp, it flourished as a gold mining center until 1942, when Congress declared that gold mining was no longer essential to the war effort. The ghost town has been kept as authentic as possible and several motion pictures have been filmed here. Turquoise and antique shops. Gunfights staged on weekends.

POWERHOUSE VISITOR CENTER

120 W. Route 66, Kingman, 928-753-6106, 866-427-7866; www.kingmantourism.org
Houses the Historic Route 66 Association of Arizona, Tourist Information Center, Carlos Elmer Memorial Photo Gallery and more. Model railroad shop, gift shop, deli.
March-November, daily 9 a.m.-6 p.m.; December-February, daily 9 a.m.-5 p.m.

SPECIAL EVENTS
ANDY DEVINE DAYS PRCA RODEO

Mohave County Fairgrounds, 2600 Fairgrounds Blvd., Kingman, 928-757-7919;
www.kingmanrodeo.com/kingsmen.html
Sports tournaments, parade and more.
Two days in late September.

MOHAVE COUNTY FAIR

Mohave County Fairgrounds, 2600 Fairgrounds Blvd., Kingman, 928-753-2636;
www.mcfafairgrounds.org
This annual event features a carnival, livestock auctions, a 4-H competition

and plenty of food.
First weekend after Labor Day.

WHERE TO STAY
★BEST WESTERN A WAYFARER'S INN AND SUITES
2815 E. Andy Devine Ave., Kingman, 928-753-6271, 800-548-5695;
www.bestwestern.com
101 rooms. Fitness center. Pets accepted. Pool. $

LAKE HAVASU CITY
See also Kingman
This is the center of a year-round resort area on the shores of 45-mile-long
Lake Havasu. The London Bridge, imported from England and reassembled
here in 1968 as part of a recreational area, connects the mainland city with a
three-square-mile island that has a marina, golf course, tennis courts, campgrounds and other recreational facilities.

WHAT TO SEE
LAKE HAVASU STATE PARK
699 London Bridge Road, Lake Havasu City, 928-855-2784; www.azstateparks.com
This park occupies 13,000 acres along 23 miles of shoreline. Windsor Beach
Unit, two miles north on old Highway 95 (London Bridge Road), has swimming, fishing, boating, hiking and camping. Cattail Cove Unit, 15 miles
south and a ½-mile west of Highway 95, has swimming, fishing, boating and
camping; 928-855-1223.
Sunrise-10 p.m.

LONDON BRIDGE RESORT & ENGLISH VILLAGE
1477 Queens Bay, Lake Havasu City, 928-855-0888, 866-331-9231;
www.londonbridgeresort.com
This English-style village on 110 acres is home to the world-famous London
Bridge. Specialty shops, restaurants, boat rides, nine-hole golf course, accommodations. Village. Daily.

TOPOCK GORGE
Lake Havasu City
Scenic (and steep) volcanic banks along the Colorado River. Migratory birds
spend winters here, while herons, cormorants and egrets nest in April and
May. Fishing, picnicking.

WHERE TO STAY
★★HAMPTON INN
245 London Bridge Road, Lake Havasu City, 928-855-4071, 800-426-7866;
www.hamptoninn.com
162 rooms. Restaurant, bar. Pets accepted. Pool. Fitness center. $

WHERE TO EAT
★★SHUGRUE'S
1425 McCulloch Blvd., Lake Havasu City, 928-453-1400; www.shugrues.com

ARIZONA ★★★★★

26

Seafood, steak. Lunch, dinner. Bar. Children's menu. $$

LITCHFIELD PARK
See also Mesa, Phoenix, Scottsdale, Tempe

WHAT TO SEE
WILDLIFE WORLD ZOO
16501 W. Northern Ave., Litchfield Park, 623-935-9453; www.wildlifeworld.com
You'll see white tigers, African lions, camels and rhinos at this zoo, which boasts a large collection of exotic animals (about 3,000, representing nearly 600 species). Daily 9 a.m.-5 p.m.

SPECIAL EVENTS
WEST VALLEY INVITATIONAL AMERICAN INDIAN ARTS FESTIVAL
The West Valley Fine Arts Council, 200 W. Fairway Drive, Litchfield Park, 623-935-6384; www.wvfac.org
Approximately 200 American Indian craft vendors display their goods. Also includes American Indian dancing and other entertainment.
Mid-January.

WHERE TO STAY
★★★THE WIGWAM GOLF RESORT AND SPA
300 Wigwam Blvd., Litchfield Park, 623-935-3811, 800-327-0396; www.wigwamresort.com
Once a private club for executives of the Goodyear Tire Company, the Wigwam Resort is one of Arizona's most storied. The rooms and suites highlight authentic regional design with whitewashed wood furniture, slate floors and Mexican ceramic tiles. The property includes award-winning golf courses, nine tennis courts, two pools with a water slide and a spa. Five restaurants and bars serve everything from filet mignon to sandwiches and salads.
331 rooms. Restaurant, bar. Spa. Pets accepted. Golf. Tennis. Business center. $$$

WHERE TO EAT
★★★ARIZONA KITCHEN
300 Wigwam East Blvd., Litchfield Park, 623-535-2598; www.wigwamresort.com
This Southwestern restaurant is a showcase for the fiery culinary techniques and flavors of the region. Using herbs grown on the premises, the kitchen pays homage to local ingredients with signature dishes like smoked corn chowder, grilled sirloin of buffalo with sweet potato pudding and mesquite-dusted Chilean sea bass. The dining room—with an adobe fireplace, red brick floors, wood-beamed ceilings and an open kitchen featuring a mesquite wood-fired hearth and grill—is the perfect setting to enjoy it.
Southwestern. Breakfast, lunch, dinner. Bar. Children's menu. Reservations recommended. Outdoor seating. $$$

MESA
See also Chandler, Litchfield Park, Phoenix, Scottsdale, Tempe
Mesa, Spanish for "table," sits atop a plateau overlooking the Valley of the

Sun and is one of the state's largest and fastest-growing cities. Mesa offers year-round golf, tennis, hiking and water sports. It also provides easy access to other Arizona and Southwest attractions and is the home of Arizona State University-Polytechnic Campus.

WHAT TO SEE
ARIZONA MUSEUM FOR YOUTH
35 N. Robson St., Mesa, 480-644-2467; www.arizonamuseumforyouth.com
Fine arts museum with changing hands-on exhibits for children.
Tuesday-Saturday 10 a.m.-4 p.m., Sunday noon-4 p.m.

ARIZONA MUSEUM OF NATURAL HISTORY
53 N. MacDonald St., Mesa, 480-644-2230;
www.mesasouthwestmuseum.com/home.aspx
Learn about the Native Americans who lived here, see a replica of a Spanish mission and more as you explore this 80,000-square-foot regional resource. Interactive center for kids. Tuesday-Friday 10 a.m.-5 p.m., Saturday 11 a.m.-5 p.m., Sunday 1-5 p.m.

BOYCE THOMPSON ARBORETUM
37615 Highway 60, Superior, 520-689-2723; www.ag.arizona.edu/bta
See a large collection of plants from arid parts of the world. Visitor center features biological and historical displays.
September-April, daily 8 a.m.-4 p.m.; May-August, daily 6 a.m.-3 p.m.

DOLLY STEAMBOAT CRUISES
Highway 88 Apache Trail, Apache Junction, 480-827-9144; www.dollysteamboat.com
Narrated tours and twilight dinner cruises of Canyon Lake follow the original path of the Salt River.
Nature Cruise: daily at noon, 2 p.m. by reservation only, arrangements can be made for 10 a.m. or 4 p.m.; Twilight Dinner Cruise: weekends.

LOST DUTCHMAN STATE PARK
6109 N. Apache Trail, Apache Junction, 480-982-4485; www.azstateparks.coml
This 300-acre park in the Superstition Mountains area offers hiking, picnicking and improved camping. There are interpretive trails and access to nearby forest service wilderness area.
Daily, sunrise-10 p.m.

VF OUTLET STORES
2055 S. Power Road, Mesa, 480-984-0697; www.vfoutlet.net
Look for deals at the 25 stores here.
Monday-Saturday 10 a.m.-8 p.m., Sunday noon-5 p.m.

SPECIAL EVENTS
CHICAGO CUBS SPRING TRAINING
Hohokam Park, 1235 N. Center St., Mesa, 480-964-4467; www.cactus-league.com
Watch the Cubs during spring training at exhibition games.
Early March-early April.

MESA TERRITORIAL DAY FESTIVAL

Sirrine House, 160 N. Center, Mesa, 480-644-2760; www.mesaaz.gov/home

Come celebrate Arizona's birthday in Old West style with Western arts and crafts, music, food, games and activities, and historical reenactments. Second Saturday in February.

WHERE TO STAY

★★★ARIZONA GOLF RESORT HOTEL & CONFERENCE CENTER

425 S. Power Road, Mesa, 480-832-3202, 800-528-8282; www.azgolfresort.com

Tropical palms and beautiful lakes surround this East Valley resort occupying 150 acres. Guest suites are arranged in clusters with courtyards, barbecue grills and heated spas. There is a golf school and the 14th hole of the championship course requires a 175 yard-shot through the trees and over water. 187 rooms. Restaurant, bar. Pets accepted. Pool. Golf. Business center. $

★★BEST WESTERN DOBSON RANCH INN

1666 S. Dobson Road, Mesa, 480-831-7000, 800-528-1356;www.dobsonranchinn.com

213 rooms. Complimentary breakfast. Restaurant, bar. Pets accepted. Fitness center. Pool. $

★BEST WESTERN SUPERSTITION SPRINGS INN

1342 S. Power Road, Mesa, 480-641-1164, 800-780-7234; www.bestwestern.com

59 rooms. Complimentary breakfast. Pets accepted. Pool. Spa. Fitness center. $

★★★HILTON PHOENIX EAST/MESA

1011 W. Holmes Ave., Mesa, 480-833-5555, 800-445-8667;
www.phoenixeastmesa.hilton.com

This newly renovated hotel is centrally located in the East Valley, allowing for easy freeway access to many attractions and business in all directions. Phoenix Sky Harbor airport is 12 miles away. Guest rooms are arranged around the large atrium lobby and are decorated in rich autumn colors with velvety textures. French doors lead to a balcony. Relax by the pool, go horseback riding or a hit the links at one of the nearby courses. The Zuni Bar & Grill serves a breakfast buffet and Sunday brunch. The bar is a good spot to meet friends for one of the micro-brewed beers or margaritas. 260 rooms. Restaurant, two bars. Pool. Business center. Fitness center. $

★LA QUINTA INN

6530 E. Superstition Springs Blvd., Mesa, 480-654-1970, 800-753-3757; www.lq.com

107 rooms. Complimentary breakfast. Pets accepted. Pool. Fitness center. Pets accepted. $

WHERE TO EAT

★★THE LANDMARK RESTAURANT

809 W. Main St., Mesa, 480-962-4652; www.lmrk.com

American. Lunch, dinner. Children's menu. $$

PAGE

See also Flagstaff

Page is at the east end of the Glen Canyon Dam, on the Colorado River. The dam, 710 feet high, forms Lake Powell, a part of the Glen Canyon National Recreation Area. The lake, 186 miles long with 1,900 miles of shoreline, is the second-largest man-made lake in the United States. The lake is named for John Wesley Powell, the intrepid and brilliant geologist who lost an arm at the Battle of Shiloh. Powell led an expedition down the Colorado in 1869 and was later director of the United States Geological Survey.

WHAT TO SEE
BOAT TRIPS ON LAKE POWELL
Lake Powell Resorts & Marinas, 100 Lakeshore Drive, Page, 928-645-2433, 888-896-3829; www.lakepowell.com
One-hour to one-day trips, some include Rainbow Bridge National Monument. Houseboat and powerboat rentals. Reservations recommended.

GLEN CANYON NATIONAL RECREATION AREA
Highway 89, Page, 928-608-6200; www.nps.gov/glca
More than one million acres, including Lake Powell. Campfire program (Memorial Day-Labor Day). Swimming, waterskiing, fishing, boating, hiking, picnicking, restaurants, lodge, camping. The visitor center on canyon rim, adjacent to Glen Canyon Bridge on Highway 89, has historical exhibits. Ranger station, seven miles north of the dam at Wahweap. Daily.

JOHN WESLEY POWELL MEMORIAL MUSEUM
6 N. Lake Powell Blvd., Page, 928-645-9496, 888-597-6873; www.powellmuseum.org
See a replica of Powell's boat, plus a fluorescent rock collection, Native American artifacts and more.
Admission: adults $5, seniors $3, children $, children under 5 free.
Monday-Friday 9 a.m.-5 p.m.

RAINBOW BRIDGE NATIONAL MONUMENT
Page, 928-608-6200; www.nps.gov/rabr
See the world's largest known natural bridge, a breathtaking phenomenon that attracts more than 300,000 visitors a year.

WILDERNESS RIVER ADVENTURES
2040 E. Frontage Road, Page, 928-645-3296, 800-992-8022;www.riveradventures.com
Specializes in multiday trips on the Colorado River in Glen Canyon in raft-like neoprene boats. Reservations are required.
April-October.

WHERE TO STAY
★BEST WESTERN LAKE POWELL
208 N. Lake Powell Blvd., Page, 928-645-5988, 888-794-2888; www.bestwesternatlakepowell.com
132 rooms. Complimentary breakfast. Pool. Spa. Fitness center. $

★TRAVELODGE
207 N. Lake Powell Blvd., Page, 928-645-2451, 800-578-7878; www.travelodge.com
132 rooms. Complimentary breakfast. Pets accepted. Pool. $

WHERE TO EAT
★★BELLA NAPOLI
810 N. Navajo Drive, Page, 928-645-2706
Italian. Dinner. Closed January. Reservations recommended. Outdoor seating. $$

PARADISE VALLEY
See also Scottsdale
A dozen resorts make this small town one of Arizona's hottest tourist destinations.

WHERE TO STAY
★★★THE HERMOSA INN
5532 N. Palo Cristi Road, Paradise Valley, 602-955-8614, 800-241-1210;
www.hermosainn.com
Built by cowboy artist Lon Megargee as his home and studio, this inn, and its onsite restaurant LON's, is a nice alternative to the bigger resorts. Situated on a half acre marked by olive and mesquite trees, towering palms and brilliant flowers, the accommodations range from cozy casitas to huge villas. Rooms feature authentic furnishings and original artwork painted by Megargee some 70 years ago.
35 rooms. Complimentary breakfast. Restaurant, bar. Pets accepted. Pool. Tennis. Fitness center. $151-250

★★★SANCTUARY ON CAMELBACK MOUNTAIN
5700 E. McDonald Drive, Paradise Valley, 480-948-2100, 800-245-2051;
www.sanctuaryoncamelback.com

This boutique hotel overlooking the valley from Camelback Mountain truly is a sanctuary. You won't find typical Southwestern décor here. Casitas are the very essence of desert chic with their spectacular contemporary design. Mountain casitas have wood block floors, glass-tiled dry bars and luxurious bathrooms with travertine marble. The multilevel spa casitas boast floor-to-ceiling windows and walk-in closets, while the spa suites have outdoor soaking tubs in case you just can't bring yourself to walk the short distance to the large infinity-edge pool. Elements restaurant offers New American fare with an Asian influence, served in a contemporary, elegant setting.
105 rooms. Pets accepted. Restaurant. Pool. Fitness room. Tennis. Business center. $251-350

ALSO RECOMMENDED
INTERCONTINENTAL MONTELUCIA RESORT & SPA
4949 E. Lincoln Drive, Paradise Valley, 480-627-3200, 888-627-3010;
www.icmontelucia.com
Nestled within the Camelback Mountains, Montelucia grounds cover 35 sprawling desert acres. There is no shortage of luxury at this Moroccan-

inspired resort. The grounds are lush, the restaurants are premier and the guestrooms are spacious. Take a dip in one or all of the five serene swimming pools. For dinner, be sure to make a reservation at Prado, Chef Claudio Urciuoli's signature restaurant. The menu features master dishes such as the Colorado lamb t-bone with black olives and wild mint and a daily paella special that serves two.

285 rooms. Restaurant, bar. Business center. Fitness center. Pool. Spa. $350 and up

WHERE TO EAT
★★EL CHORRO LODGE
5550 E. Lincoln Drive, Paradise Valley, 480-948-5170; www.elchorrolodge.com
American. Dinner, Sunday brunch. Bar. Outdoor seating. $$$

★★★ELEMENTS
5700 E. McDonald Road, Paradise Valley, 480-607-2300, 800-298-9766;
www.elementsrestaurant.com
Situated on the grounds of the Sanctuary at Camelback Mountain, Elements is a sleek spot that adds a touch of sophistication to leisurely breakfasts, power lunches and romantic dinners. Its clean, minimalist décor features stone and wood accents and expansive floor-to-ceiling windows that offer spectacular views of the sunset over Paradise Valley. The kitchen uses fresh, seasonal ingredients to create the menu of Asian-influenced New American cuisine, which has included dishes such as chilled sesame and lime noodle salad, chili-cured duck breast and braised short ribs with citrus-scented mushrooms. The Jade Bar is a great spot for a drink.
American, Asian. Breakfast, lunch, dinner, Sunday brunch. Bar. Outdoor seating. $$$

★★★LON'S
The Hermosa Inn, 5532 N. Palo Cristi Road, Paradise Valley, 602-955-7878;
www.lons.com
Built by Southwestern artist Lon Megargee in the 1930s, the inn's adobe design and rustic furnishings are a fitting setting for some of the best American comfort food in the Phoenix area. The chef grows many herbs, heirloom fruits and vegetables and grains in the onsite garden to use in fresh seasonal specials such as pork tenderloin with prickly pear braised cabbage, green beans and mashed potatoes and roasted lamb with goat cheese herb grits.
American. Lunch, dinner, Sunday brunch. Bar. Children's menu. Reservations recommended. Outdoor seating. $$$

SPA
★★★★THE SANCTUARY SPA AT SANCTUARY ON CAMELBACK MOUNTAIN
5700 E. McDonald Drive, Paradise Valley, 480-948-2100, 800-245-2051;
www.sanctuaryoncamelback.com
Originally designed as a tennis club in the 1950s by Frank Lloyd Wright protégé Hiram Hudson Benedict, the resort was renovated in 2001. The understated elegance first defined by Benedict is still here. The resort's spa was expanded and seems to include practically every treatment under the sun,

from standard facials to acupuncture. The spa menu includes several Asian-inspired treatments including Thai massage and shiatsu. The resort retains its commitment to the championship tennis courts that defined it from the start, but the grounds are also ideal for Yoga and meditation. Guided desert hikes are also available.

PARKER
See also Lake Havasu City
Parker is located on the east bank of the Colorado River, about 16 miles south of Parker Dam, which forms Lake Havasu. Popular recreational activities in the area include fishing, boating, jet and waterskiing, golfing, rock hunting and camping.

WHAT TO SEE
BUCKSKIN MOUNTAIN STATE PARK
5476 Highway 95, Parker, 928-667-3231; www.azstateparks.com
On 1,676 acres, this park features scenic bluffs overlooking the Colorado River. Swimming, fishing, boating; nature trails, hiking; picnicking, camping, riverside cabanas. River Island Unit has boating, picnicking, camping. Daily.

BLUEWATER RESORT & CASINO
11300 Resort Drive, 928-669-7000, 888-243-3360; www.bluewaterfun.com
Bluewater Casino is open 24 hours and includes slots, poker and bingo.

COLORADO RIVER INDIAN TRIBES RESERVATION
11300 Resort Drive, Parker, 928-669-7615
This reservation spans 278,000 acres in Arizona and California and offers fishing, boating, waterskiing, hunting (tribal permit required) and camping.

LA PAZ COUNTY PARK
7350 Riverside Drive, Parker, 928-667-2069; www.co.la-paz.az.us
A 540-acre park with 4,000 feet of Colorado River beachfront. Swimming, waterskiing, fishing, boating, tennis court, golf course, driving range, picnicking (shelter), playground, camping.

PARKER DAM AND POWER PLANT
Parker, 17 miles north via Highway 95, 760-663-3712
One of the deepest dams in the world—73 percent of its structural height of 320 feet is below the riverbed.
Daily.

SPECIAL EVENTS
LA PAZ COUNTY FAIR
Fairgrounds at Four Corners, 13991 Second Ave., Parker, 928-669-8100
Carnival, livestock auction, entertainment and more.
Mid-March.

PARKER 400 OFF-ROAD RACE

1217 S. California Ave., Parker

Four hundred miles of desert racing.

Late January.

PAYSON

See also Phoenix

Payson, in the heart of the Tonto National Forest, offers numerous outdoor recreational activities in a mild climate.

WHAT TO SEE
TONTO NATIONAL FOREST

Payson, 602-225-5200; www.fs.fed.us/r3/tonto

This area includes almost three million acres of desert and mountain land-scapes. Six lakes along the Salt and Verde rivers offer opportunities for fish-ing, boating, hiking and camping. Seven wilderness areas are located within the forest's boundaries, providing hiking and bridle trails. The forest also fea-tures Tonto Natural Bridge, the largest natural travertine bridge in the world. Scenic attractions include the Apache Trail, Four Peaks, the Mogollon Rim and Sonoran Desert country.

SPECIAL EVENTS
OLD-TIME FIDDLERS CONTEST & FESTIVAL

Rumsey Park, Payson, 928-970-1760

Fiddling contest, storytellers, Irish step-dancers, entertainment, food, arts and crafts and more.

Late September.

WORLD'S OLDEST CONTINUOUS PRCA RODEO

Multi-Event Center, 1400 S. Beeline Highway, Payson, 800-672-9766;
www.paysonrimcountry.com

The rodeo features calf roping, bull riding and barrel racing.

Third weekend in August.

WHERE TO STAY
★★BEST WESTERN PAYSON INN

801 N. Beeline Highway, Payson, 928-474-3241, 800-247-9477; www.bestwestern.com

99 rooms. Complimentary breakfast. Restaurant, bar. Pets accepted. Pool. Fitness center. $

PHOENIX

See also Chandler, Litchfield Park, Mesa, Payson

The capital of Arizona lies on flat desert, surrounded by mountains. People come to the Valley of the Sun for the golf, mega-resorts and spas. Phoenix has been getting bigger and better in recent years, with an influx of retirees and new industry. These days, the resorts have grown more contemporary, the spas have constantly made themselves over and the restaurants serve a lot more than Southwestern cuisine.

WHAT TO SEE
ANTIQUE GALLERY/CENTRAL ANTIQUES
5037 N. Central Ave., Phoenix, 602-241-1174
More than 150 dealers showcase heirloom-quality antiques in this 30,000-square-foot space. Shop for period furniture, silver and more.
Monday-Saturday 10 a.m.-5:30 p.m., Sunday noon-5 p.m.

ARIZONA CAPITOL MUSEUM
1700 W. Washington St., Phoenix, 602-926-3620; www.lib.az.us/museum
Built in 1899, this stately building first served as the capitol for the territorial government, then as the state capitol after Arizona was admitted to the Union in 1912. The state moved to an adjacent office building in the 1970s for more space, and the original structure has operated as a museum since its restoration in 1981. See the House and Senate chambers exactly as they looked during early statehood. Guided tours are offered daily at 10 a.m. and 2 p.m. A landscaped area includes a variety of native trees, shrubs and cacti.
Monday-Friday 8 a.m.-5 p.m., Saturday 11 a.m.-4 p.m.

ARIZONA CENTER
400 E. Van Buren St., 602-271-4000; www.arizonacenter.com
This park-like plaza, situated among palm trees, gardens and pools, includes 15 stores and kiosks.
Restaurants, bars, 24-screen theater. Monday-Saturday 10 a.m.-9 p.m., Sunday 11 a.m.-5 p.m.

ARIZONA DIAMONDBACKS (MLB)
Bank One Ballpark, 401 E. Jefferson, Phoenix, 602-462-6000; www.arizona.diamondbacks.mlb.com
Professional baseball team.

ARIZONA MINING AND MINERAL MUSEUM
1502 W. Washington, Phoenix, 602-771-1600, 800-446-4259; www.admmr.state.az.us/musgen.htm
This museum has mining exhibits and minerals, gems and petrified wood.
Monday-Friday 8 a.m.-5 p.m., Saturday 11 a.m.-4 p.m.

ARIZONA SCIENCE CENTER
600 E. Washington St., Phoenix, 602-716-2000; www.azscience.org
More than 300 hands-on exhibits on topics ranging from geology to healing make learning fun. Gaze up at the stars in the planetarium and stare wide-eyed at science films in the theater with a five-story screen.
Daily 10 a.m.-5 p.m.

BILTMORE FASHION PARK
2502 E. Camelback Road, Phoenix, 602-955-1963; www.shopbiltmore.com
Bring your oversized designer handbag to this outdoor shopping area with brick walkways and retailers such as Cartier, Escada and Saks Fifth Avenue.
Monday-Wednesday, 10 a.m.-7 p.m., Thursday-Friday 10 a.m.-8 p.m., Saturday 10 a.m.-6 p.m., Sunday noon-6 p.m.

CAMELBACK MOUNTAIN

East McDonald at Tatum Boulevard, Phoenix

Its distinctive hump makes this mountain a very visible local landmark—and a popular spot for hiking. Trails wind through desert flora and fauna. The two strenuous summit trails (each approximately 1½ miles) gain more than 1,200 feet in elevation. Two shorter ones at the base provide much easier trekking, with elevation gains of only 100 and 200 feet.

Daily dawn-dusk.

CELEBRITY THEATRE

440 N. 32nd St., Phoenix, 602-267-1600; www.celebritytheatre.com

Some of the entertainment industry's biggest names bring their music and comedy to this theater, where no seat is more than 75 feet from the revolving center stage.

CHAR'S HAS THE BLUES

4631 N. Seventh Ave., Phoenix, 602-230-0205; www.charshastheblues.com

Bands sing the blues to a diverse crowd every night at this no-frills joint.

Daily; doors open at 7:30 p.m.

DESERT BOTANICAL GARDEN

Papago Park, 1201 N. Galvin Parkway, Phoenix, 480-941-1225; www.dgb.org

This 150-acre botanical oasis is home to one of the world's foremost collections of desert plants. Thousands of plants line the 1/3-mile main trail, including more than half the world's cactus, century plant and aloe species. Music in the Gardens features performances by local bands on Friday evenings from February through June, and Saturday evenings from October through mid-November.

Admission: adults $10, seniors $9, students $5, children $4, children under 3 free. October-April, daily 8 a.m.-8 p.m.; May-September, daily 7 a.m.-8 p.m.

ENCANTO PARK AND RECREATION AREA

2605 N. 15th Ave., Phoenix, 602-261-8991; www.enchantedisland.com

Pack up the family and head to this 222-acre park just minutes from downtown. Kids can fish in a small lake, feed ducks in a pond, ride in boats, cool off in the swimming pool and hop aboard a train and eight other rides geared toward 2- to 10-year-olds at the Enchanted Island amusement park. Two public golf courses (18 holes and 9 holes) appeal to an older crowd.

Daily.

HALL OF FLAME FIREFIGHTING MUSEUM

6101 E. Van Buren St., Phoenix, 602-275-3473; www.hallofflame.org

Believed to be the largest of its kind in the world, the five galleries at this museum are packed with more than 100 pieces of awe-inspiring firefighting equipment, from antique, hand-drawn pumps dating as far back as the 1700s to snazzy, motorized fire engines.

Monday-Saturday 9 a.m.-5 p.m., Sunday noon-4 p.m.

HEARD MUSEUM

2301 N. Central Ave., Phoenix, 602-252-8848; www.heard.org

Immerse yourself in the culture and art of the Southwest at this internationally-acclaimed Native American museum. The 130,000-square-foot museum boasts 10 galleries (and a working-artist studio), all packed with items that attract nearly 250,000 visitors each year. Works include contemporary American Indian fine art, historic Hopi kachina dolls, important Navajo and Zuni jewelry and prize-winning documented Navajo textiles. The Heard also offers artist demonstrations, music and dance performances.

Daily 9:30 a.m.-5 p.m.

HERITAGE SQUARE

Heritage & Science Park, 115 N. Sixth St., Phoenix, 602-262-5071

Heritage Square is one of three sites that make up Heritage & Science Park. (The other two sites are the Arizona Science Center and Phoenix Museum of History.) Historic Heritage Park has eight turn-of-the-century houses, including the restored 1895 Victorian Rosson House (docent-guided tours: Wednesday-Saturday 10 a.m.-4 p.m., Sunday noon-4 p.m.; closed mid-August-Labor Day; fee) and Arizona Doll & Toy Museum (The Stevens House, Tuesday-Saturday 10 a.m.-4 p.m., Sunday noon-4 p.m.; closed early August-Labor Day). You'll also find the open-air Lath House Pavilion here.

Daily.

MYSTERY CASTLE

800 E. Mineral Road, Phoenix, 602-268-1581

This quirky, imaginative 18-room castle made of native stone and found objects was built by Boyce Luther Gulley for his daughter Mary Lou, who often leads tours.

October-May, Thursday-Sunday 11 a.m.-4 p.m.

★★★★★ **ARIZONA**

PAPAGO PARK

37

625 N. Galvan Parkway, Phoenix, 602-261-8318; www.phoenix.gov/parks/hikepapa.html

This 1,200-acre park with sandstone buttes is flatter than many others in the area, appealing to novice hikers and mountain bikers. (There are more than 10 miles of trails.) Families often come to enjoy its many picnic areas and fishing lagoon, while the golf course lures duffers. The park offers good views of the city, especially at sunset from the Hole-in-the-Rock Archaeological Site, a naturally eroded rock formation.

Daily 5 a.m.-11 p.m.

PHOENIX ART MUSEUM

1625 N. Central Ave., Phoenix, 602-257-1222; www.phxart.org

At more than 160,000 square feet, this is one of the largest art museums in the -Southwest. There are more than 17,000 works here—about 1,000 of which are on display at any given time, in addition to major traveling exhibits. The museum sponsors Family Sundays every third Sunday of the month for children ages 5-12, which includes imaginative art projects and self-guided explorations of the galleries.

Wednesday-Sunday 10 a.m.-5 p.m.; Tuesday 10 a.m.-9 p.m.; closed Monday.

Free admission Tuesday 3-9 p.m. First Friday events 6-10 p.m. first Friday of every month.

PHOENIX COYOTES (NHL)
Glendale Arena, 9400 W. Maryland Ave., Glendale, 486-563-7825;
www.phoenixcoyotes.com
Professional hockey team.

PHOENIX INTERNATIONAL RACEWAY
7602 S. Avondale Blvd., Avondale, 602-252-2227; www.phoenixintlraceway.com
If you've seen *Days of Thunder* with Tom Cruise, you've seen this high-octane speedway. Big-name drivers fire up their engines on six weekends throughout the year. More than 100,000 spectators pack the raceway for NA-SCAR Weekend in late fall. Other events include the Rolex Grand American Sports Car Series and the IRL Indy Car Series. No other speedway in Arizona is open to so many different classes of cars. PIR also hosts plenty of non-racing events, including a large Fourth of July celebration.

PHOENIX MERCURY (WNBA)
America West Arena, 201 E. Jefferson St., Phoenix, 602-252-9622;
www.wnba.com/mercury
Women's professional basketball team.

PHOENIX MOUNTAINS PARK
2701 E. Squaw Peak Lane, Phoenix, 602-262-6861;
www.ci.phoenix.az.us/parks/hikephx.html
This park offers more than 7,000 acres of unique desert mountain recreational activities. Hiking, horseback riding and picnicking.
Daily 5 a.m.-11 p.m. Echo Canyon, located in the park, offers hiking trails.

38

PHOENIX MUSEUM OF HISTORY
Heritage & Science Park, 105 N. Fifth St., Phoenix, 602-253-2734; www.pmoh.org
Celebrates more than 2,000 years of Arizona history. Tuesday-Saturday 10 a.m.-5 p.m. Closed Sunday-Monday.

PHOENIX SUNS (NBA)
America West Arena, 201 E. Jefferson, Phoenix, 602-379-7867; www.nba.com/suns
Professional basketball team.

PHOENIX ZOO
Papago Park, 455 N. Galvin Parkway, Phoenix, 602-273-1341; www.phoenixzoo.org
See more than 400 mammals, 500 birds and 500 reptiles and amphibians. The Arabian oryx and desert bighorn sheep are especially popular. The zoo holds special events, educational programs and outdoor recreational activities. Walk, bike (rentals available) or take a train ride around the park. November 5-January 11, daily 9 a.m.-4 p.m.; January 12-May, daily 9 a.m.-5 p.m.; June-September, Monday-Friday 7 a.m.-2 p.m., Saturday-Sunday 7 a.m.-4 p.m.

PIONEER LIVING HISTORY MUSEUM

3901 W. Pioneer Road, Phoenix, 623-465-1052; www.pioneer-arizona.com

Experience city life as pioneers in the Old West did. On these 90 acres celebrating the 1800s, you can belly up to the bar in the saloon, check out the chiseling in the blacksmith shop, eye the vintage fashions in the dress store, say a little prayer in the community church and more.

October-May, Wednesday-Sunday 9 a.m.-5 p.m.; June-September, Friday-Sunday 8 a.m.-2 p.m.

PUEBLO GRANDE MUSEUM AND ARCHAEOLOGICAL PARK

4619 E Washington St., Phoenix, 602-495-0901, 602-495-0902, 877-706-4408; www.ci.phoenix.az.us/parks/

At the ruins of a Hohokam village, revisit the past and learn how these prehistoric people lived in Arizona 1,500 years ago. You'll see an old platform mound that the Hohokam probably used for ceremonies or as an administrative center, an excavated ball court, reproductions of adobe homes and irrigation canals used for farming. Make the rounds of this 102-acre park on your own or take a guided tour on Saturday at 11 a.m. or 1 p.m. or on Sunday at 1:30 p.m. Monday-Saturday 9 a.m.-4:45 p.m., Sunday 1-4:45 p.m.; closed Sunday-Monday from May-September.

Free admission Sunday.

ROADRUNNER PARK FARMERS' MARKET

3501 Cactus Road, Phoenix, 623-848-1234; www.arizonafarmersmarkets.com

Thousands of people come to this outdoor market to stock up on fresh produce grown in the Arizona desert. As many as 60 vendors sell melons, onions, peppers, squash, tomatoes and other fresh-from-the-farm crops. A few sell arts and crafts.

Saturday 8 a.m.-noon.

SQUAW PEAK PARK

2701 E. Squaw Peak Lane, Phoenix, 602-262-7901

The views—and the hiking—will take your breath away. The demanding, 1.2-mile trek up the Summit Trail will test you every step of the way. For an easier route, opt for the Circumference Trail.

Daily.

SPECIAL EVENTS
ARIZONA OPERA

4600 N. 12th St., Phoenix, 602-266-7464; www.azopera.com

Five operas are held each year at the Phoenix Symphony Hall.

October-March, Friday-Sunday.

ARIZONA STATE FAIR

1826 W. McDowell Road, Phoenix, 602-252-6771; www.azstatefair.com

This annual event attracts big crowds. It has everything you'd expect of a good state fair: a busy midway packed with exciting rides and games, high-decibel concerts, gooey cotton candy and other carnival fare, rodeo action,

cooking contests and much more.
Mid-October-early November.

ARIZONA THEATRE COMPANY
Herberger Theater Center, 222 E. Monroe St., Phoenix, 520-622-2823; 602-257-1222;
www.aztheatreco.org
This professional company performs classic and contemporary works.
October-May.

COWBOY ARTISTS OF AMERICA SALE AND EXHIBITION
Phoenix Art Museum, 1625 N. Central Ave., Phoenix, 602-257-1222; www.phxart.org
Members of Cowboy Artists of America—a select group who produce fine
Western American art—are considered the most prestigious in the genre.
And at this annual event, they offer more than 100 of their new, never-before-
viewed works for sale—some of which command six figures. If that's more
than you can wrangle, all the painting, drawings and sculptures remain on ex-
hibit for a few weeks so everyone can enjoy them before buyers claim them.
Late October-mid-November.

FIRECRACKER SPORTS FESTIVAL
Rose Mofford, Papago and Desert West Complexes, Phoenix, 602-262-6485
About 140 teams from throughout Arizona come to play ball during this annual event, the state's largest and longest-running softball tournament. The
action features adult slow pitch and youth (girls) fast pitch in up to 13 divi-
sions. The opening-night party includes a fireworks display.
Last weekend in June.

INDIAN FAIR AND MARKET
The Heard Museum, 2301 N. Central Ave., Phoenix, 602-252-8848;
www.heardguild.org/indian-fair/indian-fair.aspx
American Indian artisans, demonstrations, dances, native foods.
First weekend in March.

NEW WORKS FESTIVAL
Phoenix Theatre's Little Theatre, 100 E. McDowell Road, Phoenix, 602-258-1974
See plays and musicals staged in their early phases. Actors perform works-
in-progress with books in hand and with minimal set decorations. Some get
produced as part of Phoenix Theatre's regular season.
Late July-mid-August.

PHOENIX SYMPHONY
Symphony Hall, 75 North Second St., Phoenix,602-495-1999, 800-776-9080;
www.phoenixsymphony.org
The symphony's annual programming includes classics, chamber orchestra,
symphonic pops and family and holiday events.

WHERE TO STAY

★★★ARIZONA BILTMORE RESORT AND SPA

2400 E. Missouri Road, Phoenix, 602-955-6600, 800-950-2575;
www.arizonabiltmore.com

The Arizona Biltmore Resort and Spa opened to great fanfare in 1929. The nice thing about it today is that it's not trying to remain great—it just is. The Frank Lloyd Wright-inspired architecture, as well as the photos of all the presidents and famous people who have stayed here, take you back to another time. Spend your days lounging at one of the eight pools, playing the adjacent golf course or relaxing in the 22,000-square-foot spa. The rooms have Mission-style furnishings and pillow-top beds.

738 rooms. Restaurant, bar. Spa. Pets accepted. Pool. Tennis. $$$

★★DOUBLETREE GUEST SUITES PHOENIX GATEWAY CENTER

320 N. 44th St., Phoenix, 602-225-0500, 800-800-3098; www.doubletree.com

242 rooms. Complimentary breakfast. Restaurant, bar. Pool. Business center. $

★★EMBASSY SUITES PHOENIX-BILTMORE

2630 E. Camelback Road, Phoenix, 602-955-3992, 800-362-2779;
www.phoenixbiltmore.embassysuites.com

232 rooms. Complimentary breakfast. Restaurant, bar. Pets accepted. Pool. Fitness center. $$

★★EMBASSY SUITES PHOENIX-NORTH

2577 W. Greenway Road, Phoenix, 602-375-1777; www.embassysuites.com

314 rooms. Complimentary breakfast. Restaurant, bar. Pets accepted. Pool. Tennis. $

★★HILTON PHOENIX AIRPORT

2435 S. 47th St., Phoenix, 480-894-1600, 800-445-8667; www.hilton.com

257 rooms. Restaurant, bar. Pool. Business center. Fitness center. $

★★★JW MARRIOTT DESERT RIDGE RESORT AND SPA

5350 E. Marriott Drive, Phoenix, 480-293-5000, 800-835-6206;
www.jwdesertridgeresort.com

This resort has it all: four sun-kissed pools, two 18-hole golf courses designed by Arnold Palmer and Tom Fazio, an eight-court tennis center, miles of hiking trails, a renowned spa and five restaurants. The rooms have balconies and patios. In summer, families can watch favorite movies like *Charlotte's Web* at the pool.

950 rooms. Restaurant, bar. Spa. Pool. Golf. Tennis. $$$

★★THE LEGACY GOLF RESORT

6808 S. 32nd St., Phoenix, 602-305-5500, 888-828-3673; www.legacygolfresort.com

328 rooms. Restaurant, bar. Pool. Golf. Tennis. $$$

★★MARICOPA MANOR BED & BREAKFAST INN
15 W. Pasadena Ave., Phoenix, 602-274-6302, 800-292-6403;
www.maricopamanor.com
7 rooms. Complimentary breakfast. Pool. $

★★★POINTE HILTON SQUAW PEAK RESORT
7677 N. 16th St., Phoenix, 602-997-2626, 800-947-9784; www.pointehilton.com
This sprawling all-suite resort at the base of Squaw Peak is great for families.
The nine-acre recreational area includes swimming pools with waterfalls and
a huge slide and an 18-hole miniature golf course. Kids will think they're in
heaven after spending a day here and then hitting the old-fashioned ice cream
parlor. For adults there's a spa with salon and fitness center, tennis courts,
shopping and hikes in the adjacent Phoenix Mountain Preserve. Accommodations range from two-bedroom suites to three-bedroom casitas.
563 rooms. Restaurant, bar. Spa. $$

★★★POINTE HILTON TAPATIO CLIFFS RESORT
11111 N. Seventh St., Phoenix, 602-866-7500, 800-947-9784; www.pointehilton.com
This resort is situated among the peaks of the Phoenix North Mountains, of-
fering dramatic views of the city and valley below. The resort boasts its own
water playground and a total of eight swimming pools, some with waterfalls.
The Lookout Mountain Golf Club is an 18-hole championship course set
along the border of an 8,000-acre Sonoran desert park. A full-service spa
offers a variety of pampering treatments. The two-room suites all have living
rooms and two TVs.
584 rooms. Restaurant, bar. Spa. Pets accepted. Golf. Tennis. $$

★★★ARIZONA GRAND RESORT
7777 S. Pointe Parkway, Phoenix, 602-438-9000, 866-267-1321;
www.arizonagrandresort.com
This upscale resort, which recently had a $52 million redesign and renova-
tion, offers spacious rooms and villas with high-quality furnishings and an
endless list of things to do. The onsite Oasis Water Park is Arizona's largest,
boasting an eight-story waterslide, wave pool and "river" for tubing. There
are also six swimming pools, lighted tennis courts, water and sand volleyball
courts, racquetball and croquet, an 18-hole golf course and horseback riding. When you exhaust all that, there's hiking and biking in South Mountain
Preserve next door.
640 rooms. Restaurant, bar. Spa. Business center. Golf. Tennis. $$$

★★★★THE RITZ-CARLTON, PHOENIX
2401 E. Camelback, Phoenix, 602-468-0700, 800-241-3333; www.ritzcarlton.com
The hotel is located in the middle of the Camelback Corridor, the exclusive
shopping, dining and financial district of Phoenix. The rooms, classically
decorated with beds topped with luxury linens, all have views of the sky-
line or the Squaw Peak Mountain Range—and of course, there's the service.
Concierges will offers tips on everything from the area's best golf courses to
the tastiest cocktail to sip in the lobby lounge. You'll find modern takes on
French classics (think steak au poivre with crisp frites) at the hotel's festive
Bistro 24. The outdoor pool sparkles and the sundeck area is cooled with

hydro-misters.

281 rooms. Restaurant, bar. Fitness center. Pool. Business center. $$$

★★★ROYAL PALMS RESORT AND SPA
5200 E. Camelback Road, Phoenix, 602-840-3610, 800-672-6011;
www.royalpalmsresortandspa.com

Constructed in the late 1920s as a private mansion, this hotel brings a bit of the Mediterranean to the Sonoran Desert. Palm trees line the entrance to this hideaway surrounded by fountains and citrus trees, where lavish casitas and guest rooms have fireplaces and balconies. The dreamy open-air spa has treatment rooms with garden areas and a villa with stone heated tables under overhead showers. T. Cook's is an award-winning restaurant.

119 rooms. Restaurant, bar. Spa. Pets accepted. Pool. Fitness center. $$$

WHERE TO EAT
★★★AVANTI
2728 E. Thomas Road, Phoenix, 602-956-0900; www.avanti-az.com

A stark, Art Deco-inspired interior of black and white provides the backdrop for this romantic restaurant specializing in fresh pasta with rich sauces. Enjoy piano music in the lounge area Thursday through Saturday.

Italian. Lunch, dinner. Bar. Reservations recommended. Outdoor seating. $$$

★BABY KAY'S CAJUN KITCHEN
2119 E. Camelback Road, Phoenix, 602-955-0011; www.babykayscajunkitchen.com

Cajun, Creole. Lunch, dinner. Closed Sunday. Bar. Outdoor seating. $$

★★BARRIO CAFE
2814 N. 16th St., Phoenix, 602-636-0240; www.barriocafe.com

Mexican. Lunch, dinner, Sunday bunch. Closed Monday. Bar. $$$

★★★BISTRO 24
The Ritz-Carlton, Phoenix, 2401 E. Camelback Road, Phoenix, 602-468-0700;
www.ritzcarlton.com

Located within the Ritz-Carlton, Bistro 24 serves classic dishes such as steak au poivre and grilled seafood such as butter-poached halibut. The restaurant is spacious and unpretentious with colorful murals and an outdoor patio, and the service is impeccable. Come for Bistro 24's happy hour which features half-priced martinis and appetizers.

French. Breakfast, lunch, dinner, Sunday brunch. Bar. Children's menu. Reservations recommended. Outdoor seating. $$$

★★★CHRISTOPHER'S
2502 E. Camelback Road, Phoenix, 602-522-2344; www.christophersaz.com

This French-influenced spot is strategically positioned in the ritzily revamped Biltmore shopping center. Opened in May 2008, Christopher's aimed to "create a sexy and ultra-chic experience enabling the perfect setting for intimate encounters." Some of the best fare in Phoenix is served here. The menu is American with a French twist (think a foie gras and brioche starter followed by an arugula, pear, and blue cheese salad before a truffle-infused filet mignon or duck confit and fig pizza). Watch it all being prepared at the bar on the sidelines of the contemporary open kitchen. For $120/head, groups up to 10 can reserve a private dining area that comes with the nightly tasting menu—just be sure that the chilled white chocolate-corn husk creation is included with that.

American, French. Lunch, dinner. Bar. Outdoor seating. $$$

★CORONADO CAFÉ
2201 N. Seventh St., Phoenix, 602-258-5149; www.coronadocafe.com
American. Lunch, dinner. Closed Sunday. Reservations recommended. $

★★COUP DES TARTES
4626 N. 16th St., Phoenix, 602-212-1082; www.nicetartes.com
American. Dinner. Closed Sunday-Monday, also Tuesday in June-August. Reservations recommended. $$

★★FISH MARKET
1720 E. Camelback Road, Phoenix, 602-277-3474; www.thefishmarket.com
Seafood. Lunch, dinner. Bar. Children's menu. Reservations recommended. Outdoor seating. $$

★★HAVANA CAFÉ
4225 E. Camelback Road, Phoenix, 602-952-1991; www.havanacafe-az.com
Cuban. Lunch (Monday-Saturday), dinner. Bar. Children's menu. Outdoor seating. $$

★★★LA FONTANELLA
4231 E. Indian School Road, Phoenix, 602-955-1213
The Italian husband-and-wife team who runs this Phoenix gem serves up recipes from their homeland, including fresh pastas and grilled meats.
Italian. Dinner. Closed two weeks in July. Bar. Reservations recommended. $$$

★★PERSIAN GARDEN CAFE
1335 W. Thomas Road, Phoenix, 602-263-1915; www.persiangardencafe.com
Mediterranean, Middle Eastern. Lunch, dinner. Closed Sunday-Monday; also late June-early July. $$

★★RUSTLER'S ROOSTE
8383 S. 48th St., Phoenix, 602-431-6474; www.rustlersrooste.com
Steak. Dinner. Bar. Children's menu. Outdoor seating. $$

★★★RUTH'S CHRIS STEAK HOUSE
2201 E. Camelback Road, Phoenix, 602-957-9600; www.ruthschris.com
Born from a single New Orleans restaurant, the chain is a favorite among steak lovers. Aged prime Midwestern beef is broiled at 1,800 degrees and served on a heated plate sizzling in butter with sides such as creamed spinach and au gratin potatoes.
Steak. Dinner. Bar. Reservations recommended. Outdoor seating. $$$

★★SOPHIE'S BISTRO

2320 E. Osborn Road, Phoenix, 602-956-8897; www.sophiesbistro.com

French. Lunch (Tuesday-Friday), dinner. Closed Sunday-Monday. Bar. Reservations recommended. $$

★★STEAMERS GENUINE SEAFOOD

2576 E. Camelback Road, Phoenix, 602-956-3631; www.steamersgenuineseafood.com

Seafood. Lunch, dinner. Bar. Children's menu. Outdoor seating. $$$

★★★T. COOK'S

Royal Palms Resort and Spa, 5200 E. Camelback Road, Phoenix, 602-840-3610, 800-672-6011; www.royalpalmsresortandspa.com

Located in the Royal Palms Resort and Spa, this stylish restaurant has deep cherry wood floors, hand-painted Italian frescoes and floor-to-ceiling windows with views of Camelback Mountain. The Mediterranean menu includes dishes such as roast duck with preserved apricots and spiced yogurt and grilled veal flank steak with warm potato salad. Some dishes are made in the restaurant's fireplace.

Mediterranean. Breakfast, lunch, dinner, Sunday brunch. Bar. $$$

★★★TARBELL'S

3213 E. Camelback Road, Phoenix, 602-955-8100; www.tarbells.com

Celebrated chef Marc Tarbell—he recently appeared on Iron Chef—continues to dazzle with fresh seasonal dishes such as hand-cut pasta with locally made chicken fennel sausage, organic tomatoes and English peas, and double-cut pork chops with Wisconsin cheddar grills, collard greens and wild boar bacon. The sophisticated restaurant features blond wood, white tablecloths and an exhibition kitchen—and somehow maintains a friendly neighborhood feel, perhaps thanks to the large curved bar that's a focal point.

American. Dinner. Bar. Reservations recommended. $$$

★★TOMASO'S

3225 E. Camelback Road, Phoenix, 602-956-0836; www.tomasos.com

Italian. Lunch, dinner. $$$

★★★VINCENT ON CAMELBACK

3930 E. Camelback Road, Phoenix, 602-224-0225; www.vincentsoncamelback.com

This intimate restaurant, which combines hearty Southwest flavors with elegant French cuisine, helped build Phoenix's culinary reputation. The flawless waitstaff and creative menu continue to attract crowds. A pianist performs every Friday and Saturday night.

French. Lunch, dinner. Closed Sunday. Bar. $$$

★★THE WILD THAIGER

2631 N. Central Ave., Phoenix, 602-241-8995; www.wildthaiger.com

Thai. Lunch, dinner. Bar. Children's menu. Outdoor seating. $$

★★★WRIGHT'S AT THE BILTMORE

Arizona Biltmore, 2400 Missouri Road, Phoenix, 602-381-7632;
www.arizonabiltmore.com

An homage to Frank Lloyd Wright, this restaurant off the lobby of the Arizona Biltmore reflects the architect's penchant for stark angles and contrasts. Muted Southwestern colors fill the comfortable room and a large paneled window frames excellent views. The American cuisine features the freshest ingredients from boutique farms across the country. The menu changes weekly and includes dishes such as aged buffalo with white cheddar and Yukon purée. Be sure to sample one of the tempting chocolate desserts. American. Breakfast, lunch (Monday-Saturday), dinner, Sunday brunch. Bar. Reservations recommended. Outdoor seating. $$$

★★ZEN 32
3160 E. Camelback Road, Phoenix, 602-954-8700; www.zen32.com
Japanese. Lunch (Monday-Friday), dinner. $$

SPAS
★★★★ALVADORA SPA AT ROYAL PALMS
Royal Palms Resort and Spa, 5200 E. Camelback Road, Phoenix, 602-840-3610, 800-672-6011; www.royalpalmshotel.com/phoenix-arizona-spas.php
Inspired by that region's native flowers, herbs and oils, this Mediterranean-style spa brings the outdoors in through its open-air design and plant-inspired therapies. The healing properties of water are a focal point here, whether you're soaking in a bath of grape seeds and herbs or floating in the Watsu pool. Indulge in the Mediterranean Wrapture, a body wrap using olive leaf, cilantro, juniper and lavender extracts. The stone therapy facial stimulates circulation and detoxifies the skin. Enjoy yoga, tai chi, meditation and mat Pilate's classes in the 24-hour fitness center.

★★★REVIVE SPA AT JW MARRIOTT DESERT RIDGE RESORT
JW Marriott Desert Ridge Resort, 5350 E. Marriott Drive, Phoenix, 480-293-3700, 800-835-6206; www.jwdesertridgeresort.com
The serenity and beauty of the desert are the true inspirations behind this spa, where outside celestial showers for men and women, private balconies—ideal for outdoor massages—and a rooftop garden with flowing water add to the atmosphere. Indigenous botanicals influence most of Revive's body treatments. Mesquite clay and desert algae body wraps detoxify and purify. Prickly pear and lime-salt body scrubs soften skin. Recharge with a workout in the spacious and well-equipped fitness center. In addition to cardio machines and free weights, this facility offers several classes, including tai chi, water fitness, golf conditioning, flexibility, yoga and mat pilates. After a workout, dine on calorie-conscious meals at Revive's Spa Bistro.

PRESCOTT
See also Flagstaff, Lake Havasu City
When President Lincoln established the territory of Arizona, Prescott became the -capital. In 1867, the capital was moved to Tucson and then back to Prescott in 1877. After much wrangling, it was finally moved to Phoenix in 1889. Tourism and manufacturing are now Prescott's principal occupations. The Prescott National Forest surrounds the city.

WHAT TO SEE
PRESCOTT NATIONAL FOREST
344 S. Cortez St., Prescott, 928-443-8000; www.fs.fed.us/r3/prescott
Minerals and varied vegetation abound in this forest of more than one million acres. Within the forest are Juniper Mesa, Apache Creek, Granite Mountain, Castle Creek, Woodchute and Cedar Bench wilderness areas, as well as parts of Sycamore Canyon and Pine Mountain wilderness areas.

SHARLOT HALL MUSEUM
415 W. Gurley St., Prescott, 928-445-3122; www.sharlot.org
Period houses include the Territorial Governor's Mansion (1864), restored in 1929 by poet-historian Sharlot Hall; Fort Misery (1864); William Bashford house (1877) and John C. Fremont house (1875). Period furnishings. Museum, library, archives. Also on the grounds is the grave of Pauline Weaver. Pioneer schoolhouse.
Admission: adults $5, children 17 and under free. All buildings May-September, Monday-Saturday 10 a.m.-5 p.m., Sunday noon-4 p.m.; October-April, Monday-Saturday 10 a.m.-4 p.m., Sunday noon-4 p.m.

SMOKI MUSEUM
147 N. Arizona St., Prescott, 928-445-1230; www.smokimuseum.org
Native American artifacts, ancient and modern, are on display.
Tuesday-Saturday 10 a.m.-4 p.m., Sunday 1-4 p.m.

SPECIAL EVENTS
BLUEGRASS FESTIVAL
Courthouse Plaza, 130 N. Cortez St., Prescott, 928-445-2000;
www.prescottbluegrassfestival.com
Features performances from local bluegrass artists.
Late June.

PHIPPEN MUSEUM WESTERN ART SHOW AND SALE
Courthouse Plaza, 130 N. Cortez St., Prescott, 928-778-1385;
www.phippenartmuseum.org
More than 50 artists participate in this event, displaying works of several different media, including watercolor, sculpture, acrylic and more.
Memorial Day weekend.

PRESCOTT FRONTIER DAYS RODEO
848 Rodeo Drive, Prescott, 928-445-3103, 800-358-1888;
www.worldsoldestrodeo.com
Spend a couple of days at the "world's oldest rodeo." Festivities and events are held throughout the city. There is also a parade and laser show.
Late June-early July.

PRESCOTT RODEO DAYS FINE ARTS AND CRAFTS SHOW
Courthouse Plaza, 130 N. Cortez St., Prescott, 928-445-2000
This citywide celebration features an art show, craft demonstrations, and old-fashioned contests. Early July.

WHERE TO STAY
★DAYS INN
7875 E. Highway 69, Prescott Valley, 928-772-8600, 800-329-7466; www.daysinn.com
59 rooms. Complimentary breakfast. Pets accepted. Pool. $

★★FOREST VILLAS HOTEL
3645 Lee Circle, Prescott, 928-717-1200, 800-223-3449; www.forestvillas.com
62 rooms. Complimentary breakfast. Pool. $

★★HASSAYAMPA INN
122 E. Gurley St., Prescott, 928-778-9434, 800-322-1927;
www.hassayampainn.com
67 rooms. Complimentary breakfast. Restaurant, bar. $

WHERE TO EAT
★★GURLEY STREET GRILL
230 W. Gurley St., Prescott, 928-445-3388; www.murphysrestaurants.com
American. Lunch, dinner. Bar. Children's menu. Outdoor seating. $$

★★MURPHY'S
201 N. Cortez, Prescott, 928-445-4044; www.murphysrestaurants.com
American. Lunch, dinner, Sunday brunch. Bar. Children's menu. Reservations recommended. $$$

SCOTTSDALE
See also Chandler, Glendale, Litchfield Park, Mesa, Phoenix, Tempe
Scottsdale is a popular resort destination located on the eastern border of Phoenix. It is renowned for outstanding art galleries, excellent shopping and dining, lush golf courses and abundant recreational activities.

WHAT TO SEE
ACACIA COURSE AT THE WESTIN KIERLAND GOLF RESORT AND SPA
15636 Clubgate Drive, Scottsdale, 480-922-9285; 480-922-9283;
www.kierlandresort.com/golf
Part of the resort's 27 perfectly manicured holes, the Acacia was created by Scott Miller, who once designed for Jack Nicklaus. Combine these nine holes with Ironwood or Mesquite's nine holes for 18 holes of great golf in one of Arizona's most beautiful resorts.

ANTIQUE TROVE
2020 N. Scottsdale Road, Scottsdale, 480-947-6074; www.antiquetrove.com
More than 150 dealers sell everything from vintage mink jackets to colonial rockers from the 1940s to claw-foot bathtubs. Daily.

CANYON COURSE AT THE PHOENICIAN
6000 E. Camelback Road, Scottsdale, 480-941-8200, 800-888-8234;
www.thephoenician.com
The Canyon is the last in the triumvirate of courses that make the Phoenician

THE TOP OF THE WORLD
HAS BEEN RELOCATED.

Experience for yourself why SKYLOFTS at MGM Grand
has been awarded the prestigious Forbes 5-Star Rating
and the AAA 5-Diamond Rating.

skyloftsmgmgrand.com | 1-877-MGM-LOFT **maximumVegas.**

a celebrated resort. This nine-hole course can be combined with either of the other two courses (Oasis or Desert) to make a challenging and enjoyable 18-hole trek through the picturesque desert.

CASINO ARIZONA AT SALT RIVER

524 N. 92nd St., Scottsdale; www.casinoaz.com

The Salt River Pima-Maricopa Indian community hit the jackpot when it opened this casino in a prime location off the 101 Freeway on the Valley's east side. They promptly opened a second location just a few miles north, off the same freeway (9700 E. Indian Bend Road). The original funhouse is larger and a notch more upscale with five restaurants—the best being the elegant Cholla Prime Steakhouse. The 250-seat cabaret-style showroom rocks with big-name entertainers. Daily.

COSANTI FOUNDATION

6433 Doubletree Ranch Road, Paradise Valley, 480-948-6145, 800-752-3187; www.cosanti.com

The famous Paolo Soleri windbells are made and sold here. Self-guided tours daily. Guided tours by reservation only.

Daily 9 a.m.-5 p.m.

CRUISE NIGHT AT SCOTTSDALE PAVILIONS

9175 E. Indian Bend Road, Scottsdale, 480-905-9111; www.scottsdalepavilions.com

While Scottsdale Pavilions may be one of the largest and most attractive shopping centers in the country, Saturday nights bring more people to the parking lot than the shops. They come for the hot rods: muscle cars, custom cars, street rods, antique roadsters, vintage trucks, motorcycles and even a few finely tuned imports.

Saturday 4-8:30 p.m.

DESERT COURSE AT THE PHOENICIAN

6000 E. Camelback Road, Scottsdale, 480-941-8200, 800-888-8234; www.thephoenician.com

This nine-hole wonder joins two other nine-hole courses (aptly named the "Oasis" and the "Canyon") to earn the swanky Phoenician some major accolades.

GRAYHAWK GOLF CLUB

8620 E. Thompson Peak Parkway, Scottsdale, 480-502-1800; www.grayhawk.com

Grayhawk has two courses: Talon (designed by David Graham and Gary Panks) and Raptor (designed by Tom Fazio). Both are nice, but Talon deserves more attention. Built in the Sonoran Desert, the course features many shots over desert brush or sand, with some water worked in for good measure. The course is good enough to host international-caliber tournaments such as the World Championship of Golf. If your game needs work, schedule some time at the Kostis McCord Learning Center, whose instructors include the two CBS commentators.

IRONWOOD COURSE AT THE WESTIN KIERLAND GOLF RESORT & SPA

15636 Clubgate Drive, Scottsdale, 480-922-9283, 888-625-5144;
www.kierlandresort.com/golf

Designed by Scott Miller (once a designer for Jack Nicklaus), the Ironwood, like the other two nine-hole courses at this resort, offers a beautiful setting for birdies, bogies and maybe even a hole-in-one.

KIERLAND COMMONS

Scottsdale Road and Greenway Parkway, Scottsdale, 480-348-1577;
www.kierlandcommons.com

This 38-acre urban village has a traditional Main Street feel and pedestrian-friendly layout. The well-landscaped streets are lined with more than 50 upscale retailers and restaurants, including Morton's Steak House and P.F. Chang's China Bistro.
Monday-Saturday 10 a.m.-9 p.m., Sunday noon-6 p.m.

LEGEND TRAIL GOLF CLUB

9462 E. Legendary Lane, Scottsdale, 480-488-7434; www.legendtrailgc.com

Drive, chip and putt your way through the Sonoran Desert on this picturesque course. Even if you don't quite shoot par, you'll enjoy the gorgeous vistas and desert landscape.

MCCORMICK-STILLMAN RAILROAD PARK

7301 E. Indian Bend Road, Scottsdale, 480-312-2312; www.therailroadpark.com

Kids will enjoy circling around this 30-acre city park aboard the Paradise and Pacific Railroad, a miniature reproduction of a Colorado narrow-gauge railroad. There's also a 1950s carousel and well-equipped playgrounds. Be sure to tour the Roald Amundsen Pullman Car, used by Herbert Hoover, Franklin Roosevelt, Harry Truman and Dwight Eisenhower. Daily.

MESQUITE COURSE AT THE WESTIN KIERLAND GOLF RESORT & SPA

15636 Clubgate Drive, Scottsdale, 480-922-9283, 888-625-5144;
www.kierlandresort.com/golf

Like its two nine-hole counterparts, this course was designed by Scott Miller (former designer for Jack Nicklaus). The resort offers three 18-hole combinations to challenge and delight duffers of all skill levels.

MONUMENT COURSE AT TROON NORTH GOLF CLUB

10320 E. Dynamite Blvd., Scottsdale, 480-585-5300; www.troonnorthgolf.com

Test your skills in the shadow of Pinnacle Peak at this beautiful course.

NORTH COURSE AT TALKING STICK GOLF CLUB

9998 E. Indian Bend Road, Scottsdale, 480-860-2221; www.talkingstickgolfclub.com

This Scottish links course stands ready to challenge golfers with its fairway bunkers, so don't let the gorgeous setting distract you.

OASIS COURSE AT THE PHOENICIAN

6000 E. Camelback Road, Scottsdale, 480-423-2450, 800-888-8234;
www.thephoenician.com
The Phoenician has earned praise from national critics and local fans alike.
Don't miss an opportunity to swing your clubs at one of three 18-hole combinations, of which the Oasis makes up nine holes.

PINNACLE COURSE AT TROON NORTH GOLF CLUB

10320 E. Dynamite Blvd., Scottsdale, 480-585-5300; www.troonnorthgolf.com
Named for Pinnacle Peak, the course is one of two you'll find at the Troon
North Golf Club. After swinging your heart out on the green—and admiring
the view—dine at the club's Grille.

RAWHIDE WILD WEST TOWN

5700 W. North Loop Road, Chandler, 480-502-5600, 800-527-1880; www.rawhide.com
Gallop into the Old West at Arizona's largest Western-themed attraction.
Roam the range on the stagecoach or train, test your aim in the shooting gallery, ride the mechanical bull, pan for gold, go horseback riding and take in
the shows—from stuntmen throwing punches and squaring off in gunfights
to performances by American Indian and Mexican dancers. The Steakhouse
serves up mesquite-grilled steaks. Browse through the many shops. Daily.

SCOTTSDALE CENTER FOR THE ARTS

7380 E. Second St., Scottsdale, 480-994-2787; www.scottsdalearts.org
Offers theater, dance and music. Lectures, outdoor festivals and concerts.
Sculpture garden; art exhibits. Daily.

SCOTTSDALE FASHION SQUARE

7014-590 E. Camelback Road, Scottsdale, 480-941-2140; www.fashionsquare.com
The largest shopping destination in the Southwest features more than 225
retailers, including Neiman Marcus, Nordstrom, Louis Vuitton, Sephora and
Tiffany & Co.Ten restaurants, food court, movies.
Monday-Saturday, 10 a.m.-9 p.m., Sunday 11 a.m.-6 p.m.

TALIESIN WEST

12621 N. Frank Lloyd Wright Blvd., Scottsdale, 480-860-2700;www.franklloydwright.org
Take a guided tour of this amazing compound and see Frank Lloyd Wright's
passion for organic architecture. In the late 1930s, Wright and his appren-
tices literally built this winter camp out of the Sonoran desert, using rocks
and sand they gathered from the rugged terrain. In true Wright fashion, the
architect designed the various buildings with terraces, gardens and walkways that link the outdoors with the indoors. Taliesin West still functions as
a school for more than 20 architectural students. Daily.

TALKING STICK GOLF CLUB-SOUTH COURSE

9998 E. Indian Bend Road, Scottsdale, 480-860-2221; www.talkingstickgolfclub.com
Unlike its counterpart, which is a Scottish links course, the South Course is
a traditional American-style golf course, punctuated with cottonwood and
sycamore trees, creeks and lakes.

TOURNAMENT PLAYERS CLUB OF SCOTTSDALE

17020 N. Hayden Road, Scottsdale, 480-585-4334, 888-400-4001; www.tpc.com
Follow in the footsteps of Tiger Woods, Vijay Singh and other big-name golfers and swing into action on the TPC's greens—home of the Phoenix Open. The club has two options: the Stadium Course (the one the pros shoot) and the Desert Course, both open for daily play.

WESTWORLD OF SCOTTSDALE

16601 N. Pima Road, Scottsdale, 480-312-6802; www.scottsdaleaz.gov/westworld
A 360-acre recreation park, equestrian center, and event facility at the base of the McDowell Mountains. Concerts, sports competitions, special events. Daily.

WILD WEST JEEP TOURS

7127 E. Becker Lane, Scottsdale, 480-922-0144; www.wildwestjeeptours.com
Three- to four-hour guided desert tour. Explore an ancient ruin. Daily.

SPECIAL EVENTS
FALL FESTIVAL ARABIAN HORSE SHOW

WestWorld, 16601 N. Pima Road, Scottsdale, 480-515-1500;www.scottsdaleshow.com
Arabian horse owners come from all over the world to show their horses. Early November.

ARTWALK

Downtown Scottsdale, 480-990-3939; www.scottsdalegalleries.com
Locals brag that Scottsdale has more art galleries per capita than most any other U.S. city. To get a taste of this thriving scene, stroll the downtown streets during ArtWalk, a weekly Thursday night tradition for more than 20 years. For two hours, galleries host special exhibits, demonstrations and meet-the-artist receptions complete with wine, champagne and hors d'oeuvres. Thursday evenings.

PARADA DEL SOL & RODEO

Scottsdale, 480-990-3179; www.paradadelsol.org
This annual festival includes a parade, rodeo and live music. Mid-February.

SAFEWAY INTERNATIONAL AT SUPERSTITION MOUNTAIN

Superstition Mountain Golf & Country Club, 3976 S. Ponderosa Drive, Superstition Mountain, 877-983-3300; www.superstitionmountain.com
Major LPGA Tour golf tournament. Late March.

SAN FRANCISCO GIANTS SPRING TRAINING

Scottsdale Stadium, 7408 E. Osborn Road, Scottsdale,480-312-2586, 800-225-2277; www.cactus-league.com/giants.html
San Francisco Giants baseball spring training, exhibition games. Early March-early April.

SCOTTSDALE CULINARY FESTIVAL

7309 E. Evans, Scottsdale, 480-945-7193; www.scottsdaleculinaryfestival.org

Indulge in some of the tastiest dishes in the region at this culinary adventure that brings the Southwest's best chefs together. Choose from any of nine individual events ranging from casual to black-tie-only. Proceeds benefit area charities. Mid-April.

WHERE TO STAY
★★CHAPARRAL SUITES RESORT
5001 N. Scottsdale Road, Scottsdale, 480-949-1414, 800-528-1456; www.chaparralsuites.com
311 rooms. Complimentary breakfast. Restaurant, bar. Pet. Fitness center. Pool. Tennis. Business center. $$

★COUNTRY INN & SUITES BY CARLSON SCOTTSDALE
10801 N. 89th Place, Scottsdale, 480-314-1200, 800-596-2375; www.countryinns.com
163 rooms. Complimentary breakfast. Pets accepted. Pool. Fitness center. $

★★★THE FAIRMONT SCOTTSDALE
7575 E. Princess Drive, Scottsdale, 480-585-4848, 800-257-7544; www.fairmont.com
The pink Spanish colonial buildings of this hotel are spread out over 450 lush acres overlooking Scottsdale and the majestic McDowell Mountains. Golfers come here to play the two championship courses—one of which hosts the PGA Tour's Phoenix Open. The Willow Stream Spa is also a big draw. Kids will love the aquatic recreation area with two water slides. The spacious rooms and suites are a blend of Mediterranean design with Southwestern accents, and offer fantastic views.
649 rooms. Restaurant, bar. Spa. Pets accepted. Pool Golf. Tennis. $$$

★★★FIRESKY RESORT AND SPA
4925 N. Scottsdale Road, Scottsdale, 480-945-7666, 800-528-7867; www.fireskyresort.com
A three-story sandstone fireplace flanked by hand-painted adobe walls is the centerpiece of this romantic resort's lobby. A traditional Western theme is reflected in the décor, while the grounds include a sandy beach pool surrounded by palm trees and flowers, as well as cozy fire pits. Rooms are stocked with small luxuries such as pillow-topped beds, in-room yoga programs and mats, fully-stocked honor bars and complimentary travel essentials you may have forgotten.
204 rooms. Restaurant, bar. Spa. Beach. Pets accepted. $$

★★★★FOUR SEASONS RESORT SCOTTSDALE AT TROON NORTH
10600 E. Crescent Moon Drive, Scottsdale, 480-515-5700, 888-207-9696; www.fourseasons.com
Located on a 40-acre nature preserve, rooms are spread across 25 Southwestern-style casitas, with views of the desert. Amenities include down duvets, CD players and baths stocked with L'Occitane products and deep soaking tubs. Spring for a suite—you'll get a plunge pool, alfresco garden shower and outdoor Kiva fireplace. A veritable mecca for golfers, the resort grants priority tee times at Troon North's two courses, considered among the best in the world. The spa offers desert nectar facials and moonlight massages,

plus salon services and a fitness center. Three restaurants serve cuisine that reflects the resort's Southwestern setting (including kiva-oven roasted pizza with carne asada, roasted peppers and jalapeno jack cheese.

210 rooms. Restaurant, bar. Spa. Pets accepted. Pool. Golf. Tennis. $$$$

★GAINEY SUITES

7300 E. Gainey Suites Drive, Scottsdale, 480-922-6969, 800-970-4666;
www.gaineysuiteshotel.com

162 rooms. Complimentary breakfast. Pool. Spa. $$

★★HILTON GARDEN INN SCOTTSDALE OLD TOWN

7324 E. Indian School Road, Scottsdale, 480-481-0400, 877-782-9444;
www.scottsdale.gardeninn.com

199 rooms. Restaurant, bar. Pool. Business center. $$

★★★HILTON SCOTTSDALE RESORT AND VILLAS

6333 N. Scottsdale Road, Scottsdale, 480-948-7750, 800-528-3119;
www.scottsdaleresort.hilton.com

Warm shades of gold, blue and apricot complement the resort's natural wood décor, creating a warm and welcoming atmosphere. The villas here recently received a total makeover. Galleries, shops and restaurants of Old Town Scottsdale are within easy walking distance, or you can take advantage of the hotel's bike rental facility. The resort has three distinct eateries, and Griff's is a nice spot for cocktails and live entertainment.

190 rooms. Restaurant, bar. Pets accepted. Pool. Business center. Fitness center. $

★★★HOTEL VALLEY HO

6850 E. Main St., Scottsdale, 480-248-2000, 866-882-4484; www.hotelvalleyho.com

A mid-century modern showpiece, this quirky hotel received a facelift in 2005, which took the property and furnishings back to their 1950s-era Jetsonian glory. Rooms now have plasma TVs, luxury bedding, CD players and Red Flower bath products. The huge outdoor pool has private cabanas for alfresco massages or simply sipping cocktails in private, while the VH Spa offers a full menu of 21st-century treatments, from lomi lomi massages to Tibetan yogic bodywork (a mix of acupressure and massage). Onsite restaurants include the retro-chic Trader Vic's and comfort-food themed Café ZuZu.

194 rooms. Restaurant, bar. Pool. Spa. Fitness center. Pets accepted. $$

★★★HYATT REGENCY SCOTTSDALE RESORT AND SPA AT GAINEY RANCH

7500 E. Doubletree Ranch Road, Scottsdale,480-444-1234, 800-554-9288;
www.scottsdale.hyatt.com

Set against the backdrop of the McDowell Mountains, the resort is nestled on 560 acres filled with shimmering pools, trickling fountains and cascading waterfalls. Desert tones and regional furnishings create contemporary havens in the rooms and suites. The grounds feature championship golf, tennis, a water playground and a camp for kids.

492 rooms. Restaurant, bar. Spa. Beach. Golf. Tennis. Business center. $$$$

★LA QUINTA INN & SUITES PHOENIX SCOTTSDALE

8888 E. Shea Blvd., Scottsdale, 480-614-5300, 800-753-3757; www.laquinta.com

140 rooms. Complimentary breakfast. Pets accepted. Pool. $

★★★CAMELBACK INN, A JW MARRIOTT RESORT & SPA

5402 E. Lincoln Drive, Scottsdale, 480-948-1700, 800-582-2169;
www.camelbackinn.com

Since the 1930s, the Camelback Inn has appealed to travelers seeking the best of the Southwest. This special hideaway is situated on 125 acres in the Sonoran Desert. The pueblo-style casitas feature wood-beamed ceilings, private patios and kitchenettes. Set at the base of Mummy Mountain, the spa is a peaceful retreat. Five restaurants satisfy every craving.

453 rooms. Restaurant, bar. Spa. Pets accepted. Pool. Golf. Tennis. $$$

★★★MARRIOTT SUITES SCOTTSDALE OLD TOWN

7325 E. Third Ave., Scottsdale, 480-945-1550, 888-236-2427; www.marriott.com

Catering mainly to business travelers, this Old Town hotel is close to Scottsdale Road and a large shopping mall. Its suites come equipped with the latest in amenities, and it has plenty of recreational facilities, including a pool and fitness center, to help guests wind down at the end of the day.

243 rooms. Restaurant, bar. Pool. Business center. $$$

★★★MILLENNIUM RESORT SCOTTSDALE, MCCORMICK RANCH

7401 N. Scottsdale Road, Scottsdale, 480-948-5050, 800-243-1332;
www.millennium-hotels.com

Situated on a 40-acre lake in the midst of the McCormick Ranch, this hotel's setting attracts couples on romantic getaways, business travelers making the most of the amenities and vacationers looking for a full-service resort experience. Proximity to the lake means easy access to paddle boats and sailboats. The resort also offers volleyball, tennis and swimming. The individually decorated villas include gas fireplaces, laundry facilities and private patios with grills.

125 rooms. Restaurant, bar. Spa. Pets accepted. Pool. Tennis. $$

★★★MONDRIAN HOTEL SCOTTSDALE

7353 E. Indian School Road, Scottsdale, 480-308-1100, 800-697-1791;
www.mondrianscottsdale.com

Following in its siblings' footsteps, the Mondrian Scottsdale caters to a young and hip crowd. Its white-on-white lobby is accented by modern furniture with sleek, clean lines. The guest rooms continue the stark coolness of the lobby; they are done entirely in black and white, save a single, strategically placed red apple. Count on your room being agreeably appointed with a 42-inch plasma TV, 300-thread count luxury bedding, a European pillow-top mattress with six pillows, Agua bath products by Korres, more than 60 movies on-demand and a deluxe CD sound system with an iPod connection. Reserve a private poolside cabana with a flat-screen TV and fireplace, or have dinner at the popular and trendy Asia de Cuba restaurant, which serves up a delicious fusion of Caribbean and Latin American cuisine.

194 rooms. Restaurant, bar. Fitness center. Pool. Spa. Business center. $$

★★★★THE PHOENICIAN

6000 E. Camelback Road, Scottsdale, 480-941-8200, 800-888-8234;
www.thephoenician.com

This resort, located at the base of Camelback Mountain, features rooms and suites with imported Italian linens and oversized bathrooms with Italian marble. Staff is always on hand to help or steer you toward one of a number of activities, including desert hikes. A resort within a resort, the Canyon Suites at the Phoenician offers sprawling, luxuriously decorated rooms and a separate pool with private cabanas. Guests are assigned ambassadors who arrange everything from in-room aromatherapy baths to chauffeured trips into town in the resort's Mercedes. There's little reason to leave the elegant, comfortable suites (which have DVD players, flat-screen TVs and Italian linen-swathed beds), but the resort's golf courses and full-service spa serve as the primary temptations.

643 rooms. Restaurant, bar. Spa. Pets accepted. Pool. Golf. Tennis. Business center. $$$

★★★SCOTTSDALE COTTONWOODS RESORT & SUITES

6160 N. Scottsdale Road, Scottsdale, 480-991-1414, 877-344-3430;
www.scottsdalecottonwoods.com

The lobby, with its Spanish colonial Monk's Tower, is both the entrance to the resort's many amenities and a buffer against the commotion of busy Scottsdale Road, located next to the Borgata Shopping Center. Lush landscaping with plenty of grass and flowers separates the lobby from the single-story guest rooms and suites. Head to one of two pools for a relaxing swim, play shuffleboard or volleyball, make use of the putting green or jog with your pooch along a trail that includes workout stations.

170 rooms. Restaurant, bar. Pets accepted. Pool. Tennis. Business center. $$

★★★SCOTTSDALE MARRIOTT AT MCDOWELL MOUNTAINS

16770 N. Perimeter Drive, Scottsdale, 480-502-3836, 800-236-2427;
www.scottsdalemarriott.com

This all-suites hotel is located in north Scottsdale. The colorful, attractive public areas and well-furnished guest rooms are designed for both families and the business traveler. Rooms have been updated with down duvets and flat-screen TVs. Some rooms have views of the TPC-Scottsdale golf course.

270 rooms. Restaurant, bar. Pets accepted. Pool. Business center. $

★HYATT SUMMERFIELD SUITES

4245 N. Drinkwater Blvd., Scottsdale, 480-946-7700, 800-889-6829; www.hyatt.com

164 rooms. Complimentary breakfast. Pets accepted. Pool. $$

★★★THE WESTIN KIERLAND RESORT AND SPA

6902 E. Greenway Parkway, Scottsdale, 480-624-1000, 800-937-8461;
www.westin.com/kierlandresort

Located in northeast Phoenix, this handsome boutique-style resort is adjacent to the 38-acre Kierland Commons, where specialty shops and restaurants attract serious shoppers and diners. The spacious rooms and suites feature soothing earth tones and regional furnishings. The resort includes two 18-hole golf courses, tennis courts, multiple pools (including a flowing river pool with landscaped waterfall), beach and volleyball courts and six restaurants. The expansive Agave Spa looks to the traditional therapies used by American Indians for inspiration.

732 rooms. Restaurant, bar. Spa. Beach. Pets accepted. Pool. Golf. Tennis. $$$

WHERE TO EAT

★★AJO AL'S MEXICAN CAFE
9393 N. 90th St., Scottsdale, 480-860-2611; www.ajoals.com
Southwestern. Lunch, dinner, Saturday-Sunday brunch. Bar. $$

★★ASIA DE CUBA
Mondrian Scottsdale, 7353 East Indian School Road, Mondrian, Scottsdale, 480-308-1131; www.mondrianscottsdale.com
If you're not into seeing and being seen, you're probably not into Asia de Cuba. The pricey plates are secondary to the stark, white contemporary décor. But that's not to say you can't get a fine lobster, rack of lamb, or pork roast here. You can, and it'll be an experience unto itself with the unique pairing of Asian and Cuban flavors that has so impressed patrons in London, Los Angeles, New York and San Francisco.
Asian, Cuban. Breakfast (Monday-Friday), dinner, Saturday-Sunday brunch. Reservations recommended. $$

★★ATLAS BISTRO
2515 N. Scottsdale Road, Scottsdale, 480-990-2433; www.atlasbistro.com
International. Dinner. Reservations recommended. $$$

★★BLOOM
8877 N. Scottsdale Road, Scottsdale, 480-922-5666; www.foxrc.com
American. Lunch, dinner. Bar. Reservations recommended. Outdoor seating. $$$

★THE BREAKFAST CLUB
4400 N. Scottsdale Road, Scottsdale, 480-222-2582; www.thebreakfastclub.us
American. Breakfast, lunch. Outdoor seating. $

★★★BOURBON STEAK SCOTTSDALE
The Fairmont Scottsdale Princess, 7575 E. Princess Drive, Scottsdale, 480-513-6002; www.bourbonsteakscottsdale.com
Just another notch on chef Michael Mina's belt, Bourbon Steak Scottsdale has received accolades since it opened in early 2008. This modern American steakhouse takes the classics and improves them. Think three types of beef—certified angus, American kobe and A5 kobe—all prepared with Mina's special touch. He poaches red meat in butter, lamb in olive oil and pork in bacon fat before grilling. Other options include whole-fried organic chicken, truffled mac and cheese, Maine lobster pot pie, and tapioca-crusted yellowtail snapper.
Contemporary American, steak. Dinner. Closed Sunday-Monday. Bar. Children's menu. Reservations recommended. Outdoor seating. $$

★★CHART HOUSE
7255 McCormick Parkway, Scottsdale, 480-951-2250; www.chart-house.com
Seafood. Dinner. Bar. Children's menu. Outdoor seating. Reservations recommended. $$$

★CHOMPIE'S
9301 E. Shea Blvd., Scottsdale, 480-860-0475; www.chompies.com
Deli. Breakfast, lunch, dinner. Bar. Children's menu. Outdoor seating. $$

★★★DESEO
The Westin Kierland Resort & Spa, 6902 E. Greenway Parkway, Scottsdale, 480-624-1000, 800-354-5892; www.kierlandresort.com
The open display kitchen is the focal point of this restaurant located in Scottsdale's Westin Keirland Resort. Choose from a variety of mojitos and be sure to order one of the signature ceviches. Other dishes include foie gras empanadas and Muscovy duck breast with Asian pear and mango.
Latin American. Dinner. Closed Monday in summer. Bar. Reservations recommended. Outdoor seating. $$$

★★★DIGESTIF
7133 E. Stetson Dr., Scottsdale, 480-425-9463; www.digestifscottsdale.com
Chef Payton Curry's handmade pasta and housemade charcuterie from locally sourced and house-butchered meat, combined with other local ingredients, are a slam dunk. The inspired cocktail menu includes absinthe, which is served with a sizable production that includes a slotted spoon, sugar cube, and water fountain. The restaurant recently moved to cozier digs, but fans need not worry: the new location is just across the street.
Italian. Lunch, dinner. Bar. Reservations recommended. $$

★★DRIFT
4341 N. 75th St., Scottsdale, 480-949-8454; www.driftlounge.com
Polynesian. Lunch, dinner. Bar. Outdoor seating. $$

★★★EDDIE V'S PRIME SEAFOOD
20715 N. Pima Road, Scottsdale, 480-538-8468; www.eddiev.com
The relaxed lodge-themed interior of this restaurant features murals, black leather chairs, crisp white table linens and brick walls. Diners are entertained nightly by a band or a vocalist, but the main draw here is the food. The Maryland-style all-lump crab cakes are a must for an appetizer, and the bananas Foster makes a memorable end to a meal.
Seafood. Dinner. Bar. Reservations recommended. Outdoor seating. $$$

★★FARRELLI'S CINEMA SUPPER CLUB
14202 N. Scottsdale Road, Scottsdale, 480-905-7200; www.farrellis.com
Continental. Dinner. Bar. Children's menu. Reservations recommended. $$

★GRAZIE PIZZERIA & WINE BAR
6952 E. Main St., Scottsdale, 480-663-9797; www.grazie.us
Italian. Lunch, dinner. Bar. Reservations recommended. Outdoor seating. $$

★★★IL TERRAZZO

6000 E. Camelback Rd., The Phoenician, Scottsdale, 480-423-2530, 800-888-8234;
www.thephoenician.com

The Phoenician's American eatery, the Terrace, recently received a $1 million facelift and a new Italian accent. Aiming to capture the rich, indigenous flavors of Italy through classic, upscale cuisine that represents all regions of the country, chef de cuisine Victor Casanova, who previously served as sous chef at New York's Ocean Grill, offers such dishes as pan seared scallops with lemon risotto and black truffle and their signature Kobe burger with crispy onions, horseradish, pickles and black truffle ketchup. The real treats are master baker Ben Hershberger's artisan loaves. Olive walnut sourdough, rosemary and farmer's rye are all baked fresh daily and are so good, you won't care much about the rest of the meal.
Italian. Breakfast, lunch, dinner, Sunday brunch. Children's menu. Reservations recommended. Outdoor seating. $$$

★★JEWEL OF THE CROWN

7373 E. Scottsdale Mall, Scottsdale, 480-949-8000; www.jewelofthecrown.net
Indian. Lunch, dinner. Bar. Reservations recommended. Outdoor seating. $$

★★★L'ECOLE RESTAURANT

8100 E. Camelback Road, Scottsdale, 480-990-3773; www.chefs.edu/scottsdale
You can be sure that the food is top-of-the-line at this training ground for the Scottsdale Culinary Institute. The student-operated, full-service restaurant is set in a lovely dining room that is booked weeks in advance. The menu changes based on the student curriculum, but it always offers a nice variety. The outdoor patio has colorful awnings and views of a golf course.
French. Lunch, dinner. Closed Saturday-Monday. Reservations recommended. Outdoor seating. $$

★LOS SOMBREROS

2534 N. Scottsdale Road, Scottsdale, 480-994-1799; www.lossombreros.com
Mexican. Dinner. Closed Monday. Bar. Outdoor seating. $$

★★★MOSAIC

10600 E. Jomax Road, Scottsdale, 480-563-9600; www.mosaic-restaurant.com
Chef/owner Deborah Knight uses ingredients and cooking techniques from around the world to create her own brand of eclectic cuisine, which has included dishes such as Louisiana spiced prawns, Thai shrimp and coconut soup, and fennel and twelve mushroom risotto. Three types of five-course tasting menus are available to suit all tastes (Mosaic, Ocean and Vegetable). Local artwork punctuates the earth-toned dining room with color, and a beautiful, custom-made mosaic floor adds sparkle.
International. Dinner. Closed Sunday-Monday; mid-August-September. Bar. Reservations recommended. Outdoor seating. $$$

★★NORTH

15024 N. Scottsdale Road, Scottsdale, 480-948-2055;
www.foxrestaurantconcepts.com
Italian. Lunch, dinner. Bar. Reservations recommended. Outdoor seating. $$

★★★PALM COURT

Scottsdale Resort & Conference Center, 7700 E. McCormick Parkway, Scottsdale, 480-991-9000, 800-548-0293; www.thescottsdaleresort.com

Although this restaurant is located on the third floor of the main building at the Scottsdale Conference Resort, you'd never know it once you enter the elegant candlelit dinning room, where tuxedo-clad waiters serve lavish French fare. A classical guitarist provides lovely background music.

French. Breakfast, lunch, dinner, Sunday brunch. Bar. Reservations recommended. $$$

★★PEPIN

7363 Scottsdale Mall, Scottsdale, 480-990-9026; www.pepinrestaurant.com

Spanish, tapas. Lunch (Friday-Saturday), dinner. Closed Monday. Bar. $$$

★QUILTED BEAR

6316 N. Scottsdale Road, Scottsdale, 480-948-7760; www.quiltedbearaz.com

American. Breakfast, lunch, dinner. Bar. Children's menu. Outdoor seating. $$

★★RA SUSHI BAR & RESTAURANT

3815 N. Scottsdale Road, Scottsdale, 480-990-9256; www.rasushi.com

Japanese, sushi. Lunch, dinner. Bar. Outdoor seating. $$

★★★RANCHO PINOT

6208 N. Scottsdale Blvd., Scottsdale, 480-367-8030; www.ranchopinot.com

Situated within the Lincoln Village Shops, Rancho Pinot offers American cuisine using the best ingredients, many of them from local farms. You might find dishes such as handmade pasta with summer squash, scallions, mint and Parmesan cheese on the menu. Art and Southwestern décor adorn the walls, and an open kitchen allows guests to watch the chef at work.

American. Dinner. Bar. Reservations recommended. Outdoor seating. $$$

★REATA PASS STEAK HOUSE

27500 N. Alma School Parkway, Scottsdale, 480-585-7277; www.reatapass.com

American. Lunch, dinner. Closed Monday. Bar. Children's menu. Outdoor seating. Reservations recommended. $$

★★★REMINGTON'S

The Scottsdale Plaza Resort, 7200 N. Scottsdale Road, Scottsdale, 480-951-5101; www.scottsdaleplaza.com

Steak. Lunch (Monday-Friday), dinner. Bar. Outdoor seating. $$$

★★★ROARING FORK

4800 N. Scottsdale Road, Scottsdale, 480-947-0795; www.eddiev.com

Executive chef Bryan Hulihee turns out Western American cooking (inspired by founding chef Robert McGrath's cuisine) at this rustic yet refined dining room filled with exposed brick and blond wood. An open display kitchen is featured, with some booths situated across the aisle for great viewing. The adjacent J-Bar is a fun place to congregate for a drink.

American. Dinner. Bar. Children's menu. Outdoor seating. $$$

★★THE SALT CELLAR RESTAURANT

550 N. Hayden Road, Scottsdale, 480-947-1963; www.saltcellarrestaurant.com
Seafood. Dinner, late-night. Bar. Reservations recommended. $$

★★★SASSI

10455 E. Pinnacle Peak Parkway, Scottsdale, 480-502-9095; www.sassi.biz
Sassi, which resembles a Tuscan villa, serves up authentic Italian cuisine including handmade pastas, fresh seafood and local organic produce. The extensive wine list offers many delicious complements. Enjoy live music Friday and Saturday evenings.
Italian. Dinner. Closed Sunday-Monday. Bar. Outdoor seating. $$$

★★SUSHI ON SHEA

7000 E. Shea Blvd., Scottsdale, 480-483-7799; www.sushionshea.com
Japanese. Lunch, dinner. Bar. Reservations recommended. Outdoor seating. $$

★★★★TALAVERA

Four Seasons Resort Scottsdale at Troon North, 10600 E. Crescent Moon Drive, Scotts-dale, 480-515-5700; www.fourseasons.com
The surrounding Sonoran Desert is palpable in this new restaurant, due to rich red loveseats, sand-colored walls and cactus-green chairs, as well as a cozy glass-enclosed fireplace. Opt to dine under the stars on the patio—all the better to behold the craggy Pinnacle Peak and the desert expanse. Start your alfresco dinner with the lobster bisque with tempura squash. For entrées, this steakhouse offers raw choices (Wagyu beef tartare), Nebraska corn-fed prime cuts, and a list of fish and chicken meals. Go for regional dishes, such as Arizona grass-fed tenderloin with savory chorizo bread pudding. A great steal is the daily two-course tasting menu that changes weekly, which in the past has included standouts such as arugula dotted with pear and Gorgonzola, halibut with tomato and couscous, and warm chocolate cake with caramel ice cream.
Steak. Dinner. Children's menu. Outdoor seating. $$$$

★★★TRADER VIC'S

6850 E. Main St., Scottsdale, 480-248-2000, 866-882-4484; www.hotelvalleyho.com
This branch of the classic 1950s Polynesian-themed restaurant serves up potent punches in bamboo coolers (and perfect Mai Tais, which they purport to have invented in 1944) plus pu-pu platters of egg rolls and crab Rangoon. Entrées include wok-fried Szechuan prawns and ginger beef, or crispy duck with moo-shu pancakes. The décor takes its cue from the tiki bars of the past (plenty of rattan, a totem here or there) but is updated.
Asian Pacific Rim. Dinner. Outdoor seating. $$

★★VILLAGE TAVERN

8787 N. Scottsdale Road, Scottsdale, 480-951-6445; www.villagetavern.com
International. Lunch, dinner, Sunday brunch. Bar. Reservations recommended. Outdoor seating. $$

★★★WINDOWS ON THE GREEN
The Phoenician, 6000 E. Camelback Road, Scottsdale, 480-941-8200;
www.thephoenician.com

Windows on the Green, located near the golf shop at the Phoenician, offers great views from the large picture windows. After undergoing a renovation, it will reopen in the fall of 2009.

Southwestern. Dinner. Bar. Children's menu. Reservations recommended. Outdoor seating. $$$

★★★ZINC BISTRO
15034 N. Scottsdale Road, Scottsdale, 480-603-0922; www.zincbistroaz.com

A high-energy spot, Zinc Bistro is located in the Kierland Commons shopping center. The Parisian-style space, decorated with a tin ceiling and solid zinc bar, serves up crêpes, omelets, steaks, onion soup and more.

French bistro menu. Lunch, dinner. Bar. Outdoor seating. $$

★★ZUZU
6850 E. Main St., 480-248-2000, 866-882-4484; www.hotelvalleyho.com

American. Breakfast, lunch, dinner, Sunday brunch. Reservations recommended. Outdoor seating. $$

SPAS

★★★★THE CENTRE FOR WELL-BEING AT THE PHOENICIAN
The Phoenician, 6000 E. Camelback Road, Scottsdale, 480-941-8200, 800-888-8234;
www.centreforwellbeing.com

This spa is always thinking big, which means services here are on the cutting edge. Want to be more Zen in the real world? Sign up for a private meditation session, where you can learn visualization and other stress-reducing techniques. Have to work 100 hours just to take a week off? The Jin Shin Jyutsu utilizes a series of holding techniques to alleviate tension blocked in the body. Tend to overdo it on the golf course? The neuromuscular treatment offers spot relief for injuries. Of course, you'll want to go home looking as great as you feel, and for that there's no shortage of wraps, facials and scrubs. Even the state-of-the-art gym is inviting.

★★★THE SPA AT CAMELBACK INN
Camelback Inn, 5402 E. Lincoln Drive, Scottsdale, 480-948-1700, 800-582-2169;
www.camelbackspa.com

Following an $8 million facelift, the Spa at Camelback Inn has swapped its old Southwest-style décor for sophisticated chocolate brown woods, flagstone walls and expansive windows to create an inviting, placid retreat. If the gas fireplace in the main relaxation room doesn't soothe your spirit, head outside to the solarium and let the sound of rippling water from a flowing fountain do the trick. Relax in your own private casita, while you choose from the menu of massages, facials and body treatments—many of which draw from Native American techniques and indigenous ingredients.

★★★★SPA AT FOUR SEASONS RESORT SCOTTSDALE AT TROON NORTH

Four Seasons Resort Scottsdale at Troon North, 10600 E. Crescent Moon Drive, Scotts-dale, 480-513-5145, 888-207-9696; www.fourseasons.com/scottsdale

You're guaranteed to relax at this 12,000-square-foot spa located in the So-noran Desert. The resort's signature moonlight massage is the perfect way to end the day. You'll also find hot stone massage and facials that feature local, seasonal ingredients, including saguaro blossom, the state flower, as well as the more common green tea and honey. Half-day and full-day -packages are available. There is also a full-service salon and fitness center here.

★★★★WILLOW STREAM SPA

Fairmont Scottsdale, 7575 E. Princess Drive, Scottsdale, 480-585-2732, 800-908-9540; www.fairmont.com

The facilities at the Fairmont Scottsdale are top-notch—from championship golf courses to award-winning restaurants—and the spa is no exception. Many of the treatments make use of the Havasupai Waterfall (inspired by the oasis of waterfalls in the Grand Canyon) located on the spa's first floor. The Havasupai Body Oasis treatment combines warm eucalyptus and herbal baths with the healing power of the waterfalls. Other treatments also reflect local surroundings. The Desert Purification features a body mask of corn-meal, clay and oats. An Ayate cloth (made from the cactus plant) is then used to exfoliate skin. Or keep it simple with a facial or massage—and hit the beauty salon for a spa pedicure.

SEDONA

See also Flagstaff

Known worldwide for the beauty of the surrounding red rocks, Sedona has grown from a pioneer settlement into a favorite film location. This is a resort area with numerous outdoor activities, including hiking, fishing and biking, which can be enjoyed all year. Also an art and shopping destination, Sedona boasts Tlaquepaque, a 4½-acre area of gardens, courtyards, fountains, galler-ies, shops and restaurants.

WHAT TO SEE

CHAPEL OF THE HOLY CROSS

780 Chapel Road, Sedona, 928-282-4069; www.chapeloftheholycross.com/store

Chapel perched between two pinnacles of uniquely colored red sandstone. Monday-Friday, 9 a.m.-5 p.m., Sunday 10 a.m.-5 p.m.

OAK CREEK CANYON

Sedona, 800-288-7336; www.visitsedona.com

A beautiful drive along a spectacular fishing stream, north toward Flagstaff.

RED ROCK JEEP TOURS

270 N. Highway 89A, Sedona, 928-282-6826, 800-848-7728; www.redrockjeep.com

Two-hour back country trips. Daily. Other tours also available.

SLIDE ROCK STATE PARK

6871 N. Highway 89A, Sedona, 928-282-3034; www.www.azstateparks.com

A 43-acre day-use park on Oak Creek. Swimming, natural sandstone water-slide, fishing, hiking, picnicking.

Summer, daily 8 a.m.-7 p.m.; winter, daily 8 a.m.-5 p.m.; fall and spring, daily 8 a.m.-6 p.m.

TLAQUEPAQUE

336 Highway 179, Sedona, 928-282-4838; www.tlaq.com

A Spanish-style courtyard, it consists of 40 art galleries and stores. Daily 10 a.m.-5 p.m.

SPECIAL EVENTS
RED ROCK FANTASY OF LIGHTS

Los Abrigados Resort & Spa, 160 Portal Lane, Sedona, 928-282-1777, 800-521-3131; www.redrockfantasy.com

This annual event features kids' activities, concerts, carriage rides and special events.

Late November-mid-January.

SEDONA JAZZ ON THE ROCKS

2020 Contractors Road, Sedona, 928-282-1985; www.sedonajazz.com

This weekend of entertainment features local and national jazz acts, and it draws more than 7,500 visitors to scenic Sedona each year.

Late September.

WHERE TO STAY
★★★AMARA HOTEL, RESTAURANT & SPA

310 N. Highway 89A, Sedona, 928-282-4828, 866-455-6610; www.amararesort.com

Located along the banks of Oak Creek, this chic, contemporary resort features well-appointed rooms and tranquil surroundings with a heated saltwater pool and fire pit. Rooms have pillow-top mattresses, Italian linens and sleek work desks. The new 4,000-square-foot spa offers a wide variety of pampering treatments.

100 rooms. Spa. Restaurant, bar. $$

★BEST WESTERN ARROYO ROBLE HOTEL & CREEKSIDE VILLAS

400 N. Highway 89A, Sedona, 928-282-4001, 800-773-3662; www.bestwesternsedona.com

65 rooms. Complimentary breakfast. Tennis. Pool. Fitness center. $

★BEST WESTERN INN OF SEDONA

1200 W. Highway 89A, Sedona, 928-282-3072, 800-292-6344; www.innofsedona.com

110 rooms. Complimentary breakfast. Pets accepted. Pool. $

★★★EL PORTAL SEDONA

95 Portal Lane, Sedona, 928-203-9405, 800-313-0017; www.innsedona.com

This secluded hacienda-style inn is conveniently located in the heart of Sedona near more than 50 shops and restaurants. The 12 luxurious rooms feature Arts and Crafts furnishings, high-beam ceilings, stained glass, whirlpool tubs, cashmere blankets and Egyptian cotton sheets. On Wednesday nights there's a cookout in the hotel's courtyard.

12 rooms. Restaurant. Pets accepted. $$$$

★★★ENCHANTMENT RESORT

525 Boynton Canyon Road, Sedona, 928-282-2900, 800-826-4180;
www.enchantmentresort.com

Located within Boynton Canyon, this resort offers spectacular views of the rugged landscape from just about everywhere. This resort is full of Southwestern charm, from the Native American furnishings and decorative accents in the rooms to the regional kick of the sensational dining. Tennis, croquet, swimming and pitch-and-putt golf are some of the activities available for adults, while Camp Coyote entertains kids with arts and crafts and special programs. The Mii Amo Spa has 16 casitas used for treatments.

220 rooms. Restaurant, bar. Spa. Tennis. Business center. $$$

★HAMPTON INN

1800 W. Highway 89A, Sedona, 928-282-4700, 800-426-7866; www.hamptoninn.com

55 rooms. Complimentary breakfast. Pool. Fitness center. $

★★★HILTON SEDONA RESORT AND SPA

90 Ridge Trail Drive, Sedona, 928-284-4040, 877-273-3763; www.hiltonsedona.com

This Southwestern-style resort is located amid the Coconino National Forest. The spacious guest rooms and suites are well decorated and have gas fireplaces, wet bars, sleeper sofas and patios or balconies with views of the Red Rock vistas. There are three pools to choose from, a full-service fitness center, tennis and racquetball and the nearby Sedona Golf Resort, featuring a 71-par championship course. The spa is located steps from the hotel's main building. The property's Grille at ShadowRock features a Southwestern menu, and with its earth tones and soft lighting, is the perfect spot for a romantic dinner. During the day, the restaurant's outdoor patio is a great place to have a hearty breakfast or a light lunch.

219 rooms. Restaurant, bar. Fitness center. Spa. Pets accepted. $$

★★★L'AUBERGE DE SEDONA

301 L'Auberge Lane, Sedona, 928-282-1661, 800-905-5745; www.lauberge.com

This secluded resort offers views of the Red Rock Canyon and Magenta Cliffs. Rooms are housed in cozy cottages with fireplaces (the staff light a juniper-infused fire nightly) and an inviting lodge. Gourmet dining is an integral part of the experience. L'Auberge Restaurant is noted for its fine French food, special five-course tasting menu and award-winning wine list. The world-class spa will banish every last bit of tension.

53 rooms. Restaurant, bar. Pool. $$$

★★★LOS ABRIGADOS RESORT AND SPA

160 Portal Lane, Sedona, 928-282-1777, 800-521-3131; www.ilxresorts.com

This Spanish-style stucco and tile-roofed hotel is set among the buttes of Oak Creek Canyon. Rooms are spacious with kitchen facilities and pullout sofas. Activities such as Jeep tours, hiking, biking and helicopter rides are nearby.

182 rooms. Restaurant, bar. Pool. Tennis. Pets accepted. $$$

★★RADISSON POCO DIABLO RESORT

1752 S. Highway 179, Sedona, 928-282-7333, 800-395-7046; www.radisson.com/sedonaaz

137 rooms. Restaurant, bar. Spa. Pool. Golf. Tennis. Business center. $$

★SEDONA REÃL INN & SUITES

95 Arroyo Pinon Drive, Sedona, 928-282-1414, 877-299-6016; www.sedonareal.com

89 rooms. Complimentary breakfast. Pets accepted. Pool. $$

★SOUTHWEST INN AT SEDONA

3250 W. Highway 89A, Sedona, 928-282-3344, 800-483-7422; www.swinn.com

28 rooms. Complimentary breakfast. Pool. $$

WHERE TO EAT

★★COWBOY CLUB

241 N. Highway 89A, Sedona, 928-282-4200; www.cowboyclub.com

American. Lunch, dinner. Bar. Children's menu. $$$

★★★HEARTLINE CAFÉ

1610 W. Highway 89A, Sedona, 928-282-0785; www.heartlinecafe.com

This intimate, cozy restaurant is located in a cottage surrounded by an English garden and showcases unique daily specials. The menu is creative, with a variety of culinary influences and vegetarian options. Dishes include smoked mozzarella ravioli and pistachio-crusted chicken with pomegranate sauce.

International. Lunch, dinner. Bar. Outdoor seating. $$$

★★★L'AUBERGE

L'Auberge de Sedona, 301 L'Auberge, Sedona, 928-282-1661; www.lauberge.com

This hotel restaurant features several separate dining rooms decorated with imported fabrics and fine china. A covered porch with large windows offers views of the creek, and an outdoor patio area is a relaxing choice in good weather. Dine on roasted duck breast with sweet potato puree, apple-fennel jam and cider reduction; or porcini crusted lamb with whipped potatoes, bacon, Swiss chad and roasted tomato jus.

American. Breakfast, lunch, dinner, Sunday brunch. Bar. Reservations recommended. Outdoor seating. $$$

★★★RENÉ AT TLAQUEPAQUE

336 Highway 179, Sedona, 928-282-9225; www.rene-sedona.com

Located in the Tlaquepaque shopping area, this local favorite has been a mainstay in Sedona since 1977. The menu is varied, offering selections such as tenderloin of venison, grilled ahi tuna salad, sweet potato ravioli and the signature dish, Colorado rack of lamb. Dine in one of two separate dining areas, where tables are topped with green and white tablecloths and flower-filled vases. Friday and Saturday entertainment includes the sounds of guitar,

piano, saxophone and Native American flutes.
French. Lunch, dinner. Bar. Children's menu. Reservations -recommended.
Outdoor seating. $$$

★★★SHUGRUE'S HILLSIDE GRILL
671 Highway 179, Sedona, 928-282-5300; www.shugrues.com
Great views of the Red Rocks can be seen from the large windows of this
modernized, Old World restaurant. Flame-broiled shrimp scampi, whiskey-
barbecued duck and herb-grilled rib-eye are among the specialty dishes.
Light jazz entertainment is offered nightly, with a pianist and guitarist per-
forming on alternate nights. A nice outdoor seating area offers guests a pic-
turesque dining experience.
American. Lunch, dinner. Bar. Children's menu. Reservations recommend-
ed. Outdoor seating. $$

SELIGMAN
See also Flagstaff, Williams
Arizona's historic Route 66 begins here, and the tiny town (population about
450) has more Route 66 kitsch than you can imagine. Stop by on your way to
the Grand Canyon (about two hours north of here) for a taste of Americana.

WHAT TO SEE
GRAND CANYON CAVERNS
Old Route 66, Peach Springs, 928-422-3223; www.gccaverns.com
This natural limestone cavern is 210 feet underground and is the largest dry
cavern in the U.S. Take an elevator down (the temperature is around 55 degrees, so bring a sweater). Guided 50-minute tours are offered and a 48-room
motel is located at the entrance along with a restaurant.
Summer, daily 9 a.m.-5 p.m.; winter, daily 10 a.m.-5 p.m.

★★★★★ ARIZONA

TEMPE
See also Chandler, Litchfield Park, Mesa, Phoenix, Scottsdale
Founded as a trading post by the father of former Senator Carl Hayden, this
city is now the site of Arizona State University, the state's oldest institution
of higher learning.

WHAT TO SEE
ARIZONA HISTORICAL SOCIETY MUSEUM
Papago Park, 1300 N. College Ave., Tempe, 480-929-0292;
www.arizonahistoricalsociety.org
Wander through this regional museum to learn more about 20th-century
life in the Salt River Valley. The 28,000 items in its collection include about
14,000 pieces in a country store and 2,800 stage props and sets from the
37-year run of the Wallace and Ladmo Show on KPHO Television. Another
exhibit focuses on the many ways World War II transformed Arizona.
Admission: adults $3, seniors $2, children $2, children under 12 free.
Tuesday-Saturday 10 a.m.-4 p.m., Sunday noon-4 p.m.

ARIZONA MILLS

5000 S. Arizona Mills Circle, Tempe, 480-491-7300; www.arizonamills.com

More than 150 stores offer tempting markdowns. Shopping diversions include a large food court, restaurants, a 24-screen cinema and an IMAX theater. Daily.

ARIZONA STATE UNIVERSITY

University Drive, and Mill Avenue, Tempe, 480-965-9011; www.asu.edu

Established in 1885, the Tempe campus has more than 51,000 students. Divided into 13 colleges. Included on the -700-acre main campus are several museums and collections: meteorites; anthropology and geology exhibits; the Charles Trumbull Hayden Library; the Walter Cronkite School of Journalism; and the Daniel Noble Science and Engineering Library. Also on campus is the Grady Gammage Memorial Auditorium, the last major work designed by Frank Lloyd Wright, and the Nelson Fine Arts Center, which features exhibits of American paintings and sculpture.

BIG SURF

1500 N. McClintock, Tempe, 480-947-2477; www.golfland.com

Check out America's original water park, a 20-acre desert oasis with a Polynesian theme. Ride some big ones in the wave pool, whoosh down 16 slippery water slides and more.

June-mid-August, daily; late May and mid-late August, weekends.

NIELS PETERSEN HOUSE MUSEUM

1414 W. Southern Ave., Tempe, 480-350-5151; www.tempe.gov/petersenhouse

Built in 1892 and remodeled in the 1930s. Restoration retains characteristics of both the Victorian era and the 1930s.

Half-hour, docent-guided tours available. Tuesday-Thursday, Saturday 10 a.m.-2 p.m.

PHOENIX ROCK GYM

1353 E. University, Tempe, 480-921-8322; www.phoenixrockgym.com

Scale 30-foot walls at Arizona's largest climbing gym. Beginners receive brief video training and a hands-on orientation. Gear is available to rent. Daily.

TEMPE BICYCLE PROGRAM

Tempe, 480-350-2775; www.tempe.gov/tim

This bicycle-friendly city has more than 165 miles of bikeways and most major destinations provide bicycle racks (including some particularly eye-catching ones designed by local artists). Several bicycle shops offer rentals for as little as $15 per day and give free bikeway maps.

TEMPE IMPROVISATION COMEDY THEATRE

930 E. University Drive, Tempe, 480-921-9877; www.symfonee.com/improv/tempe

Check out some of the country's best stand-up comedians. An optional dinner precedes the 8 p.m. shows. Thursday-Sunday.

TEMPE TOWN LAKE

620 N. Mill Ave., Tempe, 480-350-8625; www.tempe.gov/lake

Tempe Town Lake on the Rio Salado, near the Mill Avenue shopping and dining district, is a 224-acre, two-mile waterway that offers rowboats, pedal boats, kayaks and canoes for rent, along with chartered cruises. The nicely renovated 1931 Tempe Beach Park has shaded picnic groves, sandy play areas, a grassy amphitheater and the popular Splash Playground water park (late April-late September). Take the tour, or simply enjoy the shoreline.

SPECIAL EVENTS

ANAHEIM ANGELS SPRING TRAINING

Tempe Diablo Stadium, 2200 W. Alameda Drive, Tempe, 602-438-9300;
www.cactus-league.com

Anaheim Angels baseball spring training, exhibition games.
Early March-early April.

TEMPE FESTIVAL OF THE ARTS

Tempe, 480-355-6069; www.tempefestivalofthearts.com

When a three-day event attracts nearly a quarter-million people, you know you need to get there. This street party is a blast—Mill Avenue in downtown Tempe closes to traffic. Buy handmade goods from more than 500 artisans, chow down on tasty food from around the world, quench your thirst with ice-cold beer and rock to live bands. Activities for kids include arts and crafts. It's so fun the party gets crankin' twice a year.
Late March and early December.

TOSTITOS FIESTA BOWL

University of Phoenix Stadium, Cardinals Drive, Glendale, 480-350-0911;
www.tostitosfiestabowl.com

College football game.
Early January.

TOSTITOS FIESTA BOWL BLOCK PARTY

Tempe Beach Park and Mill Avenue, Tempe, 480-350-0911;
www.tostitosfiestabowl.com

Includes games, rides, entertainment, pep rally, fireworks, food.
December 31.

WHERE TO STAY

★★★THE BUTTES, A MARRIOTT RESORT

2000 Westcourt Way, Tempe, 602-225-9000, 888-867-7492; www.marriott.com/phxtm

This secluded resort sits atop a bluff overlooking Phoenix and the surrounding mountains. Take a dip in the pool or enjoy one of the four hot tubs carved out of the mountainside, relax in the spa, play some sand volleyball or horseshoes, or get in a game of tennis on the resort's eight courts. The Top of the Rock restaurant is a great spot for dining.
353 rooms. Restaurant, bar. Spa. $$

★COUNTRY INN & SUITES HOTEL TEMPE
1660 W. Elliot Road, Tempe, 480-345-8585, 888-201-1746; www.countryinns.com
138 rooms. Complimentary breakfast. Pets accepted. $

★★EMBASSY SUITES
4400 S. Rural Road, Tempe, 480-897-7444, 800-362-2779;
www.embassysuitestempe.com
224 rooms. Complimentary breakfast. -Restaurant, bar. Pool. $

★★FIESTA RESORT CONFERENCE CENTER
2100 S. Priest Drive, Tempe, 480-967-1441, 800-501-7590; www.fiestainnresort.com
270 rooms. Restaurant, bar. Fitness center. $

★HOLIDAY INN EXPRESS HOTEL & SUITES
1520 W. Baseline Road, Tempe, 480-831-9800, 800-972-3574;
www.hiexpress.com/tempeaz
128 rooms. Complimentary breakfast. Pets accepted. Pool. $

★★SHERATON PHOENIX AIRPORT HOTEL TEMPE
1600 S. 52nd St., Tempe, 480-967-6600, 800-325-3535; www.sheraton.com
210 rooms. Restaurant, bar. Pets accepted. Pool. Business center. Fitness center. $

★★TEMPE MISSION PALMS HOTEL
60 E. Fifth St., Tempe, 480-894-1400, 800-547-8705; www.missionpalms.com
303 rooms. Restaurant, bar. Fitness center. Pool. Pets accepted. $$

WHERE TO EAT
★BLUE NILE ETHIOPIAN CUISINE
933 E. University Drive, Tempe, 480-377-1113; www.bluenilecafe.net
Ethiopian. Lunch, dinner. Closed Monday. Reservations recommended. $

★★BYBLOS
3332 S. Mill Ave., Tempe, 480-894-1945; www.byblostempe.com
Mediterranean. Lunch, dinner. Closed Monday. Bar. $$

★★HOUSE OF TRICKS
114 E. Seventh St., Tempe, 480-968-1114; www.houseoftricks.com
American. Lunch (Monday-Saturday), dinner. Closed Sunday. Bar. Children's menu. Outdoor seating. $$

★MACAYO DEPOT CANTINA
300 S. Ash Ave., Tempe, 480-966-6677; www.macayo.com
Mexican. Dinner. Bar. Children's menu. Outdoor seating. $

★★MARCELLO'S PASTA GRILL
1701 E. Warner Road, Tempe, 480-831-0800; www.marcellospastagrill.com
Italian. Lunch, dinner. Closed Sunday. Bar. Children's menu. Outdoor seating. $$

GUNFIGHTS AND SALOONS

Begin exploring the town of Tombstone on Toughnut Street. At the corner of Third Street, explore the gorgeous Cochise County Courthouse, now a museum and state historic park. Built in 1882, it's a beautiful example of Victorian Neoclassical architecture. Check out the town gallows in the courtyard and browse the bookshop. To the east one block, the Rose Tree Inn Museum at Fourth and Toughnut streets occupies a 1880s home. Inside its courtyard is a century-old rose tree that blooms every April and covers an 8,000-square-foot space. At Fifth and Toughnut streets, stop in to Nellie Cashman's, the oldest restaurant in town (homemade pies are the specialty here).

Follow Third Street north one block to Allen Street, essentially the main drag of historic Tombstone. Stop at the Historama and then next door, see life-size figures in the O.K. Corral, the alleged site of the legendary gunfight between the Earp and Clanton brothers and Doc Holliday.

On the corner of Allen and Fifth streets, the Crystal Palace Saloon has been restored to its 1879 glory, looking every bit the lusty watering hole and gambling den of legend. On the block of Allen between Fifth and Sixth streets, the Prickly Pear Museum is chock-full of military history; on Allen at Sixth, find the famous old Bird Cage Theater Museum. The Pioneer Home Museum, between Eighth and Ninth streets, continues telling the rowdy-days story. From Fifth and Allen, walk north a half-block to the Tombstone Epitaph Museum to see a 1880s printing press and newsroom equipment and buy a copy of the 1881 Epitaph report of the O.K. Corral shoot-out.

★★MICHAEL MONTI'S LA CASA VIEJA

100 S. Mill Ave., Tempe, 480-967-7594; www.montis.com
American. Lunch, dinner. Bar. Children's menu. Outdoor seating. $$

★SIAMESE CAT

5034 S. Price Road, Tempe, 480-820-0406; www.thesiamesecat.com
Thai. Lunch (Monday-Friday), dinner. Reservations recommended. $$

TOMBSTONE

See also Sierra Vista

Shortly after Ed Schieffelin discovered silver, Tombstone became a rough-and-tumble town with saloons and gunfights. Tombstone's most famous battle was that of the O.K. Corral, between the Earps and the Clantons in 1881. Later, water rose in the mines and could not be pumped out. Fires and other catastrophes occurred, but Tombstone was "the town too tough to die." Now a health and winter resort, it is also a living museum of Arizona frontier life. In 1962, the town was designated a National Historic Landmark.

WHAT TO SEE

ARIZONA-SONORA DESERT MUSEUM

2021 N. Kinney Road, Tucson, 520-883-2702; www.desertmuseum.org

Live desert creatures: mountain lions, beavers, bighorn sheep, birds, tarantulas, prairie dogs, snakes, otters and many others. Nature trails through labeled desert botanical gardens. Underground earth sciences center with limestone caves; geological, mineral and mining exhibits. Orientation room provides information on natural history of deserts.

Admission: adults $9.50-13, children $2.25-4.25, children under 6 free.

June-August, Monday-Friday 7:30 a.m.-10 p.m., Saturday 7:30 a.m.-10 p.m., Sunday 7:30 a.m.-5 p.m.; March-May, September, Daily 7:30 a.m.-5 p.m.; October-February, Daily 8:30 a.m.-5 p.m.

BIRD CAGE THEATRE

517 E. Allen St., Tombstone, 520-457-3421, 800-457-3423; www.tombstoneaz.net
Formerly a frontier cabaret (1880s), this landmark was known in its heyday as "the wildest and wickedest nightspot between Basin Street and the Barbary Coast." The upstairs "cages" where feathered girls plied their trade, inspired the song "Only a bird in a gilded cage." Original fixtures and furnishings.
Daily 8 a.m.-6 p.m.

BOOTHILL GRAVEYARD

Highway 80, Tombstone, 520-457-3300
About 250 marked graves, many of famous characters, with some unusual epitaphs.

CRYSTAL PALACE SALOON

420 Allen St., Tombstone, 520-457-3611; www.crystalpalacesaloon.com
This restored saloon serves comfort food and features live music and dancing on Friday, Saturday and Sunday nights.
Daily.

O.K. CORRAL

308 Allen St. East, Tombstone, 520-457-3456; www.ok-corral.com
Restored stagecoach office and buildings surrounding the gunfight site; life-size figures; Fly's Photography Gallery (adjacent) has early photos.
Daily 9 a.m.-5 p.m.

ST. PAUL'S EPISCOPAL CHURCH

19 N. Third St., Tombstone, 520-255-3435; www.1882.org
St. Paul's, built in 1882, is the oldest Protestant church still in use in the state.
Services 10:30 a.m. every Sunday.

TOMBSTONE COURTHOUSE STATE HISTORIC PARK

223 Toughnut St., Tombstone, 520-457-3311; www.azstateparks.com
This Victorian building houses exhibits that recall Tombstone in the turbulent 1880s. Tombstone and Cochise County history.
Daily 8 a.m.-5 p.m.

TOMBSTONE EPITAPH MUSEUM

9 S. Fifth St., Tombstone, 520-457-2211; www.tombstone-epitaph.com
The oldest continuously published newspaper in Arizona, founded in 1880, is now a monthly journal of Western history. There is also collection of printing equipment.
Daily 9:30 a.m.-5 p.m.

TOMBSTONE HISTORAMA

308 Allen St. East, Tombstone, 520-457-3456; www.ok-corral.com
A film narrated by Vincent Price tells the story of Tombstone.
Daily 9:30 a.m.-4:30 p.m.; half-hourly showings.

TOMBSTONE WESTERN HERITAGE MUSEUM

Sixth St., and Fremont, Tombstone, 520-457-3800; www.thetombstonemuseum.com
This new museum has a great collection of Wyatt Earp memorabilia along
with lots of Old West artifacts and cowboy photos.
Admission: adults $5, children $3, children under 12 free, family $13.
Thursday-Tuesday 9 a.m.-6 p.m.

SPECIAL EVENTS
HELLDORADO

Tombstone, 520-457-3291; www.tombstonevigilantes.com
Three days of Old West reenactments of Tombstone events of the 1880s.
Third full weekend in October.

WILD WEST DAYS AND RENDEZVOUS OF GUNFIGHTERS

O.K. Corral, 308 Allen St. East, Tombstone, 520-457-9465; www.ok-corral.com
This annual event showcases different gunfight reenactment groups from
throughout the United States. Activities include costume contests and a parade.
Labor Day weekend.

WYATT EARP DAYS

O.K. Corral, 108 W. Allen St. East, Tombstone, 520-457-3434;
www.tombstonevigilantes.com
This annual festival is held in honor of the famous lawman. The festivities
include a barbecue, gunfights, street entertainment, dances, a chili cook-off
and more.
Memorial Day weekend.

WHERE TO EAT
★LONGHORN

501 E. Allen St., Tombstone, 520-457-3107; www.bignosekate.com
American. Breakfast, lunch, dinner. $

★NELLIE CASHMAN'S

117 S. Fifth St., Tombstone, 520-457-2212
American. Breakfast, lunch, dinner. Outdoor seating. $$

TUCSON

See also Chandler, Phoenix
Tucson offers a rare combination of delightful Western living, colorful desert
and mountain scenery and cosmopolitan culture. It is one of several U.S.
cities that developed under four flags. The Spanish standard flew first over
the Presidio of Tucson, built to withstand Apache attacks in 1776. Later, Tuc-
son flew the flags of Mexico, the Confederate States and finally, the United

States. Today, Tucson is a resort area, an educational and copper center, a cotton and cattle market, headquarters for the Coronado National Forest and a place of business for several large industries. The city has many shops, restaurants, resorts and attractions.

WHAT TO SEE

ARIZONA HISTORICAL SOCIETY FORT LOWELL MUSEUM

2900 N. Craycroft Road, Tucson, 520-885-3832; www.arizonahistoricalsociety.org
This reconstruction of a commanding officer's quarters has exhibits and period furniture.
Admission: adults $3, seniors $2, children $2, children under 12 free.
Wednesday-Saturday 10 a.m.-4 p.m.

ARIZONA HISTORICAL SOCIETY FREMONT HOUSE MUSEUM

151 S. Granada Ave., Tucson, 520-622-0956; www.arizonahistoricalsociety.org
This 19th-century adobe house, once occupied by John C. Fremont's daughter, Elizabeth, when he was territorial governor (1878-1881), has been restored. Special programs all year, including slide shows on Arizona history (Saturday) and walking tours of historic sites (November-March, Saturday; registration in advance).
Admission: adults $3, seniors $2, children $2, children under 12 free.
Wednesday-Saturday 10 a.m.-4 p.m.

ARIZONA HISTORICAL SOCIETY MUSEUM, LIBRARY, AND ARCHIVES

949 E. Second St., Tucson, 520-628-5774; www.arizonahistoricalsociety.org
Exhibits depicting state history from the Spanish colonial period to present; Arizona mining hall; photography gallery. Admission: adults $5, seniors $4, children $4, children under 12 free.
Research library Monday-Friday 10 a.m.-3 p.m., Saturday 10 a.m.-1 p.m.

BIOSPHERE 2

32540 Biosphere Road, Oracle, 520-838-6200; www.bio2.com
An ambitious attempt to learn more about our planet's ecosystems began in September 1991 with the first in a series of missions undertaken inside this 3½-acre, glass-enclosed, self-sustaining model of Earth. (The crew of researchers rely entirely on the air, water and food generated and recycled within the structure.) It contains more than 3,500 species of plants and animals in multiple ecosystems, including a tropical rain forest with an 85-foot-high mountain. Visitors are permitted within the biospherian living areas of the enclosure. Walking tours include multimedia introduction to Biosphere 2.
Daily 9 a.m.-4 p.m.

CATALINA STATE PARK

11570 N. Oracle Road, Tucson, 520-628-5798; www.azstateparks.com
A 5,500-acre desert park with a vast array of plants and wildlife; bird area (nearly 170 species). Nature and horseback riding trails.

CENTER FOR CREATIVE PHOTOGRAPHY

University of Arizona, 1030 N. Olive Road, Tucson, 520-621-7968;
www.creativephotography.org
This collection of art by more than 2,000 photographers includes the archives of Ansel Adams and Richard Avedon.
Gallery: Monday-Friday 9 a.m.-5 p.m., Saturday-Sunday 1-4 p.m.

CORONADO NATIONAL FOREST

300 W. Congress St., Tucson, 520-388-8300; www.fs.fed.us/r3/coronado
Mount Lemmon Recreation Area, part of this two-million-acre forest, offers -fishing, bird-watching, hiking, horseback riding, picnicking, skiing and camping. Madera Canyon offers recreation facilities and a lodge. Pea Blanca Lake and Recreation Area and the Chiricahua Wilderness area in the southeast corner of the state are part of the 12 areas that make up the forest. The Santa Catalina Ranger District, located in Tucson (520-749-8700), has its headquarters at Sabino Canyon, 12 miles northeast on Sabino Canyon Road; a ¼-mile nature trail begins at the headquarters, as does a shuttle ride almost four miles into Sabino Canyon.

FLANDRAU SCIENCE CENTER & PLANETARIUM

University of Arizona, 1601 E. University Blvd., Tucson, 520-621-7827;
www.flandrau.org
The center features interactive, hands-on science exhibits.
Monday-Wednesday 9 a.m.-5 p.m.; Thursday-Saturday 9 a.m.-5 p.m., 7-9 p.m.; Sunday 1-5 p.m.; planetarium shows -(limited hours). Nightly telescope viewing: Mid-August-mid-May, Wednesday-Saturday -6:40-10 p.m.; mid-May-mid-August, Wednesday-Saturday 7:30-10 p.m.

INTERNATIONAL WILDLIFE MUSEUM

4800 W. Gates Pass Road, Tucson, 520-629-0100; www.thewildlifemuseum.org
Includes hundreds of wildlife exhibits from around the world; hands-on, interactive computer displays; videos; café.
Monday-Friday 9 a.m.-5 p.m., Saturday-Sunday 9 a.m.-6 p.m.

MOUNT LEMMON SKI VALLEY

10300 Ski Run Road, Mount Lemmon, 520-576-1400; www.fs.fed.us/r3/coronado
Double chairlift, two tows; patrol, school, rentals; snack bar, restaurant. Twenty-one runs, longest run one mile; vertical drop 900 feet.
Late December-mid-April, daily. Chairlift operates the rest of the year.

OLD TOWN ARTISANS

201 N. Court Ave., Tucson, 520-623-6024, 800-782-8072; www.oldtownartisans.com
Restored adobe buildings (circa 1850s) in the historic El Presidio neighborhood serve as shops for handcrafted Southwestern and Latin American art.
September-May, Monday-Saturday 9:30 a.m.-5:30 p.m., Sunday 11 a.m.-5 p.m.; June-August, Monday-Saturday 10 a.m.-4 p.m., Sunday 11 a.m.-4 p.m.

SAGUARO NATIONAL PARK

The saguaro cactus that gives this park its name may grow as high as 50 feet and live to be 200 years old. The fluted columns with sharp, tough needles sometimes branch into fantastic shapes. During the rainy season, large saguaros can absorb enough water to sustain themselves during the dry season.

The saguaro's waxy, white blossoms (Arizona's state flower), which open at night and close the following afternoon, bloom in May and June, and the red fruit ripens in July. The Tohono O'Odham people eat this fruit fresh and used it to make jellies, jams and wines.

Wildlife in the park is abundant. Gila woodpeckers and gilded flickers drill nest holes in the saguaro trunks. Once vacated, these holes become home to many other species of birds, including the tiny elf owl. Peccaries (pig-like mammals), coyotes, mule deer and other animals are often seen. Yuccas, agaves, prickly pears, mesquite, paloverde trees and many other desert plants grow here.

The Rincon Mountain District offers nature trails, guided nature walks (winter), eight-mile self-guided drive, mountain hiking, bridle trails, picnicking (no water) and backcountry camping. Stop by the visitor center to check out the museum and see an orientation film.

The Tucson Mountain District offers nature trails, a six-mile self-guided drive, and hiking and bridle trails. Five picnic areas (no water). Visitor center; exhibits, slide program daily.

Information: Rincon Mountain District, 17 miles east of Tucson via Broadway and Old Spanish Trail; Tucson Mountain District, 16 miles west of Tucson via Speedway and Gates Pass Road, 520-733-5153; www.nps.gov/sagu

PIMA AIR & SPACE MUSEUM

6000 E. Valencia Road, Tucson, 520-574-0462; www.pimaair.org

Aviation history exhibits with an outstanding collection of more than 250 aircraft, both military and civilian. Walking tours.

Admission: adults $14-16, children $12-13, children under 7 free. Daily 9 a.m.-5 p.m.

REID PARK ZOO

1030 S. Randolph Way, Tucson, 520-881-4753; www.tucsonzoo.org

Picnicking; zoo; rose garden; outdoor performance center.

Admission: adults $6, seniors $4, $2, children under 2 free. Daily 9 a.m.-4 p.m.

TITAN MISSILE MUSEUM

1580 W. Duval Mine Road, Sahuarita, 520-625-7736; www.titanmissilemuseum.org

A deactivated Titan II missile is on display, as is a UH1F helicopter and other exhibits. A one-hour guided tour begins with a briefing and includes a visit down into the missile silo. The silo may also be viewed from a glass observation area located at the museum level.

Daily 9 a.m.-5 p.m.

TOHONO CHUL PARK

7366 N. Paseo del Norte, Tucson, 520-742-6455; www.tohonochulpark.org

A 37-acre preserve with more than 400 species of arid climate plants; nature trails; demonstration garden; geology wall; ethnobotanical garden. Many varieties of wild birds visit the park. Exhibits, galleries, tearoom and gift shops

in restored adobe house. Walking tours.
Admission: adults $7, seniors $5, children $2, children under 5 free. Daily
8 a.m.-5 p.m.

TUCSON BOTANICAL GARDENS

2150 N. Alvernon Way, Tucson, 520-326-9686; www.tucsonbotanical.org
Gardens include Mediterranean and landscaping plants; native wildflowers;
tropical greenhouse; xeriscape/solar demonstration garden. Tours, special
events. Picnic area.
Daily 8:30 a.m.-4:30 p.m.

TUCSON MOUNTAIN PARK

Ajo Way & Kinney Road, Tucson, 520-883-4200; www.co.pima.az.us
Includes more than 18,000 acres of saguaro cactus and mountain scenery.
Picnic facilities.

TUCSON MUSEUM OF ART

140 N. Main Ave., Tucson, 520-624-2333; www.tucsonarts.com
Housed in six renovated buildings within the boundaries of El Presidio Historic District (circa 1800). Pre-Columbian, Spanish Colonial and Western
artifacts; decorative arts and paintings; art of the Americas; contemporary art
and crafts; changing exhibits. Mexican heritage museum; historic presidio
room; 6,000-volume art resource library; art school.
Tuesday-Saturday 10 a.m.-4 p.m., Sunday noon-4 p.m. Free admission first
Sunday of the month.

UNIVERSITY OF ARIZONA

Campbell Avenue and Sixth Street, Tucson, 520-621-5130; www.arizona.edu
Established in 1885; 35,000 students. The 343-acre campus is beautifully
landscaped and has handsome buildings. The visitor center, located at University Boulevard and Cherry Avenue, has campus maps and information on
attractions and activities.
Tours Monday-Saturday.

SPECIAL EVENTS
ARIZONA OPERA

3501 Mountain Ave., Tucson, 520-293-4336; www.azopera.com
Five operas are produced each season.
October-March, Friday-Sunday.

ARIZONA THEATRE COMPANY

The Temple of Music and Art, 330 S. Scott Ave., Tucson, 520-622-2823;
www.aztheatreco.org
The State Theatre of Arizona performs classic and contemporary works.
Evening performances run Tuesday through Sunday; and matinees run
Wednesday, Saturday and Sunday.
September-May.

BASEBALL

Tucson Electric Park, 2500 E. Ajo Way, Tucson, 520-434-1000, 866-672-1343;
www.cactus-league.com

Tucson Electric Park is the location for Chicago White Sox and Arizona Diamondbacks baseball spring training and exhibition games from late February to late March. It is also the home of the minor league Tucson Sidewinders from April to September.

GEM & MINERAL SHOW

Tucson Convention Center, 260 S. Church Ave., Tucson,520-322-5773, 800-638-8350;
www.tgms.org

Displays of minerals and jewelry and a Smithsonian Institution collection. Mid-February.

TUCSON MEET YOURSELF FESTIVAL

El Presidio Park, Tucson, 520-792-4806; www.tucsonmeetyourself.org

Commemorates Tucson's cultural and historic heritage with a torchlight pageant, American Indian dances, children's parade, Mexican fiesta, frontier encampment and other events. October.

TUCSON SYMPHONY ORCHESTRA

Tucson Symphony Center, 2175 N. Sixth Ave., Tucson,520-882-8585;
www.tucsonsymphony.org

The symphony's eight-month season includes classic ensembles, performances by guest artists and special events such as BeatleMania! September-May.

WHERE TO STAY

★★★ARIZONA INN

2200 E. Elm St., Tucson, 520-325-1541, 800-933-1093; www.arizonainn.com

This inn was built in 1930 by Arizona Congresswoman Isabella Greenway, and is still owned by her family today. Guests who stay here are treated to quiet comfort with spacious, individually decorated rooms and 15 acres of landscaped lawns and gardens.

95 rooms. Restaurant, bar. Pool. Tennis. $$

★BEST WESTERN CONTINENTAL INN

8425 N. Cracker Barrel Road, Marana, 520-579-1099, 800-780-7234;
www.bestwestern.com

65 rooms. Complimentary breakfast. Pool. Spa. $

★★BEST WESTERN ROYAL SUN INN AND SUITES

1015 N. Stone Ave., Tucson, 866-293-9454; www.bwroyalsun.com

79 rooms. Complimentary breakfast. Restaurant, bar. Pool. $

★COUNTRY INN & SUITES BY CARLSON

7411 N. Oracle Road, Tucson, 520-575-9255, 800-456-4000; www.countryinns.com

156 rooms. Complimentary breakfast. Pets accepted. Pool. $

★★COURTYARD TUCSON AIRPORT
2505 E. Executive Drive, Tucson, 520-573-0000, 800-321-2211; www.courtyard.com
149 rooms. Restaurant, bar. Pool. $

★★DOUBLETREE HOTEL
445 S. Alvernon Way, Tucson, 520-881-4200, 800-222-8733;
www.doubletreehotels.com
295 rooms. Restaurans, bar. Pets accepted. Pool. Tennis. Fitness center. $

★★EMBASSY SUITES TUCSON-WILLIAMS CENTER
5335 E. Broadway Blvd., Tucson, 520-745-2700, 800-362-2779;
www.embassysuites.com
142 rooms. Complimentary breakfast. Pool. Fitness center. $

★HAMPTON INN
6971 S. Tucson Blvd., Tucson, 520-889-5789, 800-426-7866; www.hamptoninn.com
126 rooms. Complimentary breakfast. Pool. Fitness center. $

★★★HILTON TUCSON EL CONQUISTADOR GOLF AND TENNIS RESORT
10000 N. Oracle Road, Tucson, 520-544-5000, 800-325-7832;
www.hiltonelconquistador.com
This resort and country club has extensive golf and tennis facilities. The resort offers 45 holes of golf on three championship courses. There are 31 lighted tennis courts. Each of the newly remodeled rooms has a patio and balcony. The spa offers a full range of treatments.
428 rooms. Restaurant, bar. Spa. Pets accepted. Pool. Golf. Tennis. Business center. $$

★★★THE LODGE AT VENTANA CANYON
6200 N. Clubhouse Lane, Tucson, 520-577-1400, 800-828-5701;
www.thelodgeatventanacanyon.com
Located in the foothills of the Santa Catalina Mountains on a 600-acre desert -preserve, the Lodge is a peaceful getaway for tennis players, golfers and those in pursuit of nothing more than a day at the pool. Two 18-hole Tom Fazio-designed golf courses wind their way through the landscape of wild brush and giant saguaros, while the resort's tennis pro can help you master your serve on one of 12 hard courts. Rooms have Mission-style furniture, fully-stocked kitchens and old-fashioned freestanding bathtubs.
50 rooms. Restaurant, bar. Pets accepted. Pool. Spa. Fitness center. Golf. Tennis. $$$$

★★★LOEWS VENTANA CANYON RESORT
7000 N. Resort Drive, Tucson, 520-299-2020; www.loewshotels.com
Set on 93 acres in the Sonoran Desert, this resort recently completed a multi-million dollar room renovation. The new décor offers modern comfort with a Southwestern twist. The two award-winning Tom Fazio-designed 18-hole golf courses challenge duffers. The Spa and Tennis Center offers a full range of treatments as well as a fitness center. Five restaurants and lounges give a

taste of every kind of cuisine in a variety of settings, from poolside cafés to refined dining rooms. The Ventana Room delivers artfully presented, elegant cuisine. This intimate and romantic restaurant has floor-to-ceiling windows, which make it the perfect place to dine at sunset.

398 rooms. Pets accepted. Restaurant, bar. Fitness room, spa. Pool. Golf. Tennis. Business center. $$$

★★★MARRIOTT TUCSON UNIVERSITY PARK
880 E. Second St., Tucson, 520-792-4100; www.marriotttucson.com
This hotel is a good choice for those visiting the University of Arizona's campus. It's located right at the front gate and features rooms that are specifically designed for business travelers. New features include down duvet-topped beds, flat-screen TVs and an updated fitness center.

250 rooms. Restaurant, bar. Pool. Business center. Fitness center. $

★★★OMNI TUCSON NATIONAL GOLF RESORT AND SPA
2727 W. Club Drive, Tucson, 520-297-2271, 888-444-6664; www.omnihotels.com
Located in the foothills of the Santa Catalina Mountains, the Omni Tucson National Golf Resort and Spa has been the home to countless PGA Tours. But there's more than just golf here. There are two pools, four tennis courts, sand volleyball, lots of biking trails and the spa, which boasts 13,000 pleasure-pursuing square feet. Sign up for the terzetto massage, where two therapists perform choreographed massage. The comfortable rooms have a Southwest décor and feature views of the course or mountains. Some rooms also have full kitchens, although most people leave the cooking up to the resort's talented chefs.

129 rooms. Restaurant, bar. Spa. Pets accepted. Pool. Golf. Tennis. Business center. $

★★SHERATON TUCSON HOTEL AND SUITES
5151 E. Grant Road, Tucson, 520-323-6262, 800-325-3535; www.starwoodhotels.com
216 rooms. Complimentary breakfast. Restaurant, bar. Pets accepted. Pool. $

★★★THE WESTIN LA PALOMA RESORT AND SPA
3800 E. Sunrise Drive, Tucson, 520-742-6000, 800-937-8461;
www.westin.com/lapaloma
The large rooms here have warm, golden color schemes and feature patios or balconies and bathrooms with granite countertops and dual sinks. Golfers are drawn to the 27-hole Jack Nicklaus-designed course adjoining the resort. You'll also find tennis, pools—one with a 177-foot waterslide—and the Elizabeth Arden Red Door Spa onsite, as well as five restaurants.

487 rooms. Restaurant, bar. Spa. Pets accepted. Golf. Tennis. Business center. $$

★★★WESTWARD LOOK RESORT
245 E. Ina Road, Tucson, 520-297-1151, 800-722-2500; www.westwardlook.com
The newly renovated Westward Look Resort combines top-notch facilities, gourmet dining and sumptuous spa treatments in a naturally beautiful setting. Set on 80 acres filled with giant cacti and blooming wildflowers, this resort is home to a variety of birds and wildlife. Activities include horseback

riding, onsite tennis, and nearby golf.

241 rooms. Restaurant, bar. Spa. Pets accepted. Tennis. $$$

★WINDMILL SUITES AT ST., PHILLIPS PLAZA

4250 N. Campbell Ave., Tucson, 520-577-0007, 800-547-4747; www.windmillinns.com

122 rooms. Complimentary breakfast. Pets accepted. Pool. $

ALSO RECOMMENDED

TANQUE VERDE GUEST RANCH

14301 E. Speedway Blvd., Tucson, 520-296-6275, 800-234-3833; www.tanqueverderanch.com

74 rooms. Complimentary breakfast. Restaurant. Pool. Tennis. $$

WHITE STALLION RANCH

9251 W. Twin Peaks Road, Tucson, 520-297-0252, 888-977-2624; www.wsranch.com

41 rooms. Closed June-August. Complimentary breakfast. Restaurant, bar. Pool. Tennis. Fitness center. $$$

WHERE TO EAT

★★CAFÉ POCA COSA

110 E. Pennington St., Tucson, 520-622-6400; www.cafepocacosatucson.com

Mexican. Lunch, dinner. Closed Sunday-Monday. Bar. Reservations recommended. Outdoor seating. $$

★★CHAD'S STEAKHOUSE & SALOON

3001 N. Swan Road, Tucson, 520-881-1802; www.chadssteakhouse.com

Steak. Lunch, dinner. Bar. Children's menu. Reservations recommended. $$

★DELECTABLES

533 N. Fourth Ave., Tucson, 520-884-9289; www.delectables.com

French. Lunch, dinner. Bar. Children's menu. Reservations recommended. Outdoor seating. $$

★★EL PARADOR TROPICAL GARDEN RESTAURANT

2744 E. Broadway Blvd., Tucson, 520-881-2744, 800-964-5908; www.elparadortucson.com

Mexican. Lunch, dinner, Sunday brunch. Bar. Children's menu. Reservations recommended. Outdoor seating. $$

★★★GOLD

Westward Look Resort, 245 E. Ina Road, Tucson, 520-297-1151; www.westwardlook.com

Set at the base of the Catalina Mountains in north central Tucson at the Westward Look Resort, Gold offers a contemporary menu by chef James Wallace. You'll find options such as pinenut crusted chicken with ziti pasta, pancetta, tomato and olives; roasted butternut squash; and pancetta wrapped scallops with pasta. Wednesday night features a three-course dinner with live jazz music to enjoy while you dine.

American. Breakfast, lunch, dinner. Children's menu. Reservations recommended. Outdoor seating. $$$

★★★THE GRILL AT HACIENDA DEL SOL

5601 N. Hacienda del Sol Road, Tucson, 520-529-3500; www.haciendadelsol.com
Rustic Spanish colonial architecture, fine pottery and Mexican art adorn this beautifully restored Tucson landmark. The New American cuisine is complemented by a spectacular wine list and excellent service. The creative menu, which includes dishes like Muscovy duck breast with black quinoa pilaf, agave-glazed fennel and caramelized apple jus, makes this one of Tucson's favorite dining destinations. Jazz musicians perform every Tuesday.
American. Dinner, Sunday brunch. Bar. Children's menu. Reservations recommended. Outdoor seating. $$$

★★★JANOS RESTAURANT

The Westin Paloma Resort & Spa, 3770 E. Sunrise Drive, Tucson, 520-615-6100; www.janos.com
The legendary Janos Wilder presides over this French-inspired Southwestern masterpiece located inside the Westin La Paloma Resort & Spa. The restaurant features both tasting and à la carte menus, which are constantly changing and are inspired by influences from around the world. The emphasis is on ingredients from the region, utilizing an established network of local farmers. The romantic setting features original artwork and views of the valley.
Southwestern. Dinner. Closed Sunday; and Monday June-August. Bar. Reservations recommended. Outdoor seating. $$$

★★★KINGFISHER

2564 E. Grant, Tucson, 520-323-7739; www.kingfisherbarandgrill.com
The popular spot serves up dishes like pan-seared Atlantic salmon, spinach tagliatelle and barbecued chicken pasta. There's also a full oyster bar with 15 varieties of oysters. On Mondays and Saturdays, the sounds of jazz and blues can be heard until midnight.
American. Lunch, dinner, late-night. Bar. Reservations recommended. $$

★★LA FUENTE

1749 N. Oracle Road, Tucson, 520-623-8659; www.lafuenterestaurant.com
Mexican. Lunch, dinner, Sunday brunch. Bar. Children's menu. Reservations recommended. $$

★★LA PARRILLA SUIZA

2720 N. Oracle Road, Tucson, 520-624-4300; www.laparrillasuiza.com
Mexican. Lunch, dinner. Bar. Children's menu. Reservations recommended. $

★LA PLACITA CAFÉ

2950 N. Swan Road, Tucson, 520-881-1150; laplacitatucson.com
Mexican. Lunch, dinner. Reservations recommended. Outdoor seating. $$

★★★MCMAHON'S PRIME STEAKHOUSE

2959 N. Swan Road, Tucson, 520-327-7463; www.metrorestaurants.com
This local favorite is a perfect spot for a romantic evening or that special occasion. Original local artwork adorns the walls and a pianist performs nightly. Entrées include filet mignon with Portobello mushrooms, garlic and aged Romano cheese, and New York sirloin with onions, mushrooms, garlic

and cracked black pepper.
Steak. Lunch, dinner. Bar. Children's menu. Reservations recommended.
Outdoor seating. $$$

★MI NIDITO
1813 S. Fourth Ave., Tucson, 520-622-5081; www.minidito.net
Mexican. Lunch, dinner. Closed Monday-Tuesday. $$

★PINNACLE PEAK
6541 E. Tanque Verde Road, Tucson, 520-296-0911; www.traildusttown.com
Steak. Dinner. Bar. Children's menu. Outdoor seating. $$

★SERI MELAKA
6133 E. Broadway, Tucson, 520-747-7811; www.serimelaka.com
Pacific-Rim, Malaysian. Lunch, dinner. Reservations recommended. $$

★TOHONO CHUL TEA ROOM
7366 N. Paseo del Norte, Tucson, 520-797-1222; www.tohonochulpark.org
American. Breakfast, lunch. Children's menu. Outdoor seating. $

SPAS
★★★★THE SPA AT OMNI TUCSON NATIONAL
2727 W. Club Drive, Tucson, 520-575-7559; www.tucsonnational.com
The Spa at Omni Tucson National has a tranquil and picturesque location
in the foothills of the Santa Catalina Mountains. Whether you have half an
hour or an entire day, this spa has something to offer. In 25 minutes, the
tension reliever massage works its magic where you are most tense, while
the business facial cleanses, tones, exfoliates and hydrates in just under 30
minutes. Other facials include aromatherapy, deep-cleansing, antiaging and
deluxe hydration. Body masks smooth rough skin with a variety of ingredients, including seaweed, desert rose clay, rich mud from the Dead Sea, shea
butter and aspara, a plant that grows by the beach and is recognized for its
calming properties.

WICKENBURG
See also Phoenix
Early Hispanic families who established ranches in the area and traded with
the local American Indians first settled Wickenburg. The town was relatively
unpopulated until a Prussian named Henry Wickenburg picked up a rock to
throw at a stubborn burro and stumbled onto the richest gold find in Arizona,
the Vulture Mine. His discovery began a $30 million boom and the birth of
a town. Today, Wickenburg is the oldest town north of Tucson and is well
known for its area dude ranches.

WHAT TO SEE
DESERT CABALLEROS WESTERN MUSEUM
21 N. Frontier St., Wickenburg, 928-624-2272; www.westernmuseum.org
This museum houses a Western art gallery, diorama room, street scene (circa
1915), period rooms, mineral display and Native American exhibit. Admis-

sion: adults $7.50, seniors $6, children under 17 free, school groups free. Monday-Saturday 10 a.m.-5 p.m.,Sunday noon-4 p.m.

FRONTIER STREET
Wickenburg, 928-684-5479; www.wickenburgchamber.com
This historic street is preserved in early 1900s style. Train depot (houses the Chamber of Commerce), brick Hassayampa building (former hotel) and many other historic buildings may be toured.

GARCIA LITTLE RED SCHOOLHOUSE
245 N. Tegner St., Wickenburg, 928-684-7473; www.wco.org
This pioneer schoolhouse is on the National Register of Historic Places.

THE JAIL TREE
Tegner Street and Wickenburg Way, Wickenburg, 928-684-5479;
www.wickenburgchamber.com
This tree was used from 1863-1890 (until the first jail was built) to chain rowdy prisoners. Friends and relatives visited the prisoners and brought picnic lunches.

OLD 761 SANTA FE STEAM LOCOMOTIVE
Apache and Tegner, Wickenburg, 928-684-5479; www.wickenburgchamber.com
This engine and tender ran the track between Chicago and the West.

SPECIAL EVENTS
BLUEGRASS MUSIC FESTIVAL
Highway 60, Everett Bowman Rodeo Grounds, Wickenburg,928-684-5479;
www.wickenburgchamber.com
The Four-Corner States Championship features contests including mandolin, violin, guitar and banjo.
Second full weekend in November.

GOLD RUSH DAYS
Wickenburg, 928-684-5479; www.wickenburgchamber.com
Bonanza days are revived during this large festival, with a chance to pan for gold and keep all you find. Rodeo, contests, food, parade.
Second full weekend in February.

SEPTIEMBRE FIESTA
Wickenburg Community Center, 160 N. Valentine St., Wickenburg,928-684-5479;
www.wickenburgchamber.com
This celebration of Hispanic heritage featuring exhibits, arts and crafts, food, dancers and mariachi bands.
First Saturday in September.

WHERE TO STAY
★★BEST WESTERN RANCHO GRANDE
293 E. Wickenburg Way, Wickenburg, 928-684-5445, 800-854-7235;
www.bwranchogrande.com

78 rooms. Pets accepted. Pool. Spa. Tennis. $

ALSO RECOMMENDED
RANCHO DE LOS CABALLEROS
1551 S. Vulture Mine Road, Wickenburg, 928-684-5484, 800-684-5030; www.sunc.com
79 rooms. Closed mid-May-mid-October. Restaurant, bar. Pool. Golf. Spa.
Tennis. $$$$

WILLCOX
See also Tucson
Visit historic downtown Willcox to see the state's oldest operating store amid
antique shops, restaurants, boutiques and museums. This little town will give
you a flavor of the Old West.

WHAT TO SEE
AMERIND FOUNDATION
2100 N. Amerind Road, Dragoon, 520-586-3666; www.amerind.org
Amerind (short for American Indian) Museum contains one of the finest collections of archaeological and ethnological artifacts in the country. Paintings
by Anglo and American Indian artists are on display in the gallery. Picnic
area, museum shop.
Tuesday-Sunday 10 a.m.-4 p.m.

COCHISE STRONGHOLD
Coronada National Forest, 1500 N. Circle I Road, Willcox, 520-364-3468;
www.cochisestronghold.com
This rugged canyon once sheltered Chiricahua Apache. Unique rock formations provided protection and vantage points. Camping, picnicking, hifking,
horseback and history trails.
Daily.

FORT BOWIE NATIONAL HISTORIC SITE
3203 S. Old Fort Bowie Road, Bowie, 520-847-2500; www.nps.gov/fobo
On the way to the ruins, you'll see a stage station, cemetery and Apache Spring.
Visitor center daily 8 a.m.-4:30 p.m.

REX ALLEN ARIZONA COWBOY MUSEUM AND COWBOY
HALL OF FAME
150 N. Railroad Ave., Willcox, 520-384-4583, 877-234-4111; www.rexallenmuseum.org
This museum is dedicated to Willcox native Rex Allen, the "last of the Silver
Screen Cowboys." It details his life from ranch living in Willcox to his radio,
TV and movie days. It also has special exhibits on pioneer settlers and ranch-
ers. The Cowboy Hall of Fame pays tribute to real cattle industry heroes.
Daily 10 a.m.-4 p.m.

SPECIAL EVENTS
REX ALLEN DAYS
Rex Allen Arizona Cowboy Museum and Cowboy Hall of Fame,150 N. Railroad Ave., Willcox, 520-384-2272; www.willcoxchamber.com
PRCA Rodeo, concert by Rex Allen Jr., parade, country fair, Western dances, softball tournament.
First weekend in October.

WINGS OVER WILLCOX/SANDHILL CRANE CELEBRATION
1500 N. Circle I Road, Willcox, 520-384-2272, 800-200-2272; www.wingsoverwillcox.com
Tours of bird-watching areas, trade shows, seminars, workshops.
Third weekend in January.

WHERE TO STAY
★★BEST WESTERN PLAZA INN
1100 W. Rex Allen Drive, Willcox, 520-384-3556, 800-262-2649; www.bestwestern.com
91 rooms. Complimentary breakfast. Restaurant, bar. Pets accepted. Pool. $

WILLIAMS
See also Flagstaff, Sedona
This town lies at the foot of Bill Williams Mountain (named for an early trapper and guide) and is the principal entrance to the Grand Canyon. It is a resort town in the midst of Kaibab National Forest, which has its headquarters here. There are seven small fishing lakes in the surrounding area.

WHAT TO SEE
GRAND CANYON RAILWAY
233 N. Grand Canyon Blvd., Williams, 800-843-8724; www.thetrain.com
First operated by the Santa Fe Railroad in 1901 as an alternative to the stage-coach, this restored line carries passengers northward aboard authentically refurbished steam locomotives and coaches. Full-day round trips include a 3½-hour layover at the canyon.

SPECIAL EVENTS
BILL WILLIAMS RENDEZVOUS DAYS
Buckskinner's Park, 204 W. Railroad Ave., Williams, 928-635-1418; www.williamschamber.com
Black powder shoot, carnival, street dances, pioneer arts and crafts.
Memorial Day weekend.

LABOR DAY RODEO
200 W. Railroad, Williams, 928-635-1418; www.williamschamber.com
Professional rodeo and Western celebration.
Labor Day weekend.

WHERE TO STAY
★BEST WESTERN INN OF WILLIAMS
2600 W. Route 66, Williams, 928-635-4400, 800-635-4445; www.bestwestern.com

80 rooms. Complimentary breakfast. Pool. Pets accepted. $

★★GRAND CANYON RAILWAY HOTEL
235 N. Grand Canyon Blvd., Williams, 928-635-4010, 800-843-8724; www.thetrain.com
287 rooms. Restaurant, bar. Pool. $

★★HOLIDAY INN WILLIAMS
950 N. Grand Canyon Blvd., Williams, 928-635-4114, 877-863-4780;
www.holiday-inn.com
120 rooms. Restaurant, bar. Pets accepted. Pool. $

WHERE TO EAT
★ROD'S STEAK HOUSE
301 E. Route 66, Williams, 928-635-2671; www.rods-steakhouse.com
Steak. Lunch, dinner. Closed Sunday. Bar. Children's menu. Reservations
recommended. $$

WINDOW ROCK
See also Flagstaff
This is the headquarters of the Navajo Nation. The 88-member tribal coun-
cil, which is democratically elected, meets in an octagonal council building;
tribal officials conduct tribal business from Window Rock. Behind the town
is a natural bridge that looks like a window. It is in the midst of a colorful
group of sandstone formations called "the Window Rock."

WHAT TO SEE
CANYON DE CHELLY NATIONAL MONUMENT
Highway 191, Window Rock, 928-674-5500; www.nps.gov/cach
The smooth red sandstone walls of the canyon extend straight up as much
as 1,000 feet from the nearly flat sand bottom. When William of Normandy
defeated the English at the Battle of Hastings in 1066, the Pueblo had already
built apartment houses in these walls. Many ruins are still here. The Navajo
came long after the original tenants had abandoned these structures. In 1864,
Kit Carson's men drove nearly all the Navajo out of the area, marching them
on foot 300 miles to the Bosque Redondo in eastern New Mexico. Since
1868, Navajo have returned to farming, cultivating the orchards and graz-
ing their sheep in the canyon. In 1931, Canyon de Chelly and its tributar-
ies, Canyon del Muerto and Monument Canyon, were designated a national
monument. There are more than 60 major ruins—some dating from circa
A.D. 300—in these canyons. White House, Antelope House and Mummy
Cave are among the most picturesque. Most ruins are inaccessible but can
be seen from either the canyon bottom or from the road along the top of the
precipitous walls. Two spectacular, 16-mile rim drives can be made by car in
any season. Lookout points—sometimes a short distance from the road—are
clearly marked. The only self-guided trail (2½ miles round-trip) leads to the
canyon floor and White House ruin from White House Overlook. Other hikes
can be made only with a National Park Service permit and an authorized
Navajo guide. Only four-wheel drive vehicles are allowed in the canyons—
and each vehicle must be accompanied by an authorized Navajo guide and

requires a National Park Service permit obtainable from a ranger at the visitor center, which also has an archaeological museum and restrooms.
Daily.

NAVAJO NATION MUSEUM
Highway 64 and Loup Road, Window Rock, 928-871-7941;
www.navajonationmuseum.org
This museum was established in 1961 to preserve Navajo history, art, culture and natural history; permanent and temporary exhibits. Literature and Navajo information available.
Monday-Tuesday, Thursday-Friday 8 a.m.-5 p.m., Wednesday 8 a.m.-8 p.m., Saturday 9 a.m.-5 p.m.; closed on tribal and other holidays.

NAVAJO NATION ZOOLOGICAL AND BOTANICAL PARK
Tse Bonito Tribal Park, Window Rock, 928-871-6573; www.explorenavajo.com
Features a representative collection of animals and plants of historical or cultural importance to the Navajo people.
Daily 8 a.m.-5 p.m.

ST. MICHAEL'S
Highway 264, Window Rock, 928-871-4171; discovernavajo.com
This Catholic mission, established in 1898, has done much for the education and health of the tribe. The original mission building now serves as a museum depicting the history of the area.
Memorial Day-Labor Day, Monday-Friday 9 a.m.-5 p.m.

SPECIAL EVENTS
NAVAJO NATION FAIR
Navajo Nation Fairgrounds, Highway 264, Window Rock, 928-871-6478;
www.navajonationfair.com
Dances, ceremonials, rodeo, arts and crafts, educational and commercial exhibits, food, traditional events.
Week after Labor Day.

POWWOW AND PRCA RODEO
Navajo Nations Fairgrounds, Highway 264, Window Rock, 928-871-6478;
www.navajonationfair.com
Rodeo, carnival, fireworks, and entertainment.
July 4.

WINSLOW
See also Flagstaff
A railroad town, Winslow is also a trade center and convenient stopping point in the midst of a colorful and intriguing area; a miniature painted desert lies to the northeast. The Apache-Sitgreaves National Forests, with the world's largest stand of ponderosa pine, lie about 25 miles to the south.

WHAT TO SEE
HOMOLOVI RUINS STATE PARK
HCR 63, Winslow, 928-289-4106; www.pr.state.az.us/parks/parkhtml/homolovi.html
This park contains six major Anasazi ruins dating from A.D. 1250 to 1450. The Arizona State Museum conducts occasional excavations in June and July. The park also has trails, a visitor center and interpretive programs. Daily.

METEOR CRATER
Winslow, 20 miles west on I-40, then five miles south on Meteor Crater Road, 928-289-5898, 800-289-5898; www.meteorcrater.com
The crater is one mile from rim to rim and 560 feet deep. The world's best-preserved meteorite crater was used as a training site for astronauts. Museum, lecture; Astronaut Wall of Fame; telescope on highest point of the crater's rim offers excellent view of surrounding area.
Memorial Day-Labor Day, 7 a.m.-7 p.m.; rest of year, 8 a.m.-5 p.m.

OLD TRAILS MUSEUM
212 N. Kinsley Ave., Winslow, 928-289-5861; www.oldtrailsmuseum.org
Operated by the Navajo County Historical Society, there are exhibits of local history, Native American artifacts and early Americana here.
March-October, Tuesday-Saturday 1-5 p.m.; November-February, Tuesday, Thursday-Saturday.

YUMA
See also Chandler
The Yuma Crossing, where the Colorado River narrows between the Yuma Territorial Prison and Fort Yuma (one of Arizona's oldest military posts), was made a historic landmark in recognition of its long service as a river crossing. If the scenery looks familiar, it may be because movie producers have used the dunes and desert for location shots.

WHAT TO SEE
ARIZONA HISTORICAL SOCIETY SANGUINETTI HOUSE
240 Madison Ave., Yuma, 928-782-1841; www.arizonahistoricalsociety.org
This former home of E. F. Sanguinetti, pioneer merchant, is now a division of the Arizona Historical Society, where you can see artifacts from the Arizona Territory, including documents, photographs, furniture and clothing. Gardens and exotic birds surround museum. Historical library open by appointment.
Tuesday-Saturday 10 a.m.-4 p.m.

FORT YUMA-QUECHAN MUSEUM
350 Picacho Road, Yuma, 928-572-0661
Part of one of the oldest military posts (1855) associated with the Arizona Territory. Museum houses tribal relics of southwestern Colorado River Yuman groups.
Daily 8 a.m.-noon, 1-5 p.m.

IMPERIAL NATIONAL WILDLIFE REFUGE

100 Red Cloud Mine Road, Yuma, 928-783-3371; www.fws.gov/southwest
Bird-watching; photography. Fishing, hunting, hiking.

YUMA RIVER TOURS

1920 Arizona Ave., Yuma, 928-783-4400; www.yumarivertours.com
Narrated historical tours on the Colorado River; half- and full-day trips. Sunset dinner cruises. Also jeep tours to sand dunes.
Monday-Friday.

YUMA TERRITORIAL PRISON STATE HISTORIC PARK

1 Prison Hill Road, Yuma, 928-783-4771; www.azstateparks.com
The park includes the remains of an 1876 prison and its original cellblocks. Southwest artifacts and prison relics.
Daily 8 a.m.-5 p.m.

SPECIAL EVENTS
MIDNIGHT AT THE OASIS FESTIVAL

The Ray Kroc Complex, Desert Sun Stadium, 3500 S. Ave. A, Yuma;
www.caballeros.org
This annual event features classic cars and concerts.
First full weekend in March.

YUMA COUNTY FAIR

2520 E. 32nd St., Yuma, 928-726-4420; www.yumafair.com
Features carnival rides, live entertainment, food booths and a variety of exhibits.
Late March-early April.

WHERE TO STAY
★★QUALITY INN

711 E. 32nd St., Yuma, 928-726-4721, 800-222-2244; www.qualityinn.com
80 rooms. Complimentary breakfast. Restaurant, bar. Pets accepted. Pool. $

★★SHILO INN

1550 S. Castle Dome Ave., Yuma, 928-782-9511, 800-222-2244; www.shiloinns.com
134 rooms. Complimentary breakfast. Restaurant, bar. Pets accepted. Pool. $

WHERE TO EAT
★THE CROSSING

2690 S. Fourth Ave., Yuma, 928-726-5551; www.crossingcatering.com
American menu. Lunch, dinner. Children's menu. Outdoor seating. $$

★HUNTER STEAKHOUSE

2355 S. Fourth Ave., Yuma, 928-782-3637
Steak menu. Lunch, dinner. Bar. Children's menu. $$

COLORADO

COLORADO'S TERRAIN IS DIVERSE AND SPECTACULARLY BEAUTIFUL—AND ATTRACTS THOSE who want to venture outdoors. Throughout the state there are deep gorges, rainbow-colored canyons, grassy plains, breathtaking alpine mountains and beautiful landmass variations carved by ancient glaciers and erosion. Colorado is the highest state in the Union, with an average elevation of 6,800 feet. It has 53 peaks above 14,000 feet.

Whether you're visiting one of Colorado's booming big cities—Denver, Boulder or Colorado Springs—or heading for the glitz of Vail or Aspen, Colorado beckons people to spend more time outdoors. Hit the slopes, take a river rafting trip or drive up to the famous Pikes Peak. In between, take a trip back in time by visiting historic homes, railroad depots and ghost towns.

Colorado has a rich history. When gold was discovered near present-day Denver in 1858, an avalanche of settlers poured into the state. Then, when silver was discovered soon afterward, a new flood came. Mining camps—usually crude tent cities on the rugged slopes of the Rockies—contributed to Colorado's colorful, robust history. Some of these mines still operate, but most of the early mining camps are ghost towns today

ALAMOSA
See also Monte Vista
The settlers who came to the center of the vast San Luis Valley were pleased to find a protected area on the Rio Grande shaded by cottonwood trees, so they named their new home Alamosa, Spanish for "cottonwood." The little town quickly became a rail, agricultural, mining and educational center.

WHAT TO SEE
COLE PARK

425 Fourth St., Alamosa, 719-589-3681
See Old Denver and Rio Grande Western narrow-gauge trains on display. Chamber of Commerce located in old train station. Tennis, bicycle trails, picnicking, playgrounds.

CUMBRES & TOLTEC SCENIC RAILROAD

500 S. Terrace Ave., Antonito, 719-376-5483, 888-286-2737; www.cumbrestoltec.com
Take a round-trip excursion to Osier on a 1880s narrow-gauge steam railroad. The route passes through backwoods country and mountain scenery, including Phantom Canyon and the Toltec Gorge. Warm clothing is advised due to sudden weather changes.
Memorial Day-mid-October, daily. Also trips to Chama, New Mexico, via the New Mexico Express with van return. Reservations recommended.

FORT GARLAND MUSEUM

29477 Highway 159, Fort Garland, 719-379-3512; www.coloradohistory.org
Kit Carson held his last command at this historic Army post (1858-1883), which contains restored officers' quarters and a collection of Hispanic folk art.

April-October, daily 9 a.m.-5 p.m.; November-March, Monday and
Thursday-Sunday 10 a.m.-4 p.m.

SPECIAL EVENTS
EARLY IRON FESTIVAL
Cole Park, 425 Fourth St., Alamosa, 719-589-9170, 888-589-9170;
www.earlyironclub.com
This annual auto show attracts lovers of antique cars and hot rods.
Labor Day weekend.

SUNSHINE FESTIVAL
Cole Park, 425 Fifth St., Alamosa, 719-589-3681
Arts, crafts, food booths, bands, horse rides, contests, a pancake breakfast
and a parade are all a part of this summer celebration.
First full weekend in June.

WHERE TO STAY
★★BEST WESTERN ALAMOSA INN
2005 Main St., Alamosa, 719-589-2567, 800-459-5123; www.bestwestern.com
53 rooms. Complimentary breakfast. Restaurant, bar. Fitness center. Pool.
Pets accepted. $

★★INN OF THE RIO GRANDE
333 Santa Fe Ave., Alamosa, 719-589-5833, 800-669-1658; www.innoftherio.com
125 rooms. Restaurant, bar. Spa. Fitness center. Pets accepted. $

WHERE TO EAT
★TRUE GRITS STEAKHOUSE
100 Santa Fe Ave., Alamosa, 719-589-9954
Steak. Lunch, dinner. Bar. Children's menu. $$

ASPEN
See also Snowmass Village
The first settlers came here in 1878 in pursuit of silver and named the town
for the abundance of aspen trees in the area. They enjoyed prosperity until the
silver market crashed in 1893. By World War I, most of the local mining op-
erations had gone bust. Aspen was practically a ghost town for decades until
1946, when developer Walter Paepcke founded the Aspen Skiing Company
with the vision of a cerebral, arts-oriented community. In 1950, Aspen hosted
the Alpine Skiing World Championship, and the rest is history. Today, Aspen
is home to some of the most expensive real estate in the world and draws in
the rich and famous with immaculate ski slopes, spectacular shopping and
fine dining.

WHAT TO SEE
ASHCROFT GHOST TOWN
Castle Creek Road, Aspen, 970-925-3721; www.aspenhistorysociety.com
This partially restored ghost town and mining camp features 1880s build-
ings and a hotel. Guided tours mid-June-early September, daily 11 a.m., 1

p.m. and 3 p.m.
Self-guided tours available daily.

ASPEN HIGHLANDS

76 Boomerang Road, Aspen, 970-925-1220, 800-525-6200;
www.aspensnowmass.com/highlands

Three quads, two triple chairlifts; patrol, school, rentals, snowmaking; five restaurants, bar. One hundred twenty-five runs; longest run 3½ miles; vertical drop 3,635 feet. Snowboarding. Shuttle bus service to and from Aspen. Half-day rates.
Mid-December-early April, daily.

ASPEN HISTORICAL SOCIETY

620 W. Bleeker St., Aspen, 970-925-3721, 800-925-3721;
www.aspenhistorysociety.com

Learn all about Aspen's history with a stop at this organization's headquarters. Early June-September and mid-December-mid-April: Tuesday-Friday; rest of year: by appointment.

ASPEN MOUNTAIN

601 E. Dean, Aspen, 970-925-1220, 800-525-6200; www.aspensnowmass.com

Three quad, four double chairlifts; gondola; patrol, school, snowmaking; restaurants, bar. Seventy-six runs; longest run 3 miles; vertical drop 3,267 feet. Mid-November-mid-April, daily. Shuttle bus service to Buttermilk, Aspen Highlands and Snowmass.

BLAZING ADVENTURES

407 E. Hyman Ave., Aspen, 970-923-4544, 800-282-7238; www.blazingadventures.com

Half-day, full-day and overnight river rafting trips on the Arkansas, Roaring Fork, Colorado and Gunnison rivers. Trips range from scenic floats for beginners to exciting runs for experienced rafters. White-water rafting. May-October, reservations required. Transportation to site. Bicycle, jeep and hiking tours are also available.

BUTTERMILK MOUNTAIN

806 W. Hallam, Aspen, 970-925-9000, 888-525-6200; www.aspensnowmass.com

Two quad, three double chairlifts, surface lift; patrol, school, rentals, snowmaking; cafeteria, restaurants, bar, nursery. Forty-four runs; longest run three miles; vertical drop 2,030 feet. Snowboarding.
December-mid-April: daily 9 a.m.-3:30 p.m. Shuttle bus service from Ajax and Snowmass.

INDEPENDENCE PASS

Highway 82 from Highway 24, Aspen, 970-963-4959;

Highway 82 through Independence Pass is a spectacular visual treat, not to mention an adrenaline rush—if you're afraid of heights, opt for another route. The winding road between Highway 24 and Aspen is among the nation's highest, reaching 12,095 feet at its rocky summit—and offers beautiful vistas of Colorado's majestic forests and snow-covered peaks at every turn.

Stop at the top for the views and a short trail hike.
The pass is closed between November and May.

SPECIAL EVENTS
ASPEN MUSIC FESTIVAL
2 Music School Road, Aspen, 970-925-3254, 800-778-5542;
www.aspenmusicfestival.com
Symphonies, chamber music concerts, opera and jazz. June-August.

ASPEN THEATER IN THE PARK
110 E. Hallam St., Aspen, 970-925-9313; www.theatreaspen.org
Performances nightly and afternoons. June-August.

WINTERSKÖL CARNIVAL
Aspen, 800-670-0792; www.aspenchamber.org
Also known as the Festival of Snow, this annual four-day event features a
parade, a torchlight ski procession, contests and more.
Mid-January.

WHERE TO STAY
★★★ASPEN MEADOWS
845 Meadows Road, Aspen, 970-925-4240, 800-452-4240;
www.aspenmeadowsresort.dolce.com
This 40-acre mountain retreat with its famous Bauhaus design is made of
up six buildings and has hosted leaders from around the world since 1949
thanks to its state-of-the art conference facilities. The spacious guest suites
include study areas, wet bars and floor-to-ceiling windows with views of the
mountains or Roaring Fork River.
98 rooms. Restaurant. Pets accepted. Fitness Center. Pool. Tennis. Business
center. $$$

★ASPEN MOUNTAIN LODGE
311 W. Main St., Aspen, 970-925-7650, 800-362-7736; www.aspenmountainlodge.com
38 rooms. Closed late April-late May. Complimentary breakfast. Pets ac-
cepted. Pool. $$

★HOTEL ASPEN
110 W. Main St., Aspen, 970-925-3441, 800-527-7369; www.hotelaspen.com
45 rooms. Complimentary breakfast. Pool. Business center. Pets accepted. $$

★★★HOTEL DURANT
122 E. Durant, Aspen, 970-925-8500, 877-438-7268; www.durantaspen.com
This no-frills hotel offers wine and cheese après-ski and a rooftop hot tub
and sauna to soak your depleted muscles. The 19 cozy—some more so than
others—guest rooms are basic, but come with a complimentary continental
breakfast in the morning. The location and relatively affordable rates are the
primary pros here.
19 rooms. Complimentary breakfast. $$

★★★HOTEL JEROME

330 E. Main St., Aspen, 970-920-1000, 800-412-7625; www.hoteljerome.com

This downtown hotel was built in 1889 by Jerome B. Wheeler, co-owner of Macy's Department Store, and was one of the first buildings west of the Mississippi River to be fully lit by electricity. The boutique-style rooms here are magnificent, reflecting the hotel's Victorian heritage with carved armoires and beautiful beds. The service is superb: the ski concierge will take care of your every need, and guests are driven to the slopes in luxury SUVs. You also get access to the Aspen Club and Spa, a 77,000-square-foot exercise facility and spa. The dashing J-Bar is still one of the hottest places in town.
94 rooms. Restaurant, bar. Pets accepted. Fitness center. Pool. Business center. Spa. Golf. Tennis. $$$$

★★★HOTEL LENADO

200 S. Aspen St., Aspen, 970-925-6246, 800-321-3457; www.hotellenado.com

Value doesn't get much better than this in a town that's all about boutique and show. Fork over a fair rate (for Aspen) and you'll get a cozy room with a four-poster hickory bed, Bose radio/CD player, down comforter and terry robes. Take advantage of your access to the rooftop deck and hot tub overlooking Aspen Mountain, heated boot lockers and daily ski storage. If that's not enough to make you happy, complimentary hors d'oeuvres and hot apple cider (lemonade in the summer) in the bar after 4 p.m. will hit the spot.
19 rooms. Complimentary breakfast. Bar. Pets accepted. $$$$

★★★★★THE LITTLE NELL

675 E. Durant Ave., Aspen, 970-920-4600, 888-843-6355; www.thelittlenell.com

Tucked away at the base of a mountain, the Little Nell provides a perfect location either to hit the slopes or roam the streets in search of Aspen's latest fashions. The rooms and suites are heavenly cocoons that have been recently redecorated by famous interior designer Holly Hunt. They feature fireplaces, streamlined furnishings and luxurious bathrooms. Some suites feature vaulted ceilings showcasing glorious mountainside views, while others overlook the charming former mining town. Enjoy the well-equipped fitness center and outdoor pool and jacuzzi. Montagna restaurant is one of the most popular spots in town and serves inventive reinterpretations of American cuisine.
92 rooms. Closed late April-mid-May. Restaurant, bar. Pets accepted. Pool. Spa. Fitness center. Business center. $$$$

★MOLLY GIBSON LODGE

101 W. Main St., Aspen, 970-925-3434, 888-271-2304; www.mollygibson.com

53 rooms. Complimentary breakfast. Pool. $$

★★★SKY HOTEL

709 E. Durant Ave., Aspen, 970-925-6760, 800-882-2582; www.theskyhotel.com

This boutique hotel offers the convenience of being able to stumble upstairs from one of Aspen's trendiest bars, which is but a snowball's throw away from the rest of the city's nightlife. From the evening wine reception to to the plush animal-print terrycloth robes, the Sky Hotel has taken your every vacation need into consideration. The rooms offer amenities including L'Occitane bath products, iPod-compatible clock radios and humidifiers. Pets are welcomed with treats and their own beds and bowls in the room. The onsite ski shop will rent you equipment or store yours free of charge.

90 rooms. Restaurant, bar. Business center. Pets accepted. Pool. Fitness center. Pets accepted. $$$

★★★★THE ST. REGIS ASPEN RESORT
315 E. Dean St., Aspen, 970-920-3300, 888-454-9005; www.stregis.com/aspen

Located at the base of Aspen Mountain between the gondola and lift, this hotel's upscale, Western atmosphere is the perfect respite from skiing, shopping and warm weather activities such as fly-fishing and white-water rafting. The outdoor pool and accompanying lounge are ideal for whiling away warm afternoons, or you can relax in the lavish spa. Rooms are richly decorated in muted colors with bursts of color and oversized leather furniture. Expect complimentary water bottle service and a humidifier at turndown and Remède bath amenities, bathrobes and slippers. The Restaurant serves American cuisine with Mediterranean inspirations in an elegantly relaxed setting with an exhibition kitchen, and Shadow Mountain Lounge is a popular gathering place to enjoy a cocktail.

199 rooms. Closed late October-mid-November. Restaurant, bar. Business center. Fitness center. Pool. Spa. $$$$

WHERE TO EAT

★★AJAX TAVERN
The Little Nell, 675 E. Durant Ave., Aspen, 970-920-6334
American. Lunch, dinner. Bar. Outdoor seating. $$$

★BOOGIE'S DINER
534 E. Cooper Ave., Aspen, 970-925-6610
American. Lunch, dinner. Children's menu. $$

★★★CACHE CACHE BISTRO
205 S. Mill St., Aspen, 970-925-3835; www.cachecache.com

This eatery has become something of an Aspen institution in the last two decades. Expect the highest-quality food, wine and service from the charming owner Jodi Larner herself, not to get a bargain or a quick seat après-ski. That said, if you're not married to the white-tablecloth experience and don't mind moseying up to the bar, you can relieve your cashed legs and eat Alaskan king crab and foie gras terrine starters. Plus, with the budget-friendly bar menu, you can get out for under $20.

French. Dinner. Bar. Outdoor seating. $$

★★CANTINA
411 E. Main St., Aspen, 970-925-3663; www.cantina-aspen.com
Mexican. Lunch, dinner. Bar. Children's menu. Outdoor seating. $$

★★★JIMMY'S AN AMERICAN RESTAURANT & BAR
205 S. Mill St., Aspen, 970-925-6020; www.jimmysaspen.com

This cozy restaurant is known for both the lively bar and seriously good food, such as the dry-aged rib-eye on the bone, Chesapeake Bay crab cakes

and center-cut ahi tuna with herbed rice. The chocolate volcano cake is also a favorite.
American. Dinner. Bar. Children's menu. Outdoor seating. $$$

★★L'HOSTARIA
620 E. Hyman Ave., Aspen, 970-925-9022;
Italian. Dinner. Bar. Children's menu. Reservations recommended. Outdoor seating. $$

★★★MATSUHISA ASPEN
303 E. Main St., Aspen, 970-544-6628; www.matsuhisaaspen.com
Renowned chef Nobu Matsuhisa, who has built a mini-empire of restaurants from New York to L.A., gives Aspen a taste of his outstanding, heartfelt Japanese cuisine in this sleek restaurant located 9,000 feet above sea level. The service is polished and prompt, making for a superb experience.
Japanese. Dinner. Bar. $$$$

★★MEZZALUNA
624 E. Cooper Ave., Aspen, 970-925-5882; www.mezzalunaaspen.com
Italian. Lunch, dinner. $$$

★★★★MONTAGNA
The Little Nell, 675 E. Durant Ave., Aspen, 970-920-4600; www.thelittlenell.com
Located in the Little Nell hotel, Montagna is one of the top dining spots in Aspen. With its buttery walls, iron chandeliers and deep picture windows, the restaurant has the feeling of a chic Swiss chalet. The menu, from the pasta with housemade lamb sausage to the crispy chicken, is outstanding, and the sommelier oversees a 20,000-bottle wine cellar.
American. Breakfast, lunch, dinner, Sunday brunch. Bar. Children's menu. Outdoor seating. $$$$

★★★THE RESTAURANT
St. Regis Aspen, 315 E. Dean St., Aspen, 970-920-3300; www.stregisaspen.com
The Restaurant, located in the St. Regis Aspen, delivers American cuisine with strong Mediterranean influences. The seasonal menu contains dishes that incorporate local ingredients, such as braised Meyer ranch short ribs, Summit Creek farms brick-oven-roasted rack of lamb and wild pacific-northwest sturgeon. The warm dining room with pinewood floors, antique furniture and a Tuscan-influenced exhibition kitchen strikes just the right tone.
Mediterranean. Lunch, dinner. Children's menu. $$$

★★PACIFICA
307 S. Mill St., Aspen, 970-920-9775; www.pacificaaspen.com
American, seafood. Lunch, dinner. Bar. Children's menu. Outdoor seating. $$

★★★PINE CREEK COOKHOUSE
314 S. Second St., Aspen, 970-925-1044; www.pinecreekcookhouse.com
Dine on grilled quail salad and seared elk tenderloin in this cozy cabin located in a scenic valley in the Elk Mountains. Locals like to cycle up to the rustic location Castle Creek road for hearty lunches that might include veg-

etable paninis or grilled quail salad.
American. Lunch, dinner. Bar. Outdoor seating. $$$

★★★PINON'S
105 S. Mill St., Aspen, 970-920-2021; www.pinons.net
A reservation here is one of the most sought-after in town. Hidden away on the second floor of a shop in downtown Aspen, the contemporary restaurant is decorated with a modern mountain-style with vistas of Aspen Mountain and the atmosphere is upbeat and festive. The service is warm and the innovative and the seasonal menu delights diners.
American. Dinner. Bar. $$$

★★TAKAH SUSHI
320 S. Mill St., Aspen, 970-925-8588, 888-925-8588; www.takahsushi.com
Japanese, sushi. Dinner. Bar. $$

★★WIENERSTUBE
633 E. Hyman Ave., Aspen, 970-925-3357; www.wienerstube.com
Austrian. Breakfast, lunch. Bar. $$

AURORA
See also Denver
This Denver suburb, Colorado's third-largest city, offers plenty of opportunities to bask in Colorado's sunny weather. Visitors will enjoy Aurora's golf courses, hiking and biking trails, and Aurora Reservoir, where locals fish, swim and even scuba dive.

WHERE TO STAY
★★DOUBLETREE HOTEL DENVER-SOUTHEAST
13696 E. Iliff Place, Aurora, 303-337-2800, 800-528-0444; www.doubletree.com
248 rooms. Restaurant, bar. Pool. Business center. Fitness center. $

★★RED LION HOTEL DENVER SOUTHEAST
3200 S. Parker Road, Aurora, 303-695-1700, 888-201-1718; www.redlion.com
478 rooms. Restaurant, bar. Pets accepted. Business center. $

WHERE TO EAT
★★LA CUEVA
9742 E. Colfax Ave., Aurora, 303-367-1422; www.lacueva.net
Mexican. Lunch, dinner. Closed Sunday. Bar. Children's menu. $$

AVON
See also Beaver Creek
Avon is the gateway to Beaver Creek/Arrowhead Resort, which is located about two miles south of the town.

WHAT TO SEE
BEAVER CREEK/ARROWHEAD RESORT
137 Benchmark Road, Avon, 970-476-9090, 800-842-8062; www.beavercreek.snow.co

Ten quad, two triple, three double chairlifts; patrol, rentals, snowmaking; restaurants, bar, nursery. Longest run 2¾ miles; vertical drop 4,040 feet. Late November-mid-April, daily. Cross-country trails and rentals, November-April; ice skating, snowmobiling, sleigh rides. Chairlift rides, July-August, daily; September, weekends.

COLORADO RIVER RUNS
Rancho del Rio, 28 miles northwest of Highway 131; 800-826-1081, 970-653-4292; www.coloradoriverruns.com
Raft down the Colorado River. Tours depart from Rancho del Rio (just outside State Bridge) and last two and a half to three hours.
Admission: adults $36, children $30. May-September.

WHERE TO EAT

★★★BEAVER CREEK LODGE
26 Avondale Lane, Beaver Creek, 970-845-9800, 800-525-7280; www.beavercreeklodge.net
Located at the base of the Beaver Creek Resort, this European-style boutique hotel is close to the Centennial and Strawberry Park chairlifts. Curl up on the leather couch in front of the fireplace in one of the two-room suites, which feature kitchenettes. Condos have state-of-the-art kitchens, laundry facilities and master bedrooms with jacuzzis.
72 rooms. Restaurant, bar. Ski in/ski out. Fitness center. Spa. $$

★★★GROUSE MOUNTAIN GRILL
The Pines Lodge, 141 Scott Hill Road, Avon, 970-949-0600; www.grousemountaingrill.com
Located in the Pines Lodge, this elegant, European-style restaurant is the perfect choice for breakfast, lunch or a quiet dinner. The dark wood furnishings, nightly piano music and tables topped with crisp white linens create a warm and cozy atmosphere. The dinner menu focuses on rustic American dishes such as Meyer ranch natural beef hanger steak with horseradish potato cake, spring beans and tomato relishes, or pretzel-crusted pork chops with housemade chorizo and orange mustard sauce. The warm apple bread pudding is a perfect finish.
American. Breakfast, lunch, dinner. Bar. Children's menu. Outdoor seating. $$$

★★★THE OSPREY AT BEAVER CREEK
10 Elk Track Road, Avon, 970-845-5990, 888-485-4317; www.vbcrp.com
Formerly the Inn at Beaver Creek, The Osprey underwent a $7 million dollar renovation and is new and improved. It's all about location here: this ski in/ski out is just steps away from the Strawberry Park Express chairlift and is within walking distance of shops and eateries. The cozy and sophisticated guest rooms and suites offer an array of amenities, including high-speed Internet access, plush robes, soaking tubs and ski boot heaters.
45 rooms. Closed May, October. Bar. Ski in/ski out. Pool. Fitness center. $$$

★★★PARK HYATT BEAVER CREEK RESORT AND SPA

136 E. Thomas Place, Avon, 970-949-1234, 800-233-1234;
www.beavercreek.hyatt.com

Located at the base of the Gore Mountains, in the heart of Beaver Creek Village, the ski in/ski out resort is a classic mountain lodge, with rooms featuring oversized furniture, comfy quilts and marble bathrooms. The Performance Skiing Program helps guests improve their skiing within days. Afterward, visit Allegria Spa, which focuses on water-based treatments. In the summer, hit the links on the championship golf course. The resort has two restaurants and a café.

190 rooms. Restaurant, bar. Ski in/ski out. Golf. Tennis. Business center. Spa. Fitness center. Pool. $$$

★★★THE PINES LODGE

141 Scott Hill Road, Avon, 970-845-7900, 866-605-7625; www.rockresorts.com

Nestled among towering pines, this resort offers views of the slopes of Beaver Creek Resort. The rooms include refrigerators, marble bathrooms and ski boot heaters. Have a meal after skiing at the Lodge's elegant Grouse Mountain Grill. Amenities include Internet access and Starbucks coffee in the guest rooms.

60 rooms. Restaurant, bar. Fitness center. Spa. Pool. Golf. $$$

★★★★THE RITZ-CARLTON BACHELOR GULCH

130 Daybreak Ridge, Avon, 970-748-6200; www.ritzcarlton.com

Rugged meets refined at this resort, located at the base of the mountain at Beaver Creek. From the 10-gallon hat-clad doorman who greets you to the rustic great room, this resort captures the spirit of the Old West while incorporating polished style. The rooms and suites are comfortable and stylish, with leather chairs, dark wood furniture and wood-beamed ceilings. Iron chandeliers and twig furnishings adorn the public spaces. This family-friendly resort offers an abundance of activities, including fly-fishing, a horseshoe pit, two children's play areas, an outdoor pool, golf and skiing.

180 rooms. Restaurant, bar. Spa. Ski in/ski out. Pets accepted. Golf. Tennis. Business center. Fitness center. $$$$

SPAS

★★★★ALLEGRIA SPA AT PARK HYATT BEAVER CREEK

Park Hyatt Beaver Creek, 100 E. Thomas Place, Avon, 970-748-7500, 888-591-1234;
www.allegriaspa.com

Aged copper fountains and a crackling fireplace set the mood at this spa inside the Park Hyatt Beaver Creek, which offers a blend of locally and Eastern-inspired therapies. The hydration facial is a lifesaver for parched, wind-burned skin. Body treatments incorporate gentle exfoliation, a nourishing body wrap and a rewarding massage into one blissful experience. The body scrubs take their inspiration from the garden. The warm milk and honey sugar scrub, sweet orange and citrus salt scrub, and cranberry orange scrub render skin supple. The lavender and rose and balancing hot oil wraps are luxurious ways to hydrate skin. After a day on the slopes, treat your toes to the Allegria deluxe pedicure. $$

★★★★THE BACHELOR GULCH SPA AT THE RITZ-CARLTON

The Ritz-Carlton, Bachelore Gulch, 130 Daybreak Ridge, Avon, 970-748-6200, 800-576-5582; www.ritzcarlton.com

The Bachelor Gulch Spa captures the essence of its alpine surroundings with polished rock, stout wood and flowing water in its interiors. The rock grotto with a lazy river hot tub is a defining feature, and the fitness rooms have majestic mountain views. The beauty of the outdoors also extends to treatments that utilize ingredients indigenous to the region. Alpine berries, Douglas fir and blue spruce sap are just some of the natural components of the exceptional signature treatments. After a rigorous day on the slopes, there are also plenty of massage options, from the Roaring Rapids, which uses hydrotherapy, or the Four-Hands, where two therapists work out knots. $$

BEAVER CREEK

See also Avon

Beaver Creek's slogan is "not exactly roughing it," a perfect description for this resort town. If you're searching for great skiing, fine dining and luxury in a pristine setting, head to Beaver Creek.

WHERE TO STAY
★★★THE CHARTER AT BEAVER CREEK

120 Offerson Road, Beaver Creek, 970-949-6660, 800-525-2139; www.thecharter.com

This lodge features hotel rooms (as well as one- to five-bedroom condos) that offer guests amenities like plush robes, Aveda bath products and high-speed Internet access. Each condo also includes a fully equipped kitchen, wood-burning fireplace, private bath and TV for each bedroom as well as maid service.

80 rooms. Restaurant, bar. Spa. Ski in/ski out. Pool. $$

WHERE TO EAT
★★★BEANO'S CABIN

Beaver Creek, 970-754-3463

This log cabin restaurant is located amid the aspen trees on Beaver Creek Mountain. There are a few ways to get here: sleigh, horse-drawn wagon, van or horseback. Regardless of your mode of transport, Beano's is worth the trip. Listen to live music, sit by the crackling fire and enjoy a five-course meal, such as roasted Colorado beef tenderloin with blue cheese scalloped potatoes, asparagus salad and brandy sauce or gingerbread-crusted Colorado rack of lamb.

American. Dinner. Closed early April-late June, late September-mid-December. Bar. Children's menu. Reservations recommended. $$$$

★★★★MIRABELLE AT BEAVER CREEK

55 Village Road, Beaver Creek, 970-949-7728; www.mirabelle1.com

Love is in the air at this charming 19th-century cottage in the mountains. Each of the spacious, bright rooms is cozy and warm, while the outdoor porch, lined with colorful potted flowers, is the perfect spot for outdoor dining. The food is just as magical. The kitchen offers sophisticated French food prepared with a modern sensibility. Signature dishes include Colorado lamb chops and roasted elk medallions with fruit compote. The housemade ice cream is the perfect finish.

French. Dinner. Closed Sunday; also May, November. Bar. Children's menu. Outdoor seating. $$$

★★★SPLENDIDO AT THE CHATEAU

17 Chateau Lane, Beaver Creek, 970-845-8808; www.splendidobeavercreek.com

Locals come to this picturesque, chalet-style dining room tucked into the hills of Beaver Creek to celebrate special occasions and enjoy the wonderful piano music offered nightly. The food is splendid, too. The menu changes nightly, but seasonal signatures have included dishes like sesame-crusted Atlantic salmon with coconut basmati rice and cilantro-lemongrass sauce, and grilled elk loin with braised elk osso bucco.

American. Dinner. Closed mid-April-mid-June, mid-October-mid-November. Bar. Children's menu. Reservations recommended. $$$

BOULDER

See also Denver

Dubbed "the city between the mountains and reality," Boulder benefits from a combination of great beauty and great weather that makes the area ideal for outdoor activity. Its location between the base of the Rocky Mountains and the head of a rich agricultural valley provides an ideal year-round climate, with 300 sunny days annually. More than 30,000 acres of open, unspoiled land and 200 miles of hiking and biking paths make the city an outdoor-lover's paradise. Home to several high-tech companies, the University of Colorado, the National Institute of Standards and Technology and the National Center for Atmospheric Research, Boulder is also sophisticated and artsy, offering a wealth of cultural activities from music to dance, art and one-of-a-kind shops.

WHAT TO SEE

BOULDER CREEK PATH

Boulder, from 55th St. and Pearl Parkway to Boulder Canyon, 303-413-7200; www.boulderparks-rec.org

This nature and exercise trail runs some 16 miles through the city and into the adjacent mountains, leading past a sculpture garden, a restored steam locomotive and several parks. Daily.

BOULDER HISTORY MUSEUM

Harbeck Bergheim House, 1206 Euclid Ave., Boulder, 303-449-3464; www.boulderhistorymuseum.org

Learn about the history of Boulder from 1858 to the present. This museum includes 20,000 artifacts, 111,000 photographs and 486,000 documents. Permanent and rotating interpretive exhibits and educational programs.

Tuesday-Friday 10 a.m.-5 p.m., Saturday-Sunday noon-4 p.m.

BOULDER MUSEUM OF CONTEMPORARY ART

1750 13th St., Boulder, 303-443-2122; www.bmoca.org

View exhibits of contemporary and regional painting, sculpture and other media, along with changing exhibits featuring local, domestic and international artists. Check out the experimental performance series on Thursdays

as well as the many lectures, workshops and special events.
Tuesday, Thursday, Friday 11 a.m.-5 p.m., Wednesday 11 a.m.-8 p.m., Saturday 9 a.m.-4 p.m., Sunday noon-3 p.m.

BOULDER RESERVOIR
5565 N. 51 St., Boulder, 303-441-3468; www.bouldercolorado.gov
Swimming beach, Memorial Day-Labor Day, daily; waterskiing, fishing. Boating daily; get a power boat permit at the main gate; and boat rentals. Memorial Day-Labor Day, daily.

CELESTIAL SEASONINGS FACTORY TOUR
4600 Sleepytime Drive, Boulder, 303-581-1202, 303-530-5300;
www.celestialseasonings.com
This 45-minute tour takes visitors through the beautiful gardens that produce the herbs and botanicals used in the company's teas, with stops in the sinus-clearing Mint Room and the production area, where eight million tea bags are made every day. You can also check out the company's art gallery of original paintings, which decorate their tea boxes, and be among the first to sample some of the company's newest blends. Children must be over 5 to enter the factory. Tours are hourly.
Monday-Friday 10 a.m.-4 p.m., Saturday 10 a.m.-3 p.m., Sunday 11 a.m.-3 p.m.

ELDORA MOUNTAIN RESORT
2861 Eldora Ski Road, Nederland, 303-440-8700; www.eldora.com
Two quad, two triple, four double chairlifts; four surface lifts; patrol, school, rentals, snowmaking; cafeteria, bar, nursery. Fifty-three runs; longest run three miles; vertical drop 1,400 feet. Cross-country skiing (27 miles). Mid-November-early April.

LEANIN' TREE MUSEUM OF WESTERN ART
6055 Longbow Drive, Boulder, 303-530-1442, 800-777-8716;
www.leanintreemuseum.com
Check out the original works of art used in many of the greeting cards produced by Leanin' Tree, a major publisher. The museum also features the private collection of paintings and sculptures amassed by Edward P. Trumble, the chairman and founder of Leanin' Tree Inc.
Monday-Friday 8 a.m.-5 p.m., Saturday-Sunday 10 a.m.-5 p.m.; closed Thanksgiving Day, Christmas Day and New Year's Day.

MACKY AUDITORIUM CONCERT HALL
Pleasant Street and Macky Drive, Boulder, 303-492-8423; www.colorado.edu/macky
This 2,047-seat auditorium hosts the Boulder Philharmonic Orchestra. Concerts during the academic year.

NATIONAL CENTER FOR ATMOSPHERIC RESEARCH
1850 Table Mesa Drive, Boulder, 303-497-1000; www.ncar.ucar.edu/ncar
Designed by I. M. Pei, the center includes exhibits on global warming, weather, the sun, aviation hazards and supercomputing. There's also a 400-acre nature preserve onsite. Guided tours are also offered.

Visitor center: Monday-Friday 8 a.m.-5 p.m., Saturday-Sunday, holidays 9 a.m.-4 p.m.

PEARL STREET MALL

900 to 1500 Pearl St., Boulder, 303-449-3774; www.boulderdowntown.com
Open year-round, this retail and restaurant district is particularly appealing in the summer with its brick walkways, Victorian storefronts, lush landscaping and parade of colorful personalities. Offering four blocks of mostly upscale restaurants, galleries, bars and boutiques, the mall invites visitors to conclude a day of shopping with a meal at one of its many European-style cafes while taking in the impromptu performances of street musicians, jugglers, artists and mimes.

SOMMERS-BAUSCH OBSERVATORY

2475 Kittridge Loop Drive, Boulder, 303-492-6732; lyra.colorado.edu/sbo
Come here for an evening of stargazing. Weather permitting, school year; closed school holidays. Reservations required on Fridays.

UNIVERSITY OF COLORADO

914 Broadway St., Boulder, 303-492-1411; www.colorado.edu
This 786-acre campus, which was established in 1876, now boasts a student population of 25,000. Many buildings feature distinctive native sandstone and red-tile.
Tours of campus available.

UNIVERSITY OF COLORADO MUSEUM

Henderson Building, 15th and Broadway streets, Boulder, 303-492-6892; cumuseum.colorado.edu
See relics and artifacts of early human life in the area, plus regional geological, zoological and botanical collections. Changing exhibits.
Monday-Friday 9 a.m.-5 p.m., Saturday 9 a.m.-4 p.m., Sunday 10 a.m.-4 p.m.; closed school holidays.

VISTA RIDGE GOLF CLUB

2700 Vista Parkway, Erie, 303-665-1723; www.vistaridgegc.com
This 18-hole Jay Morrish-designed course, occupying more than 200 acres, offers golfers a lot of space to test their skills. The course's gently rolling hills and views of the Rockies take the edge off even the worst shots, while generous fairways make up for ample water hazards.

SPECIAL EVENTS
BOLDER BOULDER 10K RACE

5500 Central Ave., Boulder, 303-444-7223; www.bolderboulder.com
Join one of the largest road races in the world, with 45,000 runners and more than 100,000 spectators. Live music and entertainment along the route add to the enjoyment of this family-centered celebration.
Races begin at 7 a.m., awards at 2:30 p.m. Memorial Day.

BOULDER BACH FESTIVAL
University of Colorado, Boulder, Grusin Concert Hall, Boulder, 303-776-9666;
www.boulderbachfest.org
Listen to the music of Baroque composer Johann Sebastian Bach.
Late January.

COLORADO MUSIC FESTIVAL
Chautauqua Auditorium, 900 Baseline Road, Boulder, 303-449-1397;
www.coloradomusicfest.org
Classical music concerts featuring the CMF Chamber Orchestra.
Eight weeks in June-August.

COLORADO SHAKESPEARE FESTIVAL
University of Colorado, Mary Rippon Outdoor Theatre, Boulder, 303-492-0554;
www.coloradoshakes.org
See three Shakespeare plays in repertory.
July-August.

WHERE TO STAY
★★COURTYARD BOULDER
4710 Pearl East Circle, Boulder, 303-440-4700, 800-321-2211; www.courtyard.com
149 rooms. Restaurant. Pool. $

★★★HOTEL BOULDERADO
2115 13th St., Boulder, 303-442-4344, 800-433-4344; www.boulderado.com
Boulder was a sleepy little town of 11,000 back in 1905, when the city fa-
thers decided they could move things along by providing the comfort of a
first-class hotel. Back then, men worked 24 hours a day stoking the huge coal
furnace to keep the hotel evenly heated, and rooms went for $1 per night. The
hotel has since been restored to its original grandeur. You'll feel like you've
stepped back in time when you enter the lobby with its stained-glass ceiling,
cherry staircase, plush velvet furniture and swirling ceilings fans.
160 rooms. Restaurant, bar. Business center. $$

★★★MARRIOTT BOULDER
2660 Canyon Blvd., Boulder, 303-440-8877, 888-238-2178; www.marriott.com
This newly renovated hotel is located at the base on the Flatiron Mountains
in downtown Boulder. Rooms feature free Internet and fitness kits. Opting
for the Concierge level will get you access to two private rooftop terraces,
complimentary continental breakfast and evening appetizers. Take a dip in
the outdoor pool or hit the spa. This hotel is nonsmoking.
157 rooms. Restaurant, bar. Pool. Spa. $$

★QUALITY INN & SUITES BOULDER CREEK
2020 Arapahoe Ave., Boulder, 303-449-7550, 888-449-7550;
www.qualityinnboulder.com
46 rooms. Complimentary breakfast. Pool. Fitness center. Pets accepted. $

★★★ST. JULIEN HOTEL & SPA

900 Walnut St., Boulder, 720-406-9696, 877-303-0900; www.stjulien.com

Relax at this luxurious yet casual hotel with a 10,000-square-foot spa and fitness center, two-lane infinity pool and outdoor terrace. The elegant rooms feature custom pillow-top beds with fluffy duvets and oversized slate bathrooms with separate showers. They also include complimentary high-speed Internet access and organic coffee. The martini bar, T-Zero, is an intimate spot for a drink.

201 rooms. Restaurant, bar. Business center. Fitness center. Pool. Spa. $$

WHERE TO EAT
★★ANTICA ROMA

1308 Pearl St., Boulder, 303-449-1787; www.anticaroma.com

Italian. Lunch, dinner. Bar. Children's menu. Outdoor seating. $$

★★★★FLAGSTAFF HOUSE RESTAURANT

1138 Flagstaff Road, Boulder, 303-442-4640; www.flagstaffhouse.com

From its perch on Flagstaff Mountain, this restaurant is easily one of the most amazing spots to watch the sunset. The upscale and inspired menu changes daily, with plates like beef Wellington dressed up with black truffle sauce and Hawaiian ono with ginger, scallions and soft-shell crabs. The wine list is massive (the restaurant has a 20,000-bottle wine cellar), so enlist the assistance of the attentive sommelier for guidance. The restaurant is owned by the Monette family, which means that you'll be treated to refined service and homegrown hospitality, making dining here a delight from start to finish. If you can, arrive early and sit at the mahogany bar for a pre-dinner cocktail.

American. Dinner. Bar. Reservations recommended. Outdoor seating. $$$$

★★★THE GREENBRIAR INN

8735 N. Foothills Highway, Boulder, 303-440-7979, 800-253-1474;
www.greenbriarinn.com

Originally built in 1893, this Boulder landmark sits on 20 acres at the mouth of Left Hand Canyon. The atrium room has French doors that open up to the south garden and lawn. The mouthwatering food includes blue crab-crusted beef tournedos and maple cured duck breasts. A champagne brunch is served on Saturday and Sunday.

American. Dinner, Saturday-Sunday brunch. Closed Monday. Bar. Outdoor seating. $$$

★★★JOHN'S RESTAURANT

2328 Pearl St., Boulder, 303-444-5232; www.johnsrestaurantboulder.com

You'll feel like you're stepping into someone's home when you enter this century-old cottage with lace curtains and white tablecloths. In the spring and summer, windows open to courtyards filled with bright flowers. On the menu, you'll find contemporary European dishes with specialties like smoked Scottish salmon, filet mignon with Stilton cheese and ale sauce, and Italian-style gelato.

International menu. Dinner. Closed Sunday-Monday. $$$

★★LAUDISIO
1710 29th St., Boulder, 303-442-1300; www.laudisio.com
Italian. Lunch, dinner. Bar. Outdoor seating. $$$

★★THE MEDITERRANEAN
1002 Walnut St., Boulder, 303-444-5335; www.themedboulder.com
Mediterranean. Lunch, dinner. Bar. Children's menu. Outdoor seating. $$

★★★Q'S
2115 13th St., Boulder, 303-442-4880; www.qsboulder.com
This welcoming, bistro-style restaurant in the Hotel Boulderado offers a superb selection of seafood, meat and game. The international wine collection is eclectic and includes small barrel and boutique selections as well as a proprietor's reserve list. The service is delightful and efficient.
American. Breakfast, lunch (Monday-Friday), dinner (Monday-Friday), Saturday-Sunday brunch. Bar. Children's menu. $$$

★ROYAL PEACOCK
5290 Arapahoe Ave., Boulder, 303-447-1409; www.royalpeacocklounge.com
Indian. Lunch, dinner. Outdoor seating. $$

BRECKENRIDGE
See also Dillon
Born as a mining camp when gold was discovered along the Blue River in 1859, modern Breckenridge wears its rough-and-tumble past like a badge. With 350 historic structures, the town has the largest historic district in Colorado. The population peaked near 10,000 in the 1880s but dwindled to less than 400 in 1960, the year before the town's ski resort opened. Breckenridge now sees more than one million skier visits annually. Located on four interconnected mountains named Peaks 7, 8, 9 and 10, the terrain is revered by skiers but is especially popular with snowboarders. It's more affordable—and rowdier—than Aspen and Vail. During the summer months, outdoor enthusiasts love hiking, mountain biking, fly-fishing, white-water rafting and horseback riding in the surrounding area. The Jack Nicklaus-designed Breckenridge Golf Club offers 27 holes of world-class championship play.

WHAT TO SEE
BRECKENRIDGE SKI AREA
Ski Hill Road, Breckenridge, 970-453-5000, 800-789-7669;
www.breckenridge.snow.com
Seven high-speed quad, triple, six double chairlifts; four surface lifts, eight carpet lifts; school, rentals, snowmaking; four cafeterias, five restaurants on mountain, picnic area; four nurseries (from two months old). One-hundred twelve runs on three interconnected mountains; longest run 3½ miles; vertical drop 3,398 feet. Ski mid-November-early May, daily. Cross-country skiing (23 kilometers), heli-skiing, ice skating, snowboarding and sleigh rides. Shuttle bus service. Multiday, half day and off-season rates.
Chairlift and alpine slide operate in summer, mid-June-mid-September.

SUMMIT HISTORICAL SOCIETY WALKING TOURS

111 N. Ridge St., Breckenridge, 970-453-9022; www.summithistorical.org

Tour the historic district, which includes trips to abandoned mines.
Late June-August, Tuesday-Saturday 10 a.m.

SPECIAL EVENTS
BACKSTAGE THEATRE

121 S. Ridge St., Breckenridge, 970-453-0199;
www.backstagetheatre.org

See melodramas, musicals and comedies at this hometown theater.
July-Labor Day, mid-December-March.

BRECKENRIDGE MUSIC FESTIVAL

150 W. Adams, Breckenridge, 970-453-9142; www.breckenridgemusicfestival.com

This eight-week summer celebration includes regular full orchestra performances by Breckenridge's own highly acclaimed National Repertory Orchestra. Performances are held at Riverwalk Center in the heart of downtown Breckenridge, an 800-seat, tented amphitheater. It opens in back to allow lawn seating for an additional 1,500-2,000 symphony lovers who come to picnic and enjoy music under the stars.
Most concerts begin at 7:30 p.m. Late June-mid-August.

INTERNATIONAL SNOW SCULPTURE CHAMPIONSHIPS

Riverwalk Center, Breckenridge, 800-936-5573; www.gobreck.com

Sixteen teams from around the world create works of art from 12-foot-tall, 20-ton blocks of artificial snow.
Late January-early February.

NO MAN'S LAND DAY CELEBRATION

Breckenridge, 970-453-6018

Breckenridge was mistakenly forgotten in historic treaties when Colorado joined the Union. It became part of Colorado and the United States at a later date. This celebration emphasizes Breckenridge life in the 1880s with a parade, dance and games.
Second weekend in August.

ULLR FEST & WORLD CUP FREESTYLE

Breckenridge, 970-453-6018; www.gobreck.com

This annual celebration honors the Norse god of snow with parades, fireworks and a ski competition.
Seven days in late January.

WHERE TO STAY
★★★ALLAIRE TIMBERS INN

9511 Highway 9/South Main, Breckenridge, 970-453-7530, 800-624-4904;
www.allairetimbers.com

This charming log cabin bed and breakfast at the south end of Main Street is made from local pine. The innkeepers welcome guests with hearty home-made breakfasts, afternoon snacks and warm hospitality. Take the free shuttle from the inn to several chair lifts. After a day of activity, relax in the sunroom or retreat to the reading loft.

10 rooms. No children under 13. Complimentary breakfast. $$

★★★BEAVER RUN RESORT AND CONFERENCE CENTER

620 Village Road, Breckenridge, 970-453-6000, 800-265-3560; www.beaverrun.com

This large resort is popular with families in both winter and summer. The suites feature full kitchens and the largest ones sleep up to 10 people. The property includes eight hot tubs and an indoor/outdoor pool, tennis courts and a spa with facials by Dermalogica. There's also a ski school for the kids, as well as miniature golf and a video arcade.

567 rooms. Restaurant, bar. Ski in/ski out. Fitness center. Spa. $$

★★★GREAT DIVIDE LODGE

550 Village Road, Breckenridge, 970-547-5550, 888-906-5698;
www.greatdividelodge.com

Located just 50 yards from the base of Peak 9 and two blocks from Main Street, this lodge is excellent for winter or summer vacationing. The large guest rooms come with a wet bar, Starbucks coffee, Nintendo and wireless Internet access. Get around on the free hotel shuttle.

208 rooms. Restaurant, bar. Pool. $$

★★★SKIWAY LODGE

275 Ski Hill Road, Breckenridge, 970-453-7573, 800-472-1430; www.skiwaylodge.com

Individually designed rooms with mountain views and hearty, homemade breakfasts distinguish this Bavarian-style chalet located just blocks from Main Street. The inn offers ski-in/ski-out access.

9 rooms. No children under 10. Complimentary breakfast. $

WHERE TO EAT

★BRECKENRIDGE BREWERY

600 S. Main St., Breckenridge, 970-453-1550; www.breckenridgebrewery.com

American. Lunch, dinner, late-night. Bar. Children's menu. Outdoor seating. $$

★★CAFE ALPINE

106 E. Adams, Breckenridge, 970-453-8218; www.cafealpine.com

International. Lunch, dinner. Closed late May. Bar. Children's menu. Reservations recommended. Outdoor seating. $$$

★★HEARTHSTONE RESTAURANT

130 S. Ridge St., Breckenridge, 970-453-1148; www.stormrestaurants.com

American. Dinner. Bar. Children's menu. Reservations recommended. Outdoor seating. $$$

★★MI CASA MEXICAN CANTINA

600 S. Park Ave., Breckenridge, 970-453-2071; www.stormrestaurants.com

Mexican. Lunch, dinner. Bar. Children's menu. Outdoor seating. $$

BROOMFIELD

See also Salida

Broomfield is midway between Denver and Boulder in what is referred to as the technology corridor. The area experienced tremendous growth in the 1990s, much of it focused on technology. The biggest employers include IBM and Sun Microsystems.

WHAT TO SEE
FLATIRON CROSSING

1 W. FlatIron Circle, Broomfield, 720-887-7467, 866-352-8476; www.flatironcrossing.com

This architecturally innovative 1.5 million-square-foot retail and entertainment -complex located between Denver and Boulder was designed to reflect the natural Flatirons (rock formations), canyons and prairies of its surroundings. The result is a one-of-a-kind visual and shopping experience, with more than 200 stores and numerous restaurants for indoor and outdoor dining. Daily.

WHERE TO STAY
★★★OMNI INTERLOCKEN RESORT

500 Interlocken Blvd., Broomfield, 303-438-6600, 888-444-6664; www.omnihotels.com

Set against the backdrop of the Rocky Mountains, this 300-acre resort has something for everyone. Golfers needing to brush up on their game head for the L.A.W.s Academy of Golf for its celebrated clinics and courses before hitting the resort's three nine-hole courses. There's a well-equipped fitness center and pool and a full-service spa that offers a variety of treatments. The guest rooms are comfortable and elegant and include amenities like WebTV and high-speed Internet. Three restaurants run the gamut from traditional to pub style.

390 rooms. Restaurant, bar. Fitness center. Pool. Spa. Pets accepted. Golf. $$$

BUENA VISTA

See also Salida

Lying at the eastern edge of the Collegiate Range and the central Colorado mountain region, Buena Vista is a natural point of departure for treks into the mountains. Within 20 miles you'll find four rivers, 12 peaks with elevations above 14,000 feet and more than 500 mountain lakes and streams.

WHAT TO SEE
ARKANSAS RIVER TOURS

126 S. Main St., Buena, Vista, 719-942-4362, 800-321-4352; www.arkansasrivertours.com

The upper Arkansas River in South Central Colorado offers some of the most beautiful and challenging rafting experiences in the region. With its long, placid stretches of scenic wilderness punctuated by plunges through dramatic white-water canyons, the river accommodates all levels of river-rafting thrill-seekers. Experienced rafters won't want to miss an adrenaline-pumping ride through the magnificent Royal George Canyon. Families will love a scenic float through the gently rolling Cottonwood Rapid. Arkansas River Tours is one of several rafting outfitters along Highway 50 offering a variety of outings, from quarter-day trips to multiple-day high-adventure expeditions. Daily; weather permitting.

NOAH'S ARK WHITEWATER RAFTING COMPANY
23910 Highway 285 S, Buena Vista, 719-395-2158; www.noahsark.com
Half-day to three-day trips on the Arkansas River.
Mid-May-late August.

WILDERNESS AWARE
12600 Highway 24/285, Buena Vista, 719-395-2112, 800-462-7238; www.inaraft.com
Half-day to 10-day river rafting trips on the Arkansas, Colorado, Dolores, North Platte and Gunnison rivers.
May-September.

WHERE TO STAY
★BEST WESTERN VISTA INN
733 Highway 24 N., Buena Vista, 719-395-8009, 800-809-3495; www.bestwestern.com
51 rooms. Complimentary breakfast. Fitness center. Pool. $

CAÑON CITY

★★★★★
COLORADO

See also Colorado Springs, Cripple Creek
In 1807, Lieutenant Zebulon Pike was one of the first white men to camp on this site, which was long a favored spot of the Ute Indians. Cañon City is located at the mouth of the Royal Gorge and ringed by mountains.

WHAT TO SEE

BUCKSKIN JOE FRONTIER TOWN & RAILWAY
1193 Fremont County Road, Cañon City, 719-275-5149; www.buckskinjoes.com
This Old West theme park includes an old Western town with 30 authentic buildings. Daily gunfights, horse-drawn trolley ride, magic shows and entertainment, plus a 30-minute train ride to the rim of Royal Gorge Railway. Park open March-September, daily. Scenic railway open March-October, daily; November-December, Saturday-Sunday only.

CAÑON CITY MUNICIPAL MUSEUM
612 Royal Gorge Blvd., Cañon City, 719-276-5279
The complex includes Rudd Cabin, a pioneer log cabin constructed in 1860, and Stone House, built in 1881. Galleries display minerals and rocks, artifacts from the settlement of the Fremont County region and guns.
Early May-Labor Day, Tuesday-Sunday; rest of year, Tuesday-Saturday.

DINOSAUR DEPOT MUSEUM
330 Royal Gorge Blvd., Cañon City, 719-269-7150, 800-987-6379;
www.dinosaurdepot.com
See an entire Stegosaurus skeleton that was discovered less than 10 miles away.

Admission: adult $4, children $2, children age under 3 free. Daily 10 a.m.-4 p.m.; winter, Wednesday-Sunday only, 10 a.m.-4 p.m.

FREMONT CENTER FOR THE ARTS

505 Macon Ave., Cañon City, 719-275-2790; www.fremontarts.org
This community art center features visual art exhibits and cultural programs. Tuesday-Saturday 10 a.m.-4 p.m.

GARDEN PARK FOSSIL AREA

3170 E. Main St., Cañon City, 719-269-7150; www.dinosaurdepot.com/exhibits.htm
Fossils of well-known species of large dinosaurs have been discovered at this site over the last 120 years, many of which are on exhibit at museums around the country, including the Smithsonian. Fossils of dinosaurs, dinosaur eggs and dinosaur tracks have also been discovered in the Garden Park Fossil Area, along with fossils of rare plants. Daily.

ROYAL GORGE BRIDGE AND PARK

4218 County Road, Cañon City, 719-275-7507, 888-333-5597;
www.royalgorgebridge.com
This magnificent canyon has cliffs rising more than 1,000 feet above the Arkansas River. The Royal Gorge Suspension Bridge, 1,053 feet above the river, is the highest in the world. The Royal Gorge Incline Railway, the world's steepest, takes passengers 1,550 feet down to the bottom of the canyon. A 2,200-foot aerial tramway glides across the spectacular canyon.
Daily 10 a.m.-4:30 p.m.

ROYAL GORGE ROUTE

401 Water St., Cañon City, 303-569-1000, 888-724-5748; www.royalgorgeroute.com
Travel by train through the Royal Gorge on two-hour round-trips departing from Cañon City.

Summer, daily; call for schedule.

SPECIAL EVENTS
BLOSSOM & MUSIC FESTIVAL

Depot Park, Cañon City, 719-275-2331; www.ccblossomfestival.com
This celebration of springtime features arts and crafts, a parade and a carnival. First weekend in May.

ROYAL GORGE RODEO

1436 S. Fourth St., Cañon City, 719-275-4784
In addition to the rodeo, the weekend features a Friday night barbecue and Sunday morning pancake breakfast.
Late April-Early May.

WHERE TO STAY
★★BEST WESTERN ROYAL GORGE

1925 Fremont Drive, Cañon City, 719-275-3377, 800-231-7317; www.bestwestern.com
67 rooms. Restaurant, bar. Pool. $

WHERE TO EAT
★★LE PETIT CHABLIS
512 Royal Gorge Blvd., Cañon City, 719-269-3333
French. Lunch, dinner. Closed Sunday-Monday. $

COLORADO SPRINGS
See also Canon City, Cripple Creek
Fantastic rock formations surround Colorado Springs, located at the foot of Pikes Peak. General William J. Palmer founded the city as a summer playground and health resort. The headquarters of Pike National Forest is in Colorado Springs.

WHAT TO SEE
BROADMOOR-CHEYENNE MOUNTAIN AREA
1 Lake Ave., Colorado Springs
Broadmoor-Cheyenne Mountain Highway zigzags up the east face of Cheyenne Mountain with view of plains to the east. The Will Rogers Shrine of the Sun is nearby.
Daily.

CHEYENNE MOUNTAIN ZOOLOGICAL PARK
4250 Cheyenne Mountain Zoo Road, Colorado Springs, 719-633-9925;
www.cmzoo.org
This little gem located on the side of the Cheyenne Mountains in Colorado Springs is known for its beautiful setting and for the diversity of its animal collection. There are more than 650 animals here, including many endangered species. You can feed the giraffes and check out the monkeys. Admission includes access to the Will Rogers Shrine of the Sun.
Admission: adults $14.25, children $7.25, children under 2 free. Memorial Day-Labor Day, daily 9 a.m.-6 p.m.; Labor Day-Memorial Day, daily 9 a.m.-5 p.m.; Thanksgiving Day 9 a.m.-4 p.m., Christmas Eve 9 a.m.-3 p.m., Christmas Day 9 a.m.-4 p.m.

COLORADO SPRINGS FINE ARTS CENTER
30 W. Dale St., Colorado Springs, 719-634-5581; www.csfineartscenter.org
Permanent collections include American Indian and Hispanic art, Guatemalan textiles, 19th- and 20th-century American Western paintings, graphics and sculpture by Charles M. Russell and other American artists.
Admission: adults $10, children, students $8.50 children under 4 free.
Tuesday-Friday 10 a.m.-5 p.m., Saturday 10 a.m.-8 p.m., Sunday 10 a.m.-5 p.m.

COLORADO SPRINGS PIONEERS MUSEUM
Former El Paso County Courthouse, 215 S. Tejon St., Colorado Springs,
719-385-5990; www.cspm.org
Learn about the history of the Pikes Peak region.
Tuesday-Saturday 10 a.m.-5 p.m., Sunday 1-5 p.m. May-October.

EL POMAR CARRIAGE MUSEUM

10 Lake Circle, Colorado Springs, 719-577-7000; www.elpomar.org

An extensive collection of fine carriages, vehicles and Western articles of 1890s located next to Broadmoor Hall.

Monday-Saturday 9 a.m.-5 p.m., Sunday 1-5 p.m.

FLYING W RANCH

3330 Chuckwagon Road, Colorado Springs, 719-598-4000, 800-232-3599; www.flyingw.com

A working cattle and horse ranch with chuck-wagon suppers and a Western stage show. More than 12 restored buildings with period furniture. Reservations required.

Mid-May-September, daily; rest of year, Friday-Saturday; closed December 25-February.

GARDEN OF THE GODS

1805 N. 30th St., Colorado Springs, 719-634-6666; www.gardenofgods.com

This 1,350-acre park at the base of Pikes Peak is a showcase of geological wonders. It's best known for its outstanding red sandstone formations, including the famous Balanced Rock and Kissing Camels. The park offers eight miles of well-groomed trails to view the geological treasures, plants and wildlife. Take a free guided walking tour or hop on a bus to tour the garden. Other activities include horseback riding (Academy Riding Stables, 719-633-5667) and rock climbing (by permit only). Plan a visit at sunrise or sunset, when you'll get a true understanding of where the area gets its name.

Memorial Day-Labor Day, daily 8 a.m.-8 p.m.; rest of year, daily 9 a.m.-5 p.m.

GHOST TOWN WILD WEST MUSEUM

400 S. 21st St., Colorado Springs, 719-634-0696; www.ghosttownmuseum.com

This authentic Old West town is housed in an 1899 railroad building and includes a general store, jail, saloon, re-created Victorian home, horseless carriages and buggies and a 1903 Cadillac. Visitors can also have fun with old-time nickelodeons, player pianos, arcade "movies" and a shooting gallery. Admission: adults $6.50, children $4. June-August, Monday-Saturday 9 a.m.-6 p.m., Sunday 11 a.m.-6 p.m.; September-May, Monday-Saturday 10 a.m.-5 p.m., Sunday 11 a.m.-5 p.m.

LAKE GEORGE (ELEVEN MILE STATE PARK)

4229 Highway Road, 92, Lake George, 719-748-3401; www.parks.state.co.us/parks/elevenmile

Offering 3,400 surface acres, this reservoir is fully stocked with hungry kokanee salmon, carp, trout and northern pike. A number of local outfitters, such as 11 Mile Sports, Inc. (877-725-3172) can supply the necessary equipment as well as a guide. Daily. Ice fishing in winter.

MAY NATURAL HISTORY MUSEUM

710 Rock Creek Canyon Road, Colorado Springs, 719-576-0450, 800-666-3841; www.maymuseum-camp-rvpark.com

See a collection of more than 8,000 invertebrates from the tropics. Then,

FLORISSANT FOSSIL BEDS NATIONAL MONUMENT

Florissant Fossil Beds National Monument consists of 6,000 acres once partially covered by a prehistoric lake. Thirty-five million years ago, ash and mudflows from volcanoes in the area buried a forest of redwoods, filling the lake and fossilizing its living organisms. Insects, seeds and leaves of the Eocene Epoch are preserved in perfect detail, along with remarkable samples of standing petrified sequoia stumps. You'll also find nature trails, picnic areas and a restored 19th-century homestead. Guided tours are available. The visitor center is two miles south on Teller County Road 1. Daily.

Information: Florissant, 22 miles west of Manitou Springs on Highway 24; www.nps.gov/flfo

check out the Museum of Space Exploration, which includes NASA space photos and movies.

Admission: adults $6, children $3. May-October, daily; and by appointment.

MCALLISTER HOUSE MUSEUM

423 N. Cascade Ave., Colorado Springs, 719-635-7925;
www.nscda.org/co/mcallisterhousemuseum.html

This six-room 1873 Gothic-style cottage with Victorian furnishings has an adjacent carriage house. Guided tours.

September-April, Thursday-Saturday 10 a.m.-4 p.m.; May-August, Wednesday-Saturday noon-4 p.m.

MUSEUM OF THE AMERICAN NUMISMATIC ASSOCIATION

818 N. Cascade Ave., Colorado Springs, 719-632-2646, 800-367-9723;
www.money.org/moneymus.html

Learn all about the study of currency through the collections of coins, tokens, medals and paper money here. Changing exhibits; library.

Admission: free. Tuesday-Friday 9 a.m.-5 p.m., Saturday 10 a.m.-5 p.m., Sunday noon-5 p.m.

OLD COLORADO CITY

West Colorado Ave., between 24th Street to 28th Street, Colorado Springs,
719-577-4112; www.shopoldcoloradocity.com

This renovated historic district features more than 100 quaint shops, art galleries and restaurants.

PALMER PARK

3650 Maizeland Road, 719-578-6640

Occupying 710 acres on the Austin Bluffs, this park boasts magnificent views from its scenic roads and trails. Picnic areas.

PETERSON AIR & SPACE MUSEUM

150 E. Ent Ave., Peterson Air Force Base, 719-556-4915; www.petemuseum.org

Display of 17 historic aircraft from World War I to present, plus exhibits on the history of the Air Force base. Open on restricted basis, call for times. Tuesday-Saturday 9 a.m.-4 p.m. Closed Sunday-Monday.

PIKE NATIONAL FOREST

1920 Valley Drive, Pueblo, 719-545-8737; www.fs.fed.us/r2/psicc

This massive 1.1 million acres of national land includes world-famous Pikes Peak. Wilkerson Pass (9,507 feet) is 45 miles west on Highway 24, with a visitor information center.

Memorial Day-Labor Day.

PIKES PEAK

Pikes Peak Highway, Cascade, 719-385-7325, 800-318-9505;
www.pikespeakcolorado.com

Soaring 14,110 feet, Pikes Peak is the second most visited mountain in the world behind Mt. Fuji. To reach the peak, you can undertake an eight-hour hike or drive an hour up the 19-mile road, the last half of which is unpaved, has no guardrails and contains steep drops (a four-by-four vehicle isn't necessary but weather causes road closures even in the summer).

Daily; weather permitting. Closed during annual Hill Climb in July.

PIKES PEAK AUTO HILL CLIMB EDUCATIONAL MUSEUM

135 Manitou Ave., Manitou Springs, 719-685-4400; www.ppihc.com

More than two dozen racecars, plus numerous exhibits on the Pikes Peak race, considered America's second-oldest auto race.

Daily, shorter hours in winter.

PIKES PEAK COG RAILWAY

515 Ruxton Ave., Manitou Springs, 719-685-5401, 800-745-3773; www.cograilway.com

The surest bet to the summit of Pikes Peak is the cog railway. Trains usually depart five times daily, rain or shine, but make reservations early. Whenever you go, bundle up. Temperatures are 30-40 degrees cooler at the top. Water and aspirin help alleviate altitude sickness.

April-December, daily.

PIKES PEAK MOUNTAIN BIKE TOURS

302 S. 25th St., Colorado Springs, 888-593-3062; www.bikepikespeak.com

Tours vary in length and endurance level, and professional guides provide all the necessary equipment to make your ride safe, comfortable.

Tour schedules vary; call or visit Web site for schedule.

PRORODEO HALL OF FAME AND MUSEUM OF THE AMERICAN COWBOY

101 ProRodeo Drive, Colorado Springs, 719-528-4764; www.prorodeohalloffame.com

The Hall of Fame pays tribute to giants like nine-time world champion Casey Tibbs, while the museum will help you appreciate the life of a cowboy—try roping one of the dummy steers. Outdoor exhibits include live rodeo animals and a replica rodeo arena.

Admission: adults $6, seniors $5, youth $3, children under 6 free. Daily 9 a.m.-5 p.m.

ROCK LEDGE RANCH HISTORIC SITE

1401 Recreation Way, Colorado Springs, 719-578-6777; www.rockledgeranch.com

This living history program and working ranch demonstrates everyday life in the region. Braille nature trail.

June-Labor Day, Wednesday-Sunday 10 a.m.-5 p.m.; Labor Day-December, Saturday 10 a.m.-4 p.m., Sunday noon-4 p.m.

SEVEN FALLS

2850 S. Cheyenne Canyon Road, Colorado Springs, 719-632-0765;
www.sevenfalls.com

The only completely lighted canyon and waterfall in the world. Best seen from Eagle's Nest, reached by a mountain elevator. Native American dance interpretations occur daily in the summer. Night lighting (summer).

Daily 9 a.m.-4:15 p.m.

SHRINE OF THE SUN

4250 Cheyenne Mountain Zoo Road, Colorado Springs, 719-577-7000

This memorial to Will Rogers, who was killed in a plane crash in 1935, is built of Colorado gray-pink granite and steel. Contains memorabilia. Fee for visit is included in zoo admission price.

Memorial Day-Labor Day, daily 9 a.m.-5 p.m.; Labor Day-Memorial Day, daily 9 a.m.-4 p.m.

U.S. AIR FORCE ACADEMY

2346 Academy Drive, Colorado Springs, 719-333-2025, 800-955-4438;
www.usafa.af.mil

Established in 1955, the academy has a student population of 4,200 cadets. Cadet Chapel, located on the grounds of the academy, is the city's most famous architectural landmark, with its striking combination of stained glass and 150-foot aluminum spires. Stop by the visitor's center for a free self-guided tour map or to view films and informative exhibits about the Air Force. Also check out the planetarium, which may be offering a special program, and don't miss a chance to see a T-38 and B-52 bomber up close. Call before visiting—the chapel closes for special events, and security events may close the base unexpectedly.

Visitors Center: daily 9 a.m.-5 p.m.; Chapel: Monday-Saturday 9 a.m.-5 p.m.

U.S. OLYMPIC TRAINING CENTER

1 Olympic Plaza, Colorado Springs, 719-632-5551, 888-659-8687; www.usoc.org

Tours offer an insider's view of how Olympic-level athletes train. For most of us, the closest we'll get to a medal are the replicas available in the gift shop.

Monday-Saturday 9 a.m.-5 p.m., last tour at 4 p.m., Sunday 11 a.m.-6 p.m.

WORLD FIGURE SKATING HALL OF FAME AND MUSEUM

20 First St., Colorado Springs, 719-635-5200; www.usfsa.org

This museum features exhibits on the history of figure skating including a skate gallery and video collection.

Monday-Friday 10 a.m.-4 p.m.; November-April: Saturday 10 a.m.-4 p.m.; May-October: Saturday 10 a.m.-5 p.m.

SPECIAL EVENTS
COLORADO SPRINGS BALLOON CLASSIC
328 Bonfoy Ave., Colorado Springs, 719-471-4833; www.balloonclassic.com
This annual event features more than 100 massive balloons and entertainment.
Labor Day weekend.

LITTLE BRITCHES RODEO
5050 Edison Ave., Colorado Springs, 719-389-0333; www.nlbra.com
This roping and riding event is one of the oldest junior rodeos in the nation.
Late May.

PIKES PEAK INTERNATIONAL HILL CLIMB
1631 Mesa Ave., Colorado Springs, 719-685-4400; www.ppihc.com
The Race to the Clouds has been a part of Colorado Spring's July Fourth
celebration since 1916. Spectators of all ages marvel at those who dare steer
their racecars, trucks and motorcycles along the final 12.4 miles of Pikes
Peak Highway, a gravel route with 156 turns and a 5,000-foot rise in elevation. Vehicles can reach more than 130 mph on straightaways, and there isn't
a guardrail in sight. You need to be on the mountain at the crack of dawn to
catch the action. Those who don't take advantage of the overnight parking
the evening before the race can arrive as early as 4 a.m. to stake out a good
spot. The road closes to additional spectators at 8 a.m., so plan to spend the
day here. Those who park above the start line won't be able to leave until late
afternoon when the race is over. The best views are above the tree line.
Late June.

PIKES PEAK MARATHON
Colorado Springs, 719-473-2625; www.pikespeakmarathon.org
This race starts at Memorial Park and ends at Ruxton and Manitou avenues
in Manitou Springs.
Late August.

PIKES PEAK OR BUST RODEO
Norris-Penrose Event Center, 1045 W. Rio Grande St., Colorado Springs,
719-635-3547; www.pikespeakorbustrodeo.org
Bareback riding, bull riding, calf roping, steer wrestling and more.
Mid-July.

WHERE TO STAY
★★THE ACADEMY HOTEL
8110 N. Academy Blvd., Colorado Springs, 719-598-5770, 800-766-8524;
www.theacademyhotel.com
200 rooms. Complimentary breakfast. Restaurant, bar. Fitness center. Pool.
Pets accepted. $

★★ANTLERS HILTON COLORADO SPRINGS
4 S. Cascade Ave., Colorado Springs, 719-955-5600; www.antlers.com
292 rooms. Restaurant, bar. Pool. $

★★★★★THE BROADMOOR
1 Lake Ave., Colorado Springs, 719-634-7711; www.broadmoor.com

Located at the foot of the Rocky Mountains and surrounded by beautiful Cheyenne Lake, the Broadmoor has been one of America's favorite resorts since 1918. This all-season paradise is in Colorado Springs, yet feels a million miles away. The opulent accommodations include rooms with views of the mountains or lake. Activities include a tennis club, three championship golf courses, paddle boating on the lake and horseback riding. Kids will love the "mountain" waterslide. And the world-class spa incorporates indigenous botanicals and pure spring water. The resort includes 15 restaurants, cafés and lounges and several shops.

744 rooms. Restaurant, bar. Spa. Pets accepted. Pool. Golf. Tennis. Business center. Fitness center. $$$

★★DOUBLETREE HOTEL COLORADO SPRINGS-WORLD ARENA
1775 E. Cheyenne Mountain Blvd., Colorado Springs, 719-576-8900, 800-222-8733;
www.doubletree.com

299 rooms. Restaurant, bar. Pets accepted. Pool. $

★DRURY INN PIKES PEAK
8155 N. Academy Blvd., Colorado Springs, 719-598-2500, 800-325-8300;
www.druryhotels.com

117 rooms. Complimentary breakfast. Pets accepted. Fitness center. Pool. $

★★EMBASSY SUITES COLORADO SPRINGS
7290 Commerce Center Drive, Colorado Springs, 719-599-9100;
www.embassysuites.com

206 rooms. Complimentary breakfast. Restaurant, bar. Pool. Fitness center. Business center. $

★FAIRFIELD INN & SUITES COLORADO SPRINGS SOUTH
2725 Geyser Drive, Colorado Springs, 719-576-1717, 800-228-2800;
www.fairfieldinn.com

84 rooms. Complimentary breakfast. Pets accepted. Pool. Fitness center. Business center. $

★HOLIDAY INN EXPRESS COLORADO SPRINGS AIRPORT
1815 Aeroplaza Drive, Colorado Springs, 719-591-6000, 888-465-4329;
www.hiexpress.com

94 rooms. Complimentary breakfast. Business center. Pool. Fitness center. $

WHERE TO EAT
★★★CHARLES COURT
The Broadmoor, 1 Lake Ave., Colorado Springs, 719-577-5733, 806-634-7711;
www.broadmoor.com

One of the many restaurants at the luxurious Broadmoor Hotel, Charles Court offers progressive American fare in a relaxed and contemporary setting. In warm weather, you can dine outdoors with lakeside views. The menu features regional Rocky Mountain fare such as Colorado rack of lamb and the signature Charles Court Game Grill. The wine list boasts more than 600 selections from all around the world. For special occasions, opt for the chef's table in the kitchen (four guests minimum).

American. Breakfast, dinner (Thursday-Monday), Sunday brunch. Bar. Reservations recommended. Outdoor seating. $$$

★★EDELWEISS
34 E. Ramona Ave., Colorado Springs, 719-633-2220; www.edelweissrest.com
German. Lunch, dinner. Bar. Children's menu. Reservations recommended. Outdoor seating. $$

★★FAMOUS STEAKHOUSE
31 N. Tejon St., Colorado Springs, 719-227-7333; www.thefamoussteakhouse.net
Steak. Lunch, dinner. Bar. Reservations recommended. $$$

★★GIUSEPPE'S OLD DEPOT RESTAURANT
10 S. Sierra Madre, Colorado Springs, 719-635-3111; www.giuseppes-depot.com
American. Lunch, dinner. Bar. Children's menu. Reservations recommended. $$

★IL VICINO
11 S. Tejon St., Colorado Springs, 719-475-9224; www.ilvicino.com
Italian. Lunch, dinner, late-night. Bar. Outdoor seating. $

★★JAKE AND TELLY'S GREEK DINING
2616 W. Colorado Ave., Colorado Springs, 719-633-0406; www.greekdining.com
Greek. Lunch, dinner. Bar. Children's menu. Reservations recommended. Outdoor seating. $$

★LA CREPERIE BISTRO
204 N. Tejon, Colorado Springs, 719-632-0984; www.creperiebistro.com
French. Breakfast, lunch, dinner. Outdoor seating. $$

★★LA PETITE MAISON
1015 W. Colorado Ave., Colorado Springs, 719-632-4887; www.lapetitemaisoncs.com
French, American. Lunch, dinner. Closed Monday. Outdoor seating. $$$

★★MACKENZIE'S CHOP HOUSE
128 S. Tejon St., Colorado Springs, 719-635-3536; www.mackenzieschophouse.com
American. Lunch, dinner. Bar. Children's menu. Outdoor seating. $$$

★OLD CHICAGO PASTA & PIZZA
118 N. Tejon St., Colorado Springs, 719-634-8812; www.oldchicago.com
American, pizza. Lunch, dinner, late-night. Bar. Children's menu. Outdoor seating. $

★★★★★THE PENROSE ROOM
The Broadmoor, 1 Lake Ave., Colorado Springs, 719-577-5733, 866-381-8432; www.broadmoor.com
Located within the Broadmoor, the sophisticated and recently renovated Penrose Room offers a spectacular dining experience set against magnificent views of Colorado Springs and Cheyenne Mountain. Chef Bertrand Bouquin

serves up contemporary continental cuisine influenced by the food of Italy, Spain, Africa and France. The menu changes often and offers prix fixe meals of three, four and seven courses. Favorite appetizers include pistachio-laden warm goat cheese salad, five herbs ravioli and chilled peekytoe crab with cherry relish salad. Entrées include roasted loin of Colorado lamb with purple mustard and slowly cooked halibut in black olive oil. After dinner, enjoy live music and dancing.

French. Dinner. Closed Sunday. Bar. Children's menu. Jacket required. Reservations recommended. $$$$

★★★SUMMIT
The Broadmoor, 1 Lake Ave., Colorado Springs, 719-577-5777, 800-634-7711; www.broadmoor.com

At one of the country's premier resorts, Summit fills every bill—from impeccable service to memorable meals to the inventive interior. Chef Bertrand Bouquin was privileged enough to spend time under the tutelage of world-class chefs including Alain Ducasse, Daniel Boulud, and Jean-Pierre Bruneau before coming to Summit to create such chef d'oeuvres as the favored braised beef short ribs with rioja, baby carrots and roasted garlic mashed potatoes. The food is accented by the edgy design, which centers on a turning glass turret of wine bottles—the ultimate wine rack, if you will.

American. Dinner. Closed Monday. Bar. Children's menu. Reservations recommended. $$$

SPAS
★★★★★THE SPA AT THE BROADMOOR
The Broadmoor, 1 Lake Ave., Colorado Springs, 719-577-5770, 866-686-3965; www.broadmoor.com

With the beautiful scenery of the Rocky Mountains as a backdrop, the Spa at the Broadmoor already has an advantage over other luxury spas. But even without these surroundings, an experience at this two-level lakefront spa is pure bliss. With Venetian chandeliers, earth tones and an overall feeling of serenity, the treatment rooms perfectly set the scene for the spa's luxurious massage therapies and skin treatments. If your Rocky Mountain adventures have left you with aching muscles, the spa's variety of massage therapies will make you feel like new again, while facial therapies such as the luxe facial will get skin glowing. The Junior Ice Cream manicure and pedicure is reserved for those guests ages 11 and under. $$

CORTEZ
See also Durango

Originally a trading center for sheep and cattle ranchers, Cortez now accommodates travelers visiting Mesa Verde National Park and oil workers whose business takes them to the nearby Aneth oil field. The semi-desert area 38 miles southwest of Cortez includes the only spot in the nation where one can stand in four states (Colorado, Utah, Arizona, New Mexico) and two Native American nations (Navajo and Ute) at one time. A simple marker located approximately 100 yards from the Four Corners Highway (Highway 160) indicates the exact place where these areas meet. There are many opportunities for hunting and fishing in the Dolores River valley.

MESA VERDE NATIONAL PARK

In the far southwest corner of Colorado exists the largest—and -arguably the most interesting—archaeological preserve in the nation. Mesa Verde National Park, with 52,000 acres encompassing 4,000 known archaeological sites, is a treasure trove of ancestral Pueblo cultural artifacts, including the magnificent Anasazi cliff dwellings. Constructed in the 13th century, these huge, elaborate stone villages built into the canyon walls are spellbinding. To fully appreciate their significance, first take a walk through the park's Chapin Mesa Museum for a historical overview. A visit to the actual sites can be physically challenging but is well worth the effort. Several of the sites can be explored year-round, free of charge; others require tickets for ranger-guided tours in summer months only. Tour tickets can be purchased at the park's Far View. The visitor Center. is open daily.

Information: Mesa Verde, eight miles east of Cortez, 36 miles west of Durango on Highway 160 to park entrance, then 15 miles south to -visitor center, 970-529-4465; www.nps.gov/meve.

WHAT TO SEE

ANASAZI HERITAGE CENTER AND ESCALANTE

27501 Highway 184, Dolores, 970-882-5600; www.co.blm.gov/ahc/index.htm

This museum showcases the Anasazi and other Native American cultures. See exhibits on archaeology and local history. The Escalante site, discovered by a Franciscan friar in 1776, is within a half-mile of the center. This is also the starting point for the Canyons of the Ancients National Monument. March-October, daily 9 a.m.-5 p.m.; November-February, daily 9 a.m.-4 p.m.

HOVENWEEP NATIONAL MONUMENT

McElmo Route, Cortez, 970-562-4282; www.nps.gov/hove

This monument consists of six units of prehistoric ruins—the best preserved is at Square Tower, which includes the remains of pueblos and towers. Self-guided trail (park ranger on duty); visitor area. Daily 8 a.m.-5 p.m.

LOWRY PUEBLO

27501 Highway 184, Cortez, 970-882-5600; www.blm.gov

Part of the Canyons of the Ancients National Monument, the Lowry Pueblo was constructed by the Anasazi (circa 1075) and has 40 excavated rooms. Daily, weather and road conditions permitting.

UTE MOUNTAIN TRIBAL PARK

Highway Junction 160/491 nearCortez, 970-749-1452;
www.utemountainute.com

The Ute Mountain Tribe developed this 125,000-acre park on their tribal lands, opening hundreds of largely unexplored 800-year-old Anasazi ruins to the public. Tours begin at the Ute Mountain Visitor Center/Museum, 19 miles south of Cortez via Highway 666 (daily); reservations required. Back-packing trips in summer.

Primitive camping available.

SPECIAL EVENTS
MONTEZUMA COUNTY FAIR
Montezuma County Fairgrounds, 30100 Highway 160, Cortez, 970-565-1000; www.co.montezuma.co.us
The fair includes an antique tractor parade, barbecue and carnival. First week in August.

UTE MOUNTAIN ROUND-UP RODEO
Montezuma County Fairgrounds, 30100 Highway 160, Cortez, 970-565-8151
This weeklong extravaganza includes rodeo events as well as a children's "parade"—kids march to businesses downtown and receive treats. Early-mid-June.

WHERE TO STAY
★BEST WESTERN TURQUOISE INN & SUITES
535 E. Main St., Cortez, 970-565-3778, 800-547-3376; www.bestwestern.com
77 rooms. Complimentary breakfast. Pets accepted. Pool. Business center. $

★HOLIDAY INN EXPRESS
2121 E. Main St., Cortez, 970-565-6000, 800-626-5652; www.coloradoholiday.com
100 rooms. Complimentary breakfast. Pets accepted. Pool. Business center. $

CRESTED BUTTE
See also Gunnison
Crested Butte is a picturesque mining town in the midst of magnificent mountain country. Inquire locally for information on horseback pack trips to Aspen through the West Elk Wilderness. Guided fishing trips are also available on the more than 1,000 miles of streams and rivers within a two-hour drive of Crested Butte.

WHAT TO SEE
CRESTED BUTTE MOUNTAIN RESORT SKI AREA
12 Snowmass Road, Crested Butte, 800-810-7669; www.skicb.com
Four high-speed quad, two triple, three double chairlifts, three surface lifts, two magic carpets; patrol, school, rentals, snowmaking. Longest run 2½ miles; vertical drop 3,062 feet. Multiday, half-day rates.
Late November-mid-April, daily. Nineteen miles of groomed cross-country trails, 100 miles of wilderness trails; snowmobiling, sleigh rides.

WHERE TO EAT
★DONITA'S CANTINA
330 Elk Ave., Crested Butte, 970-349-6674; www.donitascantina.com
Mexican. Dinner. Bar. Children's menu. $$

★★LE BOSQUET
525 Red Lady St., Crested Butte, 970-349-5808
French. Dinner. Closed mid-April-mid-May. Bar. Outdoor seating. $$

CRIPPLE CREEK

See also Canon City, Colorado Springs

At its height, Cripple Creek and the surrounding area produced as much as $25 million in gold in a single year. It was nearly a ghost town when citizens voted to allow legalized gambling in the 1990s. Today it is mostly a gambling and tourist town and has managed to preserve some of its Old West charm.

WHAT TO SEE
CRIPPLE CREEK CASINOS
Cripple Creek, 877-858-4653; www.visitcripple-creek.com
Cripple Creek has nearly 20 limited-stakes ($5 bet limit) casinos along its Victorian storefront main street area. Daily.

CRIPPLE CREEK DISTRICT MUSEUM
Fifth Street and Bennett Avenue, Cripple Creek, 719-689-2634; www.cripple-creek.org
See artifacts of Cripple Creek's glory days including pioneer relics, mining and railroad displays.
June-September: daily 10 a.m.-5 p.m.; October-May: Friday-Sunday 10 a.m.-4 p.m.

CRIPPLE CREEK-VICTOR NARROW GAUGE RAILROAD
Fifth Street and Bennett Avenue, Cripple Creek, 719-689-2640
Authentic locomotive and coaches depart from Cripple Creek District Museum. The four-mile round-trip travels past many historic mines.
Late May-early October, daily, departs every 45 minutes.

IMPERIAL CASINO HOTEL
123 N. Third St., Cripple Creek, 719-689-7777, 800-235-2922;
www.imperialcasinohotel.com
This 1896 hotel-turned-casino was constructed shortly after the town's great fire and features a variety of slot machines.

MOLLIE KATHLEEN GOLD MINE
Highway 67, Cripple Creek, 719-689-2466, 888-291-5689; www.goldminetours.com
Descend 1,000 feet on a one-hour guided tour through a gold mine.
April-October: daily; tours depart every 10 minutes. Pets not accepted.

VICTOR
Cripple Creek, five miles south on Highway 67, on the southwest side of Pikes Peak, 719-689-2284; www.victorcolorado.com
This "city of mines" actually has streets paved with gold (low-grade ore was used to surface streets in the early days).

SPECIAL EVENTS
DONKEY DERBY DAYS
City Park and Bennett Avenue, Cripple Creek, 719-689-3315;
www.visitcripplecreek.com
Annual series of donkey races includes children's events and a parade.
Last full weekend in June.

VETERAN'S MEMORIAL RALLY

City Park, Cripple Creek, 719-487-8005

Four-day event honoring veterans. Mid-August.

WHERE TO STAY
★★★CARR MANOR

350 E. Carr Ave., Cripple Creek, 719-689-3709; www.carrmanor.com

A night at this boutique hotel, housed in a former 1890's schoolhouse, includes a full breakfast served in the original high school cafeteria. Rooms feature original chalkboards for messages. There's also a small fitness spa. 13 rooms. Closed January-February; also weekdays March-April. No children under 12. Complimentary breakfast. $

★★DOUBLE EAGLE HOTEL & CASINO

442 E. Bennett Ave., Cripple Creek, 719-689-5000, 800-711-7234; www.decasino.com

158 rooms. Complimentary breakfast. Restaurant, bar. Casino. $

★★IMPERIAL CASINO HOTEL

123 N. Third St., Cripple Creek, 719-689-7777, 800-235-2922;
www.imperialcasinohotel.com

26 rooms. Restaurant, bar. Casino. $

WHERE TO EAT
★★STRATTON'S STEAKHOUSE

Imperial Casino Hotel, 123 N. Third St., Cripple Creek, 719-689-7777

American. Lunch, dinner. Closed Monday-Tuesday. Bar. $$

DENVER

See also Boulder

The capital of Colorado, nicknamed the "Mile High City" because its official elevation is exactly one mile above sea level, began as a settlement of gold seekers, many of them unsuccessful. In its early years, Denver almost lost out to several booming mountain mining centers in the race to become the state's major city. In 1858, the community consisted of some 60 raffish cabins, plus Colorado's first saloon. With the onset of the silver rush in the 1870s, Denver came into its own. By 1890, the population had topped 100,000. Bolstered by the wealth that poured in from the rich mines in the Rockies, Denver rapidly became Colorado's economic and cultural center. It boomed again after World War II and in the 1990s.

Today, with the Great Plains sweeping away to the east, the foothills of the Rocky Mountains immediately to the west, and a dry, mild climate (where you'll find 300 days of sunshine), Denver is a growing city with 2.5 million people in the metropolitan area. A building boom in the 1990s resulted in a new airport, a downtown baseball park surrounded by a lively nightlife district dubbed LoDo (lower downtown), new football, basketball and hockey stadiums, and a redeveloped river valley just west of downtown with an aquarium, amusement park and shopping district.

Once economically tied to Colorado's natural resources, Denver now boasts one of the most diverse economies in the United States and is a hub for the cable and telecom industries. Parks have long been a point of civic pride in Denver. The Denver Mountain Park System covers 13,448 acres, scattered over 380 square miles. The chain begins 15 miles west of the city at Red Rocks Park, the site of a renowned musical venue, and extends 60 miles to the west to Summit Lake perched 12,740 feet above sea level.

WHAT TO SEE
16TH STREET MALL
16th Street between Civic Center and Denver Union Station, Denver, 303-534-6161; www.downtowndenver.com

This tree-lined pedestrian promenade of red and gray granite runs through the center of Denver's downtown shopping district—outdoor cafés, shops, restaurants, hotels, fountains and plazas line its mile-long walk. European-built shuttle buses offer transportation from either end of the promenade. Along the mall you'll find Larimer Square. This restoration of the first street in Denver includes a collection of shops, galleries, nightclubs and restaurants set among Victorian courtyards, gaslights, arcades and buildings. Carriage rides around square.

ANTIQUE ROW
From 300 to 2100 South Broadway, Denver; www.antique-row.com

More than 400 shops along a 14-block stretch of South Broadway sell everything from books to music to vintage Western wear to museum-quality furniture. Take the light rail to Broadway and Interstate 25 (I-25) to begin your tour. Most dealers are located between the 400 and 2000 blocks of South Broadway and the 25 and 27 blocks of East Dakota Avenue.

ARVADA CENTER FOR THE ARTS & HUMANITIES
6901 Wadsworth Blvd.,Arvada, 720-898-7200; www.arvadacenter.org

Performing arts center with concerts, plays, classes, demonstrations, art galleries and banquet hall. Amphitheater seats 1,200 (June-early September). Historical museum with old cabin and pioneer artifacts.
Museum and gallery. Monday-Friday 9 a.m.-6 p.m., Saturday 9 a.m.-5 p.m., Sunday 1-5 p.m.

BOETTCHER CONCERT HALL
1245 Champa St., Denver, 720-865-4220; www.artscomplex.com

The first fully "surround" symphonic hall in the U.S.—all of its 2,630 seats are within 75 feet of the stage. Home of the Colorado Symphony Orchestra (September-early June) and Opera Colorado with performances in the round (May).

BYERS-EVANS HOUSE MUSEUM
1310 Bannock St., Denver, 303-620-4933; www.coloradohistory.org

Restored Victorian house featuring the history of two noted Colorado pioneer families. Guided tours available.
Tuesday-Sunday 11 a.m.-3 p.m.

CHARLES C. GATES PLANETARIUM

2001 Colorado Blvd., Denver, 303-322-7009; www.dmns.org

A variety of star and laser light shows are shown here daily. The Phipps IMAX Theater has an immense motion picture system projecting images on screen 4½ stories tall and 6½ stories wide. Located in the Denver Museum of Nature and Science.

Daily showings.

CHEESMAN PARK

East Eighth Avenue and Franklin Street, Denver

This park has excellent views of nearby mountain peaks, marked off by dial and pointers. The Congress Park swimming pool is next to it and the Denver Botanical Gardens are also nearby.

THE CHILDREN'S MUSEUM OF DENVER

2121 Children's Museum Drive, Denver, 303-433-7444; www.cmdenver.org

This 24,000-square-foot, two-story hands-on museum allows children to learn and explore the world around them. Exhibits include a year-round ski slope, science center and grocery store.

Monday-Friday 9 a.m.-4 p.m., Wednesday until 7:30 p.m., Saturday-Sunday 10 a.m.-5 p.m.

COLORADO AVALANCHE (NHL)

Pepsi Center, 1000 Chopper Circle, Denver, 303-405-1100;
www.coloradoavalanche.com

Professional hockey team.

COLORADO HISTORY MUSEUM

1300 Broadway, Denver, 303-866-3682; www.coloradohistory.org

Permanent and rotating exhibits on the people and history of Colorado, including full-scale mining equipment, American Indian artifacts and photographs and a sod house.

Monday-Saturday 10 a.m.-5 p.m., Sunday noon-5 p.m.

COLORADO RAPIDS (MLS)

Dick's Sporting Goods Park, 6000 Victory Way, Commerce City, 303-727-3500;
www.coloradorapids.com

Professional soccer team. Tours.

Thursday-Saturday 10 a.m.-3 p.m., every 30 minutes.

COLORADO ROCKIES (MLB)

Coors Field, 2001 Blake St., Denver, 303-762-5437, 800-388-7625;
www.colorado.rockies.mlb.com

Professional baseball team. Tours of Coors Field available; call for fees and schedule.

COLORADO'S OCEAN JOURNEY

700 Water St., Denver, 303-561-4450, 888-561-4450

This world-class 106,500-square-foot aquarium brings visitors face to face

with more than 300 species of fish, birds, mammals and invertebrates from around the world. Check out the pool stocked with stingrays.
Sunday-Thursday 10 a.m.-10 p.m., Friday-Saturday 10 a.m.-11 p.m.

COMANCHE CROSSING MUSEUM
56060 E. Colfax Ave., Strasburg, 303-622-4322
Experience what is was like to travel via the railways in the late 1800s. This museum includes memorabilia from the completion of the transcontinental railway and includes two buildings with period rooms, a restored school-house (circa 1891) and wood-vaned windmill (circa 1880).
May-August, daily 1-4 p.m.

DENVER ART MUSEUM
100 W. 14th Ave. Parkway, Denver, 720-865-5000; www.denverartmuseum.org
Houses a collection of art objects representing almost every culture and pe-riod, including a fine collection of American Indian art; changing exhibits. Free admission first Saturday of the month.
Tuesday-Saturday 10 a.m.-5 p.m., Sunday noon-5 p.m. Closed Monday.

DENVER BOTANIC GARDENS
1005 York St., Denver, 720-865-3500; www.botanicgardens.org
This tropical paradise, which occupies 23 acres about 10 minutes east of downtown, is home to more than 15,000 plant species from around the world. The Conservatory, which holds more than 850 tropical and subtropical plants in an enclosed rainforest setting, is a soothing retreat for midwinter guests. A recent addition is the Cloud Forest Tree covered with hundreds of orchids and rare tropical plants. There are also alpine, herb, Japanese and wildflower gardens. Children particularly enjoy navigating the mazes in the Secret Path garden and climbing the resident banyan tree.
Mid-September-April: daily 9 a.m.-5 p.m.; May-mid-September: Saturday-Tuesday 9 a.m.-8 p.m., Wednesday-Friday 9 a.m.-5 p.m.

DENVER BRONCOS (NFL)
Invesco Field at Mile High, 1701 Bryant St., Denver, 720-258-3333; www.denverbroncos.com
Professional football team. Tours are available; call for fees and schedule.

DENVER FIREFIGHTERS MUSEUM
1326 Tremont Place, Denver, 303-892-1436; www.denverfirefightersmuseum.org
Housed in Fire House No. 1, this museum maintains the atmosphere of a working firehouse, with firefighting equipment from the mid-1800s.
Admission: adults $6, seniors and students $5, children under 13 $4.
Monday-Saturday 10 a.m.-4 p.m.

DENVER MUSEUM OF NATURE AND SCIENCE
City Park, 2001 Colorado Blvd., Denver, 303-322-7009, 800-925-2250; www.dmns.org
Ninety habitat exhibits from four continents are displayed against natural backgrounds. The Prehistoric Journey exhibit displays dinosaurs in recreated environments. There's also an earth sciences lab, gems and minerals, and a

Native American collection.
Daily 9 a.m.-5 p.m.

DENVER NUGGETS (NBA)

Pepsi Center, 1000 Chopper Circle, Denver, 803-405-1100; www.nba.com/nuggets
Professional basketball team. Tours of the arena are available.

DENVER PERFORMING ARTS COMPLEX

Speer Boulevard and Arapahoe Street, Denver, 720-865-4220; www.artscomplex.com
One of the most innovative and comprehensive performing arts centers in the county. The addition of the Temple Hoyne Buell Theatre makes it one of the largest under one roof. The complex also contains shops and restaurants.

DENVER PUBLIC LIBRARY

10 W. 14th Ave. Parkway, Denver, 720-865-1111; www.denverlibrary.org
This is the largest public library in the Rocky Mountain region with nearly four million items, including an outstanding Western History collection and Patent Depository Library. Programs, exhibits.
Monday-Tuesday 10 a.m.-8 p.m., Thursday-Friday 10 a.m.-6 p.m., Saturday 9 a.m.-5 p.m., Sunday 1-5 p.m.

DENVER ZOO

City Park, 2300 Steele St., Denver, 303-376-4800; www.denverzoo.org
Located in City Park just east of downtown, this 80-acre zoological wonderland is home to more than 4,000 animals representing 700 species. Founded in 1896, the zoo has evolved into one of the nation's premier animal exhibits, noted for its beautiful grounds, innovative combination of outdoor and enclosed habitats and world-class conservation and breeding programs. Don't miss the Primate Panorama, a seven-acre showcase of rare monkeys and apes. Visit the 22,000-square-foot, glass-enclosed Tropical Discovery and feel what its like to walk into a tropical rain forest complete with caves, cliffs, waterfalls and some of the zoo's most exotic (and dangerous) creatures. The Northern Shores Arctic wildlife habitat provides a nose-to-nose underwater look at swimming polar bears and sea lions. Be sure to check out the feeding schedule posted just inside the zoo's entrance. During evenings throughout December, holiday music and millions of sparkling lights transform the zoo as part of the traditional Wonderlights festival.
April-September: daily 9 a.m.-6 p.m.; October-March: daily 10 a.m.-5 p.m.

ELITCH GARDENS

2000 Elitch Circle, Denver, 303-595-4386; www.elitchgardens.com
Located in downtown Denver, this park is best known for its extreme roller coaster rides. Other favorites include a 22-story freefall in the Tower of Doom, white-water rafting and the new Flying Coaster, which simulates the experience of flying. Includes a kiddie park for younger children, the popular Island Kingdom water park and live entertainment nightly.
June-August 10 a.m.-10 p.m.; limited hours May and September.

FORNEY MUSEUM OF TRANSPORTATION

4303 Brighton Blvd., Denver, 303-297-1113; www.forneymuseum.com

This museum houses more than 300 antique cars, carriages, cycles, sleighs, steam locomotives and coaches. One of the most notable permanent exhibits is that of Union Pacific "Big Boy" locomotive X4005, which was involved in a horrific crash in 1953, but has been restored and sits on the museum's grounds. You can also see the "Gold Bug" Kissel automobile once owned by Amelia Earhart and Crown Prince Aly Khan's Rolls Royce.

Monday-Saturday 10 a.m.-4 p.m.

FOUR MILE HISTORIC PARK

715 S. Forest St., Denver, 720-865-0800; www.fourmilehistoricpark.org

Once a stage stop, this 14-acre living history museum encompasses the oldest house still standing in Denver (circa 1859), plus other outbuildings and farm equipment from the late 1800s. Guides in period costume reenact life on a farmstead. And it's a great place for a picnic.

April-September, Wednesday-Friday noon-4 p.m., Saturday-Sunday 10 a.m.-4 p.m.; October-March, Wednesday-Sunday noon-4 p.m.

HALL OF LIFE

2001 Colorado Blvd., Denver, 303-370-6453; www.dmns.org

This health education center has permanent exhibits on genetics, fitness, nutrition and the five senses.

Daily 9 a.m.-5 p.m.

THE HELEN BONFILS THEATRE COMPLEX

Denver, 303-572-4466; www.denvercenter.org

Home of the Denver Center Theatre Company. Contains three theaters: the Stage, seating 547 in a circle around a thrust platform; the Space, a theater-in-the-round seating 450; and the Source, a small theater presenting plays by American playwrights. Also contains the Frank Ricketson Theatre, a 195-seat theater available for rental for community activities, classes and festivals.

HYLAND HILLS WATER WORLD

1800 W. 89th Ave., Federal Heights, 303-427-7873; www.waterworldcolorado.com

Ranked among the nation's largest water parks, this 64-acre aquatic extravaganza is a great time for all ages. Water World's beautifully landscaped grounds include a wave pool the size of a football field, 16 water slides, nine inner-tube rides and a splash pool for tots. Hours vary according to season and weather, so be sure to call ahead.

Late May-early September: daily 10 a.m.-6 p.m.

MOLLY BROWN HOUSE MUSEUM

1340 Pennsylvania St., Denver, 303-832-4092; www.mollybrown.org

This museum stands as an enduring tribute to Margaret Molly Brown, the "unsinkable survivor" of the Titanic. A spectacular example of Colorado Victorian design, the fully restored 1880s sandstone and lava stone mansion—designed by one of Denver's most famous architects, William Lang—is filled with many of the lavish furnishings and personal possessions of Brown's.

September-May, Monday-Saturday 10 a.m.-3:30 p.m., Sunday noon-3:30 p.m.; June-August, Monday-Saturday 9 a.m.-4 p.m., Sunday noon-4 p.m.

PEARCE-MCALLISTER COTTAGE

1880 Gaylord St., Denver, 303-322-1053; www.coloradohistory.org
This 1899 Dutch Colonial Revival house contains original furnishings. The second floor houses the Denver Museum of Dolls, Toys and Miniatures. Tuesday-Saturday 10 a.m.-4 p.m., Sunday 1-4 p.m.

SAKURA SQUARE

Larimer Street between 19th and 20th streets, Denver
Denver's Japanese Cultural and Trade Center features Asian restaurants, shops, businesses, authentic Japanese gardens and it's also the site of a famed Buddhist Temple.

SKI TRAIN

Union Station, 555 Seventh St., Denver, 303-296-4754; www.skitrain.com
A ride on the Ski Train from downtown Denver to Winter Mountain Ski Resort in Winter Park has been a favorite day trip for skiers, hikers, bikers and family vacationers since 1940. Operating on weekends year-round, the 14-car train takes you on a spectacular 60-mile wilderness ride through the Rockies and across the Continental Divide, climbing 4,000 feet and passing through 28 tunnels before dropping you off at the front entrance of beautiful Winter Park Resort. Tickets are for round-trip, same-day rides only, and reservations are highly recommended.
Winter: Saturday-Sunday; June-August: Saturday.

STATE CAPITOL

200 E. Colfax Ave., Denver, 303-866-2604; www.milehighcity.com/capitol
This magnificent edifice overlooking Civic Center Park is a glorious reminder of Denver's opulent past. Designed by architect Elijah Myers in the classical Corinthian style, it was 18 years in the making before its official dedication in 1908. The building is renowned for its exquisite interior details and use of native materials such as gray granite, white marble, pink Colorado onyx and of course, the gold that covers its dome. Tours include a climb to the dome, 272 feet up, for a spectacular view of the surrounding mountains. Look for the special marker on the steps outside noting that you are, indeed, a mile high.
Monday-Friday 7 a.m.-5:30 p.m.

TEMPLE HOYNE BUELL THEATER

1050 13th St., Denver, 303-893-4100; www.denvercenter.org
This 1908 theater—which has hosted operas, political conventions, revivalist meetings and more—is now the stage for Broadway productions and the Colorado Ballet. It's also the home of Colorado Contemporary Dance.

UNIVERSITY OF DENVER

South University Boulevard and E. Evans Avenue, Denver, 303-871-2000; www.du.edu
Established in 1864; 8,500 students. Handsome 125-acre main campus with

historic buildings dating back to the 1800s. The 33-acre Park Hill campus at Montview Boulevard and Quebec Street is the site of the University of Denver Law School (Lowell Thomas Law Building) and the Lamont School of Music (Houston Fine Arts Center). For a schedule of performances, call 303-871-6400. Campus tours. The University also includes the Chamberlin Observatory, which houses a 20-inch aperture Clark-Saegmuller refractor in use since 1894.

WASHINGTON PARK
Downing Street between East Virginia and East Louisiana avenues, Denver,
303-698-4962
This 165-acre park features a large recreation center with an indoor pool and floral displays, and a replica of George Washington's gardens at Mount Vernon.

SPECIAL EVENTS
CHERRY CREEK ARTS FESTIVAL
Cherry Creek North, on Second and Third avenues between Clayton and Steele streets,
303-355-2787; www.cherryarts.org
Features works by 200 national artists, plus culinary and performing arts. July Fourth weekend.

DENVER FILM FESTIVAL
Starz FilmCenter at the Tivoli, 900 Auraria Parkway, Denver, 303-595-3456;
www.denverfilm.org
Movie junkies will get more than their fill of flicks at this 10-day festival, which showcases 175 films, including international feature releases, independent fiction and documentaries, experimental productions and children's programs. All films are shown at the Starz FilmCenter at the Tivoli. Fall.

DENVER LIGHTS AND PARADE OF LIGHTS
Denver, downtown starting at Civic Center Park in front of the City and County Building,
303-478-7878; www.denverparadeoflights.com
From early December through January, downtown Denver is ablaze with what is possibly the largest holiday light show in the world. Locals and tourists drift down to Civic Center Park after dark to view the incredible rainbow display covering the buildings. A spectacular Parade of Lights that winds for two miles through Denver's downtown kicks off the holiday season.

THE INTERNATIONAL AT CASTLE PINES GOLF CLUB
8480 E. Orchard Road, Greenwood Village, 303-660-8000; www.golfintl.com
The International is a week-long, world-class golf event that attracts some of the top professional golfers. The Jack Nicklaus-designed course is renowned for the beauty of its pine-strewn mountain setting and the challenge of its terrain. The tournament begins in earnest on Thursday, but spectators are welcome to watch practice rounds as well as the junior and pro-am tournaments held earlier in the week.
One week in August.

NATIONAL WESTERN STOCK SHOW, RODEO & HORSE SHOW

National Western Complex, 4655 Humboldt St., Denver, 303-297-1166, 888-551-5004;
www.nationalwestern.com

This two-week extravaganza—which includes 600,000 exhibitors and spectators—is packed with nonstop shows and demonstrations, from sheep shearing to steer -wrestling. Daily rodeos showcase the horse- and bull-riding skills of some of the best riders in the country before cheering, sellout crowds in the National Western Complex. Other favorites include barrel races, show-horse contests, a junior rodeo (where some of the riders are as young as three years old), Wild West shows and the colorful Mexican Rodeo Extravaganza. Take a break from the action and tour the exhibition hall for demonstrations in wool spinning and goat milking, or walk the grounds to see what a yak looks like up close.

Mid-January.

WHERE TO STAY

★★★★THE BROWN PALACE HOTEL

321 17th St., Denver, 303-297-3111, 800-321-2599; www.brownpalace.com

Denver's most celebrated and historic hotel, the Brown Palace has hosted presidents, royalty and celebrities since 1892. The elegant lobby features a magnificent stained-glass ceiling that tops off six levels of cast-iron balconies. The luxurious guest rooms have two styles—Victorian or Art Deco. The award-winning Palace Arms restaurant features signature favorites like rack of lamb and pan-roasted veal. Cigar aficionados take to the library-like ambience of the Churchill Bar. Afternoon tea is accompanied by live harp music. And Ellygnton's Sunday brunch is legendary. After a busy day of exploring nearby attractions like the 16th Street Mall and the Museum of Natural History, the full-service spa is the perfect place to unwind with a deep massage, body treatment or facial.

241 rooms. Restaurant, bar. Spa. Pets accepted. Fitness center. Business center. Pool. $$$

★COMFORT INN CENTRAL DOWNTOWN

401 17th St., Denver, 303-296-0400, 877-424-6423; www.comfortinn.com

161 rooms. Complimentary breakfast. Pool. Business center. Fitness center. Pets accepted. $$

★★★GRAND HYATT

1750 Welton St., Denver, 303-295-1234, 888-591-1234; www.grandhyattdenver.com

The beautiful lobby of this centrally located hotel has a 20-foot sandstone fireplace and cozy seating areas with touches of mahogany, granite and wrought iron. Stay fit with the rooftop tennis courts surrounded by a jogging track, indoor pool and health club. The hotel's restaurant 1876, which is the year Colorado became a state, is a nice spot for dinner.

513 rooms. Complimentary breakfast. Restaurant, bar. Pool. Business center. Fitness center. $$$

★★HISTORIC CASTLE MARNE INN

1572 Race St., Denver, 303-331-0621, 800-926-2763; www.castlemarne.com

9 rooms. Complimentary breakfast. $$

★★★HOTEL MONACO DENVER

1717 Champa St., Denver, 303-296-1717, 800-990-1303; www.monaco-denver.com

The lobby feels like an elegant, somewhat exotic living room with cushy couches, recessed bookshelves and potted palms. But the scene stealer at this hotel is the domed ceiling, described as a Russian Circus Tent, with diamond shapes in blue, green and gold. The punchy décor carries through to the hallways and guest rooms, with bold, colorful stripes on the walls and very glam black and white ottomans. The rooms also include plush duvet covers, bathroom phones and terrycloth shower curtains.

189 rooms. Pets accepted. Restaurant. Spa. Fitness center, Business center. $$$

★★★HOTEL TEATRO

1100 14th St., Denver, 303-228-1100, 888-727-1200; www.hotelteatro.com

Located across from the Denver Center for the Performing Arts, the Hotel Teatro inspires its guests with creative design and contemporary flair. Down comforters, Frette linens, Aveda bath products and Starbucks coffee keep you feeling relaxed, while the staff attends to your every whim. Want someone to draw you an aromatherapy bath? This is the place. Even pets get the VIP treatment, with a doggie dish with his name on it and Fiji water. Chef Kevin Taylor, who oversees two restaurants here, is something of a local sensation.

110 rooms. Restaurant, bar. Pets accepted. Business center. Fitness center. $$$

★★★JET HOTEL

1612 Wazee St., Denver, 303-572-3300, 877-418-2462; www.thejethotel.com

The dimly lit lobby gives you an idea of what you can expect from this ultra-modern boutique hotel. To the right is the open counter of Velocity, where you can get crêpes and organic coffee each morning. To the left, stretching almost the entire length of the lobby, is the futuristic Flow Bar, backlit in soft colors that change every few minutes. Step around a handful of tall, round cocktail tables to get to the inconspicuous reception desk. There are just 19 rooms, in which standard amenities are anything but. No coffeemakers—just French plunge pots. No ice buckets—only funky insulated pitchers. No clock radios, either. Instead, there's a CD alarm clock with a library of CDs.

19 rooms. Complimentary breakfast. Restaurant, bar. $$$

★★★JW MARRIOTT DENVER AT CHERRY CREEK

150 Clayton Lane, Denver, 303-316-2700; www.jwmarriottdenver.com

There is plenty to do right outside the doors of this property located just a few miles east of downtown in Cherry Creek. The area is filled with high-end boutiques, art galleries and trendy restaurants. This luxury boutique hotel has modern décor and features comfortable guest rooms with 32-inch flat-screen TVs and minibars—though you may wind up hanging out in the lobby, which has a waterfall, fireplace and live jazz. Pets are welcomed with sheepskin beds, their own dining menus and designer bowls.

196 rooms. Restaurant, bar. Spa. Business center. $$$

★★LOEWS DENVER HOTEL

4150 E. Mississippi Ave., Denver, 303-782-9300, 800-345-9172; www.loewshotels.com

Saying this hotel caters to the entire family is an understatement. Kids get Frisbees, backpacks and games. The hotel also offers a variety of amenities for babies, including tubs, electric bottle warmers and invisible outlet plugs. For parents, there's a menu of comfort items like chenille throws, a pillow menu and CDs. Everyone will appreciate the fitness center and restaurant.

183 rooms. Restaurant, bar. Fitness center. Business center. $$

★★★THE MAGNOLIA HOTEL

818 17th St., Denver, 303-607-9000, 888-915-1110; www.magnoliahoteldenver.com

Many visitors to Denver make the Magnolia their home for extended stays. It's easy to see why. Set back from busy 17th Street, the Magnolia says cozy, from the wingback chairs and fireplace in its lobby to the full-size kitchens in its suites. Access to a snazzy health club is included with your stay. Upgrading to the Magnolia Club gets you wireless Internet access, access to a nightly cocktail reception and continental breakfast and late-night milk and cookies. Pets are welcome and receive a goodie bag at check-in.

246 rooms. Complimentary breakfast. Restaurant, bar. $$$

★★★MARRIOTT DENVER CITY CENTER

1701 California St., Denver, 303-297-1300, 800-228-9290; www.denvermarriott.com

You'd be hard-pressed to find a better health club in an urban hotel than this one. There is a wide variety of equipment, personal trainers, massage therapy, body treatments and a pool and whirlpool—all of which will come in handy if you're here on business. Located on the first 20 floors of an office building in downtown Denver, this property is within walking distance of Coors Field, as well as several restaurants and shops.

627 rooms. Restaurant, bar. Business center. Fitness center. Pool. $$$

★★★OXFORD HOTEL

1600 17th St., Denver, 303-628-5400, 800-228-5838; www.theoxfordhotel.com

Built in 1891, this restored hotel is touted as the city's "oldest grand hotel." The luxurious property is filled with antiques, marble floors, stained glass and beautiful paintings. It's also near many attractions, including Coors Field, the 16th Street Mall, Larimer Square and many shops and galleries. Spend the day getting pampered at the hotel's full-service spa.

80 rooms. Restaurant, bar. Spa. Pets accepted. Business center. Fitness center. $$$

★★★RENAISSANCE DENVER HOTEL

3801 Quebec St., Denver, 303-399-7500; www.denverrenaissance.com

This atrium hotel has Rocky Mountain views and large rooms with mini-refrigerators, free laundry and porches, making it a good choice for families looking for a full-service hotel while trying to stay within a budget, or business travelers who prefer to stay near the airport. Downtown Denver is about a 10-minute drive. There's also a pool and exercise facility.

400 rooms. Complimentary breakfast. Restaurant, bar. Business center. Fitness center. Pool. Spa. $$

★★★THE RITZ-CARLTON, DENVER

1881 Curtis St., Denver, 303-312-3800; www.ritzcarlton.com

It's the numbers that speak for this Ritz-Carlton's luxury: 400 thread-count Frette linens, 550 square-foot and larger guest rooms, and 24-hour room service. Rooms hold a number of other treats, including featherbeds, plush Frette terry robes, flat-panel HD TVs, cappuccino makers, iPod alarm clocks, rain showerheads and Bulgari bath amenities. This outpost of the Ritz was designed with a focus on the state's natural beauty, with red rocks, stones and water features incorporated into the construction.

202 rooms. Restaurant, bar. Fitness center. Tennis. Pool. Spa. Business Center. Pets accepted.

★★★THE WESTIN TABOR CENTER, DENVER

1672 Lawrence St., Denver, 303-572-9100, 800-937-8461; www.starwoodhotels.com

Located in downtown Denver, adjacent to the 16th Street Mall, this hotel boasts some of the largest guest rooms in the city, many with panoramic views of the Rocky Mountains. The signature Heavenly Beds and Baths and nightly wine service ensure a relaxing stay. Get a massage, hit the rooftop pool or whirlpool, work out in the outstanding fitness center (with a personal flatscreen TV on each piece of cardio equipment) or get in a game at the indoor half-basketball court. Afterward, relax in the lobby with Starbucks coffee.

430 rooms. Restaurant, bar. Pool. Fitness center. Business center. Spa. Pets accepted. $$$

WHERE TO EAT

★ANNIE'S CAFE AND BAR

3100 E. Colfax Ave., Denver, 303-355-8197; www.annies-cafe.com

American. Breakfast, lunch, dinner. Children's menu. $

★★★BAROLO GRILL

3030 E. Sixth Ave., Denver, 303-393-1040; www.barologrilldenver.com

This upscale Italian farmhouse, named after the famous wine, serves authentic Northern Italian food. The interior is rustic and romantic, with grapevines covering one corner and hand-painted porcelain on display throughout, and the fireplace casts a warm glow. Be sure to ask about the daily tasting menu. And yes, the extensive wine list includes more than Barolo, but why bother?

Italian. Dinner. Closed Sunday-Monday. Bar. Reservations recommended. $$$

★★BENNY'S

301 E. Seventh Ave., Denver, 303-894-0788; www.bennysrestaurant.com

Mexican. Breakfast, lunch, dinner. Bar. Children's menu. Outdoor seating. $

★★★THE BROKER RESTAURANT

821 17th St., Denver, 303-292-5065; www.thebrokerrestaurant.com

Located in downtown Denver in what was once the Denver National Bank, the Broker is a fun place to dine. Private parties can take over one of the old boardrooms. The restaurant's centerpiece is a huge bank vault, now a dining room. Go down some stairs and through what seems like it might have been a secret passageway, and you find yourself in the restaurants massive wine cellar, which has a dining table that can seat up to 20—or just two, if you're feeling romantic.

Steak. Lunch (Monday-Friday), dinner. Bar. Children's menu. Reservations recommended. $$$

★★BUCKHORN EXCHANGE
1000 Osage St., Denver, 303-534-9505; www.buckhorn.com

Steak. Lunch (Monday-Friday), dinner. Bar. Children's menu. Reservations recommended. Outdoor seating. $$$

★★DENVER CHOPHOUSE & BREWERY
1735 19th St., Denver, 303-296-0800; www.chophouse.com

Steak, seafood. Lunch, dinner, Sunday brunch. Bar. Outdoor seating. $$

★★★ELWAY'S
The Ritz-Carlton, Denver, 1881 Curtis St., Denver, 303-312-3107; www.elways.com

Because it wouldn't be a Colorado vacation without a hearty steak dinner, and Denver wouldn't be Denver without Bronco Hall-of-Famer John Elway, add Elway's to your must-do list. This restaurant is a touchdown all around. The smart décor features a floor-to-ceiling wine wall holding thousands of bottles. The lamb fondue appetizer, Elway's salmon, and the bone-in rib-eye are sure bets. Try the Bison burger or sliced prime rib sandwich.

Steak. Breakfast, lunch, dinner. Bar. Reservations recommended. $$

★EMPRESS DIM SUM SEAFOOD RESTAURANT
2825 W. Alameda Ave., Denver, 303-922-2822; www.empressseafoodrestaurant.com

Chinese. Lunch, dinner. Bar. $$

★★★HIGHLANDS GARDEN CAFÉ
3927 W. 32nd Ave., Denver, 303-458-5920; www.highlandsgardencafe.com

This unique Denver mainstay is actually two converted Victorian houses from about 1890. The main dining room has exposed brick, polished hardwood floors and crisp white tablecloths, but other rooms have a different feel. The country room is painted white and has French doors leading out to the gardens. The eclectic American menu takes advantage of seasonal ingredients.

American. Lunch, dinner, Sunday brunch. Closed Monday. Outdoor seating. $$$

★★★IMPERIAL CHINESE
431 S. Broadway, Denver, 303-698-2800; www.imperialchinese.com

From the giant fish tank at the entrance to the inventive Szechwan, Cantonese and Mandarin menu, this restaurant dazzles. The large dining room is segmented with partitions that provide a sense of privacy. The service is unobtrusive, and the dishes are as eye-catching as they are delicious.

Chinese. Lunch, dinner. Bar. Reservations recommended. $$

★★INDIA'S RESTAURANT
3333 S. Tamarac Drive, Denver, 303-755-4284; www.indiasrestaurant.com

Indian. Lunch, dinner. Bar. $$

★JAPON RESTAURANT
1028 S. Gaylord St., Denver, 303-744-0330; www.japonsushi.com
Japanese. Lunch, dinner. $$

★★LE CENTRAL
112 E. Eighth Ave., Denver, 303-863-8094; www.lecentral.com
French. Lunch, dinner, brunch. Reservations recommended. $$

★★★MORTON'S, THE STEAKHOUSE
1710 Wynkoop St., Denver, 303-825-3353; www.mortons.com
This national chain fits right into the upscale Denver meat-and-potatoes scene. It's very simple here: Order a martini, listen to the server recite the menu, dig in. And go home stuffed.
Steak. Dinner. Bar. $$$

★★★PALACE ARMS
The Brown Palace Hotel, 321 17th St., Denver, 303-297-3111, 800-321-2599;
www.brownpalace.com
The Palace Arms opened its doors in 1892—and has carried on a tradition of culinary excellence ever since. Located on the ground level of the Brown Palace Hotel, the majestic Palace Arms' dining room has a unique Western charisma, with rich wood, brocade-upholstered seating, wood shutters and antiques. The delicious international cuisine is prepared with regional accents. Taste some of the oldest known blended cognac, which dates back to Napoleonic times.
International. Dinner. Bar. Children's menu. Reservations recommended. $$$

★★★★RESTAURANT KEVIN TAYLOR
Hotel Teatro, 1106 14th St., Denver, 303-820-2600; www.ktrg.net
Located inside the stylish Hotel Teatro and across from the Denver Center for Performing Arts, this 70-seat restaurant brings French style to downtown Denver. Vaulted ceilings are offset with Versailles mirrors and alabaster chandeliers. Chairs are covered in green-and-yellow-striped silk fabric, and tables are topped with yellow Frette linens, Bernardaud china and Christofle silver. Chef Kevin Taylor earns applause for his unpretentious contemporary cuisine. Start with seared Grade A French foie gras, and then try one of the signature dishes such as butter-poached Maine lobster, Serrano ham roasted Berkshire pork tenderloin and Colorado lamb sirloin. Top it off with a killer dessert like the German chocolate ice cream sandwich. The restaurant features seasonal menus that change every two months, four-, five- and seven-course tasting menus and a prix fixe pre-theatre menu. There are also 900 vintages here—ask for a private table in the wine cellar.
American, French. Dinner. Closed Sunday. Bar. Reservations recommended. $$$

★ROCKY MOUNTAIN DINER
800 18th St., Denver, 303-293-8383; www.rockymountaindiner.com
American. Lunch, dinner, Saturday-Sunday brunch. Bar. Children's menu. Outdoor seating. $$

★★★STRINGS

1700 Humboldt St., Denver, 303-831-7310; www.stringsrestaurant.com

Strings is like no other restaurant in Denver. The locals know it—and so do the scores of celebrities and politicians who have dined here, many of whom have left autographed pictures on the wall. Some love it for the unusual, eclectic cuisine served in the light and airy dining room with an open kitchen. Others are admirers of owner Noel Cunningham, a well-known humanitarian who constantly holds fundraisers at the restaurant to help fight illiteracy and hunger.

International. Lunch, dinner. Bar. Reservations recommended. Outdoor seating. $$$

★★3 SONS ITALIAN RESTAURANT

14805 W. 64th Ave.,Arvadar, 303-455-4366; www.threesons.net

Italian. Lunch, dinner. Closed Monday. Bar. Children's menu. $$

★★★TUSCANY

Loews Denver Hotel, 4150 E. Mississippi Ave., Denver, 303-639-1600;
www.loewshotels.com

Located in the Loews Denver Hotel, Tuscany is decorated in creamy earth tones and luxurious fabrics with soft lighting. Pen-and-ink drawings and paintings of the Tuscan countryside dot the walls, and a central, marble fireplace serves to divide the room. The feeling is contemporary and comfortable, and the restaurant uses only the freshest ingredients to create its outstanding fare paired with wines from the exceptional list.

Italian. Breakfast, lunch, dinner. Bar. Children's menu. Reservations recommended. $$$

★WAZEE SUPPER CLUB

1600 15th St., Denver, 303-623-9518; www.wazeesupperclub.com

American. Lunch, dinner, late-night. Bar. Children's menu. $

★★★WELLSHIRE INN

3333 S. Colorado Blvd., Denver, 303-759-3333; www.wellshireinn.com

The tables at this restaurant are topped with crisp white linens and beautiful china that was created exclusively for the Wellshire and based on the Tudor period, a theme that is richly executed here. Built in 1926 as a clubhouse for the exclusive Wellshire Country Club, the castle-like building fell into disrepair. Today, it has been restored with four intimate dining rooms. Classics like shrimp cocktail and Maryland crab cakes are featured as appetizers, while entrées include steak Oscar, pan-roasted Cornish game hen and grilled North Atlantic salmon.

American. Lunch, dinner, Sunday brunch. Bar. Children's menu. Reservations recommended. Outdoor seating. $$$

★ZAIDY'S DELI

121 Adams St., Denver, 303-333-5336; www.zaidysdeli.com

American, deli. Breakfast, lunch, dinner. Children's menu. Outdoor seating. $

SPAS
★★★★THE RITZ-CARLTON SPA, DENVER
The Ritz-Carlton, Denver, 1881 Curtis St., Denver, 303-312-3830; www.ritzcarlton.com

Spending the day in the mountains and heading back to the city to rest? Then wind down at this elegant spa. With eight treatment rooms, including a VIP Suite, the spa is Denver's largest full-service luxury spa. Choose from all manner of treatments, including massage therapies, body treatments, skin care, nail services and makeup application; or skip the slopes and spend the whole day in the spa, indulging in the only-in-Denver hops n' honey ultimate pedicure, which pays homage to the city's brewery roots; it'll leave your skin fragrant with notes of amber, caramel, oats and honey. And your pampering comes with tastings of three local microbrews (or herbal teas, but c'mon, you're in Denver—drink the beer), just another Rocky Mountain twist.

★★★★THE SPA AT THE BROWN PALACE
The Brown Palace Hotel, 321 17th St., Denver, 303-312-8940, 800-321-2599;
www.brownpalace.com

An artesian well has supplied the Brown Palace Hotel since it opened in 1892. The soothing natural rock waterfall at its spa's entrance speaks to this history. The Spa at the Brown Palace's six massage, facial and water treatment rooms, separate men's and women's lounges, and private couples' suite are spread over two floors. The facility also has a full-service hair and nail salon. This commitment to guest pampering isn't new—the spa occupies the same space as a spa that opened with the hotel more than a century ago. The treatment menu offers five distinct soaks, and the artesian plunge is 20 minutes of tub time followed by a sea algae masque.

DURANGO
See also Cortez

Will Rogers once said of Durango, "It's out of the way and glad of it." For more than 100 years, this small Western city has profited from its secluded location at the base of the San Juan Mountains. Durango has been the gateway to Colorado's riches for Native Americans, fur traders, miners, prospectors, ranchers and engineers. Founded by the Denver & Rio Grande Railroad, Durango was a rowdy community during its early days. The notorious Stockton-Eskridge gang once engaged local vigilantes in an hourlong gun battle in the main street. In the 1890s, the Durango Herald-Democrat was noted for the stinging, often profane, wit of pioneer editor "Dave" Day, who once had 42 libel suits pending against him.

WHAT TO SEE
DIAMOND CIRCLE THEATRE
Durango Arts Center, Eighth and Second avenues, Durango, 970-247-3400;
www.diamondcirclemelodrama.com

Professional turn-of-the-century melodrama and vaudeville performances. June-September, nightly; closed Sunday. Advance reservations recommended.

COLORADO'S GOLD MINES

The San Juan Skyway is a scenic 236-mile loop out of Durango that ranges over five mountain passes as it wanders through the San Juan Mountains. From Durango, head west on Highway 160 to Hesperus, where you can take a side trip into La Plata Canyon to see mining ruins and a few ghost towns. Continuing west, you'll pass Mesa Verde National Park and come to Highway 145 shortly before Cortez. Head north to the town of Dolores and the Anasazi Heritage Center, which features a large display of artifacts, most more than 1,000 years old. The road now follows the Dolores River, a favorite of trout anglers, and climbs the 10,222-foot-high Lizard Head Pass, named for the imposing rock spire looming overhead.

Descending from the pass, take a short side trip into Telluride, a historic mining town and ski resort nestled in a beautiful box canyon. Follow the San Miguel River valley to Highway 62, and turn north to cross the 8,970-foot Dallas Divide. After passing the historic railroad town of Ridgway and Ridgway State Park, where you might stop for a swim or picnic, turn south on Highway 550 and drive to Ouray, a picturesque old mining town. Continue over the 11,008-foot Red Mountain Pass—there is a monument here dedicated to snowplow operators who died while trying to keep the road open during winter storms. Next stop is Silverton, a small mining town and the northern terminus of the Durango and Silverton Narrow Gauge Railroad. South of Silverton is the 10,910-foot Molas Divide, after which the road almost parallels the rails as they follow the Animas River back to Durango. This tour can be done in one long day by those who want to see only the mountain scenery, but is better over two or three days, with stops at Mesa Verde National Park and the historic towns along the way.

Approximately 236 miles.

DURANGO & SILVERTON NARROW GAUGE RAILROAD

479 Main Ave., Durango, 970-247-2733, 877-872-4607; www.durangotrain.com

This historic Narrow Gauge Railroad, in operation since 1881, links Durango in southwest Colorado with the Victorian-era mining town of Silverton, 45 miles away. A journey on this coal-fired, steam-powered locomotive up the Animas River and through the mountainous wilderness of the San Juan National Forest gives you the chance to relive history while taking in some of the most breathtaking scenery Colorado has to offer. Round-trip travel takes approximately nine hours. Same-day travelers may opt to return by bus; others can stay overnight in historic Silverton with a return train ride the next day. During the winter season, the train makes a shorter, round-trip journey to and from Cascade Canyon.

May-October; shorter routes during the winter months.

DURANGO MOUNTAIN RESORT (ALSO KNOWN AS PURGATORY)

1 Skier Place, Durango, 970-247-9000, 800-982-6103; www.ski-purg.com

Quad, four triple, three double chairlifts; patrol, school, rentals; five restaurants, five bars, nursery, lodge, specialty stores.

85 runs; longest run two miles; vertical drop 2,029 feet. Late November-early April. Cross-country skiing. Multiday, half-day rates. Chairlift and alpine slide also operate mid-June-Labor Day.

SAN JUAN NATIONAL FOREST

15 Burnett Court, Durango, 970-247-4874; www.fs.fed.us/r2/sanjuan

This forest consists of nearly two million acres and includes the Weminuche

Wilderness, Colorado's largest designated wilderness area, with several peaks topping 14,000 feet. The Colorado Trail begins in Durango and traverses the backcountry all the way to Denver. Recreation includes fishing in high mountain lakes and streams, boating, whitewater rafting, hiking, biking and camping. The San Juan Skyway is a 232-mile auto loop through many of these scenic areas. Daily.

SOUTHERN UTE INDIAN CULTURAL MUSEUM

Southern Ute Indian Reservation, Ignacio, 23 miles southeast via Highways 160 and 172, 970-563-9583; www.southernutemuseum.org

This historical museum contains archival photos, turn-of-the-century Ute clothing, tools and accessories. Multimedia presentation.

Monday-Friday 8 a.m.-5 p.m., Saturday 10 a.m.-3 p.m.; closed Sunday.

SPECIAL EVENTS
DURANGO COWBOY GATHERING

Stater Hotel, 699 Main Ave., Durango, 970-382-7494; www.durangocowboygathering.org

A clebration of the American cowboy, enjoy poetry and vocal performances. First weekend in October.

IRON HORSE BICYCLE CLASSIC

346 S. Camino Del Rio, Durango, 970-259-4621; www.ironhorsebicycleclassic.com

Cyclists race the Silverton narrow-gauge train (47 miles).
Late May.

SNOWDOWN WINTER CARNIVAL

Durango, 970-247-8163; www.snowdown.org

Winter festival features entertainment, contests, food and more.
Late January-February.

WHERE TO STAY
★★★APPLE ORCHARD INN

7758 County Road 203, Durango, 970-247-0751, 800-426-0751; www.appleorchardinn.com

This lovely inn is just 15 minutes from town and a 20-minute drive to Durango Mountain Resort. The property includes beautiful gardens, trout ponds, waterfalls and streams. All rooms feature featherbeds. Homemade baked goods and jam at breakfast—as well as fresh chocolate chip cookies anytime—make visits extra sweet. Gourmet dinners are also available with a reservation.

10 rooms. Complimentary breakfast. $$

★BEST WESTERN DURANGO INN AND SUITES

21382 US Highway 160, Durango, 970-247-3251, 800-547-9090; www.durangoinn.com

71 rooms. Complimentary breakfast. Restaurant, bar. Pool. $

★★DOUBLETREE HOTEL DURANGO

501 Camino Del Rio, Durango, 970-259-6580, 800-222-8733; www.doubletree.com
159 rooms. Restaurant, bar. Pets accepted. Fitness center. Pool. $

★★STRATER HOTEL

699 Main Ave., Durango, 800-247-4431; www.strater.com
93 rooms. Complimentary breakfast. Restaurant, bar. $

★★★LIGHTNER CREEK INN

999 County Road 207, Durango, 970-259-1226, 800-268-9804;
www.lightnercreekinn.com
This inn, built in 1903, resembles a French country manor and offers finely decorated rooms. The mountain getaway feels very secluded but is only five minutes from downtown. Guests are encouraged to make themselves at home here—grab a drink from the kitchen and watch a movie in the living room.
9 rooms. $$

★★★THE ROCHESTER HOTEL

721 E. Second Ave., Durango, 970-385-1920, 800-664-1920; www.rochesterhotel.com
Built in 1892, this Victorian hotel has been authentically restored and evokes the Old West, and it's only one block from downtown Durango. It bills itself as a "green" hotel—Electra Cruiser bikes are available for guests to get around and all-natural Aveda products are provided.
15 rooms. Complimentary breakfast. Pets accepted. $$

★★★THE LODGE AT TAMARRON

40292 Highway 550 North, Durango, 970-259-2000, 800-982-6103
Pine trees surround this scenic resort, located on a 750-acre site in the San Juan Mountains. The property is just a short drive or shuttle from Durango and Purgatory Village and the chairlifts. Accommodations range from studios and lofts to suites, and amenities include tennis and indoor/outdoor pools.
210 rooms. Restaurant, bar. Fitness center. Pool. Spa. Pets accepted. $

★★★★★ COLORADO

143

WHERE TO EAT
★★ARIANO'S ITALIAN RESTAURANT

150 E. College Drive, Durango, 970-247-8146
Italian. Dinner. Bar. Children's menu. $$

★CARVER BREWING CO.

1022 Main Ave., Durango, 970-259-2545; www.carverbrewing.com
American, Southwestern. Breakfast, lunch, dinner. Bar. Children's menu. $

★★FRANCISCO'S

619 Main Ave., Durango, 970-247-4098
Mexican, American. Lunch, dinner. Bar. Children's menu. $$

★★THE PALACE RESTAURANT

505 Main Ave., Durango, 970-247-2018; www.palacedurango.com
American. Lunch, dinner. Closed Sunday, November-May. Bar. $$

★★RED SNAPPER
144 E. Ninth St., Durango, 888-259-2714; www.redsnapperdurango.com
Seafood, steak. Lunch (Monday-Friday), dinner. Bar. Children's menu. $$

EDWARDS
See also Vail
Not far from tony Vail Valley and Beaver Creek, Edwards has all of the ski resorts' beauty without the hype. With a charming shopping and dining district, proximity to resorts and plenty of Colorado's natural beauty nearby, Edwards is a good option for visitors looking to spend some time on a Rocky Mountain high.

WHERE TO STAY
★★INN AND SUITES AT RIVERWALK
27 Main St., Edwards, 970-926-0606, 888-926-0606; www.innandsuitesatriverwalk.com
59 rooms. Restaurant, bar. $

★★★THE LODGE & SPA AT CORDILLERA
2205 Cordillera Way, Edwards, 970-926-2200, 866-650-7625; www.cordilleralodge.com
The French-chateau architecture and beautiful mountaintop location make this one of the most exclusive resorts in the area. A lovely rustic style dominates the accommodations, where wood-burning or gas fireplaces add warmth and terraces offer views of the Vail Valley. The lodge also includes award-winning golf and a full-service spa. Four restaurants feature everything from steaks and seafood to traditional Irish fare at Grouse-on-the-Green, where even the interiors were constructed in Ireland.
56 rooms. Restaurant, bar. Pool. Golf. Tennis. Business center. $$

WHERE TO EAT
★★★MIRADOR
The Lodge & Spa at Cordillera, 2205 Cordillera Way, Edwards, 970-926-2200; www.cordilleralodge.com
Located in the luxurious Lodge & Spa at Cordillera, Mirador features breathtaking views of the Rocky Mountains and an elegant atmosphere. Its innovative menu of regional Colorado fare has won critical acclaim. It's complemented by an impressive wine list. If you'd like to dine privately with a group, you can reserve the 24-seat private dining area or the 12-seat family table in the wine cellar.
French. Dinner. Bar. Outdoor seating. $$$

ENGLEWOOD
See also Denver
Englewood is located in Denver's south metro area and is home to the Denver Technological Center.

WHAT TO SEE
FIDDLER'S GREEN AMPHITHEATRE
6350 Greenwood Plaza Blvd.,Greenwood Village, 303-220-7000;
www.livenation.com/amphitheatre

Fiddler's Green Amphitheatre, formerly Coors Amphitheatre, is located 15 minutes south of downtown Denver. The park-like setting is an inviting venue for a wide variety of musical performances during the summer months, from marquee names to classical orchestras. Come early to enjoy the mountain sunset. Bring a blanket or tarp (no lawn chairs are allowed) and a picnic, or reserve an indoor seat, purchase dinner from one of the many vendors and watch the acts up close.

June-August.

THE MUSEUM OF OUTDOOR ARTS
1000 Englewood Parkway, Englewood, 303-806-0444; www.moaonline.org

Outdoor sculpture garden on 400 acres. Guided tours available. Lunchtime summer performance series (Wednesday).

WHERE TO STAY
★★EMBASSY SUITES DENVER-TECH CENTER
10250 E. Costilla Ave., Centennial, 303-792-0433, 800-362-2779;
www.embassysuites.com

236 rooms. Complimentary breakfast. Restaurant, bar. Pool. $

★HAMPTON INN
9231 E. Arapahoe Road, Greenwood Village, 303-792-9999, 800-426-7866;
www.hamptoninn.com

149 rooms. Complimentary breakfast. Pool. $

★★★THE INVERNESS HOTEL AND CONFERENCE CENTER
200 Inverness Drive West, Englewood, 303-799-5800, 800-832-9053;
www.invernesshotel.com

This hotel and conference center, with 60,000 square feet of function space, is the perfect choice for corporate retreats, thanks to naturally lit boardrooms, "fatigue-free" chairs, built-in audiovisual equipment and more. All rooms feature views of the golf course or the Rocky Mountains and suites on the Club Floor have sunken living rooms. The spa offers a variety of treatments. 302 rooms. Restaurant, bar. Fitness center. Pool. Spa. Golf. Tennis. Business center. $$

★★★SHERATON DENVER TECH CENTER HOTEL
7007 S. Clinton, Greenwood Village, 303-799-6200, 800-325-3535;
www.starwoodhotels.com

The spacious guest rooms at this hotel will appeal to both business and leisure travelers. Nearby attractions include the Denver Museum of Natural History, the Denver Zoo and the Coors Brewery. There is also complimentary shuttle service provided within a five-mile radius. 262 rooms. Restaurant, bar. Pets accepted. Pool. $

ESTES PARK

See also Fort Collins, Loveland

Estes Park occupies an enviable swath of land at the eastern edge of the Rockies. Many claim that Estes Park offers the quintessential Colorado experience. History certainly would support this. The area has been a vacation destination for thousands of years. Archaeological evidence indicates that Native Americans were drawn here to escape the summer heat. Situated 7,500 feet above sea level, the town's elevation manages to keep summertime temperatures comfortably cool—and also brings an average of 63 inches of snow during the winter months. The snowfall draws hordes of skiers and snowboarders to the area, with a season that typically lasts from November until April. During the warmer months, Estes Park becomes even more crowded. The city's downtown area features an array of shops, restaurants and accommodations, including the Stanley Hotel, constructed nearly 100 years ago in the neoclassical Georgian style—where Stephen King stayed while he was writing *The Shining* in 1973.

WHAT TO SEE

AERIAL TRAMWAY

420 Riverside Drive, Estes Park, 970-586-3675

Two cabins suspended from steel cables move up or down Prospect Mountain at 1,400 feet per minute. You get a superb view of the Continental Divide during the trip. Picnic facilities at 8,896-foot summit; panoramic dome shelter; snack bar.

Mid-May-mid-September, daily.

BIG THOMPSON CANYON

Estes Park, east on Highway 34

One of the most beautiful canyon drives in the state.

ENOS MILLS ORIGINAL CABIN

6760 Highway 7, Estes Park, 970-586-4706

On this family-owned 200-acre nature preserve stands the 1885 cabin of Enos Mills, regarded as the father of Rocky Mountain National Park. In the shadow of Longs Peak, the cabin contains photos, notes and documents of the famed naturalist. Nature guide and self-guided nature trails.

Memorial Day-Labor Day, Wednesday-Friday 10 a.m.-3 p.m.; rest of year by appointment.

ESTES PARK AREA HISTORICAL MUSEUM

200 Fourth St., Estes Park, 970-586-6256; www.estesnet.com/museum

Three facilities including a building that served as the headquarters of Rocky Mountain National Park from 1915 to 1923. See exhibits on the history of the park and surrounding area.

Gallery: May-October, Monday-Saturday 10 a.m.-5 p.m., Sunday 1-5 p.m.; November-April, Friday-Saturday 10 a.m.-5 p.m., Sunday 1-5 p.m.

FUN CITY AMUSEMENT PARK

455 Prospect Village Drive, Estes Park, 970-586-2828; www.funcityofestes.com

There's plenty of fun here—bumper cars, a 15-lane giant slide and spiral slide, an arcade, miniature golf, two 18-hole golf courses and go-karts. Mid-May-mid-September, daily.

ROOSEVELT NATIONAL FOREST

240 W. Prospect Road, Fort Collins, 970-498-1100; www.fs.fed.us/r2/arnf

On the reserve's more than 780,000 acres of icy streams, mountains and beautiful scenery, visitors can enjoy trout fishing, hiking trails, a winter sports area, picnicking and camping. The Cache la Poudre River, five wilderness areas and the Peak-to-Peak Scenic Byway are all nearby.

SPECIAL EVENTS
ESTES PARK MUSIC FESTIVAL

Performance Park Pavilion, Estes Park, 970-586-9519; www.estesparkmusicfestival.org

Chamber, symphonic and choral concerts.
Early June-late August.

HORSE SHOWS

Estes Park, 800-443-7837; www.estes-park.com

Includes an Arabian and Hunter-Jumper horse shows.
July-August.

LONGS PEAK SCOTTISH-IRISH HIGHLAND FESTIVAL

Estes Park, 970-586-6308, 800-903-7837; www.scotfest.com

Athletic and dance competitions, arts and crafts, magic shows, folk dancing.
Weekend after Labor Day.

ROOFTOP RODEO

Stanley Park Fairgrounds, Estes Park, 970-586-6104

Rodeo parade, nightly dances, kids jamboree, steer wrestling, bull riding.
Five days in mid-July.

WHERE TO STAY
★BEST WESTERN SILVER SADDLE

1260 Big Thompson Ave., Estes Park, 970-586-4476, 800-780-7234;
www.bestwestern.com

55 rooms. Complimentary breakfast. Pool. $

★BOULDER BROOK ON FALL RIVER

1900 Fall River Road, Estes Park, 970-586-0910, 800-238-0910;
www.boulderbrook.com

16 rooms. $

★COMFORT INN
1450 Big Thompson Ave., Estes Park, 970-586-2358, 800-424-6423;
www.comfortinn.com
75 rooms. Closed November-April. Complimentary breakfast. Pool. $

★★HOLIDAY INN-ROCKY MOUNTAIN PARK
101 S. St. Vrain Ave., Estes Park, 970-586-2332, 877-863-4780; www.holiday-inn.com
150 rooms. Restaurant, bar. Pool. Fitness center. Business center. Pets accepted. $

★PONDEROSA LODGE
1820 Fall River Road, Estes Park, 970-586-4233, 800-628-0512;
www.ponderosa-lodge.com
25 rooms. $

★★★THE STANLEY HOTEL
333 Wonderview Ave., Estes Park, 970-577-4000, 800-976-1377;
www.stanleyhotel.com
The inspiration behind *The Shining*, the Stanley Hotel was built in 1909 by automaker F. Stanley and is only six miles from Rocky Mountain National Park. Multimillion dollar renovations have restored the gorgeous white hotel, which occupies 35 acres surrounded by the Rocky Mountains, to its original grandeur. The cozy rooms are classically styled and feature pillow-top mattresses and free wireless Internet.
138 rooms. Restaurant, bar. Pool. Spa. Tennis. $

WHERE TO EAT
★MAMA ROSE'S
338 E. Elkhorn Ave., Estes Park, 970-586-3330, 877-586-3330;
www.mamarosesrestaurant.com
Italian. Dinner. Bar. Children's menu. Outdoor seating. $$

★★NICKY'S
1360 Fall River Road, Estes Park, 970-586-5377, 866-464-2597; www.nickysresort.com
American. Breakfast, lunch, dinner. Closed Monday, mid-October-mid-May. Bar. Children's menu. Outdoor seating. $$

★★TWIN OWLS STEAKHOUSE
800 MacGregor Ave., Estes Park, 970-586-9344; www.twinowls.net
Steak. Dinner. Bar. Reservations recommended. $$

FORT COLLINS
See also Estes Park, Loveland
Founded as a military post in 1864, Fort Collins is a large college town—home to Colorado State University. It's a thriving community these days because of great schools, low crime, jobs in the high-tech field and great outdoor living. Many high-tech companies have moved here, and three microbreweries and Anheuser-Busch are located here as well. Old Town is a historic shopping district with red brick pedestrian walkways and street lamps.

ROCKY MOUNTAIN NATIONAL PARK

Straddling the Continental Divide, the 415-square-mile park contains a staggering profusion of peaks, upland meadows, sheer canyons, glacial streams and lakes. Dominating the scene is Longs Peak, with its east face towering 14,255 feet above sea level. The park's forests and meadows provide sanctuary for more than 750 varieties of wildflowers, 260 species of birds and such indigenous mammals as deer, wapiti (American elk), bighorn sheep and beaver. There are five campgrounds, two of which take reservations from May to early September. Some attractions are not accessible in the winter months.

Information: Rocky Mountain National Park, 1000 US Highway 36, Estes Park, 970-586-1206; www.nps.gov/romo

WHAT TO SEE
ANHEUSER-BUSCH BREWERY TOUR

2351 Busch Drive, Fort Collins, 970-490-4691; www.budweisertours.com

The Anheuser-Busch Brewery in Fort Collins produces 2.6 million cans of beer a day. The tour includes an overview of the company's history (which dates back to the mid-1800s), a walking tour of the brewing and control rooms and a visit with the famous Budweiser Clydesdales, housed with their Dalmatian companions in picturesque stables on the beautiful Busch estate. Enjoy complimentary beer tasting at the end of the tour.

January-May, Thursday-Monday 10 a.m.-4 p.m.; June-August, daily 9:30 a.m.-4.30 p.m.; September, daily 10 a.m.-4 p.m.; October-December, Thursday-Monday 10 a.m.-4 p.m.

★★★★★ COLORADO

COLORADO STATE UNIVERSITY

Fort Collins, West Laurel and Howes streets, 970-491-4636;
www.welcome.colostate.edu

Established in 1870, this campus now has 24,500 students. Land-grant institution with an 833-acre campus. Pingree Park, adjacent to Rocky Mountain National Park, is the summer campus for natural resource science education and forestry program.

149

DISCOVERY SCIENCE CENTER

703 E. Prospect Road, Fort Collins, 970-472-3990; www.dcsm.org

This hands-on science and technology museum features more than 100 educational exhibits.

Admission: adults $7.00, children $5.00, seniors $5.50, children under 3 free. Tuesday-Saturday 10 a.m.-5 p.m.

FORT COLLINS MUSEUM

Library Park, 200 Mathews St., Fort Collins, 970-221-6738;
www.ci.fort-collins.co.us/museum

Exhibits include a model of the army post, a fine collection of Folsom points and American Indian beadwork, plus displays of historic household, farm, and business items and three historic cabins.

Tuesday-Saturday 10 a.m.-5 p.m., Sunday noon-5 p.m.

LINCOLN CENTER

417 W. Magnolia, Fort Collins, 970-221-6735; www.ci.fort-collins.co.us/lctix

Includes a theater for the performing arts, concert hall, sculpture garden, art gallery and display areas with changing exhibits.

Daily.

LORY STATE PARK

708 Lodgepole Drive, Bellvue, 970-493-1623; www.parks.state.co.us/Parks/lory

Approximately 2,500 acres near Horsetooth Reservoir. Waterskiing, boating, nature trails, hiking, stables, picnicking.

Daily.

WHERE TO STAY
★BEST WESTERN KIVA INN

1638 E. Mulberry St., Fort Collins, 970-484-2444, 888-299-5482;
www.bestwestern.com

62 rooms. Complimentary breakfast. Pool. Fitness center. Pets accepted. $

★★★MARRIOTT FORT COLLINS

350 E. Horsetooth Road, Fort Collins, 970-226-5200, 800-342-4398; www.marriott.com

Located just three miles from Colorado State University, this hotel is a great place to stay during CSU parents' weekend. Rooms feature new luxury bedding with down comforters and fluffier pillows. Take a swim in the indoor or outdoor pool and hit the gym for a workout. This hotel is nonsmoking.

229 rooms. Restaurant, bar. Pool. Business center. $

★★RAMADA FORT COLLINS

3836 E. Mulberry St., Fort Collins, 970-484-4660, 800-272-6232; www.ramada.com

197 rooms. Restaurant, bar. Pets accepted. Pool. Fitness center. $

GEORGETOWN

See also Dillon

Georgetown is named for George Griffith, who discovered gold in this valley in 1859 and opened up the area to other gold seekers. The area around Georgetown has produced almost $200 million worth of gold, silver, copper, lead and zinc. Numerous 19th-century structures remain standing.

WHAT TO SEE
GEORGETOWN LOOP HISTORIC MINING AND RAILROAD PARK

Georgetown, 888-456-6777; www.georgetownlooprr.com

The reconstructed Georgetown Loop Railroad was used in the late 1800s for shipping ore and was hailed as an engineering marvel. It now carries visitors on a scenic 6½-mile trip, which includes a stop at the mine area for tours. The train leaves from Devil's Gate Viaduct (west on Interstate 70 to exit 228, then a half mile south on Old US 6) or Silver Plume (I-70, exit 226).

Five or six round-trips per day. Late May-early October, daily.

HAMILL HOUSE MUSEUM

305 Argentine St., Georgetown, 303-569-2840

Early Gothic Revival house acquired by William A. Hamill, Colorado silver magnate and state senator, with period furnishings.

Late May-September, daily; rest of year, by appointment.

HOTEL DE PARIS MUSEUM

409 Sixth St., Georgetown, 303-569-2311; www.hoteldeparismuseum.org

This internationally known hostelry was built in 1875 and is elaborately decorated with original furnishings.

Admission: adults $4, seniors $3, students $2, children under 6 free. Memorial Day-Labor Day, daily 10 a.m.-4:30 p.m.; May, September-December, Saturday-Sunday noon-4 p.m.

LOVELAND SKI AREA

Loveland Pass, Georgetown, 303-569-3203, 800-736-3754; www.skiloveland.com

Three quad, two triple, four double chairlifts, Poma lift, Mighty-mite; patrol, school, rentals, snowmaking; cafeteria, restaurants, bars; nursery; 60 runs; longest run two miles; vertical drop 2,410 feet.

Mid-October-mid-May, Monday-Friday 9 a.m.-4 p.m., Saturday-Sunday 8:30 a.m.-4 p.m.

SPECIAL EVENTS
GEORGETOWN CHRISTMAS MARKET

Sixth Street, Georgetown, 303-569-2405, 303-569-2888;
www.georgetowncolorado.com

For a delightful old-fashioned Christmas experience, visit the little Victorian hamlet of Georgetown during the first two weekends in December. The streets and shops come alive with holiday lights, music, dancing and carolers.

Early December.

WHERE TO EAT
★THE HAPPY COOKER

412 Sixth St., Georgetown, 303-569-3166

American. Breakfast, lunch. Children's menu. Outdoor seating. $

GLENWOOD SPRINGS

See also Aspen

Doc Holliday, the famous gunman, died here in 1887. Today, Glenwood Springs is a popular year-round health spa destination, thanks to its famous hot springs. The town is located between Aspen and Vail on the forested banks of the Colorado River and is the gateway to White River National Forest. Excellent game and fishing country surrounds Glenwood Springs, and camping areas are sprinkled throughout the region. The nearby town offers museums, art galleries, specialty shops and restaurants in a relaxed, Western-style setting.

WHAT TO SEE
GLENWOOD HOT SPRINGS POOL
Hot Springs Lodge and Pool, 415 Sixth St., Glenwood Springs, 970-945-6571,
800-537-7946; www.hotspringspool.com

For centuries, visitors have traveled to the hot springs in Colorado to soak in their soothing—and many say healing—mineral-rich waters. Today, those same legendary springs feed this hot spring pool—the world's largest. The main pool, more than two blocks long, circulates 3.5 million gallons of naturally heated, spring-fed water each day. The complex includes lap lanes, a shallow play area, diving area, two water slides and a therapy pool.

Late May-early September, daily 7:30 a.m.-10 p.m.; early September-late May, daily 9 a.m.-10 p.m.

SCENIC DRIVES
Glenwood Springs, on Highway 133, visit Redstone, Marble and Maroon peaks; Interstate 70 provides access to Lookout Mountain and Glenwood Canyon

Just a two-mile hike from the road, you'll find beautiful Hanging Lake and Bridal Veil Falls. The marble quarries in the Crystal River Valley are the source of stones for the Lincoln Memorial in Washington, D.C. and the Tomb of the Unknown Soldier in Arlington National Cemetery.

SUNLIGHT MOUNTAIN RESORT
10901 County Road 117, Glenwood Springs, 970-945-7491, 800-445-7931;
www.sunlightmtn.com

Triple, two double chairlifts; surface tow; patrol, school, rentals; cafeteria, bar; nursery. 67 runs; longest run 2½ miles; vertical drop 2,010 feet. Snowmobiling half-day rates. Late November-early April, daily. Also cross-country touring center, 10 miles.

WHITE RIVER NATIONAL FOREST
900 Grand Avenue, Glenwood Springs, 970-945-2521; www.fs.fed.us/r2/whiteriver

More than 2,500,000 acres in the heart of the Colorado Rocky Mountains. Recreation at 70 developed sites with boat ramps, picnicking, campgrounds and observation points; Holy Cross, Flat Tops, Eagles Nest, Maroon Bells-Snowmass, Raggeds, Collegiate Peaks and Hunter-Frying Pan wildernesses. (Check with local ranger for information before entering wildernesses or any backcountry areas.) Many streams and lakes with trout fishing; large deer and elk populations. Dillon, Green Mountain and Ruedi reservoirs.

SPECIAL EVENTS
STRAWBERRY DAYS FESTIVAL
Sayre Park, Glenwood Springs, 970-945-6589; www.strawberrydaysfestival.com

Arts and crafts fair, rodeo, parade. Third weekend in June.

WHERE TO STAY
★BEST WESTERN ANTLERS
171 W. Sixth St., Glenwood Springs, 970-945-8535, 800-626-0609;
www.bestwestern.com

99 rooms. Complimentary breakfast. Pool. $

★GLENWOOD HOT SPRINGS LODGE

415 E. Sixth St., Glenwood Springs, 970-945-6571, 800-537-7946;
www.hotspringspool.com
107 rooms. Complimentary breakfast. Business center. Fitness center. Pool. $

WHERE TO EAT
★★FLORINDO'S
721 Grand Ave., Glenwood Springs, 970-945-1245
Italian. Dinner. Bar. Children's menu. $$

★★RIVER'S RESTAURANT
2525 S. Grand Ave., Glenwood Springs, 970-928-8813; www.theriversrestaurant.com
American. Dinner, Sunday brunch. Bar. Outdoor seating. $$

GOLDEN

See also Denver, Georgetown
Not surprisingly, Golden was founded during Colorado's gold rush. A mere 15 miles from downtown Denver, Golden has done a good job preserving its small-town charm.

WHAT TO SEE
ASTOR HOUSE HOTEL MUSEUM
822 12th St., Golden, 303-278-3557; www.astorhousemuseum.org
The first stone hotel west of the Mississippi, the Astor House was built in 1867. Period furnishings Self-guided and guided tours (reservations required). Tuesday-Saturday 10 a.m.-4:30 p.m..

BUFFALO BILL MUSEUM & GRAVE
987-1/2 Lookout Mountain Road, Golden, 303-526-0744; www.buffalobill.org
Lookout Mountain is the final resting place of the man who virtually defined the spirit of the Wild West: William F. "Buffalo Bill" Cody, whose life included stints as a cattle driver, fur trapper, gold miner, Pony Express rider and scout for the U.S. Cavalry. He became world famous with his traveling Buffalo Bill's Wild West Show. At the Buffalo Bill Museum & Grave, Cody still draws crowds who come to see the museum's Western artifacts collection, take advantage of the beautiful hilltop vistas and pay homage to this legendary Western hero.
May-October: daily 9 a.m.-5 p.m.; November-April: Tuesday-Sunday 9 a.m.-4 p.m.

COLORADO RAILROAD MUSEUM
17155 W. Fourth Ave., Golden, 303-279-4591, 800-365-6263; www.crrm.org
This 1880s-style railroad depot houses memorabilia and an operating model railroad. More than 50 historic locomotives and cars from old railroads are displayed outside.
Daily 9 a.m.-5 p.m.

COLORADO SCHOOL OF MINES

1500 Illinois St., Golden, 303-273-3000, 800-446-9488; www.mines.edu

World-renowned institution devoted exclusively to the education of mineral, energy and material engineers and applied scientists.

Tours of campus.

COORS BREWERY TOUR

13th and Ford streets, Golden, 303-277-2337, 866-812-2337; www.coors.com

For a fun, free factory tour, visit Coors Brewing Company—the nation's third-largest brewer—to see how beer is made. The 40-minute walking tour reviews the malting, brewing and packaging processes and ends with a free sampling in the hospitality room (proper ID required). Visitors under 18 must be accompanied by an adult.

Monday-Saturday 10 a.m.-4 p.m.

GOLDEN GATE CANYON STATE PARK

Crawford Gulch Road, Golden, 303-582-3707;

www.parks.state.co.us/goldengatecanyon

On 12,000 acres. Nature and hiking trails, cross-country skiing, snowshoeing, biking, horseback riding, ice skating, picnicking, camping. Visitor center. Panorama Point Overlook provides a 100-mile view of the Continental Divide. Daily.

GOLDEN PIONEER MUSEUM

923 10th St., Golden, 303-278-7151; www.goldenpioneermuseum.com

This museum houses more than 4,000 items dating from Golden's days as the territorial capital, including household articles, clothing, furniture, mining, military and ranching equipment.

Monday-Saturday 10 a.m.-4:30 p.m.; Memorial Day-Labor Day: Sunday 11 a.m.-5 p.m.

HERITAGE SQUARE

18301 W. Colfax Ave., Golden, 303-279-2789; www.heritagesquare.info

Heritage Square family entertainment park is reminiscent of a 1870s Colorado mining town with its Old West streetscapes and Victorian façades. In addition to specialty shops, restaurants, museums and a theater, there are amusement rides, a waterslide, a 70-foot bungee tower, go-karts and a miniature golf course. Heritage Square is also home to Colorado's longest Alpine slide.

Winter, Monday-Saturday 10 a.m.-5 p.m., Sunday noon-5 p.m.; summer, Monday-Saturday 10 a.m.-8 p.m., Sunday noon-8 p.m.

LARIAT TRAIL

Golden, also known as Lookout Mountain Road, trail begins west of Sixth Avenue at 19th Street, 720-971-9649; www.lariatloop.org

Leads to Denver Mountain Parks. Lookout Mountain (five miles west off Highway 6) is the nearest peak.

SPECIAL EVENT
BUFFALO BILL DAYS
Golden, 303-279-8141; www.buffalobilldays.com

Held in honor of "Buffalo Bill" Cody, this event features a parade, golf tournament, children's rides and games, a car show, food and arts and crafts. July.

WHERE TO STAY
★LA QUINTA INN DENVER GOLDEN
3301 Youngfield Service Road, Golden, 303-279-5565, 800-753-3757;
www.laquinta.com

129 rooms. Complimentary breakfast. Pets accepted. Pool. $

★★★MARRIOTT DENVER WEST
1717 Denver West Blvd., Golden, 303-279-9100, 888-238-1803; www.marriott.com

Rooms at this hotel feature new Revive bedding and high-speed Internet access. The renovated health club is stocked with cutting-edge equipment. The sports bar has 37 flatscreen high-definition TVs.

305 rooms. Restaurant, bar. Fitness center. Pool. $

★★TABLE MOUNTAIN INN
1310 Washington Ave., Golden, 303-277-9898, 800-762-9898;
www.tablemountaininn.com

74 rooms. Restaurant, bar. $

WHERE TO EAT
★★CHART HOUSE
25908 Genesee Trail Road, Golden, 303-526-9813; www.chart-house.com

American. Dinner. Bar. Children's menu. $$

★★SIMMS STEAKHOUSE
11911 W. Sixth Ave., Golden, 303-237-0465; www.simmssteakhouse.com

Seafood. Dinner, Sunday brunch. Bar. Children's menu. Outdoor seating. $$

★★TABLE MOUNTAIN INN GRILL & CANTINA
Table Mountain Inn, 1310 Washington Ave., Golden, 303-216-8040;
www.tablemountaininn.com

Southwestern. Breakfast, lunch, dinner, Sunday brunch. Bar. Children's menu. Outdoor seating. $$

GRANBY
See also Estes Park

The Arapaho National Recreation Area, developed by the Department of Interior as part of the Colorado-Big Thompson Reclamation Project, is northeast of Granby. Several national forests, lakes and big-game hunting grounds are within easy reach. Two ski areas are also nearby.

WHAT TO SEE
ARAPAHO NATIONAL RECREATION AREA
9 Ten Mile Drive, Granby, 970-887-4100; www.fs.fed.us/r2/arnf
The area includes Shadow Mountain and several lakes. Boating, fishing, hunting, camping, picnicking, horseback riding.
Daily.

BUDGET TACKLE
255 E. Agate Ave., Granby, 970-887-9344
Rent ice-fishing equipment, get advice on techniques and request directions to the best places to fish.

GRAND ADVENTURE BALLOON TOURS
127 Fourth St., Granby, 970-887-1340; www.grandadventureballoon.com
Take a sunrise hot air balloon flight over the Rockies from the Winter Park/ Fraser Valley area.

SILVERCREEK SKI AREA
1000 Village Road, Granby
Two triple, double chairlifts; Poma lift; patrol, school, rentals, snowmaking; concession, cafeteria, bar; nursery; day-lodge. 22 runs; longest run 1½ miles; vertical drop 1,000 feet.
December-mid-April.

WHERE TO EAT
★LONGBRANCH & SCHATZI'S PIZZA
165 E. Agate Ave., Granby, 970-887-2209
German. Lunch, dinner. Closed Sunday. Bar. Children's menu. Reservations recommended. $$

GRAND JUNCTION
See also Glenwood Springs
Grand Junction's name stems from its location at the junction of the Colorado and Gunnison rivers. The altitude and warm climate combine to provide a rich agricultural area, which produces peaches, pears and grapes for the local wine industry. The city serves as a trade and tourist center for Western Colorado and Eastern Utah, as well as a gateway to two national parks, six national forests and seven million acres of public land.

WHAT TO SEE
ADVENTURE BOUND RIVER EXPEDITIONS
2392 H. Road, Grand Junction, 970-245-5428, 800-423-4668; www.raft-colorado.com
Take a two- to five-day whitewater rafting trip on the Colorado, Green and Yampa rivers.

CROSS ORCHARDS HISTORIC FARM
3073 F Road, Grand Junction, 970-434-9814; www.wcmuseum.org/crossorchards.htm
Costumed guides interpret the social and agricultural heritage of Western Colorado. Restored buildings and equipment on display; narrow gauge rail-

DINOSAUR NATIONAL MONUMENT

This 325-square-mile monument on the Utah/Colorado border holds one of the largest concentrations of fossilized Jurassic-era dinosaur bones in the world. Visitors can get a close-up view of a quarry wall containing at least 1,500 fossil bones dating back 150 million years. The wall was once part of an ancient riverbed. The monument itself is distinguished by its beautiful landscape of high plateaus and river-carved canyons. Access to the Colorado backcountry section, a land of deeply eroded canyons of the Green and Yampa Rivers, is via the Harper's Corner Road, starting at monument headquarters on Highway 40 (two miles east of Dinosaur). At the end of this 32-mile surfaced road, a one-mile foot trail leads to a promontory overlooking the Green and Yampa rivers.

The entrance to the Dinosaur Quarry section in Utah is at the junction of Highways 40 and 149 in Jensen, Utah (13 miles east of Vernal). Dinosaur Quarry is seven miles north on Highway 149. The Green River campground is about five miles from there. No lodgings are available other than at campgrounds. The visitor's centers and one quarry-section campground are open all year; the remainder are often closed by snow from mid-November-mid-April. Information: 4545 E. Highway 40, Dinosaur, 435-781-7700; www.nps.gov/dino.

road exhibit and country store. Demonstrations, special events.
Admission: adults $4, seniors $3, children $2.50 and family groups $10.
May-October, Tuesday-Saturday 9 a.m.-4 p.m.

MUSEUM OF WESTERN COLORADO

462 Ute Ave., Grand Junction, 970-242-0971, 888-488-3466; www.wcmuseum.org
Features exhibits on regional, social and natural history of the Western Slope, plus a collection of small weapons and wildlife exhibits.
Admission: adults $5.50-$12, seniors $4.50-$10, children $3-$8 and family groups $16. Tuesday-Saturday 10 a.m.-3 p.m. Tours by appointment.

RABBIT VALLEY TRAIL THROUGH TIME

2815 H. Road, Grand Junction, 970-244-3000
This 1½-mile self-guided walking trail takes you through a paleontologically significant area where you can see fossilized flora and fauna from the Jurassic Age. No pets allowed.
Daily.

RIGGS HILL

South Broadway and Meadows Way, Grand Junction, 970-241-9210
A ¾-mile, self-guided walking trail in an area where the bones of the Brachiosaurus dinosaur were discovered in 1900.
Daily.

SPECIAL EVENTS

COLORADO MOUNTAIN WINEFEST

2785 Highway 50, Grand Junction, 970-464-0111, 800-704-3667;
www.coloradowinefest.com
Wine tastings, outdoor events.
Late September.

WHERE TO STAY
★BEST WESTERN SANDMAN MOTEL
708 Horizon Drive, Grand Junction, 970-243-4150; www.bestwestern.com
80 rooms. Pets accepted. Pool. $

★★DOUBLETREE HOTEL GRAND JUNCTION
743 Horizon Drive, Grand Junction, 970-241-8888; www.doubletree.com
273 rooms. Restaurant, bar. Pool. Tennis. Business center. Fitness center. $

★★GRAND VISTA HOTEL
2790 Crossroads Blvd., Grand Junction, 970-241-8411, 800-800-7796;
www.grandvistahotel.com
158 rooms. Restaurant, bar. Business center. Pets accepted. Pool. Fitness center. $

★★CLARION INN
755 Horizon Drive, Grand Junction, 970-243-6790, 888-489-9796;
www.holiday-inn.com
290 rooms. Restaurant, bar. Pets. Fitness center. Pool. $

WHERE TO EAT
★★WINERY RESTAURANT
620 Main St., Grand Junction, 970-242-4100; www.thewineryrestaurant.net
American. Dinner. Bar. $$

GRAND LAKE
See also Estes Park, Granby
Grand Lake is on the northern shore of the largest glacial lake in Colorado. As one of the state's oldest resort villages, Grand Lake boasts the world's highest yacht club, a full range of water recreation and horseback riding and pack trips on mountain trails. Grand Lake is at the terminus of Trail Ridge Road at the west entrance to Rocky Mountain National Park.

SPECIAL EVENTS
ROCKY MOUNTAIN REPERTORY THEATRE
Community Building, Town Square, Grand Lake, 970-627-3421;
www.rockymountainrep.com
Three musicals change nightly, Monday-Saturday. Reservations advised. Late June-late August.

WINTER CARNIVAL
Grand Lake, 970-627-3372; www.winter-carnival.com
Ice skating, snowmobiling, snow sculptures, ice fishing derby, ice-golf tournament. February.

WHERE TO EAT
★★★CAROLINE'S CUISINE
9921 Highway 34, Grand Lake, 970-627-8125, 800-627-9636;
www.sodaspringsranch.com
At this cozy restaurant, large windows offer views of either the mountain or

the hills, and the bistro-style menu includes steak frites and roasted duck. The menu has classic American fare such as grilled steaks and roasted chicken. French, American. Dinner. Bar. Children's menu. Outdoor seating. $$

GUNNISON

See also Crested Butte

With 2,000 miles of trout-fishing streams and Colorado's largest lake within easy driving range, Gunnison has long been noted as an excellent fishing center.

WHAT TO SEE
ALPINE TUNNEL

500 E. Tomichi Ave., Gunnison, 36 miles northeast via Highway 50

Completed in 1881 and abandoned in 1910, this railroad tunnel—nearly 12,000 feet above sea level—is 1,771 feet long.
July-October.

CURECANTI NATIONAL RECREATION AREA

102 Elk Creek, Gunnison, 970-641-2337; www.nps.gov/cure

This area includes Blue Mesa, Morrow Point and Crystal reservoirs. Elk Creek -Marinas, Inc., offers boat tours on Morrow Point Lake (Memorial Day-Labor Day, daily; 970-641-0402 for reservations). Blue Mesa Lake has water-skiing, windsurfing, fishing, boating; picnicking, camping. The Elk Creek visitor center is 16 miles west (mid-April-October, daily).

GUNNISON NATIONAL FOREST

216 N. Colorado St., Gunnison, 970-641-0471; www.fs.fed.us/r2/gmug

This forest contains 27 peaks. Activities include fishing, hiking, picnicking and camping. Includes West Elk Wilderness and portions of the Maroon Bells-Snowmass, Collegiate Peaks, La Garita and Raggeds wilderness areas.

TAYLOR PARK RESERVOIR

216 N. Colorado St., Gunnison, 970-641-2922

The road runs through this 20-mile canyon.
Fishing, boating, hunting, camping. Memorial Day-September, daily.

SPECIAL EVENT
CATTLEMEN'S DAYS, RODEO AND COUNTY FAIR

275 S. Spruce, Gunnison, 970-641-4160; www.visitgunnison.com

The oldest rodeo in Colorado.
Mid-July.

WHERE TO STAY
★★BEST WESTERN VISTA INN

733 Highway 24 N., Buena Vista, 719-395-8009, 800-809-3495; www.bestwestern.com

52 rooms. Restaurant. Pool. $

★HOLIDAY INN EXPRESS-GUNNISON

910 E. Tomichi Ave., Gunnison, 970-641-1288, 877-863-4780; www.holiday-inn.com
107 rooms. Complimentary breakfast. Pool. $

WHERE TO EAT
★★TROUGH

37550 Highway 50, Gunnison, 970-641-3724
American. Dinner. Bar. Children's menu. $$

KEYSTONE

See also Dillon
This tiny town is best known for its skiing and scenic setting, so strap on your
sticks and enjoy.

WHAT TO SEE
KEYSTONE RESORT SKI AREA

1254 Soda Ridge Road, Keystone, 800-344-8878; www.keystone.snow.com
Four ski mountains (Arapahoe Basin, Keystone, North Peak and the Out-
back). Patrol, school, rentals. Snowmaking at Keystone, North Peak and the
Outback. Late October-early May. Cross-country skiing, night skiing, ice
skating, snowmobiling and sleigh rides. Shuttle bus service. Combination
and half-day ski rates; package plans. Summer activities include boating,
rafting and gondola rides, plus golf, tennis, horseback riding, bicycling and
jeep riding.

WHERE TO STAY
★★★KEYSTONE LODGE & SPA

22101 Highway 6, Keystone, 970-496-3000, 877-753-9786;
www.keystonelodge.rockresorts.com
Keystone Lodge is a perfect Rocky Mountain getaway, thanks to a variety
of activities, comfortable accommodations and enjoyable dining. The guest
rooms and suites are the picture of mountain chic, with large windows fram-
ing unforgettable views of snow-capped peaks and the Snake River. You'll
never be at a loss for something to do, with an onsite ice-skating rink, BMW
driving tours, nearby skiing and golf and a complete fitness center. After an
action-packed day, head to the Spa at Keystone Resort, which offers a variety
of soothing treatments.
152 rooms. Restaurant, bar. Pool. Fitness center. Business center. Spa. $$$

WHERE TO EAT
★★★SKI TIP LODGE

764 Montezuma Road, Keystone, 800-354-4386; www.skitiplodge.com
This charming bed and breakfast has been served American regional cuisine
for more than 50 years.
Dinner. Bar. Children's menu. $$$

LAKEWOOD

See also Denver

Lakewood is a suburban community west of Denver.

WHAT TO SEE
COLORADO MILLS

14500 W. Colfax Ave., Lakewood, 303-384-3000; www.coloradomills.com

This brand-new 1.2-million-square-foot state-of-the-art retail and entertainment complex is just 10 minutes from downtown Denver, and brings a vast array of value-oriented stores, restaurants and entertainment venues together. Movie theaters, shops, restaurants, an interactive play area for kids and a 40,000-square-foot ESPN X Games Skatepark for older kids form the core of the entertainment center.

Monday-Saturday 10 a.m.-9 p.m., Sunday 11 a.m.-6 p.m.

CROWN HILL PARK

West 26th Avenue and Kipling Street, Lakewood, 303-271-5925

This 242-acre nature preserve includes Crown Hill Lake and a wildlife pond. Fishing, hiking, bicycle, bridle trails.

Daily.

LAKEWOOD'S HERITAGE CENTER

801 Yarrow St., Lakewood, 303-987-7850

This 127-acre park includes nature, art and historical exhibits. Turn-of-the-century farm; one-room schoolhouse; vintage farm machinery; Barn Gallery with permanent and changing exhibits, interpretive displays. Lectures, workshops. visitor center.

Admission: adults $5, seniors $4, children $3, children under 3 free.

Tuesday-Saturday 10 a.m.-4 p.m.

WHERE TO STAY
★HAMPTON INN DENVER-SOUTHWEST/LAKEWOOD

3605 S. Wadsworth Blvd., Lakewood, 303-989-6900, 800-426-7866;
www.hamptoninn.com

150 rooms. Complimentary breakfast. Pool. Business center. Fitness center. $

★★HOLIDAY INN DENVER LAKEWOOD

7390 W. Hampden Ave., Lakewood, 303-980-9200, 888-565-6159;
www.hilakewood.com

166 rooms. Restaurant, bar. Pets accepted. Pool. $

★★★SHERATON DENVER WEST HOTEL

360 Union Blvd., Lakewood, 303-987-2000, 800-325-3535; www.sheraton.com

Adjacent to the Denver Federal Center, this hotel is a perfect launching pad to explore nearby attractions, including Coors Brewery and Red Rocks Concert Amphitheater. The 10,000-square-foot health club includes a heated indoor lap pool and the spa offers a variety of relaxing treatments. The rooms are warm and cozy in deep maroons and traditional décor. And even dogs get the Sheraton Sweet Sleeper beds.

242 rooms. Restaurant, bar. Business center. Pool. Spa. Fitness center. $$

WHERE TO EAT
★★★240 UNION
240 Union Blvd., Lakewood, 303-989-3562; www.240union.com
This contemporary American grille with a large open kitchen is known for having some of the best seafood in the Denver area. Other favorites include wood-fired oven pizzas, Colorado lamb sirloin with camembert potatoes and beef tenderloin with black garlic butter, asparagus and three onion mashed potatoes. The wine list features a number of good selections, and desserts include classics like key lime pie and chocolate mousse cake.
American. Lunch, dinner. Bar. Reservations recommended. $$

★CASA BONITA OF DENVER
6715 W. Colfax Ave., Lakewood, 303-232-5115; www.casabonitadenver.com
Mexican. Lunch, dinner. Bar. Children's menu. $$

LEADVILLE
See also Buena Vista, Dillon, Vail
Located just below the timberline, Leadville's high altitude contributes to its reputation for excellent skiing, cool summers and beautiful fall colors. First a rich gold camp, then an even richer silver camp, the town boasts a lusty, brawling past in which millionaires were made and destroyed in a single day, a barrel of whiskey could net $1,500 and thousands of dollars could be won and lost in a card game in the town's saloons and smoky gambling halls. Leadville's lively history is intertwined with the lives of Horace Tabor and his two wives, Augusta and Elizabeth Doe, whose rags-to-riches-to-rags story is the basis of the American opera The Ballad of Baby Doe. The "unsinkable" Molly Brown (of Titanic fame) made her fortune here, as did David May, Charles Boettcher, Charles Dow and Meyer Guggenheim. Until 1950, Leadville was a decaying mining town. However, a burst of civic enthusiasm has led to the rebirth of many attractions that date back to the town's glory days, including several museums and a Victorian downtown area.

WHAT TO SEE
EARTH RUNS SILVER
Fox Theater, 115 West Sixth St., Leadville, 719-486-3900
Video presentation featuring Leadville's legendary mining camp with music and narration.
Daily.

HEALY HOUSE-DEXTER CABIN
912 Harrison Ave., Leadville, 719-486-0487; www.coloradohistory.org
The restored Healy House, built in 1878, contains many fine Victorian-era furnishings. Dexter Cabin, built by early mining millionaire James V. Dexter to entertain wealthy gentlemen, looks like an ordinary two-room miner's cabin from the outside but is surprisingly luxurious.
Memorial Day-Labor Day, daily.

HERITAGE MUSEUM AND GALLERY
Ninth Street and Harrison Avenue, Leadville, 719-486-1878
Learn all about local history at this museum, which houses Victorian costumes, memorabilia of mining days and changing exhibits of American art.
Mid-May-October, daily.

LEADVILLE, COLORADO & SOUTHERN RAILROAD TRAIN TOUR
326 E. Seventh St., Leadville, 719-486-3936, 866-386-3936; www.leadville-train.com
Depart from the old depot for a 23-mile round trip scenic ride following the headwaters of the Arkansas River through the Rocky Mountains.
Memorial Day-October, daily.

THE MATCHLESS MINE
East Seventh Street, Leadville, 719-486-1899; www.matchlessmine.com
When Horace Tabor died in 1899, his last words to his wife were "hold on to the Matchless," which produced as much as $100,000 a month in its bonanza days. Faithful to his wish and ever hopeful, the once fabulously rich Baby Doe lived on in poverty in the little cabin next to the mine for 36 years, where she was found frozen to death in 1935. The cabin is now a museum.
June-Labor Day, daily.

NATIONAL MINING HALL OF FAME AND MUSEUM
120 W. Ninth St., Leadville, 719-486-1229; www.mininghalloffame.org
This Museum is dedicated to those who have made significant contributions to the mining industry. It includes history and technology exhibits.
May-October, daily; rest of year, Monday-Friday.

SKI COOPER
Highway 24, Leadville, 800-707-6114; www.skicooper.com
Triple, double chairlift; Poma lift, T-bar; patrol, school, rentals; snowcat tours; cafeteria, nursery; 26 runs; longest run 1½ miles; vertical drop 1,200 feet. Groomed cross-country skiing (15 miles).
Late November-early April, daily.

TABOR OPERA HOUSE
308 Harrison Ave., Leadville, 719-486-8409; www.taboroperahouse.net
Now a museum, this 1879 theater played host to the Metropolitan Opera, the Chicago Symphony and most of the famous actors and actresses of the period. Their photos line the corridors. Many of the original furnishings, scenery and the dressing areas are still in use and on display. Summer shows.
Memorial Day-September, daily.

SPECIAL EVENTS
BOOM DAYS & BURRO RACE
Leadville, 719-486-3900, 888-532-3845; www.leadvilleboomdays.com
Celebrates the town's 1880s Old West heritage with mining skill competitions, gunslingers, a parade and the 21-mile International Pack Burro Race.
Early August.

CRYSTAL CARNIVAL WEEKEND
Harrison Ave., Leadville, 719-486-0739; www.colorado.com/events
There is no actual carnival at this event. Instead, it features a skijoring competition in which dogs draw a person on skis over a snowy obstacle course. First full weekend of March.

WHERE TO EAT
★★★TENNESSEE PASS COOKHOUSE
1892 Highway 25, Leadville, 719-486-8114; www.tennesseepass.com
This ski-oriented dining room serves one prix fixe meal nightly with entrées ordered 24 hours in advance. The restaurant can only be reached by a one mile hike, bike or off-road vehicle ride through the woods to access the secluded mountain top location.
American. Dinner. Reservations recommended. $$$

LONGMONT
See also Boulder, Denver, Loveland
Considered one of the top small communities in the country, Longmont has found its own place in the spotlight outside the shadow of Boulder, its better-known neighbor.

WHAT TO SEE
LONGMONT MUSEUM
400 Quail Road, Longmont, 303-651-8374; www.ci.longmont.co.us/museum
Changing and special exhibits on art, history, space and science; permanent exhibits on the history of Longmont and the St. Vrain Valley.
Tuesday-Saturday 9 a.m.-5 p.m., Wednesday until 8 p.m, Sunday 1-5 p.m.; closed Monday, holidays.

SPECIAL EVENTS
BOULDER COUNTY FAIR AND RODEO
Longmont, 303-441-3927
Fairgrounds. Nine days in early August.

RHYTHM ON THE RIVER
Roger's Grove, Hover Street. and Boston Avenue, Longmont, 303-776-5295;
www.ci.longmont.co.us/rotr
Honoring Roger Jones, who preserved this riverside grove for generations to enjoy, this festival features music, an art show and children's activities. Early July.

WHERE TO STAY
★★RADISSON HOTEL & CONFERENCE CENTER
LONGMONT-BOULDER
1900 Ken Pratt Blvd., Longmont, 303-776-2000, 800-395-7046; www.radisson.com
210 rooms. Restaurant, bar. Pets accepted. Pool. $

LYONS

See also Boulder, Estes Park, Longmont, Loveland

In the foothills of the Rocky Mountains, this small town is known for the beautiful red cliffs that surround it.

SPECIAL EVENT
GOOD OLD DAYS CELEBRATION

350 Broadway Ave., Lyons, 303-823-5215; www.lyons-colorado.com/goodolddays

Parade, flea market, craft fair, food.

Last weekend in June.

WHERE TO EAT
★ANDREA'S HOMESTEAD CAFE

216 E. Main St., Lyons, 303-823-5000; www.andreashomesteadcafe.com

German. Breakfast, lunch, dinner, brunch. Closed Wednesday. Bar. Children's menu. Reservations recommended. $$

★★★BLACK BEAR INN

42 E. Main St., Lyons, 303-823-6812; www.blackbearinn.com

Since 1977, owners Hans and Annalies Wyppler have welcomed guests to their cozy Alpine-style restaurant. The menu features hearty dishes such as roasted duck and pork schnitzel.

American. Lunch, dinner. Closed Monday-Thursday. Bar. Outdoor seating. $$$

★★★LA CHAUMIÈRE

Highway 36, Lyons, 303-823-6521; www.lachaumiere-restaurant.com

This charming French restaurant offers friendly service and a simple but delicious menu of French cuisine. The menu changes with the seasons, but you might see filet mignon with red wine sauce, stuffed quail with wild mushrooms and a port wine demi-glaze. One mainstay is the chef's award-winning Maryland crab soup. The mountain setting adds to the relaxing atmosphere.

French. Dinner. Closed Monday. Children's menu. $$

MANITOU SPRINGS

See also Colorado Springs, Cripple Creek

Nestled at the foot of Pikes Peak, only seven miles west of downtown Colorado Springs, Manitou Springs is one of the state's definitive—and most accessible—mountain communities. The many mineral springs gave nearby Colorado Springs its name. The natives, attributing supernatural powers to the waters (Manitou is an American Indian word for "Great Spirit"), once marked off the surrounding area as a sanctuary. Today, the town is a National Historic District and a popular tourist resort. Manitou Avenue has many artists' studios, restaurants and boutiques.

WHAT TO SEE
CAVE OF THE WINDS

Cave of the Winds Road, Manitou Springs, 719-685-5444; www.caveofthewinds.com

This fascinating 45-minute guided tour—which goes through underground passageways filled with beautiful stalactites, stalagmites and flowstone formations created millions of years ago—leaves every 15 minutes and includes a laser light show.

Summer, 9 a.m.-9 p.m.; winter, 10 a.m.-5 p.m.

IRON SPRINGS MELODRAMA DINNER THEATER

444 Ruxton Ave., Manitou Springs, 719-685-5104; www.pikes-peak.com

Dinner theater featuring a traditional "olio" show. Named for the mineral-rich water beneath the ground.

Monday-Saturday.

MANITOU CLIFF DWELLINGS MUSEUM

Highway 24 W., Manitou Springs, 719-685-5242, 800-354-9971;
www.cliffdwellingsmuseum.com

See the architecture of the cliff-dwelling natives, circa 1100 to 1300. American Indian dancing June-August.

March-November, daily.

MIRAMONT CASTLE MUSEUM

9 Capitol Hill Ave., Manitou Springs, 719-685-1011; www.miramontcastle.org

A 46-room, four-story Victorian house (circa 1895) featuring nine styles of architecture, a miniatures and doll collection, a tea room, a soda fountain and gardens.

Admission: adults $6, seniors $5.50, children $2, children under 6 free.

Tuesday-Sunday.

WHERE TO STAY

★AMERICAS BEST VALUE INN VILLA MOTEL

481 Manitou Ave., Manitou Springs, 719-685-5492, 888-315-2378; www.villamotel.com

47 rooms. Complimentary breakfast. Pool. $

★★★THE CLIFF HOUSE AT PIKES PEAK

306 Canon Ave., Manitou Springs, 719-685-3000, 888-212-7000;
www.thecliffhouse.com

Built in 1873—before Colorado was even a state—this hotel has retained every charming detail of the Victorian age while adding modern touches. Each room is different and may include a gas fireplace, steam shower and towel warmers. Galleries, shops, restaurants and museums surround the hotel, and bicycles are available for rent. The dining room and wine cellar repeatedly win awards.

55 rooms. Complimentary breakfast. Restaurant. $$$

★★★RED CRAGS BED & BREAKFAST COUNTRY INN

302 El Paso Blvd., Manitou Springs, 719-685-1920, 800-721-2248; www.redcrags.com

Housed in an 1884 mansion that was originally built as a clinic, this charming and elegant inn, surrounded by the Rocky Mountains, has high ceilings, hardwood floors and beautiful antiques. In-room fireplaces provide a romantic atmosphere. All rooms also have plasma TVs.

8 rooms. No children under 10. Complimentary breakfast. $$

★★★ROCKLEDGE COUNTRY INN

328 El Paso Blvd., Manitou Springs, 719-685-4515, 888-685-4515;
www.rockledgeinn.com

Situated atop a hill and surrounded by lush juniper and pine trees, the Rockledge Country Inn is located at the foot of Pikes Peak and has a beautiful view of the Rocky Mountains. Built in 1912, the inn is built in an Arts and Crafts style. The living room has leather couches, a marble fireplace and a grand piano. And there's plenty on hand here, from bike rentals to hiking trails to croquet.

7 rooms. Complimentary breakfast. $$

WHERE TO EAT

★★★BRIARHURST MANOR ESTATE

404 Manitou Ave., Manitou Springs, 719-685-1864, 877-685-1448; www.briarhurst.com

Located in a pink sandstone Tudor manor house built in 1876 by the founder of -Manitou Springs, this elegant fine-dining restaurant's kitchen is headed up by executive chef Tyler Peoples, who uses homegrown vegetables and herbs in his recipes. Menu items include artisan cheeses, trout amandine, salmon filet, calamari steak piccata, and bison short ribs. The dessert sampler is the perfect ending to a delicious meal.

American. Dinner. Bar. Children's menu. Outdoor seating. $$$

★★★THE CLIFF HOUSE DINING ROOM

306 Canon Ave., Manitou Springs, 719-685-3000, 888-212-7000;
www.thecliffhouse.com

Located in the historic Cliff House hotel, this elegant dining room serves up new American cooking presented with flair. Look for dishes like Colorado lamb loin with Fuji apples, apricots and spinach in filo dough, rosemary rissolée potatoe and balsamic reduction. The ingredients in each dish are fresh and local, and there are more than 700 bottles of wine to accompany them.

American. Breakfast, lunch, dinner. $$

★★★CRAFTWOOD INN

404 El Paso Blvd., Manitou Springs, 719-685-9000; www.craftwood.com

This romantic restaurant located in a 1912 Tudor manor house serves Southwestern-influenced cuisine. The focus is on steaks, elk, pheasant, venison, quail and seafood. When in season, the kitchen also uses Colorado vegetables and produce. Dining here is an adventure. Dishes include Colorado elk steak, grilled blue Russian wild boar and aged buffalo ribeye.

American. Dinner. Bar. Outdoor seating. $$$

★★MISSION BELL INN

178 Crystal Park Road, Manitou Springs, 719-685-9089; www.missionbellinn.com

Mexican. Dinner. Closed Monday; also Tuesday in winter. Children's menu. Outdoor seating. $$

★★STAGECOACH INN

702 Manitou Ave., Manitou Springs, 719-685-9400; www.stagecoachinn.com

American. Lunch, dinner. Bar. Children's menu. Reservations recommended. Outdoor seating. $$

MONTE VISTA

See also Alamosa

Located in the heart of the high-altitude San Luis Valley, Monte Vista means "mountain view" in Spanish.

WHAT TO SEE
MONTE VISTA NATIONAL WILDLIFE REFUGE

9383 El Rancho Lane, Alamosa, 719-589-4021; www.fws.gov/alamosa

Created as a nesting, migration and wintering habitat for waterfowl and other migratory birds. Marked visitor tour road.

SPECIAL EVENTS
MONTE VISTA CRANE FESTIVAL

Ski-Hi Park, 2345 Sherman Ave., Monte Vista, 719-852-2731; www.cranefest.com

Tour this refuge to view cranes and other wildlife. Arts, crafts, workshops. Mid-March.

SKI-HI STAMPEDE

Ski-Hi Park, 2345 Sherman Ave., Monte Vista, 719-852-2055; www.skihistampede.com

Rodeo, carnival, arts and crafts show, street parade, barbecue, Western dances. Last weekend in July.

WHERE TO STAY
★★BEST WESTERN MOVIE MANOR

2830 W. Highway 160, Monte Vista, 719-852-5921, 800-771-9468; www.bestwestern.com

59 rooms. Restaurant, bar. Pets accepted. $

MONTROSE

See also Ouray

Montrose is a trading center for a rich mining, agricultural and recreational area in the Uncompahgre Valley. Several fishing areas are nearby, including the Gunnison River east of town and Buckhorn Lakes southeast.

WHAT TO SEE
BLACK CANYON OF THE GUNNISON NATIONAL MONUMENT

102 Elk Creek, Gunnison, 970-641-2337; www.nps.gov/blca

Within this monument, 12 of the most spectacular miles of the rugged gorge of the Gunnison River slice down to a maximum depth of 2,660 feet. At one point, the river channel is only 40 feet wide. The narrowest width between the north and south rims at the top is 1,100 feet. The combination of dark, weathered rock and lack of sunlight due to the narrowness of the canyon give the monument its name. The spectacular scenery includes pine trees—some more than 800 years old. There are scenic drives along the south rim (the road is plowed to Gunnison Point in winter) and the north rim (approximately May-October). There are also hiking areas and concessions (June-Labor Day). The visitor center is located at Gunnison Point on the south rim. A descent into the canyon requires a free hiking permit from the visitor center. Cross-country skiing is open in winter from Gunnison Point to High Point.

MONTROSE COUNTY HISTORICAL MUSEUM

Depot Building, 21 N. Rio Grande, Montrose, 970-249-2085

View collections of antique farm machinery; archaeological artifacts; pioneer cabin; tool collection; early electrical equipment; and Montrose newspapers 1896-1940.

May-September, daily.

WHERE TO STAY
★★BEST WESTERN RED ARROW

1702 E. Main St., Montrose, 970-249-9641, 800-468-9323;
www.bestwestern.com/redarrow

57 rooms. Complimentary breakfast. Fitness center. Pool. Pets accepted. $

WHERE TO EAT
★WHOLE ENCHILADA

44 S. Grand Ave., Montrose, 970-249-1881

Mexican. Lunch, dinner. Closed Sunday. Bar. Outdoor seating. $

MORRISON

See also Lakewood

This tiny town has played a big role in paleontologists' search for dinosaur bones. In the late 19th century, scientists found fossil remains of a Stegosaurus and an Apatosaurus in and around Morrison, and recent discoveries include preserved adult Stegosaurus tracks.

WHAT TO SEE
RED ROCKS PARK AND AMPHITHEATER

18300 W. Alameda Parkway, Morrison, 720-865-2494; www.redrocksonline.com

Red Rocks Amphitheater is located in the majestic 816-acre Red Rocks Park, 15 miles west of Denver. Two 300-foot sandstone monoliths serve as stadium walls for this open-air arena. During the summer months, the 8,000-seat amphitheater, with its perfect acoustical conditions, awe-inspiring beauty and panoramic view of Denver, serves as a stunning stage for performers ranging from chart-topping rock bands to world-renowned symphony orchestras.

WHERE TO EAT
★★★THE FORT

19192 Highway 8, Morrison, 303-697-4771; www.thefort.com

Sam Arnold's popular, kitschy restaurant has been serving buffalo steaks for 30 years. The menu also features other game, such as elk chops, as well as beef and seafood. The adobe re-creation of the historic Bent's Fort is reason enough to come here.

American. Dinner. Bar. Children's menu. Outdoor seating. $$$

OURAY

See also Montrose, Silverton

Ouray's location in a natural basin surrounded by the majestic 12,000 to 14,000-foot peaks of the San Juan Mountains has made it a nice spot for visitors. Ouray, named for a Ute chief, is reached by the magnificent Million

Dollar Highway section of the San Juan Skyway, which was blasted from cliff walls high above the Uncompahgre River.

WHAT TO SEE
BACHELOR-SYRACUSE MINE TOUR
1222 County Road 14, Ouray, 970-325-0220, 888-227-4585;
www.bachelorsyracusemine.com
This mine has been in continuous operation since 1884. Guided tours are aboard a mine train that advances 3,350 feet horizontally into Gold Hill (mine temperature 47°F) where you can see mining equipment, visit work areas and learn how explosives are used. Gold panning.
Late May-September, daily.

BEAR CREEK FALLS
1230 Main, Ouray, 970-325-4746; www.ouraycolorado.com
An observational point lets you take in the 227-foot falls.

BOX CANON FALLS PARK
Highway 550, Ouray, 970-325-7080; www.ouraycolorado.com/boxcanyon
Canyon Creek has cut a natural canyon 20 feet wide and 400 feet deep. Take the stairs and a suspended bridge to the floor of the canyon, where you can see the thundering falls.
Daily.

HOT SPRINGS POOL
Ouray City Park, 1220 Highway 50, Ouray, 970-325-7073; www.cityofouray.com
Outdoor, million-gallon pool fed by natural mineral hot springs (sulphur-free). Bathhouse; spa.
Daily.

SPECIAL EVENTS
ARTISTS' ALPINE HOLIDAY & FESTIVAL
1230 Main St., Ouray, 970-325-4746; www.ouraycolorado.com
Each year, artists from across the country come to Ouray to enter their work in this juried art show.
One week in mid-August.

IMOGENE PASS MOUNTAIN MARATHON
100 Fifth St., Ouray, 970-728-0251; www.imogenerun.com
The 18-mile course, which follows an old mining trail, starts at Ouray's 7,800-foot elevation, crosses over Imogene Pass (13,114 feet) and ends at Main Street, Telluride (8,800 feet).
September.

WHERE TO STAY
★COMFORT INN
191 Fifth Ave., Ouray, 970-325-7203, 800-438-5713; www.ouraycomfortinn.com
33 rooms. Restaurant, bar. Complimentary breakfast. Pool. Pets accepted. $

★★★ST. ELMO HOTEL
426 Main St., Ouray, 970-325-4951; www.stelmohotel.com
The guest rooms at this restored 1898 hotel are individually decorated in Victorian style and feature period antiques. Enjoy a wine and cheese social hour every afternoon in the parlor and a full breakfast every morning in the sun room.
9 rooms. Complimentary breakfast. Restaurant. $

WHERE TO EAT
★★BON TON RESTAURANT
St. Elmo Hotel, 426 Main St., Ouray, 970-325-4951; www.stelmohotel.com
American, Italian. Dinner. Bar. Children's menu. Outdoor seating. $$$

★BUEN TIEMPO RESTAURANT
515 Main St., Ouray, 970-325-4544; www.stelmohotel.com
Mexican. Lunch, dinner. Bar. Children's menu. Outdoor seating. $$

PAGOSA SPRINGS
See also Durango
People come here for the remarkable mineral springs. The town is surrounded by the San Juan National Forest, and deer and elk hunting are popular activities.

WHAT TO SEE
CHIMNEY ROCK ARCHAEOLOGICAL AREA
180 N. Pagosa Blvd., Pagosa Springs, 970-883-5359; www.chimneyrockco.org
This area features twin pinnacles, held sacred by the Anasazi. The Fire Tower offers a spectacular view of nearby ruins. Four guided scheduled tours daily.

FRED HARMAN ART MUSEUM
85 Harman Park Drive, Pagosa Springs, 970-731-5785; www.harmanartmuseum.com
See original paintings by Fred Harman—best known for his famous Red Ryder and Little Beaver comic strip. Rodeo, movie and Western memorabilia is found here.
Admission: adults $4, children under 6 $.50. Monday-Saturday 10:30 a.m.-5 p.m., Sunday noon-4 p.m.; Winter, Monday-Friday 10:30 a.m.-5 p.m.

ROCKY MOUNTAIN WILDLIFE PARK
4821 Highway 84, Pagosa Springs, 970-264-5546; www.alldurango.com/wildlife
This park features animals indigenous to the area along with a wildlife museum and photography displays.
Summer, daily 9 a.m.-6 p.m.; winter, daily noon-4 p.m.

TREASURE MOUNTAIN

Pagosa Springs

Begin at the Wolf Creek Pass, just east of summit marked where Continental Divide Trail winds southward and connects with the Treasure Mountain Trail. Legend states that in 1790, 300 men mined five million dollars in gold and melted it into bars but were forced to leave it behind. The gold has never been found.

WOLF CREEK PASS

Pagosa Springs, 20 miles northeast on Highways 160 and 84

Take a scenic drive across the Continental Divide. The eastern approach is through the Rio Grande National Forest, the western approach through the San Juan National Forest. The best time to drive through is September, when you'll see spectacular views of the aspens changing color. Drive takes approximately one hour.

WOLF CREEK SKI AREA

Pagosa Springs, 20 miles northeast of Highways 160 and 84, 970-264-5639;
www.wolfcreekski.com

Two triple, two double chairlifts; Poma lift; patrol, school, rentals; cafeteria, restaurant, bar, day lodge; 50 runs; longest run two miles; vertical drop 1,604 feet. Shuttle bus service.
Early November-April, daily.

WHERE TO STAY
★★HIGH COUNTRY LODGE

3821 E. Highway 160, Pagosa Springs, 800-862-3707; www.highcountrylodge.com

32 rooms. Complimentary breakfast. Restaurant. Pets accepted. $

WHERE TO EAT
★★TEQUILA'S

439 San Juan St., Pagosa Springs, 970-264-9989; www.chatosytequilas.com

Mexican. Lunch, dinner. Children's menu. Outdoor seating. $

PUEBLO

See also Canon City, Colorado Springs

Pueblo began as a crossroad for Native Americans, Spaniards and fur traders. When the Rio Grande Railroad reached here in 1872, Pueblo was the leading center for steel and coal production west of the Mississippi. Today, Pueblo is a major transportation and industrial center—more than half of all goods manufactured in Colorado are produced in Pueblo.

WHAT TO SEE
EL PUEBLO MUSEUM

301 N. Union, Pueblo, 719-583-0453; www.coloradohistory.org

Check out this full-size replica of Old Fort Pueblo, which served as a base for fur traders and other settlers from 1842-1855. Daily.

LAKE PUEBLO STATE PARK

640 Pueblo Reservoir Road, Pueblo, 719-561-9320; www.parks.state.co.us

Swimming, water-skiing, boating, hiking, camping.
Daily.

MINERAL PALACE PARK

1500 N. Santa Fe, Pueblo

In addition to a pool, this park has a rose garden and green house. The Pueblo
Art Guild Gallery, which showcases the work of local artists, is also here.
Saturday-Sunday; closed December-February.

PUEBLO WEISBROD AIRCRAFT MUSEUM

Pueblo Memorial Airport, 31001 Magnuson Ave., Pueblo, 719-948-9219;
www.pwam.org

This outdoor museum features static aircraft displays. Adjacent is the B-24
Aircraft Memorial Museum, with displays of the history of the B-24 bomber.
Monday-Saturday 10 a.m.-4 p.m., Sunday 1-4 p.m.

ROSEMOUNT VICTORIAN HOUSE MUSEUM

419 W. 14th St., Pueblo, 719-545-5290; www.rosemount.org

This 37-room mansion contains original Victorian furnishings and the Mc-
Clelland Collection of World Curiosities.
Tuesday-Sunday; closed in January.

SAN ISABEL NATIONAL FOREST

2840 Kachina Drive, Pueblo, 719-553-1400

This forest, spread over 1,109,782 acres, offers camping and two winter
sports areas, Monarch and Ski Cooper. In the southern part of the forest is the
Spanish Peaks National Natural Landmark. Collegiate Peaks, Mount Massive and Holy Cross Wilderness areas are also within the forest, as well as
four wilderness study areas. Colorado's highest peak, Mount Elbert (14,433
feet), is within the forest south of Leadville.

SANGRE DE CRISTO ARTS AND CONFERENCE CENTER

210 N. Santa Fe Ave., Pueblo, 719-295-7200; www.sdc-arts.org

The four art galleries here include the Francis King Collection of Western
Art, currently on permanent display. Children's museum, workshops, dance
studios, theater.
Monday-Saturday.

SPECIAL EVENTS
COLORADO STATE FAIR

Fairgrounds, 1001 Beulah Ave., Pueblo, 719-561-8484, 800-876-4567;
www.coloradostatefair.com

Annual event includes rodeo, grandstand and amphitheater entertainment,
agricultural and technological displays, arts and crafts and a carnival.
August-September.

WHERE TO STAY
★LA QUINTA INN & SUITES
4801 N. Elizabeth St., Pueblo, 719-542-3500; www.laquinta.com
101 rooms. Complimentary breakfast. Fitness center. Pets accepted. Pool. $

★★★MARRIOTT PUEBLO CONVENTION CENTER
110 W. First St., Pueblo, 719-542-3200, 800-228-9290; www.marriott.com
This hotel is connected to the convention center downtown and is surrounded by beautiful landscaping. Guest rooms feature modern furnishings and include microwaves and ergonomic desk chairs.
164 rooms. Restaurant, bar. Fitness center. Pets accepted. Pool. Business center. $$

WHERE TO EAT
★★★LA RENAISSANCE
217 E. Routt Ave., Pueblo, 719-543-6367; www.larenaissancerestaurant.com
This award-winning restaurant was originally built in 1886 as a Presbyterian church and still includes the pews and stained-glass windows. It's an interesting atmosphere, and the food is superb, from lobster tail to prime rib.
American. Dinner. Closed Sunday. Bar. Reservations recommended. $$

SALIDA
See also Buena Vista
Located on the eastern slope of the Rocky Mountains, Salida is surrounded by San Isabel National Forest. A pleasant climate makes it ideal for recreational activities throughout the year, including river rafting, fishing, mountain biking, hiking and hunting.

WHAT TO SEE
ANGEL OF SHAVANO

Salida
Every spring, the snow melts on the 14,239-foot slopes of Mount Shavano leaving an outline called "the Angel."

ARKANSAS HEADWATERS STATE RECREATION AREA
307 W. Sackett Ave., Salida, 719-539-7289
This outstanding waterway cuts its way through rugged canyons for 148 miles, from Leadville to Pueblo, making it one of the world's premier places for kayaking and white-water rafting. Fishing, boating, hiking, bridle trails, picnicking, camping.

MONARCH SCENIC TRAM
Chamber of Commerce, 406 W. Rainbow Blvd., Salida, 719-539-4789, 888-996-7669
This trip to an observatory at 12,000 feet offers panoramic views of the beautiful Rocky Mountains.
May-September, daily.

MONARCH SKI & SNOWBOARD AREA

1 Powder Place, Monarch, 719-539-3573, 888-996-7669; www.skimoarch.com

Four double chairlifts; patrol, school, rentals; 63 runs; longest run one mile; vertical drop 1,170 feet.

Multiday, half-day rates. Mid-November-mid-April, daily. Cross-country skiing.

MOUNTAIN SPIRIT WINERY

16150 County Road 220, Salida, 719-539-1175, 888-679-4637;
www.mountainspiritwinery.com

This family-operated boutique winery is located on five acres with apple orchard, homestead, tours and tastings.

Memorial Day-Labor Day, Monday-Saturday 10 a.m.-5 p.m.

SALIDA MUSEUM

406 Highway 50, Salida, 719-539-2068, 877-772-5432;
www.salidachamber.org/museum

Museum features a mineral display, American Indian artifacts, an early pioneer household display and mining and railroad displays.

Late May-early September, daily.

TENDERFOOT DRIVE

Salida, west on Highway 291

This spiral drive encircling Mount Tenderfoot offers view of the surrounding mountain area and the upper Arkansas Valley.

SPECIAL EVENTS

ARTWALK

Downtown Historic District, 406 W. Rainbow Blvd., Salida, 877-772-5432;
www.salidaartwalk.org

Local artists, craftspeople and entertainers display artwork to celebrate Colorado's largest historic district.

Last weekend in June.

CHRISTMAS MOUNTAIN USA

406 W. Rainbow Blvd., Salida, 719-539-2068; www.salidachamber.org

This three-day event kicks off the holiday season. More than 3,500 lights outline a 700-foot Christmas tree on Tenderfoot Mountain. Parade.

Day after Thanksgiving.

FIBARK WHITEWATER FESTIVAL

240 N. F St., Salida, 719-539-6918; www.fibark.com

International experts compete in a 26-mile kayak race. Other events include slalom, raft, foot and bicycle races.

Father's Day weekend.

NEW OLD-FASHIONED CHAFFEE COUNTY FAIR

10165 County Road 120, Poncha Springs, 719-539-6151; www.chaffeecounty.org

This annual event features a rodeo, live entertainment, arts and crafts, food, a

★★★★★ COLORADO

175

beer garden, livestock auctions, tractor-pull contests and much more. Late July-early August.

WHERE TO EAT
★WINDMILL
720 E. Rainbow Blvd., Salida, 719-539-3594
American. Lunch, dinner. Bar. Children's menu. $

SILVERTON
See also Durango, Ouray
Situated in the San Juan Mountains, Silverton is nicknamed "the mining town that never quits." The last mine in Silverton closed in 1991. Since then, tourists have discovered the natural beauty, historic ghost towns and many recreational opportunities of the area.

WHAT TO SEE
CIRCLE JEEP TOUR
414 Greene St., Silverton, 970-387-5654, 800-752-4494; www.silvertoncolorado.com
Take in the history of the area, including information on mines and ghost towns, on a jeep tour.

OLD HUNDRED GOLD MINE TOUR
721 County Road 4 A, Silverton, 970-387-5444, 800-872-3009; www.minetour.com
Learn all about the methods of hard rock mining. This guided one-hour tour of an underground mine offers views of the equipment and crystal pockets. Memorial Day-September, daily.

RED MOUNTAIN PASS
Silverton, Highway 550 between Ouray and Silverton
Stretching through the towering San Juan Mountains, the 23-mile stretch of Highway 550 between Ouray and Silverton passes through some of Colorado's wildest country. The road rises to 11,075 feet to cross the Red Mountain Pass, a favorite spot for hikers, rock climbers, mountain bikers and backcountry ski enthusiasts. Along the way you'll see numerous gorges and falls, as well as abandoned log cabins and mining equipment.

SAN JUAN COUNTY HISTORICAL SOCIETY MUSEUM
1315 Snowden, Silverton
Located in an old three-story jail, this museum showcases mining and railroad artifacts from Silverton's early days.
Memorial Day-mid-October, daily.

SPECIAL EVENTS
GREAT WESTERN ROCKY MOUNTAIN BRASS BAND CONCERTS
Silverton, 800-752-4494; www.silvertoncolorado.com
Nationally recognized musicians—and Silverton's own brass band—perform concerts throughout the weekend.
Mid-August.

WHERE TO STAY
★★THE WYMAN HOTEL & INN
1371 Greene St., Silverton, 970-387-5372, 800-609-7845; www.thewyman.com
17 rooms. Closed late March-early May, mid-October-mid-December. Complimentary breakfast. Restaurant. Pets accepted. $

SNOWMASS VILLAGE
See also Aspen, Glenwood Springs
Snowmass Village, only eight miles from Aspen, is best known as the location of Snowmass Ski Area, a popular winter resort. (The village is located at the base of the ski area.) There's also much to do in summer, including swimming (there are 50 outdoor heated pools and hot tubs), rafting, hiking, horseback riding, golf, tennis, hot air balloon rides and free outdoor concerts. The village includes more than 20 restaurants. A free shuttle bus runs throughout the village.

WHAT TO SEE
ASPEN SNOWMASS SKIING COMPANY
40 Carriage Way, Snowmass Village, 970-923-1220; www.aspensnowmass.com
Seven quad, two triple, six double chairlifts; two platter pulls; patrol, school, rentals, snowmaking; restaurants, bar, nursery. 91 runs; longest run five miles, vertical drop 4,406 feet. Cross-country skiing (50 miles). Shuttle bus service from Aspen.
Late November-mid-April, daily.

BICYCLE TRIPS AND JEEP TRIPS
48 Snowmass Village Mall, Snowmass Village, 970-923-4544, 800-282-7238;
www.blazingadventures.com
These trip travel throughout the Snowmass/Aspen area. Transportation and equipment is provided.
June-September.

WHERE TO STAY
★★★SILVERTREE HOTEL SNOWMASS VILLAGE
100 Elbert Lane, Snowmass Village, 970-923-3520, 800-837-4255;
www.silvertreehotel.com
This year-round mountain resort offers ski in/ski out access, two heated pools and a fitness center with a steam room and massage services as well as family-style suites.
260 rooms. Restaurant. Fitness center. Pets accepted. Business center. Pool. $$$

★★★SNOWMASS CLUB
0239 Snowmass Club Circle, Snowmass Village, 970-923-5600, 800-525-0710;
www.snowmassclub.com
This year-round resort is located in the Elk Mountain range area and offers one-, two- and three-bedroom villas with daily maid service. All of the villas have full kitchens and high-speed Internet access, and most feature a fireplace, deck with barbecue grill and laundry. The 19,000-square-foot health club includes four pools, spa services and dozens of fitness classes. Sage

Restaurant and Black Saddle Bar & Grille serve everything from barbecue to New York-style cuisine.

55 rooms. Restaurant. Spa. Golf. Tennis. Business center. $$$$

★★THE STONEBRIDGE INN

300 Carriage Way, Snowmass Village, 970-923-2420, 800-213-3214; www.stonebridgeinn.com

92 rooms. Closed mid-April-May. Complimentary breakfast. Restaurant. Fitness center. Pool. $$

★★WILDWOOD LODGE

100 Elbert Lane, Snowmass Village, 970-923-3520, 800-837-4255; www.silvertreehotel.com

140 rooms. Closed early April-May. Complimentary breakfast. Restaurant. Pets accepted. Fitness center. Pool. $$

WHERE TO EAT

★★★KRABLOONIK

4250 Divide Road, Snowmass Village, 970-923-3953; www.krabloonik.com

Celebrate the dog days of winter at this log restaurant with ski-in access and large picture windows framing the mountain views. More than 200 sled dogs live in the kennel next door—take a sled ride after a lunch of wild mushroom soup, fresh baked bread and smoked meat from the onsite smokehouse. (No lunch during summer.) At night, the sunken fire pit keeps everyone warm and toasty.

American, seafood. Lunch, dinner. Closed mid-April-mid-June, October-Thanksgiving. Children's menu. Reservations recommended. $$$

★★★SAGE

Snowmass Club, 239 Snowmass Circle, Snowmass Village, 970-923-0923; www.snowmassclub.com

Located in the Snowmass Club, this restaurant offers simple classics with fresh ingredients. In the summer, the patio is a lovely spot for lunch, thanks to unobstructed views of Mount Daly.

American. Breakfast, lunch, dinner. Bar. Children's menu. Outdoor seating. $$$

STEAMBOAT SPRINGS

See also Craig

In 1913, Norwegian Carl Howelsen introduced ski jumping here. Since then, 10 national ski-jumping records have been set on Steamboat Springs' Howelsen Hill. The area has produced 47 winter Olympians. Summer activities include camping, fishing, hot air ballooning, horseback riding, hiking, bicycling, river rafting, canoeing and llama trekking. One of the largest elk herds in North America ranges near the town. There are more than 100 natural hot springs in the area.

WHAT TO SEE
HOWELSEN HILL SKI COMPLEX
245 Howelsen Parkway, Steamboat Springs, 970-879-8499
International ski jump complex includes a double chairlift, Poma lift, rope tow, five ski-jumping hills; patrol; ice skating, snowboarding. December-March, daily.

STEAMBOAT
2305 Mount Werner Circle, Steamboat Springs, 970-879-6111, 800-922-2722;
www.steamboat.com
High-speed gondola; four high-speed quad (two covered), quad, six triple, seven double chairlifts; two surface tows; patrol, school, rentals, snowmaking; cafeterias, restaurants, bars, nursery; 142 runs; longest run more than three miles; vertical drop 3,668 feet. Snowboarding. Cross-country skiing (14 miles). Multiday, half-day rates.
Late November-early April, daily. Gondola: Mid-June-mid-September (also).

STEAMBOAT LAKE STATE PARK
61105 Routt County Road 129, Steamboat Springs, 970-879-3922;
www.parks.state.co.uss
Swimming, water-skiing, fishing, boating, picnicking, camping.
Daily.

STRAWBERRY PARK NATURAL HOT SPRINGS
44200 County Road 36, Steamboat Springs, 970-879-0342;
www.strawberryhotsprings.com
Mineral springs feed four pools (water cooled from 160 F to 105 F). Changing area, picnicking, camping, cabins.
Sunday-Thursday 10 a.m.-10.30 p.m., Friday-Saturday 10 a.m.-midnight.

STEAMBOAT SPRINGS HEALTH & RECREATION ASSOCIATION
136 Lincoln Ave., Steamboat Springs, 970-879-1828; www.sshra.org
Three hot pools fed by 103-degree mineral water. Lap pool, saunas, exercise classes, massage, weight room, tennis courts (summer). Daily.

TREAD OF PIONEERS MUSEUM
800 Oak St., Steamboat Springs, 970-879-2214; www.treadofpioneers.org
Check out the permanent ski exhibit tracing the evolution of skiing and a Victorian house with period furnishings and cattle-ranching artifacts.
Admission: adults $5, seniors $4 children. Tuesday-Saturday 11 a.m.-5 p.m.

SPECIAL EVENTS
COWBOY ROUNDUP DAYS
Steamboat Springs
Rodeos, parade, entertainment.
July Fourth weekend.

ROCKY MOUNTAIN MUSTANG ROUND-UP

1255 S. Lincoln Ave., Steamboat Springs, 970-879-0880; www.steamboatchamber.com
Car fanatics will enjoy this parade of more than 350 Ford Mustangs. Timed
driving event.
Mid-June.

WHERE TO STAY
★FAIRFIELD INN & SUITES STEAMBOAT SPRINGS
3200 S. Lincoln Ave., Steamboat Springs, 970-870-9000, 800-325-3535;
www.fairfieldinn.com
66 rooms. Pets accepted. Complimentary breakfast. Business center. $

★HAMPTON INN & SUITES STEAMBOAT SPRINGS
725 S. Lincoln Ave., Steamboat Springs, 970-871-8900; www.hamptoninn.com
68 rooms. Business center. Fitness center. Pool. $

★★PTARMIGAN INN
2304 Après Ski Way, Steamboat Springs, 970-879-1730, 800-538-7519;
www.steamboat-lodging.com
77 rooms. Closed late mid-April-late May. Restaurant, bar. Pets accepted. Pool. $

★★★SHERATON STEAMBOAT RESORT
2200 Village Inn Court, Steamboat Springs, 970-879-2220, 800-325-3535;
www.starwoodhotels.com
This hotel is a great choice for families and business travelers—it's the only
conference hotel in the area with ski in/ski out access. After a day on the
slopes, enjoy the rooftop hot tubs or get a massage at the spa. The elegant and
comfortable rooms include Sweet Sleeper beds. Ask for a slope view room.
The resort has boutiques and an art gallery.
239 rooms. Closed mid-April-May, fall season. Restaurant, bar. Business
center. Fitness center. Spa. Golf. Pool. $$

★★★THE STEAMBOAT GRAND RESORT HOTEL
2300 Mount Werner Circle, Steamboat Springs, 970-871-5500, 877-366-2628;
www.steamboatgrand.com
The accommodations here range from studios to private residences with Al-
der cabinets and granite countertops. The spa offers a wide variety of treat-
ments, from hot stone massage to herbal hibernation body wraps. The fitness
center has lots of equipment but, more important, a eucalyptus steam room,
perfect after a day on the slopes. The Cabin restaurant has an extensive wine
list and serves Midwestern beef aged at least 30 days in controlled cellars and
native Colorado game.
327 rooms. Restaurant, bar. Fitness center. Pool. Spa. $$$

WHERE TO EAT
★★ANTARES
57 1/2 Eighth St., Steamboat Springs, 970-879-9939

American. Dinner. Closed mid-April-early June. Bar. Children's menu. $$$

★★★HARWIGS-L'APOGEE
911 Lincoln Ave., Steamboat Springs, 970-879-1919; www.lapogee.com
Housed in a former saddlery store, L'Apogee has become local favorite. The interesting American menu features favorites like black Angus filet and lamb chops, as well as less traditional dishes such as venison. The large wine cellar is filled with many reasonably priced choices from around the world.
American, Thai. Dinner. Bar. Children's menu. Outdoor seating. $$$

★★ORE HOUSE AT THE PINE GROVE
1465 Pine Grove Road, Steamboat Springs, 970-879-1190, 800-280-8310;
www.orehouseatthepinegrove.com
American. Dinner. Closed mid-April-mid-May. Bar. Children's menu. Outdoor seating. $$$

★TUGBOAT GRILL & PUB
1860 Mt Werner Road, Steamboat Springs, 970-879-7070
America. Lunch, dinner. Closed mid-April-early June. Bar. Children's menu. Outdoor seating. $

★WINONA'S DELI-BAKERY
617 Lincoln Ave., Steamboat Springs, 970-879-2483
American. Breakfast, lunch. Children's menu. Outdoor seating. $

STERLING
See also Fort Collins
Sterling is known as the "City of Living Trees" because of the unique carved trees found throughout town.

WHAT TO SEE
OVERLAND TRAIL MUSEUM
210533 CR 26.5, Sterling, 970-522-3895
This village of seven buildings includes collections of American Indian artifacts, cattle brands, farm machinery, archaeological and paleontological exhibits, a one-room schoolhouse, a fire engine and more.
April-October, daily; rest of year, Tuesday-Saturday.

WHERE TO STAY
★BEST WESTERN SUNDOWNER
125 Overland Trail St., Sterling, 970-522-6265; www.bestwestern.com
58 rooms. Complimentary breakfast. Pets accepted. Spa. Fitness center. Pool. $

★★RAMADA STERLING
22140 E. Highway 6, Sterling, 970-522-2625, 800-272-6232; www.ramada.com
100 rooms. Restaurant, bar. Pool. Fitness center. Pets accepted. $

WHERE TO EAT
★T. J. BUMMER'S
203 Broadway St., Sterling, 970-522-8397
American. Breakfast, lunch, dinner. Children's menu. $$

TELLURIDE
See also Ouray, Silverton
Gray granite and red sandstone mountains surround this mining town, named for the tellurium ore containing precious metals found in the area. Telluride, proud of its bonanza past, has not changed its façade. Because of its remoteness and small size, Telluride is a favorite getaway spot for celebrities. Summer activities include fly-fishing, mountain biking, river rafting, hiking, Jeep trips, horseback riding and camping, as well as many annual events and festivals from May to October.

WHAT TO SEE
BEAR CREEK TRAIL
South end of Pine Street, Telluride
This two-mile canyon walk features a view of a tiered waterfall.
May-October.

BRIDAL VEIL FALLS
Telluride, 2½ miles east on Highway 145
These falls are the the highest in Colorado.

TELLURIDE GONDOLA
Aspen and San Juan, Telluride
Passengers are transported from downtown Telluride to Mount Village.
Early June-early October and late November-mid-April, daily.

TELLURIDE HISTORICAL MUSEUM
201 W. Gregory Ave., Telluride, 970-728-3344; www.telluridemuseum.org
Built in 1893 as the community hospital, this historic building houses artifacts, historic photos and exhibits that show what Telluride was like in its Wild West days.
Tuesday-Saturday 11 a.m.-5 p.m., Sunday 1-5 p.m.

TELLURIDE SKI RESORT
565 Mountain Village Blvd., Telluride, 800-778-8581; www.tellurideskiresort.com
Three-stage gondola; seven quad, two triple, two double chairlifts; two surface lift; patrol, school, rentals; restaurants, nursery. 92 runs; longest run 4½ miles; vertical drop 3,530 feet. Thanksgiving-early April, daily.

SPECIAL EVENTS
BALLOON FESTIVAL
Colorado Avenue, Telluride, 970-728-4769; www.tellurideballoonfestival.com
See the balloons launch in the morning, or come in the evening to see them lined up on Colorado Avenue.
Early June.

JAZZ CELEBRATION

Town Park, Telluride, 970-728-7009; www.telluridejazz.com

After the daytime concerts with the San Juan Mountains as a backdrop, several of the musicians can be found in the Main Street saloons mingling with visitors and fans.

Early August.

MOUNTAIN FILM FESTIVAL

109 E. Colorado Ave., Telluride, 970-728-4123; www.mountainfilm.org

In addition to showing films, the Mountain Film Festival is a unique conglomeration of filmmakers, authors, political activists and other thinkers who host seminars and symposiums throughout the weekend. These highbrow hosts discuss the films with the public and discuss how they relate to the festival's theme.

Late May.

TELLURIDE BLUEGRASS FESTIVAL

Telluride; www.bluegrass.com/telluride

Thousands of music lovers come to Telluride for what many agree is the nation's premier bluegrass festival. The festival draws top bluegrass and folk performers. But the best part might be the spontaneous jams that break out in the wee hours at local drinking spots. The festival includes amateur competitions and workshops and is a favorite destination for campers seeking high-spirited fun in a natural setting.

Mid-June.

WHERE TO STAY

★★★HOTEL COLUMBIA, TELLURIDE

300 W. San Juan Ave., Telluride, 970-728-0660, 800-201-9505;
www.columbiatelluride.com

Situated on the San Miguel River at the base of the Telluride Ski Resort, this hotel feels more like a small inn, with only 21 Victorian-style rooms, each with a gas fireplace. (Columbia was Telluride's original name.) Spring for the penthouse—it has a steam shower and two-person jetted tub surrounded by windows overlooking the mountains and river.

21 rooms. Restaurant, bar. Fitness room. Pets accepted. Spa. $$

★★★THE PEAKS RESORT & GOLDEN DOOR SPA

136 Country Club Drive, Telluride, 866-282-4557, 800-789-2220;
www.thepeaksresort.com

This is the perfect home for outdoor enthusiasts who like to rough it a bit outdoors—and live it up indoors. Situated on top of the mountain, Peaks Resort is a skier's heaven with ski in/ski out access and a ski valet who will warm and tune your equipment. The guest rooms and suites are cocoons of luxury, with huge picture windows with plantation shutters, fluffy duvets and glass-enclosed showers with separate tubs. Suites boast leather furniture and stone fireplaces. The centerpiece of this first-class resort is the Golden Door Spa, an outpost of the legendary California destination spa featuring a variety of restorative treatments. If you're here in summer, challenge yourself on one of the country's highest golf courses.

175 rooms. Closed mid-April-mid-May, mid-October-mid-November. Restaurant, bar. Spa. Ski in/ski out. Fitness center. Pool. Pets accepted. Tennis. $$$

★★★NEW SHERIDAN HOTEL

231 W. Colorado Ave., Telluride, 970-728-4351, 800-200-1891; www.newsheridan.com

Built in 1891, this hotel is located in the heart of Telluride. Many of the elegant guest rooms feature mountain views and separate sitting rooms. Warm up with a hearty gourmet breakfast and then relax in the afternoon with a complimentary glass of Pine Ridge wine at the New Sheridan Bar.

26 rooms. Closed mid-April-mid-May. Complimentary breakfast. Restaurant. $$

WHERE TO EAT

★★★ALLRED'S

2 Coonskin Ridge, Telluride, 970-728-7474; www.allredsrestaurant.com

At more than 10,000 feet above sea level, Allred's offers mountain views to complement its delicious culinary creations. The menu is made up of regional Colorado cuisine with international accents such as free-range chicken breast with creamy polenta, Manchego, spinach and roasted peppers and elk short loin with summer squash and braised figs. If you're looking for a special treat, reserve the Chef's Table (for four to six guests), where you'll be treated to a five-course, chef-prepared menu with the option to pair wines with each course.

American. Dinner. Closed mid-April-mid-June, late September-mid-December. Bar. Children's menu. Reservations recommended. $$$

★★★COSMOPOLITAN

Hotel Columbia, 300 W. San Juan, Telluride, 970-728-1292; www.cosmotelluride.com

Housed in the luxurious Hotel Columbia, Cosmopolitan is an elegant restaurant where fresh ingredients and flavors from around the world are blended together to create an innovative contemporary American menu. Dishes, which change on a weekly basis, have included creations such as crab-stuffed roasted chicken breast with risotto, mushrooms, Gruyere cheese, asparagus, truffle oil and chicken jus and barbequed wild king salmon with fried sweet potatoes, sweet corn broth and bacon braised Swiss chard.

French, American. Dinner. Closed mid-April-mid-May and the last week in October. Bar. Children's menu. Reservations recommended. $$

★★FLORADORA

103 W. Colorado Ave., Telluride, 970-728-8884

Southwestern, American. Lunch, dinner. Bar. Children's menu. $$

VAIL

See also Beaver Creek, Dillon

Built to resemble a Bavarian village, Vail is the world's largest single-mountain ski resort. Known for having vast and varied terrain for every skill level of skier or snowboarder, Vail often tops ski resort lists and gets rave reviews for its legendary powder. Summer has also emerged as a prime recreation season on Vail Mountain, with mountain biking being the sport of choice. Today, ski conglomerate Vail Resorts owns numerous ski resorts in Colorado, including Beaver Creek, Breckenridge and Arapahoe Basin, and many passes work at all the properties.

WHAT TO SEE
COLORADO SKI MUSEUM & SKI HALL OF FAME
In Vail Village Transportation Center, 231 S. Frontage Road E., Vail, 970-476-1876; www.skimuseum.net

Learn everything you ever wanted to know about skiing. The museum traces the history of skiing in Colorado back more than 120 years.

Memorial Day-late September and late November-mid April, Tuesday-Sunday.

GERALD R. FORD AMPHITHEATER VILAR PAVILION/BETTY FORD ALPINE GARDENS
Ford Park and the Betty Ford Alpine Gardens, Vail, 970-845-8497, 888-920-2797; www.vvf.org

Enjoy top-notch entertainment under Vail's crystal-clear starlit skies at this open-air theater surrounded by the Betty Ford Alpine Gardens—a public botanical garden with more than 500 varieties of wildflowers and alpine plants. Performances throughout the summer normally include classical music, rock and roll, jazz, ballet, contemporary dance and children's theater. June-August.

VAIL SKI RESORT
137 Benchmark Road, Avon, 970-476-9090, 800-503-8748; www.vail.com

Gondola; 14 high-speed quad, seven fixed-grip quad, three triple, five double chairlifts; ten surface lifts; patrol, school, rentals, snowmaking; cafeterias, restaurants, bars, nursery. Longest run four miles; vertical drop 3,450 feet. Late November-mid-April, daily. Cross-country trails, rentals November-April; ice skating, snowmobiling, sleigh rides. Gondola and Vista Bahn June-August, daily; May and September, weekends.

SPECIAL EVENTS
TASTE OF VAIL
Vail, 970-926-5665; www.tasteofvail.com

This unique food festival combines tastings, competitions and cooking seminars. Sample premium desserts, or watch the annual bartender mix-off. Listen to winemakers talk about their craft—and then taste the fruits of their labor. Past demonstrations have explained how to pair wine with Japanese cuisine. Early April.

WHERE TO STAY
★★HOTEL GASTHOF GRAMSHAMMER
231 E. Gore Creek Drive, Vail, 970-476-5626, 800-610-7374; www.pepis.com

34 rooms. Closed mid April-June. Complimentary breakfast. Restaurant, bar. Fitness center. Spa. $

★★LION SQUARE LODGE

660 W. Lionshead Place, Vail, 970-476-2281, 800-525-1943; www.lionsquare.com

108 rooms. Restaurant. Pool. $$

★★★THE LODGE AT VAIL

174 E. Gore Creek Drive, Vail, 970-476-5011, 877-528-7625; www.rockresorts.com

This lodge perfectly marries the charm of an alpine inn with the amenities of a world-class resort. The individually decorated rooms are the ideal blend between Western style and European elegance. Located at the base of Vail Mountain, the lift—as well as boutiques and shops of Vail Village—are just steps away. Mickey's Piano Bar is a great spot for a drink.

165 rooms. Restaurant, bar. Ski in/ski out. Pool. $$$

★★★MARRIOTT VAIL MOUNTAIN RESORT

715 W. Lionshead Circle, Vail, 970-476-4444, 800-648-0720; www.marriott.com

This newly renovated hotel is in a great location at the base of Vail Mountain near the lift and many boutiques and restaurants. The rustic guest rooms contain wood furnishings and marble and granite baths. Privately owned condos are also available. The new Golden Leaf Spa offers body wraps and massages. The full-service retail shop has rental equipment.

344 rooms. Restaurant, bar. Pool. Spa. Fitness center. $$

★★THE SITZMARK LODGE

183 Gore Creek Drive, Vail, 970-476-5001, 888-476-5001; www.sitzmarklodge.com

35 rooms. Complimentary breakfast. Restaurant, bar. Ski in/ski out. Pool. $

★★★SONNENALP RESORT OF VAIL

20 Vail Road, Vail, 970-476-5656, 800-654-8312; www.sonnenalp.com

This charming family-owned and -operated resort recalls the Bavarian countryside. Located in Vail Village within walking distance of the ski lift, it's a natural choice for winter sports lovers while the 18-hole championship golf course and European style makes it a treasure any time of the year. A variety of dishes—from contemporary American to ski favorites such as fondue at the Swiss Chalet—promise to keep your stomach happy. The King's Club fireside lounge is perfect for live entertainment and après ski, serving everything from burgers to caviar.

127 rooms. Restaurant, bar. Spa. $$$

★★★VAIL CASCADE RESORT & SPA

1300 Westhaven Drive, Vail, 970-476-7111, 800-282-4183; www.vailcascade.com

Located on Gore Creek at the base of Vail Mountain, this European-style alpine village contains a combination of standard guest rooms, condominiums and private residences. This huge property boasts the largest athletic facility in the Vail Valley, a shopping arcade, two movie theaters, a beauty shop, two outdoor pools and five whirlpools. Camp Cascade keeps kids entertained throughout the day.

292 rooms. Restaurant, bar. Spa. Pool. Ski in/ski out. Fitness center. $$

★★VAIL MOUNTAIN LODGE & SPA
352 E. Meadow Drive, Vail, 970-476-0700, 866-476-0700; www.vailmountainlodge.com
28 rooms. Complimentary breakfast. Restaurant, bar. Fitness center. Spa. $$

★★VAIL'S MOUNTAIN HAUS
292 E. Meadow Drive, Vail, 970-476-2434, 800-237-0922; www.mountainhaus.com
75 rooms. Complimentary breakfast. Restaurant, bar. Spa. Pool. Fitness center. $$$

WHERE TO EAT
★BLU'S
193 E. Gore Creek Drive, Vail, 970-476-3113; www.blusrestaurant.com
American. Breakfast, lunch, dinner. Bar. Children's menu. Outdoor seating. $$

★★THE GOLDEN EAGLE INN
118 Beaver Creek Place, Vail, 970-949-1940; www.thegoldeneagleinn.com
American. Dinner. Bar. Children's menu. Outdoor seating. $$

★★LANCELOT RESTAURANT
201 E. Gore Creek Drive, Vail, 970-476-5828; www.lancelotinn.com
Seafood, steak. Lunch, dinner. Bar. Reservations recommended. Outdoor seating. $$$

★★★LEFT BANK
183 Gore Creek Drive, Vail, 970-476-3696; www.leftbankvail.com
As the name suggests, this restaurant serves classic French cuisine in a friendly, casual atmosphere in the heart of the Village. The restaurant serves all the classics from escargot to steak au poivre. Start off with a Kir Royale. French, Mediterranean. Dinner. Closed Sunday. Bar. Reservations recommended. $$$

★★MONTAUK SEAFOOD GRILL
549 W. Lionshead Circle, Vail, 970-476-2601; www.montaukseafoodgrill.com
Seafood. Dinner. Reservations recommended. $$$

★★★RESTAURANT KELLY LIKEN
12 Vail Road, Vail, 970-479-0175; www.kellyliken.com
The warm burgundy and champagne colors, custom-made furniture, slate and glass tile floors and hand-blown glass chandelier create an elegant and romantic atmosphere. Chef Kelly Liken uses mostly locally produced and cultivated products for the seasonal American menu, including elk carpaccio, potato-crusted trout and Colorado lamb.
American. Dinner. Bar. Children's menu. Reservations recommended. $$$

★★★SWEET BASIL
193 E. Gore Creek Drive, Vail, 970-476-0125; www.sweetbasil-vail.com
This contemporary American restaurant has been a local favorite since it opened in 1977. Understated modern décor with cherry wood accents and colorful artwork provides a comfortable setting in which to enjoy the inventive menu. The culinary adventure begins with starters like Dungeness crab

salad and Spanish almond gazpacho with olive oil sorbet, flashed grapes and aged sherry vinegar. Entrées might include sea scallops with wild arugula, Spanish chorizo, warm artichoke salad, sunchoke puree and romesco sauce; or dry-aged Heritage pork chops with grilled Colorado peaches, fried green tomatoes, frisee and whiskey bacon jus. An award-winning wine list complements the full menu, and desserts can provide the perfect ending.

Contemporary American. Lunch, dinner, Saturday-Sunday brunch. Bar. Reservations recommended. Outdoor seating. $$$$

★★★THE WILDFLOWER

The Lodge at Vail, 174 Gore Creek Drive, Vail, 877-528-7625; www.lodgeatvail.rockresorts.com

If you're searching for a memorable dining experience, head to the Wildflower, a beautiful restaurant located inside the Lodge at Vail. Filled with baskets of wildflowers and massive floral arrangements, the room boasts wonderful views and tables lined with country-style floral linens. The restaurant features a delicious and innovative selection of seafood, game and poultry (such as ostrich), accented with global flavors like lemongrass, curry and chilies, and local fruits and vegetables, including herbs grown in the Wildflower's garden. An extensive and reasonably priced wine list concentrates on Italy and matches the distinctive menu.

American. Lunch, dinner. Closed Monday. Bar. Reservations recommended. Outdoor seating. $$$$

WINTER PARK

See also Granby

Winter Park is located in the Arapaho National Forest on the western slope of Berthoud Pass, one of the nation's highest and oldest ski areas. It is an easy 90-minute drive from Denver, or a two-hour ride on the popular weekend Ski Train. In addition to its many winter activities, Winter Park is gaining a reputation as a year-round recreational area with dozens of activities available during the spring, summer and fall. Winter Park, Granby and Hot Sulphur Springs are part of the Sulphur Ranger District of the Arapho and Roosevelt National forests.

WHAT TO SEE

DEVIL'S THUMB RANCH

3530 County Road 83, Tabernash, 800-933-4339; www.devilsthumbranch.com

Set on 3,700 acres at the foot of the Continental Divide, Devil's Thumb Ranch is a year-round resort with an abundance of activities in every season. In summer, visitors enjoy fly-fishing, horseback riding, river rafting, hiking, bird/nature walks and inflatable kayaking. Winter brings opportunities for cross-country skiing, sleigh rides, winter horseback riding, ice skating and snowshoeing.

DOG SLED RIDES

505 Zerex, Fraser, 970-726-8326; www.dogsledrides.com/winterpark

Thirty-minute, one-hour and two-hour rides on a sled pulled by eight Siberian and Alaskan huskies. Guides give talks on wildlife, trees and mountains.

FRASER RIVER TRAIL

Winter Park, one mile southeast off Highway 40, 970-726-4118; www.allwinterpark.com

This wide, flat, five-mile trail runs between the Winter Park Resort and the towns of Winter Park and Fraser, and is a haven for walkers, bikers and in-line skaters who want to enjoy the scenery without worrying about crosswalks or traffic lights. The route between Winter Park and Fraser has picnic tables.

POLE CREEK GOLF CLUB

6827 County Road 51, Tabernash, 970-887-9195, 800-511-5076; www.polecreekgolf.com

The Rocky Mountain News ranked this 27-hole course the best mountain golf course. It is also the only nationally ranked course open to the public.

WINTER PARK RESORT

85 Parsenn Road, Winter Park, 970-726-5514, 800-979-0332; www.skiwinterpark.com

In winter, skiers make full use of the resort's eight high-speed quad, five triple and seven double chairlifts and 143 runs—longest is five miles, vertical drop 2,610 feet. Patrol, school, equipment rentals and snowmaking; cafeterias, restaurants and bars. NASTAR and coin-operated racecourses. Mid-November–mid-April, daily. In summer, the Zephyr Express chairlift takes mountain bikers and their bikes to the top of a summit where they can access the resort's 50-mile network of interconnected trails. Colorado's longest Alpine Slide takes riders on heavy-duty plastic sleds equipped with hand-held brakes 3,030 feet down the side of a mountain. An outdoor climbing wall, bungee jumping, disc golf (18 holes that wrap around the top of Winter Park Mountain) and miniature golf are also available.

WHERE TO STAY
★★GASTHAUS EICHLER HOTEL

78786 Highway 40, Winter Park, 970-726-5133, 800-543-3899; www.gasthauseichler.com

15 rooms. Restaurant, bar. $$

WHERE TO EAT
★★★THE LODGE AT SUNSPOT

239 Winter Park Drive, Winter Park, 970-726-1564; www.skiwinterpark.com

This dining room at the Winter Park Ski Resort can be reached only by chairlift—and it's worth the trip. The restaurant has the feel of a mountain lodge, built with logs from Grand County. The windows are eight feet high, so you have magnificent views of the Continental Divide. It is a glorious setting to enjoy the satisfying American menu.

American. Lunch, dinner. Bar. Children's menu. Reservations recommended. $$$

NEVADA

THERE'S MORE TO NEVADA THAN LAS VEGAS AND GAMBLING. NEVADA ALSO HAS A RICH history, magnificent scenery and some of the wildest desert country on the continent. You'll find large mountain peaks and beautiful lakes, including Lake Tahoe. Ghost towns hint at earlier days filled with fabulous gold and silver streaks that made men millionaires overnight.

Nevada became part of U.S. territory after the Mexican-American War in 1846. It became a state in 1864 (for a while, it was part of Utah). Gold was found along the Carson River in Dayton Valley in May of 1850. A decade later, the impressive Comstock Lode (silver and gold ore) was discovered. The gold rush was on, and Virginia City mushroomed into a town of 20,000.

Unregulated gambling (called "gaming" here) was common in these early mining towns but was outlawed in 1909. It was legalized in 1931, when construction on the Hoover Dam began and there was a population boom. This was also the same year residency requirements for obtaining a divorce were relaxed. Soon, Las Vegas transformed from a sleepy desert town to become the world's top gaming and entertainment destination. And Las Vegas keeps reinventing itself. These days, it's perhaps known for being home to some of the best dining in the country as much as it is for gambling. You'll also find some of the best shopping and spas.

Outside of Las Vegas and Reno, development can be sparse. The government owns much of the land in Nevada, and the area about one hour northwest of Las Vegas has been the site of much nuclear testing.
www.travelnevada.com

BOULDER CITY
See also Henderson, Las Vegas

A mere 20 miles from Las Vegas, Boulder City is also a world away from the bright lights of Sin City. This quiet town is a haven for visitors seeking thrills outside the casinos. Its proximity to Lake Mead National Recreation Area makes it a perfect spot to rest after a day of fishing, swimming, hiking and sightseeing in one of the Southwest's most beautiful playgrounds.

WHAT TO SEE
HOOVER DAM
Highway 93, Boulder City, 702-494-2517, 866-730-9097; www.usbr.gov/lc/hooverdam/

It took 6.6 million tons of concrete—enough to pave a highway between New York and San Francisco—to stop the mighty Colorado River at Hoover Dam, which was completed in 1935 and is now a National Historic Landmark. Check out the visitor center where you can watch a short film that tells the story of the dam's construction in Black Canyon. An elevator plunges 500 feet down the canyon wall, depositing passengers in a tunnel that leads to the power plant and its eight enormous generators. The observation deck takes in both sides of the dam, including Lake Mead and the Colorado River. Parking. Daily 9 a.m.-6 p.m.

LAKE MEAD CRUISES

Lake Mead Marina, 480 Lakeshore Road, Boulder City, 702-293-6180;
www.lakemeadcruises.com

Paddle wheelers take you on a 90-minute sightseeing cruise to the Hoover Dam. Breakfast and dinner cruises available. Daily.

LAKE MEAD NATIONAL RECREATION AREA

601 Nevada Highway, Boulder City, 702-293-8906; www.nps.gov/lame

Lake Mead was formed when Hoover Dam was completed in 1935. Located 30 miles from the Strip, visitors come here for boating and fishing. You can catch trout, bass and bluegill. Several marinas around the lake and on neighboring Lake Mojave offer rentals, everything from kayaks to houseboats that sleep up to 14 people (because of the great demand for the latter, call six months prior to your visit). Hikers can take in the desert basins, steep canyons, rainbow-hued rocks and wildlife including bighorn sheep in the recreation area surrounding the lake.

Open 24 hours; visitors center 8:30 a.m.-4:30 p.m.

CARSON CITY

See also Reno

The state capital is situated near the edge of the forested eastern slope of the Sierra Nevada in Eagle Valley. The town was named for the nearby Carson River, which in turn was named for pioneer Christopher "Kit" Carson.

WHAT TO SEE
BOWERS MANSION

4005 Highway, 775-849-0201

The Bowers, Nevada's first millionaires, built this $200,000 granite house with the profits from a gold and silver mine. Half-hour guided tours of 16 rooms with many original furnishings.

Memorial Day-Labor Day, daily 11 a.m.-4:30 p.m.

CHILDREN'S MUSEUM OF NORTHERN NEVADA

813 N. Carson St., Carson City, 775-884-2226; www.cmnn.org

This excellent kids' museum provides 8,000 square feet of education and playground-style fun. A grocery store, arts and crafts station, and a walk-in kaleidoscope are among the permanent exhibits.

Daily 10 a.m.-4:30 p.m.

NEVADA STATE MUSEUM

600 N. Carson St., Carson City, 775-687-4810; www.nevadaculture.org

The former site of the U.S. Mint contains varied exhibits showcasing Nevada's natural history and anthropology, including life-size displays of a Nevada ghost town and an American Indian camp. A 300-foot mine tunnel with displays runs beneath the building.

Daily 8:30 a.m.-4:30 p.m.

NEVADA STATE RAILROAD MUSEUM

2180 S. Carson St., Carson City, 775-687-6953; www.nsrm-friends.org

This museum houses more than 600 pieces of railroad equipment. It exhibits 50 freight and passenger cars, as well as five steam locomotives that once belonged to the Virginia and Truckee railroad, and also houses a pictorial history gallery and artifacts of the famed Bonanza Road.

Daily 8:30 a.m.-4:30 p.m.

STATE CAPITOL

101 N. Carson St., Carson City, 775-684-5700; www.nv.gov

The capitol building is a large Classical Revival structure with Doric columns and a silver dome. It houses portraits of past Nevada governors. Self-guided tours.

Daily 8 a.m.-5 p.m.

STATE LIBRARY BUILDING

100 N. Stewart, Carson City, 775-684-3360; www.nevadaculture.org

Files of Nevada newspapers and books about the state.

Monday-Friday 8 a.m.-5 p.m.

WARREN ENGINE COMPANY NO. 1 FIRE MUSEUM

777 S. Stewart St., Carson City, 775-887-2210; www.visitcarsoncity.com

See the old photographs, antique fire-fighting equipment, the state's first fire truck (restored), an 1847 four-wheel cart and more.

Children under 18 must be accompanied by an adult.

SPECIAL EVENTS
NEVADA DAY CELEBRATION

Carson Street and Highway 50 East, Carson City, 775-882-2600, 866-683-2948; www.nevadaday.com

Commemorates Nevada's admission to the Union with a grand ball, parades, and exhibits. Four days in late October.

WHERE TO EAT
★★ADELE'S

1112 N. Carson St., Carson City, 775-882-3353; www.adelesrestaurantandlounge.com

American. Lunch (Monday-Friday), dinner, late-night. Closed Sunday. Bar. Outdoor seating. $$

GREAT BASIN NATIONAL PARK

Established as a national park in 1986, Great Basin consists of 77,092 acres of diverse scenic, ecologic and geologic attractions. It includes Lehman Caves (formerly Lehman Caves National Monument), Wheeler Peak, a glacier and Lexington Arch, a natural limestone arch more than six stories tall.

Of particular interest is Lehman Caves, a large limestone solution cavern. The cave contains numerous limestone formations, including shields and helictites. The 12-mile Wheeler Peak Scenic Drive reaches to the 10,000-foot elevation mark of Wheeler Peak. From there, you can hike to the summit. Backcountry hiking and camping are permitted. The Lexington Arch is located at the south end of the park. Camping is allowed at three campgrounds located along the Wheeler Peak Scenic Drive: the Wheeler Peak Campground, the Upper Lehman Creek Campground and the Lower Lehman Campground. Baker Creek Campground is located approximately five miles from park headquarters. Picnic facilities are available near park headquarters.

FALLON
See also Reno

Fallon is one of the westernmost cities on what is often called "the Loneliest Road in America," a segment of Route 50 that runs through Nevada and is known for its relative seclusion.

WHAT TO SEE
LAHONTAN STATE RECREATION AREA
16799 Lahontan Dam, Fallon, 775-867-3500; www.parks.nv.gov/lah.htm
Approximately 30,000 acres with a 16-mile-long reservoir. Water sports, fishing, boating (launching, ramps), picnicking, camping.

SPECIAL EVENTS
ALL INDIAN RODEO AND POW WOW
Churchill County Fairgrounds, Sheckler Street and U.S. 95 South, Fallon, 775-427-2014
Rodeo events, parade, powwow, Native American dances, arts, games. Third weekend in July.

FALLON AIR SHOW
Fallon Naval Air Station, 4755 Pasture Road, Fallon, 775-426-2880;
www.fallontourism.com
Part of the state's "Aerial Triple Crown," this event includes military exhibition flying, civilian aerobatics and aircraft displays. Ground events and static displays of vintage and modern aircraft. September.

WHERE TO STAY
★COMFORT INN FALLON
1830 W. Williams Ave., Fallon, 775-423-5554, 877-424-6423; www.comfortinn.com
82 rooms. Complimentary breakfast. Restaurant. Pool. Business center. Pets accepted. $

★SUPER 8 FALLON
855 W. Williams Ave., Fallon, 775-423-6031; www.super8.com
75 rooms. Restaurant, bar. Casino. Pool. Fitness center. Business center. Pets accepted. $

HENDERSON
See also Boulder City, Las Vegas
The fastest growing city in Nevada, Henderson has become the third-largest city in the state, thanks to its proximity to Las Vegas. Many of the area's most

luxurious resorts are actually located in Henderson.

WHAT TO SEE

CLARK COUNTY HERITAGE MUSEUM

1830 S. Boulder Highway, Henderson, 702-455-7955; www.co.clark.nv.us

Learn all about the history of southern Nevada. You'll see replicas of Native American dwellings, historic houses and businesses from the early 20th century, a ghost town, vintage automobiles, a 1932 train depot, old photos of the Strip and more. A detailed timeline charts the region's evolution from prehistoric times.

Daily 9 a.m.-4:30 p.m.

ETHEL M. CHOCOLATES FACTORY & CACTUS GARDEN

2 Cactus Garden Drive, Henderson, 702-435-2655, 888-627-0990; www.ethelm.com

Take the self-guided tour of this factory, where everything from chewy caramels to crunchy nut clusters roll off the assembly line.

Daily 8:30 a.m.-6 p.m.

GALLERIA AT SUNSET

1300 W. Sunset Road, Henderson, 702-434-0202; www.galleriaatsunset.com

This mall has 140 shops and restaurants and a free rock climbing wall.

Monday-Saturday 10 a.m.-9 p.m., Sunday 11 a.m.-6 p.m.

MONTELAGO VILLAGE

1600 Lake Las Vegas, Henderson, 702-564-4700, 866-564-4799;
www.montelagovillage.com

Escape to this development reminiscent of a centuries-old seaside village. About 35 unique shops and restaurants line the cobblestone streets of MonteLago, which borders the Ritz-Carlton Las Vegas. Retailers offer everything from fine art and custom-made jewelry to women's apparel and handcrafted home furnishings.

REFLECTION BAY GOLF CLUB

1605 Lake Las Vegas Parkway, Henderson, 702-740-4653, 877-698-4653;
www.lakelasvegas.com

Designed by golf great Jack Nicklaus, the public, par-72 resort course follows the rugged desert contours with the final holes along the shore of the 320-acre man-made Lake Las Vegas. Arroyo-meets-grass flora, maddening bunkers and interesting (and frustrating) water features make the course memorable. Afterward, kick back at the Mediterranean-style clubhouse with patio dining under a colonnade.

Winter 7 a.m.-sunset, summer 6:30 a.m.-sunset.

RIO SECCO GOLF CLUB

2851 Grand Hills Drive, Henderson, 702-777-2400; www.riosecco.net

Rio Secco is an expensive course, but its variety makes it well worth playing. The course is essentially divided into thirds, with six holes in small canyons, six on plateaus with views of the local skyline and six built to resemble the Nevada desert. The course is more than 7,300 yards long, so be prepared to swing for the fences. Number 9 is a long par-5 with bunkers surrounding the green. Make the turn facing the city and count yourself lucky if you've played 8 and 9 (back-to-back par-fives measuring 1,150 yards combined) at one or two over.

SPECIAL EVENTS
HERITAGE PARADE AND FESTIVAL
Henderson Events Plaza, 200 S. Water St., Henderson, 702-565-8951;
www.visithenderson.com
This annual festival is one of the largest in Henderson. It lasts nine days and features food, a carnival, appraisal fair and more. Late April.

WHERE TO STAY
★★★GREEN VALLEY RANCH RESORT AND SPA
2300 Paseo Verde Parkway, Henderson, 702-617-7777, 866-782-9487;
www.greenvalleyranchresort.com
A Mediterranean-style oasis in the middle of the desert, the Green Valley Ranch Resort is situated between the Strip and the Lake Las Vegas resorts in Henderson. The sprawling property feels more like one of your rich uncle's estates than a Vegas hotel, with personal touches like one-of-a-kind furnishings, plush sitting areas and textured accents. The casino does have a solid supply of dinging slot machines, but it's all done with a level of class that is rarely found on the Strip. Goose-down pillows, separate tubs and showers, twice-daily housekeeping service, and plush, terry-cloth robes turn guest rooms into refuges. Whether you spend your day at The Beach (with actual sand) or The Pond, you'll be treated to pools that promote excess. Of course, the property would be lost without an equally luxuriant spa that includes tempting treatments and a private lap pool.
490 rooms. Restaurant, bar. Fitness center. Pool. Spa. Business center. $$

★★★LOEWS/LAKE LAS VEGAS RESORT

101 Montelago Blvd., Henderson, 702-567-6000; www.loewshotels.com
Golf, kayaking, fishing, hiking and spa treatments? Is this Vegas? Well, technically, it's Lake Las Vegas, a 320-acre man-made and privately owned lake that is closer to the town of Henderson than Las Vegas proper (it is 17 miles from the Strip, for those who want to take in a show after all the outdoor recreation). The resort has a Moroccan theme and guest rooms offer amenities that include flat-screen TVs, plush terry robes, Bloom bath products and twice-daily maid service. Entertainment in the area includes a concert series in the summer and a floating skating rink (yes, ice skating, in the desert) in the nearby MonteLago Village during winter. Duffers will enjoy the Reflection Bay Golf Course and the Falls Golf Course. And, lest the kids and pets feel left out, Loews offers onsite specialty programs for both.
493 rooms. Restaurant, bar. Fitness center. Pool. Spa. Business center. Pets accepted. $$

★★★M RESORT SPA CASINO
12300 Las Vegas Blvd. S., Henderson, 702-797-1000, 877-673-7678;
www.themresort.com
The newest addition to Henderson, the M Resort provides a refreshing al-

ternative to typical Vegas. Instead of the constant dinging of slot machines and flashing of neon signs, the M Resort is a study in natural light, trickling waterfalls and the subtle scent of eucalyptus, which is filtrated through the hotel. Lest you forget you're in Las Vegas, guest rooms offer views of the Strip through floor-to-ceiling windows, as well as Bose sound systems, flat-screen TVs and marble vanities. The sprawling 100,000-square-foot Villaggio Del Sole Pool and Entertainment Piazza includes two pools, cabanas, an outdoor cocktail lounge and a stage for live music performances. Nine onsite restaurants and bars ensure that you're well fed throughout your stay.

390 rooms. Wireless Internet access. Restaurant, bar. Business center. Fitness center. Pool. Spa. $

★★★★THE RITZ-CARLTON, LAKE LAS VEGAS

1610 Lake Las Vegas Parkway, Henderson, 702-567-4700; www.ritzcarlton.com

The Ritz-Carlton's motto is "ladies and gentlemen serving ladies and gentlemen," and that commitment to service is found at this Tuscan-style property in the resort community of Lake Las Vegas, known for the Reflection Bay Golf Course (designed by Jack Nicklaus) and the Falls Golf Course (designed by Tom Weiskopf). Relaxation takes precedence in the guest rooms and suites, which feature soft colors, oversized marble bathrooms with Bulgari amenities and luxurious bed linens. Located 17 miles from the Strip, the resort has a private beach located alongside a waterfall and a 30,000-square-foot spa and fitness center.

349 rooms. Complimentary breakfast. Restaurant, bar. Fitness center. Pool. Spa. Business center. Pets accepted. $$

★★SUNSET STATION HOTEL CASINO

1301 W. Sunset Road, Henderson, 702-547-7777, 888-786-7389;
www.sunsetstation.com

457 rooms. Restaurant, bar. Casino. Business center. Fitness center. Pool. $

WHERE TO EAT

★★SETTEBELLO

140 Green Valley Parkway, Henderson, 702-222-3556; www.settebello.net

It isn't easy finding good pizza in Las Vegas. Located in a strip mall, like most Vegas venues off the Strip, this Henderson eatery is a hit with locals for its honest-to-goodness Naples-style pizza (but not the back-to-basics décor). The brick oven, imported from Italy, is what makes these thin-crust beauties so tasty. It gets up to temperatures of 950 degrees Fahrenheit, which chars the bottom of the pizza, while keeping the top warm and gooey. Simple toppings like crushed tomatoes, luscious fresh mozzarella and fruity olive oil are all you need to satisfy your pizza craving.

Pizza. Lunch, dinner. $$

SPAS

★★★★THE RITZ-CARLTON SPA, LAKE LAS VEGAS

The Ritz-Carlton, Lake Las Vegas,1610 Lake Las Vegas Parkway, Henderson, 702-567-
4700, 800-241-3333; www.ritzcarlton.com

Though only 17 miles off the Strip, this spa feels a million tranquil miles away, especially after wading in hot and cold plunge pools and luxuriating in a massage treatment outside by a waterfall. Facial treatments—with True products—are highly advanced (in other words, they actually do something) and range from anti-acne to anti-aging. While the high-end, Italian-style structures may be anything but natural, the spa draws some inspiration from its desert surroundings. For post-sun exposure, try Desert Radiance ($160), which uses natural ingredients to fight nasty sunspots. You'll be over the moon for the unusual Lunar Rhythms massage ($350), which supposedly takes cues from heavenly cycles.

INCLINE VILLAGE

See also Carson City

Swanky and affluent, Incline Village sits on the north rim of Lake Tahoe. It derives its name from the Great Incline Tramway built by loggers in 1878, but today the town is primarily a haven for those seeking outdoor fun.

WHAT TO SEE
DIAMOND PEAK SKI RESORT

1210 Ski Way, Incline Village, 775-832-1177; www.diamondpeak.com

Three quads, three double chairlifts; patrol, school, rentals, snowmaking. Thirty runs; longest run approximately 2½ miles; vertical drop 1,840 feet. Mid-December-mid-April, daily.

LAKE TAHOE NEVADA STATE PARK

2005 Highway 28, Incline Village, 775-831-0494; www.parks.nv.gov/lt.htm

Approximately 14,200 acres on the eastern shore of beautiful Lake Tahoe. Gently sloping sandy beach, swimming, fishing, boating (ramp), hiking, mountain biking, cross-country skiing. No camping. Daily.

SPECIAL EVENTS
LAKE TAHOE SHAKESPEARE FESTIVAL

Sand Harbor State Park, 948 Incline Way, Incline Village, 775-832-1616, 800-747-4697; www.laketahoeshakespeare.com

This event has grown into one of the premier Shakespeare festivals in the West. The troupe performs nightly from mid-July to late August in a natural amphitheater on the water's edge at Sand Harbor. A food court serves tasty fare from several outstanding local eateries, as well as beer and wine. Mid-July-late August.

WHERE TO STAY
★★★HYATT REGENCY LAKE TAHOE RESORT, SPA & CASINO

1111 Country Club Drive, Incline Village, 775-832-1234; www.hyatt.com

This resort is a top pick for rustic, upscale accommodations on the North Shore of Lake Tahoe. It's not located on mountain, but the resort will shuttle you to the slopes. Spa services are offered through the fitness center. The hotel also houses a small but charming old-style casino, a private hotel beach and a destination restaurant with arguably one of the best dining views of the lake.

422 rooms. Restaurant, bar. Spa. Casino. Pool. Business center. Fitness center. $$

LAS VEGAS

See also Boulder City, Henderson

Plan a visit to Vegas these days and you'll still see "world wonders," glitzy showgirls and plenty of dice-throwing. But today's version of Las Vegas is more haute. The kitsch has been toned down a bit and world-class spas, more refined accommodations and some of the country's best restaurants have moved in. In the last few years, Las Vegas has morphed into one of the top cities for dining in the country.

You'll still hear plenty of dinging slot machines all day long. But today it's as much about the pool (as in, which resort has the best one), championship golf and Cirque du Soleil. Check out one of the best aquariums (at Mandalay Bay) and browse the collection at the Bellagio Gallery of Fine Art.

Bring your hiking shoes. You'll find numerous canyons, valleys and man-made lakes around the city. Enjoy spectacular scenery and a wide range of recreational activities, including hiking, swimming, fishing, biking, boating, horseback riding, rock climbing, camping and whitewater rafting.

WHAT TO SEE
A PERMANENT TRIBUTE TO HEROES
New York-New York Hotel and Casino, 3790 Las Vegas Blvd. S., Las Vegas, 800-689-1797; www.nynyhotelcasino.com

This memorial of September 11, 2001 includes display cases showing some of the thousands of T-shirts, notes and other mementos left by mourning tourists in the months following the terror attacks.

ADVENTUREDOME
Circus Circus Hotel and Casino, 2880 Las Vegas Blvd. S., Las Vegas, 702-794-3939, 866-634-8894; www.adventuredome.com

The Adventuredome is the largest indoor amusement park in the United States. The operative word is, of course, "indoor"; it offers rides and respite from the desert's brutal summer heat. With 25 rides and attractions, there are options for kids of all ages and heights. Canyon Blaster, the world's only indoor double-loop, double-corkscrew coaster, is one of the most popular thrill rides.

Admission: $4-$7 per ride. All-day passes adults $24.95, children 33"-47" tall $14.95. Summer, 10 a.m.-midnight; school year, Monday-Thursday 11 a.m.-6 p.m., Friday-Saturday 10 a.m.-midnight, Sunday 10 a.m.-9 p.m.

THE ATOMIC TESTING MUSEUM
755 E. Flamingo Road, Las Vegas, 702-794-5161; www.atomictestingmuseum.org

Few states have such an explosive history as Nevada. The Atomic Testing Museum, in association with the Smithsonian Institute, educates visitors about the Nevada Test Site, which is a piece of land the size of Rhode Island that witnessed the bulk of American nuclear tests from 1951 to 1992, only 65 miles from Las Vegas. Get a better understanding of the nuclear world through simulations, artifacts, films and a glimpse into what it was like to work at the test site, as told by the former employees. Be sure to stop by the gift shop to see the assortment of nuclear-themed gifts—including an Albert Einstein action figure.

Admission: adults $12, seniors, military, students, Nevada residents and youth 7-17 $9, children 6 and under free. Monday-Saturday 9 a.m.-5 p.m., Sunday 1-5 p.m

BADLANDS GOLF CLUB

9119 Alta Drive, Las Vegas, 702-363-0754; www.badlandsgc.com

Designed by Chi Chi Rodriguez and Johnny Miller, Badlands is an example of an increasing trend of three sets of nine holes, offering different combinations of courses. The three nines (Diablo, Desperado and Outlaw) are markedly different. The Outlaw course is more forgiving than the other two, which are the usual tournament 18.

BALI HAI GOLF CLUB

5160 Las Vegas Blvd. S., Las Vegas, 888-427-6678; www.balihaigolfclub.com

Your first thought might be that golf and the desert don't make a great pair. But when that desert happens to be in Las Vegas, they do. Courses like Bali Hai show mans' triumph over nature (and then nature's triumph over man, when it comes to the $200 to $300 rates, to keep up the greens). The name elicits visions of a tropical paradise immortalized in the Rodgers and Hammerstein musical South Pacific, and this lush golf club doesn't disappoint. The Lee Schmidt and Brian Curley-designed course has seven acres of water features and the type of service you'd expect in paradise.

BELLAGIO CONSERVATORY AND BOTANICAL GARDENS

Bellagio Las Vegas, 3600 Las Vegas Blvd. S., Las Vegas, 702-693-7111, 888-987-3456; www.bellagiolasvegas.com

Picture an organic art museum, where the displays are made of flowers, shrubs, plants and trees, and change with the seasons. The Bellagio Conservatory and Botanical Gardens does just that, and it's even more beautiful than it sounds. The 13,500-square-foot palatial setting, located across from the resort's lobby, is home to five alternating displays throughout the year, with themes that include the holidays, Chinese New Year, spring, summer and fall. Each season manages to outdo the last. In winter, you might find reindeers made of whole pecans, giant greeting cards comprised of thousands of flowers and a 21-foot wreath built from pinecones. Come spring, a whole new world awaits with a live butterfly garden, leaping fountains and butterfly shaped topiaries. On average, each display consists of 40 trees, 1,500 shrubs and 10,000 blooming plants. Considering that the hotel spends $8 million annually on the Conservatory, this free attraction is a jackpot all around. Daily, 24 hours.

BELLAGIO GALLERY OF FINE ART

Bellagio, 3600 Las Vegas Blvd. S., Las Vegas, 702-693-7871, 877-957-9777; www.bellagiolasvegas.com

If you think a casino is a strange bedfellow for a museum, you haven't been to the Bellagio Gallery of Fine Art. Critics harrumphed when they heard about a highbrow museum in "low-brow" Las Vegas, but they've since given BGFA an approving nod. Exhibits at this small space, located near the pool area, change throughout the year, and display paintings, sculpture and other artistic mediums. Past exhibits have included American modernism, Claude Monet's masterworks, Faberge treasures (of the egg variety), Picasso's ceramics and more. With the local Guggenheim's closure in 2008, Bellagio's gallery is now the only art gallery on the Strip.

Admission: adults $15, seniors $12, students, teachers and military $10, children 12 and under free. Sunday-Thursday 10 a.m.-6 p.m., Friday-Saturday 10 a.m.-7 p.m.

BODIES: THE EXHIBITION

Luxor, 3900 Las Vegas Blvd. S., Las Vegas, 800-288-1000;
www.bodiestheexhibition.com

This show is something between art, science and just plain macabre. BODIES: The Exhibition is just what it sounds like: human cadavers displayed for all to see. The polymer-preserved bodies, each with its dermis removed, demonstrate everything from the muscular to the vascular systems of the body, so you can see just what you and your muscles look like from the inside when you're, say, playing baseball or throwing darts. Partial-body specimens show what a smoker's lung looks like compared to a healthy lung, and what kind of damage over-eating can do to your organs. The exhibition is educational, but has raised some controversy since its inception because the bodies were acquired from the Chinese police (visit the Website if you're curious). Originally housed at the Tropicana, BODIES recently signed a 10-year agreement with Luxor.

Admission: adults $31, seniors $29, children 4-14 $23. Daily 10 a.m.-10 p.m.

BONANZA "THE WORLD'S LARGEST GIFT SHOP"

2440 Las Vegas Blvd. S., Las Vegas, 702-385-7359;

The self-proclaimed "world's largest gift shop" has far more than the typical tourist knickknacks you'd expect. You'll find fuzzy dice (just begging for a rearview mirror to call their own) and miniature, lighted "Welcome to Fabulous Las Vegas" signs, but there's also an array of bachelor and bachelorette gag gifts, and even a sombrero-wearing dog that sings "La Bamba" when activated. Located at the corner of Las Vegas Boulevard and Sahara Avenue, this 40,000-square-foot space is a Sin City staple even locals frequent. Daily 8 a.m.-midnight.

BONNIE SPRINGS OLD NEVADA

1 Gunfighter Lane, Blue Diamond, 702-875-4191; www.bonniesprings.com

Gunfights break out in the streets and public hangings are common in Bonnie Springs, a replica of an 1880s mining town, where the spirit of the Old West is still kicking. Located just outside of Red Rock Canyon, about 25 miles from Las Vegas, this 115-acre ranch is a wild spot for the family, with a petting zoo, miniature train, stage coaches and even a cemetery. Wander the shops, check out the shows and enjoy a "Bonnie burger" at the restaurant or a beer at the saloon. The circular fire pit is the perfect spot for a mug of hot chocolate in winter—it does occasionally get cold in the desert.

Admission: $20 per car. Wednesday-Sunday 10:30 a.m.-5 p.m.

THE COLOSSEUM SHOWS

Caesars Palace, 3570 Las Vegas Blvd. S., Las Vegas, 702-866-1400;
www.caesarspalace.com

Divas have taken over the Colosseum at Caesars Palace yet again. Cher, Bette Midler and Jerry Seinfeld rotate performances at the venue (formerly the dominion of über-diva Celine Dion) and continue to pack them in. With such impressive costumes and choreography, it's easy to forgive the singers for their occasional vocal lapses—they are all in their sixties, after all. See Cher with her countless costume changes; admire the divine Ms. M and her showgirls in *The Showgirl Must Go On*; or laugh constantly with the hilarious Jerry Sienfeld.

Tickets: $95-$250; see Website for information. Daily 7:30 p.m.

DESERT FOX TOURS

6265 Dean Martin Road, Las Vegas, 866-740-3332; www.vegashummertours.com

If you're the adventurous type, go off-road in a Hummer and see the desert in all its rugged glory. Various tours last from three to six hours and take you to Red Rock National Conservation Area, the Valley of Fire, or a gold mine and ghost town.

DESERT PINES GOLF CLUB

3415 E. Bonanza Road, Las Vegas, 888-427-6678; www.desertpinesgolfclub.com

Desert Pines strives to emulate the seaside designs found in the Carolinas. Pine trees line most of the narrow fairways, and several ponds can increase a score in short order. The Desert Pines golf center is comprehensive, even offering target areas shaped like famous holes such as the 17th island green at Sawgrass and the second hole at Pinehurst.

THE EIFFEL TOWER EXPERIENCE

Paris Las Vegas, 3655 Las Vegas Blvd. S., Las Vegas, 877-603-4386;
www.parislasvegas.com

Las Vegas is a city obsessed with replication—and we're not talking carbon copies and model airplanes. Though the Eiffel Tower at Paris Las Vegas is half the size of the original at 460 feet, the view from the top is equally stunning. A dizzying windowed elevator ride takes guests up nearly 50 floors to the open-air (well, fence-enclosed) observation deck, which allows for 360-degree views of Las Vegas. It's intimate up here, and gets packed with tourists on the weekends. But if you can get to the border of the deck facing west, you're in for perhaps the best view of the Fountains of Bellagio water show in town. Avoid tripping over men down on one knee. This is a popular spot for marriage proposals.

FASHION SHOW LAS VEGAS

3200 Las Vegas Blvd. S., Las Vegas, 702-784-7000; www.thefashionshow.com

One of the first malls on the Strip to feature high-end retailers, the Fashion Show underwent a multimillion dollar expansion in 2002 to keep up with its neighbors. An 80-foot-long runway and stage were built right down the center of the two-story mall to host live fashion shows, and it's already been put to use during press conferences by Mayor Oscar Goodman, flanked by

★☆★☆★ NEVADA

his entourage of usual showgirls, and local charity fundraisers. It's the shopping that attracts fashionistas from around the world. The nearly two million-square-foot mall has six anchor stores: Neiman Marcus, Saks Fifth Avenue, Macy's, Dillard's, Nordstrom and Bloomingdale's Home. Other shopping-mall standbys include J. Crew, Banana Republic, Lacoste and Gap. A massive food court boasts everything from pizza to Mediterranean food, as well as the usual Wendy's and KFC.

Monday-Saturday 10 a.m.-9 p.m., Sunday 11 a.m.-7 p.m.

FORUM SHOPS AT CAESARS PALACE

Caesars Palace, 3500 Las Vegas Blvd. S., Las Vegas, 702-893-4800;
www.caesarspalace.com

The cobblestone faux-Roman streets that intersect inside Caesars' Forum Shops carry travelers from around the world to such shopping meccas as Harry Winston, Burberry, Gucci, Louis Vuitton, Versace and Christian Dior. This is definitely one of the more upscale malls in the Las Vegas valley, but calling it a mall is not giving it all its due. Aside from shopping at this tony spot, there's the entertainment. The free Atlantis Show brings Roman gods and a simple story to life with animatronic "actors" that spring to action every hour. A Festival Fountain show also entertains guests; but don't miss the restaurants. Although there is much to choose from in Vegas, many stars still go back to their favorites at the Forum Shops. The Palm, Spago, BOA Steakhouse and Joe's Seafood, Prime Steak & Stone Crab are a few of the many fine food finds scattered throughout this 636,000-square-foot mall. A winding circular escalator carries shoppers from the marbled first floor to the top third floor, where you will find some of the best views of the Strip at Sushi Roku.

Monday-Thursday 10 a.m.-11 p.m., Friday-Saturday 10 a.m.–midnight.

FOUNTAINS OF BELLAGIO

Bellagio Las Vegas, 3600 Las Vegas Blvd. S., Las Vegas, 702-693-7111;
www.bellagiolasvegas.com

Romance is anything but watered down at Lake Bellagio, as the trinity of water, music and light meld together in an aquatic ballet. The water echoes human motion seen in dance, swaying while spraying more than 460 feet into the air. The jets' moves are perfectly choreographed to music, with scores from Broadway, the classics and more. If you can't snag a prime place along the Bellagio Lake railing, head to Paris, located across the street from Bellagio, for an equally stellar view. Or book a veranda table inside the Bellagio at Olives restaurant, have a glass of wine (and some freshly made pasta), and enjoy multiple shows throughout your meal. It's one of the most mesmerizing sights in Vegas and since it's free, you're saving up blackjack dollars every time you watch.

Monday-Friday 3-8 p.m. (every half hour), 8 p.m.-midnight. (every 15 minutes; Saturday-Sunday noon-8 p.m. (every half hour), 8 p.m.-midnight (every 15 minutes).

FREMONT STREET EXPERIENCE

425 Fremont St., Las Vegas, 702-678-5777; www.vegasexperience.com

The Fremont Street Experience light canopy typifies vintage Las Vegas. Located downtown, the production spans five football fields and a whole host of historic casinos and neon signs. Despite the live music and street-fair atmosphere on the ground, the real action is in the sky. Six times nightly, the canopy springs into a vibrant show, as 12 million lights draw all eyes up. Music ranging from classic rock to classic Vegas blasts from surrounding speakers, and is choreographed to match the illumination. One of the best spots to watch is at Gold Diggers, the second-story nightclub at the Golden Nugget. Their patio is directly under the canopy, affording great views of the show, and the tourists swigging beer from football-shaped containers. Show hours vary. See Website for details.

GONDOLA RIDES

The Venetian Resort Hotel Casino, 3355 Las Vegas Blvd. S., Las Vegas, 702-414-4300,
877-883-6423; www.venetian.com

Who needs the murky waterways of Venice when you can take a gondola ride through the pristine, chlorinated canals of the Venetian Resort Hotel Casino? Choose the indoor canal or the outdoor one, and float in a gondola modeled after the real deal. Of course, rather than floating under historic bridges and sidewalk cafes, you'll be floating past stores (like Banana Republic and Ann Taylor) and a Wolfgang Puck restaurant. Don't let that detract from the romantic lilt of your gondolier's serenades. The ride takes you through the Grand Canal Shoppes, which cover 500,000 feet of retail space and restaurants—not that you have much buying power from the confines of your romantic vessel (which could be a very good thing for your wallet).

Admission: adults and children $16, children 2 and under free. Sunday-Thursday 10 a.m.-11 p.m., Friday-Saturday 10 a.m.-midnight

THE GRAND CANAL SHOPPES AT THE VENETIAN

The Venetian Resort Hotel Casino, 3355 Las Vegas Blvd. S., Las Vegas, 702-414-4500;
www.venetian.com

This elegant space simply sings of Italy: It boasts painted frescos, polished marble, gondoliers and, of course, exceptional shopping. Aside from the luxury retailers you'll find at other shopping destinations such as Venetzia and Movado, there is also a nice array of independent boutiques. History buffs can have their pick of authentic Spanish galleons, coins and other finds at Ancient Creations; delicate, handblown Venetian glass sits pretty at Ripa de Monti; handmade Venetian masks and period pieces await you at Il Prato, and Ca'd'Oro is the place to go for exquisite jewelry. A winding indoor canal below the cobblestoned walkways links the shops together, and if you've always dreamed of having a gondolier steer you from storefront to storefront, now's the time to make it a reality, as rides with singing gondoliers are available. Throughout St. Mark's Square, the center of the Grand Canal Shoppes, actors, musicians and strolling singers entertain guests, and living statues come to life. The Grand Canal Shoppes connect to the newly opened Palazzo, housing the first Barneys New York in Vegas, complete with its own valet and entrance on the Strip. You won't find any steals here, but you can definitely find some serious designer duds that will impress the pals back home.

Sunday-Thursday10 a.m.-11 p.m., Friday-Saturday 10 a.m.-midnight.

IMPERIAL PALACE AUTO COLLECTION

Imperial Palace Hotel & Casino, 3535 Las Vegas Blvd., Las Vegas, 702-794-3174; www.autocollections.com

We all know money and nice cars go hand-in-hand. So it makes sense that Imperial Palace houses one of the largest collections of classic cars in the world. The Auto Collection includes more than $100 million in inventory, and over 250 cars of all varieties—muscle, classic, historic and more. From Johnny Carson's 1939 Chrysler Royal Sedan to the 1928 Mercedes-Benz S Tourer valued at more than $5.5 million, the vintage variety is endless. Buy, sell or just stroll through the 125,000-square-foot showroom at your leisure. Admission: adults $8.95, seniors and children under 12 $5, children under 3 free. Daily 10 a.m.-6 p.m.

THE JOINT

Hard Rock Hotel & Casino, 4455 Paradise Road, Las Vegas, 800-693-7625; www.hardrockhotel.com

Considering its location in the Hard Rock, a resort built around the theme of good music, the bar remains high for talent at The Joint. The rocking stage and sound system have blasted the likes of Bob Dylan, The Killers, Tom Petty and Coldplay, and succeed in bringing in varied acts of a high caliber (don't expect to find lesser known bands and singers here, unless they're an opening act). The space blends down-home charm with state-of-the-art technology—25-foot-tall speaker bays and multiple plasma screens—to create an authentic rock club vibe. But charm aside, be prepared to pay big bucks for the privilege. Shows in Vegas rank among the highest priced in the nation.

JUBILEE! BACKSTAGE TOUR

Bally's, 3645 Las Vegas Blvd. S., Las Vegas, 800-237-7469; www.harrahs.com

There's a lot more to being a showgirl than having a knockout body. It takes stamina, style and an incredibly strong neck to hoist up those headdresses. Peek into the showgirl's world with the Donn Arden's Jubilee! backstage tour. A showgirl leads you across the stage, around the set and through the costume room, sharing fun facts about the current production. Did you know that the heaviest headdress weighs 35 pounds? Or that there is a minimum of nine costume changes for each person throughout the show, and that five different kinds of feathers are used? As more and more traditional showgirl-themed shows are replaced by Cirque du Soleil and other large-scale productions, this is your chance to check out a Vegas icon, before she hits the road for good.

Admission: adults and children 13-18 $15, with purchase of Jubilee! show ticket $10. Monday, Wednesday and Saturday 11 a.m.

LAKE OF DREAMS

Wynn Las Vegas, 3131 Las Vegas Blvd. S., Las Vegas, 877-321-9966; www.wynnlasvegas.com

No multi-star hotel on Las Vegas Boulevard is worth its weight without a manmade lake, and the one at Wynn is particularly special. Surrounded by a 120-foot-tall artificial mountain that shields it from Las Vegas Boulevard, the Lake of Dreams breathes an air of exclusivity, just like the rest of Wynn re-

sort. But the lake's true purpose is to wow onlookers throughout the evening, as it plays host to a variety of surreal shows: statues of men and women arise from the water, light and music spring to life, and there's even a giant inflatable frog (seriously) whose mouth moves in sync with Louis Armstrong's "What a Wonderful World." For the best view of the show, make a reservation on the patio at SW Steakhouse or Daniel Boulud Brasserie. The free shows begin after dark and occur approximately every half hour.
Daily 7 p.m.-12:30 a.m., times vary seasonally.

LAS VEGAS ART MUSEUM
9600 W. Sahara Ave., Las Vegas, 702-360-8000; www.lasvegasartmuseum.org
One of the biggest challenges the Las Vegas Art Museum faces is how to lure people off the Strip to its west side location. With powerhouse executive director Libby Lumpkin at the helm, the museum manages to shake people successfully from their slot-machine comas by showing provocative contemporary art by local and interna-tionally renowned artists. The works are hung in four airy rooms within the 11,000-square-foot facility, which is housed in a contemporary building shared with the Sahara West Library. Past exhibitions included a survey of Southern California Minimalists including Robert Irwin, Larry Bell and James Turrell, a collection of Roy Lichtenstein's prints, and an exhibition of models by the architect Frank Gehry.
Admission: adults $6, seniors $5, students $3, children under 12 free.
Tuesday-Saturday 10 a.m.-5 p.m., Sunday 1-5 p.m.

LAS VEGAS MOTOR SPEEDWAY
7000 Las Vegas Blvd. N., Las Vegas, 800-644-4444; www.lvms.com
You may not understand the appeal, but that shouldn't deter you from feeling the power, smelling the oil and reveling in the grit of NASCAR at the Las Vegas Motor Speedway. Every March the city's neck turns a touch redder, as more than 100,000 fans fire up their grills and head to NASCAR's Sprint Cup and Nationwide Series races. The $200 million track, which was built in 1995, extends 1,500 acres and includes the 1.5-mile super speedway, in addition to a 2.5-mile road course, a half-mile dirt oval and a drag strip.
Tours: Daily adults $8, children under 12 and seniors $6. Race prices vary.

LAS VEGAS OUTLET CENTER
7400 Las Vegas Blvd. S., Las Vegas, 702-896-5599; www.lasvegasoutletcenter.com
This enclosed mall was the first true outlet mall on the Strip, luring tourists from the high-end shops to the tail end of the Boulevard to save their pennies. Offering deep discounts at more than 130 stores, including Bass, Lenox, Wedgwood, Liz Claiborne, Etienne Aigner, Mikasa, Nike, Oneida, Reebok, Tommy Hilfiger, Waterford and more, you can take home serious steals at up to 65 percent off. What's the catch? Good question. Try to avoid visiting on the weekends, when tourists descend by the busload. Also, eat before you come. There's a basic food court to please those with a penchant for fried foods, but save your money for the tastier stuff at your hotel.
Monday-Saturday 10 a.m.-9 p.m., Sunday 10 a.m.-8 p.m.

LAS VEGAS PREMIUM OUTLETS

875 S. Grand Central Parkway, Las Vegas, 702-474-7500; www.premiumoutlets.com
Stroll the wide sidewalks at this sister to the Outlet Center and take advantage of discounts at stores such as Coach, Lacoste, A|X Armani Exchange, Dolce & Gabbana, Catherine Malandrino and more. Burberry always has a nice selection of accessories, including hats, headbands and scarves with the signature plaid pattern to spruce up your wardrobe. Check the clearance area in the back for some truly good finds. On Tuesday there is a 50 Plus Shoppers special, giving anyone older than 50 an extra 10 percent off. Monthly sales are also listed on the Website, so check before you drop in. When your stomach starts rumbling, bypass all the usual suspects at the food court and head straight to Makino, a sprawling sushi buffet.
Monday-Saturday 10 a.m.-9 p.m., Sunday 10 a.m.-8 p.m.

THE LIBERACE MUSEUM

1775 E. Tropicana Ave., Las Vegas, 702-798-5595; www.liberace.org
Spend an afternoon celebrating Liberace and all of the sequins, furs and glitz that he loved. Opened by Mr. Showmanship himself in 1979, the museum is a walk through the glamour of the pianist's life. Be sure to head across the parking lot to Carluccio's Tivoli Gardens. Liberace once owned this Italian restaurant (and decorated it), and was technically one of the first celebrity chefs in Las Vegas. Ask the bartender to fill you in on some ghost stories, too. It seems Liberace is about as gregarious in death as he was in life.
Admission: adults $15, seniors and students $10, children under 10 free.
Monday-Saturday 10 a.m.-5 p.m., Sunday noon-4 p.m.

LION HABITAT

MGM Grand Hotel & Casino, 3799 Las Vegas Blvd. S., Las Vegas, 877-880-0880;
www.mgmgrand.com

Superstitious folks may choose to toss their chips at MGM Grand, and it's not because the dealers are better or the drinks are more potent. It's because of the lions. An Asian good-luck symbol, lions have made a home at MGM Grand for years, frolicking in their own expansive habitat, just a few feet from the slots. The multi-level dwelling hosts a handful of lions, and even a translucent tunnel that makes you feel as though you're in with the beasts. The lions only spend "shifts" in the habitat. When they're not here, lying amid the waterfalls and foliage, they live on an 8.5-acre ranch nearby. Because they're in the habitat for such a limited time, trainers engage them in play or feed them, keeping them on their paws.
Daily 11 a.m.-10 p.m.

MIRACLE MILE SHOPS

Planet Hollywood Resort & Casino, 3663 Las Vegas Blvd. S., Las Vegas, 888-800-8284;
www.miraclemileshopslv.com
Recently redesigned with a contemporary flair, this meandering mall is filled with 170 stores, including French Connection, Ann Taylor Loft, bebe and Lucky Brand Jeans. You'll notice many shoppers with Alpaca Pete's shopping bags, an odd little store filled with the softest alpaca (a cousin of the llama) sweaters and slippers, as well as sheepskin rugs, car seat covers and home décor from around the world. Catch the free entertainment at small podiums

around the mall while you sip a coffee or gelato from the Aromi d'Italia, or at the V Theater in the middle of the mall. A favorite attraction for families is the live indoor rainstorm near Merchants' Harbor. Thunder, lightning and a light rain that turns torrential create a dramatic effect as you pass. If you're hungry, you won't find the usual food court choices here. Instead they've concentrated on high-end restaurants such as Pampas Churrascaria Brazilian Grille or Trader Vic's. If you just want a casual bite, you can pop into La Salsa Cantina, Sbarro pizza or the fun, frenzied Cheeseburger Las Vegas. Sunday-Thursday 10 a.m.-11 p.m., Friday-Saturday 10 a.m.-midnight.

MYSTERE BY CIRQUE DU SOLEIL

Treasure Island, 3300 Las Vegas Blvd. S., Las Vegas, 702-894-7111, 800-392-1999; www.treasureisland.com

This is classic Cirque du Soleil, with bright costumes, intriguing sets and acrobatics that make soaring through the air and scaling the walls look effortless. The show is a whirlwind of activity: cast members hop up ropes feet first, flip atop human totem poles and swing horizontally across the stage, and that's just in the opening number.

Saturday-Wednesday 7:30 and 9:30 p.m.

THE NEON MUSEUM

509 E. McWilliams Ave., Las Vegas, 702-387-6366; www.neonmuseum.org

It's referred to as The Boneyard for a reason. The Neon Museum holds the vestiges of vintage Vegas. This is where the history comes to rest—that which avoided implosion, that is. The signs and architecture date back to the 1940s, and include relics such as the Golden Nugget sign. The most recent addition is La Concha, a shell-shaped building designed by Paul Revere Williams that was saved from demolition and painstakingly moved here. Eventually, La Concha will serve as the hub of the museum and regular hours will be posted. For now, though, tours are by appointment only and must be made at least one day in advance (check Website or call for updates).

Admission: $15. Tours: Tuesday-Saturday, by appointment; June-July 10 a.m.

O BY CIRQUE DU SOLEIL

Bellagio, 3600 Las Vegas Blvd. S., Las Vegas, 702-693-7722, 888-488-7111; www.bellagiolasvegas.com

Fans of grace and fluidity (over sheer strength) fall in love with O at the Bellagio. The show focuses on the concept of infinity and how it applies to time and water (and, on a more literal level, the letter O and the French word for water, eau). The cast of Cirque characters are complemented by world-class synchronized swimmers and divers who take to a 1.5 million gallon pool, which doubles as a stage. Bodies slip in and out of the water like amphibians, and the high-dive takes on an entirely new meaning. Comic relief in the form of two oddly paired clowns reminds you that you're still at a circus, but as sideshows go, this certainly is the big top for waterworks.

Wednesday-Sunday 7:30 and 10:30 p.m.

THE ROLLER COASTER

New York-New York, 3790 Las Vegas Blvd. S., Las Vegas, 800-689-1797;

If you're going to ride one coaster in Las Vegas, it should be the roller coaster at New York-New York. Zip through the faux New York skyline, past the Statue of Liberty, while admiring the view of Las Vegas Boulevard from 200 feet up. With barrel rolls, a loop and multiple heart-wrenching drops at speeds nearing 70 mph, this coaster is good old nail-biting fun. For those afraid of heights (and speed), New York-New York's Coney Island Emporium allows you to keep your feet on the ground and still relish in the flavor of the Big Apple with 12,000 square feet of games and carnival-style entertainment. Admission: $14. Sunday-Thursday 11 a.m.-11 p.m., Friday-Saturday 10:30 a.m.-midnight; Coney Island Emporium: Sunday-Thursday 8 a.m.-midnight, Friday-Saturday 8 a.m.-2 a.m.

SECRET GARDEN AND DOLPHIN HABITAT

The Mirage, 3400 Las Vegas Blvd. S., Las Vegas, 800-374-9000;

The cats here hold magical secrets behind their eerie blue eyes—literally. These are the white tigers that once performed in Siegfried and Roy's magic show, prior to the incident in which their brother, Montecore, attacked magician and trainer Roy Horn in 2003. Though they're no longer disappearing and reappearing on stage, the cats lead a pretty luxurious life, surrounded by exotic plants and waterfalls and other felines, such as snow leopards, lions, golden tigers and black panthers. Following the cats, flip for Flipper at the nearby Dolphin Habitat. It's home to six Atlantic bottlenose dolphins, whom you'll spot leaping, "walking" on water, swimming and doing whatever it is that dolphins do. Because it's primarily a research facility, the Dolphin Habitat doesn't host regular "shows," but the trainers interact with the creatures throughout the day for the public to see. To get even more up-close, inquire about the Trainer for a Day program. Visitors can suit up and rub dorsal fins with some of the earth's smartest creatures.

Admission: adults $15, children 4-12 $10, children 3 and under free. Memorial Day-Labor Day: Daily 10 a.m.-7 p.m.; Labor Day-Memorial Day: Monday-Friday 11 a.m.-5:30 p.m., Saturday-Sunday 10 a.m.-5:30 p.m.

SHARK REEF AQUARIUM

Mandalay Bay, 3950 Las Vegas Blvd. S., Las Vegas, 877-632-7800;

Mandalay Bay's stunning aquarium holds more than 2,000 animals, including a variety of sharks, giant sting rays, piranha, golden crocodiles and its newest addition, an 87-pound, 7-foot-long Komodo dragon. With 1.6 million gallons of water, the cool, cavernous shark reef is a quiet, yet thrilling escape from the buzzing of the slots. Be sure to swing by the sting ray petting pool before settling in for an underwater aquatic ballet, as floor-to-ceiling glass walls show sea turtles, sharks and a variety of fish frolicking about in their impressive Vegas digs. Part of the floor is glass, too, allowing an eerie view of the sharks as they swim below.

Admission: adults $16.95, children under 12 $10.95, children 4 and under free. Daily 10 a.m.-11 p.m.

SHOWCASE MALL

3785 Las Vegas Blvd. S., Las Vegas; www.vegas.com

The words "Showcase Mall" should be code for sugar kingdom. Kids love the place as it boasts a slew of family-friendly activities. (There are a few shops, too.) At M&M's World (702-736-7611) you'll find every color of M&M imaginable—purple, gray, black, pink, turquoise. Head to Everything Coca-Cola (702-270-5952) for a fizzy drink made by an old-fashioned soda jerk as you browse the Coca-Cola memorabilia. Once the kids are fully buzzed on sugar, head upstairs to GameWorks (702-432-4263) and let them play video games to their hearts' content. When they start crashing, the United Artists movie theater (702-225-4828) provides the perfect respite (and relief from the desert sun thanks to constantly cranked air conditioning).

Store hours vary. M&M's World: Sunday-Thursday 9 a.m.-11 p.m., Friday-Saturday 9 a.m.-midnight. Everything Coca-Cola: Daily 10 a.m.-11 p.m. GameWorks: Sunday-Thursday 10 a.m.-midnight, Friday-Saturday 10 a.m.-1 a.m.

RED ROCK CANYON NATIONAL CONSERVATION AREA

West Charleston Blvd. (State Route 159), Las Vegas, 702-515-5350;
www.nv.blm.gov/redrockcanyon

Grab that karabiner and hightail it to Red Rock Canyon National Conservation Area. Located just 17 miles from the Las Vegas Strip, Red Rock Canyon is a popular spot for rock climbing, but it's also a naturalist's heaven with nearly 200,000 acres, and miles and miles of hiking and biking trails complemented by waterfalls, springs, wild burros, creosote bushes, pinion pine trees and more. The canyon is one of the world's largest wind-deposited formations, and is part of the Navajo Formation, created nearly 200 million years ago. A 13-mile paved scenic road circles through Red Rock, with stops and lookout points marked along the way.

Admission: $5 per car, $2 per motorcycle. Park: Daily 6 a.m.-7 p.m. Hours vary seasonally; call for details. Visitor center: Daily 8 a.m.-4:30 p.m.

ROYAL LINKS GOLF CLUB

5995 E. Vegas Valley Drive, Las Vegas, 702-450-8123, 888-427-6678;
www.royallinksgolfclub.com

Royal Links does its best to create the atmosphere of a traditional Scottish or Irish course. Each hole was inspired by one on which the British Open is contested each year. Designs were taken from Royal Troon, Prestwick and Royal Birkdale, among others. The club suggests that you let the caddies on staff carry your bag to get the full British Isles golf experience right here in the states.

SCENIC AIRLINES

2705 Airport Drive, North Las Vegas, 702-638-3300, 800-634-6801; www.scenic.com

Board one of this company's twin-engine planes for a bird's-eye view of the glorious Grand Canyon. More than 20 different tours are offered, ranging from one hour to three days of sightseeing. Depending on which tour you choose, you'll also see other popular natural attractions, such as Bryce Canyon, the Hoover Dam, Lake Mead, Monument Valley and the Valley of Fire. On some tours, you'll also spend some time exploring on foot or in a boat.

Plane wings are up high, so no aerial views are obstructed, and oversized panoramic windows give you an even better look at what's down below.

SHADOW CREEK GOLF CLUB

5400 Losee Road, North Las Vegas, 866-260-0069; www.shadowcreek.com

Probably the most exclusive course in town, a tee time here will cost a couple hundred dollars and you might find yourself playing behind George Clooney or Michael Jordan. The views of the surrounding mountains are breathtaking. (Because it's so pricey, the course isn't crowded.) Pine trees make for an interesting site in the Nevada desert, as do crystal-clear lagoons and streams along holes like the signature 15th, which runs toward the mountains.

SIRENS OF TI

Treasure Island, 3300 Las Vegas Blvd. S., Las Vegas, 702-894-7111, 800-288-7206; www.treasureisland.com

Stand your ground early for the Sirens of TI show because it fills up quickly. This battle between buff young pirates and barely clad sirens takes place in the lake in front of TI (formerly called Treasure Island, and once with a family-friendly pirate show), on Las Vegas Boulevard—you can imagine the rubber-necking delays. There are powerful pyrotechnics, amazing acrobatics and nearly 12 minutes of dialogue. Back in the days of Odysseus, Sirens were best seen, not heard, and that adage hasn't changed, but the visual charade is entertaining nevertheless. Spoiler alert: The sinking of the ship at the end of the melee makes it worth the wait (and maybe even the banter).

Daily at 5:30, 7, 8:30, 10 and 11:30 p.m.

SPRINGS PRESERVE

333 S. Valley View Blvd., Las Vegas, 702-822-7700; www.springspreserve.org

The Mojave Desert isn't all browns and grays. At the Springs Preserve, it's actually green—in more ways than one. This 180-acre historic preservation project is lo-cated just a couple of miles from the Strip, and embraces the concept of sustainability—a positive step in a city known for its frequent building implosions. Without these historic springs, Las Vegas wouldn't be what it is today. Originally, this central spot in the valley was the water source for residents and travelers. The springs dried up in 1962, but the Las Vegas Valley Water District has re-created them. The $250 million project hosts a variety of LEED-certified buildings that include museums, galleries and interactive displays, including a flash flood, an actual fossil digging area, animal exhibits and more. With eight acres of gardens, miles of walking paths, a play area for kids, an amphitheater and even a Wolfgang Puck restaurant (and you thought all the good grub was on the Strip), the Springs Preserve celebrates the history and culture of Southern Nevada, while also keeping its sights on the future.

Special exhibits: adults $18.95, seniors $17.95, children $10.95, children under 5 free. Daily 10 a.m.-6 p.m.

STRATOSPHERE RIDES

The Stratosphere, 2900 Las Vegas Blvd. S., Las Vegas, 702-380-7777, 800-998-6937;www.stratospherehotel.com

The screams carry for miles from the top of the Stratosphere, as riders dangle, shoot and blast over Las Vegas Boulevard, nearly 900 feet up. The Big Shot propels pas-sengers up at 45 miles per hour, losing their stomachs and then catching them as they fall back down. X-Scream is like a giant teeter-totter that shoots passengers off the edge of the Stratosphere. And Insanity, the Ride is a giant arm that twirls riders off the edge of the tower, spinning at 3 Gs. For those less inclined to heighten their heart rates, an enclosed 109th-floor observation deck gives a tremendous view of the Las Vegas Valley—and the horrified faces of riders as they're hurled over the edge.

Tower tickets: adults $13.95, seniors and hotel guests $10, children $8. Sunday-Thursday 10-1 a.m., Friday-Saturday 10-2 a.m.

THE TANK

The Golden Nugget, 129 E. Fremont St., Las Vegas, 800-634-3454;
www.goldennugget.com

This may be as close as you'll ever come to swimming with the fishes. The $30 million tank at the Golden Nugget is a 200,000-gallon aquarium full of sharks, sting rays and fish—and a three-story, translucent waterslide goes right through the center of it. The Tank is located smack-dab in the middle of the hotel's swimming pool, so even non-sliders can go head-to-head with the sharks, swimming loops around the Tank and making faces at the toothsome fin-flappers. Those who get their fill of sharks from Discovery Channel's "Shark Week" can lounge in the partially submerged chaises that line the pool.

Admission: adults $20, children under 11 $15, children under 2 free. Hotel guests free. Daily 10 a.m.-8 p.m.

TITANIC: THE ARTIFACT EXHIBITION

Luxor, 3900 Las Vegas Blvd. S., Las Vegas, 800-288-1000; www.titanictix.com

This exhibit gives colorful insight into the 1912 tragedy, boasting an extensive collection of artifacts discovered two and a half miles under the sea, including snippets from the last night's dinner menu, luggage, floor tiles and other items salvaged from "the ship of dreams." The exhibit moved from Tropicana to Luxor in 2008, where it will gained a themed bar and a replicated bow, which can be reached by lifeboat.

Admission: adults $2, seniors $25, children 4-12 $20, children 3 and under free. Daily 10 a.m.-10 p.m.

TOURNAMENT PLAYERS CLUB LAS VEGAS

9851 Canyon Run Drive, Las Vegas, 702-256-2000; www.tpc.com/lasvegas

Codesigned by PGA legend Raymond Floyd, the Canyons features short fairways and rough that's consistent but tough. The course hosts the Las Vegas Senior Classic on the PGA's Champions Tour each year. There are fairway bunkers on many holes to penalize golfers for hitting errant tee shots, and the greens make it challenging to get your approach shots close enough to have consistent birdie opportunities. It's a difficult course, but one that shouldn't be missed.

VEGAS INDOOR SKYDIVING

200 Convention Center Drive, Las Vegas, 877-545-8093;
www.vegasindoorskydiving.com

This indoor simulation skydiving gig is not for the faint of heart. First, you watch a video and sign a lengthy disclaimer. Then you step into a one-piece jumpsuit, put on your flight goggles and enter the chamber. Once inside an instructor works with you as you lie, facedown, on what feels like metal fencing. Then they start the DC-3 propeller, and it makes enough wind (up to 120 mph) for you to float. So if the thought of jumping from an airplane is too terrifying to stomach, you can still experience the (simulated) thrill of freefall at this unique attraction.

First flight $75, second flight on same day $40. Minimum weight to fly is 40 pounds. Daily 9:45 a.m.-8 p.m.

VIA BELLAGIO

Bellagio Las Vegas, 3600 Las Vegas Blvd. S., Las Vegas, 702-693-7111;
www.bellagiolasvegas.com

Overlooking the Bellagio lake where the famed fountain show blasts off throughout the day, Via Bellagio offers a wide selection of luxury shopping options. When you seek out the roster here—Hermès, Dior, Prada, Giorgio Armani, Gucci, Tiffany & Co., Yves Saint Laurent, Chanel and Fendi—you can pretty much guarantee that dropping a wad of benjamins won't be hard to do. After browsing the shops of Via Bellagio, head to the Via Fiore shops outlining the Conservatory and Botanical Gardens. For luminous artwork, Chihuly offers paintings and original glass blown by artist Dale Chihuly, who created the glass chandelier in the hotel's lobby. Or put a bit of beauty in your yard with a decorative gift from the Giardini Garden Store. If you're a sucker for hotel gear, visit Essentials, which sells Bellagio-themed clothing, accessories and gifts. Not only can you pick up the typical tourist t-shirt, but there are hand towels and other household items to show off the tasteful places you've been to in your travels.

Daily 10 a.m.-midnight. Essentials: Daily 24 hours.

WYNN GOLF COURSE

3131 Las Vegas Blvd. S., Las Vegas, 888-320-7122; www.wynnlasvegas.com

With its $500 fee (summer rates are less expensive), you would hope that this golf outing includes a down payment on a car, but no. Just the links. Built in 2003, Wynn Golf Course actually has a historic reputation. It's located on the former Desert Inn Golf Club site that for 50 years hosted PGA, Senior PGA and LPGA tournaments. Nearly 1,200 of the 50-year-old trees still stand on the 7,042-yard par-70 course, which was designed by Tom Fazio and Steve Wynn. A 37-foot waterfall is just one of the many water details that meander throughout the course. Wynn has something of the Midas touch when it comes to development, and Wynn Golf Club is no exception (hence, the 500 smack-ers). To emphasize its exclusivity, the course was previously open to Wynn hotel guests and invited visitors only, though that requirement was lifted in November of 2007.

WYNN LAS VEGAS ESPLANADE

Wynn Las Vegas, 3131 Las Vegas Blvd. S., Las Vegas, 702-770-7000, 888-320-7123; www.wynnlasvegas.com

Since opening in 2005, Wynn has added even more luxury to its list of high-end boutiques. Some of the most exclusive names in haute couture have found a home in Wynn's elegant Esplanade. Owner Steve Wynn first brought high-end shops to Las Vegas when he opened the Bellagio more than a decade ago, and he's continued that trend in his eponymous luxe resort. Elaine Wynn secured many of the big names to round out what might just be the most upscale shopping in the world concentrated in one spot. Shops include Las Vegas' first Oscar de la Renta boutique fashion store, Alexander McQueen's second shop in the U.S., Manolo Blahnik, as well as Vertu, the luxury-phone creator that starlets covet (at up to $20,000 each), Louis Vuitton, Cartier and more. Even if you can't afford any of the retail, the Wynn Esplanade is worth the trip for its beauty. Skylights bathe shoppers in soft, natural light in this high-ceilinged posh palace, and stained-glass accents round out the experience.

Sunday-Thursday 10 a.m.-11 p.m., Friday-Saturday 10 a.m.-midnight.

SPECIAL EVENTS

JUSTIN TIMBERLAKE SHRINERS HOSPITALS FOR CHILDREN OPEN

Tournament Players Club at Summerlin, 1700 Village Center Circle, Las Vegas, 702-873-1010; www.tpcatsummerlin.com

All proceeds of this tournament benefit the Shriners Hospitals for children. October.

WRANGLER NATIONAL FINALS RODEO

Thomas & Mack Center, 4505 S. Maryland Parkway, Las Vegas, 719-593-8840, 888-388-3267; www.prorodeo.com

For 10 days in December, the Old West rides into Las Vegas with a round up of events, including bull riding, calf roping, barrel racing and steer wrestling. Only the top 15 money winners per event on the Professional Rodeo Cowboys Association competitive circuit earn the right to compete in this championship event, vying for millions in prize money. Despite being somewhat of a novelty act, this rodeo is one of the most sought-after tickets in Vegas. Ten days in early December.

WORLD SERIES OF POKER

Las Vegas, 702-382-1600; www.worldseriesofpoker.com

The number of competitors in this tournament has increased dramatically from fewer than 100 in the early days to more than 7,000 in recent years. The prize money has climbed proportionally to $20 million, more than $7.5 million of which the champion pocketed in 2005. A wide variety of games are played, and anyone age 21 or older can enter the competition, which continues for five suspenseful, nerve-wracking weeks.

May-July.

WHERE TO STAY
★★★BALLY'S LAS VEGAS
3645 Las Vegas Blvd., Las Vegas, 877-603-4390; www.ballyslv.com
If Vegas conjures images of showgirls, then look to Bally's, which offers the quintessential showgirl sensation, Donn Arden's Jubilee! Like the show, Bally's epitomizes classic Vegas with its center-Strip location and traditional-style guest rooms (think floral bedspreads instead of duvets). The beige-on-beige décor can feel a bit dated, but the rooms are comfortable and the floor-to-ceiling windows provide nice views of the Strip. The North Tower rooms have been renovated more recently, so be sure to specify when you book. Eight tennis courts (illuminated for night play) and access to two nearby golf courses motivates those who thought they'd spend all their time at the pool (which is a great option, especially if you squeeze one of the luxe cabanas). Movie buffs may remember Bally's as the spot where Nicholas Cage and the Flying Elvis' skydivers landed in the film Honeymoon in Vegas.
2,814 rooms. Restaurant, bar. Tennis. Fitness center. Pool. Spa. Business center. $$

★★★★BELLAGIO
3600 Las Vegas Blvd. S., Las Vegas, 702-693-7111, 888-987-6667;
www.bellagiolasvegas.com
With its world-class art offerings—from the Chihuly glass sculpture over-looking the lobby to the masterpieces gracing the walls of The Bellagio Gallery of Fine Art—the Bellagio continues to hail as the class act of the Strip. Water is the element of choice here, with the magical Fountains of Bellagio, Cirque du Soleil's awe-inspiring water-themed performance O, and five beautifully manicured courtyard pool areas. The guest rooms continue the aquatic adventure with Italian marble deep soaking tubs and glass-enclosed showers. If the water's got you "pruned," dry off in a luxurious terrycloth robe and slip between the triple-sheeted linens for a rest. Flat-screen TVs, a fully stocked minibar and electronic drapes round out the contemporary décor. For those looking to raise the stakes, the Bellagio Tower suites flaunt deep, dark wood furnishings, extra-spacious floor plans and a striking panoramic view of the city.
3,421 rooms. Restaurant, bar. Fitness Center. Pool. Spa. Business center. $$

★★BILLS' GAMBLIN' HALL & SALOON
3595 Las Vegas Blvd. S., Las Vegas, 702-737-2100, 866-245-5745;
www.billslasvegas.com
Formerly the Barbary Coast Hotel & Casino, Bill's Gamblin' Hall & Saloon is named for casino impresario Bill Harrah and offers a small casino-hotel experience with a Gold Rush theme amid the mega resorts of the central Strip. Recreation amenities are limited, but you have access to the tennis courts, spa and a fitness center and the pools next door at the Flamingo if you can pull yourself away from the low-minimum tables. Guest rooms are small and somewhat dated, but they embrace a style reminiscent of the Old West and still find a way to incorporate plasma TVs and high-speed Internet access. For a real kick, reserve the John Wayne Suite; purple padded ceiling panels, detailed French doors and antique furnishings that look like they were plucked straight from Lily Munster's parlor can only add to your Sin

City experience. All in all, Bill's offers a casual, fun (and cheaper) alternative to the mega-wattage found front and center on the Strip.
198 rooms. Restaurant, bar. $

★★★CAESARS PALACE
3570 Las Vegas Blvd. S., Las Vegas, 702-731-7110, 866-227-5938;
www.caesarspalace.com
With a name like Caesars, you'd expect a bit of Roman excess—but that's an understatement, considering the Palace's 85 acres, 26 restaurants, five (soon to be six) towers and three pools. Your only problem will be deciding where to go first. The original circular casino is still popular and offers a 14,000-square-foot poker room and a Pussycat Dolls-themed area with go-go dancers performing in bronze cages. No matter which of the towers you retreat to, your room is guaranteed to give a lesson in tasteful opulence with plush linens, modern décor, LCD TVs (including one embedded in the bathroom mirror) and oversized walk-in showers with dual rain showerheads. A sixth tower, the Octavius, is expected to open soon with 665 guest rooms that include the latest in amenities. Until then, the Augustus Tower has the newest and most up-to-date rooms, with views of the Garden of the Gods pool complex or the Strip.
3,289 rooms. Wireless Internet access. Restaurant, bar. Fitness center. Pool. Spa. Business center. $$

★★EMBASSY SUITES LAS VEGAS
4315 Swenson St., Las Vegas, 702-795-2800, 800-362-2779; www.embassysuites.com
Embassy Suites is all about consistency; if you've stayed at an Embassy Suites in the past, you know what to expect: a free cooked-to-order breakfast, complimentary happy hour and a separate bedroom and sitting area in each room. This particular Embassy Suites was recently renovated and also offers flat-screen TVs, work spaces with ergonomic chairs and sleek black and tan décor. The hotel is across from über-hip Hard Rock, the University of Nevada, Las Vegas campus and close to the gay-friendly district nicknamed "the Fruit Loop," if you're looking to ditch your computer for a night.
220 rooms. Complimentary breakfast. Restaurant, bar. Fitness center. Pool. Business center. $$

★★★★ENCORE LAS VEGAS
3131 Las Vegas Blvd. S., Las Vegas, 702-770-7000, 877-321-9966;
www.wynnlasvegas.com
The newest resort in Steve Wynn's luxury Vegas repertoire, Encore delivers the same exceptional service and class as its flagship property with more of a boutique vibe. The casual elegance of the décor is both playful and intimate, from the vibrant red chandeliers in the casino to the alluring golden buddha in the spa to the signature butterfly motif fluttering throughout the property (said to portend good luck). Guest suites are awash in neutrals, reds and blacks, and have floor-to-ceiling windows with views of the Strip, swiveling flat-screen TVs and limestone and marble baths. With five restaurants onsite, your taste buds will want for nothing. An evening at Sinatra will have you crooning between bites of house-made pasta, while Botero is sure to have you seeing food as a higher art form. The spa gets top billing in Las Vegas

with 37 treatment rooms in which to enjoy a transformation ritual or fusion massage. And if the tables have been good to you, leaving you money to burn, book a VIP table at XS, one of Vegas' hottest nightclubs, where a wading pool and a ten-foot rotating chandelier over the dance floor are just part of the experience.

1,767 rooms. Restaurant, bar. Business center. Fitness center. Pool. Spa. $$$$

★★FLAMINGO LAS VEGAS

3555 Las Vegas Blvd. S., Las Vegas, 702-733-3111, 888-902-9929; www.flamingolasvegas.com

The Flamingo was Bugsy Siegel's dream project realized when it opened in 1946 and according to legend, the name comes from the long legs of his showgirl girlfriend, not the bird itself. Still, six-foot flamingos flank the European-style "GO" pool, while the newly renovated Flamingo Go Rooms feature retro furnishings that include white vinyl headboards and splashes of Flamingo pink throughout the space—chromophobes might be more comfortable in the less colorful deluxe rooms. Go rooms have also been updated with the latest in high-tech devices, such as iPod docking stations, flat-screen HDTVs and motorized drapes.

3,460 rooms. Restaurant, bar. Fitness center. Tennis. Pool. Spa. Business center. $$

★★★★FOUR SEASONS HOTEL LAS VEGAS

3960 Las Vegas Blvd. S., Las Vegas, 702-632-5000, 877-632-5000;
www.fourseasons.com

Tranquility isn't a word often used to describe the Las Vegas Strip, but it can be found at the Four Seasons. Located on floors 35 through 39 of the Mandalay Bay resort, this non-gaming hotel has its own entrance, restaurants and a pool with attendants at the ready to provide the requisite Evian spritz, fresh fruit and chilled water. They'll even provide you with a swimsuit to keep in case you hadn't planned on taking a dip during your trip. The elegance of the hotel extends to the guest rooms, which start at 500 square feet of luxury with down duvets and pillows, floor-to-ceiling windows overlooking the city and twice-daily housekeeping service. If this sybaritic lifestyle ever gets stale, Mandalay Bay's 135,000-square-foot casino is downstairs, and then it's back upstairs to your tranquil quarters.

424 rooms. Restaurant, bar. Fitness center. Pool. Spa. Business center. Pets accepted. $$$$

★★★GOLDEN NUGGET HOTEL AND CASINO

129 E. Fremont St., Las Vegas, 702-385-7111, 800-846-5336; www.goldennugget.com

More than $160 million has been spent on renovations to the Golden Nugget since it was purchased by the Landry's Restaurants company in 2005, and now the hotel—which originally opened in 1946 and retains its Gold Rush-kitsch design—is the closest thing to a Strip-style property in the downtown area. The most striking addition is the hotel's Tank pool, which features a 200,000-gallon aquarium filled with sharks—no more dangerous than the poker variety you'll find in the casino—and a 30-foot waterslide that runs right through it. You won't find any fresh flowers in your room, but if you're staying in the North or South Towers, the tacky floral prints on the bedspread and drapes will surely make up for it. Try to snag a room in the newly refurbished Spa Tower suites instead. These rooms run 1,500 square feet on two levels and offer whirlpool baths, floor-to-ceiling windows, wet bars and even a shoeshine machine. Before getting cozy at the tables, pay a visit to the hotel's "Hand of Faith," a gold nugget found in 1980 with an estimated worth of $425,000 and a weight of 61 pounds, 11 ounces.

1,915 rooms. Restaurant, bar. Fitness center. Pool. Spa. Business center. $$

★★★HARD ROCK HOTEL CASINO
4455 Paradise Road, Las Vegas, 702-693-5000, 800-473-7625; www.hardrockhotel.com

If you've never jammed on air guitar in your basement, the charms of The Rock may be lost on you. This rock 'n' roll-themed hotel is awash in memorabilia, but it's the rockers themselves (plus actors, models and sports stars) who really pull in the crowds. A center for stag parties, the Hard Rock attracts a moneyed 20-something set that's eager to hang out at the Tahitian-style pool wearing as little as possible. The standard guest rooms offer Bose stereo systems, plasma TVs, lots of plush linens and French doors that open onto either a pool or a mountain view. The 1,300-square-foot Celebrity Suite features a lounge area with a circular couch, a wet bar and a pool table, while the Penthouse ups the ante even more by adding a single-lane automated bowling alley and a mosaic hot tub with a view of the Strip.

713 rooms. Restaurant, bar. Fitness center. Pool. Spa. Business center. $$

★★★HARRAH'S HOTEL & CASINO LAS VEGAS
3475 Las Vegas Blvd. S., Las Vegas, 800-214-9110; www.harrahslasvegas.com

Bill Harrah opened his first bingo parlor in Reno in 1937, but never lived to see his eponymous hotel-casino open in the middle of the Las Vegas Strip (it would have been a long wait; Harrah's opened as a replacement for the Holiday Casino in 1992). The rooms are pretty much what you'd expect from a hotel built in the early nineties (muted colors, standard-issue furniture) but they're spacious and clean, and some even have Nintendo (just don't expect Wiis). The most updated rooms are in the Mardi Gras Tower, but even these are frill-free. The Carnaval theme spills out onto the street, where the outdoor Carnaval Court Bar & Grill offers a stage with live bands, a busy bar featuring "flair" bartenders and blackjack tables (on weekends).

2,550 rooms. Restaurant, bar. Fitness center. Pool. Spa. Business center. $

★★★JW MARRIOTT LAS VEGAS RESORT & SPA AT SUMMERLIN
221 N. Rampart Blvd., Las Vegas, 702-869-7777, 877-869-8777; www.marriott.com

When the JW Marriott first opened in Summerlin in 1999, it was one of the only hotels in the town, a suburb better known for its golf offerings and proximity to Red Rock Canyon. The resort is only a 20-minute drive from the Strip, but you'll have little reason to stray. The hotel has its own restaurant row with everything from Italian to Asian to Irish, 54 acres of gardens, an 11,000-square-foot pool with a cascading waterfall and a 50,000-square-foot casino (which caters to locals who prefer it to the tourist-trodden gaming rooms on the Strip). If you have yet to realize that square footage is no object here, the 40,000-square-foot spa, 100,000 square feet of function space and

11 championship golf courses, including the TPC Las Vegas, should do the trick. The oversized guest rooms range from 560 to 1,950 square feet and offer views of the garden, the Strip or the surrounding mountains. Marble bathrooms with Jacuzzi tubs and separate rain showers, walk-in closets, ceiling fans and triple-sheeted beds make the time spent in your room nearly as enjoyable as that spent outdoors.

545 rooms. Restaurant, bar. Fitness center. Pool. Spa. Business center. $$$

★★★LAS VEGAS HILTON

3000 Paradise Road, Las Vegas, 702-732-5111, 888-732-7117; www.lvhilton.com

The place where Elvis Presley broke concert attendance records, the Hilton is now home to Barry Manilow's Ultimate Manilow: The Hits show and even has a shop selling Manilow collectibles, including a bottle of wine emblazoned with his face. Sports fans should enjoy the Hilton's Race and Sports SuperBook, which is considered one of the best in town for those who love putting bets down on everything from ponies to pugilists. The guest rooms have been recently renovated with a neutral color scheme, contemporary furnishings and new beds. If you can, upgrade to a premium room, which has high-end linens and plasma TVs. Business travelers no longer have to worry about perspiring through their suits, thanks to the addition of a skybridge connecting the hotel to the Las Vegas Convention Center.

3,000 rooms. Restaurant, bar. Fitness center. Tennis. Pool. Spa. $$

★★★LUXOR

3900 Las Vegas Blvd. S., Las Vegas, 702-262-4444, 888-777-0188; www.luxor.com

Boasting the world's brightest beam of light, the Luxor is becoming even brighter with a much needed makeover of the formerly tired rooms. The hotel's 30 stories are serviced by "inclinators" that run at a 39-degree angle in each corner of the pyramid. The décor is contemporary and simple with warm colors, Egyptian-themed bedspreads and work spaces—just watch your head when you're near the window (that slanted wall will get you every time). The rooms in the twin 22-story towers are larger and offer better views of the city lights with floor-to-ceiling (non-slanted) windows. Luxor has jumped on the Cirque bandwagon, opening the newest Cirque du Soleil show featuring magician Criss Angel. The LAX Nightclub is one of the sultriest spots on the Strip.

4,405 rooms. Restaurant bar. Fitness center. Pool. Spa. Business center. $

★★MAIN STREET STATION CASINO BREWERY & HOTEL

200 N. Main St., Las Vegas, 702-387-1896, 800-465-0711; www.mainstreetcasino.com

The Main Street Station is located, appropriately, on Main Street where it connects with Fremont at the beginning of the Fremont Street Experience. The hotel has a Victorian theme and is filled with unique artifacts that include Buffalo Bill Cody's private rail car, a fireplace from Scotland's Prestwick Castle and a piece of the Berlin Wall (found in the men's bathroom off the casino floor). Guest rooms have been recently renovated with a few of the same Victorian touches as the casino, including sconces and dark mahogany headboards. The rooms are still basic and can feel cramped.

406 rooms. Restaurant, bar. Pool. $

★★★MANDALAY BAY RESORT AND CASINO

3950 Las Vegas Blvd. S., Las Vegas, 702-632-7777, 877-632-7800;
www.mandalaybay.com

From the 14-foot-high salt-water aquarium in the lobby to the 11-acre Mandalay Bay Beach, which includes 2,700 tons of real sand, waves and a lazy river, this hotel offers more than most Las Vegas resorts for non-gamblers. Families traveling with kids are big business for Mandalay Bay, but the hotel covers the adult playground concept, too, with THEhotel at Mandalay Bay, a boutique-style hotel-within-a-hotel that has a separate entrance, check-in and spa. And why not? Space isn't an issue at this mega-resort, which almost feels like a small city—a city with its own 135,000-square-foot casino, 1.8 million-square-foot convention center and 12,000-seat event center that hosts everything from boxing to Beyoncé. The guest rooms recently got a facelift and now are outfitted in classic neutral tones, chic modern furnishings and enormous marble baths. You can even pick your room—maybe an unobstructed Strip view, or one with a spa tub, or perhaps a room with a "playpen couch" that allows for face-to-face seating.

4,752 rooms. Restaurant, bar. Fitness center. Pool. Spa. Business center. $$

★★★LAS VEGAS MARRIOTT SUITES LAS VEGAS

325 Convention Center Drive, Las Vegas, 702-650-2000, 800-228-9290;
www.marriott.com

A smoke-free non-gambling hotel set directly across from the Las Vegas Convention Center, the Las Vegas Marriott Suites offers a convenient location for those attend-ing a conference. The adjacent Monorail Station affords easy access to several stops along the Strip for those who simply can't resist throwing down a few chips between meetings. Some of the newly renovated guest rooms have separate living and sleeping areas, while all offer work stations with high-speed Internet access, cotton-rich linens and custom duvets. Essentially, this is a very pleasant stay for those who want to be in Vegas without really being in Vegas.

278 rooms. Restaurant, bar. Fitness center. Pool. Business center. $

★★★MGM GRAND HOTEL & CASINO

3799 Las Vegas Blvd. S., Las Vegas, 702-891-7777, 877-880-0880;
www.mgmgrand.com

With more than 5,000 hotel rooms in four 30-story towers, 170,000-square-feet of casino space and a 6.6-acre pool complex, the MGM takes the "Grand" in its name seriously. Even the entrance looms large with its icon, a 45-foot-tall, 100,000-pound bronze lion (the largest bronze statue in the country), greeting guests from atop a 25-foot pedestal. Guest rooms vary based on the tower, but all include comfortable pillow-top mattresses, oversized bathrooms with marble vanities and work spaces. Rooms in the West Wing have been recently renovated and up the ante with Bose Wave radios, sleek modern furnishings and flat-screen TVs in the bathrooms. It's nearly impossible to choose from more than a dozen signature restaurants onsite, but Joël Robuchon should be at the top of any foodie's list.

3,044 rooms. Restaurant, bar. Fitness center. Pool. Spa. Business center. $

★★★MONTE CARLO RESORT AND CASINO

3770 Las Vegas Blvd. S., Las Vegas, 702-730-7777, 888-529-4828;
www.montecarlo.com

As the name suggests, Monte Carlo is all about the suave sophistication of the Riviera. Water takes center stage with a 21,000-square-foot pool, waterfalls, a lazy river and wave pool. And when the desert sun gets the best of you, retreat to one of the private cabanas, complete with a flat-screen TV, radio, phone and refrigerator. The Lido-like atmosphere carries into the monochromatic guest rooms with cherry wood furniture and Italian marble baths. For a more spacious experience, upgrade to a Monaco suite and enjoy a clean, modern design with black chrome and shades of gray, dark brown and white—essentially what you'd expect if you were to spend your holiday in Monte Carlo. New restaurant offerings include the BRAND Steakhouse, and for the all-nighter crowd, there's a 24-hour Starbucks in the lobby. The recently opened Hotel 32 occupies the top floor of the Monte Carlo and offers VIP airport transport service and sleek suites stocked with HDTVs and iPod docking stations.

5,044 rooms. Restaurant, bar. Pool. Fitness center. Spa. Business center. $$

★★★NEW YORK-NEW YORK HOTEL AND CASINO

3790 Las Vegas Blvd. S., Las Vegas, 800-689-1797, 866-815-4365;
www.nynyhotelcasino.com

Only in Las Vegas can the Big Apple be so accessible. Best known for its checker-cab roller coaster, New York-New York whirls guests through the city's most recognizable monuments, including the Empire State Building and the Statue of Liberty, in a matter of minutes. Guest rooms are given appropriate names like Park Avenue and Broadway Deluxe, which offers nearly 450 square feet of space and includes marble counter tops and a glass tub enclosure. When space is available, you can upgrade to a spa suite for a nominal fee. Entertainment options run the gamut from dueling pianos at the Bar at Times Square to Cirque's "sensual" show, Zumanity to rockin' djs at the ROK Vegas nightclub.

2,024 rooms. Restaurant, bar. Fitness center. Pool. Spa. Business center. $$

★★THE ORLEANS HOTEL & CASINO LAS VEGAS

4500 W. Tropicana Ave., Las Vegas, 702-365-7111, 800-675-3267;
www.orleanscasino.com

The Big Easy is the inspiration for this off-Strip hotel-casino-convention center, with giant Mardi Gras masks decorating the lobby and the Canal Street steakhouse among the dining options. Though the rooms are basic and unremarkable, they do contain touches of French Quarter charm, like floral bedspreads and gilded mirrors. But with many entertainment options, you'll have little reason to stay in your room. In addition to headliners like Steve Miller Band and Gladys Knight, Orleans also books its share of comedians, from Bill Maher to the Smothers Bothers. There is an 18-screen movie theater, a 70-lane bowling center and shuttle service to Orleans' sister hotel, the Gold Coast.

1,862 rooms. Restaurant, bar. Fitness center. Pool. Spa. Business center. $$

★★★PALMS CASINO RESORT

4321 W. Flamingo Road, Las Vegas, 702-942-7777, 866-942-7777; www.palms.com

Home to MTV's Real World: Las Vegas and Bravo's Celebrity Poker Showdown, the Palms is known for its Hollywood-hip credentials—and for its themed "fantasy" suites. Sports fans will enjoy the Hardwood Suite, which has its own basketball court, or Kingpin Suite, which offers two regulation bowling lanes. The Palms has also revived the classic Playboy Club, which includes a lounge and gaming venues and Playboy Bunnies wearing both vintage and updated Roberto Cavalli-designed attire. It's the closest thing you can get to a Sunset Strip hotel in Las Vegas, and it hits home with the 30-something hipster crowd. The three-acre pool complex features an air-conditioned gaming area and a catwalk for swimsuit shows. The Palms Place tower has 599 condominium suites (many of which are available to rent as hotel rooms) and is attached to the Palms by the SkyTube, an elevated, enclosed moving walkway (to avoid that oppressive desert heat).

703 rooms. Restaurant, bar. Fitness center. Pool. Spa. Business center. $$

★★★★THE PALAZZO RESORT HOTEL CASINO

3325 Las Vegas Blvd. S, Las Vegas, 702-607-7777; www.palzzolasvegas.com

One of the newest kids on the block—if a megaresort with more than 3,000 rooms can be considered a kid—this sister property of the Venetian opened in January 2008 at an estimated cost of $1.9 billion. The guest rooms in the 50-story tower start at 720 square feet and are decorated in a contemporary Italian style complete with remote-controlled Roman shades and curtains to block out that searing desert sun. The rooms also offer Egyptian linens from Anichini and have been reviewed by a feng shui master for proper energy flow (always good to have before hitting the slots). The Shoppes at Palazzo has more than 50 stores, including an 85,000-square-foot Barneys New York, with the New York vibe continuing in the Broadway musical Jersey Boys in the Palazzo Theater. Celebrity chefs such as Mario Batali, Wolfgang Puck, Emeril Lagasse and Charlie Trotter have all opened signature restaurants here, bringing with them a hip crowd of hungry, happy revelers.

3,066 rooms. Restaurant, bar. Fitness center. Pool. Spa. Business center. $$

★★★PARIS LAS VEGAS

3655 Las Vegas Blvd. S., Las Vegas, 877-603-4386; www.parislasvegas.com

With a half scale version of the Eiffel Tower (built using Gustav Eiffel's original drawings) dotting the skyline, Paris Las Vegas offers a Vegas version of the City of Lights. Francophiles will be either entranced or dismayed (the bar at the sports book is called Le Bar du Sport). The 34-floor tower is modeled after Paris's Hotel de Ville (the city hall) and features guest rooms ranging from 750 to 4,180 square feet in size and decorated using European-style furniture and fabrics in warm colors. The 85,000-square-foot casino is surrounded by Paris street scenes and features a ceiling painted to emulate the city's sky. At 100 feet up, the Eiffel Tower Restaurant offers skyline views of the Strip, while the street-side Mon Ami Gabi supplies a great vantage point for the Bellagio fountains.

2,916 rooms. Restaurant, bar. Fitness center. Pool. Spa. Business center. $$

★★★PLANET HOLLYWOOD RESORT & CASINO

3667 Las Vegas Blvd. S., Las Vegas, 702-785-5555, 866-919-7472;
www.planethollywood.com

Previously the Aladdin, this hotel brings La La Land to Sin City. Focused on the cult of celebrity, there is plenty of movie memorabilia to go around in the rooms decorated in shades of black and white with red highlights. Three acres of gaming include the Playing Field race and sports book and the Pleasure Pit, which features lingerie-clad blackjack dealers presiding over the tables as go-go dancers frolic around them—we never said this was family-friendly. Restaurants include Koi (a paparazzi favorite in Los Angeles) and the Strip House from New York. A newly constructed all-suites luxury tower is schedule to open in 2010.

2,916 rooms. Restaurant, bar. Fitness center. Pool. Spa. Business center. $$

★★★THE PLATINUM HOTEL & SPA

211 E. Flamingo Road, Las Vegas, 702-365-5000, 877-211-9211;
www.theplatinumhotel.com

With no gaming and a no-smoking policy throughout the hotel, the sleek Platinum would seem almost anti-Vegas. But that doesn't mean it isn't hip. The guest rooms, which run between 900 and 2,200 square feet, are all residential-style suites and include living rooms, gourmet kitchens, sound systems, double vanities and whirlpool tubs in the bathroom and private balconies offering views of the Strip or the nearby mountains. Chef Tim Perkins oversees the restaurant, which is on the fifth floor and adjoins a lounge and pool deck area with outdoor fire pits and cabanas.

255 rooms. Restaurant, bar. Fitness center. Pool. Spa. Business center. $$

★★★RED ROCK CASINO, RESORT & SPA

11011 W. Charleston Blvd., Las Vegas, 702-797-7777, 866-767-7773;
www.redrocklasvegas.com

A favorite among local hipsters, the Red Rock is located in the Summerlin neighborhood, which had been known more for its golf courses and proximity to Red Rock Canyon (hence the name) than its dinging slot machines and thumping nightclubs. That all changed when the Red Rock opened in 2006. Roomy suites provide a respite from the gaming scene, with dark chocolate-brown tones and oversized, overstuffed pillows. Ask for a room facing the canyon for a spectacular sunset view. Grab a drink at the Cherry Nightclub or throw a few rocks at the 72-lane Red Rock Lanes bowling center. With its suburban locale, Red Rock can afford to spread out, claiming three acres of space for the pools, including 19 private cabanas and the Sand Bar offering refreshing drinks.

814 rooms. Restaurant, bar. Fitness center. Pool. Spa. Business center. Pets accepted. $$

★★★RIO ALL-SUITE HOTEL AND CASINO

3700 W. Flamingo Road, Las Vegas, 866-746-7671; www.playrio.com

Although the Rio has an Off-Strip location that prohibits you from casino-hopping, you'll find there's plenty to keep you occupied here. People-watching takes the top spot on the list, thanks to the hundreds of sunglass-donning, stone-faced players flocking to the World Series of Poker tournaments. Penn

& Teller entertain nightly and the Village Seafood Buffet gets high marks—as does the new adults-only pool that is open to the public (but charges a cover) and features DJ Madam Malixa spinning Top 40 and hip hop throughout the day. The guest rooms are all suites and while the décor leaves something to be desired, you'll have plenty of room to spread out with more than 600 square feet of space.

2,522 rooms. Restaurant, bar. Fitness center. Pool. Spa. Business center. $$

★★SANTA FE STATION HOTEL & CASINO

4949 N. Rancho Drive, Las Vegas, 702-658-4900; www.santafestationlasvegas.com

There's nothing quite like staying at the Station. Located on more than 38 acres in northwest Las Vegas just off U.S. 95, the Santa Fe Station is popular with locals for its 16-screen movie theater and 60-lane bowling alley. A recent expansion added a new race and sports book, updated restaurants and lounges and additional meetings and convention space. You get what you pay for when it comes to the guest rooms, but there are pillow-top mattresses and wireless Internet access.

200 rooms. Restaurant, bar. Pool. Business center. $

★★★★THE SIGNATURE AT MGM GRAND LAS VEGAS

145 E. Harmon Ave., Las Vegas, 877-612-2121; www.signaturemgmgrand.com

Luxury properties have been popping up along the Las Vegas Strip for years, so it should come as no surprise that one of Sin City's biggest players has an über-luxe offering all its own. The Signature at MGM is associated with the palatial MGM Grand Las Vegas in name and proximity only (although guests do get access to all MGM Grand amenities). The seductive, all-suite three-tower hotel has no casino, and a no smoking policy, to ensure a relaxing getaway atmosphere for its guests. Whether you book a junior suite or a gargantuan two-bedroom, you'll be treated to a deluxe king-sized bed, 300-count Anichini cotton sheets, a marble and granite bathroom with dual sinks and a spa tub, a kitchenette with Sub-Zero stainless steel appliances and wireless Internet throughout. But the perks go beyond the guest rooms; a 24-hour concierge is there to attend to your every request, private fitness centers for Signature guests only are outfitted with the latest state-of-the-art equipment and each tower boasts its own private pool with cabanas and cocktail service, so you'll never be vying for that last chaise lounge. From the moment you enter through the grand private entrance, you'll be whisked away to a pleasantly un-Vegas Vegas experience.

1,728 suites. Restaurant, bar. Fitness center. Pool. Business center. $$$

★★SILVERTON CASINO LODGE

3333 Blue Diamond Road, Las Vegas, 702-263-7777, 866-946-4373;
www.silvertoncasino.com

It's not clear whether this is the first Bass Pro Shop connected to a casino-hotel or the first casino-hotel connected to a Bass Pro Shop (a 165,000-square-foot Bass Pro Shop at that), but either way, it's a first and allows those who feel more comfortable with a rod, bow or gun in hand to also feel at home in Las Vegas. The lobby of the lodge-themed Silverton wouldn't be complete without a deer head hanging from the walls, but it also gives a nod to its Sin City locale with a huge 117,000-gallon saltwater aquarium filled with more than 5,000 tropical fish—and, occasionally, live mermaids—to greet you. A $150 million renovation has upped the ante for this budget oasis, but the rooms are still relatively basic and small. You're guaranteed a good night's sleep, though, since all the rooms boast the same beds used at the Bellagio. 300 rooms. Restaurant, bar. Fitness center. Pool. $

★★★★★SKYLOFTS AT MGM GRAND

3799 Las Vegas Blvd. S., South Strip, 877-711-7117;
www.skyloftsmgmgrand.com

With thousands of guests streaming through the doors of the MGM Grand each day, it can be hard to get personalized attention, which is why the clever people at MGM created Skylofts, an ultra-luxury, stylish boutique hotel within the hotel. Occupying the top two floors of the MGM Grand, Skylofts is the brainchild of designer Tony Chi, and evokes an urban bachelor pad with modern furniture, steam rooms, flat-screen TVs in the bathrooms and custom Bang & Olufsen entertainment systems. A 24-hour butler is at your beck and call, offering everything from lifts from the airport in a custom Maybach limousine to custom chef-prepared gourmet room service. Check-in takes place in the privacy of your own room (rather than in line at the MGM below), a luxury that in Las Vegas is worth its weight in casino chips. 51 suites. Fitness center. Spa. Business center. $$$$

★★★THEHOTEL AT MANDALAY BAY

3950 Las Vegas Blvd. S., Las Vegas, 702-632-7777, 877-632-7800;
www.mandalaybay.com

THEhotel's odd naming convention is just about its only showy, Vegas-style gimmick. This all-suite boutique hotel located within the Mandalay Bay is all about class. Its slicker-than-thou décor (minimalist with Art Deco touches and a Mid-Century Modern aesthetic) seems to have been plucked from the pages of a magazine, and the sizable suites (they start at 725 square feet) feature elegant marble and granite bathrooms, down comforters and 42-inch flat-screen TVs, and stunning views of the Strip and the Las Vegas valley mountains. The clientele isn't far behind, either—you can find young and sophisticated types cutting through the gleaming black-and-white lobby to get to their suite or to Mix, a scenester's dream of a restaurant outfitted in stark white and a canopy of hanging glass globes. It's gorgeous enough to make you forget about any grammatical gambits.
1,117 suites. Spa. Fitness center. Restaurant, bar. $$$

★★★★★TOWER SUITES AT ENCORE

3131 Las Vegas Blvd. S., Las Vegas, 702-770-8000, 877-321-9966;
www.encorelasvegas.com

Taking its cues from its flagship property (and next door neighbor), Tower Suites at Wynn Las Vegas, this exceptional hotel within a hotel delivers the utmost in luxury, making you feel more at home than ever—assuming your home includes panoramic views of the Strip and a flat-screen TV in the bathroom. A private entrance and registration lounge lets you to bypass the mayhem of the casino floor before being whisked up to your hotel room. Suites are cosmopolitan and modern with neutral and black tones, signature Encore artwork and high-tech features such as one-touch climate controls and wireless office equipment. Access to a private pool reserved for Tower Suites guests guarantees that you'll always find an empty chaise lounge with your name on it. Restaurants run by celebrity chefs, an electric club scene and ritzy shopping options on The Esplanade round out the Encore experience. 267 rooms. Restaurant, bar. Fitness center. Pool. Spa. Business center. $$$$

★★★★★TOWER SUITES AT WYNN LAS VEGAS

3131 Las Vegas Blvd. S., Las Vegas, 702-770-7100, 877-321-9966; www.wynnlasvegas.com

Located within Wynn Las Vegas, the luxurious Tower Suites offer not only the ultimate in intimate hotel experiences, but also the amenities to round out the perfect stay (think fine cuisine, high-end shops, an exclusive golf club, a Ferrari dealership). Guests of the Tower Suites enter from the south gate entrance, which means no walking through a casino floor or fighting crowds to get to check-in. Instead, you're greeted by an army of smiling Wynn employees standing at attention to take care of your every desire. Additional amenities include a personal shopper, an exclusive restaurant and a private pool with personal cabanas outfitted with ceiling fans, lounge chairs, mini-bars and flat-screen TVs. Guest rooms have the feel of residential apartments and feature wall-to-wall and floor-to-ceiling windows; automatic drapery and lighting controls; the pillow-top Wynn Dream Bed featuring 100 percent Egyptian cotton linens with a 310 thread count; and enormous bathrooms with soaking tubs, glass-enclosed showers and nightlights under his and her sinks. With more high-end properties opening in Vegas, there's sure to be competition to be the best, but at the moment, this is considered the crème de la crème on the Las Vegas Strip, and it deserves every bit of that title. 296 rooms. Restaurant. Fitness center. Pool. Spa. Business center. $$$$

★★★TREASURE ISLAND (TI)

3300 Las Vegas Blvd. S., Las Vegas, 702-894-7111, 800-288-7206; www.treasureisland.com

While visitors to Treasure Island—now called simply TI—won't find any real pirates here, they will find a unique band of pirates frolicking about the front entrance every 90 minutes from 7 to 11:30 p.m. The free nightly show has been transformed from its earlier, more family-friendly, incarnation into the more adult-themed Sirens of TI, but the swordplay and pyrotechnics are still cool for all ages. The guest rooms have all been renovated to include floor-to-ceiling windows, marble bathrooms and pillow-top beds. A new nightclub from designer Christian Audigier features rhinestone-encrusted skulls and an outdoor terrace facing the Siren show in case you don't want to fight the crowds that gather on the Strip. The hotel's tropical pool provides cabanas and the TI Party Tub, an over-sized hot tub that can hold up to 25 people. 2,885 rooms. Restaurant, bar. Fitness center. Tennis. Pool. Spa. Business center. $$

★★★TROPICANA LAS VEGAS

3801 Las Vegas Blvd. S., Las Vegas, 702-739-2222; www.tropicanalv.com

An affordable alternative to neighboring hotels MGM Grand and New York-New York, the Tropicana delivers a prime location and an old-school Vegas feel at a bargain price. For the novice gambler, the casino offers instruction (in case you want to brush up on your craps skills) and a casual and less-stressful environment in which to learn how to play—not to mention lower minimums. Ask for a room in the Paradise Tower since these tend to be more elegant. If you're more in the mood for a jungle theme, opt for the Island Tower—the rooms have tropical-printed bedspreads and faux bamboo furnishings.

1,876 rooms. Restaurant, bar. Fitness center. Pool. Spa. Business center. $

★★★TRUMP INTERNATIONAL HOTEL & TOWER LAS VEGAS

2000 Fashion Show Drive, Las Vegas, 702-982-0000, 877-878-6711;
www.trumplasvegashotel.com

The newest high-rise to spring from the desert ground, Trump International Hotel & Tower Las Vegas has The Donald's signature gold gilding written all over it—here in the form of the 24-karat gold glass windows that wrap around the 64-story building. Located just off the Strip adjacent to the Fashion Show mall, the non-gaming Trump is another jewel in a neighborhood that also houses Wynn. The condominium suites feature floor-to-ceiling windows offering panoramic views of the city, custom-designed furnishings in warm earth tones that play off the white duvets, and a marble bathroom with a separate shower and jet-stream tub. Not only is the refrigerator custom stocked, but each guest is assigned a Trump Attaché to make sure every whim is granted. If you're curious about what fills the Trump table at home, book a table at DJT, a restaurant that puts many of Ivanka and Donald's favorite dishes on the menu. Otherwise, you can request an in-room chef to prepare a meal in your personal kitchen—which has appliances by Sub-Zero, Wolf and Bosch—and serve them course by course. The Spa at Trump also comes with an attaché, who can customize everything from the infused elixir tonics to the music selections on your iPod.

1,282 rooms. Restaurant, bar. Fitness center. Pool. Spa. Business center. Pets accepted. $$$

226

NEVADA ★★★★

★★★★THE VENETIAN RESORT HOTEL CASINO

3355 Las Vegas Blvd. S., Las Vegas, 702-414-1000, 877-883-6423; www.venetian.com

Built on the former site of the historic Sands Hotel in the center of the Las Vegas Strip, the Venetian takes the idea of a mega-resort to a new level. The Italy-themed property features two towers comprising more than 4,000 suites, more than 1.9 million square feet of meeting space, 80-some-odd stores in its Grand Canal Shoppes and 20 restaurants from celebrated chefs such as Thomas Keller, Wolfgang Puck and Emeril Lagasse. The newest suites are found in the Venezia Tower, which has a separate check-in area and offers access to the private Venezia Garden Pool Deck. But the best part? The bathrooms. Nearly a third of the size of the room itself, each bathroom includes a Roman tub with a separate glass-enclosed shower, marble countertops and intricate gold detailing. Additional amenities include a private work area with fax/printer/copier, dual-line telephone, wireless Internet access and flat-screen TVs in both the bedroom and living room.

4,027 rooms. Restaurant, bar. Fitness center. Pool. Spa. Business center. $$

★★★THE WESTIN CASUARINA HOTEL CASINO & SPA

160 E. Flamingo Road, Las Vegas, 702-836-5900, 866-837-4215; www.westin.com

The Westin Casuarina offers a relaxing Westin experience just a block from the Strip. For businesspeople or meeting-goers, it's a mile from the Las Vegas Convention Center (in one direction) and the convention complex at Mandalay Bay (in the other), to leave you plenty of time to either relax by the pool or rev up your gambling guns before and after your business. The hotel's Heavenly Bed, Heavenly Bath and cool muted tones in the guest rooms and a Westin Kids Club onsite in case you brought the kids along make for a comfortable stay. The 20,000-square-foot casino in the lobby acts as a nice (and not so subtle) reminder that you're still in Vegas.

826 rooms. Restaurant, bar. Fitness center. Pool. Spa. Business center. Pets accepted. $$

★★★★WYNN LAS VEGAS

3131 Las Vegas Blvd. S., Las Vegas, 702-770-7100, 888-320-9966;
www.wynnlasvegas.com

In his most personal resort to date, Steve Wynn has put his name, voice and signature on just about everything you could think of—including an 18-hole golf course attached to the back of the resort, designed by Tom Fazio and Wynn himself. Wynn's penchant for fusing nature, art and luxury is also on display, with flowers and trees, waterfalls and lagoons scattered about the property along with original fine art draping the walls. Resort rooms average 640-square-feet in space (nearly twice as large as standard Vegas hotel rooms) and, like the more expensive rooms in the Tower Suites, include wall-to-wall and floor-to-ceiling windows, the pillow-top Wynn Dream Bed (covered in 100 percent Egyptian Cotton and 300-plus-thread-count sheets) and Desert Bambu bath amenities. Entertainment includes the unique show LE RÊVE ("the Dream") and the Blush Boutique Nightclub overlooking the casino, while shopaholics will enjoy window shopping along the Wynn Esplanade, which also includes a Manolo Blahnik boutique and a Ferrari-Maserati dealership.

2,063 rooms. Restaurant, bar. Fitness center. Pool. Spa. Business center. $$$

ALSO RECOMMENDED
ARIA RESORT & CASINO

3730 Las Vegas Blvd. S., Center Strip, 866-359-7757; www.arialasvegas.com

With more than 4,000 guest rooms and suites, Aria is set to give Vegas's heavy hitters a run for their money, or at least their occupancy levels, when it opens in CityCenter in December 2009. Everything is big at Aria, from the three-story lobby to the gargantuan 215,000-square-foot pool area. Guest rooms will offer modern décor and one-touch technology, controlling everything from the curtains to the room temperature. Entertainment options promise to be equally enticing. The casino will incorporate natural sunlight into its design, and include exclusive high-limit salons for VIP guests. Cirque du Soleil's newest theatrical sensation based on the life of Elvis Presley will find a home here as well, shortly after the hotel opens.

4,004 rooms. Restaurant, bar. Fitness center. Pool. Spa. Business center. Casino. $$$

MANDARIN ORIENTAL LAS VEGAS

3950 Las Vegas Blvd. S., Las Vegas, 702-632-7777, 877-632-7800;
www.mandalaybay.com

The smallest of the new CityCenter hotels, this 47-story, non-gaming hotel promises to deliver the same sophisticated elegance and top-notch service that its namesake properties have been providing for years. When it opens in early December 2009, guests will be awed by the spacious rooms with floor-to-ceiling windows and state-of-the-art entertainment systems. The 27,000-square-foot spa will include 17 treatment rooms with seven couples suites, as well as a fitness center with yoga and Pilates studios. If you'd rather get your exercise outdoors, try one of the hotel's two lap pools before grabbing lunch at the café or one of the premier restaurants onsite.
392 rooms. Restaurant, bar. Fitness center. Pool. Spa. Business center. $$$$

VDARA

3950 Las Vegas Blvd. S., Las Vegas, 702-632-7777, 877-632-7800;
www.mandalaybay.com

Guest suites with open-floor plans, custom-designed artwork and a champagne bar in the spa are just a few of the details that will set this new non-gaming CityCenter property apart from the rest on the Strip. As one of the major players in the massive CityCenter venture, this all-suite hotel, slated to open in December 2009, is modern and luxurious in design (the brainchild of famed architect Rafael Vinoly) with large picture windows and frameless glass-enclosed showers in each of the guest rooms. The Sky Pool and Lounge, occupying space above the entrance to the hotel, is posing to be Vegas' newest twenty-something hotspot with made-to-order cocktails and semi-private plunge pools alongside spa cabanas.
1,495 rooms. Restaurant, bar. Fitness center. Pool. Spa. Business center. $$$

WHERE TO EAT

★★★★★ALEX

Wynn Las Vegas, 3131 Las Vegas Blvd. S., Las Vegas, 702-248-3463, 888-352-3463;
www.wynnlasvegas.com

Perhaps it is the walls lined in mother of pearl and the 22 karat gold sand-casted candelabras at the entrance, or the custom-carved mahogany ceiling and boiserie wood marquetry. Whatever the secret, Alessandro Stratta's namesake restaurant has awed diners and garnered accolades since settling in at Wynn Las Vegas in 2005. The richly appointed dining room is only a hint of the luxury and grandeur that await you on the plate. The cuisine of the French Riviera is what Stratta focuses on, and he executes it with such style and grace you'll think you're in the South of France. You will find entrées such as roasted squab and seared foie gras or olive oil poached kanpachi that concentrate on enhancing natural flavors with subtle touches and aromatic sauces. The seasonal tasting menu, which runs at $185 per person, or $295 if you include wine pairings, travels through seven courses from a tangy heirloom tomato and octopus carpaccio amuse-bouche to a rich Wagyu strip loin with wild mushrooms to a perfectly subtle toasted vanilla custard topped with maple-poached peaches. Service is attentive and pleasant, but not overwhelming. A meal at Alex will certainly be one of those long marathon dining evenings, where you'll likely leave fuzzy from the wine pairings and, above all, pleasantly satiated.

French. Dinner. Closed Sunday-Tuesday. $$$$

★★★ALIZE

Palms Casino Resort, 4321 W. Flamingo Road, Las Vegas, 702-951-7000; www.alizelv.com

André Rochat of Alizé is one of the first star chefs to bring his knives to Las Vegas. His restaurant at the top of the Palms features a 180-degree view of the Strip through 16-foot floor-to-ceiling windows. A two-story wine cellar in the middle of the dining room houses more than 1,700 bottles, with a healthy mix of New World and Old, top dollar price points and affordable finds. The intimate bar isn't the place to sling cosmopolitans or Red Bulls and vodkas; serious spirits await you, including an impressive collection of cognac gathered by Rochat himself. The menu is a study in contemporary French cuisine and elegant presentation with dishes such as escargots Burgogne with garlic herb butter and pan-seared duck breast with sautéed foie gras in a raspberry vinaigrette. Tasting menus are available and are a nice place to start for those being initiated into French fine dining.

French. Dinner. $$$

★★★AQUAKNOX

The Venetian Resort Hotel & Casino, 3355 S. Las Vegas Blvd. S., Las Vegas, 702-414-3772; www.venetian.com

Contrary to what you might think, seafood is big business in the desert, especially at places like Aquaknox, which has its own selections flown in daily. The restaurant lets you know from start to finish that they're serious about underwater delicacies, from the lights bathing the whole space in aquatic blue hues to the water cascading down around the bottles in the wine wall. Though the menu varies between Mediterranean and Asian influences, both treatments take full advantage of beautiful seafood sourced from around the world. Executive chef Tom Moloney's signature fish soup, much more than a solution for leftover scraps, is chock full of the choicest lobster, John Dory, mussels and clams in a fragrant and rich tomato saffron broth.

Seafood. Dinner. $$$

★★★★AUREOLE

Mandalay Bay Resort and Casino, 3950 Las Vegas Blvd. S., Las Vegas, 702-632-7401; www.aureolerestaurant.com

When you come to Aureole, come thirsty. The 42-foot steel and glass wine tower that greets you at the door holds 10,000 bottles of wine and comes complete with "Wine Angel Stewards," servers who float on wires to snag your bottle of choice from the towers. Throw in one of the foremost chefs in American contemporary cuisine and a soaring modern interior, and you've got Aureole. But this restaurant isn't all big names and acrobatic wait staff; there's soul in the cooking, too. Charlie Palmer's menu treats fresh-off-the-farm ingredients with elegance and sophistication, evidenced in dishes such as the scallop sandwiches in a crisp potato crust and monkfish osso buco with chanterelles and pork belly stuffed cabbage. A handheld computer gives you access to the expansive wine list, which is directly sent to the aerialists in the tower. It's worth ordering a bottle just to watch the show, which is part Cirque

du Soleil, part Mission: Impossible.
American. Dinner. $$$$

★★★B&B RISTORANTE

The Venetian Resort Hotel Casino, 3355 Las Vegas Blvd. S., 702-266-9977;
www.venetian.com

It used to be you could only find celebrity chef Mario Batali's restaurants in New York City, but he has expanded to Las Vegas with a few new ventures. B&B Ristorante (the other "B" stands for his partner, winemaker Joe Bastianich) is a small space where you might bump elbows with your neighbors, but the coziness adds to the jovial atmosphere. Batali's menu at this spot is simple, rustic Italian with a gourmet edge. The salumi are a must-try—all are made fresh in house by executive chef Zach Allen or cured in house with the exception of the prosciutto di San Danielle which is imported from Italy. More adventurous options include a light and airy lambs' brain francobolli. A pasta tasting menu is available for those who can't decide which dish to order. The wine list, featuring some Bastianich private label bottles, is extensive, especially as far as—you guessed it—Italian wines go.

Italian. Dinner. Bar. Reservations recommended. $$$

BARTOLOTTA RISTORANTE DI MARE

Wynn Las Vegas, 3131 Las Vegas Blvd. S., Las Vegas, 702-248-3463, 888-352-3463;
www.wynnlasvegas.com

Italian preparations of seafood usually revolve around the freshest fish available treated with the simplest of ingredients. Bartolotta Ristorante di Mare upholds that practice by flying in shellfish and seafood daily straight from the Mediterranean, which means you're most likely getting choices that aren't available elsewhere on the Strip. The warm and friendly waitstaff walks diners through chef Paul Bartolotta's newest creations and can aptly suggest the perfect wine pairing to complete any meal. The elegant dining room overlooks a romantic lagoon, and the mood is further enhanced by dim lighting and sparkling crystal chandeliers. If the weather is nice, and you can secure a table, dine in one of the chic outdoor private cabanas overlooking the lagoon. Serene, quiet and secluded, this intimate space is a breath of fresh air in Las Vegas. Combine the impossibly fresh seafood with the homemade pastas, or opt for a whole fish simply grilled with minimal accoutrement and a glass of wine, and it's the perfect light, yet still decadent, Italian meal.

Italian, seafood. Dinner. $$$

★★BLUE AGAVE

Palms Casino Resort, 4321 W. Flamingo Road, Las Vegas, 702-942-7777;
www.thepalmslasvegas.com

Latin flavors collide with prime raw seafood at the Palms' Blue Agave. Top that off with a margarita made from any one of their 150 tequilas behind the bar and you've got yourself the perfect Mexican meal. The circular bar is festive, with stars hanging from the ceiling, and always draws a crowd (we assume the tequila has something to do with it). Expect bold tastes in almost everything that comes out of the kitchen, from the pastas to the roasted seafood, including our favorite: the spicy lobster, shrimp, crab and scallop

gumbo. Be sure to utilize the chile bar, a wide assortment of fresh chilies and salsas, to add extra heat and even more flavor to your plate.
Mexican. Lunch, dinner, Sunday brunch. $$

★★★BOUCHON
The Venetian Resort Hotel Casino, 3355 Las Vegas Blvd. S., Las Vegas, 702-414-6200; www.bouchonbistro.com
Star chef Thomas Keller has dreamed up his version of a French bistro, and it's appropriately elegant and tasteful, yet completely comfortable (the original is in Napa Valley). The room, designed by Adam Tihany, is spacious and simple, trimmed in dark woods against white walls and brass rails, and feels like an authentic brasserie. The dress code is Las Vegas chic, meaning that just about anything goes. Men in suits sit next to tourists in jeans and flip-flops, and everyone focuses on the simple flavors of the food. It's not about pretentious, tiny eats at Bouchon; it's about a solid meal of bistro standards, from steak frites to roasted lamb in thyme jus. Every dish comes with pommes frites, which is a good thing, since these French fries are revered as some of the best in Las Vegas. A casual brunch on weekends on the patio overlooking the pool and its sunbathers is a good way to get some fresh desert air.
French. Breakfast, dinner, Saturday-Sunday brunch. $$$

★★★★BRADLEY OGDEN
Caesars Palace, 570 Las Vegas Blvd. S., Las Vegas, 877-346-4642; www.caesarspalace.com
Located off the casino floor at Caesars Palace, chef Bradley Ogden's eponymous restaurant, with its décor accented by rich wood, feels a million miles away from the Strip. Ogden is best known for his farm-to-table culinary philosophy, as well as his passion for using organic products from sustainable resources. Though the menu changes seasonally, you can be sure that you're getting the freshest ingredients prepared so that their true flavors shine through. This is definitely an upscale restaurant, but the affable waitstaff makes the experience comfortable, inviting and warm. The menu is an honest reflection of simple American cuisine, so dishes will be ones you recognize. The burger, available at the bar, is often cited as one of the best in Las Vegas. Another mainstay, the twice-baked Maytag blue cheese soufflé—fluffy, rich and savory—is divine and a necessary indulgence every time you find yourself in this dining room.
American. Dinner. $$$$

★★★CARNEVINO
The Palazzo Resort Hotel Casino, 3325 Las Vegas Blvd. S., Palazzo Hotel, Las Vegas, 702-789-4141; www.carnevino.com
If you are equal parts carnivore and oenophile, bring both to Carnevino, a place where you can get a juicy slab of steak and a glass of wine to match it. And while there are Italian dishes on the menu (such as pappardelle with porcini trifolati), made-in-the-Midwest meat is the main attraction. You're guaranteed a good cut, as the steaks are all-natural and free of hormones and antibiotics. The Italian villa-inspired dining room is decked out in dark wood, plump cushions, a marble bar and a big old bronze bull, just in case you didn't know it was a steakhouse. Order the 2005 Nero d'Avola, Planeta

"Santa Cecilia," a reliably good bottle, from the never-ending wine list and share the slightly charred Florentine porterhouse, which is rubbed with sea salt, pepper and fresh rosemary. This succulent steak is one of the highlights of Mario Batali's menu.

Steak, Italian. Lunch, dinner. $$$

★★★CHINOIS

Forum Shops, Caesars Palace, 3500 Las Vegas Blvd. S., Las Vegas, 702-737-9700; www.wolfgangpuck.com

Wolfgang Puck's culinary empire expands all the way into Asian cuisine with Chinois. Located in the middle of the Forum Shops at Caesars Palace, Chinois is elegant and modern, with décor that's a mixture of marble and natural woods with Asian-themed touches. Based on the name, you may think the food would be predominantly Chinese, but Puck takes diners on a whirlwind tour of pan-Asian cuisines, with Thai, Malaysian, Vietnamese and Indian influences. Classic dishes maintain flavors you'll be familiar with but are presented with contemporary flair. General Tso's chicken may be your stand-by at your favorite Chinese restaurant, but at Chinois, you'll find a version made with organic chicken and spiced with Thai chilies and sweet soy. The food at your neighborhood Chinese place may never taste the same again.

Asian. Lunch, dinner. Bar. $$$

THE COUNTRY CLUB

Wynn Las Vegas, 3131 Las Vegas Blvd. S., Las Vegas, 702-248-3463, 888-352-3463; www.wynnlasvegas.com

Down a long hallway far away from the casino, The Country Club feels exactly as it should: exclusive. But that doesn't mean the space is stuffy. With gorgeous views of the waterfalls on the 18th hole of the Wynn golf course, the restaurant has a supper club vibe to it, with dark woods, plaid carpeting and low lighting. The friendly staff makes you feel like a long-standing member from the moment you enter to your last sip of wine. For lunch, you'll find excellent burgers and more casual offerings like a French dip and a grilled hot dog. Dinner is more subdued and slightly more formal, with a variety of steaks, including a charbroiled 20-ounce rib chop and a veal T-bone, making an appearance. If you've ever wanted to feel like you're part of the club, this place is sure to take you there.

Steak. Lunch, dinner, Saturday-Sunday brunch. $$$$

★★★CRAFTSTEAK

MGM Grand Hotel & Casino, 3799 Las Vegas Blvd. S., Las Vegas, 702-891-7318; www.mgmgrand.com

Meat purists will want to sink their teeth into the prime cuts here. Chef Tom Colicchio, who also moonlights as the exacting head judge on Bravo's Top Chef, goes by the philosophy that simpler is better. That goes for the dining room too, which is plainly decorated with wooden tables sans cloth, bare branches in vases and spare bulbs dangling from the ceiling. When it comes to food, Colicchio refuses to let fancy sauces or complicated preparations take away from the meat. But fewer ingredients don't mean fewer choices: You can have your hunk of meat roasted, grilled or braised; you can get cuts from Idaho, New York or Australia; you can opt for corn-fed or grass-fed beef; and you'll have to pick from sizes ranging from six to 32 ounces. A solid option is the Kobe skirt steak, and if you're not a meat fan, go for the shellfish sampler, a tempting platter teeming with fresh chilled lobster salad, Alaskan king crab, oysters and clams. At a back-to-basics joint like this, when it comes time for dessert, stick to the classics and get the sinful chocolate soufflé with espresso ice cream doused with caramel sauce. Steak. Dinner. $$$$

★★★CUT

The Palazzo Resort Hotel Casino, 3325 Las Vegas Blvd. S., 702-607-6300; www.palazzolasvegas.com

Wolfgang Puck's at it again. This time it is in the form of a steakhouse at the Palazzo that some are saying is the best new meat market in Las Vegas. The 160-seat metallic dining room manages to feel simultaneously industrial and warm thanks to well-chosen appointments and lamp-lit chandeliers. In the adjacent bar, sample custom cocktails and dishes from the smaller "Rough Cuts" bar menu. The classic steakhouse offerings are given the Puck treatment, including the use of Wagyu and pure Japanese Kobe beef, but innovative dishes such as double thick pork chop atop an apple and nectarine moustarda allow the chef's true talents to shine through. Other hits from the menu include the Indian-spiced Kobe short ribs, slow cooked for eight hours and finished with a purée of curried corn. Steak. Dinner. $$$$

DANIEL BOULUD BRASSERIE

Wynn Las Vegas, 3131 Las Vegas Blvd. S., Las Vegas, 702-248-3463, 888-352-3463; www.wynnlasvegas.com

Wynn Las Vegas's version of a French bistro is, of course, more than just a simple affair. It involves one of the finest French chefs in the country doing his version of bistro cuisine. Classic, rustic dishes that you'd find in any restaurant in France, including onion soup, mussels or steak frites, are all on this bistro's menu. The signature DB Burger is Boulud's homage to decadence: red-wine braised short rib, foie gras and truffle mixed with ground sirloin and grilled. It's more than a mouthful. Though the room seems to be built for intimate, romantic encounters, there's still a sense of conviviality around the restaurant, promoted by the affable, efficient staff. The Lake of Dreams is just outside the floor-to-ceiling windows, adding a musically driven light and water show to the mix. It all adds up to a brasserie that offers a fine dining experience without the fine dining stuffiness. French. Dinner. $$$$

★★★DAVID BURKE

The Venetian Resort Hotel Casino, 3355 Las Vegas Blvd. South, Las Vegas, 702-414-7111; www.davidburkelasvegas.net

When you enter the bold, sleek purple, red and white dining room and see water cascading from the ceiling into a hand-blown glass sculpture of red branches, you know the food is going to be equally showy. And it is. But this meat mecca offers more than steak; everything from chicken to salmon makes an appearance on the menu. Start with the amazing pretzel-crusted crab cake with confit orange and a touch of poppy seed honey. Then move on to the main event with either the inventive day boat sea scallops Benedict with chorizo oil and lobster foam or the juicy Bronx-style filet mignon of

veal with jack cheese polenta, cipollini onions and tarragon jus. Cap your meal off with the fun cheesecake lollipop tree. Complete with leaves and lollipop branches, the tasty dessert fits right in among the flashy environs.
Contemporary American. Lunch (Monday-Friday), dinner. $$$

★★★DELMONICO STEAKHOUSE
The Venetian Hotel Resort Casino, 3355 Las Vegas Blvd. S., Las Vegas, 702-414-3737; www.venetian.com
Celebrity chef Emeril Lagasse is best known for his talent with Creole cuisine, but Delmonico, his steakhouse concept, takes it to a different level. The dining room, with its high-backed chairs and padded banquettes, vaulted ceilings and track-lighting, is comfortable enough to enjoy the kind of meal Lagasse can provide. The steaks and chops themselves are standard steakhouse fare, but some options, such as bone-in rib eye or a chateaubriand for two, are carved and presented tableside. Don't overlook the appetizers: a Creole boiled gulf shrimp cocktail with a piquant horseradish sauce will call your taste buds to attention. To wash it all down, choose something from their spectacular wine list, which has garnered many awards for its vast and high-quality selections.
Steak, Creole. Lunch, dinner. $$$

★★DIEGO
MGM Grand Hotel & Casino, 3799 Las Vegas Blvd. S., Las Vegas, 702-891-3200; www.mgmgrand.com
With hues of red, pink and orange, Diego's atmosphere is vivacious and sexy, adding excitement to your impending night out. You'll find traditional Mexican flavors and dishes given contemporary twists, such as the Diego carne asada, a rib eye steak marinated in red chile adobo and topped with tequila-laced roasted cactus and tangy onion salsa. Guacamole custom-prepared tableside isn't only entertaining, but tasty, too. With an unparalleled tequila selection, Diego makes going out for a taco a livelier experience. If you're looking for a post-meal, pre-club boost, one sip of the Mexican coffee (with Herradura Reposado tequila, Kahlua and fresh whipped cream) will perk you up.
Mexican. Dinner. $$$

★★★DJT
Trump International Hotel & Tower Las Vegas,2000 Fashion Show Drive, Las Vegas, 702-476-7358; www.trumplasvegashotel.com
It's all about the art of the meal at this handsome restaurant inside Trump International Hotel & Tower. The dining room, with rich colors and intimate seating, recalls the glamour of the 1930s. Upscale and sophisticated contemporary American cuisine blends flavors and cooking styles from France, Asia and the Mediterranean. Even if you can't make a deal like a Trump, you can eat like one—Ivanka's caviar breakfast and the Donald's favorite ice cream sundae are among the selections on the menu.
American. Breakfast, lunch, dinner, Sunday brunch. $$$

★★EMBERS

Imperial Palace Hotel & Casino, 3535 Las Vegas Blvd. S., Las Vegas, 702-731-3311; www.imperialpalace.com

Those looking for a real Vegas steakhouse experience without having to pay exorbitant prices will find great value in Embers—where else could you find escargot for $11? The cozy dining room is comfortable and unfussy, though some might argue plain, and the menu presents classic offerings like shrimp scampi and broiled filet mignon. Steaks are the focus here, whether you go with the Delmonico steak, the petite filet or the lobster tail. Embers may not have the trendiest menu or décor on the Strip, but it delivers with the food. Steak, seafood. Dinner. $$$

★★★EMERIL'S NEW ORLEANS FISH HOUSE

MGM Grand Hotel & Casino, 3799 Las Vegas Blvd. S., Las Vegas, 702-891-7374; www.mgmgrand.com

The restaurant that started the Emeril Lagasse empire in New Orleans now has a home at MGM Grand. The same spunk that Lagasse exudes on television is present in the fun dining room (complete with a 14-foot wrought-iron fish sculpture to greet you at the entrance), even if its namesake chef isn't always behind the burners. Focused heavily on Creole and Cajun flavors, the menu is both home-style and sophisticated, elevating low country cuisine. The seafood gumbo is a standout starter, as is the signature New Orleans barbecue shrimp. A hearty lunch requires little more than the seafood pan roast, which is full of fresh seafood, jambalaya and a butter sauce spiked with Emeril's own herb essence.

Seafood, Cajun. Lunch, dinner. $$

★★★ENOTECA SAN MARCO

The Venetian Resort Hotel Casino, 3355 Las Vegas Blvd. S., 702-677-3390; www.enotecasanmarco.com

Yet another success in the Bastianich-Batali empire—which includes Babbo, Del Posto, Otto and others in New York—Enoteca San Marco excels in serving casual dishes, like small plates and pizzas, made for sharing. There are, of course, more substantial entrées and pastas as well—for those who didn't learn how in kindergarten. The laidback atmosphere is as appropriate for a long, leisurely lunch as it is for a friendly, informal dinner. Very similar to the menu at Otto in New York, this restaurant is best sampled with a slightly adventurous spirit and an appreciation for the quality ingredients and simple Italian cooking that has won Batali so many fans.

Italian. Lunch, dinner. Bar. $$

★★★FIAMMA TRATTORIA & BAR

MGM Grand Hotel & Casino, 3799 Las Vegas Blvd. S., Las Vegas, 702-891-7600; www.mgmgrand.com

This cozy, chic trattoria encourages lingering. Clusters of bamboo form nests of lighting that hang above chocolate banquettes with honey-hued pillows. You'll want to sit near the undulating sculptural wave wall in front of the glass-enclosed, blazing fireplace, a nod to the restaurant's name, which means "flame" in Italian. The menu isn't as contemporary as the décor, but it updates old-school Italian faves. Spaghetti comes with Kobe meatballs, raviolini is stuffed with short ribs and splashed with Barbera wine sauce

and sprinkled with pecorino romano, and gnocchi become puffs of lobster instead of potato. If you're not in the mood for pasta, choose entrées like the involtino di coniglio (roasted rabbit leg) or the brasato (Piemontese braised beef short ribs). Be sure to leave room for the Italian desserts. Cheesecake gelato and basil-lime sorbetto give fresh alternatives to the usual flavors, but a real treat is the crochette, crispy amaretti doughnuts that come with a trio of dunking sauces: chocolate ganache, vanilla bean glaze and strawberry jam. If you can't eat another bite, opt for a glass of Italian wine and huddle in front of the beautiful fireplace.
Italian. Dinner. $$$

★★HACHI

Red Rock Casino, Resort & Spa, 11011 W. Charleston Blvd., Las Vegas, 702-797-7576; www.ilovehachi.com

Modern Japanese has found its way into the suburbs under the capable hands of Nobu alum chef Linda Rodriguez. One of the few female executive chefs at a major property in Las Vegas, Rodriguez' touch can be seen and felt throughout the dining room and in the kitchen. Hachi's décor is both modern and feminine, with Japanese cherry blossoms incarnated not only in photographs on the wall, but also in the form of 2,500 hand-blown glass blossoms hanging from the ceiling. Presentations of dishes are dynamic, yet delicate and thoughtful. Drawing on her training from Nobu as well as cultural influences from Europe and Latin America, the menu offers twists on classics like seafood ceviche with guava-yuzu sauce and seared tuna tataki with warm bacon vinaigrette. With an outstanding sushi selection and amazing hot dishes under her belt, Rodriguez also is willing to do an omakase tasting menu for tables of six or fewer (a must if you have the time). With her making the decisions based on your personal likes and dislikes, you're in good hands.
Japanese. Dinner. $$$

★★HAMADA OF JAPAN

365 E. Flamingo Road, Las Vegas, 702-733-3005; www.hamadaofjapan.com

With three locations close to each other by the Las Vegas Strip, Hamada of Japan must be doing something right. Sure, it might play into the stereotypes of what a Japanese restaurant looks like, in addition to pushing specialty cocktails with names like "Geisha" and "Banzai," but they definitely do traditional Japanese cuisine well, if not a little kitschy. Favorites such as teriyakis, tempura and sushi dinners are popular, and special platters groaning under the weight of seafood or shabu shabu prepared tableside can be ordered for two or more to share. With private, low-seated tatami rooms and teppanyaki dinner grilled tableside, Hamada of Japan is great for groups who want to have a good time during their meal, at a decent price point.
Japanese. Lunch (Monday-Friday), dinner. $$$

★★★JASMINE

Bellagio Las Vegas, 3600 Las Vegas Blvd. S., Las Vegas, 702-693-8166; www.bellagiolasvegas.com

Going out for Chinese has never felt so refined. With a great view of Lake Bellagio, this dining room is regal and elegant with warm pastel tones and glowing chandeliers. Chef Phillip Lo's menu includes traditional Cantonese,

Szechwan and Hunan fare as well as nouveau Hong Kong cuisine. Traditional dishes like hot and sour soup are done with panache. The Maine lobster dumplings with a ginger dipping sauce are excellent, as is the caramelized pork tenderloin. Be sure to specify that you'd like a table by the open windows to ensure an uninterrupted view of the famed Bellagio fountains. Chinese. Dinner. $$$

★★★★★JOËL ROBUCHON

MGM Grand Hotel and Casino, 3799 Las Vegas Blvd. S., Las Vegas, 702-891-7925; www.mgmgrand.com

One of the world's greatest chefs, Joël Robuchon has come to epitomize fine, French cuisine. The intimate dining room is regal, from the black and white tiled entryway to the chandelier in the middle of the room. There is even an indoor patio where a façade of flowing greenery transforms a windowless side room into a classical garden. The 16-course tasting menu will set you back $385, but it's worth it. What makes his food so special is the innovative ways he shows his respect for ingredients. Take Le Caviar Oscietre, one of Robuchon's signature dishes, for example. Elevating the ingredient beyond typical blinis and crème fraîche, he combines thin slices of warm scallops with lime zest, smooth cauliflower cream, avocado and Osetra caviar to create a total sensory explosion of surprisingly complementary textures and flavors. You'd never think to mix these ingredients yourself, but when you bite into his creations, they just make sense. Service may is formal and it's flawless—exactly what you'd expect from a restaurant of this caliber. French. Dinner. $$$$

★★★L'ATELIER DE JOËL ROBUCHON

MGM Grand Hotel & Casino, 3799 Las Vegas Blvd. S., Las Vegas, 702-891-7358; www.mgmgrand.com

It might be safe to call L'Atelier ("workshop" in French) a more casual offering from master chef Joël Robuchon, as a meal here is somewhat more interactive than at the formal Joël Robuchon located right next door. The dining room, decorated in reds and blacks, features an open-air kitchen and counter seating where you can watch chefs prepare your food. No surprise here: The cuisine is all French, and signature dishes include a langoustine fritter with basil pesto and free-range quail stuffed with foie gras. Two tasting menus are available, though you can order à la carte to mix and match your own personal Robuchon experience. French. Dinner. $$$

★★★LAVO

The Palazzo Resort Hotel Casino, 3325 Las Vegas Blvd. S., Las Vegas, 702-791-1800; www.lavolv.com

Before the party people head upstairs to bathhouse-inspired club LAVO, they pre-game with dinner and drinks at this first-floor restaurant. Join the clubbers and order up a bunch of the Mediterranean small plates to share with your party, like the kobe stuffed rice balls with garden peas, mozzarella and spicy marinara; and the ultimate pizza topped with roasted lobster, fingerling potatoes and garlic oil. You'll want to linger with your crew in this dining room; the high ceilings with coned chandeliers, low leather booths and

Moroccan tables make it a cozy social spot. But soon the lure of the dance floor above will get the better of you, and you'll make your way to the gorgeous glass-and-wood-screened bridge flanked with ancient Turkish sinks that leads to the thumping club.

Mediterranean. Dinner. $$$

★★★★LE CIRQUE

Bellagio Las Vegas, 3600 Las Vegas Blvd. S., Las Vegas, 702-693-8135, 866-259-7111;www.bellagiolasvegas.com

The original Le Cirque in New York City is legendary because the food is spectacular, and because the service, often led by family patriarch Sirio Maccioni himself, is stellar and welcoming, not stuffy and snobby. Le Cirque at Bellagio holds to the same principles. Maccioni's sons are Las Vegas residents these days, and they can be seen daily at Le Cirque, running the restaurant to the same exacting standards as its East Coast sibling. In the vibrantly colored, circus-tent-like dining room, expertly executed French cuisine is served. Le Cirque's signature dish, the potato-crusted sea bass with a red wine reduction, lives up to its reputation as an outstanding offering. The three-course, $98 prix fixe menu is a smart choice.

French. Dinner. Closed Monday. $$$$

★★★MARCHÉ BACCHUS

2620 Regatta Drive #106, Las Vegas, 702-804-8008; www.marchebacchus.com

You don't have to be relegated to the Strip to find excellent French bistro fare. Marché Bacchus, located in the community of Summerlin 10 miles from downtown, is a perfect way to get a feel for just how good the locals have it here. The restaurant is part wine shop, part restaurant, and diners can select from the shop's 950 labels and have the bottle with their meal at only $10 over the retail price. The outdoor patio sits alongside one of the city's many man-made lakes, and cooling misters and rustic trellises offer a nice respite from the Vegas heat. Executive chef Jean Paul Labadie recently joined the restaurant after stints as head chef at Emeril's in the MGM Grand and Table 10. Labadie's menu features French bistro favorites such as croque monsieur sandwiches, steak frites (which they call "La Bavette de Bacchus") and baked escargot in garlic herb butter. With a selection of wine platters offering everything from imported cheeses and olives to pâté and French salami, Marché Bacchus is also a stellar pick if you're looking to get out of dodge for an afternoon.

French. Lunch, dinner, Sunday brunch. $$$

★★★★MICHAEL MINA

Bellagio Las Vegas, 3600 Las Vegas Blvd. S., Las Vegas, 702-693-7223, 877-234-6358; www.bellagiolasvegas.com

Tucked behind the Bellagio's stunning Conservatory, Michael Mina feels like a nice little secret. The restaurant is the perfect storm of design and cuisine, from its chic décor with floor-to-ceiling blond wood shelves to its innovative menu and equally sleek wine collection. Michael Mina, one of the few restaurants on the Strip that does a vegetarian tasting menu, is well-known for its tasting trios, which feature a singular product presented three different ways, ideal for those who want to expand their palates. Ingredients such as

boneless Colorado rack of lamb, American Kobe rib eye and Nantucket Bay scallops get Mina's signature trio treatment. Seafood also factors in heavily on this menu, done primarily in the style of contemporary California cuisine. If you have a soft spot for foie gras, order a dish of whole foie gras which is carved tableside and proves as savory for the eyes as the taste buds. Michael's signature root beer float, a swimmingly icy blend of sassafras ice cream and root beer sorbet, seals the deal on this American classic.
Contemporary American. Dinner. $$$$

★★MING'S TABLE
Harrah's Las Vegas, 3475 Las Vegas Blvd. S., Las Vegas, 702-369-5000, 800-214-9110; www.harrahslasvegas.com

Sometimes you just need a break from the latest in fusion cuisine. For hearty classics, head to Ming's Table. The restaurant provides a casual and authentic Chinese dining experience in a comfortable setting. The bright room takes on a minimalist mystique with a few Asian accents tossed about, but the food is decidedly authentic Chinese. We're not talking cutting-edge cuisine here, but the traditional dishes are still local favorites, and include crab Rangoon, roast duck with plum sauce, Peking duck, spicy hot and sour soup, and kung pao shrimp and scallops. If you're familiar with the more adventurous dishes, Ming's Table serves dan dan noodles and shark's fin stir fried with black bean or ginger scallion sauce. Sushi and Southeast Asian cuisine is also available, but the Chinese fare is definitely the way to go.
Asian. Lunch, dinner. Closed Wednesday-Thursday. $$$

★★★★MIX IN LAS VEGAS
Mandalay Bay, 3950 Las Vegas Blvd., Las Vegas, 702-632-9500; www.mandalaybay.com

Alain Ducasse's artful restaurant atop THEHotel at Mandalay Bay offers one of the most stunning views of the Strip. Walking into the restaurant is truly like entering into a modern art museum with its sleek, white décor and enormous chandelier, made of 15,000 hand-blown Murano glass balls. With the glitter of the lights of the Mandalay Bay sign outside the windows and surrounded by the glass bubbles, you'll feel like you've entered a flute of champagne. The chic design of the restaurant is reflected on the plate as well. American cuisine is interpreted using contemporary haute French technique, producing dishes such as lobster salad served with a tangy apple and vegetable mosaique, and surf and turf made with halibut and foie gras rather than the standard lobster and steak.
French. Dinner. $$$$

★★★N9NE STEAKHOUSE
Palms Casino Resort, 4321 W. Flamingo Road, Las Vegas, 702-933-9900; www.n9negroup.com

It may feel like a nightclub when you walk in, complete with loud, thumping music and a modern metal décor lit by blacklights, but if you can get past the trendy aspect, you're in for a good meal. Starters such as the N9NE rock shrimp are always fun to munch on, and are served in a carnival-style cardboard box with two dipping sauces. Prime aged steaks are expertly done, and sides, such as macaroni and cheese and loaded baked potatoes, are above average. There's a high likelihood of a celebrity sighting here as sports stars like to come before heading out to the big parties. So if part of your Vegas experience includes a solid steak and some star gazing, you'd better get used to the pulsating house music.

Steak. Dinner. $$$

★★★NOBHILL TAVERN

MGM Grand Hotel & Casino, 3799 S. Las Vegas Blvd., Las Vegas, 702-891-7337; www.mgmgrand.com

As Michael Mina's culinary homage to San Francisco, Nobhill is one of the great contemporary American restaurants on the Strip. Many ingredients on the menu are sourced from the Bay Area and all over the country, including poultry and organic produce. Nobhill Tavern offers Mina's "trio concept," which offers guests the choice of proteins prepared in three different and unique ways. Ingredient selections include shellfish, poultry, greens, American Kobe beef, finfish and caviar. Try one of Mina's specialties, like the San Francisco cioppino with steamed shellfish, tomato broth and basil oil, or chicken and dumplings served with roasted cauliflower, carrots and baby leeks. Finish with desserts such as a pecan-praline sundae or apple crisp with cinnamon ice cream. The restaurant's design takes its cues from the best Bay City spots, complete with dark wood accents, intimate booths and a soothing, earthy color palette.

Contemporary American. Dinner. $$$$

★★★NOBU

Hard Rock Hotel, 4455 Paradise Road, Las Vegas, 702-693-5000; www.hardrockhotel.com

There's sushi in Las Vegas, and then there's Nobu. One of the pioneers of modern Japanese cuisine, chef Nobu Matsuhisa takes traditional Japanese ingredients and technique and applies to them the knowledge he acquired while working in South America. There may now be about 20 versions worldwide of Matsuhisa's original restaurant, but this outpost at the Hard Rock Hotel is particularly welcoming, with calming green walls behind bamboo stalks, small birch trees and an onyx-tiled sushi bar. The yellowtail sashimi with jalapeños simply melts in your mouth and the lobster salad includes a spicy lemon dressing that will kick-start any meal. You know that black cod with miso that you find on every menu in every trendy Japanese restaurant across the country? This is one of Matsuhisa's original signature dishes, and there's nothing quite like the original.

Japanese. Dinner. $$$

OKADA

Wynn Las Vegas, 3131 Las Vegas Blvd. S., Las Vegas, 702-248-3463, 888-352-3463; www.wynnlasvegas.com

Japanese cuisine is traditionally elegant, precise and simple, and the food served at Okada at Wynn Las Vegas falls in line with those aesthetics. The dining room has an excellent flow to it (if you're thinking feng shui), and is accented by blond woods and natural stone, with a giant window offering a view of the waterfall just outside. Sushi is the main attraction, with expert sushi chefs behind the bar preparing some of the freshest raw fish available in Las Vegas. Teppanyaki-style cooking is also a good bet, but don't expect

these chefs to theatrically clang their knives against the grill—this is a much more reserved forum, ideal for group dinners.
Japanese. Dinner. $$$

★★OLIVES

Bellagio Las Vegas, 3600 S. Las Vegas Blvd., Las Vegas, 702-693-7223, 877-234-6358;
www.bellagiolasvegas.com

Celebrity chef Todd English is best known for his take on rustic Italian and Mediterranean cuisine. His dim and sexy, Jeffrey Beers-designed restaurant at the Bellagio overlooks the famed fountains, and features outdoor patio seating for those wanting an even closer look. Like the original Olives in Boston, the menu focuses on the best of his Italian cooking, including brick-oven flatbreads and pastas made in-house. The brick oven roasted chicken with avocado purée and fried polenta is particularly tasty and surprisingly light. This is one of those restaurants that is not only consistent every time you have a meal at the same outpost, but state to state as well. The waitstaff is upbeat and knowledgeable, so they feel like family, and strive to help you feel the same way.
Mediterranean. Lunch, dinner. $$$

★★OSTERIA DEL CIRCO

Bellagio Las Vegas, 3600 S. Las Vegas Blvd., Las Vegas, 702-693-8150;
www.osteriadelcirco.com

The famed Maccioni family may have made their mark with French cuisine in New York, but at Osteria del Circo, they return to their Italian roots with a Tuscan menu inspired by their matriarch, Egidiana Maccioni. Circo is referred to as the more "casual" sister to Le Cirque next door, but it's still fine dining in our book. The whimsical, colorful décor adds an air of playfulness, making the ambience less stuffy. The menu may look intimidating but in reality, this is pure, honest Italian food at its best. Simple preparations of seafood, such as grilled sea bass served with fennel, cherry tomatoes and zucchini, are presented with style and elegance, allowing the flavors of each dish to shine. If you think all pizza is created equal, forgo the heartier dishes and opt for pizza alla crema bianca, which incorporates Norwegian smoked salmon, onions, capers, crème fraîche and American caviar into a clay oven-baked, thin-crust masterpiece. Overlooking Lake Bellagio, Circo makes you feel as if you're on Lake Como itself, complete with the authentic Tuscan aromas streaming from the kitchen.
Italian. Dinner. $$$

★★★THE PALM

Forum Shops, Caesars Palace, 3500 Las Vegas Blvd. S., Las Vegas, 702-732-7256;
www.thepalm.com

Vegas bigwigs love The Palm. It has that classic steakhouse vibe and a staff that remembers your name. But you don't have to be a bigwig or a regular to enjoy a meal here. There are no frills, no fancy presentations, just hon-est-to-goodness solid steakhouse fare, as well as some traditional Italian-American dishes, staying true to the original New York City concept. The veal scallopini with Milanese, piccata or Marsala sauce is one of the best Italian dishes you'll find in Nevada (though competition drops off once you

leave the Strip). If you're more inclined for a steak, you're in good company. The 32-ounce prime rib for two is fantastic; smaller appetites are well sated with the 9-ounce filet mignon. And since you were always taught to eat your vegetables, a side of creamed spinach balances out the meal.
Steak. Lunch, dinner. $$

★★PEARL
MGM Grand Hotel & Casino, 3799 Las Vegas Blvd. S., Las Vegas, 702-891-7380; www.mgmgrand.com
True elegance and sophistication is what Pearl exudes in both its traditional menu and minimalist, but stunning décor. With red lanterns hanging from the ceiling, black lacquered tables and serene blue walls surround the dining room, it demonstrates a combination of modern and classic Asian aesthetics. Here you'll discover that Chinese food is more than egg foo young and General Tso's chicken. Live seafood is exceptional, dispatched only before it's going to be cooked, and prepared simply to allow the ingredients' true flavors to surface. If you're not ready to take the plunge with live fare, signature (and more recognizable) items, such as spider prawn dumplings and roasted Peking duck, showcase the chef's talent for Cantonese and Beijing cuisine.
Chinese. Dinner. $$$

★★★★PICASSO
Bellagio Las Vegas, 3600 Las Vegas Blvd. S., Las Vegas, 702-693-7223, 866-259-7111; www.bellagiolasvegas.com
Only in Las Vegas can you sit and eat a full meal among priceless works of art by a legendary artist. Picasso, with its stunning view of the Fountains of Bellagio, is by far one of the most elegant and awe-inspiring dining rooms in the world. And if all the Picassos surrounding you aren't enough, culinary artist Julian Serrano prepares his own masterpieces for you to enjoy. The sublime degustation and prix fixe menus are predominantly French and Spanish influenced, and the wines, with more than 1,500 selections to choose from, are sourced exclusively from European vineyards. The menu changes almost daily based on what's fresh each morning. If you can catch the pan-seared sea scallops with potato mousseline and leeks, you're in for a flavorful culinary treat.
French, Spanish. Dinner. Closed Tuesday. $$$$

★★PINOT BRASSERIE
The Venetian Resort Hotel Casino, 3355 S. Las Vegas Blvd. S., Las Vegas, 702-414-8888; www.patinagroup.com
As a classically-trained French chef, Eric Lhuillier feels right at home with the traditional brasserie fare on the menu here. The charming space looks as if it came straight from Paris, with its red leather chairs and banquettes, brass rails and wood walls. Like the décor, the bistro menu is comfortable, yet elegant. Dishes such as the roasted chicken with garlic French fries and braised short rib with potato mousseline are comfort foods at their best. If your evenings are already booked up, try Pinot Brasserie for lunch, as there are hearty sandwiches, including a croque monsieur, which hit the right note every time.
French. Breakfast, lunch, dinner. $$$

★★POSTRIO BAR & GRILL

The Venetian Resort Hotel Casino, 3377 Las Vegas Blvd. S., Las Vegas, 702-796-1110;
www.wolfgangpuck.com

Located in St. Mark's Square at the Grand Canal Shoppes at The Venetian, Postrio is a perfect spot to enjoy a casually elegant meal, with some priceless people-watching to boot. The interior of the restaurant is subtle, with intimate booths around the floor and deep red décor. Sitting on the faux patio (you're still inside a mall) allows you to watch not only passers-by, but also the entertainment (in the way of jugglers, singers and musicians) that roams around the plaza. Postrio is Wolfgang Puck's blend of American and Mediterranean cuisine, so expect plenty of fresh flavors and ingredients prepared in unexpected ways. Try the lobster club sandwich; it's one of the best on the Strip. For a heartier dish, opt for the kurobuta pork schnitzel with Austrian potatoes. No matter which main course you get, it's not complete without Puck's famous 13-layer tiramisu with coffee anglaise and chocolate sorbet. American. Lunch, dinner. $$$

★★★PRIME STEAKHOUSE

Bellagio Las Vegas, 3600 Las Vegas Blvd. S., Las Vegas, 702-693-7223, 877-234-6358;
www.bellagiolasvegas.com

A concept by celebrity chef and restaurateur Jean-Georges Vongerichten, Prime delivers a true luxury steakhouse experience. From its plush brown and blue décor to the contemporary art hanging on the walls, the room sings decadence. The menu offers standard steakhouse dishes, but it's the detailed presentation that sets it apart from other steak places. Vongerichten is known for the Asian influences and flavors in his dishes, and he continues this theme in dishes such as grilled diver scallops in a soy-yuzu broth, or filet mignon over shishito peppers. The wine list is impressive, featuring the best of the big reds of California. If you forgot to secure a reservation weeks in advance, try your luck on the outdoor terrace, where you can sample tasty appetizers and desserts without calling ahead.
Steak. Dinner. $$$

RED 8

Wynn Las Vegas, 3131 Las Vegas Blvd. S., Las Vegas, 702-248-3463, 888-352-3463;
www.wynnlasvegas.com

Red 8 is the more casual Asian restaurant at Wynn, offering a wider variety of cuisines, but that doesn't mean it resembles your average Chinese take-out place. The red and black dining room is often bustling, as guests schmooze around cozy booths and polished stone tables. In case there's any doubt left as to the cuisine of choice here, a large red lantern hangs majestically in the middle of the restaurant with tiny lamps around the perimeter of the space. Red 8 offers heartier, more common dishes than its shark's fin-serving counterparts, including Hong Kong-style barbecued beef and soups containing fresh noodles and meaty dumplings. Don't miss the dim sum menu, offering 20 choices of deliciously dense dumplings. And with this more casual dining experience, comes a smaller bill—in case you haven't had luck at the tables. Chinese. Lunch, dinner. $$$

★★★★RESTAURANT CHARLIE

The Palazzo Hotel Resort Casino, 3325 Las Vegas Blvd. S., 702-607-6336;
www.palazzolasvegas.com

Charlie Trotter has long held ranks as one of the chefs who helped define contemporary American cuisine at his eponymous Chicago restaurant. Restaurant Charlie, at the Palazzo, is Trotter's second attempt on the Las Vegas culinary stage since his first restaurant at MGM Grand in the early 1990s. The main dining room, with its high ceilings and contemporary, clean lines, is almost church-like in its hushed silence. The menu is seafood-centric, with hints of Asian influences executed with European technique, evident in dishes like sea bream served with a bright addition of lemon, chile and cilantro, and slow-poached Arctic char enhanced by savoy cabbage and a rich but delicate trout roe and shiso vinaigrette. Bar Charlie, Trotter's restaurant-within-a-restaurant, looks like a sushi bar lined with a team of chefs, but you won't find a rainbow roll on the menu here. The narrow room is serene and calm, and features Japanese-style kaiseki dining with either an eight- or 14-course tasting menu of some of the most divine sushi and sashimi done in Trotter's trademark style.
Seafood, contemporary American. Dinner. $$$$

★★★★RESTAURANT GUY SAVOY

Caesars Palace, 3570 Las Vegas Blvd. S., Las Vegas, 877-346-4642;
www.caesarspalace.com

Located in the Augustus Tower of Caesars Palace, Guy Savoy's only American venture is quiet, cool and sophisticated. Run by Guy's son Franck, you can be assured that you'll get the same quality treatment and meal here that you would at the original Guy Savoy in Paris—minus the Eiffel Tower view. Two tasting menus (one 10-course and one four-course) are available, and both offer Savoy's signature dish of artichoke and black truffle soup, a divine concoction served with toasted mushroom brioche and an earthy truffle butter. For a more casual experience, grab a seat at the Bites & Bubbles bar where you can order smaller tasting portions of the menu.
French. Dinner. Closed Monday-Tuesday. Bar. $$$$

★★★SEABLUE

MGM Grand Hotel & Casino, 3799 Las Vegas Blvd. S., Las Vegas, 702-891-3486;
www.mgmgrand.com

Delicious seafood is the theme at Seablue, one of two Michael Mina-helmed restaurants at MGM Grand. Watch the chefs in the open-air kitchen from the aquatic-themed dining room, complete with water cascading down the walls. The menu changes with the season, and all the seafood is caught wild and flown in daily. The kitchen draws from traditional Mediterranean cooking techniques, including the use of tagines, or Moroccan clay ovens, and simple grilling to make the seafood shine. The Seablue paella is not traditional Spanish paella, but it's loaded with fresh seafood, rabbit and chorizo and finished with a saffron risotto. One of the biggest hits on the menu is the lobster corndog, a luxurious version that puts the original to shame. Delicate lobster sausage is dipped in batter, fried and served with a pungent but refreshing mustard crème fraîche. Not the healthiest option, but how often do you come across lobster corn dogs? Besides, you're on vacation.
Seafood. Dinner. $$$$

★★SHANGHAI LILLY

Mandalay Bay Resort and Casino, 3950 Las Vegas Blvd. S., Las Vegas, 702-632-7409;
www.mandalaybay.com

With long curtains and walls adorned with vintage photos of Chinese beauties, Shanghai Lilly simultaneously examines the past while looking forward to the future. They don't tell you if Shanghai Lilly was an actual woman or not, but the black and white 1920s-era portraits of anonymous ladies hanging throughout the space make you hope she was. The award-winning design of the room was imagined by Tony Chi, who sought to simulate the elegance and ease of ancient Chinese luxury. The Imperial Peking duck is second to none, as are the lobster lettuce wraps. If you're more of a traditionalist, go for the black-peppered beef tenderloin or kung pao chicken; you won't be disappointed. The four private dining rooms, apart from the main dining area, are ideal for a private affair or a special celebration—just book months out because those tables are often hard to nab.
Chinese. Dinner. $$$

★★★SHIBUYA

MGM Grand Hotel & Casino, 3799 Las Vegas Blvd. S., Las Vegas, 702-891-3001;
www.mgmgrand.com

MGM Grand's Japanese restaurant is so much more than just a sushi bar. Taking its name from a popular neighborhood in Tokyo, Shibuya features traditional Japanese cuisine executed with contemporary twists and techniques. The interior is chic and almost clubby; the cool physique of the glass cube wall behind the sushi bar at the entrance is balanced by the appearance of natural woods throughout the space. High quality ingredients make for interesting preparations, including the toro tartare, which features gorgeous tuna belly enhanced with achiote oil and made more decadent with the addition of caviar and gold leaf. If you're feeling adventurous, opt for the live Maine lobster served three ways: the tail as sashimi, the claws as tempura and the rest in a silky miso soup. Boasting the only certified sake sommelier in Las Vegas, Shibuya has the Japanese fine dining experience covered.
Japanese. Dinner. $$$$

STRATTA

Wynn Las Vegas, 3131 Las Vegas Blvd. S., Las Vegas, 702-770-3463;
www.wynnlasvegas.com

Chef Alessandro Stratta's second restaurant at the Wynn is his more casual concept of rustic, regional Italian fare. Red-backed chairs, an open fire hearth and a clear view into the kitchen create an atmosphere that is laid back and welcoming. Formerly known as Corsa Cucina, the restaurant's lounge is a smart place to meet for drinks, and the location makes it an ideal spot to grab a bite before or after catching a show at Wynn. The wood-fired pizzas are great noshes (we particularly liked the Bosco with roasted mushroom purée, white truffle oil and Bel Paese cheese), and the pastas definitely have enough variety to make everyone in your group happy. For a more substantial meal, roasted pork chop stuffed with fontina cheese and prosciutto is heavenly.
Italian. Dinner. $$$

SW STEAKHOUSE

Wynn Las Vegas, 3131 Las Vegas Blvd. S., Las Vegas, 702-248-3463, 888-352-3463;
www.wynnlasvegas.com

SW at Wynn Las Vegas rises above and beyond a classic Vegas steakhouse. You won't find a dimly lit, smoky room here. Instead, an airy dining room opens onto the Lake of Dreams, where light and music shows play nightly. The prime steaks come from corn-fed Nebraskan cows, which result in great tasting beef. Side dishes are where steakhouses always differentiate themselves, and SW's offerings—truffled creamed corn, broccolini, garlic and aged goat cheese, and an excellent potato rosti—are what set it apart. The fairground-gone-luxe funnel cake is a good way to end an indulgent experience—crisp, fluffy funnel cake slices are presented on the branches of a metal tree, served with sauces of crème anglaise, salty caramel and fudge. Steak. Dinner. $$$$

★★★TABLE 10

The Palazzo Resort Hotel Casino, 3327 Las Vegas Blvd. S., Las Vegas, 702-607-6363;
www.emerils.com

Enter the French Quarter-inspired iron gates of Table 10 to get a taste of Emeril "Bam!" Lagasse's Cajun-flavored, seafood-heavy comfort cuisine. Watch all of the action at the Food Bar, which gives you a glimpse of the chefs manning the grills and flitting about the busy kitchen. Watching them cook will make your stomach rumble, so start off with the traditional gumbo with bits of andouille sausage or the crab trinity, a holy union of snow crab cocktail, lump crab rémoulade and jumbo lump citrus onion salad. Keep the fresh-from-the-ocean theme going with the to-die-for lobster dome, with chunks of Maine lobster, sweet corn, mushrooms, leeks and spinach in truffle-sherry cream sealed in a flaky crust. For dessert, get the white chocolate malassadas, doughnut-like cousins to native-to-New-Orleans beignets, with cinnamon sugar and vanilla bean crème anglaise.
Cajun, American. Lunch, dinner. $$$

TABLEAU

Wynn Las Vegas, 3131 Las Vegas Blvd. S., Las Vegas, 702-248-3463, 888-352-3463;
www.wynnlasvegas.com

Don't think you can't secure a table at Tableau just because it's tucked away in the Tower Suites at Wynn. This spacious, airy dining room offers American cuisine for breakfast, lunch and weekend brunch along with prime views of the Tower Suites pool and gardens. You won't find any frou frou nouveau fare here—deep down the menu is meat and potatoes, albeit more elegantly presented. The organic roast chicken BLT sandwich is far from your run-of-the-mill lunch option, with cipolini onions and a warm bacon-shallot dressing. For sweeter palates, the wild blueberry buttermilk pancakes slathered in orange blossom butter is a cure all for hangover headaches. Service is personable and outgoing, but not obsequious. Tableau certainly offers fine dining, but it's not hard to feel comfortable here.
American. Breakfast (Monday-Friday), lunch (Monday-Friday), Saturday-Sunday brunch. $$$$

★★★TAO

The Venetian Resort Hotel Casino, 3355 Las Vegas Blvd. S., Las Vegas, 702-388-8338;
www.taorestaurant.com

Part nightclub, part Asian restaurant, Tao packs crowds in nightly with its alluringly sexy Buddha-filled décor, a koi pond and weathered wood, a harmonious combination of ancient culture and contemporary life. You'll find a pan-Asian menu with elements of Chinese, Japanese and Thai cuisine figuring prominently. Sushi is a good choice, and the menu is heavy on trendy maki creations. Entrées are boldly flavored, but still familiar, including the wasabi-crusted filet mignon. If you want to linger after your meal, head upstairs to the nightclub—it's one of the hottest Vegas spots for bass thumping music and celebrity sightings.

Pan-Asian. Dinner. $$$

★★★TOP OF THE WORLD

Stratosphere Las Vegas, 2000 Las Vegas Blvd. S., Las Vegas, 702-380-7711;
www.stratospherehotel.com

It may not literally be the top of the world, but when the Strip includes the Empire State Building, the Eiffel Tower and the great Pyramids of Giza, it's pretty darn close. Perched atop the Stratosphere, the tallest point in Las Vegas, Top of the World is best known for its revolving dining room, which offers a complete 360-degree view of the city. On a clear day, you can see straight to Nellis Air Force Base, and at night, spy one of the best views of downtown Sin City. You'll find classic continental cuisine on the menu executed with quality ingredients, such as the veal chop served with roma artichoke and mushroom demi-glace. Old favorites like surf and turf are a big hit with diners looking for the optimum "high-end" Vegas dining experience. But in Vegas you get what you pay for, so don't expect the food to be quite as good as some of the celeb-chef haunts down below. Top of the World can also get tourist-heavy, with gawkers wanting to see that perfect view of Vegas.

American, continental. Lunch, dinner. $$$

★★★VALENTINO LAS VEGAS

The Venetian Resort Hotel & Casino 3355 Las Vegas Blvd., S., Las Vegas, 702-414-
3000; www.valentinolv.com

Italian cuisine can either be very humble and rustic, or it can be highly refined and extravagant. Sometimes, however, there is a pleasant blending of the two, and Valentino is it. This signature Venetian spot is spacious and beautifully appointed, and has six private dining rooms in addition to the main rooms, including an intimate wine cellar room that can seat four and an exclusive chef's table for up to six people. The menu is, of course, Italian, concentrating on traditional flavors with elegant presentations. Many ingredients are imported directly from Italy for optimum authenticity in flavor, and the menu changes seasonally. One of the mainstays, the pollo al mattone is a simple, flavorful roast chicken butterflied and cooked flat under a brick, served with a creamy spinach risotto. While you're piling on the carbs, go for the three-color gnocchi with rabbit sausage, mushrooms and a cream demiglace sauce—it's actually lighter than it sounds. The wine list is staggering, with about 2,500 selections, and service is impeccable.

Italian. Dinner, late-night. $$$$

★★★THE VERANDAH

Four Season Hotel Las Vegas, 3960 Las Vegas Blvd. S., Las Vegas, 702-632-5000;
www.fourseasons.com

Four Seasons Hotel Las Vegas is one of those rare spots on the Strip where you don't feel like you're on the Strip at all. Verandah, an open, airy restaurant, with plenty of lush greenery and overlooking the exclusive Four Seasons pool, is a common destination for both ladies who lunch and those looking for a little break from daily Las Vegas shenanigans. Afternoon tea (you can opt for champagne as well), complete with tiered platters of delicate finger sandwiches, scones and pastries, is popular, as Verandah is one of the few places where you can enjoy this genteel activity without the sound of slot machines in the background. Though the restaurant serves breakfast, lunch and dinner, the weekend breakfast buffet, with its create-your-own-doughnut station, is most popular. Instead of focusing on quantity for the masses, the staff delivers quality for those who are smart enough to dine here rather than the cattle calls that can be found at other hotel buffets.

American. Breakfast, lunch, dinner, Saturday-Sunday brunch. $$$

★★VOODOO STEAK & LOUNGE

Rio Hotel & Casino, 3700 W. Flamingo Road, Las Vegas, 702-777-7923;
www.harrahs.com

As if the nightclub at the top of the Rio wasn't enough, you can have a fantastic steak up there as well. Formerly known as VooDoo Café, VooDoo Steak has a more refined menu, with premium reserve and dry-aged beefs as the specialties. With a gorgeous view of the entire Strip, the restaurant features Creole and Cajun bites such as ham and andouille sausage beignets and delta frog legs and mussels. The VooDoo "Menage a Trois," a surf and turf offering of petite filet mignon, prawns and lobster, puts a sexy spin on your meal. Head out on to the terrace for an after-dinner cocktail, but don't look down (the view of the ground below is not for the weak).

Steak, Cajun, Creole. Dinner. $$$

WING LEI

Wynn Las Vegas, 3131 Las Vegas Blvd. S., Las Vegas, 702-248-3463, 888-352-3463;
www.wynnlasvegas.com

The meaning of the Chinese characters that represent Wing Lei is twofold: not only does it mean "forever prosperous" but it also represents "Wynn" itself (Wing in English is "Wynn"). This upscale Chinese offering pulls out all the stops with its decadent menu and French- and Chinese-inspired décor. Red, the color of luck in China, accents the room in the form of curtains and on the backs of chairs, emphasizing the handcrafted black onyx bar in the corner. Chef Richard Chen's menu is a blend of traditional Shanghai, Szechwan and Cantonese cuisines, including a five-course Peking duck extravaganza which starts with Peking duck salad with orange truffle vinaigrette and wild duck soup and carries into pan-seared duck noodles and the famed table-carved roasted duck presentation. The honey glazed barbecue spare ribs with Shanghai pickled cabbage are phenomenal and braised pork belly with twice-cooked tofu and steamed Chilean sea bass are solid entrées. If you simply can't decide (the menu is lengthy), the chef's tasting menu features

seven progressive courses of his greatest hits.
Chinese. Dinner. $$$$

★★★WOO
The Palazzo Resort Hotel Casino, 3325 Las Vegas Blvd. S., Las Vegas, 702-699-8966;
www.woorestaurant.com
Woo—run by mom Ming See Woo, proprietor and chef de cuisine, and son
Peter, executive chef (along with other family members working behind the
scenes)—is the only family-run business in the palatial Palazzo, and the clan
was the only one to receive an exclusive invite from the hotel's president to
set up a kitchen. In that kitchen the family is churning out Chinese cuisine
with Thai and Japanese influences and fresh California ingredients. Take
a seat in the eco-friendly designed dining room, where bamboo sticks line
some walls and hover above the bar, and dive into the fusion goodness with
the delicious cold Alaskan king crab with orange-jicama salsa and the lettuce
wraps stuffed with spicy Thai shrimp bursting with garlic and basil. For entrées, try the juicy lobster atop forbidden Bhutanese rice or the scrumptious
grilled beef tenderloin doused with zesty Mongolian sauce. Of course, true
to Woo's own we-are-family philosophy, everything is served family-style.
Pan-Asian. Lunch, dinner. $$$

JUST OPENED
BOTERO
Encore Las Vegas, 3131 Las Vegas Blvd. S., Center Strip, 702-248-3463;
www.encorelasvegas.com
If you ever doubted the link between food and fine art, an evening spent at
Botero is certain to change your mind. This poolside space is visually stun-
ning with a soaring arched ceiling, padded white columns and, of course, lots
of original works of art by Fernando Botero. Celebrity chef Mark LoRusso
ensures that the food is equally artistic. Ahi tuna tartare is a study in color
and texture with creamy avocado and crispy ginger, while the pinwheel of
wild salmon is almost too pretty to eat. There is no lack of masterpieces
on the dessert menu either. The signature ice cream cupcakes will have you
reminiscing back to your early days, as will the PB & J brioche doughnuts. If
you're in search of a more adult treat (for those looking to start the night off
right), order the 21 & over sorbet.
Contemporary American. Lunch, dinner. $86 and up

SINATRA
Encore Las Vegas, 3131 Las Vegas Blvd. S., Center Strip, 702-248-3463;
www.encorelasvegas.com
Encore's signature restaurant pays homage to Ol' Blue Eyes in more than
name alone. Framed images of the famous crooner line the cream colored
walls and his voice provides a pleasant backdrop for dinner conversation.
Celebrated chef Theo Schoenegger continues the salute with sophisticated
Italian fare fit for the Rat Packer himself. Pastas read simple and straightfor-
ward, though taste anything but. The lasagna Bolognese incorporates veal,
pork and beef between layers of heavenly hand-rolled pasta, and the agnolotti
stuffed with bufala ricotta is surprisingly light and airy. The chicken saltim-
bocca is another sure bet, only improved upon with a side of herb-potato
gnocchi. The intimate dining room is often filled with two-tops looking for a

romantic alternative to the frenzied pulse of Vegas. And what's more romantic than spending a night with Frank?
Italian. Dinner. $86 and up

SWITCH
Encore Las Vegas, 3131 Las Vegas Blvd. S., Center Strip, 702-248-3463; www.encorelasvegas.com
If anything at Encore is kitschy, this restaurant might be it. But as with all things Wynn, even kitsch is done with style, sophistication and a touch of playfulness. The concept behind Switch is that the walls constantly rotate to provide changing ambience throughout your meal. You won't get through dessert without seeing a few repeats, but at that point your full attention will be on your plate, not the walls around you. Chef René Lenger has created a menu that is as animated as the décor. Jumbo lump crab cakes come alongside a quail egg and fried pickles, while the salmon filet is bathed in a champagne sauce. Serious carnivores will appreciate the charbroiled steak selection, and the black truffle creamed spinach is a side worth splurging on. The service is warm and informed, especially on questions regarding the lengthy wine list.
American. Dinner. $86 and up

SPAS

★★★THE BATHHOUSE
Thehotel at Mandalay Bay Resort & Casino, 3950 Las Vegas Blvd. S., Las Vegas, 702-632-7777; www.mandalaybay.com
The Bathhouse makes its home inside Mandalay Bay's boutique sidekick THEhotel, giving the spa a very intimate feel (by Vegas standards, at least). Designed with simple stripped-down European aesthetics in mind, the imposing slate gray walls throughout the space have an almost industrial, gallery-like vibe. Luxuriating in the Jacuzzi pool, for instance, you feel almost as if you've sneaked into a heated museum fountain. Even the Jacuzzi warnings look artistic and cool, printed on the wall in an interesting typeface. Every once in a while, though, a bright, geometric-patterned pillow or flower arrangement offers a pop of color. Crème Brûlée Body Treatments ($145-$205) and Hot Spiced Rum Stone Massages ($95-$215) demonstrate a propensity towards intermingling the senses (taste, smell and touch). If you need to look bikini-ready upon arrival, treatments like the Cell-U-Less Herbal Wrap ($145-205) offer a skin-sucking boost.

★★★★CANYON RANCH SPACLUB
The Palazzo Resort Hotel Casino, 3325 Las Vegas Blvd. S., Las Vegas, 702-414-3600, 877-220-2688; www.canyonranch.com
The newly renovated and expanded Canyon Ranch SpaClub—at 134,000 square feet—is a monster. In fact, as you wander past the impressive Palazzo into the Venetian and towards the neutral-toned spa (festooned with raw organic design elements like bamboo) you'll enter the biggest spa in North America (with more than 100 treatment rooms). Canyon Ranch's wellness reputation—as the foremost pioneer of modern day ultra-luxury health resorts—precedes the Sin City addition (the first Canyon Ranch opened in 1979 in Tucson, Arizona). And it has unveiled something exclusive and

brand new: The Aquavana pre-treatment plunging experience allows lollers to move between invigorating spaces such as a Wave Dream, Salt Chamber, Igloo, Rasul mud room and Snow Cabin, in addition to the usual steam and sauna. No appointment is necessary, as long as you buy a day pass to the spa ($35 or less per pass if purchased for several days). Not for cynics are new-age signatures like Vibrational Therapy ($160), which combines crystal sounding bowls, essential oils, Chakra stone placements, acupoints and negative ionization of the Cavitosonic chamber to balance the body's energy fields. A Yamuna Hands-On Treatment ($200), in which muscles are massaged with a special ball, may offer more tangible satisfaction. And while the fitness center is an afterthought at many spas, Canyon Ranch SpaClub offers holistic wellness programs. The multi-colored climbing wall is also the spa's aesthetic centerpiece, so be aware that if you scale it you might attract some attention.

★★★QUA BATHS AND SPA
Caesars Palace, 3570 Las Vegas Blvd. S., Las Vegas, 702-731-7110, 866-782-0655; www.harrahs.com/qua

Mile-high ceilings and lavish azure décor—mimicking an underwater world—welcome you to Qua Baths & Spa at Caesars Palace. After slipping on your robe, stroll around the corner to the sizeable relaxation lounge. If you're thirsty, head to the Tea Room, where an herbal sommelier will find the perfect concoction to ease you into a mellow mood before your treatment. Signature experiences like the Hawaiian Lomi Lomi ($225) and Chakra Balancing ($275)—with aromatherapy oil dripped onto the third eye (that's "forehead" to you) and energetic stones arranged on your back—may seem a bit far-fetched but are actually very relaxing. "Social spa-ing" is also a priority here and shared amenities truly deliver: Three Roman baths (separate pools ranging in temperature from 76° to 104°) sit poised atop polished stone steps and surrounded by opalescent walls, just waiting for a group to soak and chit-chat. But a favorite is the amazing Arctic Ice Room (best used as cooling relief after a sauna and/or a Laconium steam), where a water and moisturizer mix, posing as snow, falls upon heated seats and floors—a truly refreshing winter wonderland.

★★★★★THE SPA AT ENCORE LAS VEGAS
Encore Las Vegas, 3131 Las Vegas Blvd. S., Las Vegas, 702-770-3900, 877-321-9966; www.encoreasvegas.com

The wow-factor is certainly in play at this ritzy rejuvenation center. Taking pointers from the Spa at Wynn, Encore carries the Asian theme further with glowing gold lanterns, life-size Buddhas and blossoming orchids. The expansive reception area looks like the lobby of a luxury hotel rather than a sterile spa environment (with plenty of pillow-laden couches for lounging), while the locker rooms are unusually bright and airy. The separate men's and women's spaces are sprawling in size, with large saunas and steams rooms, as well as just about any amenity you might need to refresh post-treatment. But it's not just about the décor; technology plays a part as well. State-of-the-art waterfall showers use digital screens to let you control water temperature, water pressure from the six shower heads, and mood lighting, and the personal lockers don't require keys. A transformation ritual might be just what you need after a long losing battle in the casino. Try the lavender stone ritual ($250), which incorporates lavender and sea salt to calm frayed nerves, or the vitamin infusion facial ($200), giving your system a boost of vitamins and collagen to heal damaged skin. The onsite salon offers everything from manicures and pedicures to cuts and colors, as well as a full menu of traditional barbershop services. You can also buy a day pass and enjoy all of the outrageous amenities of the spa without a treatment. It may be the best $30 you spend in Vegas.

★★★★THE SPA AT FOUR SEASONS HOTEL LAS VEGAS
Four Seasons Hotel Las Vegas, 3960 Las Vegas Blvd. S., Las Vegas, 702-632-5000, 800-819-5053; www.fourseasons.com

You'd never know you were in Sin City at The Spa at The Four Seasons Hotel Las Vegas, as there's no casino and, hence, no stroll—on the road to relaxation—through intentionally disorienting chaos. Once you wander into the hotel's tasteful lobby, a representative immediately leads you to your destination. The Spa's subdued décor is seamless. This intimate refuge swathed in mild tones is on the smaller side, so personal attention (in concert with The Four Seasons' usual impeccable service) is a plus. Shuffling to the Zen lounge in one of the city's plushest robes, you sip cucumber water or herbal tea and nibble on an array of treats from dried fruit to pastries. Don't be surprised by the smell of fresh-baked goods either; fresh doughnuts are served in the lobby café, and sinful mini-chocolate muffins are omnipresent in the spa (finally, snacks you can get behind). The Spa's services are some of the most effective and clinical of the Vegas bunch, so you're asked to fill out a health information form at onset. Opt for a unique results-oriented facial like the signature Vitality of the Glaciers ($275), an anti-aging RNA, DNA and collagen treatment that jump starts your cellular metabolism. Think you liked hot rocks on your back? You'll leave the new Everlasting Flower Stone facial ($230), with poppy seed exfoliation, hibiscus extract and rhodochrosite rocks, feeling relaxed.

★★★THE SPA AT RED ROCK
Red Rock Casino, Resort & Spa, 11011 W. Charleston Blvd., Las Vegas, 702-797-7777; www.redrocklasvegas.com

As Red Rock is situated closer to a national park than the Strip, spa services extend outside their casino-adjacent digs and into the great outdoors. "Adventure Spa" activities include horseback riding and rock climbing, as well as location-specific experiences like rafting down the Colorado River and hiking to natural hot springs. Inside, mosaic pebble fountains, a bright red relaxation area with a faux snakeskin centerpiece and a chocolate and turquoise color scheme lend a "boutique" feel to the ultra-modern (yet-retro '60s/mod-style) spa. If you're up for something different, try the Ashiatsu massage ($190), where a masseuse actually suspends from the ceiling to walk on your back, or the Radiance facial ($195), which uses a cinnamon enzyme peel and active protein enzymes to improve skin's elasticity.

★★★★ THE SPA AT TRUMP

Trump International Hotel & Tower Las Vegas,2000 Fashion Show Drive, Las Vegas,
702-476-8000; www.trumplasvegashotel.com

The Spa at Trump International Hotel & Tower is among Vegas' newest, most intimate and, of course, swankiest refuges. A spa attaché guides you through 11,000 square feet of Rain Shower and Eucalyptus steam-laden space to help discern your signature intention: Calm, Balance, Purify, Heal or Revitalize. Special gemstone-infused oil massages ($275) are meant to heal internally and externally—we'll take rubies, emeralds, sapphires and diamonds in any form. To get event-ready, try the Dermal Quench ($250): hydration with oxygen and hyaluronic serum delivered with hyperbaric pressure for extra absorption. Or, for long-lasting benefits, sample the Dermalucent ($150) with LED skin rejuvenation; or a hotel-exclusive Ultimate Kate facial (combining both of the above and a foot massage, $350). Late-night partiers flock to the Morning-After Eye Cure ($50) to refresh before starting the cycle again. Of course, The Donald wouldn't open a spa without some kind of service for luscious locks, so try an Espresso Yourself hair treatment ($95) for damage control.

★★★★★THE SPA AT WYNN LAS VEGAS

Wynn Las Vegas, 3131 Las Vegas Blvd. S., Las Vegas, 702-770-3900, 877-321-9966;
www.wynnlasvegas.com

No need to feel a pang of guilt as you pass exercise bikes between treatments. At The Spa at Wynn, the fitness center sits outside the pampering area, unlike at many other spas. The décor is grand, and the waiting room—adorned with fireplaces—feels plush and regal. You could lounge here on one of the ultra-comfortable couches sipping herbal tea and flipping through magazines for hours post-treatment. The truly gorgeous Jacuzzi room harkens to a mermaid's lair, with its lily pad-covered walls inset with stones, Deluge showers that simulate waterfalls, and a central soaking bath. Exotic Asian- and Middle Eastern-inspired treatments are signatures here, but the real attraction is the ultra-indulgent 80-minute Stone Ritual ($250), a soothing full-body massage using heated stones to melt the knots in overworked muscles. Other treatments include Thai massage, shiatsu, and facials that will do everything from boost the collagen in your visage to impart a glow to tired, dull skin. Male estheticians are plentiful here, so make sure to specify if you have a gender preference. If the views in your room at Wynn are too difficult to pull yourself away from (and at night, they are alluring, no matter which direction your room faces), you can opt to have a massage performed in the privacy of your own retreat. Manicures and pedicures at the onsite salon are performed in comfortable chairs cordoned off by curtains that provide extra privacy. An army of black-clad, top-notch stylists are on hand to offer cuts, coloring and even makeup application, which makes the salon a favorite for visiting brides and their bridal parties celebrating their big day.

★★★★SPA BELLAGIO LAS VEGAS

Bellagio Las Vegas, 3600 Las Vegas Blvd. S., Las Vegas, 702-693-7472, 888-987-6667;
www.bellagio.com

Bellagio's spa is a well-oiled machine, albeit a large machine that runs well thanks to the efficiency of its technology-aided staff, who don headsets to subtly communicate with each other as they whisk you into the spa. Once checked in at the second story spa (having wandered past the full-service salon, enormous manicure/pedicure area and a gentlemen's "Barber Shop"), disrobe and re-robe in the large changing area, then head to the coed waiting area. (At last, you can sit with your significant other before a couple's treatment.) The designers adorned the space with spectacular natural elements like wall-mounted orchid installations complete with waterfalls; enormous terra cotta pots; and backlit jade inlaid in fossilized sandstone floors. An extensive menu offers options from the luscious Deep Coconut Surrender massage ($210), which features lovely scented warm coconut milk drizzled on your back amidst hot stones, to more experimental world treatments like spinal realignment essential oil Raindrop Therapy ($205). But the mosaic Watsu massage ($210) is the spa's major claim to fame: In a large, steamy, sea blue- and green-tiled private space, submerged in 94-degree water, you experience a Zen Shiatsu-technique massage, which some say mirrors the experience of being born.

LAUGHLIN

See also Boulder City

This resort community offers a pleasant change of pace from the glitz of Las Vegas. In many ways, it resembles Las Vegas in its earlier days. Hotels and casinos line the Colorado River, and some provide ferry service to and from parking facilities on the Arizona side. Laughlin offers other diversions such as fishing, waterskiing and swimming in nearby Lake Mohave.

WHERE TO STAY

★★★AQUARIUS CASINO RESORT

1900 S. Casino Drive, Laughlin, 702-298-5111, 888-662-5825; www.aquariuscasinoresort.com

The largest resort on the Colorado River, this enormous property offers activities for every member of the family. Visitors will enjoy the 3,300-seat outdoor amphitheater and 60,000-square-foot casino as well as recently renovated hotel rooms.

1,907 rooms. Restaurant, bar. Spa. Casino. Tennis. Fitness center. Pool. Business center. $

★★DON LAUGHLIN'S RIVERSIDE RESORT HOTEL & CASINO

1650 Casino Drive, Laughlin, 702-298-2535, 800-227-3849; www.riversideresort.com
1,400 rooms. Restaurant, bar. Pool. Casino. $

★★★GOLDEN NUGGET LAUGHLIN

2300 S. Casino Drive, Laughlin, 702-298-7111, 800-955-7278; www.goldennugget.com/laughlin

This resort is like a tropical oasis in the desert. A jungle theme is carried from the rain-forest-inspired lobby to the tropical themed rooms. Tarzan's Night Club completes the illusion.

300 rooms. Restaurant, bar. Pool. Casino. $

RENO

See also Carson City, Incline Village, Virginia City

Reno, "the biggest little city in the world," is renowned as a gambling and vacation center. Between the steep slopes of the Sierra and the low eastern hills, Reno spills across the Truckee Meadows. The neon lights of the nightclubs, gambling casinos and bars give it a glitter that belies its many quiet acres of fine houses, churches and schools. The surrounding area is popular for sailing, boating, horseback riding and deer and duck hunting. The downtown Riverwalk along the Truckee's banks is loaded with coffee shops, art galleries, chic eateries, eclectic boutiques, antique stores, salons and theaters.

WHAT TO SEE

ANIMAL ARK

1265 Deerlodge Road, Reno, 775-970-3111; www.animalark.org

Tucked in the forested hills north of Reno, Animal Ark is not a zoo, but a sanctuary for animals that cannot be returned to the wild. Many were disabled or orphaned, and others were unwanted exotic pets. The residents include big cats (tigers, snow leopards and cougars), gray wolves, black bears and a few reptiles and birds. Each has a name and is presented as an "ambassador" for its species.

April-October, Tuesday-Sunday 10 a.m.-4:30 p.m.

FLEISCHMANN PLANETARIUM AND SCIENCE CENTER

1650 N. Virginia St., Reno, 775-784-4811; www.planetarium.unr.edu

This facility projects public shows on the inside of its 30-foot dome. The museum here also houses all four of the meteorites that have landed in Nevada (including a massive specimen that weighs more than a ton) and scales rigged to reflect the gravity on Jupiter or a neutron star. On cloudless Friday nights, guests can peer through telescopes with members of the Astronomical Society of Nevada.

★★★★★ NEVADA

255

GREAT BASIN ADVENTURE

Rancho San Rafael Regional Park, 1595 N. Sierra St., Reno, 775-785-4064;
www.maycenter.com

Part of the Wilbur D. May Center in Rancho San Rafael Regional Park, Great Basin Adventure consists of several attractions designed to educate and entertain kids. At Wilbur's Farm, pint-sized visitors can take a pony ride or explore the 1½-acre petting zoo. Guests can pan for gold at a replica mine building, with faux mine shafts that double as slides and displays on minerals and the area's mining history.

Tuesday-Saturday 10 a.m.-5 p.m., Sunday noon-5 p.m.

HUMBOLDT-TOIYABE NATIONAL FOREST

1200 Franklin Way, Sparks, 775-331-6444; www.fs.fed.us/r4htnf

At 6.3 million acres, this is the largest national forest in the lower 48 states. It extends across Nevada from the California border in a scattershot pattern, comprising 10 ranger districts that encompass meadows, mountains, deserts and canyons. Just northwest of the Reno city limits, Peavine Mountain is crisscrossed by a number of old mining roads now reserved for hikers and mountain bikers. Other Humboldt-Toiyabe highlights include scenic

SCENIC NEVADA

This tour from Reno, which can be accomplished over one or two days, combines the scenic beauty and recreational opportunities of Lake Tahoe with historic sites from Nevada's mining days. From Reno, go south on Highway 395 to Highway 431 (the Mount Rose Scenic Byway), which heads west and southwest as it climbs to an 8,911-foot pass and then drops down to Lake Tahoe, providing splendid panoramic views of the lake. Continue on Highway 431 to Highway 28 and Incline Village, a good base from which to enjoy the beach, swimming, fishing and the spectacular views at Lake Tahoe Nevada State Park. The beach at the park's Sand Harbor section is delightful—and also very popular. If you're looking for a little more seclusion, opt for Memorial Point and Hidden Beach. Those visiting from late July through August might want to experience the Lake Tahoe Shakespeare Festival, with shows at an outdoor theater at Sand Harbor. Also in Incline Village is the Ponderosa Ranch, a Western theme park where the popular television series Bonanza was filmed from 1959 to 1973.

From Incline Village, continue south on Highway 28 along Lake Tahoe's eastern shore, and then take Highway 50 east to Carson City. Part of the Lake Tahoe Scenic Byway, this route offers panoramic views of the lake and nearby mountains. Carson City, Nevada's capital, is roughly the halfway point of this tour and is a good spot to spend the night. Founded in 1858, Carson City features numerous historic sites, including the handsome state capitol, built in 1871 with a dome of silver. Attractions also include the 1864 Bowers Mansion, built of granite and furnished with many original pieces; the Warren Engine Company No. 1 Fire Museum, where you'll see a variety of historic firefighting equipment; and the Nevada State Railroad Museum, with three steam locomotives and numerous freight and passenger cars.

Now head northeast on Highway 50 to Highway 341, which you follow north to picturesque Virginia City, a historic mining town that had its heyday in the 1870s. Beautifully restored, Virginia City today offers a glimpse into its opulent and sometimes wicked past with historic buildings, a mine and a working steam train. To see the epitome of 19th-century extravagance, stop at the Castle, an 1868 Victorian mansion known for its marble fireplaces, crystal chandeliers and silver doorknobs. Other attractions include Piper's Opera House, which hosted the major stars of the late 1800s, and the Mackay Mansion, built in 1860 as the headquarters of mining magnate John Mackay. To return to Reno, take Highway 341 north to Highway 395 north. Approximately 100 miles.

Lamoille Canyon and the Ruby Mountains, southeast of Elko; the rugged, isolated Toiyabe Range, near the geographic center of Nevada; and Boundary Peak, the state's highest point at 13,143 feet, southeast of Reno on the California-Nevada border.

Monday-Friday.

MEADOWOOD MALL

5000 Meadowood Mall Circle, Reno, 775-827-8451, www.simon.com

The most contemporary shopping center in the region, this is actually the city's most-visited tourist attraction.

Monday-Saturday 10 a.m.-9 p.m., Sunday 11 a.m.-6 p.m.

MOUNT ROSE SKI AREA

22222 Mt. Rose Highway, Reno, 775-849-0704, 800-754-7673; www.mtrose.com

Of all the ski resorts in the Reno-Tahoe area, Mount Rose has the highest base elevation (a precipitous 7,900 feet above sea level), making it the best bet for late-season skiing. Eight lifts, including two six-person, high-speed chairlifts, take skiers and snowboarders to the 9,700-foot summit to 1,200 acres of terrain nearly evenly split among skill levels (20 percent beginner, 30 percent intermediate and 40 percent advanced) and a pair of snowboarding parks. Located northwest of Lake Tahoe, Mount Rose is also known for its excellent beginners' program. There are no on-mountain accommodations. Mid-November-mid-April, daily.

NATIONAL AUTOMOBILE MUSEUM (THE HARRAH COLLECTION)

10 Lake St. S., Reno, 775-333-9300; www.automuseum.org
The brainchild of car collector and gaming titan Bill Harrah, this excellent facility covers more than a century of automotive history in detail. Four galleries house the museum's collection of more than 200 cars: The first gallery details the late 19th and early 20th century (complete with a blacksmith's shop, the garage of the day); the second covers 1914 to 1931; the third, 1932 to 1954; and the fourth, 1954 to modern day. The Masterpiece Circle Gallery in the fourth gallery also accommodates temporary themed exhibits on subjects ranging from Porsches to pickup trucks. The oldest car in the museum dates from 1892, and there are a number of collector's trophies (such as the 1949 Mercury Coupe driven by James Dean in Rebel Without a Cause) and one-of-a-kind oddities (the steam-powered 1977 Steamin' Demon). Monday-Saturday 9:30 a.m.-5:30 p.m., Sunday 10 a.m.-4 p.m.

NEVADA HISTORICAL SOCIETY MUSEUM

1650 N. Virginia St., Reno, 775-688-1190; www.nevadaculture.org
Founded in 1904, this is both Nevada's oldest museum and one of its best. On permanent display is "Nevada: Prisms and Perspectives," which examines the Silver State's five biggest historical stories: the Native American perspective, the mining boom, the neon-lit story of gaming, transportation and the "Federal Presence" (the federal government owns 87 percent of the land). Wednesday-Saturday 10 a.m.-5 p.m.

NEVADA MUSEUM OF ART

160 W. Liberty St., Reno, 775-329-3333; www.nevadaart.org
The only nationally accredited art museum in the entire state, the Nevada Museum of Art would be a top-notch facility no matter where it was located. Perhaps the most distinctive architectural specimen in all of artsy Reno, the curved, sweeping structure is a work of art in and of itself: modern (it opened in 2003) and monolithic (60,000 square feet), evoking the image of the legendary Black Rock of the Nevada desert. The collection housed within is equally impressive, broken into five different themes: contemporary art, contemporary landscape photography (one of the best of its kind anywhere), regional art, American art from 1900 to 1945, and the E. L. Weigand Collection, American art with a work-ethic theme.
Tuesday-Wednesday, Friday-Sunday 10 a.m.-5 p.m., Thursday 10 a.m.-8 p.m.; Galleries closed Mondays and national holidays.

RENO ARCH

Virginia St., downtown Reno

In 1926, Reno commemorated the completion of the first transcontinental highway in North America, which ran through the city en route to San Francisco, with an arch that traverses Virginia Street downtown. Three years later, locals adopted the tagline "the biggest little city in the world" and added it to the landmark. The arch has since been replaced twice, in 1964 and in 1987.

RENO-SPARKS THEATER COALITION

528 W. First St., Reno, 775-786-2278; www.theatercoalition.org

Consisting of more than 20 separate companies in the Reno-Sparks area, this organization is a cooperative effort to market a varied slate of theater, dance and other performing arts. Member troupes range from the avant-garde to the kid-friendly, and the Coalition puts together an up-to-date events schedule for all of them.

SIERRA SAFARI ZOO

10200 N. Virginia St., Reno, 775-677-1101; www.sierrasafarizoo.org

The largest zoo in Nevada, Sierra Safari is home to 150 animals representing more than 40 species. The majority of the animals were selected for the rugged Reno climate, including a Siberian tiger and a number of other felines, but there are also tropical birds, a few reptiles and a number of primates. A petting zoo and a picnic area are onsite.

April-October, daily 10 a.m.-5 p.m.

UNIVERSITY OF NEVADA, RENO

1664 N. Virginia St., Reno, 775-784-1110; www.unr.edu

Established in 1874; 12,000 students. The campus covers 200 acres on a plateau overlooking the Truckee Meadows, in the shadow of the Sierra Nevada Mountains. Opened in Elko, it was moved to Reno and reopened in 1885. Nevada enrolled 16,336 students in fall 2005.

Tours of campus.

W. M. KECK EARTH SCIENCES AND ENGINEERING MUSEUM

Mackay School of Mines Building, 1664 N. Virginia St., Reno, 775-784-4528;
www.mines.unr.edu/museum

Located in the Mackay School of Mines Building, the Keck Museum focuses on the state's mining history. The collection of specimens originated from Nevada's most renowned mining districts—the Comstock Lode, Tonopah and Goldfield—but exotic minerals from all over the world share the space. There are also displays of fossils, vintage mining equipment and a collection of fine silver donated by the family of mining tycoon John Mackay.

Monday-Friday 9 a.m.-4 p.m.

SPECIAL EVENTS
ARTOWN FESTIVAL

Reno, 775-322-1538; www.renoisartown.com

Held annually in July (with a newer holiday counterpart in November and December), Reno's Artown Festival is a monthlong extravaganza that includes more than 200 events and exhibitions and 1,000 artists in all—making it the largest arts festival in the United States. Not surprisingly, it has won its fair share of national acclaim since it launched in 1996. The artists span the disciplines of ballet, opera, theater, film and the visual arts. There are flamenco dancers, comedy troupes and internationally known performers of all stripes not to mention myriad gallery openings and historical tours. Multiple down-town venues host various aspects of the festival. Wingfield Park is the setting of an outdoor film every week. "Rollin' on the River" is a weekly concert series. July.

ELDORADO GREAT ITALIAN FESTIVAL

Fourth and Virginia streets, Reno, 775-786-5700, 800-879-8879; www.eldoradoreno.com

Put on by the Eldorado Hotel and Casino, the two-day event includes several buffets, a farmers market and live entertainment. But the contests, including a spaghetti sauce cook-off, gelato-eating contest for kids and a grape-stomping competition, are the real attraction.

Early October.

HOT AUGUST NIGHTS

1425 E. Greg St., Sparks, 775-356-1956; www.hotaugustnights.net

This retro event pays homage to the 1950s and 1960s. Highlights include a series of concerts by nostalgia acts (past performers have included Chuck Berry, the Turtles, and Jan and Dean) and a classic car parade. There are street dances and sock hops, and casinos get in on the action by awarding a classic car or two to a few lucky winners.

Early August.

NEVADA OPERA

Pioneer Center for the Performing Arts, 100 S. Virginia St., Reno, 775-786-4046; www.nevadaopera.org

Founded in 1967, the Nevada Opera stages several noteworthy operas each year in its fall/spring calendar such as *Carmen* and *Aida*.

NEVADA STATE FAIR

1350 N. Wells Ave., Reno, 775-688-5767; www.nvstatefair.com

A Reno area tradition since 1874, the Nevada State Fair features rodeo events, livestock competitions and a carnival midway. The event also includes a kid-oriented science festival, an aerial motorcycle stunt show and contests for the best homemade pies, cookies and salsa.

Late August.

RENO BASQUE FESTIVAL*Wingfield Park, Reno, 775-762-3577*

Basques from Northern Spain and Southern France immigrated to Nevada's Great Basin in the early 20th century to herd sheep, and they have been a visible part of the Reno community ever since. The Reno Basque Festival started in 1959 with the goal of preserving Basque culture in the United States. Today, it's one of the largest events of its kind in the country, kicked off by a parade that snakes around downtown before coming to a stop at Wingfield

Park along the Truckee River. From there, the festival takes over with food, dancing, singing and athletic competitions. Basque cuisine available for sampling includes sheepherder bread, Basque beans, lamb stew and other hearty staples, and there's also a market. Crowds gather for the traditional games: soka tira (a Basque tug-of-war), woodcutting and weightlifting.
Late July.

RENO FILM FESTIVAL
925 Riverside Drive, Reno, 775-334-6707;
www.renofilmfestival.com
Drawing a handful of celebrities to downtown Reno, this film -festival screens Hollywood productions, independent features, world premieres and retrospective revivals. Movies are shown at various downtown venues (casinos, museums and theaters), and there are also a number of film-related workshops, demonstrations and lectures. June.

RENO JAZZ FESTIVAL
University of Nevada, Reno, 775-784-4046; www.unr.edu/rjf
Held on the University of Nevada at Reno campus since 1963, this three-day event is one of the biggest of its kind, drawing hundreds of school bands (junior high to college) from Nevada, California, Oregon, Idaho and Washington. The top bands and soloists play at a concluding encore performance, and the first two nights are highlighted by sets from nationally known artists.
Late April.

RENO PHILHARMONIC ORCHESTRA
925 Riverside Drive, Reno, 775-323-6393; www.renophilharmonic.com
Reno's symphony orchestra plays a September-to-April Master Classics Series (as well as a July 4th pops concert) at a number of venues in town, with Pioneer Center for the Performing Arts serving as its home stage. The orchestra plays works from composers such as Mozart, Beethoven, Copland and Gershwin. A free one-hour lecture is given immediately beforehand.

RENO RODEO
Reno Livestock Events Center, 1350 N. Wells Ave., Reno, 775-329-3877, 800-225-2277; www.renorodeo.com
Known as the wildest, richest rodeo in the west—with a total purse in excess of $1 million—the Reno Rodeo has been a big event since its inaugural year in 1919. Includes bull riding, barrel racing and roping events.
Late June.

WHERE TO STAY
★★★ATLANTIS CASINO RESORT SPA
3800 S. Virginia St., Reno, 775-825-4700, 800-723-6500; www.atlantiscasino.com
Located about three miles south of downtown, Atlantis is among Reno's top resorts, with several smoke-free gaming areas in the casinos, a top-notch business center and an array of rooms. A highlight is the spa, which offers a variety of treatments using Ahava and Dermalogica products.
973 rooms. Restaurant, bar. Spa. Casino. Pets accepted. $

★★BEST WESTERN AIRPORT PLAZA HOTEL

1981 Terminal Way, Reno, 775-348-6370, 800-648-3525; www.bestwestern.com

269 rooms. Restaurant, bar. Casino. Fitness center. Pets accepted. Pool. $

★★★ELDORADO HOTEL AND CASINO

345 N. Virginia St., Reno, 800-879-8879; www.eldoradoreno.com

Of the casinos in downtown Reno, Eldorado attracts the youngest crowd, thanks to its myriad nightspots, which include a microbrewery with live rock and blues, a martini/piano bar and BuBinga, a popular dance club with DJs and live bands. Eldorado has some of the most updated rooms in town.

17 rooms. Restaurant, bar. Business center. Pool. Casino. $

★★★HARRAH'S HOTEL RENO

219 N. Center St., Reno, 775-786-3232; www.harrahsreno.com

Located downtown next to the Reno Arch, Harrah's Reno is one of the glitziest casinos in the city, a distinction it has held since opening in the early 1960s. The casino is immense and diverse, featuring more than 1,000 slot machines, table games of all kinds and a sports book. Sleek hotel rooms range from standard rooms to skyline suites. There are seven restaurants, including the renowned Steak House at Harrah's Reno. Entertainers work the crowd onstage at Sammy's Showroom, named after Sammy Davis, Jr., who performed here 40 times.

928 rooms. Restaurant, bar. Casino. Pets accepted. Pool. Spa. $

★LA QUINTA INN

4001 Market St., Reno, 775-348-6100, 800-531-5900; www.laquinta.com

130 rooms. Complimentary breakfast. Pool. Pets accepted. $

★★★PEPPERMILL HOTEL AND CASINO RENO

2707 S. Virginia St., Reno, 775-826-2121, 800-648-6992; www.peppermillreno.com

Consistently ranked one of the best casinos in the city, Peppermill's flagship resort is a fixture in the entertainment district near the airport, about two miles south of downtown. The property features 2,000 slot machines, the full spectrum of table gaming, poker and sports betting, plus nightly live entertainment in the swanky cabaret and the more intimate piano lounge. In addition to seven restaurants, the resort boasts a dozen nightspots, including Oceano, with large aquariums, and the domed-shaped Romanza Bar.

1,635 rooms. Restaurant, bar. Casino. Pool. Spa. Fitness center. Business center. $

★★★SIENA HOTEL SPA CASINO

1 S. Lake St., Reno, 775-327-4362, 877-743-6233; www.sienareno.com

Designed to resemble a Tuscan village, this comprehensive resort, located along the banks of the Truckee River, includes a 23,000-square-foot casino and a full-service spa with a variety of treatments. The bright and comfortable rooms include custom fabrics reflecting the sun-drenched palette of Tuscany and have views of the mountains or river. Among the three restaurants, Lexie's offers view of the water.

214 rooms. Restaurant, bars. Spa. Pool. Casino. $

★★★SILVER LEGACY RESORT CASINO RENO
407 N. Virginia St., Reno, 775-325-7401, 800-687-7733; www.silverlegacyreno.com
This Victorian-themed resort has a steel and brass dome and a façade designed to resemble an 1890s storefront. Beyond the gaming—2,000 slots, table games, sports book and a keno lounge—there's a comedy club and a rum bar with dueling pianos. And the showroom attracts big-name entertainers. 1,720 rooms. Restaurant, bar. Pool. Spa. Business center. $

WHERE TO EAT
★★BRICKS RESTAURANT AND WINE BAR
1695 S. Virginia St., Reno, 775-786-2277
American. Lunch, dinner. Closed Sunday. Bar. $$

★★PALAIS DE JADE
960 W. Moana Lane, Reno, 775-827-5233; www.palaisdejadereno.com
Chinese. Lunch, dinner. Bar. $$

★★RAPSCALLION
1555 S. Wells Ave., Reno, 775-323-1211, 877-932-3700; www.rapscallion.com
Seafood. Dinner, Sunday brunch. Bar. Outdoor seating. Reservations recommended. $$

★★WASHOE GRILL
4201 W. Fourth St., Reno, 775-786-1323; www.washoesteakhouse.com
Seafood, steak. Dinner. Bar. Reservations recommended. $$$

SPARKS
See also Reno
Located in the Truckee Meadows of northern Nevada, Sparks is close to Reno. Its desert climate makes it a perfect destination if you want to head outdoors or enjoy some of Reno's high-stakes fun.

WHAT TO SEE
SPARKS HERITAGE MUSEUM
820 Victorian Ave., Sparks, 775-355-1144
Housed in a former courthouse, the museum's exhibits follow Sparks' progression from a train depot to a mining hub to a municipality of more than 80,000 people. Highlights include a vintage model train set and a pump-powered antique player piano.
Tuesday-Friday 11 a.m.-4 p.m., Saturday-Sunday 1-4 p.m.

WILD ISLAND FAMILY ADVENTURE PARK
250 Wild Island Court, Sparks, 775-359-2927; www.wildisland.com
Primarily known as a summer water park, Wild Island is now a year-round facility with the 2003 addition of Coconut Bowl, a state-of-the-art 20-lane bowling alley, and the surprisingly chic Smokin' Marlin Grill. The water park is huge, with a wave pool, tubing river and myriad slides. Hours vary by attraction and season.

SPECIAL EVENTS
BEST OF THE WEST RIB COOK-OFF
John Ascuaga's Nugget Casino Resort,1100 Nugget Ave., Sparks, 775-356-3428; www.nuggetribcookoff.com
Nearly 300,000 barbecue lovers flock to this annual event. In recent years, about 150,000 pounds of ribs have been consumed at this five-day cook-off where two dozen of the West's most revered barbecue pros (all of whom are invited) compete for the first-prize trophy. There is also a lineup of live entertainment on numerous outdoor stages.
Labor Day weekend.

SPARKS HOMETOWNE FARMERS MARKET
Victorian Square, Sparks, 775-353-2291; www.ci.sparks.nv.us
Every Thursday evening between June and August, more than 100 vendors gather and offer everything from rhubarb to pastries to tacos. Also includes cooking demonstrations, kids' area, and home and garden vendors.
June-August.

WHERE TO STAY
★★★JOHN ASCUAGA'S NUGGET
1100 Nugget Ave., Sparks, 775-356-3300, 800-648-1177; www.janugget.com
An anchor in downtown Sparks, the Nugget is located right on the doorstep of Victorian Square, the site of numerous special events. The casino is loaded with all of the standards: slots, table games, poker room and sports book. The Celebrity Showroom is the place to go for entertainment. The hotel itself is a landmark, with a pair of 29-story towers flanking the casino, and a slate of amenities that includes everything from an arcade to a wedding chapel.
1,407 rooms. Restaurant, bar. Casino. Pool. Spa. Business center. $

STATELINE

See also Carson City, Incline Village
This area is best known for its famous high-rise casino/hotels, cabarets and fine dining, but as an integral part of Tahoe's "south shore," it is also appreciated for its spectacular natural beauty. Alpine beaches and Sierra forests afford visitors an endless variety of year-round recreation. There are several excellent public golf courses in the area.

WHERE TO STAY
★★LAKESIDE INN AND CASINO
168 Highway 50, Stateline, 775-588-7777, 800-624-7980; www.lakesideinn.com
124 rooms. Restaurant, bar. Casino. Pool. Pets accepted. $

★★★HARRAH'S LAKE TAHOE
15 Highway 50, Stateline, 775-588-6611, 800-427-7247; www.harrahstahoe.com
This property offers 18,000 square feet of function space and plenty of recreation options for leisure visitors. Shop at the Galleria, swim in the glass-domed pool and, of course, hit the casino.
532 rooms. Restaurant, bar. Casino. Pets accepted. Pool. Spa. $

★★★HARVEY'S LAKE TAHOE
Stateline Ave., Stateline, 775-588-2411, 800-427-8397; www.harveys.com

Most rooms at this resort, the first built in South Lake Tahoe, have a view of Lake Tahoe or the Sierra Nevada mountains. The resort offers a variety of ski packages in the winter and the outdoor arena draws top music guests (including Beyoncé and Diana Krall) in the summer.

740 rooms. Restaurant, bar. Casino. Pool. Fitness center. $

WHERE TO EAT
★★CHART HOUSE
392 Kingsbury Grade, Stateline, 775-588-6276; www.chart-house.com

American. Dinner. Bar. Children's menu. Outdoor seating. Reservations recommended. $$$

★★★FRIDAY'S STATION STEAK & SEAFOOD GRILL
15 Highway 50, Stateline, 775-588-6611; www.harrahs.com

The view of the lake from this restaurant, located on the 18th floor, is memorable. Several steak and seafood combos are offered, such as filet mignon and Alaskan king crab or blackened shrimp.

Seafood, steak. Dinner. Reservations recommended. Bar. $$$

★★★SAGE ROOM
Highway 50, Stateline, 775-588-2411; www.harrahs.com

Since 1947, the Sage Room Steak House has been world-renowned for its old Western ambience and fine cuisine. Dine among the works of Russell and Remington while enjoying traditional steak house dining highlighted by tableside flambé service. Top off your meal with the Sage Room's famous bananas Foster.

American. Dinner. Bar. $$$

★★★THE SUMMIT
15 Highway 50, Stateline, 775-588-6611; www.harrahs.com

Located on the 16th and 17th floors of Harrah's, this restaurant has stunning views and sophisticated cuisine. Try the filet mignon with truffled parsnip purée or pistachio-encrusted rack of lamb.

American. Dinner. Bar. $$$$

VIRGINIA CITY
See also Carson City, Reno

Nevada's most famous mining town once had a population of about 35,000 people and was one of the richest cities in North America. Its dazzling career coincided with the life of the Comstock Lode, which yielded more than $1 billion worth of silver and gold. In the 1870s, Virginia City had four banks, six churches, 110 saloons, an opera house, numerous theaters and the only elevator between Chicago and San Francisco. Great fortunes, including those of Hearst and Mackay, were founded here. Virginia City is perched on the side of Mount Davidson, where a diagonal slit marks the Comstock Lode. The site is beautiful and the air is so clear that the blue and purple masses of the Stillwater Range can be seen 120 miles away. Visitors can tour mines and old mansions, some of which have been restored (Easter week, Memorial Day-October, daily); visit several museums and saloons (daily); stroll through the local shops; and ride on the steam-powered V&T Railroad (May-September).

WHAT TO SEE
THE CASTLE

70 South B St., Virginia City

Built by Robert N. Graves, a mine superintendent of the Empire Mine, the building was patterned after a castle in Normandy, France. Filled with international riches and original furnishings.

Memorial Day weekend-October; daily.

★
★
★
★
★
NEVADA

NEW MEXICO

NEW MEXICO IS A LAND OF CONTRASTS. ITS HISTORY DATES BACK FAR BEFORE THE FIRST
Spanish explorers arrived in 1540 in search of gold. One day you might be
on a Native American reservation, the next you may be taking in the many art
galleries and restaurants in Santa Fe.

New Mexico was first occupied by Native Americans and had been a territory of Spain and then Mexico before becoming a state in 1912. Today, it still
has the highest percentage of Hispanic Americans and the second-highest
population of Native Americans, making for a unique culture.

The landscape ranges from desert in the south to forest and mountain country with clear streams and snow in the north. The Sangre de Cristo (Blood of
Christ) Mountains run north and south along the east side of the Rio Grand in
the north. There are many national parks in New Mexico and several reservations, which are popular with tourists. The government built the Los Alamos
Research Center during World War II, where the atomic bomb was developed
and first detonated in the desert in 1954. There are atomic museums in Albuquerque. Experiments near Roswell caused some people to believe that a
UFO landed here after headlines reported that a "flying disk" was found. The
government said this was a research balloon, but this hasn't stopped specula-
tion of a cover-up, although that theory has never been proven. The capital,
Santa Fe, has a large artistic community. There are many art galleries and
museums, including one honoring Georgia O'Keefe.

ALAMOGORDO

See also Cloudcroft

Alamogordo is a popular tourist destination because of its proximity to Mescalero Apache Indian Reservation, Lincoln National Forest and White Sands
National Monument. A branch of New Mexico State University is located
here. Surrounded by desert and mountains, the first atomic bomb was detonated nearby.

WHAT TO SEE
ALAMEDA PARK ZOO

1321 N. White Sands Blvd., Alamogordo, 505-439-4290

Built in 1898, this is the oldest zoo in the Southwest. It has 300 native and
exotic animals.

Daily 9 a.m.-5 p.m.

LINCOLN NATIONAL FOREST

3463 Las Palomas Road, Alamogordo, 505-434-7200; www.fs.fed.us/r3/lincoln

This forest is known as the birthplace of Smokey Bear. Fishing, hunting,
picnicking, camping, wild cave tours and winter sports in the Sacramento,
Capitan and Guada-lupe mountains. Backpack in the White Mountain Capitan Wildernesses. Camping.

NEW MEXICO MUSEUM OF SPACE HISTORY
Highway 2001, Alamogordo, 575-437-2840, 877-333-6589; www.nmspacemuseum.org
This museum has space-related artifacts, exhibits and an IMAX theater.
Daily 9 a.m.-5 p.m.

OLIVER LEE STATE PARK
409 Dog Canyon Road, Alamogordo, 505-437-8284;
www.emnrd.state.nm.us/PRD/oliverlee.htm
Mountain climbers, photographers and history buffs will enjoy this state
park, the site of at least five major battles. The box canyon is protected by a
2,000-foot bluff. Also includes Frenchy's Place, a substantial rock house with
miles of stone fence. Hiking, camping.
Visitor center, museum, tours of restored Lee Ranch House.

THREE RIVERS PETROGLYPH SITE
County Road B-30, Three Rivers, 505-525-4300; www.blm.gov
Twenty-thousand rock carvings were made here between A.D. 900-1400 by
the Jornada Branch of the Mogollon Indian Culture. Semi-desert terrain includes interpretive signs, a reconstructed prehistoric village, six picnic sites
and tent and trailer sites.

TOY TRAIN DEPOT
1991 N. White Sands Blvd., Alamogordo, 888-207-3564;
www.toytraindepot.homestead.com
More than 1,200 feet of model railroad track and hundreds of model and toy
trains are on display in this five-room, 100-year-old train depot, as well as a
two-mile outdoor miniature railroad track.

SPECIAL EVENT
TRINITY SITE TOUR
1301 N. White Sands Blvd., Alamogordo, 505-437-6120, 888-843-3441;
www.alamogordo.com
Visit the site of the first atomic bomb explosion (open only twice a year).
First Saturday in April and October, 9 a.m.-2 p.m.

WHERE TO STAY
★BEST WESTERN DESERT AIRE HOTEL
1021 S. White Sands Blvd., Alamogordo, 505-437-2110; www.bestwestern.com
92 rooms. Complimentary breakfast. Pets accepted. Pool. Spa. $

ALBUQUERQUE
See also Rio Rancho
In 1706, Don Francisco Cuervo y Valdes, then-governor of New Mexico,
moved 30 families from Bernalillo to a spot some 15 miles south on the Rio
Grande where the pasturage was better.
Catholic missionaries began to build churches in the area and inadvertently
brought diseases that afflicted the Pueblo Indians. The settlers fought with
the Native Americans for many years, but Albuquerque now celebrates the
cultural heritage of groups like the Pueblo, the Anasazi and other tribes. By

1790, the population had grown to almost 6,000 (a very large town for New Mexico at the time). Today, Albuquerque is the largest city in New Mexico. Albuquerque was an important U.S. military outpost from 1846 to 1870. In 1880, when a landowner near the Old Town refused to sell, the Santa Fe Railroad chose a route two miles east, forming a new town called New Albuquerque. It wasn't long before the new town had enveloped what is still called "Old Town," now a popular tourist shopping area.

Surrounded by mountains, Albuquerque continues to grow. The largest industry is Sandia National Laboratories, a laboratory engaged in solar and nuclear research and the testing and development of nuclear weapons.

Dry air and plenty of sunshine (more than 75 percent of the time) have earned Albuquerque a reputation as a health center. Adding to that reputation is the Lovelace Medical Center (similar to the Mayo Clinic in Rochester, Minnesota), which gave the first United States astronauts their qualifying examinations. The University of New Mexico is also located in Albuquerque.

Local attractions such as the annual Albuquerque Balloon Fiesta and several nearby vineyards make it a place for all to visit and enjoy. The culture is an active one and the people of Albuquerque enjoy as many outdoor activities as they can fit into their schedules.

WHAT TO SEE
ALBUQUERQUE BIOLOGICAL PARK
903 10th St. S.W., Albuquerque, 505-764-6200; www.cabq.gov/biopark
This biological park consists of the Albuquerque Aquarium, the Rio Grande Botanic Garden and the Rio Grande Zoo. The aquarium features a shark tank, eel tunnel and shrimp boat. The botanic garden displays formal walled gardens and a glass conservatory. The zoo exhibits include koalas, polar bears, sea lions and shows.
Daily 9 a.m.-5 p.m., until 6 p.m. summer weekends and holidays.

ALBUQUERQUE LITTLE THEATRE
224 San Pasquale Ave. S.W., Albuquerque, 505-242-4750;
www.albuquerquelittletheatre.org
This historic community theater troupe stages Broadway productions. September-May.

ALBUQUERQUE MUSEUM
2000 Mountain Road N.W., Albuquerque, 505-243-7255; www.cabq.gov/museum
Located in a solar-heated building across from the New Mexico Museum of Natural History and Science, this museum displays regional art and history.
Tuesday-Sunday 9 a.m.-5 p.m.

CIBOLA NATIONAL FOREST
2113 Osuna Road N.E., Albuquerque, 505-346-3900; www.fs.fed.us/r3/cibola
This forest has more than 1.5-million acres and stretches throughout Central New Mexico. The park includes Mount Taylor (11,301 feet), several mountain ranges and four wilderness areas: Sandia Mountain (where you'll see bighorn sheep), Manzano Mountain, Apache Kid and Withington.

CORONADO STATE MONUMENT

485 Kuaua Road, Bernalillo, 505-867-5351

Francisco Vásguez de Coronado is said to have camped near this excavated pueblo in 1540 on his famous quest for the seven golden cities of Cibola. Reconstructed, painted kiva; visitor center devoted to Southwestern culture and the Spanish influence on the area.
Wednesday-Monday 8:30 a.m.-4:30 p.m.

FINE ARTS CENTER, UNIVERISTY OF NEW MEXICO

Central Avenue and Stanford Drive, Albuquerque, 505-277-4001; www.unm.edu

Houses the University Art Museum, which features more than 23,000 pieces in its collection. Tuesday-Friday 9 a.m.-4 p.m., Sunday 1-4 p.m.; the Fine Arts Library, which contains the Southwest Music Archives; the Rodey Theatre; and Popejoy Hall, home of the New Mexico Symphony Orchestra and host of the Best of Broadway International Theatre seasons of plays, dance and music.

INDIAN PUEBLO CULTURAL CENTER

2401 12th St. N.W., Albuquerque, 505-843-7270, 866-855-7902; www.indianpueblo.org

Owned and operated by the 19 pueblos of New Mexico, exhibits in the museum tell the story of the Pueblo culture. The gallery showcases handcrafted art; Native American dance and craft demonstrations (weekends).
Daily 9 a.m.-5 p.m.

JONSON GALLERY

1909 Las Lomas Road N.E., Albuquerque, 505-277-4967; www.unm.edu/~jonsong

This gallery, owned by the University of New Mexico and part of its art museums, houses the archives and work of modernist painter Raymond Jonson (1891-1982) and a few works by his contemporaries.
Tuesday-Friday 10 a.m.-4 p.m.

MAXWELL MUSEUM OF ANTHROPOLOGY

1 University of New Mexico, Albuquerque, 505-277-4405; www.unm.edu/~maxwell

The museum displays permanent and changing exhibits of early man and Native American cultures with an emphasis on the Southwest.
Tuesday-Friday 9 a.m.-4 p.m., Saturday 10 a.m.-4 p.m.

MUSEUM OF GEOLOGY AND INSTITUTE OF METEORITICS METEORITE MUSEUM

Northrop Hall, 200 Yale Blvd. N.E., Albuquerque, 505-277-4204

The Museum of Geology contains numerous samples of ancient plants, minerals, rocks and animals while the meteorite museum has a major collection of more than 550 meteorites.
Monday-Friday 7:30 a.m.-4:30 p.m.

NATIONAL ATOMIC MUSEUM

1905 Mountain Road N.W., Albuquerque, 505-245-2137; www.atomicmuseum.com

This nuclear energy science center, the nation's only such museum, features exhibits depicting the history of the atomic age, including the Manhattan

Project, the Cold War and the development of nuclear medicine. See replicas of Little Boy and Fat Man, the world's first two atomic weapons deployed in Japan in World War II, as well as B-52 and B-29 aircraft. Guided tours and audiovisual presentations are offered.

Daily 9 a.m.-5 p.m.; closed holidays.

NEW MEXICO MUSEUM OF NATURAL HISTORY AND SCIENCE

1801 Mountain Road N.W., Albuquerque, 505-841-2800;
www.museums.state.nm.us/nmmnh

Those interested in dinosaurs, fossils and volcanoes will love this museum, with exhibits on botany, geology, paleontology and zoology. The LodeStar Astronomy Center gives guests a view of the heavens in its observatory.

Daily 9 a.m.-5 p.m.; closed. Thanksgiving Day, Christmas Day, New Years Day and nonholiday Mondays in September and January.

OLD TOWN

Old Town and Romero roads, Albuquerque

The original settlement is one block north of Central Avenue, the city's main street, at Rio Grande Boulevard. Old Town Plaza retains a lovely Spanish flavor with many interesting shops and restaurants.

PETROGLYPH NATIONAL MONUMENT

6001 Unser Blvd., Albuquerque, 505-899-0205; www.nps.gov/petr

This park contains concentrated groups of rock drawings experts believe ancestors of the Pueblo carved on lava formations. Three hiking trails wind along the 17-mile escarpment.

Daily 8 a.m.-5 p.m.

RIO GRANDE NATURE CENTER STATE PARK

2901 Candelaria Road N.W., Albuquerque, 505-344-7240; www.emnrd.state.nm.us

The highlight here is a glass-enclosed observation room overlooking a three-acre pond that is home to birds and other wildlife; interpretive displays on the wildlife of the bosque (cottonwood groves) along the Rio Grande; two miles of nature trails.

Guided hikes, hands-on activities. Daily 8 a.m.-5 p.m.

RIO GRANDE ZOO

903 10th St. S.W., Albuquerque, 505-764-6200; www.cabq.gov/biopark/zoo

Visit more than 1,200 exotic animals, including white tigers.

Daily 9 a.m.-5 p.m., until 6 p.m. weekends in summer.

SANDIA PEAK AERIAL TRAMWAY

Albuquerque, 505-856-7325; www.sandiapeak.com

The tram travels almost three miles up the west slope of the Sandia Mountains to 10,378 feet, with amazing 11,000-square-mile views. Hiking trail; restaurant at summit and Mexican grill at base.

Memorial Day-Labor Day, daily 9 a.m.-9 p.m.; shorter hours rest of year; closed two weeks in April and two weeks in October.

SANDIA PEAK TRAMWAY SKI AREA

Albuquerque, in Cibola National Forest, Crest Scenic Byway, Sandia Mountains, 505-856-7325; www.sandiapeak.com

Four double chairlifts, surface lift; patrol, school, rentals, snowmaking. Aerial tramway on the west side of the mountain meets lifts at the top. Longest run is more than 2½ miles; vertical drop 1,700 feet.

Mid-December-March, daily. Chairlift also operates July-Labor Day. Friday-Sunday.

TELEPHONE PIONEER MUSEUM

110 Fourth St. N.W., Albuquerque, 505-842-2937

Displays trace the development of the telephone from 1876 to the present. More than 400 types of telephones, plus switchboards, early equipment and old telephone directories.

Monday-Friday 10 a.m.-2 p.m.; weekends by appointment.

UNIVERSITY OF NEW MEXICO

Central Avenue and University Boulevard, Albuquerque, 505-277-1989, 800-225-5866; www.unm.edu

Established 1889; 25,000 students. This campus has both Spanish and Pueblo architectural influences. It is one of the largest universities in the Southwest.

SPECIAL EVENTS
ALBUQUERQUE INTERNATIONAL BALLOON FIESTA

Balloon Fiesta Park, North Albuquerque, 505-821-1000, 888-422-7277; www.aibf.org

As many as 100,000 people attend this annual event, the largest of its kind in the world. Attendees can catch their own balloon rides from Rainbow Ryders Inc. (505-823-1111).

First Saturday in October through the following Sunday.

FOUNDERS DAY

Old Town, Albuquerque, 505-768-3556; www.cabq.gov

The holiday celebrates the city's founding in 1706 with traditional New Mexican festivities.

Late April.

INDIAN PUEBLO CULTURAL CENTER

2401, 12th St., Albuquerque, 505-843-7270; www.indianpueblo.org

Traditional Native American dances, races, contests.

Late May-mid-June.

MUSICAL THEATER SOUTHWEST

2401 Ross Ave. S.E., Albuquerque, 505-265-9119; www.musicaltheatresw.com

This troupe produces five Broadway-style musicals each season at the historic Hiland Theater in the Frank A. Peloso Performing Arts Center.

NEW MEXICO ARTS & CRAFTS FAIR

303 Romero St. N.W., Albuquerque, 505-884-9043; www.nmartsandcraftsfair.org

The fair features exhibits and demonstrations by more than 200 craftsworkers representing Spanish, Native American and other North American cultures. Artists sell their wares, which range from paintings to sculpture to jewelry. Last weekend in June.

NEW MEXICO STATE FAIR

Expo New Mexico State Fairgrounds, 300 San Pedro Blvd., Albuquerque, 505-265-3976; www.exponm.com

Horse shows and racing, rodeo, midway, flea market; entertainment. September.

NEW MEXICO SYMPHONY ORCHESTRA

University of New Mexico, Popejoy Hall, 4407 Menaul Blvd., Albuquerque, 505-881-9590, 800-251-6676; www.nmso.org

September-May.

TAOS PUEBLO DANCES

Taos Pueblo, Albuquerque, 505-758-1028; www.taospueblo.com

Several Native American dances are held throughout the year. For a schedule of annual dances, contact the pueblo.

WHERE TO STAY

★★BEST WESTERN RIO GRANDE INN

1015 Rio Grande Blvd. N.W., Albuquerque, 505-843-9500, 800-959-4726; www.riograndeinn.com

173 rooms. Restaurant, bar. Business center. Fitness center. Pool. Pets accepted. $

★★COURTYARD ALBUQUERQUE AIRPORT

1920 S. Yale Blvd., Albuquerque, 505-843-6600, 800-321-2211; www.marriott.com

150 rooms. Restaurant, bar. Fitness center. Pool. $

★★DOUBLETREE HOTEL ALBUQUERQUE

201 Marquette Ave. N.W., Albuquerque, 505-247-3344; www.albuquerque.doubletree.com

295 rooms. Restaurant, bar. Pool. Business center. Fitness center. $$

★★★HILTON ALBUQUERQUE

1901 University Blvd. N.E., Albuquerque, 505-884-2500, 800-445-8667; www.hilton.com

With its arched doorways, Native American rugs and local art, this hotel on 14 acres near the university fits right in. The hotel includes indoor and outdoor heated pools, a sauna and lighted tennis courts. Rooms feature sliding glass doors and balconies with great views of the high desert.

261 rooms. Restaurant, bar. Pool. Fitness center. Business center. Pets accepted. $

★★★HOTEL ALBUQUERQUE AT OLD TOWN

800 Rio Grande Blvd. N.W., Albuquerque, 505-843-6300, 800-237-2133; www.hhandr.com

With its large, open lobby and tiled floors, this hotel offers a casual yet el-

egant environment. Located in historic Old Town across from the New Mexico Museum of Natural History, it is close to more than 200 specialty stores. All guest rooms feature furniture made by local artists.
188 rooms. Restaurant, bar. Pets accepted. Fitness center. Pool. Spa. Business center. $

★HOMEWOOD SUITES BY HILTON ALBUQUERQUE UPTOWN

7101 Arvada Ave. N.E., Albuquerque, 505-881-7300; www.homewoodsuites.com
151 rooms. Business center. Fitness Room. Pool. Complimentary breakfast. Pets accepted. $

★★★HYATT REGENCY ALBUQUERQUE

330 Tijeras N.W., Albuquerque, 505-842-1234, 800-233-1234; www.hyatt.com
Adjacent to the convention center, this 22-story tower is centrally located near Old Town and the Rio Grande Zoo and is only five miles from the airport. One of the city's newest high-rise hotels, the property offers a health club, sauna and outdoor pool. Business rooms include separate work areas and dual line phones. All rooms have Southwestern décor and views of the city or mountains.
395 rooms. Restaurant, bar. Fitness center. Pool. Business center. $$

WHERE TO EAT
★66 DINER

1405 Central Ave. N.E., Albuquerque, 505-247-1421; www.66diner.com
American, Southwestern. Breakfast, lunch, dinner. Children's menu. $

★★ANTIQUITY

112 Romero St. N.W., Albuquerque, 505-247-3545
American, Southwestern. Dinner. Reservations recommended. $$

★★★ARTICHOKE CAFÉ

424 Central St., Albuquerque, 505-243-0200; www.artichokecafe.com
This pleasant eatery, which has tables set with fresh flowers, serves a mix of French, Italian and creative American cuisine. Dishes include steamed artichokes with three dipping sauces, or housemade pumpkin ravioli and scallops wrapped in prosciutto.
American. Lunch, dinner. Reservations recommended. $$

★★BARRY'S OASIS

4451 Osuna Road N.E., Albuquerque, 505-884-2324; www.barrysoasis.com
Mediterranean. Dinner. Reservations recommended. $

★CHRISTY MAE'S

1400 San Pedro Drive N.E., Albuquerque, 505-255-4740; www.christymaes.com
American. Breakfast, lunch, dinner. Closed Sunday. Children's menu. $

★COOPERAGE

7220 Lomas Blvd. N.E., Albuquerque, 505-255-1657
American. Lunch, dinner. Bar. $$

★GARDUÑO'S OF MEXICO RESTAURANT & CANTINA

10551 Montgomery Blvd. N.E., Albuquerque, 505-298-5000;
www.gardunosrestaurants.com

Mexican. Lunch, dinner, Sunday brunch. Bar. Children's menu. Outdoor seating. $$

★★HIGH NOON

425 San Felipe St. N.W., Albuquerque, 505-765-1455; www.999dine.com

Southwestern, steak. Lunch, dinner. Bar. Children's menu. $$

★★★SCALO NOB HILL

3500 Central Ave. S.E., Albuquerque, 505-255-8781; www.scalonobhill.com

Chef Steven Lemon has taken over the kitchen of this more than 20-year-old Italian grill that offers dining areas on several levels. From the wood-fired pizzas to the freshly made pastas, Lemon relies on organic, seasonal local ingredients. Classic Italian desserts such as tiramisu and bread pudding make for a sweet end to a meal.

American. Lunch, dinner. Closed Monday. Bar. Reservations recommended. Outdoor seating. $$

★★TROMBINO'S BISTRO ITALIANO

5415 Academy Road N.E., Albuquerque, 505-821-5974

Italian. Lunch, dinner, brunch. Bar. Children's menu. $$

CARLSBAD

See also Carlsbad Caverns National Park

On the lovely Pecos River, Carlsbad is an excellent place to get out and explore, thanks to nearby Carlsbad Caverns and the Guadalupe Mountains National Park.

WHAT TO SEE

CARLSBAD MUSEUM & ART CENTER

Halagueno Park, 418 W. Fox St., Carlsbad, 505-887-0276; www.nmculture.org

The center showcases Pueblo pottery, art and meteorite remains; pioneer and Apache relics; bird carvings by Jack Drake; mineral exhibits and more. Summer: Monday-Saturday 10 a.m.-6 p.m.; winter until 5 p.m.

LAKE CARLSBAD WATER RECREATION AREA

Carlsbad, off Green Street on the Pecos River, 575-887-2702

CAPULIN VOLCANO NATIONAL MONUMENT

This dormant volcano last erupted approximately 10,000 years ago. The strikingly symmetrical cinder cone rises more than 1,500 feet from plains, with a crater one mile in circumference and 415 feet deep. Visitors can spiral completely around the mountain on paved road to rim (Daily); five states can be seen on clear days. Picnic area. Visitor center with exhibits of geology, flora and fauna of the area.

Daily. Uniformed personnel on duty at the crater rim (summer only).

CARLSBAD CAVERNS NATIONAL PARK

One of the largest and most remarkable in the world, this cavern extends approximately 30 miles and extends as deep as 1,037 feet below the surface. It was once known as Bat Cave because of the spectacular bat flights, still a daily occurrence at sunset during the warmer months.

Cowboy and guano miner Jim White first explored and guided people through the caverns in the early 1900s, later working for the National Park Service as the Chief Park Ranger. Carlsbad Cave National Monument was established in 1923 and in 1930 the area was enlarged and designated a national park. The park contains 46,755 acres and more than 80 caves. Carlsbad Cavern was formed by the dissolving action of acidic water in the Tansill and Capitan limestones of the Permian age. When an uplift drained the cavern, mineral-laden water dripping from the ceiling formed the stalactites and stalagmites.

The main cavern has two self-guided routes, a Ranger-guided Kings Palace tour and several "off-trail" trips. The "Cavern Guide," an audio tour rented at the visitor center, enhances self-guided tours with interpretations of the caverns, interviews and historic re-creations. Tours are also available in two backcountry caves: Slaughter Canyon Cave and Spider Cave. All guided tours require reservations. Bat flight programs are held each evening during the summer at the cavern entrance amphitheater. Information: 727A Carlsbad Caverns Highway, Carlsbad, 505-785-2232;

Swimming, water sports, fishing, boating; tennis, golf, picnic area.

LIVING DESERT ZOO AND GARDENS STATE PARK

1504 Miehls Drive, Carlsbad, 505-887-5516; www.emnrd.state.nm.us
This 1,100-acre park is an indoor/outdoor living museum of the Chihuahuan Desert's plants and animals. The Desert Arboretum has an extensive cactus collection and the zoo has more than 60 animal species native to the region, including mountain lions, bear, wolf, elk, bison and an extensive aviary. Summer: daily 8 a.m.-8 p.m.; winter: daily 9 a.m.-5 p.m.

WHERE TO STAY
★★BEST WESTERN STEVENS INN

1829 S. Canal St., Carlsbad, 505-887-2851; www.bestwestern.com
220 rooms. Complimentary breakfast. Restaurant, bar. Pets accepted. Pool. Fitness center. $

★★HOLIDAY INN EXPRESS HOTEL & SUITES CARLSBAD

2210 I W. Pierce St., Carlsbad, 575-234-1252, 877-863-4780; www.holiday-inn.com
80 rooms. Complimentary breakfast. Restaurant, bar. Pool. Business center. Fitness center. $

CLOUDCROFT

See also Alamogordo
Cloudcroft has one of the highest golf courses in North America, but this is also a recreation area for nongolfers. It is located at the crest of the Sacramento Mountains in the Lincoln National Forest, among fir, spruce, pine and aspen trees. The area is popular with writers, photographers and artists.

CHACO CULTURE NATIONAL HISTORICAL PARK

From A.D. 900 to 1150, Chaco Canyon was a major center of Anasazi culture. A prehistoric roadway system, which included stairways carved into sandstone cliffs, extends for hundreds of miles in all directions. Ancient roads up to 30 feet wide represent the most developed and extensive road network of this period north of Central America. Researchers speculate that Chaco Canyon was the center of a vast, complex and interdependent civilization in the American Southwest. There are five self-guided trails with tours conducted Memorial Day-Labor Day, as well as evening campfire programs in summer. Daily. Camping.

Information: Nageezi, from Highway 44, 25 miles south on country road 7900; three miles south of Nageezi Trading Post; from Interstate 40, 60 miles north of Thoreau on Highway 57. Check road conditions locally; may be extremely difficult when wet;.

Several art schools conduct summer workshops here. There are also many miles of horseback trails through the mountains and skiing, snowmobiling and skating in winter. Several campgrounds are located in the surrounding forest. During the day temperatures seldom reach 80 F, and nights are always crisp and cool.

WHAT TO SEE
SACRAMENTO MOUNTAINS HISTORICAL MUSEUM

1000 Highway 82, Cloudcroft, 505-682-2932; www.cloudcroftmuseum.com

Exhibits depict life from 1880 to 1910 in the Sacramento Mountains area. Monday, Tuesday, Friday-Sunday.

SKI CLOUDCROFT

1920 Highway 82, East of Cloudcroft, Cloudcroft, 575-682-2333; www.skicloudcroft.net

Double chairlift, beginner tows; patrol, school, rentals, snowmaking, lodge, snack bar, cafeteria, restaurant. Vertical drop 700 feet. Mid-December-mid-March, daily. Snowboarding. Elevations of 8,350-9,050 feet.

WHERE TO STAY
★★★THE LODGE RESORT AND SPA

1 Corona Place, Cloudcroft, 505-682-2566, 800-395-6343; www.thelodgeresort.com

This historic 1899 building is surrounded by 215,000 acres of the Lincoln National Forest and features a challenging golf course, full-service spa and lawn games including croquet, horseshoes and volleyball. Individually appointed rooms are decorated with antiques.

59 rooms. Restaurant, bar. Spa. Pets accepted. Pool. Golf. Business center. Fitness center. $$

CLOVIS

See also Portales

A mid-sized city in Eastern New Mexico, Clovis calls itself the gateway to the Land of Enchantment.

WHAT TO SEE
CLOVIS DEPOT MODEL TRAIN MUSEUM
221 W. First St., Clovis, 505-762-0066, 888-762-0064; www.clovisdepot.com
Built in 1907 by the Atchison, Topeka and Santa Fe Railway, the Depot has been restored to its condition in the 1950s, and features working model train layouts, railroad memorabilia, historical displays and an operating telegraph station. Real train operations along one of the busiest rail lines in the U.S. can be viewed from a platform.

HILLCREST PARK AND ZOO
1201 Sycamore and 10th streets, Clovis, 575-769-7873
The second-largest zoo in New Mexico has more than 500 animals, most of which are exhibited in natural environments. Also includes a park with amusement rides, outdoor and indoor swimming pool, golf course, picnic areas and sunken garden.

SPECIAL EVENTS
PIONEER DAYS & PRCA RODEO
1002 W. McDonald, Clovis, 575-763-3435
Parade, Little Buckaroo Rodeo. First week in June.

WHERE TO EAT
★GUADALAJARA CAFÉ
916 L Casillas St., Clovis, 505-769-9965
Mexican. Lunch, dinner. Closed Sunday. Outdoor seating. $

★LEAL'S MEXICAN RESTAURANT
2115 N. Prince St., Clovis, 505-763-9069; www.lealsmexicanfoods.com
Mexican. Lunch, dinner. Children's menu. $$

DEMING
The old Butterfield Trail, route of an early stagecoach line to California, passed through about 12 miles north of here; there is a marker on Highway 180. Hunting enthusiasts will find deer, antelope, ibex, bear and blue quail plentiful in the surrounding mountains.

WHAT TO SEE
DEMING-LUNA MIMBRES MUSEUM
301 S. Silver St., Deming, 505-546-2382
See mining, military, ranching, railroad, Native American and Hispanic artifacts of the Southwest. Includes Mimbres pottery, Indian baskets, chuckwagon with equipment, quilt room gems and minerals and more.

ROCK HUNTING
Deming Gem and Mineral Society, 4200 Raymond Road, Deming, 575-546-2445
Check out the jasper, onyx, nodules and many other types of semiprecious stones found in the area.

EL MORRO NATIONAL MONUMENT (INSCRIPTION ROCK)

The towering cliff that served as the guest book of New Mexico is located here on the ancient trail taken by the conquistadores from Santa Fe to Zuni. Don Juan de Oñate carved his name here in 1605; scores of other Spaniards and Americans added their names to the cliff at later dates. The rock is pale buff Zuni sandstone. The cliff, 200 feet high, has pueblo ruins on its top and pre-Columbian petroglyphs. Visitor center and museum. Daily. Trail, picnic facilities.

ROCKHOUND STATE PARK

Highway 143, Deming, 575-546-6182; www.emnrd.state.nm.us/prd/Rockhound.htm
This 1,000-acre park is on the rugged western slope of the Little Florida Mountains and has an abundance of agate, geodes and other semiprecious stones for collectors (limit 15 pounds). Display of polished stones. Hiking, picnicking, playground, camping.
Daily.

SPECIAL EVENTS
OLD WEST GUN SHOW

4335 Salvador Road S.E., Deming, 800-848-4955
Western artifacts, jewelry, military equipment, guns, ammunition.
Third weekends in February and August.

ROCKHOUND ROUNDUP

4335 Salvador Road S.E., Deming, 800-848-4955
Guided field trips for agate, geodes, candy rock, marble and honey onyx attract more than 6,000 participants.
Auctions; exhibitions; demonstrations.
Mid-March.

SOUTHWESTERN NEW MEXICO STATE FAIR

Deming, Done Ana Country Fairgrounds, 505-524-8602; www.snmstatefair.com
Livestock shows, midway, parade.
Early-mid-October.

WHERE TO STAY
★★HOLIDAY INN

Interstate 10 E., Deming, 505-546-2661, 877-863-4780; www.holiday-inn.com
117 rooms. Restaurant. Pets accepted. Pool. Business center. Fitness center. $

ESPAÑOLA

See also Los Alamos, Santa Fe
First settled 700 years ago by the Pueblo, then by Don Juan de Oñate in 1598, Española was claimed by the United States in 1846. Espanola is situated between Taos and Santa Fe.

WHAT TO SEE
FLORENCE HAWLEY ELLIS MUSEUM OF ANTHROPOLOGY
Mile Post 224, Highway 84, Española, 505-685-4333, 877-804-4678;
www.ghostranch.org
Exhibits of Native American/Spanish history.
Memorial Day-Labor Day, Tuesday-Sunday; rest of year, Tuesday-Saturday;
closed December.

RUTH HALL MUSEUM OF PALEONTOLOGY
Mile Post 224, US-84, Española, 505-685-4333, 877-804-4678
Exhibits on Triassic animals and Coelophysis, the New Mexico state fossil.
Memorial Day-Labor Day, Tuesday-Sunday; rest of year, Tuesday-Saturday.

SPECIAL EVENTS
FIESTA DEL VALLE DE ESPAÑOLA
Española
The festival celebrates the establishment of New Mexico's first Spanish set-
tlement in 1598. Torch relay, vespers, candlelight procession, street dancing,
arts and crafts, food, entertainment, parade.
Second week in July.

SAINTE CLAIRE FEAST DAY
One Kee St., Santa Clara Pueblo, Española, 505-753-7326; www.espanolaonline.com
Dancing, food, market. Mid-August.

SAN JUAN FEAST DAY
Española, San Juan Pueblo, 505-852-4400, 800-793-4955;
www.espanolaonline.com/events.htm
Dancing, food, carnival. Late June.

TRI-CULTURAL ARTS FESTIVAL
Northern New Mexico Community College, 921 Paseo de Onte Road, Española
Features local artisans and their works, including potters, weavers, wood-
workers, photographers, painters, singers and dancers.
Usually first weekend in October.

WHERE TO STAY
★★★RANCHO DE SAN JUAN COUNTRY INN
Highway 285, Española, 505-753-6818; www.ranchodesanjuan.com
Situated between Taos and Santa Fe, this inn is spread over 225 scenic acres.
Designed in the Spanish tradition, the décor is both rustic and refined with
wildflower-filled courtyards, exposed beams, tile floors and Southwestern art
and antiques. Rooms feature views of the mountains and river valley, as well
as wood-burning fireplaces.
17 rooms. No children under 8. Restaurant. Spa. $$

WHERE TO EAT
★★EL PARAGUA
603 Santa Cruz Road, Española, 505-753-3211, 800-929-8226; www.elparagua.com
Southwestern. Lunch, dinner. Bar. Children's menu. $$

★★★RANCHO DE SAN JUAN
Highway 285, Española, 505-753-6818; www.ranchodesanjuan.com
The elegant, cheerful dining room of this inn overlooks the Ojo Caliente River Valley and the Jemez Mountains. The tranquil setting is an attractive backdrop for chef/owner John Johnson's Southwest-inspired international cuisine, including dishes such as roasted coriander quail and coconut-crusted white shrimp.
International. Dinner. Closed Sunday-Monday. Bar. Reservations recommended. Outdoor seating. $$$

FARMINGTON
See also Dulce, Shiprock
The Navajos call it Totah, the meeting place at the convergence of three rivers in the colorful land of the Navajo, Ute, Apache and Pueblo. Once the home of the ancient Anasazi, Farmington is now the largest city in the Four Corners area and supplies much of the energy to the Southwest. From Farmington, visitors may explore Mesa Verde, Chaco Canyon and the Salmon and Aztec ruins. You can enjoy some of the best year-round fishing in the state at Navajo Lake State Park and in the San Juan River. There are many shops offering traditional Native American crafts in the immediate area—baskets, jewelry, pottery, rugs and sand paintings. Obtain a list of local art galleries and trading posts at the Convention and Visitors Bureau.

WHAT TO SEE
BISTI BADLANDS
Highway 371, Farmington, 505-599-8900
A federally protected wilderness area of strange geologic formations; large petrified logs and other fossils are scattered among a few scenic landforms. No vehicles permitted beyond boundary.

FOUR CORNERS MONUMENT
Navajo Reservation, Farmington, 64 miles northwest via Highway 64, Highway 504, Highway 160, 928-871-6647; www.navajonationparks.org
This is the only point in the country common to four states: Arizona, Colorado, New Mexico and Utah.

SPECIAL EVENTS
BLACK RIVER TRADERS
Lions Wilderness Park Amphitheater, Pinon Hills and College boulevards, Farmington, 505-326-7602
Historical drama about the Southwest's multicultural heritage presented in an outdoor amphitheater. Contact the Convention and Visitors Bureau to get a schedule.
Mid-June-mid-August.

CONNIE MACK WORLD SERIES BASEBALL TOURNAMENT

Ricketts Park, 1101 Fairgrounds Road, Farmington
Annual 17-game series involves teams from the U.S. and Puerto Rico.
August.

FARMINGTON INVITATIONAL BALLOON RALLY

3041 E. Main St., Farmington, 800-448-1240
Hare and hound races; competitions.
Memorial Day weekend.

SAN JUAN COUNTY FAIR

41 Road 5568, Farmington
Parade; rodeo; fiddler contest; chili cook-off; exhibits.
Mid-late August.

WHERE TO STAY
★★BEST WESTERN INN & SUITES

700 Scott Ave., Farmington, 505-327-5221; www.bestwestern.com
192 rooms. Complimentary breakfast. Restaurant, bar. Pets accepted. Pool.
Business center. Fitness center. Spa. $

★COMFORT INN

555 Scott Ave., Farmington, 505-325-2626, 800-341-1495; www.comfortinn.com
60 rooms. Complimentary breakfast. Pets accepted. Pool. Business center. $

WHERE TO EAT
★CLANCY'S PUB

2703 E. 20th St., Farmington, 505-325-8176; www.clancys.net
Mexican, American. Lunch, dinner. Bar. Children's menu. Outdoor seating. $

GRANTS

See also Albuquerque
More than half of the known domestic reserves of uranium ore are found in
this area. About four miles east, Interstate 40 (I-40/Route 66) crosses one of
the most recent lava flows in the continental United States. Native American
pottery has been found under the lava, which first flowed about four million
years ago from Mount Taylor to the north. Lava also flowed less than 1,100
years ago from fissures that today are near the highway. The lava is sharp and
hard; heavy shoes are advisable for walking on it.

WHAT TO SEE
CASAMERO PUEBLO RUINS

Grants, 505-761-8700
The Chaco Anasazi occupied Casamero Pueblo between A.D. 1000 and 1125
as a community building that served a number of nearby farmsteads. It was
used for social and religious activities aimed at uniting individual families
into a cohesive community. It is included on the World Heritage List.

EL MALPAIS NATIONAL MONUMENT AND NATIONAL CONSERVATION AREA

123 East Roosevelt Ave., Grants, 505-783-4774; www.nps.gov/elma

These two areas total 376,000 acres of volcanic formations and sandstone canyons. Monument features splatter cones and a 17-mile-long system of lava tubes. The Conservation area, which surrounds the monument, includes La Ventana Natural Arch, one of the state's largest freestanding natural arches; Cebolla and West Malpais wildernesses; and numerous Anasazi ruins. The Sandstone Bluffs Overlook, off Highway 117, offers an excellent view of the lava-filled valley and surrounding area. Facilities include hiking, bicycling, scenic drives, primitive camping (acquire Backcountry Permit at information center or ranger station). Most of the lava tubes are accessible only by hiking trails; check with the information center in Grants before attempting any hikes. Information center and visitor facility on Highway 117.
Daily.

ICE CAVE AND BANDERA VOLCANO

Highway 53, 28 miles southwest of Grants, 888-423-2283; www.icecaves.com

See an example of volcanic activity and hike on lava trails. The ice cave is part of a collapsed lava tube. The temperature never rises above 31 degrees, but reflected sunlight creates beautiful scenery. A historic trading post displays and sells artifacts and American Indian artwork.
Daily 8 a.m.-one hour before sunset.

NEW MEXICO MINING MUSEUM

100 N. Iron Ave., Grants, 505-287-4802, 800-748-2142; www.grants.org

This is the only underground uranium mining museum in the world. Native American artifacts and relics; native mineral display.
Monday-Saturday.

282

WHERE TO STAY

★★BEST WESTERN INN & SUITES

1501 E. Santa Fe Ave., Grants, 505-287-7901, 800-528-1234; www.bestwestern.com

126 rooms. Complimentary breakfast. Restaurant, bar. Fitness center. Pool. Pets accepted. $

LAS CRUCES

See also Deming

In 1830 a group of people from Taos were traveling on the Spanish highway El Camino Real. They camped here and were massacred by the Apache. They were buried under a field of crosses; hence the name Las Cruces ("the crosses"). Situated in the vast farming area of the fertile lower Rio Grande Valley, this region is especially noted for its homegrown green chiles. There are ghost mining towns, extinct volcanoes, frontier forts, mountains and pecan orchards in the area.

THE WILD WEST

This two- to three-day tour from Las Cruces offers a combination of scenic wonders, hiking and fishing opportunities and a glimpse into the old West. From Las Cruces, head northeast on Highway 70 to White Sands National Monument, a seemingly endless expanse of sparkling white gypsum dunes. You'll drive past the dunes along a 16-mile scenic drive, which also provides access to the monument's four hiking trails. Or just take off on foot into the dunes, where kids will have endless hours of fun sliding down the mountains of sand on plastic saucers (available at the monument's gift shop). Visiting the monument is best either early or late in the day, when the dunes display mysterious and often surreal shadows.

Continue northeast on Highway 70 to Alamogordo, a good spot to spend the night. Attractions here include the Space Center, where you can test your skills as a pilot in a Space Shuttle simulator, explore the International Space Hall of Fame and visit the Toy Train Depot, which has a fascinating collection of toy trains—some dating from the 1800s. About 12 miles south of Alamogordo via Highway 54 is Oliver Lee Memorial State Park, with a short, pleasant nature trail along a shaded stream, plus a rugged hiking trail that climbs up the side of a mountain and offers spectacular views. The park also includes the ruins of a pioneer cabin and a museum that tells the story of the site's violent past.

From Alamogordo, go north on Highway 54 to Tularosa, where you can visit Tularosa Vineyards. Then head east on Highway 70 up into the Sacramento Mountains to the resort community of Ruidoso, whose name (Spanish for "noisy") comes from the babbling Ruidoso Creek. Surrounded by the Lincoln National Forest, this picturesque town is a good base for hiking. Head east out of Ruidoso Downs to Hondo and then turn back to the northwest on Highway 380, which leads to Lincoln. This genuine Wild West town, which is preserved as a state monument, was the site of a jail break by famed outlaw Billy the Kid. Continue west on Highway 380 to the town of Capitan for a visit to Smokey Bear Historical State Park, with exhibits and the grave of the orphaned bear cub who was found in a forest fire near here and became a symbol of forest fire prevention. Leaving Capitan, drive west on Highway 380 to the town of Carrizozo and cross Highway 54. Continue four miles to Valley of Fires National Recreation Site, where a short trail provides close-up views of numerous jet-black lava formations. Return to Carrizozo and head south on Highway 54 to the turnoff to Three Rivers Petroglyph Site, one of the best places in the Southwest to see prehistoric rock art. An easy trail meanders along a hillside where there are thousands of images, ranging from geometric patterns to handprints to a variety of animals (some pierced by arrows or spears) created by the Mogollon people at least 1,000 years ago. To return to Las Cruces, take Highway 54 south through Tularosa and Alamogordo; turn southwest on Highway 70. Approximately 349 miles.

WHAT TO SEE
BRANIGAN CULTURAL CENTER

501 N. Main St., Las Cruces, 505-541-2155; www.las-cruces.org
This complex includes the Las Cruces Museum of Fine Art & Culture and the Bicentennial Log Cabin Museum.
Monday-Friday 10 a.m.-4 p.m., Saturday 9 a.m.-1 p.m.

NEW MEXICO FARM AND RANCH HERITAGE MUSEUM

4100 Dripping Springs Road, Las Cruces, 505-522-4100; www.frhm.org
Interactive 47-acre museum that brings to life Mexico's 3,000-year history and farming and ranching life. Hands-on exhibits including plowing, blacksmithing and cow-milking. Outdoor animal and plant life.

Monday-Saturday 9 a.m.-5 p.m., Sunday noon-5 p.m.

NEW MEXICO STATE UNIVERSITY

University Avenue, Las Cruces, 505-646-0111, 800-662-6678; www.nmsu.edu

Established in 1888; 15,500 students. The 950-acre campus includes a history museum (Tuesday-Sunday), art gallery and an 18-hole public golf course.

WHITE SANDS MISSILE RANGE

Las Cruces, 20 miles east on Highway 70, 575-678-1134; www.wsmr.army.mil

The range where missiles are tested is closed to the public but visitors are welcome at the outdoor missile park and museum.

Missile Park: daily 8 a.m.-4 p.m. Museum: Monday-Friday 8 a.m.-4:30 p.m.

SPECIAL EVENT
WHOLE ENCHILADA FIESTA

Downtown Mall, Main and Las Cruces streets, Las Cruces, 505-526-1938;
www.enchiladafiesta.com

This fiesta includes street dancing, entertainment, parade, crafts and food including world's largest enchilada.

Last weekend in September.

WHERE TO STAY
★★BEST WESTERN MESILLA VALLEY INN

901 Avenida De Mesilla, Las Cruces, 505-524-8603, 800-327-3314;
www.mesillavalleyinn.com

160 rooms. Restaurant, bar. Pets accepted. Pool. Spa.

★FAIRFIELD INN

2101 Summit Court, Las Cruces, 505-522-6840; www.fairfieldinn.com

77 rooms. Complimentary breakfast. Pool. $

★★★HOTEL ENCANTO DE LAS CRUCES

705 S. Telshor Blvd., Las Cruces, 575-522-4300; www.hhandr.com

This hotel located close to New Mexico State University, Las Cruces International Airport, White Sands Missile Range and Historic Old Mesilla. Activities such as golfing, bowling, horseback riding and fishing are nearby. All of the guest rooms feature a warm Southwestern style.

203 rooms. Restaurant, bar. Pets accepted. Pool. Fitness center. $$

★★RAMADA PALMS DE LAS CRUCES

201 E. University Ave., Las Cruces, 505-526-4411; www.ramada.com

114 rooms. Restaurant, bar. Pets accepted. Business center. Complimentary breakfast. Fitness center. Pool. $

WHERE TO EAT
★★★MESON DE MESILLA

1803 Avenida de Mesilla, Las Cruces, 505-525-9212; www.mesondemesilla.com

This romantic restaurant located in an adobe-style bed and breakfast combines continental cuisine with Italian and Southwestern accents for an unusual menu. Entrées include almond crusted trout and linguine with clams. French. Dinner. Closed Monday. Bar. Reservations recommended. $$$

LOS ALAMOS
See also Española, Santa Fe
Situated on high mesas between the Rio Grande Valley floor and the Jemez Mountain peaks, Los Alamos offers spectacular views and outdoor activities. The city was originally the site of a boys' school. It was acquired by the government in 1942 to develop the first atomic bomb. In 1967, the city property was turned over to Los Alamos County. The scientific laboratory, where research continues, remains a classified installation.

WHAT TO SEE
BRADBURY SCIENCE MUSEUM
15th Street and Central Avenue, Los Alamos, 505-667-4444; www.lanl.gov
Displays artifacts relating to the history of the laboratory and the atomic bomb. Exhibits on modern nuclear weapons, life sciences, materials sciences, computers, particle accelerators, geothermal, fusion and fission energy sources.
Daily.

FULLER LODGE ART CENTER AND GALLERY
2132 Central Ave., Los Alamos, 505-662-9331; www.artfulnm.org
This historic log building is the setting for changing exhibits featuring arts and crafts of northern New Mexico.
Monday-Saturday.

LOS ALAMOS HISTORICAL MUSEUM
Fuller Lodge Cultural Center, 1921 Juniper, Los Alamos, 505-662-6272; www.losalamoshistory.org
See artifacts, photos, other material tracing local history from prehistoric to present times; exhibit on the Manhattan Project. Daily.

PAJARITO MOUNTAIN SKI AREA
397 Camp May Road, Los Alamos, 505-662-5725; www.skipajarito.com
Despite being a small resort (280 acres), Pajarito offers some excellent and challenging terrain, making it a well-kept secret for local ski buffs.
Friday-Sunday, 9 a.m.-4 p.m.

WHERE TO STAY
★BEST WESTERN HILLTOP HOUSE HOTEL
400 Trinity Drive, Los Alamos, 505-662-2441, 800-462-0936; www.bestwestern.com
92 rooms. Complimentary breakfast. Business center. Pets accepted. Fitness center. Pool. $

RED RIVER

See also Cimarron, Taos

This was a gold-mining boomtown with a population of 3,000 in the early days of the 20th century. Today it is a summer vacation and winter ski center. Trout fishing, hunting (deer, elk and small game), snowmobiling, horseback riding and backpacking are all popular.

WHAT TO SEE
RED RIVER SKI AREA

400 Pioneer Road, Red River, 505-754-2223; redriverskiarea.com

Two triple, three double chairlifts, surface tow; patrol, school, rentals; snow-making. Fifty-seven runs; vertical drop 1,600 feet.

Thanksgiving-late March, daily. Chairlift: Memorial Day-Labor Day (also).

SPECIAL EVENTS
MARDI GRAS IN THE MOUNTAINS

Red River; www.redriver.org

Ski slope parades, Cajun food. February.

WHERE TO STAY
★★ALPINE LODGE

417 W. Main, Red River, 575-754-2952, 800-252-2333; www.thealpinelodge.com

45 rooms. Restaurant, bar. $

★BEST WESTERN RIVER'S EDGE

301 W. River St., Red River, 505-754-1766, 877-600-9990; www.bestwestern.com

30 rooms. Complimentary breakfast. Pets accepted. $

WHERE TO EAT
★★SUNDANCE

401 E. High St., Red River, 505-754-2971; www.redrivernm.com

Mexican. Dinner. Children's menu. $

BANDELIER NATIONAL MONUMENT

A major portion of this 32,000-acre area is designated wilderness. The most accessible part is in Frijoles Canyon, which features cave dwellings carved from the soft volcanic turf and houses built out from the cliffs. There's also a great circular pueblo ruin (Tyuonyi) on the floor of the canyon. These houses and caves were occupied from about A.D. 1150 to 1550. The depletion of resources forced residents to abandon the area. Some of the modern pueblos along the Rio Grande are related to the prehistoric Anasazi people of the canyon and the surrounding mesa country. There is a paved one-mile self-guided trail to walk and view these sites. The monument is named after Adolph Bandelier, ethnologist and author of the novel, The Delight Makers, which used Frijoles Canyon as its locale.

There are 70 miles of trails (free permits required for overnight trips; pets not accepted on the trails). Visitor center with exhibits depicting the culture of the pueblo region, ranger-guided tours (summer), campfire programs (Memorial Day-Labor Day). Campground (March-November, daily).

ROSWELL

See also Carlsbad

Did a UFO crash here in 1947? That has been the question for decades. The government maintains that materials recovered were from a top-secret research balloon. UFO proponents believe it was wreckage of an alien spacecraft and that the military has been covering it up. You decide after a visit to the International UFO Museum, located in Roswell.

WHAT TO SEE

BITTER LAKE NATIONAL WILDLIFE REFUGE
4067 Bitter Lakes Road, Roswell, 505-622-6755; www.fws.gov
Wildlife observation, auto tour. Daily.

BOTTOMLESS LAKES STATE PARK
Roswell, 10 miles east on Highway 380, then six miles south on Highway 409, 575-624-6058; www.emnrd.state.nm.us/PRD/bottomless.htm
Bordered by high red bluffs, seven small lakes were formed when circulating underground water formed caverns that collapsed into sinkholes. Headquarters at -Cottonwood Lake has displays and a network of trails. Beach and swimming at Lea Lake only; some lakes have fishing (trout), paddleboat rentals; picnicking, camping. Daily.

HISTORICAL CENTER FOR SOUTHEAST NEW MEXICO
200 N. Lea, Roswell, 575-622-8333
See turn-of-the-century furnishings, communications exhibits and more; research library and archives.
Daily, afternoons; Friday, by appointment.

INTERNATIONAL UFO MUSEUM & RESEARCH CENTER
114 N. Main St., Roswell, 505-625-9495, 800-822-3545; www.iufomrc.org
Check out the exhibits here on various aspects of UFO phenomena; video viewing room.
Daily 9 a.m.-5 p.m.

NEW MEXICO MILITARY INSTITUTE
101 W. College Blvd., Roswell, 575-622-6250, 800-421-5376; www.nmmi.edu
This state-supported high school and junior college was established in 1891. Alumni Memorial Chapel, near the entrance, has beautiful windows. Also here is the General Douglas L. McBride Military Museum with an interpretation of 20th-century American military history.
Tuesday-Friday. Occasional marching formations and parades. Tours.

ROSWELL MUSEUM AND ART CENTER
100 W. 11th St., Roswell, 575-624-6744; www.roswellmuseum.org
The center features a Southwest arts collection including Georgia O'Keeffe, Peter Hurd, Henriette Wyeth; Native American, Mexican-American and western arts. Robert H. Goddard's early liquid-fueled rocketry experiments are on display.
Monday-Saturday, also Sunday and holiday afternoons.

SPECIAL EVENTS
UFO ENCOUNTERS FESTIVAL

International UFO Museum & Research Center, 114 Main St., Roswell, 505-625-9495;
www.iufomrc.org

The festival includes the UFO Expo trade show, alien chase, alien parade, costume contest, guest speeches.

July Fourth weekend.

WHERE TO STAY
★★BEST WESTERN SALLY PORT INN & SUITES

2000 N. Main St., Roswell, 505-622-6430; www.bestwestern.com

124 rooms. Complimentary breakfast. Fitness center. Restaurant, bar. Pool. $

RUIDOSO

See also Alamagordo

This resort town in the Sierra Blanca Mountains, surrounded by the trees of the Lincoln National Forests, has seen spectacular growth. It is a year-round resort with skiing in winter and fishing and horseback riding in summer. If you're planning to visit in the summer, secure confirmed reservations before leaving home. The forested mountain slopes and streams are idyllic, the air is clear and cool and there are many interesting things to do.

WHAT TO SEE
HUBBARD MUSEUM OF THE AMERICAN WEST

841 Highway 70 West, Ruidoso Downs, 575-378-4142; www.hubbardmuseum.org

Western-themed exhibits relating to horses and pioneer life.

Daily.

LINCOLN STATE MONUMENT

Ruidoso, 30 miles east on Highway 70, then 10 miles northwest on Highway 380

Lincoln was the site of the infamous Lincoln County War and a hangout of Billy the Kid. Several properties have been restored, including the Old Lincoln County Courthouse and the mercantile store of John Tunstall.

Tours: summer; reservations required. Daily.

SKI APACHE RESORT

Highway 532, Ruidoso, 505-464-3600; www.skiapache.com

The resort has a four-passenger gondola; two quad, five triple, one double chairlift; surface lift; patrol, school, rentals. Fifty-five runs, longest run more than two miles; vertical drop 1,800 feet.

Thanksgiving-Easter, daily.

THE SPENCER THEATER FOR THE PERFORMING ARTS

108 Spencer Road, Airport Highway 220, Alto, 575-336-4800, 888-818-7872;
www.spencertheater.com

This stunning $22 million structure was created from 450 tons of Spanish limestone; breathtaking blown glass installations by Seattle artist Dale Chihuly are inside.

Tours Tuesday, Thursday.

SPECIAL EVENTS
ASPENFEST
Ruidoso, 505-257-7395, 877-784-3676; www.ruidosonow.com/aspenfest
The festival includes a motorcycle convention, the official state chili cook-off, arts and crafts.
Early October.

HORSE RACING
Ruidoso Downs, 1461 Highway 70 West, 573-378-4431; www.ruidownsracing.com
Thoroughbred and quarter horse racing; pari-mutuel betting. Home of All-American Futurity, the world's richest quarter horse race (Labor Day); All-American Derby and All-American Gold Cup.
Thursday-Sunday and holidays. Early May-Labor Day.

RUIDOSO ART FESTIVAL
Paradise Canyon Road and Sudderth Drive, Ruidoso, 505-257-7395;
www.ruidosonow.com/artfestival
See more than 125 artists exhibits displaying painting, drawings, photography, glass, porcelain, woodwork, jewelry, pottery and sculpture.
Last full weekend in July.

SMOKEY BEAR STAMPEDE
8 Fifth St., Ruidoso
Fireworks, music festival, parade, dances, barbecue.
Early July.

WHERE TO STAY
★SWISS CHALET INN
1451 Mechem Drive, Ruidoso, 505-258-3333; www.sciruidoso.com
82 rooms. Restaurant, bar. Complimentary breakfast. Bar. Pets accepted. Pool. $

SANTA FE
See also Española, Las Vegas, Los Alamos
This picturesque city, the oldest capital in the United States, is set at the base of the Sangre de Cristo Mountains. A few miles south, these mountains taper down from a height of 13,000 feet to a rolling plain, marking the end of the North American Rockies. Because of the altitude, the climate is cool and bracing. There's much to do and see here all year.

Don Pedro de Peralta, who laid out the plaza and built the Palace of the Governors in 1610, founded Santa Fe. In 1680, the Pueblo revolted and drove the Spanish out. In 1692, led by General Don Diego de Vargas, the Spanish made a peaceful reentry. The opening of the Santa Fe Trail followed Mexico's independence from Spain in 1821. In 1846, General Stephen Watts Kearny led U.S. troops into the town without resistance and hoisted the American flag. During the Civil War, Confederate forces occupied the town for two weeks before they were driven out.

In addition to its own attractions, Santa Fe is also the center of a colorful area, which can be reached by car. The Pueblos, farmers for centuries, are also extremely gifted craftworkers and painters. Their pottery, basketry and jewelry are especially beautiful. At various times during the year, especially on the saint's day of their particular pueblo, they present dramatic ceremonial dances. Visitors are usually welcome.

WHAT TO SEE
ATALAYA MOUNTAIN HIKING TRAIL
St. John's College, 1160 Camino Cruz Blanca, Santa Fe
The Atalaya Mountain Trail, accessible from the parking lot at St. John's College, is one of the most popular and easily accessible hiking trails in Santa Fe. Hikers have the option of taking the longer route (Trail 174), which is approximately seven miles round-trip, or parking further up near the Ponderosa Ridge development and doing a 4.6-mile loop (Trail 170). Both trails eventually join and take you toward the top of Atalaya Mountain, a 9,121-foot peak. The first few miles of the trail are relatively easy, but it becomes increasingly steep and strenuous as you near the summit, which offers great views of the Rio Grande valley and the city below.

CANYON ROAD TOUR
Canyon Road, Santa Fe
Many artists live on this thoroughfare, and there is no better way to savor the unique character of Santa Fe than to travel along its narrow, picturesque old streets, which includes the famous Camino del Monte Sol. Stop in the Cristo Rey Church, the largest adobe structure in the U.S., with beautiful ancient stone reredos (altar screens).
Monday-Friday.

CATHEDRAL OF ST. FRANCIS
Santa Fe Plaza, 231 Cathedral Place, Santa Fe, 505-982-5619
This French Romanesque cathedral was built in 1869 under the direction of Archbishop Jean-Baptiste Lamy, the first archbishop of Sante Fe (the novel Death Comes for the Archbishop is based on his life). Also here is La Conquistadora Chapel, said to be the country's oldest shrine to the Virgin Mary. Daily 8 a.m.-5:45 p.m., except during mass. Tours: summer.

COLLEGE OF SANTA FE
1600 St., Michael's Drive, Santa Fe, 505-473-6133, 800-456-2673; www.csf.edu
Established in 1947; 1,400 students. Includes the Greer Garson Theatre Center, Garson Communications Center and Fogelson Library.

CROSS OF THE MARTYRS
Paseo de la Loma, 545 Canyon Road, Santa Fe, 505-983-2567;
www.historicsantafe.org/popcross.html
This large, hilltop cross weighs 76 tons, stands 25 feet tall and honors the memory of more than 20 Franciscan priests and numerous Spanish colonists who were killed during the 1680 Pueblo Revolt against Spanish dominion. Dedicated in 1920, this cross shouldn't be confused with the newer one at nearby Fort Marcy Park. Vistas from the old cross include those of the Sangre de Cristos mountain range immediately northeast, the Jemez about 40 miles west and the Sandias, 50 miles south near Albuquerque.

EL RANCHO DE LAS GOLONDRINAS

334 Los Pinos Road, Santa Fe, 505-471-2261; www.golondrinas.org

This living history museum is set in a 200-acre rural valley and depicts Spanish Colonial life in New Mexico from 1700 through 1900. It was once a stop on El Camino Real and is one of the most historic ranches in the Southwest. Original colonial buildings date from the 18th century. Special festivals offer visitors a glimpse of the music, dance, clothing, crafts and celebrations of Spanish Colonial New Mexico.

June-September: Wednesday-Sunday 10 a.m.-4 p.m.

FEDERAL COURT HOUSE

Federal Place and Paseo De Peralta, Santa Fe

A monument to American frontiersman Kit Carson stands in front of the courthouse.

GEORGIA O'KEEFFE MUSEUM

217 Johnson St., Santa Fe, 505-946-1000; www.okeeffemuseum.org

One of the most important American artists of the 20th century, Georgia O'Keeffe lived and worked at Ghost Ranch near Abiqui for much of her career, drawing inspiration from the colors and forms of the surrounding desert environment. This museum houses the world's largest permanent collection of her artwork and is also dedicated to the study of American Modernism, displaying special exhibits of many of her contemporaries.

November-June, Monday-Tuesday, Thursday, Saturday-Sunday 10 a.m.-5 p.m., Friday 10 a.m.-8 p.m.; daily rest of year.

HYDE MEMORIAL STATE PARK

740 Hyde Park Road, Santa Fe, 505-983-7175; www.emnrd.state.nm.us

Perched 8,500 feet up in the Sangre de Cristo Mountains near the Santa Fe Ski Basin, this state park serves as a base camp for backpackers and skiers in the Santa Fe National Forests. Cross-country skiing, rentals, picnicking, camping. Daily.

HYDE PARK HIKING/BIKING TRAILS

Hyde Memorial State Park, Santa Fe; www.emnrd.state.nm.us

One of the closest hiking opportunities to Santa Fe is available in the Hyde Park area on the road to the ski basin. From the Hyde Park parking lot, you can access a loop covering three different trails offering easy hiking that's popular with dog walkers and locals on weekends. The loop consists of switchbacks, moderate grades and creek crossings and has good views of the mixed conifer forest. If you come during the fall, you can view the spectacularly colorful changing of the Aspen leaves. Start with the common trailhead at the far side of the parking lot. Look for the Borrego Trail (150), Bear Wallow Trail (182) and Winsor Trail (254) markings. A loop covering all three is about four miles long.

INSTITUTE OF AMERICAN INDIAN ARTS MUSEUM

108 Cathedral Place, Santa Fe, 505-983-8900; www.iaiancad.org

The Institute of American Indian Arts, established in 1962, runs a college in south Santa Fe in addition to a museum just off the Plaza. The museum is the only one in the country dedicated solely to collecting and exhibiting contemporary Native American art, much of it produced by the staff and faculty of the college.

June-September, daily 9 a.m.-5 p.m.; October-May, daily 10 a.m.-5 p.m.

KOKOPELLI RAFTING ADVENTURES

551 W. Cordova Road, Santa Fe, 505-983-3734, 800-879-9035; www.kokopelliraft.com

Kokopelli Rafting offers a full range of white-water rafting trips to the Rio Grande and Rio Chama rivers, as well as sea kayaking trips to Cochiti and Abiqui lakes and Big Bend National Park in Texas. Excursions include half-day, full-day, overnight and two- to eight-day wilderness expeditions. Transportation from Santa Fe included.

April-September.

LAS COSAS SCHOOL OF COOKING

DeVargas Center, 181 Paseo de Peralta, Santa Fe, 877-229-7184;
www.lascosascooking.com

Located within a store stocked with gourmet kitchen tools and elegant tableware, this cooking center offers hands-on culinary education experiences that fill a morning or evening. Taught by school director John Vollertsen and chefs from New Mexico's leading restaurants, the classes cover a wide range of topics.

Classes usually start at 10 a.m. and 6 p.m.

LENSIC PERFORMING ARTS CENTER

211 W. San Francisco St., Santa Fe, 505-988-1234; www.lensic.com

The Lensic Theater is one of Santa Fe's historical and architectural gems, reopened after a full restoration in 2001. The structure was first built in 1931 in a Moorish/Spanish Renaissance style and has always been Santa Fe's premiere theater space, having played host to celebrities such as Roy Rogers and Judy Garland over the years. Since reopening, it has provided a constantly changing schedule of theater, symphony and performing arts events.

LORETTO CHAPEL

207 Old Santa Fe Trail, Santa Fe, 505-982-0092; www.lorettochapel.com

Modeled after St. Chapelle Cathedral in Paris, this chapel, built in 1873, was the first Gothic building built west of the Mississippi. The chapel itself is not particularly impressive, but what draws countless tourists is the miraculous stairway, a two-story spiral wooden staircase built without any nails or central supports that seems to defy engineering logic.

Summer, Monday-Saturday 9 a.m.-6 p.m., Sunday 10:30 a.m.-5 p.m.; winter, Monday-Saturday 9 a.m.-5 p.m., Sunday 10:30 a.m.-5 p.m.

MUSEUM OF FINE ARTS

107 W. Palace Ave., Santa Fe, 505-476-5072; www.museumofnewmexico.org

Designed by Isaac Hamilton Rapp in 1917, the museum is one of Santa Fe's earliest Pueblo revival structures and its oldest art museum. It contains more than 20,000 holdings, with an emphasis on Southwest regional art and the artists of Santa Fe and Taos from the early 20th century. The St. Francis Auditorium inside the museum also presents lectures, musical events, plays and various other performances.

Free admission on Friday evenings. Tuesday-Sunday 10 a.m.-5 p.m., Friday 5-8 p.m.

MUSEUM OF INDIAN ARTS AND CULTURE

710 Camino Lejo, Santa Fe, 505-476-1250; www.indianartsandculture.org

When the Spanish arrived in the Southwest in the 16th century, they found many sprawling towns and villages, which they referred to as pueblos, a name that is still used to identify Native American communities here. The Museum of Indian Arts and Culture houses an extensive collection of historic and contemporary Pueblo art from throughout the Southwest. The highlight is an excellent interpretive section where you can encounter Pueblo cultures from the viewpoint and narrative of modern-day natives and exhibit designers. The museum itself is housed in a large, adobe-style building that blends architecturally into the surroundings and also houses many outstanding examples of Pueblo textiles, pottery, jewelry, contemporary paintings and other rotating exhibits.

Tuesday-Sunday10 a.m.-5 p.m.

MUSEUM OF INTERNATIONAL FOLK ART

706 Camino Lejo, Santa Fe, 505-476-1200; www.moifa.org

The Museum of International Folk Art, first opened in 1953, contains more than 130,000 objects, billing itself as the world's largest folk museum dedicated to the study of traditional cultural art. Much of the massive collection was acquired when the late Italian immigrant and architect/designer Alexander Girard donated his 106,000-object collection of toys, figurines, figurative ceramics, miniatures and religious/ceremonial art, which he had collected from more than 100 countries around the world. This is a rich museum experience and can easily take several hours to explore. Two museum shops offer a wide variety of folk-oriented books, clothing and jewelry to choose from.

Tuesday-Sunday 10 a.m.-5 p.m.

MUSEUM OF SPANISH COLONIAL ART

750 Camino Lejo, Santa Fe, 505-982-2226; www.spanishcolonial.org

This small museum, housed in a building designed in 1930 by famous local architect John Gaw Meem, holds some 3,000 objects showcasing traditional Hispanic art in New Mexico dating from conquest to present day. The collection includes many early works in wood, tin and other local materials, as well as numerous works by contemporary New Mexican artists.

The galleries are open Tuesday-Sunday 10 a.m.-5 p.m.

PALACE OF THE GOVERNORS

105 Palace Ave., Santa Fe, 505-476-5100; www.palaceofthegovernors.org

Built in 1610, this is the oldest public building in continuous use in the U.S. It was the seat of government in New Mexico for more than 300 years. Lew Wallace, governor of the territory (1878-1881), wrote part of *Ben Hur* here in 1880. It is now a major museum of Southwestern history. The Palace,

Museum of Fine Arts, Museum of Indian Arts and Culture, Museum of International Folk Art and state monuments all make up the Museum of New Mexico. Free admission Friday evenings. Tours.
Monday-Saturday 10:15 a.m.-noon, Tuesday-Sunday 10 a.m.-5 p.m., Friday 5-8 p.m.

PLAZA

100 Old Santa Fe Trail, Santa Fe

The Santa Fe Plaza, steeped in a rich history, has been a focal point for commerce and social activities in Santa Fe since the early 17th century. The area is marked by a central tree-lined park surrounded by some of Santa Fe's most important historical landmarks, many of which hail from Spanish colonial times. The most important landmark is the Palace of the Governors. Native American artists from nearby Pueblos sell handmade artwork in front of the Palace and various museums, shops and dining establishments surround the Plaza, making it the top tourist destination in Santa Fe. Numerous festivals and activities are held throughout the year.

SAN ILDEFONSO PUEBLO

Santa Fe, 505-455-2273

This pueblo is famous for its beautiful surroundings and its black, red and polychrome pottery made famous by Maria Poveka Martinez. Daily; closed winter weekends; visitors must register at the visitor center. Various festivals take place here throughout the year. The circular structure with the staircase leading up to its rim is a kiva or ceremonial chamber. There are two shops in the pueblo plaza and a tribal museum adjoins the governor's office.

SAN MIGUEL MISSION

401 Old Santa Fe Trail, Santa Fe, 505-983-3974

Built in the early 1600s, this is the oldest church in the U.S. still in use. Construction was overseen by Fray Alonso de Benavidez, along with a group of Tlaxcala Indians from Mexico, who did most of the work. The original adobe still remains beneath the stucco walls and the interior has been restored along with Santa Fe's oldest wooden reredos (altar screen). Church services are still held on Sundays.
Sunday 1-4:30 p.m.; summer, Monday-Saturday 9 a.m.-4:30 p.m.; winter, Monday-Saturday 10 a.m.-4 p.m.

SANTA FE CHILDREN'S MUSEUM

1050 Old Pecos Trail, Santa Fe, 505-989-8359; www.santafechildrensmuseum.org

The hands-on exhibits invite kids to make magnetic structures, route water streams, create paintings, illustrate cartoon movies, discover plants on a greenhouse scavenger hunt, scale an 18-foot-high climbing wall, use an old-fashioned pitcher pump and weave beads and fabric on a loom. Local artists and scientists make appearances.
Wednesday-Saturday 10 a.m.-5 p.m., Sunday noon-5 p.m.

SANTA FE FASHION OUTLETS

8380 Cerrillos Road, Santa Fe, 505-474-4000; www.fashionoutletssantafe.com

This is New Mexico's only outlet center. More than 40 stores include Bose, Brooks Brothers and more.

SANTA FE NATIONAL FOREST

1474 Rodeo Road, Santa Fe, 505-438-7840; www.fs.fed.us/r3/sfe

This forest covers more than 1.5 million acres. Fishing is excellent in the Pecos and Jemez rivers and tributary streams and hiking trails are close to unusual geologic formations. You'll find hot springs in the Jemez Mountains. Four wilderness areas within the forest total more than 300,000 acres. Campgrounds are provided by the Forest Service at more than 40 locations.

SANTA FE RAFTING COMPANY

1000 Cerrillos Road, Santa Fe, 505-988-4914, 888-988-4914; www.santaferafting.com

The Rio Grande and Rio Chama rivers north of Santa Fe provide excellent opportunities for river running and white-water rafting. Santa Fe Rafting Company offers several rafting trips including half-day, full-day and multi-day camping excursions, some of which include a boxed lunch. The biggest rapids are found on their Taos Box full-day trip, open to anyone over age 12. All trips include roundtrip transportation from Santa Fe.
April-September.

SANTA FE SCHOOL OF COOKING

116 W. San Francisco St., Santa Fe, 505-983-4511, 800-982-4688;
www.santafeschoolofcooking.com

Sign up for classes offered several times weekly in traditional and contemporary Southwestern cuisine. Culinary tours involve classes with nationally renowned chefs and trips to local farms and wineries.

SANTA FE SOUTHERN RAILWAY

410 S. Guadalupe St., Santa Fe, 505-989-8600, 888-989-8600; www.sfsr.com

Several scenic train rides in restored vintage cars are offered to the public, following the original high desert route to and from Lamy. The rides range from short scenic roundtrips to longer outings that include picnics, barbecues and various holiday-themed events, such as the Halloween Highball Train and New Year's Eve Party Train. The start of the route is housed in the old Santa Fe Depot, where you can view vintage railcars and shop for gifts and memorabilia in the original mission-style train depot.

SANTA FE TRAIL MUSEUM

614 Maxwell Ave., Springer, 505-483-2682

The Santa Fe Trail Museum displays artifacts and exhibits about pioneer life on and around the trail from 1880 to 1949.
Open daily 9 a.m.-4 p.m., summer only.

SENA PLAZA AND PRINCE PLAZA
Washington and East Palace avenues, Santa Fe
Both plazas include small shops and old houses, built behind portals and around central patios.

SHIDONI BRONZE FOUNDRY AND GALLERY
1508 Bishop's Lodge Road, Santa Fe, 505-988-8001; www.shidoni.com
A fantastic resource for art collectors and sculptors, Shidoni consists of a bronze foundry, art gallery and outdoor sculpture garden set in an eight-acre apple orchard. Artists from around the country come to work at Shidoni's 14,000-square-foot foundry, open to the general public for self-guided tours. Explore the lovely sculpture garden during daylight hours or shop for works of bronze and metal in the adjacent gallery.
Gallery: Monday-Saturday 9 a.m.-5 p.m. Foundry: Monday-Friday noon-1 p.m., Saturday 9 a.m.-5 p.m.

SHONA SOL SCULPTURE GARDEN
Turquoise Trail, Highway 14, Santa Fe, 505-473-5611
See exhibits of some of the world's finest stone sculptors.
Saturday-Sunday 10 a.m.-6 p.m.

SKI SANTA FE
2209 Brothers Road, Santa Fe, 505-982-4429; www.skisantafe.com
World-class skiing and snowboarding in the majestic Sangre de Cristo Mountains is only a 20-minute drive from the downtown Santa Fe Plaza. Ski Santa Fe is a family-owned resort catering to skiers and snowboarders of all levels. In addition to great views of the city, the 12,075-foot summit offers six lifts and 67 runs (20 percent easy, 40 percent more difficult, 40 percent most difficult), with a total of 660 acres of terrain. The longest run is three miles and the mountain offers a vertical drop of 1,725 feet. The average yearly snowfall is 225 inches. A PSIA-certified ski school offers group and private lessons for adults and children and there are restaurants, rental shops and a clothing boutique onsite. The Chipmunk Corner offers activities and lessons for children ages 4-9.
Late November-early April, daily.

STATE CAPITOL
Old Santa Fe Trail at Paseo de Peralta, Santa Fe, 505-986-4589
This round building in modified Territorial style is intended to resemble a Zia Sun symbol.
Mid-May-August, Monday-Saturday 8 a.m.-7 p.m.; September-mid-May, Monday-Friday 8 a.m.-7 p.m.

TEN THOUSAND WAVES
3451, Hyde Park Road, Santa Fe, 505-982-9304; www.tenthousandwaves.com
This exquisite Japanese-themed spa and bathhouse is a genuine treat. Located in a unique Zen-like setting in the Sangre de Cristo Mountains, Ten Thousand Waves offers soothing hot tubs, massages, facials, herbal wraps and other spa treatments. Includes coed public hot tubs (where clothing is op-

tional before 8:15 p.m.), a women-only tub, secluded private tubs and large private tubs that can accommodate up to 20. All the tubs are clean and chlorine-free and amenities such as kimonos, towels, sandals, lotion and lockers are provided for you. Be sure to call ahead for reservations, especially for massage services.

TURQUOISE TRAIL
Highway 14, Santa Fe; www.turquoisetrail.org
Undeniably the most interesting path between Albuquerque and Santa Fe, this poetically named route is the 50-mile reach of New Mexico 14 that parallels Interstate 25 north from Interstate 40 and is a National Scenic Byway. Cutting a course along the backside of the Sandias just north of Albuquerque, the trail winds through a rolling countryside of sumptuous, cactus-lined hills populated by tiny burgs. Along the way, watch for crumbling rock houses, ancient family cemeteries and long-abandoned ranch houses and barns. Stops include the town of Golden, where the first discovery of gold west of the Mississippi was made and where a silver boom once employed more than 1,200 workers, and Madrid, once rich in coal mines but today the refuge of artists whose galleries and shops have become lucrative businesses. The wonderful Mine Shaft Tavern offers burgers, buffalo steaks and cold beer, along with live entertainment on weekends.

WHEELWRIGHT MUSEUM
704 Camino Lejo, Santa Fe, 505-982-4636, 800-607-4636; www.wheelwright.org
Founded in 1937 by Mary Cabot Wheelwright and Navajo singer/medicine man Hastiin Klah to help preserve Navajo art and traditions, the Wheelwright now devotes itself to hosting major exhibits of Native American artists from tribes throughout North America. The Case Trading Post in the basement sells pottery, jewelry, textiles, books, prints and other gift items.
Monday-Saturday 10 a.m.-5 p.m., Sunday 1-5 p.m.

SPECIAL EVENTS
CHRISTMAS EVE CANYON ROAD WALK
Santa Fe Plaza, Canyon Road, Santa Fe, 800-777-2489; www.newmexico.org
This major Santa Fe tradition is not to be missed. Adorned with thousands of farolitos (paper bag lanterns), the streets and homes around Canyon Road play host to a unique and colorful festival each Christmas Eve. Thousands of pedestrians stroll up and down the streets while singing Christmas carols, lighting bonfires and enjoying hot apple cider.
December 24.

EIGHT NORTHERN PUEBLOS ARTS & CRAFTS SHOW
San Juan Pueblo, Santa Fe, 505-747-1593
This annual festival features traditional and contemporary American Indian art at more than 500 booths. Approximately 1,500 artists attend and have their work judged for prizes before being displayed for sale.
Third weekend in July.

FIESTA AT SANTO DOMINGO PUEBLO

Santo Domingo Pueblo, Santa Fe, 505-465-2214

This is probably the largest and most famous of the Rio Grande pueblo fiestas. Includes a corn dance.

Early August.

INDIAN MARKET

Santa Fe Plaza, Santa Fe, 505-983-5220

Buyers and collectors from all over the world come to the largest and oldest Native American arts show and market in the world. More than 1,200 artists from 100 North American tribes participate in the show, with around 600 outdoor booths set up in the middle of the ancient Santa Fe Plaza. The market is a great opportunity to meet the artists and buy directly. Numerous outdoor booths sell food. The event draws an estimated 100,000 visitors to Santa Fe during the weekend.

Late August.

INTERNATIONAL FOLK ART MARKET

Milner Plaza, Camino Lejo, Santa Fe, 505-476-1189; www.folkartmarket.org

This new two-day event brings together 75 master folk artists from Bangladesh to Zimbabwe in a celebration of color, music and cuisine. Includes everything from textiles to woodblock prints to ceramics and sculptures. In addition to shopping for works to take home, visitors can attend demonstrations and lectures, tour local folk art collections, bid on works at an auction and participate in children's activities.

Mid-July.

INVITATIONAL ANTIQUE INDIAN ART SHOW

Sweeney Center, 201 W. Marcy, Santa Fe

This large show attracts dealers, collectors and museum curators. Includes pre-1935 items.

Two days in mid-August.

MOUNTAIN MAN RENDEZVOUS AND FESTIVAL

105 W. Palace Ave., Santa Fe, 505-476-5100; www.santafe.org

Costumed mountain men ride into town on horseback for the Museum of New Mexico's annual buffalo roast, part of a large gathering of trappers and traders from the pre-1840 wilderness. Participants sell primitive equipment, tools and trinkets and compete in period survival skills such as knife and tomahawk throwing, muzzleloader rifle shooting and cannon firing.

Early August.

RODEO DE SANTA FE

Santa Fe Rodeo Grounds, Santa Fe, 505-471-4300; www.rodeodesantafe.org

The Santa Fe rodeo offers a chance to see real cowboys and bucking broncos in action. Various professional competitions and public exhibitions are put on during the brief summer season. Rodeo events generally happen during evening and weekend matinee hours.

A downtown rodeo parade takes place in mid-June at the start of the season.

SANTA FE CHAMBER MUSIC FESTIVAL

St. Francis Auditorium, Museum of Fine Arts and the Lensic Performing Arts Center,
Santa Fe, 505-983-2075, 888-221-9836; www.sfcmf.org
Since the first season of the festival in 1973, this artistic tradition has grown into a major event consisting of more than 80 performances, open rehearsals, concert previews and roundtable discussions with composers and musicians during the annual summer season. Performances are frequently heard on National Public Radio.
July-August.

SANTA FE FIESTA

Santa Fe Plaza, Santa Fe, 505-988-7575; www.santafefiesta.org
This ancient folk festival dating back to 1712 features historical pageantry, religious observances, arts and crafts shows and street dancing. It also celebrates the reconquest of Santa Fe by Don Diego de Vargas in 1692.
First weekend in September.

SANTA FE OPERA

Highways 84/285, Santa Fe, 505-986-5900, 800-280-4654; www.santafeopera.org
Founded in 1957, this opera company presents one of the world's most famous and respected opera festivals each summer. The company stages five works per season, including two classics, a lesser-known work by a well-known composer, a Richard Strauss offering and a world premiere or new American staging. What's more, the Santa Fe Opera performs in a gorgeous hilltop amphitheater. Designed by Polshek & Partners of New York, who refurbished Carnegie Hall in Manhattan, the Opera incorporates bold, swooping lines with excellent sight lines and is known for superb acoustics.
Backstage tours early July-late August: Monday-Saturday at 1 p.m. Performances begin between 8 and 9 p.m.

SANTA FE PRO MUSICA

Lensic Performing Arts Center, 211 W. San Francisco St., Santa Fe, 505-988-4640,
800-960-6680; www.santafepromusica.com
This chamber orchestra and ensemble performs classical and contemporary music. A performance of Messiah takes place during Christmas season.
September-May.

SANTA FE SYMPHONY AND CHORUS

Lensic Performing Arts Center, 211 W. San Francisco St., Santa Fe, 505-983-1414,
800-480-1319; www.sf-symphony.org
Santa Fe's orchestral company presents works in classical and jazz music, as well as specialty programs that may include the music of Spain and Mexico. The season generally runs from early October through Memorial Day, with matinée and evening performances at the Lensic Performing Arts Center.
Early October-late May.

SANTA FE STAGES

Lensic Performing Arts Center, Santa Fe, 505-982-6680; www.santafestages.org
With presentations offered primarily at the wonderfully renovated and his-

toric Lensic Performing Arts Center, Santa Fe Stages hosts a season of dance, music and theater with national appeal. The season typically begins before Memorial Day and ends in late September and may offer Irish folk dance, classical ballet, opera, jazz, drama, comedy and cabaret.
Late May-late September.

SANTA FE WINE AND CHILE FIESTA
551 W. Cordova Road, Santa Fe, 505-438-8060; www.santafewineandchile.org
Begun in 1991, this wildly popular festival honoring the best in food and drink brings in some 2,000 appreciative fans from around the state and across the country. Roughly 30 local restaurants and 90 wineries from around the globe team up with a half-dozen or so of America's top celebrity chefs and cookbook authors to present a culinary extravaganza in a variety of venues around town. Includes wine seminars, cooking demonstrations, special vintners lunches and dinners and the gastronomic circus called the Grand Tasting, staged in mammoth tents on the Santa Fe Opera grounds.
Late September.

SPANISH MARKET
Museum of Spanish Colonial Art, 750 Camino Lejo, Santa Fe, 505-982-2226;
www.spanishmarket.org
The rich and colorful Hispanic art traditions of Northern New Mexico are celebrated twice a year during Spanish Market, the oldest and largest exhibition and sale of traditional Hispanic art in the U.S. The smaller winter market in December is held indoors in the Sweeney Convention Center (201 W. Marcy St.), while the larger summer market occupies the entire Santa Fe Plaza for one weekend in July. As many as 300 vendors sell and display santos (carved saints), hide paintings, textiles, furniture, jewelry, tinwork, basketry, pottery, bonework and other locally produced handicrafts reflecting the unique and deeply religious traditional art that still flourishes in this part of New Mexico. Sponsored by the Spanish Colonial Arts Society.
December and late July.

TESUQUE PUEBLO FLEA MARKET
Highway 84/285, Santa Fe, 505-670-2599; www.tesuquepuebloffleamarket.com
You'll find hundreds of vendors offering antiques, gems, jewelry, pottery, rugs and folk art, all at very competitive prices, at this flea market. Plan on devoting a couple of hours to browse all the various treasures and myriad of vendor booths stretching for several acres.

ZOZOBRA FESTIVAL
Fort Marcy Park, 490 Washington Ave., Santa Fe, 505-660-1965; www.zozobra.com
Each year on the Thursday before Labor Day, the Kiwanis Club of Santa Fe hosts the burning of Zozobra, a 50-foot effigy of Old Man Gloom, whose passing is designed to dispel the hardships and travails of the previous year. Zozobra started in 1924 as part of the Fiesta's celebration when a local artist conceived a ritual based on a Yaqui Indian celebration from Mexico. Over the years, Zozobra caught on and the crowd sizes have grown, making it Santa Fe's largest and most colorful festival. Lasting for several hours, as many as

60,000 visitors crowd into a large grassy field in Fort Marcy Park to listen to live bands, watch spectacular fireworks displays and cheer the ritual burning. The celebration continues through the Labor Day weekend with booths and activities set up in the nearby plaza.

Thursday before Labor Day.

WHERE TO STAY

★★★THE BISHOP'S LODGE RANCH RESORT & SPA

1297 Bishop's Lodge Road, Santa Fe, 505-983-6377, 800-419-0492; www.bishopslodge.com

This lodge is a Santa Fe treasure. The historic resort dates back to 1918 and its chapel, listed on the National Register of Historic Places, remains a popular site for weddings. This resort is vintage chic, with rooms decorated either in an old Sante Fe style or with more modern décor. The ShaNah Spa and Wellness Center is influenced by Native American traditions—each treatment begins with a soothing drumming and blessing. Modern seasonal American cuisine is the focus at the lodge's restaurant, Las Fuentes Restaurant & Bar. 111 rooms. Restaurant, bar. Fitness center. Pool. Spa. Pets accepted. Tennis. $$$

★COMFORT INN SANTA FE

4312 Cerrillos Road, Santa Fe, 505-474-7330, 877-424-6423; www.comfortInn.com

83 rooms. Complimentary breakfast. Pets accepted. Pool. $

★★★ELDORADO HOTEL & SPA

309 W. San Francisco St., Santa Fe, 505-988-4455, 800-955-4455; www.eldoradohotel.com

The Pueblo Revival-style building is one of Santa Fe's largest and most important landmarks. Its lobby and interiors are lavishly decorated with an extensive collection of original Southwest art. Rooms have private balconies and kiva fireplaces. Head over to the Nidah Spa (Nidah is the Native American word for "your life") to get treatments such as the turquoise gem massage or the blue corn and Anasazi bean cleansing body wrap. The Eldorado Court and Lounge, near the main lobby, is a great spot for snacking, people-watching and enjoying live entertainment.

219 rooms. Restaurant, bar. Pets accepted. Pool. Spa. Business center. Fitness center. $$$

★★★★ENCANTADO RESORT

198 State Road 592, Santa Fe, 505-988-9955; www.encantadoresort.com

Tucked in the foothills of the Sangre de Cristo Mountains, Encantado is an oasis of serenity, privacy and luxury. Tapping into the mystic energies that New Mexico is known for, it was designed as a destination for wellness and rejuvenation. And you can find just that at the new Spa at Encantado, which provides treatments from massage to ayurvedic rituals, Eastern medicine and aesthetic arts. Complementing the New Mexico landscape, Encantado has a main lodge and 65 private and cozy casitas with kiva fireplaces and outdoor terraces which are scattered throughout the 57-acre property. Terra, Encantado's signature restaurant, features American cuisine made with or-

ganic ingredients (and much of is also local) and offers alluring views of the surrounding vistas.
65 rooms. Restaurant, bar. Fitness room. Pool. $$$$

★★★HILTON SANTA FE HISTORIC PLAZA
100 Sandoval St., Santa Fe, 505-988-2811, 800-445-8667; www.hiltonofsantafe.com
Located just two blocks from the historic Plaza, this hotel is located in a 380-year-old family estate, and takes up an entire city block. The hotel has the city's largest pool. Guest rooms feature locally handcrafted furnishings.
157 rooms. Restaurant, bar. Business center. Fitness center. Pool. Pets accepted. $$

★★HOTEL PLAZA REAL
125 Washington Ave., Santa Fe, 505-988-4900; www.sterlinghotels.com
56 rooms. Restaurant, bar. Pets accepted. $$

★★HOTEL SANTA FE
1501 Paseo De Peralta, Santa Fe, 800-825-9876; www.hotelsantafe.com
129 rooms. Restaurant, bar. Pets accepted. Spa. Pool. $$

★★HOTEL ST. FRANCIS
210 Don Gaspar Ave., Santa Fe, 505-983-5700, 800-529-5700; www.hotelstfrancis.com
80 rooms. Fitness room. Restaurant, bar. $$

★★★HYATT REGENCY TAMAYA RESORT & SPA
1300 Tuyuna Trail, Santa Ana Peublo, 505-867-1234, 800-554-9288;
www.tamaya.hyatt.com
Located on 500 acres of unspoiled desert, the Hyatt Regency Tamaya Resort & Spa has striking views of the Sandia Mountains. The property blends right in with its Pueblo-style buildings and open-air courtyards and includes punches of turquoise and bright oranges throughout the public and private spaces. Golf, tennis and hot air ballooning are among the activities available at this family-friendly resort, where programs for kids are available. The restaurants are a showcase of Southwestern flavors, offering sophisticated takes on local favorites.
350 rooms. Restaurant, bar. Business center. Fitness center. Spa. Pets accepted. Golf. Tennis. $$

★★★INN AND SPA AT LORETTO
211 Old Santa Fe Trail, Santa Fe, 505-988-5531, 800-727-5531; www.hotelloretto.com
This boutique hotel, which rests at the end of the Sante Fe Trail, is a recreation of an ancient adobe. Rooms feature a charming Southwestern motif with hand-carved furniture and Native American art. The property includes a heated pool and 12 specialty stores, including many art galleries.
129 rooms. Restaurant, bar. Spa. Fitness room. Pool. $$

★★★INN OF THE GOVERNORS
101 W. Alameda, Santa Fe, 505-982-4333, 800-234-4534; www.innofthegovernors.com
First-rate amenities are the draw at this cozy inn. Guests are treated to a

complimentary full breakfast each morning, and a heated outdoor pool with poolside service. Rooms are decorated Southwestern style and feature hand-crafted furniture, Spanish artwork, fireplaces and French doors that open to a patio. Amenities include wireless Internet access, feather pillows, down comforters and plush towels and robes. The rustic Del Charro Saloon, a popular gathering place for locals and tourists alike, offers cocktails and a full bar menu, including what many say are the best burgers in town.
100 rooms. Complimentary breakfast. Restaurant, bar. Pool. $$

★★★LA POSADA DE SANTA FE RESORT AND SPA
330 E. Palace Ave., Santa Fe, 505-986-0000, 866-331-7625; www.rockresorts.com
Located on six landscaped acres, La Posada easily blends past and present. The original Staab House, dating to 1870, is the focal point of the resort. The attractive Spanish Colonial-style rooms and suites are scattered throughout the gardens in a village setting. The fantastic Avanyu Spa features Native American-themed treatments using local ingredients. Fuego Restaurant is a standout for its innovative food with Spanish and Mexican inflections, while the historic Staab House is an inviting setting for American classics.
157 rooms. Restaurant, bar. Spa. Fitness room. Pool. $$$

★★★★ROSEWOOD INN OF THE ANASAZI
113 Washington Ave., Santa Fe, 505-988-3030; www.innoftheanasazi.com
Located just off the historic Plaza, the inn was designed to resemble the traditional dwellings of the Anasazi. Enormous handcrafted doors open to a world of authentic artwork, carvings and textiles synonymous with the Southwest. The lobby sets a sense of place for arriving guests with its rough-hewn tables, leather furnishings, unique objects and huge cactus plants in terra cotta pots. The region's integrity is maintained in the guest rooms, where fireplaces and four-poster beds rest under ceilings of vigas and latillas and bathrooms are stocked with toiletries made locally with native cedar extract. The restaurant earns praise for honoring the area's culinary heritage.
58 rooms. Restaurant, bar. Buiness center. Pets accepted. Fitness center. $$$

★★★SUNRISE SPRINGS
242 Los Pinos Road, Santa Fe, 505-471-3600, 800-955-0028; www.sunrisesprings.com
Get your chakras in order at Santa Fe's Zen-chic Sunrise Springs. This eco-conscious resort proves that it's easy being green with biodynamic gardens, organic produce and locally harvested spa products. Sunrise Springs takes its cues from the East for its activity menu, offering tai chi, Raku ceramics and Yoga, as well as traditional tea ceremonies in its authentic Japanese tea house, but the guestrooms and casitas are definitively Southwestern.
56 rooms. Fitness center. Pool. Spa. $$

WHERE TO EAT
★★AMAYA RESTAURANT
Hotel Santa Fe, 1501 Paseo de Peralta, Santa Fe, 800-825-9876;
www.hotelsantafe.com
Southwestern. Breakfast, lunch, dinner. Bar. Children's menu. Outdoor seating. $$$

★★★THE ANASAZI RESTAURANT & BAR
Rosewood Inn of the Anasazi, 113 Washington Ave., Santa Fe, 505-988-3236;
www.innoftheanasazi.com
The creators of the memorable cuisine at this Plaza mainstay like to point
out that the Navajo definition of Anasazi has come to embody an ancient
wisdom that encourages living in peace with the environment. That philosophy is translated in the petroglyph-inspired art on the walls. Executive chef
Oliver Ridgeway devotes himself to finding inventive uses for organic, locally grown products in dishes such as chile and mustard braised rabbit with
spring pea fettuccine, baby heirloom carrots and lemon thyme gremolata,
and blue corn crusted salmon with crimini mushroom, spring squash suc-
cotash and citrus jalapeño sauce.
Southwestern. Breakfast, lunch, dinner, Sunday brunch. Bar. $$$

★★ANDIAMO
322 Garfield St., Santa Fe, 505-995-9595; www.andiamoonline.com
Italian. Dinner. Outdoor seating. $$

★BLUE CORN CAFÉ & BREWERY
133 Water St., Santa Fe, 505-984-1800; www.bluecorncafe.com
Southwestern. Lunch, dinner. Bar. Outdoor seating. $$

★★CAFE PARIS
31 Burro Alley, Santa Fe, 505-986-1688; www.cafeparisnm.com
French. Breakfast, lunch, dinner. Outdoor seating. $$

★★CAFE PASQUAL'S
121 Don Gaspar, Santa Fe, 505-983-9340; www.pasquals.com
Southwestern. Breakfast (Monday-Saturday), lunch (Monday-Saturday),
dinner, Sunday brunch. Reservations recommended. $$$

★★CELEBRATIONS
1620 St. Michael's Drive, Santa Fe, 505-989-8904 ; www.celebrationssantafe.com
American. Breakfast (Monday-Saturday), lunch (Monday-Saturday), dinner
(Tuesday-Saturday), Sunday brunch. Outdoor seating. $$

★CHOW'S ASIAN BISTRO
720 St. Michaels Drive, Santa Fe, 505-471-7120; www.mychows.com
Chinese. Lunch, dinner. $$

★★★THE COMPOUND RESTAURANT
653 Canyon Road, Santa Fe, 505-982-4353; www.compoundrestaurant.com
The setting of this landmark restaurant is casual yet elegant, with minimalist
décor, neutral tones and white-clothed tables. Patios surrounded by flower
gardens and a marble fountain make for a relaxing outdoor dining experi-
ence. The contemporary American menu features specialties such as grilled
beef tenderloin and tuna tartar topped with Osetra caviar and preserved lem-
on. The warm bittersweet liquid chocolate cake is a star dessert.
American. Lunch (Monday-Saturday), dinner. Bar. Outdoor seating. $$

★★★COYOTE CAFE
132 W. Water St., Santa Fe, 505-983-1615; www.coyotecafe.com

Famed cookbook author and Southwestern cuisine pioneer Mark Miller enjoyed nothing but success at this super-cool restaurant decorated with folk art and located just a block off the Plaza. But when he decided to sell it, chef Eric DiStefano (who was the executive chef of Santa Fe hotspot, Geronimo) stepped in to save the popular spot. Although the menu changes seasonally, regulars know they'll find a whimsical mingling of the cuisines of New Mexico, Mexico, Cuba and Spain. Look for slow braised prime beef short ribs with red pepper risotto and brandy shallot sauce and elk tenderloin with roasted garlic potatoes, applewood smoked bacon and brandied mushroom sauce. The rooftop Cantina is a festive spot to enjoy cocktails and lighter fare.

Southwestern. Dinner. Bar. Children's menu. Reservations recommended. Outdoor seating. $$$

★★EL FAROL
808 Canyon Road, Santa Fe, 505-983-9912; www.elfarolsf.com

Spanish. Lunch, dinner. Bar. Outdoor seating. $$$

★★EL MESÓN—LA COCINA DE ESPAÑA
213 Washington Ave., Santa Fe, 505-983-6756; www.elmeson-santafe.com

Spanish, tapas. Dinner. Closed Sunday-Monday. Bar. Children's menu. $$

★★GABRIEL'S
Highway 285/84, Santa Fe, 505-455-7000; www.restauranteur.com/gabriels

Southwestern. Lunch, dinner. Bar. Outdoor seating. $$

★★★★GERONIMO
724 Canyon Road, Santa Fe, 505-982-1500; www.geronimorestaurant.com

Housed in a restored 250-year-old landmark adobe building, Geronimo (the name of the restaurant is an ode to the hacienda's original owner, Geronimo Lopez) offers robust Southwestern-spiked global fusion fare in a stunning and cozy space. Owners Cliff Skoglund and Chris Harvey treat each guest like family. The interior is like a Georgia O'Keeffe painting come to life, with its wood-burning cove-style fireplace, tall chocolate-and-garnet-leather seating and local Native American-style artwork decorating the walls. The food is remarkable, fusing the distinct culinary influences of Asia, the Southwest and the Mediterranean. Vibrant flavors, bright colors and top-notch seasonal and regional ingredients come together in such dishes as peppery elk tenderloin and applewood smoked bacon with roasted garlic fork-mashed potatoes, sugar snap peas and creamy brandied mushroom sauce; or sweet chile and honey grilled Mexican white prawns with Jasmine-almond rice cakes and frisée red onion salad. When it's warm outside, sit on the patio for prime Canyon Road people-watching.

International. Dinner. Bar. Reservations recommended. Outdoor seating. $$$

★★IL PIATTO CUCINA ITALIANA
95 W. Marcy St., Santa Fe, 505-984-1091; www.ilpiattosantafe.com

Italian. Lunch, dinner. Bar. Children's menu. Reservations recommended. Outdoor seating. $$

★★INDIA PALACE

227 Don Gaspar Ave., Santa Fe, 505-986-5859; www.indiapalace.com
Indian. Lunch, dinner. Children's menu. Outdoor seating. $$

★★★LAS FUENTES RESTAURANT & BAR

The Bishops Lodge Ranch Resort & Spa, 1297 Bishop's Lodge Road, Santa Fe, 505-983-6377, 800-419-0492; www.bishopslodge.com
Executive chef Brian Shannon brings an explosion of Continental American cuisine to the Bishop's Lodge at this inviting restaurant. Stand-out dishes include tomatillo chipotle glazed pork ribs with mango slaw and grilled sweet corn succutash and grilled ruby trout with tagliatelle pasta with lemon, olives, artichoke hearts, capers, piquillo peppers and fresh oregano. The interior has ranch-like Southwestern décor, Navajo rugs, and murals by a local Santa Fe artist.
American. Breakfast, lunch, dinner, Sunday brunch. Bar. Outdoor seating. $$$

★★MARIA'S NEW MEXICAN KITCHEN

555 W. Cordova Road, Santa Fe, 505-983-7929; www.marias-santafe.com
Southwestern. Lunch, dinner. Bar. Children's menu. Outdoor seating. $$

★★★THE OLD HOUSE RESTAURANT

Eldorado Hotel & Spa, 309 W. San Francisco St., Santa Fe, 505-988-4455, 800-955-4455; www.eldoradohotel.com
Located in the Eldorado Hotel & Spa, the Old House Restaurant serves up International cuisine with a southwestern twist. For example, try the bistro steak served with duck fat fries and creamed spinach or the chicken with wild mushrooms, green chile and corn flan and chicken jus. Take a moment to look up and take in the candlelit stucco room, part of one of the city's oldest buildings, which is adorned with Mexican folk art and bold, oversized paintings. To enjoy your meal somewhere more intimate, reserve the private wine room.
Southwestern. Dinner. Bar. Reservations recommended. $$$

★★THE ORE HOUSE ON THE PLAZA

50 Lincoln Ave., Santa Fe, 505-983-8687; www.orehouseontheplaza.com
Southwestern. Lunch, dinner. Bar. Children's menu. Outdoor seating. $$

★★OSTERIA D'ASSISI

58 S. Federal Place, Santa Fe, 505-986-5858; www.osteriadassisi.net
Italian. Lunch, dinner. Bar. Children's menu. Reservations recommended. Outdoor seating. $$$

★★THE PINK ADOBE

406 Old Santa Fe Trail, Santa Fe, 505-986-9558; www.thepinkadobe.com
Southwestern. Lunch, dinner. Bar. Reservations recommended. Outdoor seating. $$$

★THE PLAZA CAFÉ
54 Lincoln Ave., Santa Fe, 505-982-1664; www.thefamousplazacafe.com
Southwestern. Breakfast, lunch, dinner. $$

★★PRANZO ITALIAN GRILL
540 Montezuma, Santa Fe, 505-984-2645; www.pranzosantafe.com
Italian. Lunch (Monday-Saturday), dinner, late-night. Bar. $$

★★RISTRA
548 Agua Fria St., Santa Fe, 505-982-8608; www.ristrarestaurant.com
French, Southwestern. Dinner. Outdoor seating. $$$

★★★SANTACAFÉ
231 Washington Ave., Santa Fe, 505-984-1788; www.santacafe.com
Situated a block from the Plaza in the restored Padre Gallegos House, Santa-café offers dishes such as shiitake and cactus spring rolls with southwestern ponzu, shrimp-spinach dumplings in a tahini sauce, filet mignon with asparagus, green chile mashed potatoes and truffle oil butter; or roasted free-range chicken with gorgonzola creamy polenta, applewood smoked bacon, capers, olives and sage. The patio dining in warmer weather is a treat.
American, Southwestern. Lunch, dinner, Sunday brunch. Bar. Children's. Reservations recommended. Outdoor seating. $$$

★THE SHED
113 1/2 E. Palace Ave., Santa Fe, 505-982-9030; www.sfshed.com
Southwestern. Lunch, dinner. Closed Sunday. Bar. Children's menu. Reservations recommended. Outdoor seating. $$

★★SHOHKO CAFÉ
321 Johnson St., Santa Fe, 505-982-9708; www.shohkocafe.com
Japanese. Lunch (Monday-Friday), dinner. Closed Sunday. Reservations recommended. $$

★STEAKSMITH AT EL GANCHO
104 B Old Las Vegas Highway, Santa Fe, 505-988-3333; www.santafesteaksmith.com
Steak. Lunch (Monday-Friday), dinner. Bar. Children's menu. $$$

★★★TERRA
Encantado Resort, 198 State Road 592, Santa Fe, 877-262-4666;
www.encantadoresort.com
Terra is the signature restaurant at the Encantado Resort. The minimalistic and modern design uses natural materials such as stone, leather and wood, as well as poured concrete and steel, which contrast nicely with the crisp white linens topping the tables. Executive Chef Charles Dale uses many ingredients from the restaurants own 10,000-square-foot on-site biodynamic garden to create dishes such as miso-baked Wild Tasmanian Salmon with bamboo rice, poached Shiitake mushrooms and soy vinaigrette, as well as the Three Little Pigs, which consists of grilled tenderloin in adobo, crispy belly over edamame purée and pork cheek casuela with pumpkin seed mole. A well-edited list of specialty cocktails and wines round out the offerings.

American. Breakfast, lunch, dinner. Bar. $35-86

★★★TRATTORIA NOSTRANI
304 Johnson St., Santa Fe, 505-983-3800; www.trattorianostrani.com
Guests can dine in one of four semi-private dining rooms at Trattoria Nostrani, a northern Italian restaurant housed in an 1883 territorial-style house. The interior retains much of its historical atmosphere, with tin ceilings and adobe archways. Entrées include Diver scallops with quail porchetta, white wine and tomatoes; roasted chicken with mushrooms and marsala wine; and duck ravioli with plums and red wine. More than 400 wines are offered on the extensive European wine list and a knowledgeable staff will assist in selecting the perfect one.
Italian. Dinner. Closed Sunday. Reservations recommended. $$$

★★VANESSIE OF SANTA FE
434 W. San Francisco St., Santa Fe, 505-982-9966; www.vanessiesantafe.com
American. Dinner. Bar. Reservations recommended. $$

SPAS
★★★THE SPA AT ENCANTADO
198 State Road 592, Santa Fe, 877-262-4666; www.encantadoresort.com
Reflecting the uniquely modern and earthy décor of the resort, The Spa at Encantado is a peaceful and luxurious retreat. If you're with someone special, book one of the two couple's massage rooms, which are actually more like private retreats that feature their own personal Jacuzzi, steam bath and shower. Without or without a private treatment room, allow enough time to take full advantage of the elegant and inviting "Warming Room." Here guests can relax by the fire while enjoying some tea, hot chocolate, appetizers and a good book before or after a treatment. Signature treatments are inspired by the surroundings. The Blue Corn and Honey Renewal, for example, uses Native blue corn and wildflower honey to exfoliate and revive tired skin. Prior to beginning any treatment, follow the spa's well detailed "purification ritual" to maximize your enchanting spa experience at this foothill retreat.

SANTA ROSA
See also Las Vegas
In grama-grass country on the Pecos River, Santa Rosa has several natural and man-made lakes.

WHAT TO SEE
BILLY THE KID MUSEUM
1435 E. Sumner Ave., Fort Sumner, 575-355-2380;
www.billythekidmuseumfortsumner.com
The museum contains 60,000 items, including relics of the Old West, Billy the Kid and Old Fort Sumner.
Admission: adults $5, seniors $4, children $3, children under 7 free. Summer, daily 8.30 a.m.-5 p.m.; winter, Monday-Saturday 8:30 a.m.-5 p.m.

BLUE HOLE
Blue Hole Road, Santa Rosa; www.santarosanm.org
This clear blue lake set in a rock setting is fed by natural artesian spring; and many people enjoy scuba diving here.

FORT SUMNER STATE MONUMENT
RR 1, Fort Sumner, 575-355-2573
The monument is the original site of the Bosque Redondo, where the U.S. Army held thousands of Navajo and Mescalero Apache captive from 1863 through 1868. The military established Fort Sumner to oversee the containment. Visitor center has exhibits relating to the period.
Monday, Wednesday-Sunday.

GRZELACHOWSKI TERRITORIAL HOUSE
Santa Rosa
Billy the Kid frequently visited this store and mercantile, which was built in 1800.
Daily, mid-morning-early evening.

PUERTA DE LUNA
Puerta de Luna
Founded in approximately 1862, this Spanish-American town of 250 people holds to old customs in living and working.

SANTA ROSA DAM AND LAKE
Highway 91, Santa Rosa, 505-472-3115; www.spa.usace.army.mil
An irrigation pool is often available for recreation. Fishing, boating; nature trails; camping.

SPECIAL EVENTS
OLD FORT DAYS
Santa Rosa, Fort Sumner, downtown and County Fairgrounds
Parade, rodeo, bank robbery, barbecue, contests, exhibits.
Second week in June.

SANTA ROSA DAY CELEBRATION
Santa Rosa
Sports events, contests, exhibits.
Memorial Day weekend.

WHERE TO STAY
★BEST WESTERN ADOBE INN
1501 Historic Route 66 St., Santa Rosa, 505-472-3446; www.bestwestern.com
58 rooms. Complimentary breakfast. Pets accepted. Pool. $

SILVER CITY

See also Deming

The rich gold and silver ores in the foothills of the Mogollon Mountains are running low, but copper mining has now become important to the economy. Cattle ranching thrives on the plains. The forested mountain slopes to the north are the habitat of turkey, deer, elk and bear and the streams and lakes provide excellent trout fishing.

WHAT TO SEE

GILA CLIFF DWELLINGS NATIONAL MONUMENT

Highway 15, Silver City, 505-536-9461; www.nps.gov/gicl

More than 40 rooms in six caves are accessible by a one-mile hiking trail. The Mogollon circa 1300 occupied the caves. Self-guided tour; camping. Forest naturalists conduct programs Memorial Day-Labor Day.

Admission: adult $3, children under 16 free, family $10. Ruins and visitor center, daily.

GILA NATIONAL FOREST

Silver City, 505-388-8201; www.fs.fed.us/r3/gila

The Gila National Forest covers about three million acres. Blue Range Wilderness and Aldo Leopold Wilderness are within its borders. Hunting, backpacking, horseback riding. Also includes several lakes (Quemado, Roberts, Snow) ideal for fishing, boating and camping.

PHELPS DODGE COPPER MINE

Highway 15, Silver City, 575-538-5331

This historic mining town is home to forts and other historic buildings.

SILVER CITY MUSEUM

312 W. Broadway, Silver City, 505-538-5921, 877-777-7947; www.silvercitymuseum.org

This museum is located in the restored 1881 house of H. B. Ailman, owner of a rich silver mine. Includes Victorian antiques and furnishings; artifacts; memorabilia from mining town of Tyrone.

Admission: $3. Tuesday-Sunday.

WESTERN NEW MEXICO UNIVERSITY MUSEUM

Fleming Hall, 1000 College Ave., Silver City, 575-538-6386; www.wnmu.edu

This museum depicts the contributions of Native American, Hispanic, African American and European cultures to the history of region; largest display of Mimbres pottery in the nation; photography, archive and mineral collections. Daily.

SPECIAL EVENT

FRONTIER DAYS

Silver City

Parade, dances, exhibits, food. Western dress desired. Fourth of July.

SALINAS PUEBLO MISSIONS NATIONAL MONUMENT

This monument was established to explore European-Native American contact and the resulting cultural changes. The stabilized ruins of the massive 17th-century missions are basically unaltered, preserving the original design and construction. All three units are open and feature wayside exhibits, trails and picnic areas. Monument Headquarters, one block west of Highway 55 on Highway 60 in Mountainair, has an audiovisual presentation and an exhibit depicting the Salinas story. There are three units of this monument.

Gran Quivira, includes the massive walls of the 17th-century San Buenaventura Mission (begun in 1659 but never completed), as well as San Isidro Church (circa 1639) and 21 pueblo mounds, two of which have been excavated. A self-guided trail and museum and visitor center combine to vividly portray Native American life over the past 1,000 years. Various factors led to the desertion of the pueblo and the mission around 1671. Tompiro Indians occupied this and the Ab site, 25 miles southeast of Mountainair on Highway 55, 505-847-2770.

Ab contains the ruins of the mission church of San Gregorio de Ab (circa 1622), built by Native Americans under the direction of Franciscan priests. This is the only early church in New Mexico with 40-foot buttressed curtain walls—a style typical of medieval European architecture. The pueblo adjacent to the church was abandoned around 1673 because of drought, disease and Apache uprisings. The Ab and others from the Salinas jurisdiction eventually moved south with the Spanish to El Paso del Norte, where they established the pueblo of Ysleta del Sur and other towns still in existence today. There are self-guided trails throughout the mission compound and pueblo mounds. Located nine miles west of Mountainair on Highway 60, then ¾-mile north on Highway, 505-847-2400.

Quarai encompasses the ruins of the Mission de la Pursima Concepción de Cuarac, other Spanish structures and unexcavated American Indian mounds, all built of red sandstone. Built about 1630, it was abandoned along with the pueblo about 1677, most likely for the same reasons. Unlike the other two, Tiwa-speaking people occupied this site. Much of the history is related to the Spanish-Indian cultural conflict. The church ruins have been excavated and it is the most complete church in the monument. The visitor center has a museum and interpretive displays. Eight miles north of Mountainair on Highway 55, then one mile west on a county road from Punta.

WHERE TO STAY
★COMFORT INN
1060 E. Highway 180, Silver City, 505-534-1883; www.comfortinn.com
52 rooms. Complimentary breakfast. Pets accepted. $

SOCORRO
See also Abuquerque
Socorro is located in the Rio Grande Valley. Originally a Piro Indian town, Socorro had a Franciscan mission as early as 1598. It is the home of a very large astronomy observatory.

WHAT TO SEE
MINERAL MUSEUM
801 Leroy Place, Socorro, 505-835-5140; geoinfo.nmt.edu/museum
See more than 12,000 mineral specimens from around the world. Free rockhounding and prospecting information.
Monday-Saturday.

NATIONAL RADIO ASTRONOMY OBSERVATORY

1003 Lopez Ville Road, Socorro, 505-835-7000; www.nrao.edu
The main component here is the VLA (Very Large Array), a radio telescope that consists of 27 separate antennas situated along three arms of railroad track. The VLA is used to investigate all kinds of astronomical topics. Self-guided walking tour of grounds and visitor center. Daily.

OLD SAN MIGUEL MISSION

403 El Camino Real Northwest, Socorro, 505-835-1620; www.sdc.org/~smiguel
This restored 17th-century mission has carved ceiling beams and corbels and walls that are five feet thick. Daily.
Artifacts on display in church office (building south of church). Monday-Friday.

WHERE TO STAY
★BEST WESTERN SOCORRO

1100 N. California St., Socorro, 575-838-0556; www.bestwestern.com
120 rooms. Complimentary breakfast. Pets accepted. Pool. Fitness center. Business center. $

TAOS

See also Red River
As early as 1615, a handful of Spanish colonists settled in this area. In 1617 a church was built. After the Pueblo Rebellion of 1680, the town was a farming center plagued by Apache raids and disagreements with the Taos Indians and the government of Santa Fe. The first artists came in 1898; since then it has flourished as an art colony. Many people come here for the clear air, magnificent surroundings and exciting and congenial atmosphere.

Taos is actually three towns: the Spanish-American settlement into which Anglos have infiltrated, which is Taos proper; Taos Pueblo, two and a half miles north; and Ranchos de Taos, four miles south. Many farming communities and fishing resorts can be found in the surrounding mountains. Taos Ski Valley, 19 miles northeast, is a popular spot for winter sports. The town has a few famous residents, including Julia Roberts, Val Kilmer and Donald Rumsfeld.

WHAT TO SEE
CARSON NATIONAL FOREST

208 Cruz Alta Road, Taos, 575-758-6200; www.fs.fed.us/r3/carson
This forest occupies 1½ million acres and includes Wheeler Peak, New Mexico's highest mountain at 13,161 feet. Lots of small mountain lakes and streams provide good fishing. There's also hunting, hiking, winter sports, picnicking, camping. Daily.

ERNEST L. BLUMENSCHEIN HOME

222 Ledoux St., Taos, 575-758-0505; www.taosmuseums.org
This restored adobe house includes furnishings and exhibits of paintings by

the Blumenschein family and other early Taos artists.
May-October: daily 9 a.m.-5 p.m.; call for winter hours. Combination tickets to seven Taos museums available.

FORT BURGWIN RESEARCH CENTER
6580 Highway 518, Taos, 505-758-8322; www.smu.edu/taos
The First Dragoons of the U.S. Calvary (1852-1860) occupied this restored
fort. Summer lecture series, music and theater performances. Operated by
Southern Methodist University.
Schedule varies.

GOVERNOR BENT HOUSE MUSEUM AND GALLERY
117 Bent St., Taos, 505-758-2376; www.laplaza.org/art/museums_bent.php3
Visit the home of New Mexico's first American territorial governor (and the
scene of his death in 1847). Includes Bent family possessions, Native American artifacts, Western American art.
Summer, daily 9 a.m.-5 p.m.; winter, daily 10 a.m.-4 p.m.

HACIENDA DE LOS MARTINEZ
708 Ranchitos Road, Taos, 505-758-0505; www.taoshistoricmuseums.com
Contains early Spanish Colonial hacienda with period furnishings; 21 rooms,
two large patios. Early Taos, Spanish culture exhibits. Used as a fortress during raids. Living museum demonstrations.
Summer, daily 9 a.m.-5 p.m., call for winter hours. Combination tickets to
seven Taos museums available.

HARWOOD MUSEUM OF ART
238 Ledoux St., Taos, 505-758-9826; www.harwoodmuseum.org
Founded in 1923, this museum features paintings, drawings, prints, sculp-
tures and photographs by artists of Taos from 1800 to the present.
Tuesday-Saturday 10 a.m.-5 p.m., Sunday noon-5 p.m.; closed Monday.
Combination tickets to seven Taos museums available.

KIT CARSON HOME AND MUSEUM
113 Kit Carson Road, Taos, 505-758-4945; www.kitcarsonhome.com
Restored 1825 home of the famous frontiersman with artifacts, including a
gun exhibit.
Summer: daily 9 a.m.-5 p.m., call for winter hours.

KIT CARSON PARK
211 Paseo del Pueblo Norte, Taos, 575-758-8234
This 25-acre park includes a bicycle and walking path, picnic tables, a playground and a sand volleyball pit. No camping. The graves of Kit Carson and
his family are also here.

ORILLA VERDE RECREATION AREA
Highway 570 and Highway 68, Taos, 505-758-8851; www.blm.gov/nm
This park runs along the banks of the Rio Grande, offering some of the fin-
est trout fishing in the state; as well as white-water rafting. Enjoy hiking,

picnicking and spectacular views.
Daily.

RANCHOS DE TAOS

60 Ranchos Plaza Road, Taos, 575-758-2754

This adobe-housed farming and ranching center has one of the most beautiful churches in the Southwest—the San Francisco de Asis Church. Its huge buttresses and twin bell towers echo the beauty of its interior.
Monday-Saturday 9 a.m.-4 p.m.

RIO GRANDE GORGE BRIDGE

Taos, 12 miles northwest on Highway 64

This bridge is 650 feet above the Rio Grande; observation platforms, picnic and parking areas.

SIPAPU SKI & SUMMER RESORT

Highway 518, three miles west of Tres Ritos, 800-587-2240; www.sipapunm.com

Area has two triple chairlifts, two Pomalifts; patrol, school, rentals, snowmaking; 39 runs, the longest two miles; vertical drop 1,055 feet.
Mid-December-March, daily.

TAOS PUEBLO

Taos, 505-758-1028; www.taospueblo.com

With a full-time population of 150, this is one of the most famous Native American pueblos and has been continuously inhabited for more than 1,000 years. Within the pueblo is a double apartment house. The north and south buildings, separated by a river, are five stories tall and form a unique communal dwelling. Small buildings and corrals are scattered around these impressive architectural masterpieces. The residents here live without modern utilities such as electricity and plumbing and get their drinking water from the river. The people are independent, conservative and devout in their religious observances. There are fees for parking and photography permits. In order to photograph individual Native Americans, you must get their consent first.
Daily 8 a.m.-4 p.m.; closed for special occasions in spring.

TAOS SKI VALLEY

103A Suton Place, Taos Ski Valley, 866-968-7386; www.skitaos.org

The ski area has 12 chairlifts, two surface lifts; patrol, school, rentals; cafeteria, restaurants, bar; nursery, lodges. Longest run more than four miles; vertical drop 2,612 feet.
November-April, daily.

SPECIAL EVENTS
ANNUAL POW WOW

Taos Pueblo, Taos, 505-758-1028; www.taospueblopowwow.com

Intertribal dancers from throughout U.S., Canada and Mexico participate in this competition.
Second weekend in July.

CHAMBER MUSIC FESTIVAL

145 Paseo del Pueblo, Taos, 505-776-2388; www.taosschoolofmusic.com
Mid-June-early August.

FIESTAS DE TAOS

Taos Plaza, Taos, 505-741-0909; www.fiestasdetaos.com
This traditional festival honoring the patron saints of Taos includes a candle-light procession, parade, crafts, food and entertainment. Late July.

SAN GERONIMO EVE SUNDOWN DANCE

Taos Pueblo, Taos, 505-758-1028; www.taospueblo.com/calendar.php
See a traditional men's dance, which is followed the next day by San Geronimo Feast Day, with intertribal dancing, trade fair, pole climb and foot races. Last weekend in September.

TAOS ARTS FESTIVAL

Taos, 505-758-1028; www.taosguide.com
Arts and crafts exhibitions, music, plays, poetry readings. Mid-September-early October.

TAOS PUEBLO DANCES

Taos Pueblo, Albuquerque, 505-758-1028; www.taospueblo.com
Several Native American dances are held throughout the year. For a schedule of annual dances, contact the pueblo.

YULETIDE IN TAOS

Taos, 800-348-0696; www.taosvacationguide.com
The celebration includes area farolito (paper bag lantern) tours, food and craft fairs, art events and dance performances.
Late November-late December.

WHERE TO STAY
★COMFORT INN

1500 Paseo Del Pueblo Sur, Taos, 505-751-1555; www.comfortinn.com
60 rooms. Complimentary breakfast. Pool. $

★★★EL MONTE SAGRADO

317 Kit Carson Road, Taos, 505-758-3502, 800-828-8264; www.elmontesagrado.com
This unique resort, tucked away in alluring Taos, celebrates the natural beauty of New Mexico while highlighting its rich Native American heritage. The themed guestrooms and suites, which display local and international artwork, are seductive retreats. Taos, well known for its world-class skiing, is a year-round playground, offering everything from rock climbing and fly fishing to llama trekking and mountain biking. The onsite spa focuses on renewal of body and mind. The award-winning De La Tierra restaurant is a feast for the eyes and the palate.
36 rooms. Restaurant, bar. Spa. Pool. Fitness center. Business center. $$$$

★★★THE HISTORIC TAOS INN

125 Paseo Del Pueblo Norte, Taos, 505-758-2233, 888-518-8267; www.taosinn.com

This inn offers a comfortable Old West atmosphere and modern amenities. The grounds include an outdoor heated pool and greenhouse whirlpool. The unique guest rooms feature Southwestern décor and many offer kiva fireplaces. Be sure to dine at the acclaimed Doc Martin's Restaurant.

44 rooms. Restaurant, bar. Pool. $

★★★SAGEBRUSH INN

1508 Paseo Del Pueblo Sur, Taos, 505-758-2254, 800-428-3626;
www.sagebrushinn.com

Built in 1929, this 100-room adobe inn houses a large collection of paintings, Native American rugs and other regional art. The most recent addition, an 18,000-square-foot conference center, features hand-hewn vigas and fireplaces. Visitors will enjoy the outdoor pool and two whirlpools. Guest rooms have handmade furniture.

100 rooms. Complimentary breakfast. Restaurant, bar. Pets accepted. Pool. $

WHERE TO EAT

★★APPLE TREE

123 Bent St., Taos, 505-758-1900; www.appletreerestaurant.com

American, Southwestern. Lunch, dinner, Sunday brunch. Reservations recommended. Outdoor seating. $$

★★★DE LA TIERRA

El Monte Sagrado, 317 Kit Carson Road, Taos, 505-758-3502, 800-828-8267;
www.elmontesagrado.com

From its unique décor to its Southwestern cuisine, De la Tierra, located inside Taos' El Monte Sagrado resort, practically begs for special occasions. Towering ceilings capped by an enormous wrought iron chandelier, high-backed, tapestry-covered chairs make this dining room romantic. Chef John Cox focuses on creative International farm-to-table dishes. Everything from roasted bison filet with blue corn posole and warm sopapillas; and lamb with barbecued eggplant, goat cheese timbale, arugula, olives and lemon is given his unique stamp.

Southwestern, International. Dinner. Reservations recommended. $$$

★★★DOC MARTIN'S

The Historic Taos Inn, 125 Paseo Del Pueblo, Taos, 505-758-1977; www.taosinn.com

Chef Zippy White serves organic Southwestern cuisine in an adobe setting. Specialties include grilled shrimp on blue corn cakes with green onion and pineapple firecracker sauce; the chef's mixed grill of rattlesnake sausage, buffalo steak, whole quail and ancho chile sauce; and Doc's classic chile rellenos with green chile, salsa fresca, pumpkin seeds and goat cheese cream. The wine list, with more than 400 selections, is one of the best in the area.

American, Southwestern. Breakfast, lunch, dinner, Saturday-Sunday brunch. Bar. Children's menu. Reservations recommended. Outdoor seating. $$$

★★★LAMBERT'S OF TAOS

309 Paseo Del Pueblo Sur, Taos, 505-758-1009; www.lambertsoftaos.com

Zeke and Tina Lambert came to Taos years ago on their honeymoon and never left. This restaurant serves contemporary cuisine. The produce is local when possible and all the sauces are made from scratch. Dishes include breaded Kurobuta pork cutlet with chipotle cream sauce, braised red cabbage and apples with smashed sweet potatoes; and grilled filet mignon with horseradish crème, steak fries and grilled asparagus. The extensive wine list, with is primarily from California. Contemporary

American. Dinner. Bar. Children's menu. Reservations recommended. Outdoor seating. $$$

★★OGELVIE'S TAOS BAR AND GRILLE

103-I E. Plaza, Taos, 505-758-8866; www.ogelvies.com

American, Southwestern. Lunch, dinner. Bar. Children's menu. Outdoor seating. $$

★★★OLD BLINKING LIGHT

Mile Marker One, Ski Valley Road, Taos, 505-776-8787; www.oldblinkinglight.com

American, Southwestern. Dinner. Bar. Children's menu. Outdoor seating. $$

★★STAKEOUT GRILL AND BAR

101 Stakeout Drive, Taos, 505-758-2042; www.stakeoutrestaurant.com

Seafood, steak. Dinner. Bar. Children's menu. Outdoor seating. $$

TRUTH OR CONSEQUENCES

See also Las Cruces

Formerly called "Hot Springs" for the warm mineral springs nearby, the town changed its name in 1950 to celebrate the tenth anniversary of Ralph Edwards' radio program, Truth or Consequences.

In the early 1500s, the Spanish Conquistadores came through this area and legends of lost Spanish gold mines and treasures in the Caballo Mountains persist today. There are numerous ghost towns and old mining camps in the area.

WHAT TO SEE

CABALLO LAKE STATE PARK

Truth or Consequences, 18 miles south on Interstate 25, 575-743-3942;
www.emnrd.state.nm.us

The Caballo Mountains form a backdrop for this lake. Swimming, windsurfing, waterskiing, fishing, boating (ramp); hiking, picnicking, playground, camping. Daily.

GERONIMO SPRINGS MUSEUM

211 Main St., Truth or Consequences, 505-894-6600;
www.geronimospringsmuseum.com

See exhibits of Mimbres pottery, fossils and photographs, as well as articles on local history.

Gift shop (Monday-Saturday).

WHERE TO EAT
★★LOS ARCOS STEAK HOUSE AND LOBSTER HOUSE
1400 N. Date St., Truth or Consequences, 575-894-6200
American. Dinner. Bar. Children's menu. Outdoor seating. $$

ZUNI PUEBLO
Thirty-nine miles south of Gallup, via Highway 602 and west on Highway 53, is one of Coronado's "Seven Cities of Cibola." Fray Marcos de Niza reported that these cities were built of gold. When looking down on the Zuni pueblo from a distant hilltop at sunset, it does seem to have a golden glow.

The people here make beautiful jewelry, beadwork and pottery. They also have a furniture and woodworking center with colorful and uniquely painted and carved items. Ashiwi Awan Museum and Heritage Center displays historical photos and exhibits. The pueblo, built mainly of stone, is one story high. The old Zuni mission church has been restored and its interior painted with murals of Zuni traditional figures. A tribal permit is required for photography; certain rules must be observed.

UTAH

UTAH'S NATURAL DIVERSITY HAS MADE IT A STATE OF MAGNIFICENT BEAUTY, WITH MORE than 3,000 lakes, miles of mountains, acres of forests and large expanses of desert. In northern Utah, the grandeur of the Wasatch Range, one of the most rugged mountain ranges in the United States, cuts across the state north to south. The Uinta Range, capped by the white peaks of ancient glaciers, is the only major North American range that runs east to west. In the western third of the state is the Great Basin. Lake Bonneville extended over much of western Utah leaving behind the Great Salt Lake, Utah Lake and Sevier Lake. To the east and west extends the Red Plateau. This red rock country, renowned for its brilliant coloring and fantastic rock formations, is home to one of the largest concentrations of national parks and monuments. Utah is definitely the place for those who love the western outdoors and can appreciate the awesome accomplishments of the pioneers who developed it.

This natural diversity created an environment inhospitable to early settlers. Although various groups explored much of the state, it took the determination and perseverance of a band of religious fugitives, members of the Church of Jesus Christ of Latter-Day Saints, to settle the land permanently. Brigham Young, leader of the Mormons, once remarked, "If there is a place on this earth that nobody else wants, that's the place I am hunting for." On July 24, 1847, on entering the forbidding land surrounding the Great Salt Lake, Young exclaimed, "This is the place!" The determined settlers immediately began to plow the unfriendly soil and build dams for irrigation. During 1847, as many as 1,637 Mormons came to Utah, and by the time the railroad made its way here, more than 6,000 had settled in the state. Before his death in 1877, 30 years after entering the Salt Lake Valley, Brigham Young had directed the founding of more than 350 communities.

The LDS church undoubtedly had the greatest influence on the state, developing towns in an orderly fashion with wide streets, planting straight rows of poplar trees to provide wind breaks and introducing irrigation throughout the desert regions. But the church members were not the only settlers. In the latter part of the 19th century, the West's fabled pioneer era erupted. The gold rush of 1849 to 1850 sent gold seekers pouring through Utah on their way to California. The arrival of the Pony Express in Salt Lake City in 1860 brought more immigrants, and when the mining boom hit the state in the 1870s and 1880s, Utah's mining towns appeared almost overnight. In 1900, the population was 277,000. It now stands at more than 1.7 million, with more than 75 percent living within 50 miles of Salt Lake City. The LDS church continues to play an important role and close to 60 percent of the state's population are members.

ALTA

See also Park City, Salt Lake City, Snowbird
Founded around silver mines in the 1870s, Alta was notorious for constant shoot-outs in its 26 saloons. With the opening of Utah's first ski resort in 1937, the town became the center of a noted resort.

ARCHES NATIONAL PARK

This natural landscape of giant stone arches, pinnacles, spires, fins and windows was once the bed of an ancient sea. Over time, erosion laid bare the skeletal structure of the earth, making this 114-square-mile area a spectacular outdoor museum. This wilderness, which contains the greatest density of natural arches in the world, was named a national monument in 1929 and a national park in 1971. More than 2,000 arches have been cataloged, ranging in size from three feet wide to the 105-foot-high, 306-foot-wide Landscape Arch. The arches, other rock formations and views of the Colorado River canyon (with the peaks of the La Sal Mountains in the distance) can be reached by car, but hiking is the best way to explore. Petroglyphs from the primitive peoples who roamed this section of Utah from A.D. 700 to 1200 can be seen at the Delicate Arch trailhead.

Hiking, rock climbing or camping in isolated sections should not be undertaken unless first reported to a park ranger at the visitor center (check locally for hours). Twenty-four miles of paved roads are open year-round. Graded and dirt roads should not be attempted in wet weather. Devils Garden Campground, 18 miles north of the visitor center off Highway 191, provides 52 individual and two group campsites (year-round; fee; water available only March-mid-October).

Information: Five miles northwest of Moab on Highway 191 to paved entrance road. 435-719-2299; www.nps.gov/arch

WHAT TO SEE
ALTA SKI AREA
Highway 210, Little Cottonwood Canyon Alta, 801-359-1078; www.alta.com

Two quad, two triple, three double chairlifts; four rope tows; patrol, school, rentals, snowmaking. Longest run 3.5 miles, vertical drop 2,020 feet. Half-day rates. No snowboarding.
Mid-November-April, daily.

WHERE TO STAY
★ALTA LODGE
10230 East State Highway 210, Alta, 801-742-3500, 800-707-2582; www.altalodge.com

57 rooms. Closed mid-late October, May. Restaurant, bar. Ski in/ski out. $

★★★ALTA'S RUSTLER LODGE
10380 Highway 210, Alta, 801-742-2200, 888-532-2582; www.rustlerlodge.com

With its ski in/ski out access to all of Alta's lift base facilities and a full-service ski shop onsite, the Rustler Lodge is all about the slopes. A complimentary shuttle takes guests wherever they want to go in Alta and Snowbird. The new business center offers wireless Internet access for those who need to get some work done between runs. The lodge also has a steam room and offers manicures, pedicures and other spa treatments. The children's programs will keep kids occupied.

85 rooms. Closed May-October. Business center. Restaurant, bar. Ski in/ski out. Fitness center. Pool. $$$

BRIGHAM CITY

See also Logan, Ogden

Renamed for Brigham Young in 1877 when he made his last public address
here, this community, situated at the base of the towering Wasatch Mountains, was first known as Box Elder because of the many trees of that type
that grew in the area. Main Street, which runs through the center of this city,
is still lined with these leafy trees.

WHAT TO SEE
BRIGHAM CITY MUSEUM-GALLERY
24 N. 300 W. Brigham City, 435-723-6769; www.brighamcity.utah.govt
Displays include furniture, clothing, books, photographs and documents reflecting the history of the Brigham City area since 1851. Also showcases
rotating art exhibits.
Tuesday-Friday 11 a.m.-6 p.m., Saturday 1-5 p.m.; closed Sunday-Monday.

GOLDEN SPIKE NATIONAL HISTORIC SITE
Brigham City, 435-471-2209; www.nps.gov/gosp
This is the site where America's first transcontinental railroad was completed
when the Central Pacific and Union Pacific lines met on May 10, 1869. At the
visitor center, you'll find movies and exhibits. There's also a self-guided auto
tour along the old railroad bed. The summer interpretive program includes
presentations and operating replicas of steam locomotives.
Daily 9 a.m.-5 p.m.

TABERNACLE
251 S. Main St., Brigham City, 435-723-5376; www.ldsces.org
The Box Elder tabernacle, one of the most architecturally interesting buildings in Utah, has been in continuous use since 1881. Gutted by fire and rebuilt in the late 1890s, it was restored in the late 1980s. Guided tours are
given in the summer months.

SPECIAL EVENTS
DRIVING OF THE GOLDEN SPIKE
Brigham City, 435-471-2209
The reenactment of the driving of the golden spike (the ceremonial nail
driven to mark the completion of a railroad) takes place at the site where the
Central Pacific and Union Pacific railroads met in 1869. Locomotive replicas
are used. Mid-May.

PEACH DAYS CELEBRATION
Brigham City; www.boxelder.org/tourism/events
Parade, arts and crafts, carnival, car show, entertainment.
First weekend after Labor Day.

WHERE TO STAY
★CRYSTAL INN, A RODEWAY INN
480 Westland Drive, Brigham City, 435-723-0440, 877-462-7978; www.crystalinns.com
30 rooms. Pets accepted. Business center. Pool. Fitness center. $

BRYCE CANYON NATIONAL PARK

See also Cedar City

Bryce Canyon is a 56-square-mile area of colorful, fantastic cliffs created by millions of years of erosion. Towering rocks worn down into odd, sculptured shapes stand grouped in striking sequences. The Paiute, who once lived nearby, called this "the place where red rocks stand like men in a bowl-shaped canyon." Although labeled as a canyon, Bryce is actually a series of "breaks" in 12 large amphitheaters—some plunging as deep as 1,000 feet into the multicolored limestone. The formations appear to change color as the sunlight strikes from different angles and seem incandescent in the late afternoon. The famous Pink Cliffs were carved from the Claron Formation; shades of red, orange, white, gray, purple, brown and soft yellow appear in the strata. The park road follows 17 miles along the eastern edge of the Paunsaugunt Plateau, where the natural amphitheaters are spread out below. Plateaus covered with evergreens and valleys filled with sagebrush stretch into the distance.

The visitor center at the entrance station has information about the park, including orientation shows, geologic displays and detailed maps. The park is open 24 hours a day year-round; in winter, the park road is open to most viewpoints. Lodging is also available from April to October.

WHAT TO SEE
CAMPING

Bryce Canyon

Camping is available at the North Campground (year-round), east of park headquarters; Sunset Campground, two miles south of park headquarters. Fourteen-day limit at both sites; fireplaces, picnic tables, restrooms, water available.

WHERE TO STAY
★★BEST WESTERN RUBY'S INN

26 S. Main, Bryce Canyon City, 435-834-5341, 866-866-6616; www.rubysinn.com
368 rooms. Restaurant. Pets accepted. Pool. $

WHERE TO EAT
★FOSTER'S STEAK HOUSE

1150 Highway 12, Bryce, 435-834-5227; www.fostersmotel.com
Steak. Breakfast, lunch, dinner. Children's menu. $$

CEDAR CITY

See also Beaver

In 1852, Cedar City produced the first iron made west of the Mississippi. The blast furnace operation was not successful, however, and stock-raising soon overshadowed it. A branch line of the Union Pacific entered the region in 1923 and helped develop the area. Now a tourist center because of its proximity to Bryce Canyon and Zion national parks, Cedar City takes pride in its abundant natural wonders. Streams and lakes have rainbow trout and the Markagunt Plateau provides deer and mountain lion hunting.

NATURAL BRIDGES NATIONAL MONUMENT

This 7,439-acre area of colorful, fantastically eroded terrain was made a national monument in 1908. It features three natural bridges (formed through erosion by water), all with Hopi names. Sipapu, a 268-foot span, and Kachina, a 204-foot span, are both in White Canyon, a major tributary gorge of the Colorado River. Owachomo, a 180-foot span, is near Armstrong Canyon, which joins White Canyon. Sipapu is the second-largest natural bridge in the world. From 2,000 to 650 years ago, the ancestral Puebloan people lived in this area, leaving behind cliff dwelling ruins and pictographs that visitors can view today. The major attraction is Bridge View Drive, a nine-mile-loop road open daily from early morning to 30 minutes past sunset, providing views of the three bridges from rim overlooks. There are also hiking trails to each bridge within the canyon.

The park also has a visitor center (Daily 8 a.m.-5 p.m.) and primitive campground with 13 tent and trailer sites (all year). Car and passenger ferry service across Lake Powell is available.

Information: Blanding, four miles south on Highway 191, then 36 miles west on Highway 95, then four miles north on Highway 275, 435-692-1234; www.nps.gov/nabr

WHAT TO SEE

DIXIE NATIONAL FOREST

1789 N. Wedgewood Lane, Cedar City, 435-865-3700; www.fs.fed.us/dxnf

This two-million-acre forest provides opportunities for camping, fishing, hiking, mountain biking and winter sports.
Daily.

IRON MISSION STATE PARK

635 N. Main, Cedar City, 435-586-9290; www.stateparks.utah.gov/stateparks

The museum at the park is dedicated to the first pioneer iron foundry west of the Rockies and features an extensive collection of horse-drawn vehicles and wagons from Utah pioneer days.
Daily.

SOUTHERN UTAH UNIVERSITY

351 W. Center, Cedar City, 435-586-5432; www.suu.edu

Established in 1897; 7,000 students. Visit the Braithwaite Fine Arts Gallery.

SPECIAL EVENTS

RENAISSANCE FAIR

City Park, Cedar City; www.umrf.net

Entertainment, food and games, all in the style of the Renaissance. Held in conjunction with opening of Utah Shakespearean Festival.
Early July.

UTAH SHAKESPEAREAN FESTIVAL

Southern Utah University Campus, 351 W. Center St., Cedar City, 435-586-7884; www.bard.org

Shakespeare is presented on an outdoor stage (a replica of 16th-century Tir-

CEDAR BREAKS NATIONAL MONUMENT

Cedar Breaks National Monument's major formation is a spectacular, multicolored, natural amphitheater created by the same forces that sculpted Utah's other rock formations. The amphitheater, shaped like an enormous coliseum, is 2,000 feet deep and more than three miles in diameter. It is carved out of the Markagunt Plateau and is surrounded by Dixie National Forest. Cedar Breaks, at an elevation of more than 10,000 feet, was established as a national monument in 1933. It derives its name from the surrounding cedar trees; "breaks" means "badlands." Although similar to Bryce Canyon National Park, the formations here are fewer but more vivid and varied in color. Young lava beds, resulting from small volcanic eruptions and cracks in the earth's surface, surround the Breaks area. The heavy forests include bristlecone pines, one of the oldest trees on earth. As soon as the snow melts, wildflowers bloom profusely and continue to bloom throughout the summer.

Rim Drive, a five-mile scenic road through the Cedar Breaks High Country, provides views of the monument's formations from four different overlooks. The area is open late May through mid-October, weather permitting. Point Supreme Campground, two miles north of south entrance, provides 30 tent and trailer sites (mid-June-mid-September). The visitor center offers geological exhibits (June-mid-October, daily).

Information: Cedar City, 23 miles east of Cedar City via Highway 14, 435-586-0787; www.nps.gov/cebr

ing House) and 750-seat indoor facility.
Monday-Saturday evenings; pre-play activities. Children over five years only; babysitting at festival grounds. Late June-early October.

UTAH SUMMER GAMES
351 W. Center St., Cedar City, 435-865-8421; www.utahsummergames.org
Olympic-style athletic events for amateur athletes. June.

WHERE TO STAY
★ABBEY INN
940 W. 200 N. Cedar City, 435-586-9966, 800-325-5411; www.abbeyinncedar.com
83 rooms. Complimentary breakfast. Pool. Spa. $

★BEST WESTERN TOWN AND COUNTRY INN
189 N. Main St., Cedar City, 435-586-9900, 800-493-0062; www.bestwesternutah.com
156 rooms. Complimentary breakfast. Pool. $

GARDEN CITY
See also Logan
This small resort town on the western shore of Bear Lake offers many water-based activities.

WHAT TO SEE
BEAR LAKE
Garden City
Covering 71,000 acres on the border of Utah and Idaho, this body of water is the state's second-largest freshwater lake. Approximately 20 miles long and

200 feet deep, it offers good fishing for mackinaw, rainbow trout and the rare Bonneville cisco. Boat rentals at several resorts.

BEAR LAKE STATE PARK
1030 N. Bear Lake Road, Garden City, 435-946-3343; www.utah.com/stateparks
Three park areas include State Marina on the west shore of the lake, Rendezvous Beach on the south shore and Eastside area on the east shore. Swimming, beach, waterskiing, fishing, ice fishing, boating (ramp, dock), sailing; hiking, mountain biking, cross-country skiing, snowmobiling, picnicking, tent and trailer sites.
Visitor center: daily.

BEAVER MOUNTAIN SKI AREA
40000 E. Highway 89, Garden City, 435-753- 4822; www.skithebeav.com
Three double chairlifts, two surface lifts; patrol, school, rentals; day lodge, cafeteria. Twenty-two runs; vertical drop 1,600 feet. Half-day rates.
December-early April, daily.

HEBER CITY
See also Alta, Park City, Salt Lake City
Located in a fertile, mountain-ringed valley, Heber City is the bedroom community for Orem, Provo, Park City and Salt Lake City. Unusual crater mineral springs, called hot pots, are located four miles west near Midway. Mount Timpanogos, one of the most impressive mountains in the state, is to the southwest in the Wasatch Range.

WHAT TO SEE
HEBER VALLEY RAILROAD
450 S. 600 W., Heber City, 435-654-5601, 800-888-7499; www.hebervalleyrr.org
A 100-year-old steam-powered excursion train takes passengers through the -farmlands of Heber Valley, along the shore of Deer Creek Lake and into Provo Canyon on various one-hour to four-hour trips. Restored coaches and open-air cars. Reservations are required.
May-mid-October, Tuesday-Sunday; mid-October-November, schedule varies; December-April, Monday-Saturday.

WASATCH MOUNTAIN STATE PARK
Heber City, two miles northwest off Highway 224, 435-654-1791;
www.stateparks.utah.gov/stateparks
This park covers approximately 25,000 acres in Heber Valley, offering fishing, hiking, golf, snowmobiling, cross-country skiing, picnicking and camping.
Visitor center: daily.

SPECIAL EVENTS
WASATCH COUNTY FAIR
2843 S. Daniels Road, Heber City; www.co.wasatch.ut.us/fair
Parades, exhibits, country market, livestock shows, rodeos, dancing.
First weekend in August.

TIMPANOGOS CAVE NATIONAL MONUMENT

Timpanogos Cave National Monument consists of three small, beautifully decorated underground chambers within limestone beds. The cave entrance is on the northern slope of Mount Timpanogos. A filigree of colorful crystal formations covers much of the cave's interior, where stalactites and stalagmites are common. But what makes Timpanogos unique is its large number of helictites—formations that appear to defy gravity as they grow outward from the walls of the cave. The temperature in Timpanogos Cave is a constant 45 fahrenheit, and the interior is electrically lighted.

The cave's headquarters are located on Highway 92, eight miles east of American Fork. There is picnicking at Swinging Bridge Picnic Area, ¼ mile from the headquarters. The cave entrance is 1½ miles from headquarters via a paved trail with a vertical rise of 1,065 feet. Allow three to five hours for a guided tour. Tours limited to 20 people (late May-early-September, daily). Purchase tickets in advance by calling 801-756-5238 or stopping at the visitor center. Monday-Friday 8 a.m.-4:30 p.m. Information: Heber City, 26 miles south of Salt Lake City on I-15, then 10 miles east on Highway 92, 801-756-5238; www.nps.gov/tica

WHERE TO STAY
★HOLIDAY INN EXPRESS
1268 S. Main St., Heber City, 435-654-9990, 877-863-4780; www.ichotelsgroup.com
75 rooms. Pool. Complimentary breakfast. $

KANAB

See also Bryce Canyon National Park

Since 1922, more than 200 Hollywood productions have used the sand dunes, canyons and lakes surrounding Kanab as their settings. Some movie-set towns can still be seen. Kanab is within a 1½-hour drive from the north rim of the Grand Canyon, Zion and Bryce Canyon national parks, Cedar Breaks and Pipe Spring national monuments and Glen Canyon National Recreation Area.

WHAT TO SEE
CORAL PINK SAND DUNES STATE PARK
Yellow jacket and Hancock Roads, Kanab, 435-648-2800;
www.stateparks.utah.gov/stateparks
The park includes six square miles of very colorful, windswept sand hills. Hiking, picnicking, tent and trailer sites. Off-highway vehicles allowed. Daily.

LAKE POWELL

See also Page

Lake Powell is the second largest man-made lake in the United States, with more than 1,900 miles of shoreline. The lake is named for John Wesley Powell, the one-armed explorer who, in 1869, successfully navigated the Colorado River through Glen Canyon and the Grand Canyon and later became director of the U.S. Geological Survey.

WHAT TO SEE
BOAT TRIPS ON LAKE POWELL
Bullfrog Marina, Highway 276, Lake Powell, 435-684-3000; www.lakepowell.com
Trips include the Canyon Explorer tour (2½ hours) and the half-day and all-day Rainbow Bridge tours. (Due to the current level of the lake, these tours involve a 1¼-mile hike to see the monument.) Visitors can also take wilderness float trips and rent houseboats and powerboats. Reservations are advised. Daily.

GLEN CANYON NATIONAL RECREATION AREA (BULLFROG MARINA)
Highway 276, Lake Powell, 435-684-3010; www.lakepowell.com
Additional access and recreational activities are available at Hite Marina, at the north end of lake. This boasts more than a million acres with year-round recreation area, including swimming, fishing, boating, boat tours and trips, boat rentals; picnicking, camping, tent and trailer sites, lodgings.
April-October, daily.

LOGAN
See also Brigham City, Garden City
Situated in the center of beautiful Cache Valley, Logan is surrounded by snowcapped mountains and is home to Utah State University.

WHAT TO SEE
DAUGHTERS OF THE UTAH PIONEERS MUSEUM
160 N. Main, Logan, 435-752-5139; www.dupinternational.org/histDep.html
Exhibits depict Utah's past. Monday-Friday.

HYRUM STATE PARK
405 W. 300 S. Logan, 435-245-6866; www.stateparks.utah.gov/stateparks

---

RAINBOW BRIDGE NATIONAL MONUMENT
Rainbow Bridge, which rises from the eastern shore of Lake Powell, is the largest natural rock bridge in the world. It was named a national monument in 1910. This natural bridge stands 290 feet tall, spans 275 feet and stretches 33 feet wide at the top. One of the natural wonders of the world, Rainbow Bridge is higher than the nation's capitol dome and nearly as long as a football field. The monument is predominantly salmon pink in color, modified by streaks of iron oxide and manganese. In the light of the late afternoon Sunday, the bridge is a brilliant sight. American Indians consider the area a sacred place; legend holds that the bridge is a rainbow turned to stone.

The easiest way to reach Rainbow Bridge is a half-day round-trip boat ride across Lake Powell from Page, Arizona, or a full-day round-trip boat ride from Bullfrog and Halls Crossing marinas. The bridge also can be reached on foot or horseback via the Rainbow Trail through the Navajo Indian Reservation. Fuel and camp supplies are available at Dangling Rope Marina, accessible by boat only, 10 miles south down lake.

Information: Rainbow Bridge National Monument, 928-608-6200;
www.nps.gov/rabr

A 450-acre reservoir with beach swimming, waterskiing, fishing, ice fishing, boating (ramp, dock), sailing; picnicking, camping.
Year-round. Summer, 6 a.m.-10 p.m.; winter, 8 a.m.-5 p.m.

MORMON TABERNACLE

50 N. Main St., Logan, 435-755-5598
A gray limestone example of an early Mormon building. Genealogy library. Monday-Friday.

MORMON TEMPLE

175 N. 300 E. Logan, 435-752-3611
The site for this massive, castellated limestone structure was chosen by Brigham Young, who broke ground here in 1877.
Grounds are open all year, but the temple is closed to the general public.

UTAH STATE UNIVERSITY

1400 Old Main Hill, Logan, 435-797-1000; www.usu.edu
Established in 1888; 20,100 students. On campus is the Nora Eccles Harrison Museum of Art. Monday-Friday.

WASATCH-CACHE NATIONAL FOREST, LOGAN CANYON

1500 E. Highway 89, Logan, 435-755-3620; www.fs.fed.us/r4/uwc
This national forest offers fishing, backcountry trails, hunting, winter sports, picnicking and camping. Daily.

WILLOW PARK ZOO

419 W. 700 S. Logan, 435-716-9265; www.loganutah.org
This small but attractive zoo has shady grounds and especially good bird-watching of migratory species, with more than 100 captive species and 80 species of wild birds visiting and nesting at the zoo.
Daily 9 a.m.-dusk.

UTAH FESTIVAL OPERA COMPANY

59 S. 100 W., Logan; www.ufoc.org
July-August.

WHERE TO STAY
★★BEST WESTERN BAUGH MOTEL

153 S. Main St., Logan, 435-752-5220, 800-462-4154; www.bestwestern.com
76 rooms. Complimentary breakfast. Restaurant. Pool. $

★QUALITY INN LOGAN

447 N. Main St., Logan, 435-752-9141, 866-537-6459; www.choicehotels.com
83 rooms. Complimentary breakfast. Fitness center. Pool. $

WHERE TO EAT
★THE COPPER MILL
55 N. Main St., Logan, 435-752-0647
American. Lunch, dinner. $

★★LE NONNE
129 N. 100 East, Logan, 435-752-9577; www.lenonne.net
Italian. Lunch (Thursday-Friday), dinner. Closed Sunday. $$

MIDWAY
See also Salt Lake City
This town recalls its Swiss roots with Swiss architecture and an annual festival that celebrates the town's heritage. Less than an hour's drive from Salt Lake, Midway is near Wasatch Mountain State Park.

SPECIAL EVENTS
SWISS DAYS
Midway Town Square; www.midwayswissdays.com
Old country games, activities, costumes.
Friday and Saturday before Labor Day.

WHERE TO STAY
★★★THE BLUE BOAR INN
1235 Warm Springs Road, Midway, 435-654-1400, 888-650-1400;
www.theblueboarinn.com
Decorated in a unique Austrian-influenced style, the guest rooms at this inn feature themes inspired by famous authors and poets. From the handmade willow bed of the Robert Frost room to the English cottage style of the William Butler Yeats, each room attempts to capture its namesake's distinctive personality. The restaurant serves fresh American cuisine.
12 rooms. Complimentary breakfast. Restaurant, bar. Business center. $$

★★★HOMESTEAD RESORT
700 N. Homestead Drive, Midway, 435-654-1102, 888-327-7220;
www.homesteadresort.com
Surrounded by gardens and the Wasatch Mountains, this historic country resort on 200 acres features quaint cottages that make up the majority of the accommodations. Amenities include an Aveda spa, adventure center with billiards, board games, video library and a championship golf course. The resort also rents cross-country skis and snowshoes and provides transportation to nearby Deer Valley's Jordanelle Express Gondola.
144 rooms. Restaurant, bar. Spa. Golf. Tennis. Business center. Pets accepted. $$

★★★INN ON THE CREEK
375 Rainbow Lane, Midway, 435-654-0892, 800-654-0892; www.innoncreek.com
Picturesque landscaping and hot springs surround this full-service inn. Located at the base of the Wasatch Mountains in Heber Valley, the inn is near popular ski resorts and golf courses. Guests can choose from rooms in the

main inn or luxury chalets. All are spacious and most rooms feature fireplaces and balconies or private decks. The inn's restaurant, which serves American-French cuisine, utilizes garden vegetables and herbs, and has an extensive wine selection.

40 rooms. Restaurant, bar. Pool. $$

WHERE TO EAT
★★★THE BLUE BOAR INN RESTAURANT
The Blue Boar Inn, 1235 Warm Springs Road, Midway, 435-654-1400, 888-650-1400; www.theblueboarinn.com

This charming Tyrolean chalet offers some of the best New American cuisine in Utah. The menu changes periodically to capture the best produce and fresh seafood available, but you might see entrées like herb-crusted salmon with roasted fingerling potatoes, spring vegetables and a roasted red bell pepper sauce or braised lamb shank with pine nut cous cous, spring vegetables, white wine and tomato sauce.

American. Lunch, dinner, Sunday brunch. Bar. Outdoor seating. $$$

★★★FANNY'S GRILL
Homestead Resort, 700 N. Homestead Drive, Midway, 435-654-1102, 800-327-7220; www.homesteadresort.com

Dine on Western cuisine (steaks, hearty side dishes) in an elegant country setting, either inside the dining room by the fireplace or outside on the deck, with beautiful views of the valley. The outdoor patio is a comfortable spot to dine in warm weather.

American. Breakfast, lunch, dinner. Bar. Children's menu. Outdoor seating. $$

MOAB
See also Monticello

The first attempt to settle this valley was made in 1855, but Moab, named after an isolated area in the Bible, was not permanently settled until 1880. Situated on the Colorado River at the foot of the La Sal Mountains, Moab was a sleepy agricultural town until after World War II, when uranium and oil exploration created a boom. Today, tourism and moviemaking help make it a thriving community.

WHAT TO SEE
ADRIFT ADVENTURES
378 N. Main St., Moab, 435-259-8594, 800-874-4483; www.adrift.net

This outfitter offers oar, paddle and motorized trips of lengths from one to seven days. Jeep tours and horseback rides are also offered.

Early April-late October.

CANYON VOYAGES ADVENTURE COMPANY
211 N. Main St., Moab, 435-259-6007, 800-733-6007; www.canyonvoyages.com

Kayaking, white-water rafting, canoeing, biking or four-wheel drive tours.

Early April-October.

CANYONLANDS BY NIGHT

1861 S. Highway 191, Moab, 435-259-2628, 800-394-9978;
www.canyonlandsbynight.com

This two-hour boat trip with sound-and-light presentation highlights the history of area. April-mid-October, daily, leaves at sundown, weather permitting. Reservations required.

CANYONLANDS FIELD INSTITUTE

1320 S. Highway 191, Moab, 435-259-7750, 800-860-5262;
www.canyonlandsfieldinst.org

Adult and family-oriented educational seminars and trips feature geology, natural and cultural history, endangered species and Southwestern literature. Many programs use Canyonlands and Arches national parks as outdoor classrooms.
Monday-Friday.

DAN O'LAURIE CANYON COUNTRY MUSEUM

118 E. Center St., Moab, 435-259-7985; www.discovermoab.com

See exhibits on local history, archaeology, geology, uranium and minerals of the area. Walking tour information.
Summer, Monday-Friday 10 a.m.-6 p.m., Saturday-Sunday noon-6 p.m.; winter, Monday-Friday 10 a.m.-3 p.m., Saturday-Sunday noon-5 p.m.

DEAD HORSE POINT STATE PARK

313 State Road, Moab, 435-259-2614, 800-322-3770;
www.stateparks.utah.gov/parks/dead-horse

This island mesa offers views of the La Sal Mountains, Canyonlands National Park and the Colorado River.
Daily 6 a.m.-10 p.m.

HOLE 'N THE ROCK

11037 S. Highway 191, Moab, 435-686-2250; www.moab-utah.com/holeintherock

See a 5,000-square-foot home carved into huge sandstone rock. Picnic area with stone tables and benches.
Tours: daily 8 a.m.-dusk.

MANTI-LA SAL NATIONAL FOREST, LA SAL DIVISION

599 W. Price River Drive, Price, 435-637-2817; www.fs.fed.us/r4/mantilasal

The land here is similar in color and beauty to some parts of the Grand Canyon and also includes high mountains nearing 13,000 feet, as well as pine and spruce forests. Enjoy swimming, fishing hiking and hunting.

PACK CREEK RANCH TRAIL RIDES

La Sal Mountain Loop Road, Moab, 435-259-5505; www.packcreekranch.com

Go horseback riding through the foothills of the La Sal Mountains. Guided tours for small groups; reservations required.
March-October; upon availability.

REDTAIL AVIATION SCENIC AIR TOURS

North Highway 191, Moab, 435-259-7421, 800-842-9251; www.moab-utah.com/redtail

Offers flights over Canyonlands National Park and various other tours.
Daily.

RIM TOURS

1233 S. Highway 191, Moab, 435-259-5223, 800-626-7335; www.rimtours.com

Guided mountain bike tours in canyon country and the Colorado Rockies.
Vehicle support for camping tours.
Daily and overnight trips; combination bicycle/river trips available.

SHERI GRIFFITH RIVER EXPEDITIONS

2231 S. Highway 191 Moab, 435-259-8229, 800-332-2439; www.griffithexp.com

Take your pick and ride oar boats, motorized rafts, paddleboats or inflatable
kayak for one- to five-day trips. Instruction available.
May-October.

TAG-A-LONG EXPEDITIONS

452 N. Main St., Moab, 435-259-8946, 800-453-3292; www.tagalong.com

Choose from one- to seven-day white-water rafting trips on the Green and
Colorado rivers; jet boat trips on the Colorado River; and jet boat trips and
four-wheel-drive tours into Canyonlands National Park. Winter four-wheel
drive tours, November--February. One-day jet boat trips with cultural performing arts programs are offered part of the year as well.
April-mid-October.

TEX'S RIVERWAYS

691 N. 500 W., Moab, 435-259-5101; www.texsriverways.com

Flatwater canoe trips, four to 10 days. Confluence pick-ups available, jet boat
cruises.
March-October.

SPECIAL EVENTS
BUTCH CASSIDY DAYS PRCA RODEO

Moab, 800-635-6622

Second weekend in June.

MOAB MUSIC FESTIVAL

58 E. 300 S. Moab, 435-259-7003; www.moabmusicfest.org

This festival features classical music performed in natural settings throughout southeastern Utah.
First two weeks in September.

WHERE TO STAY
★★BEST WESTERN CANYONLANDS INN

16 S. Main St., Moab, 435-259-2300; www.bestwestern.com

77 rooms. Complimentary breakfast. Business center. Pool. Fitness center. $

MOAB AND BEYOND

This three- to four-day tour out of Moab includes magnificent vistas, unique rock formations and the upper reaches of Lake Powell. From Moab, head south on Highway 191 to Highway 211; follow 211 west to Newspaper Rock, a huge sandstone panel with petroglyphs that are up to 1,500 years old. Prehistoric peoples such as the Fremonts and ancestral Puebloans, as well as the Utes, Navajo and European-American settlers, left images etched into this wall of stone. From Newspaper Rock, it is an easy drive west on Highway 211 to the Needles District of Canyonlands National Park. You probably visited the Island in the Sky District of Canyonlands during your stay in Moab, but this section of the park offers a different perspective. Although best explored by mountain bike or in a high-clearance four-wheel-drive vehicle, there are several roadside viewpoints from which you can see the district's namesake red-and-white-striped rock pinnacles and other formations. Several easy hikes offer additional views.

Retrace your route back to Highway 191 and continue south to Highway 95, where you will head west to Natural Bridges National Monument. This easy-to-explore monument has a scenic drive with overlooks that offer views of three awe-inspiring natural stone bridges and some 700-year-old ancestral Puebloan cliff dwellings. There is also prehistoric rock art and a demonstration of how solar energy is used to produce the monument's electricity. The viewpoints are short walks from parking areas. You can also hike to all three of the natural bridges, which were created over millions of years as water cut through solid rock. Returning to Highway 95, head northwest to the Hite Crossing section of Glen Canyon National Recreation Area. Encompassing the northern end of Lake Powell, this is one of the least developed (and least crowded) sections of the recreation area. Hite Crossing has scenic views, boat rentals and plenty of available lodging (including houseboats).

From Hite, continue northwest on Highway 95 across rock-studded terrain to Hanksville; head north on Highway 24 to the turnoff to Goblin Valley State Park. This delightful little park is a fantasyland where whimsical stone goblins seem to be frozen in mid-dance. From Goblin Valley, return to Highway 24 and continue north to Interstate 70 (I-70). Head east to the community of Green River, where you'll find several motels. Here you'll discover Green River State Park, a good spot for a picnic under the Russian olive and cottonwood trees along the river, or perhaps a round of golf at the park's nine-hole championship course. Nearby, the John Wesley Powell River History Museum tells the incredible story of explorer Powell, a one-armed Civil War veteran who did what was considered impossible when he charted the Green and Colorado rivers in the late 1800s. From Green River continue east on I-70 to Highway 191, which leads south back to Moab. Approximately 448 miles.

★★★★ **UTAH**

333

★★BEST WESTERN GREENWELL INN

105 S. Main St., Moab, 435-259-6151; www.bestwestern.com
72 rooms. Pool. Fitness center. $

★BOWEN MOTEL

169 N. Main St., Moab, 435-259-7132, 800-874-5439; www.bowenmotel.com
40 rooms. Complimentary breakfast. Pets accepted. Pool. $

★★★SORREL RIVER RANCH RESORT & SPA

Highway 128, Moab, 435-259-4642, 877-359-2715; www.sorrelriver.com
Set in a dramatic landscape of red rock formations, this full-service resort is just 30 minutes from Arches National Park. Many of the Western-themed guest rooms, all of which have kitchenettes, overlook the Colorado River.

Family loft suites are also available and fireplaces and jetted hydrotherapy tubs are found in the deluxe suites. Also offered are horseback tours, tennis and a spa. After a busy day, enjoy an upscale meal at the Sorrel River Grill. 59 rooms. Restaurant. Spa. Tennis. $$

WHERE TO EAT
★★CENTER CAFÉ
60 N. 100 W., Moab, 435-259-4295; www.centercafemoab.com
International. Dinner. Outdoor seating. $$

★MOAB BREWERY
686 S. Main St., Moab, 435-259-6333; www.themoabbrewery.com
American. Lunch, dinner. $$

★★SLICKROCK CAFÉ
5 N. Main St., Moab, 435-259-8004; www.slickrockcafe.com
American. Lunch, dinner. $

OGDEN
See also Brigham City, Salt Lake City
Brigham Young laid out the streets of Ogden, the fourth-largest city in Utah, in traditional Mormon geometrical style: broad, straight and bordered by poplar, box elder, elm and cottonwood trees. In 1846, Miles Goodyear, the first white settler, had built a cabin and trading post here, which he sold to the Mormons a year later. During the last 30 years of the 19th century, Ogden was an outfitting center for trappers and hunters heading north. Its saloons and gambling halls were typical of a frontier town, and there was considerable friction between the Mormons and the "gentiles." With the arrival of the railroad, Ogden became one of the few cities in Utah whose inhabitants were not primarily Mormons.

Today, Ogden is a commercial and industrial center. Hill Air Force Base is nearby. Mount Ben Lomond, north of the city in the Wasatch Range, was the inspiration for the logo of Paramount Pictures.

WHAT TO SEE
DAUGHTERS OF UTAH PIONEERS MUSEUM AND RELIC HALL
4046 South 895 E., Ogden, 801-621-4891; www.dupinternational.org
See old handicrafts, household items and portraits of those who came to Utah prior to the railroad of 1869. This is also the site of Miles Goodyear's cabin, the first permanent house built in Utah.
Mid-May-mid—September, Monday-Saturday.

ECCLES COMMUNITY ART CENTER
2580 Jefferson Ave., Ogden, 801-392-6935; www.ogden4arts.org
This 19th-century castle-like mansion hosts changing art exhibits. It also has a dance studio and outdoor sculpture and floral garden.
Monday-Saturday.

FORT BUENAVENTURA STATE PARK

2450 A. Ave., Ogden, 801-399-8099; www.utah.com/stateparks

The exciting era of mountain men is brought to life on this 32-acre site, where Miles Goodyear built Ogden's first settlement in 1846. The fort has been reconstructed according to archaeological and historical research. No nails were used in building the stockade; wooden pegs and mortise and tenon joints hold the structure together.
April-November.

GEORGE S. ECCLES DINOSAUR PARK

1544 E. Park Blvd., Ogden, 801-393-3466; www.dinosaurpark.org

This outdoor display contains more than 100 life-size reproductions of dinosaurs and other prehistoric creatures. There's also an educational building with a working paleontological lab, as well as fossil and reptile displays.
Daily. Closed November-March.

HILL AEROSPACE MUSEUM

7961 Wardleigh Road, Hill Air Force Base, 801-777-6868; www.hill.af.mil

More than 55 aircraft on display here, including the SR-71 "Blackbird" reconnaissance plane and the B-52 bomber. Helicopters, jet engines, missiles, uniforms and other memorabilia are also featured.
Daily.

PINE VIEW RESERVOIR

Wasatch-Cache National Forest, Ogden, 801-625-5306; www.fs.fed.us

See some of the world's largest locomotives. The Browning-Kimball Car Museum and Browning Firearms Museum are also here (John Browning was the inventor of the automatic rifle), plus a 500-seat theater for musical and dramatic productions, art gallery and restaurant. Visitors Bureau for Northern Utah is located here.
Monday-Saturday. 10 a.m.-5 p.m.

UNION STATION

2501 Wall Ave., Ogden, 801-393-9886; www.theunionstation.org

See some of the world's largest locomotives. The Browning-Kimball Car Museum and Browning Firearms Museum are also here (John Browning was the inventor of the automatic rifle), plus a 500-seat theater for musical and dramatic productions, art gallery and restaurant. Visitors Bureau for Northern Utah is located here.
Monday-Saturday. 10 a.m.-5 p.m.

WEBER STATE UNIVERSITY

3848 Harrison Blvd., Ogden, 801-626-6000; www.weber.edu

Established in 1889; 17,000 students. On campus is the Layton P. Ott Planetarium with Foucault pendulum; shows Wednesday; no shows summer. The Stewart Bell Tower, with 183-bell electronic carillon, offers performances.
Daily. Campus tours.

WILLARD BAY STATE PARK
900 West 650 N., Ogden, 435-734-9494; www.stateparks.utah.gov/stateparks
This park has a 9,900-acre lake for swimming, fishing, boating, and picnicking. Daily.

SPECIAL EVENTS
PIONEER DAYS
Ogden Pioneer Stadium, 1875 Monroe Blvd., Ogden; www.ogdenpioneerdays.com
Rodeo, concerts, vintage car shows, fireworks, chili cook-off. Mid-late July.

UTAH SYMPHONY POPS CONCERT
Lindquist Fountain/Plaza, 1875 Monroe Blvd., Ogden
Music enhanced by a fireworks display. Late July.

WHERE TO STAY
★BEST WESTERN HIGH COUNTRY INN
1335 W. 12th St., Ogden, 801-394-9474, 800-594-8979; www.bestwestern.com
109 rooms. Restaurant, bar. Pets accepted. Pool. Fitness center. $

★COMFORT SUITES OGDEN
2250 S. 1200 W. Ogden, Ogden, 801-621-2545; www.ogdencomfortsuites.com
142 rooms. Complimentary breakfast. Pool. Fitness center. Pets accepted. $

★HAMPTON INN & SUITES OGDEN
2401 Washington Blvd., Ogden, 801-394-9400; www.hamptoninn.com
124 rooms. Complimentary breakfast. Fitness center. Business center. $

★★MARRIOTT OGDEN
247 24th St., Ogden, 801-627-1190, 888-825-3163; www.marriott.com
292 rooms. Restaurant, bar. Fitness center. Pool. Business center. $

PARK CITY
See also Alta, Heber City, Salt Lake City, Snowbird
Soldiers struck silver here in 1868, starting one of the nation's largest silver mining camps, which reached a population of 10,000 before declining to a near ghost town when the silver market collapsed. Since then, however, Park City has been revived as a four-season resort with skiing, snowboarding, golf, tennis, water sports and mountain biking.

WHAT TO SEE
BRIGHTON SKI RESORT
12601 E. Big Cottonwood Canyon Road, Brighton, 801-532-4731, 800-873-5512; www.skibrighton.com
The resort includes 16 high-speed quad, triple, and double chairlifts; a gondola; ski patrol, school, and rentals; and a restaurant, bar, and lodge.
155 trails. Winter lift daily 9 a.m.-4 p.m. Thanksgiving-April, daily.

THE CANYONS

4000 The Canyons Resort Drive, Park City, 435-649-5400; www.thecanyons.com
This ski resort features 16 high-speed quad, triple, and double chairlifts; a gondola; a ski patrol, school, and rentals; and restaurant, bar, and lodge. 155 trails. Winter lift daily 9 a.m.-4 p.m. Thanksgiving-April, daily.

DEER VALLEY RESORT

2250 Deer Valley Drive S., Park City, 435-649-1000, 800-424-3337; www.deervalley.com
The resort has eight high-speed quads, eight triple, and two double chairlifts; rental, patrol, school, snowmaking; restaurants, lounge, lodge, and nursery. Approximately 1,750 skiable acres. Vertical drop 3,000 feet. Summer activities include mountain biking, hiking and horseback riding.

EGYPTIAN THEATRE

328 Main St., Park City, 435-649-9371; www.egyptiantheatrecompany.org
Originally built in 1926 as a silent movie and vaudeville house, this is now a year-round performing arts center with a semi-professional theater group. Wednesday-Saturday; some performances other days.

KIMBALL ART CENTER

638 Park Ave., Park City, 435-649-8882; www.kimball-art.org
Exhibits in various media by local and regional artists.
Admission: free. Gallery, Monday, Wednesday-Friday 10 a.m.-5 p.m., Saturday-Sunday noon-5 p.m.

PARK CITY MOUNTAIN RESORT

1310 Lowell Ave., Park City, 435-649-8111, 800-222-7275; www.pcski.com
The ski resort has a gondola; two quads, four doubles, five triples, and four six-passenger chairlifts; patrol, school, rentals, snowmaking; restaurants, cafeteria, bar. Approximately 3,300 acres; 104 trails; 750 acres of open-bowl skiing. Lighted snowboarding.
Mid-November-mid-April, daily.

ROCKPORT STATE PARK

9040 N. Highway 302, Peoa, 435-336-2241; www.stateparks.utah.gov/stateparks
This 1,000-acre park along east side of Rockport Lake offers great opportunities for viewing wildlife, including bald eagles (winter) and golden eagles. Swimming, waterskiing, sailboarding, fishing, boating; cross-country ski trail (six miles), camping, tent and trailer sites.
Daily.

SOLITUDE MOUNTAIN RESORT

12000 Big Cottonwood Canyon, Solitude, 801-534-1400; www.skisolitude.com
Dining, lodging, solitude community, mountain biking are available daily.

TANGER FACTORY OUTLET

6699 N. Landmark Drive, Park City, 435-645-7078, 866-665-8681;
www.tangeroutlet.com

The more than 45 outlet stores here include Gap, Nike and Eddie Bauer. Daily.

UTAH WINTER SPORTS PARK

3419 Olympic Parkway, Park City, 435-658-4200; www.olyparks.com

Recreational ski jumping is available at this $25-million park built for the 2002 Olympic Winter Games. Lessons are offered, followed by two-hour jumping session and an Olympic bobsled and luge track are available. Wednesday-Sunday.

WHITE PINE TOURING CENTER

1790 Bonanza Drive, Park City, 435-649-8710; www.whitepinetouring.com

Groomed cross-country trails (12 miles), school, rentals; guided tours. November-April, daily.

SPECIAL EVENTS
ART FESTIVAL

Main St., Park City

This open-air market features more than 200 visual artists and entertainment. First weekend in August.

SUNDANCE FILM FESTIVAL

Park City, 435-776-7878; www.sundance.org/festival

This 10-day festival for independent filmmakers has become famous for its groundbreaking works and celebrity attendance. Workshops, screenings and special events.
Mid-January.

WHERE TO STAY
★★★THE CANYONS GRAND SUMMIT HOTEL

4000 The Canyons Resort Drive, Park City, 435-649-5400, 888-226-9667;
www.thecanyons.com

This mountain lodge, one of three at the Canyons Resort, is set at the foot of Park City's ski slopes. Guest rooms, most of which have balconies and fireplaces, have excellent views of the mountains and the valley below. If you need a break from skiing, check out the resort's Village Shops, where regularly scheduled concerts and other events are held. Summer brings warm-weather activities like horseback riding, hiking and fly-fishing and the gondola remains open for scenic rides.

358 rooms. Restaurant, bar. Spa. Ski in/ski out. Pool. $$$$

★★★THE CHATEAUX AT SILVER LAKE

7815 E. Royal St., Park City, 435-658-9500, 800-453-3833;
www.chateaux-silverlake.com

Situated in the heart of Deer Valley Resort's Silver Lake Village, the Chateaux at Silver Lake offers guests a comfortable stay in an elegant and picturesque setting. Rooms are decorated with custom-designed furniture and feature pillow-top mattresses and feather beds, gas fireplaces and wet bars. Onsite amenities include a full-service spa, heated covered parking, free local shuttle service and winter sports equipment rentals.

95 rooms. Restaurant, bar. Fitness center. Spa. Pool. Business center. $$$$

★★★CLUB LESPRI BOUTIQUE INN & SPA

1765 Sidewinder Drive, Park City, 435-645-9696; www.clublespri.com

The suites here all of which feature fireplaces, hand-carved furniture, custom beds, oversize tubs and full kitchens. The onsite spa offers a full range of massages, and two restaurants serve steaks and more in an upscale setting.

10 rooms. Restaurant, bar. Fitness center. Spa. $$$

★★★GOLDENER HIRSCH INN

7570 Royal St. E. Park City, 435-649-7770, 800-252-3373; www.goldenerhirschinn.com

Warm and inviting, this ski resort blends the services of a large hotel with the charm of a bed and breakfast. The romantic guest rooms and suites have warm colors and hand-painted furniture. All-day dining and après-ski service are available at the hotel's Austrian-themed restaurant.

20 rooms. Closed mid-April-early June, early October-early December. Complimentary breakfast. Restaurant, bar. Ski in/ski out. $$$$

★HOLIDAY INN EXPRESS

1501 W. Ute Blvd., Park City, 435-658-1600, 888-465-4329; www.hieparkcity.com

76 rooms. Fitness center. Pool. Pets accepted. Complimentary breakfast. $

★★★HOTEL PARK CITY

2001 Park Ave., Park City, 435-200-2000, 888-999-0098; www.hotelparkcity.com

This all-suite resort pampers its guests. The amenities are top notch, from triple-head showers and jetted tubs to Bose audio systems and Bulgari bath products. The suites have a residential feel with cozy fireplaces and traditional alpine-style furnishings. Set at the base of the Wasatch Mountains, this hotel has a scenic location that's ideal for skiers.

100 rooms. Restaurant, bar. Pool. Spa. Ski in/ski out. Golf. Skiing. $$

★★★PARK CITY MARRIOTT

1895 Sidewinder Drive, Park City, 435-649-2900, 800-234-9003; www.marriott.com

This newly renovated hotel is located a mile from downtown Park City and the historic Main Street. Take the complimentary shuttle to Utah Olympic Park, outlet stores and old Main Street. Starbucks fans will find a coffee kiosk in the lobby, as well as rental ski equipment and bicycles.

191 rooms. Restaurant, bar. Pets accepted. Pool. Business center. $$

★★★★★STEIN ERIKSEN LODGE

7700 Stein Way, Park City, 435-649-3700, 800-453-1302; www.steinlodge.com

Situated mid-mountain at Utah's Deer Valley ski resort, this Scandinavian resort calls a magnificent alpine setting home. Heated sidewalks and walkways keep you toasty, while the ski valet service takes care of all your needs on the slopes. The dining at Glitretind is outstanding, and the Sunday Brunch is a

local favorite. Be sure to try the housemade chocolates from executive pastry chef Raymond Lammers in the Chocolate Atelier, where the gourmet treats are made. The fireplace and inviting ambience of the Troll Hallen Lounge make it a cozy spot for après-ski or light fare. Rooms are all distinctive and feature jetted tubs; suites have gourmet kitchens and stone fireplaces.
180 rooms. Restaurant, bar. Spa. Pool. Ski in/ski out. Fitness center. Business center. $$$$

WHERE TO EAT
★★★THE CABIN
The Canyons Grand Summit Hotel, 4000 The Canyons Resort Drive, Park City, 435-649-8060; www.thecanyons.com
This upscale restaurant at the Canyons Grand Summit Hotel has rustic décor and a friendly staff. The restaurant serves dishes from an eclectic Western menu, including buffalo tenderloin, lamb osso bucco and their signature crispy trout.
American. Breakfast, lunch, dinner. Bar. Children's menu. $$$

★★CHEZ BETTY
1637 Short Line Drive, Park City, 435-649-8181; www.chezbetty.com
American. Dinner. Outdoor seating. $$$

★★★CHIMAYO
368 Main St., Park City, 435-649-6222; www.chimayorestaurant.com
Tucked on Main Street in downtown Park City, this restaurant serves creative Southwestern cuisine. Dishes include scallops wrapped in wild boar bacon and served with a tortilla tomato casserole with salsa verde and seared trout fajitas. A fireplace enhances the warm, colorful atmosphere.
Southwestern. Dinner. Children's menu. Reservations recommended. $$$

★★★★GLITRETIND RESTAURANT
Stein Eriksen Lodge, 7700 Stein Way, Park City, 435-645-6455; www.steinlodge.com
Executive chef Zane Holmquist prepares acclaimed New American cuisine at this restaurant inside the Stein Eriksen Lodge. Try the Berkshire pork porterhouse with pecan grits, baby beans, watermelon and bourbon sacue; or the filet of Colorado beef with smoked blue cheese, fingerling potatoes, peas and veal jus. The wine selection is managed by Sommelier Cara Schwindt, and includes more than 750 types of wine that total more than 10,000 bottles. The restaurant also provides a wide selection of dessert and after dinner drinks, including a wide range of single malt scotch, bourbon, Cognac and brandy.
American. Breakfast, lunch, dinner, Sunday brunch. Bar. Children's menu. Reservations recommended. Outdoor seating. $$$

★★★GRAPPA
151 Main St., Park City, 435-645-0636; www.grapparestaurant.com
Tucker inside a former boarding house on Park City's historic Main Street, this upscale restaurant offers dining on three levels. Many of the dishes feature fresh herbs and flowers from the adjacent gardens, such as the salmon encrusted in horseradish, garlic, herbed breadcrumbs and chopped shallots with housemade fettuccine, mushrooms, tomatoes and sherry butter sauce.

Italian. Dinner. Children's menu. Outdoor seating. $$$

★★★★RIVERHORSE ON MAIN
540 Main St., Park City, 435-649-3536; www.riverhorsegroup.com

Even ski bunnies (and bums) must eat, and when they do, they come to Riverhorse on Main, a bustling scene. Located in the renovated historic Masonic Hall on Main Street, this modern restaurant, with dark woods, soft candlelight and fresh flowers offers lots of fun, Asian-inspired eats such as chicken satay, shrimp potstickers, crispy duck salad, macadamia-crusted halibut, poached lobster tail and grilled rack of lamb. While the dress code is informal, reservations are a must.

American. Dinner. Children's menu. Reservations recommended. Outdoor seating. $$$

SPAS

★★★★THE SPA AT STEIN ERIKSEN LODGE
Stein Eriksen Lodge, 7700 Stein Way, Park City, 435-649-3700; www.steinlodge.com

The Spa at Stein Eriksen Lodge was designed to appeal to guests needing remedies for sore and tired muscles after skiing, or those affected by the resort's high altitude. With a new renovation (revealed in December 2009), you'll find a larger spa, at 20,000 square-feet, with an expanded fitness center and larger pool deck, among other things. All spa services grant complimentary use of the fitness center, steam room, sauna, whirlpool, and relaxation room. Aromatic and exhilarating treatments refresh and renew at this European-style spa, where Vichy showers and kurs are de rigueur. The extensive

---

CANYONLANDS NATIONAL PARK

Set aside by Congress in 1964 as a national park, this 337,570-acre area is largely undeveloped and includes spectacular rock formations, canyons, arches, ancestral Puebloan ruins and more. Road conditions vary; primary access roads are paved and maintained while others are safe only for high-clearance four-wheel-drive vehicles.Island in the Sky, North District, south and west of Dead Horse Point State Park, has Grand View Point, Upheaval Dome and Green River Overlook. This section is accessible by passenger car via Highway 313 and by four-wheel-drive vehicles and mountain bikes on dirt roads.

Needles, South District, has hiking trails and four-wheel-drive roads to Angel Arch, Chesler Park and the confluence of the Green and Colorado rivers. You'll also see prehistoric ruins and rock art here. This section is accessible by passenger car via Highway 211, by four-wheel-drive vehicle on dirt roads and by mountain bike. Maze, West District, is accessible by hiking or by four-wheel-drive vehicles using unimproved roads. The most remote and least-visited section of the park, this area received its name from the many mazelike canyons. Horseshoe Canyon., a separate unit of the park nearby, is accessible via Highway 24 and 30 miles of two-wheel-drive dirt road. Roads are usually passable only in mid-March-mid-November.

Canyonlands is excellent for calm-water and white-water trips down the Green and Colorado rivers. Permits are required for private and commercial trips. Campgrounds, with tent sites, are located at Island in the Sky and at Needles; water is available only at Needles. Visitor centers are in each district and are open daily. Information: Canyonlands National Park, 2282 S. West Resource Blvd., Moab, 435-719-2313; www.nps.gov/cany

massage menu includes Swedish, deep tissue, aromatic, stone, reflexology, and a special massage for mothers-to-be. In-room massages are available for additional privacy.

PAYSON

See also Provo

Payson sits at the foot of the Wasatch Mountains, near Utah Lake. Mormons first settled the area after spending a night on the banks of Peteneet Creek.

WHAT TO SEE
MOUNT NEBO SCENIC LOOP DRIVE

Payson

This 45-mile drive around the eastern shoulder of towering Mount Nebo (elevation 11,877 feet) is one of the most thrilling in Utah. Mount Nebo's three peaks are the highest in the Wasatch Range. The road travels south through Payson and Santaquin canyons and then climbs 9,000 feet up Mount Nebo, offering a view of Devil's Kitchen, a brilliantly colored canyon. (This section of the drive is not recommended for those who dislike heights.) The forest road continues south to Highway 132; take Highway 132 east to Nephi, and then drive north on I-15 back to Payson.

PETEETNEET CULTURAL MUSEUM AND ARTS CENTER

10 N. 600 East, Payson, 801-465-5265; www.peteetneetacademy.org

Named after Ute leader Chief Peteetneet, the center and museum (also called the Peteetneet Academy) is housed in a historic Victorian-style building, which includes an art gallery, photography exhibit, blacksmith shop and visitor's center.

Open Monday-Friday 10 a.m.-4 p.m.

SPECIAL EVENT
GOLDEN ONION DAYS

Payson; www.payson.org

The festival includes community theater presentations, 5K and 10K runs, horse races, demolition derby, parade, fireworks and picnic.

Labor Day weekend.

WHERE TO STAY
★COMFORT INN

830 N. Main St., Payson, 801-465-4861; www.comfortinn.com

62 rooms. Complimentary breakfast. Pets accepted. Pool.

WHERE TO EAT
★DALTON'S FINE DINING

20 S. 100 W. Payson, 801-465-9182; www.daltonsrestaurant.com

American. Lunch, dinner. Closed Sunday. $

PRICE

See also Provo

Price, the seat of Carbon County, bases its prosperity on coal. More than 30 mine properties are within 30 miles. Several parks are located here.

WHAT TO SEE

CLEVELAND-LLOYD DINOSAUR QUARRY

125 S. 600 W. Price, 435-636-3600; www.blm.gov

Since 1928, more than 12,000 dinosaur bones representing at least 70 different animals have been excavated on this site.

Visitor center, nature trail, picnic area. Memorial Day-Labor Day, daily; Easter-Memorial Day, weekends only.

COLLEGE OF EASTERN UTAH PREHISTORIC MUSEUM

155 E. Main St., Price, 435-613-5060, 800-817-9949; www.museum.ceu.edu

This museum includes dinosaur displays and archaeology exhibits.

Memorial Day-Labor Day, daily; rest of year, Monday-Saturday.

GEOLOGY TOURS

90 N. 100 E., Price

Self-guided tours of Nine Mile Canyon, San Rafael Desert, Cleveland-Lloyd Dinosaur Quarry, Little Grand Canyon and more.

Maps available at Castle Country Travel Region or Castle Country Regional Information Center, 155 E. Main, 800-842-0784.

MANTI-LA SAL NATIONAL FOREST, MANTI DIVISION

599 W. Price River Drive, Price, 435-637-2817; www.fs.fed.us/r4/mantilasal

This 1,413,111-acre area offers scenic mountain drives, riding trails, campsites, winter sports and deer and elk hunting. Joe's Valley Reservoir on Highway 29 and Electric Lake on Highway 31 have fishing and boating. .

PRICE CANYON RECREATION AREA

Price, 15 miles north on Highway 6, then three miles west on unnumbered road, 435-636-3600; www.blm.gov/utah/price/pricerec.htm

Scenic overlooks, hiking, picnicking, camping. Roads have steep grades. May-mid-October, daily.

SCOFIELD STATE PARK

Highways 6 and 96, Price, 435-448-9449 (summer), 435-687-2491 (winter); www.stateparks.utah.gov

Utah's highest state park has a 2,800-acre lake that lies at an altitude of 7,616 feet. Fishing, boating, ice fishing; camping; snowmobiling; cross-country skiing in winter.

May-October.

WHERE TO STAY
★BEST WESTERN CARRIAGE HOUSE INN
590 E. Main St., Price, 435-637-5660, 800-937-8376; www.bestwestern.com
40 rooms. Complimentary breakfast. Pool. $

★★HOLIDAY INN
838 Westwood Blvd., Price, 435-637-8880, 877-863-4780; www.holiday-inn.com
151 rooms. Restaurant, bar. Pool. $

PROVO
See also Heber City, Payson, Salt Lake City

Provo received its name from French-Canadian trapper Etienne Provost, who arrived in the area in 1825. But it wasn't until 1849 that the first permanent settlement, begun by a party of Mormons, was established. The Mormon settlers erected Fort Utah as their first building, and despite famine, drought, hard winters and the constant danger of attack, they persisted and the settlement grew. Today, Provo is the seat of Utah County and the state's third-largest city. An important educational and commercial center, Provo's largest employer is Brigham Young University.

Provo lies in the middle of a lush, green valley: to the north stands 12,008-foot Mount Timpanogos; to the south is the perpendicular face of the Wasatch Range; to the east Provo Peak rises 11,054 feet; and to the west lies Utah Lake, backed by more mountains. Provo is the headquarters of the Uinta National Forest, and many good boating, camping and hiking spots are nearby.

WHAT TO SEE
BRIGHAM YOUNG UNIVERSITY
Provo, 801-422-4636; www.byu.edu
Founded in 1875 by Brigham Young and operated by the Church of Jesus Christ of Latter-day Saints, this is one of the world's largest church-related institutions of higher learning, with students from every state and more than 90 foreign countries. Free guided tours can be arranged at the Hosting Center. Monday-Friday; also by appointment.

EARTH SCIENCE MUSEUM
1683 North Canyon Road, Provo, 801-422-3680; cpms.byu.edu
Geological collection, extensive series of minerals and fossils.

HARRIS FINE ARTS CENTER
HFAC Campus Drive, Provo, 801-422-4322; cfac.byu.edu
The center includes periodic displays of rare instruments and music collection. Concert, theater performances.

MONTE L. BEAN LIFE SCIENCE MUSEUM
645 E. 1430 N., Provo, 801-442-5051; mlbean.byu.edu
The museum features exhibits and collections of insects, fish, amphibians, reptiles, birds, animals and plants.
Closed Sunday.

MUSEUM OF ART

North Campus Drive, Provo, 801-422-8287; moa.byu.edu

Exhibits from the BYU Permanent Collection are on display, along with traveling exhibits.

MUSEUM OF PEOPLES AND CULTURES

105 Allen Hall, Provo, 801-422-0020; mpc.byu.edu

The museum displays material from South America, the Near East and the Southwestern United States. Admission: free.

Monday, Wednesday, Friday 9-5 a.m., Tuesday, Thursday 9-7 a.m.

PIONEER MUSEUM

500 W. 500 N. Provo, 801-852-6609; www.provo.org

This museum includes an outstanding collection of Utah pioneer relics and Western art. Pioneer Village.

May-August, Wednesday, Friday and Saturday 1-4 p.m.

UINTA NATIONAL FOREST

88 W. and 100 N. Provo, 801-342-5100; www.fs.fed.us/r4/uwc

Scenic drives through the forest give an unsurpassed view of colorful landscapes, canyons and waterfalls. Stream and lake fishing; hunting for deer and elk, camping, picnicking. Reservations accepted.

UTAH LAKE STATE PARK

4400 W. Center St., Provo, 801-375-0731; www.stateparks.utah.gov/parks/utah-lake

The park is situated on the eastern shore of Utah Lake, a 150-square-mile, freshwater remnant of ancient Lake Bonneville that created the Great Salt Lake. Fishing, boating (ramp, dock); ice skating; picnicking, camping. Visitor center. Summer daily 6 a.m.-10 p.m.; winter 8 a.m.-5 p.m.

SPECIAL EVENTS
FREEDOM FESTIVAL

4626 N. 300 W., Provo, 801-818-1776; www.freedomfestival.org

Bazaar, carnival, parades.

Early July.

WHERE TO STAY
★BEST WESTERN COTTONTREE INN

2230 N. University Parkway, Provo, 801-373-7044, 800-662-6886;
www.bestwestern.com

80 rooms. Complimentary breakfast. Pool. Fitness center. Pool. $

★★COURTYARD PROVO

1600 N. Freedom Blvd., Provo, 801-373-2222; www.marriott.com

100 rooms. Restaurant, bar. Pool. $

CAPITOL REEF NATIONAL PARK

Capitol Reef, at an elevation ranging from 3,900 to 8,800 feet, is composed of red sandstone cliffs capped with domes of white sandstone. It was named Capitol Reef because the rocks formed a natural barrier to pioneer travel and the white sandstone domes resemble that of the U.S. Capitol.

Located in the heart of Utah's slickrock country, the park is actually a 100-mile section of the Waterpocket Fold, an upthrust of sedimentary rock created during the formation of the Rocky Mountains. Pockets in the rocks collect thousands of gallons of water each time it rains. From A.D. 700-1350, this 378-square-mile area was the home of an ancient people who grew corn along the Fremont River. Petroglyphs can be seen on some of the sandstone walls. A schoolhouse, farmhouse and orchards, established by early Mormon settlers, are open to the public in season.

The park can be approached from either the east or the west via Highway 24, a paved road. There is a visitor center on this road about seven miles from the west boundary and eight miles from the east (Daily). A 25-mile round-trip scenic drive, some parts unpaved, starts from this point. There are evening programs and guided walks Memorial Day-Labor Day. Three campgrounds are available: Fruita, approximately one mile south off Highway 24, provides 70 tent and trailer sites year-round; Cedar Mesa, 23 miles south off Highway 24, and Cathedral, 28 miles north off Highway 24, offer five primitive sites with access depending on the weather. The Visitor Center is open daily (except for some major holidays) from 8 a.m.-4:30 p.m. with extended hours during the summer season. Ripple Rock Nature Center is open from Memorial Day-Labor Day from 10 a.m.-3 p.m. Tuesday-Saturday, closed Sundays and Mondays. Information: Torrey, 10 miles east of Richfield on Highway 119, then 65 miles southeast on Highway 24, 435-425-3791; www.nps.gov/care

★FAIRFIELD INN PROVO

1515 S. University Ave., Provo, 801-377-9500; www.marriott.com
72 rooms. Complimentary breakfast. Pool. $

★★★MARRIOTT PROVO HOTEL AND CONFERENCE CENTER

101 W. 100 N. Provo, 801-377-4700, 800-777-7144; www.marriott.com
Nearby attractions include two shopping malls, as well as the Seven Peaks Water Park and Ice Rink, where the ice hockey competition and practices for the 2002 Winter Olympics were held. The comfortable rooms feature views of the Wasatch Mountains, duvet-topped beds and flat-screen TVs.
330 rooms. Restaurant, bar. Pool. Business center. Fitness center. $$

WHERE TO EAT
★★BOMBAY HOUSE
463 N. University Ave., Provo, 801-373-6677; www.bombayhouse.com
Indian. Dinner. Closed Sunday. $

SALT LAKE CITY

See also Alta, Heber City, Ogden, Park City, Provo, Snowbird
Salt Lake City, with its 10-acre blocks, 132-foot-wide, tree-lined streets and mountains rising to the east and west, is one of the most beautifully planned cities in the country.

On a hill at the north end of State Street stands Utah's classic Capitol building. Three blocks south is Temple Square, with the famed Mormon Temple and Tabernacle. The adjacent block houses the headquarters of the

Church of Jesus Christ of Latter-Day Saints, whose members are commonly called Mormons.

Once a desert wilderness, Salt Lake City was built by Mormon settlers who sought refuge from religious persecution. Followers of Brigham Young arrived and named their new territory Deseret. In the early days, the Mormons began a variety of experiments in farming, industry and society, many of which were highly successful. Today, Salt Lake City is an industrious, businesslike city, a center for electronics, steel, missiles and a hundred other enterprises.

West of the city is the enormous Great Salt Lake, stretching 48 miles one way and 90 miles the other. It is less than 35 feet deep and between 15 and 20 percent salt—almost five times as salty as the ocean. You can't sink in the water—instead you'll just bob up and down. The lake is what remains of ancient Lake Bonneville, once 145 miles wide, 350 miles long and 1,000 feet deep. As Lake Bonneville's water evaporated over thousands of years, a large expanse of perfectly flat, solid salt was left. Today, the Bonneville Salt Flats stretch west almost to Nevada.

Salt Lake City was laid out in grid fashion, with Temple Square at the center. Most street names are coordinates on this grid: Fourth South Street is four blocks south of Temple Square, Seventh East is seven blocks east. These are written as 400 South and 700 East.

WHAT TO SEE
ASSEMBLY HALL
500 W. North Temple, Salt Lake City, 801-240-3318; www.lds.org
Victorian gothic congregation hall.

BRIGHAM YOUNG MONUMENT
Salt Lake City, Main and South Temple streets
This statue honoring the church leader was first seen at the Chicago World's Fair in 1893.

CLARK PLANETARIUM
110 S. 400 W., Salt Lake City, 801-456-7827; www.hansenplanetarium.net
The Hansen Dome Theatre and the IMAX Theatre are the two main attractions here. Daily. Free exhibits include images from the Hubble Space telescope and a fully functioning weather station.

COUNCIL HALL
300 N. State St., Salt Lake City, 801-538-1900; www.utah.com
Council Hall was once the meeting place of the territorial legislature and city hall for 30 years. It was dismantled and then reconstructed in 1963 at its present location. Visitor information center and office; memorabilia. Daily.

SALT LAKE CITY'S MORMON HERITAGE

The centerpiece of downtown Salt Lake City is Temple Square, the city block bordered by three streets named Temple West, North and South and Main Streets on the east side. Utah's top tourist attraction, Temple Square is the hub for the Church of Jesus Christ of the Latter-Day Saints, where guests are invited to join a free guided tour that offers a glimpse of several architectural and cultural landmarks, including the Mormon Tabernacle, the Museum of Church History and Art and the Joseph Smith Memorial Building. (Tours start at the flagpole every few minutes.) If your timing is right, you can also take in a film, choir rehearsal or organ recital here.

From Temple Square, head east on South Temple to a pair of historic homes, the Lion House (63 E. South Temple) and the Beehive House (67 E. South Temple). No tours are available of the Lion House, which served as Brigham Young's home during the mid-19th century, but there is a restaurant on the lower level that is a good spot for a lunch break. Next door, the Beehive House, another former Young residence and a National Historic Landmark, offers free tours every day. Just east of these houses on South Temple is Eagle Gate (at the intersection of State Street), an impressive arch capped by a 2-ton sculpture of an eagle with a 20-foot wingspan.

South of Eagle Gate on the east side of State Street are two of Salt Lake City's standout cultural facilities: the Hansen Planetarium (15 South State St.) and the Social Hall Heritage Museum (39 South State St.). The former features daily star shows and a free space museum with hands-on exhibits. The latter includes remnants of Utah's first public building and the West's first theater. From the museum, it's best to reverse course and walk north on State Street, passing under Eagle Gate. Just beyond North Temple, hop on the paths that run through the lush City Creek Park and head north to the adjoining Memory Grove Park. From here, it's only a two-block walk west to the Utah State Capitol (just north of the intersection of State Street and 300 North St.), an exemplary Renaissance Revival-style structure built from Utah granite in 1915. The building is open to the public daily and guided tours are offered on weekdays.

Two blocks west of the State Capitol is the Pioneer Memorial Museum (300 North Main St.), a majestic replica of the original Salt Lake Theater (demolished in 1928) with 38 rooms of relics from the area's past, including photographs, vehicles, dolls and weapons. The museum is on the eastern edge of one of the city's oldest neighborhoods, the tree-lined Marmalade District (between 300 and 500 North Streets to the north and south and Center and Quince Streets to the east and west), a good place to meander and gaze at historic homes.

FAMILY HISTORY LIBRARY

35 N.W., Temple, Salt Lake City, 801-240-2584, 800-346-6044;
www.familysearch.org/eng
This genealogical library is the largest such facility in the world.
Monday 8 a.m.-5 p.m., Tuesday-Saturday 8 a.m.-9 p.m.

GOVERNOR'S MANSION

603 E. South Temple St., Salt Lake City, 801-538-1005; www.utah.gov/governor
Built by Thomas Kearns, a wealthy Utah senator in the early 1900s, this mansion is the official residence of Utah's governor. It was painstakingly restored after a fire in 1993. President Theodore Roosevelt, a personal friend of Senator Kerns, dined here often.
June-September, Tuesday and Thursday 2-4 p.m.

INNSBROOK TOURS

Salt Lake City, 801-534-1001; www.saltlakecitytours.org

This is the best way to see all the famous sites in Salt Lake City. Pick-up begins at 9:15 a.m., and then you're off to see landmarks like the Mormon Tabernacle, the Salt Lake Temple and the Olympic Stadium and Village. Daily.

LAGOON AMUSEMENT PARK, PIONEER VILLAGE
AND WATER PARK

Salt Lake City, 17 miles north on Interstate 15, 800-748-5246; www.lagoonpark.com

Besides fun rides and waterslides, the village includes a re-creation of a 19th-century Utah town with stagecoach and steam-engine train rides. There are also camping sites and picnicking areas here.

Memorial Day-August, daily; mid-April-late May and September, Saturday-Sunday only.

LIBERTY PARK

1300 South St., Salt Lake City, 801-972-7800; www.slcgov.com

This 100-acre park is Salt Lake's largest. Go for a run, play tennis or enjoy a picnic. There's a playground and paddleboats are available in summer.

Park: daily 7 a.m.-10 p.m. Aviary: daily 9 a.m-6 p.m.; November-March: daily 9 a.m.-4:30 p.m.

LION HOUSE

63 E. South Temple, Salt Lake City, 801-363-5466

Lion House was home to Brigham Young's family. Today it houses a restaurant. Next door is another residence, Beehive House, which is open to the public for tours.

Monday-Saturday 11 a.m.-8 p.m.

MAURICE ABRAVANEL CONCERT HALL

123 W. South Temple, Salt Lake City, 801-355-2787; www.finearts.slco.org

Home to the Utah Symphony, this building is adorned with more than 12,000 square feet of 24-karat gold leaf and a mile of brass railing. It has been rated one of the best halls in the U.S. for acoustics. Free tours by appointment.

MOKI MAC RIVER EXPEDITIONS

6006 S. 1300 E. Salt Lake City, 801-268-6667, 800-284-7280; www.mokimac.com

Offers one to 14-day white-water rafting and canoeing trips on the Green and Colorado rivers

Check Web site for schedule.

MUSEUM OF CHURCH HISTORY AND ART

45 N. West Temple St., Salt Lake City, 801-240-4615; www.lds.org

Exhibits of Latter-Day Saints church history from 1820 to present.

Admission: free. Monday-Friday 9 a.m.-9 p.m., Saturday-Sunday 10 a.m.-7 p.m.

PARK CITY MOUNTAIN RESORT

1310 Lowell Ave., Park City, 435-649-8111, 800-331-3178; www.pcski.com

Ski and snowboard resort also open daily during the summer season.
Monday-Thursday noon-6 p.m., Friday-Sunday 11 a.m.-6 p.m.

PIONEER MEMORIAL MUSEUM

300 N. Main St., Salt Lake City, 801-532-6479; www.dupinternational.org

This extensive collection of pioneer relics includes a carriage house, with exhibits relating to transportation, including Brigham Young's wagon and Pony Express items. One-hour guided tours by appointment.
Monday-Saturday 9 a.m.-5 p.m.; June-August, also Sunday 1-5 p.m.

PIONEER THEATRE COMPANY

300 S. 1400 E. Salt Lake City, 801-581-6961; www.pioneertheatre.org

Two auditoriums host dramas, musicals, comedies.
Mid-September-mid-May.

RED BUTTE GARDEN AND ARBORETUM

300 Wakara Way, Salt Lake City, 801-581-4747; www.redbuttegarden.org

Includes more than 9,000 trees on 150 acres, representing 350 species; conservatory. Self-guided tours. Special events in summer.
Daily.

SALT LAKE ART CENTER

20 S. West Temple, Salt Lake City, 801-328-4201; www.slartcenter.org

Changing exhibits feature photographs, paintings, ceramics and sculptures. The school hosts lectures and shows films.
Tuesday-Thursday, Saturday 11 a.m.-6 p.m., Friday 11 a.m.-9 p.m. Closed Sunday-Monday.

UTAH

350

SOLITUDE RESORT

12000 Big Cottonwood Canyon, Salt Lake City, 801-534-1400; www.skisolitude.com

Three quad, one triple, four double chairlifts; racecourse, patrol, school, rentals. Longest run 3½ miles, vertical drop 2,047 feet.
November-April, daily.

TEMPLE SQUARE

50 W. North Temple Street, Salt Lake City, 801-240-1245, 800-537-9703;
www.mormon.org

This 10-acre square is owned by the Church of Jesus Christ of Latter-Day Saint. Two visitors' centers provide information, exhibits and guided tours.

TABERNACLE

50 W. North Temple, Salt Lake City, 801-240-4150, 866-537-8457;
www.mormontabernaclechoir.org

The self-supporting roof, an elongated dome, is 250 feet long and 150 feet wide. The tabernacle organ has 11,623 pipes, ranging from 5/8 inch to 32 feet in length. The world-famous Tabernacle Choir may be heard at rehearsal (Thursday 8 p.m.) or at broadcast time (Sunday 9:30 a.m.).

Organ recitals: Monday-Saturday noon, Sunday afternoon.

TEMPLE
50 W. North Temple, Salt Lake City, 801-240-4150, 866-537-8457;
www.mormontabernaclechoir.org
Used for sacred ordinances, such as baptisms and marriages. Closed to non-Mormons.

THIS IS THE PLACE HERITAGE PARK
2601 E. Sunnyside Ave., Salt Lake City, 801-582-1847; www.thisistheplace.org
This historic park is located at the mouth of Emigration Canyon, where Mormon pioneers first entered the valley, and includes Old Deseret Pioneer Village and This Is the Place Monument (1947), commemorating Brigham Young's words upon first seeing the Salt Lake City site. Hundreds of people depict pioneer life. Admission to the monument and visitors' center, which includes an audio presentation and murals of the Mormon migration, is free. Monument and grounds, daily, dawn-dusk.
Visitor center Monday-Saturday 9 a.m.-6 p.m. Village late May-early September, Monday-Saturday 10 a.m.-6 p.m.

TROLLEY SQUARE
600 S. 700 East St., Salt Lake City, 801-521-9877; www.trolleysquare.com
This 10-acre complex of trolley barns has been converted into an entertainment/shopping/dining center.
Monday-Saturday 10 a.m.-9 p.m., Sunday noon-5 p.m.

★
★★ **UTAH**
★★
★

UNIVERSITY OF UTAH
201 S. Presidents Drive, Salt Lake City, 801-581-7200; www.utah.edu
Established in 1850. On campus is the J. Willard Marriott Library, named for the hotel magnate, it includes a vast Western Americana collection.
Monday-Thursday 7 a.m.-midnight, Friday 7 a.m.-8 p.m., Saturday 9 a.m.-8 p.m., Sunday 10 a.m.-midnight; closed holidays, also July 24.

351

UTAH MUSEUM OF FINE ARTS
410 Campus Center Drive, Salt Lake City, 801-581-7332; www.umfa.utah.org
Representations of artistic styles from Egyptian antiquities to contemporary American paintings are displayed here as well as 19th-century French and American paintings and furniture.
Tuesday-Friday 10 a.m.-5 p.m., Saturday-Sunday 11 a.m.-5 p.m., Wednesday 10 a.m.-8 p.m.

UTAH MUSEUM OF NATURAL HISTORY
1390 E. Presidents Circle, Salt Lake City, 801-581-6927; www.umnh.utah.edu
The museum shows exhibits of the Earth's natural wonders and honors Utah's native cultures.
Monday-Saturday 9:30 a.m.-5:30 p.m., Sunday noon-5 p.m.; closed July 24.

UTAH JAZZ (NBA)

301 W. South Temple, Salt Lake City, 801-325-2500; www.nba.com/jazz
Professional basketball team.

UTAH OPERA COMPANY

123 W. South Temple, Salt Lake City, 801-533-5626; www.utahopera.org
Grand opera. October-May.

UTAH STARZZ (WNBA)

301 W. South Temple, Salt Lake City, 801-355-3865; www.utah.com/sports/starzz.htm
Women's professional basketball team.

WASATCH-CACHE NATIONAL FOREST

125 S. State St., Salt Lake City, 801-236-3400; www.fs.fed.us/r4/uwc
This wilderness area has alpine lakes, rugged peaks and several canyons.
Fishing, boating, deer and elk hunting, winter sports and camping.

WHEELER HISTORIC FARM

6351 S. 900 E. St., Salt Lake City, 801-264-2241; www.wheelerfarm.com
This living history farm on 75 acres depicts rural life from 1890 to1918 and
includes a farmhouse, farm buildings, animals, crops and hay rides. Tour.
Visitors can feed the animals, gather eggs and milk cows. There is a small fee
for various activities and events.
Monday-Saturday dawn-dusk.

ZCMI (ZION'S CO-OPERATIVE MERCANTILE INSTITUTION) CENTER

Main and South Temple, Salt Lake City
A department store established in 1868 by Brigham Young anchors this 85-
store, enclosed downtown shopping mall.
Monday-Saturday.

SPECIAL EVENTS
UTAH ARTS FESTIVAL

230 S. 500 W., Salt Lake City, 801-322-2428; www.uaf.org
This four-day festival featuring visual, performing and culinary artists, draws
more than 80,000 people every year.
Last week in June.

WHERE TO STAY
★DAYS INN SALT LAKE CITY/AIRPORT

1900 W. North Temple, Salt Lake City, 801-539-8538, 800-329-7466; www.daysinn.com
110 rooms. Complimentary breakfast. Business center. Fitness center. Pets
accepted. Pool. $

★★EMBASSY SUITES SALT LAKE CITY

110 W. 600 S., Salt Lake City, 801-359-7800; www.embassysuites.com
241 rooms. Complimentary breakfast. Restaurant, bar. Pool. $

★★★★THE GRAND AMERICA HOTEL

555 S. Main St., Salt Lake City, 801-258-6000, 800-621-4505; www.grandamerica.com

Set against the beautiful backdrop of the Wasatch Mountains, the Grand America is a tribute to the Old World Europe. The guest rooms are classically French, with luxurious fabrics, fine art and Richelieu furniture. The spa offers a full menu of treatments, from massages to facials and body wraps, and includes a full-service salon. The hotel's Sunday brunch is a Salt Lake City institution, with a sprawling buffet of breakfast dishes and a huge array of desserts.

775 rooms. Restaurant, bar. Spa. Pool. $$$

★★HILTON SALT LAKE CITY AIRPORT

5151 Wiley Post Way, Salt Lake City, 801-539-1515, 800-999-3736; www.hilton.com

278 rooms. Restaurant, bar. Pets accepted. Pool. Business center. Fitness center. $

★★★HILTON SALT LAKE CITY CENTER

255 S. West Temple, Salt Lake City, 801-328-2000; www.hilton.com

Located downtown, this large hotel caters to business travelers with updated rooms with large work areas and wireless access. The fitness center includes first-rate cardio machines, a sauna and an indoor pool. The onsite restaurant serves grilled steaks and seafood, along with an expansive wine list.

499 rooms. Restaurant, bar. Spa. Pets accepted. Pool. $

★★★HOTEL MONACO SALT LAKE CITY

15 W. 200 S., Salt Lake City, 801-595-0000, 877-294-9710; www.hotelmonaco.com

This hotel stands out for its contemporary décor and personalized services. Located in downtown Salt Lake City, the refurbished 14-story landmark hotel has rooms with beds swathed in Frette linens. Tall rooms are available with eight-foot beds and heightened showerheads. Amenities include coffeemakers with Starbucks coffee, Yoga programs (grab a mat from the basket and flip on the Yoga channel) and gourmet minibars. If all you're missing is a travel companion, you can adopt a goldfish during your stay.

225 rooms. Restaurant, bar. Pets accepted. $

★★★LITTLE AMERICA HOTEL

500 S. Main St., Salt Lake City, 801-596-5700, 800-453-9450;
www.littleamerica.com/slc

This hotel offers a variety of accommodations. Rooms in the tower are decorated in rich French brocade fabrics and English wool carpets, and offer large parlor areas with views of the city. There's also a separate dressing area and bathroom with an oval-shaped tub. Garden rooms are spacious and have private entrances. The hotel includes a large indoor pool and salon.

850 rooms. Restaurant, bar. Spa. Pool. $

★★★MARRIOTT SALT LAKE CITY DOWNTOWN

75 S. West Temple, Salt Lake City, 801-531-0800; www.marriott.com

Located across from the Salt Palace Convention Center, this hotel caters to business travelers and is close to the airport and major ski resorts. Everything is on hand here, including a heated pool, fitness center and a Starbucks. 514 rooms. Restaurant, bar. Business center. $$

★★★MARRIOTT SALT LAKE CITY-CITY CENTER
220 S. State St., Salt Lake City, 801-961-8700, 866-961-8700; www.marriott.com
Situated adjacent to the Gallivan Center, which hosts concerts in summer and skating in winter, this hotel is within walking distance to numerous restaurants and shops. The contemporary guest rooms are decorated in a relaxing palette and feature down comforters, large marble baths and views of either the city or the mountains. The hotel's restaurant, Piastra, serves up continental cuisine in a sophisticated setting.
359 rooms. Restaurant, bar. $

★★PEERY HOTEL
110 W. Broadway, Salt Lake City, 801-521-4300, 800-331-0073; www.peeryhotel.com
73 rooms. Restaurant, bar. Business center. Fitness center. $

★★★RADISSON HOTEL SALT LAKE CITY DOWNTOWN
215 W. S. Temple, Salt Lake City, 801-531-7500, 800-333-3333; www.radisson.com
Located downtown next to the Salt Palace Convention Center, all rooms in this hotel have spacious work areas with Herman Miller-designed ergonomic chairs and complimentary high-speed Internet access. There's also an indoor pool, fitness center, sauna and whirlpool.
381 rooms. Restaurant, bar. Fitness center. Pool. Pets accepted. $

WHERE TO EAT
★★★BAMBARA
202 S. Main St., Salt Lake City, 801-363-5454; www.bambara-slc.com
This chic new American bistro housed in a former bank serves up creations based on whatever is fresh and seasonal. Entrées include seared halibut with sweet corn and crab hash, smokey bacon and green chili butter, and housemade angel hair pasta with Maine lobster, seared oyster mushrooms, basil and sweet corn butter.
American. Breakfast, lunch, dinner. Children's menu. Reservations recommended. $$$

★★★FRESCO ITALIAN CAFE
1513 S. 1500 E., Salt Lake City, 801-486-1300; www.frescoitaliancafe.com
A winding brick walkway lined with flowers leads the way to this neighborhood bistro, where you'll find a fireplace in winter and alfresco dining during the summer. Standout dishes include the chef's nightly risotto and freshly made herb gnocchi.
Italian. Dinner. Reservations recommended. Outdoor seating. $$

★★★LA CAILLE
9565 S. Wasatch Blvd., Little Cottonwood Canyon, 801-942-1751; www.lacaille.com
This country French chateau is surrounded by beautiful gardens populated by peacocks, llamas, ducks and a host of other exotic animals. The menu features innovative fare such as roasted rack of venison with a venison cabernet

sauvignon glaze and lingon berries.

French. Dinner, Sunday brunch. Bar. Children's menu. Reservations recommended. Outdoor seating. $$$

★★★LOG HAVEN

6451 E. Millcreek Canyon Road, Salt Lake City, 801-272-8255; www.log-haven.com

This rustic log mansion is one of Utah's most innovative restaurants. The fresh specialties change daily, but you might see chilled edamame soup with sake steamed clams, tomato coulis and lime aioli; grilled lamb lollipops with truffled potatoe salad, arugula and tarragon aioli; or tarragon-crusted sea scallops with English pea risotto, lemon-carrot butter and watermelon radish salad. The restaurant also has an extensive wine list.

International. Dinner. Bar. Reservations recommended. Outdoor seating. $$$

★★MARKET STREET GRILL UNIVERSITY

260 S. 1300 E., Salt Lake City, 801-583-8808; www.gastronomyinc.com

Seafood. Lunch (Monday-Saturday), dinner. Outdoor seating. $$

★★MARKET STREET GRILL

48 W. Market St., Salt Lake City, 801-322-4668; www.gastronomyinc.com

Seafood. Breakfast, lunch, dinner, Sunday brunch. Children's menu. $$

★★★METROPOLITAN

173 W. Broadway, Salt Lake City, 801-364-3472; www.themetropolitan.com

This contemporary restaurant specializes in new American cuisine. Indulge in dishes such as mahi mahi with purple potatoes, peas, kumquat and lychee-lavender foam; or potato gnocchi with caramelized sunchokes, heirloom cauliflower and macadamia nut pesto. End with a soufflé in a variety of flavors, including spicy chocolate and kumquat.

American. Lunch, dinner. Closed Sunday. Bar. $$$

★★★THE NEW YORKER

60 W. Market St., Salt Lake City, 801-363-0166; www.gastronomyinc.com

Recognized as one of Salt Lake's top dining spots since 1978, this elegant restaurant located in the historic New York hotel, serves traditional fare. The menu sticks to the classics, including bouillabaisse, grilled rib-eye with bearnaise sacue, and caesar salad.

Steak. Lunch (Monday-Friday), dinner. Closed Sunday. Bar. Reservations recommended. $$$

★★RINO'S ITALIAN RISTORANTE

2302 Parleys Way, Salt Lake City, 801-484-0901; www.rinositalianrestaurant.com

Italian. Dinner. Reservations recommended. Outdoor seating. $$

★RIO GRANDE CAFE

270 S. Rio Grande St., Salt Lake City, 801-364-3302

Southwestern. Lunch, dinner. Bar. Children's menu. Outdoor seating. $

★SQUATTERS PUB BREWERY

147 W. Broadway, Salt Lake City, 801-363-2739; www.squatters.com

American. Lunch, dinner, late-night, brunch. Bar. Children's menu. Outdoor seating. $$

★★TUCCI'S CUCINA ITALIA

515 S. 700 E., Salt Lake City, 801-533-9111; www.tuccis.qwestoffice.net

Italian. Lunch, dinner, brunch. Children's menu. Outdoor seating. $$

★★★TUSCANY

2832 E. 6200 S., Salt Lake City, 801-277-9919; www.tuscanyslc.com

This tremendously popular place maintains a high quality of service and offers authentic Tuscan fare while incorporating modern American culinary trends. Tasty items on the menu include risotto with sauteed sea scallops, bacon, sweet peas and basil with a carbonara parmesan cream sauce; or steak with fresh-cut haystack potatoes.

Italian. Lunch, dinner, Sunday brunch. Bar. Outdoor seating. $$$

SNOWBIRD

See also Alta, Park City, Salt Lake City

In 1971, a Texas oilman recognized the potential of Little Cottonwood Canyon in the Wasatch National Forest and developed the area as a ski resort. Once home to thriving mining communities, the resort village of Snowbird, 29 miles east of Salt Lake City, now offers year-round recreational activities. With an average of 500 inches of snowfall annually, Snowbird claims to have the world's best powder.

WHAT TO SEE

SNOWBIRD SKI AND SUMMER RESORT

Highway 210, Snowbird, 801-933-2222, 800-232-9542; www.snowbird.com

Includes 89 runs on 2,500 acres; 27 percent beginner, 38 percent intermediate, 35 percent advanced/expert. Elevations of 7,800 to 11,000 feet. Six double chairlifts, four high-speed quads, 125-passenger aerial tram. Patrol, school, rentals. Four lodges. Night skiing, Wednesday, Friday. Heli-skiing, half-pipe. Snowboarding, snowshoeing, ice skating. Summer activities include rock climbing, hiking, mountain biking, tennis, tram rides and concerts.

Mid-November-early May, daily.

WHERE TO STAY

★★CLIFF LODGE & SPA

Little Cotton Canyon, Snowbird, 801-933-2222, 800-232-9542; www.snowbird.com

511 rooms. Restaurant, bar. Ski in/ski out. $$$

★★LODGE AT SNOWBIRD

Little Cottonwood Canyon, Snowbird, 801-933-2222, 800-232-9542;
www.snowbird.com

125 rooms. Restaurant, bar. $$

WHERE TO EAT
★★STEAK PIT
Snowbird Center, Snowbird, 801-933-2260; www.snowbird.com
Steak. Dinner. Children's menu. $$

ST. GEORGE
See also Kanab

Extending themselves to this hot, arid corner of southwest Utah, members of the LDS Church built their first temple here and struggled to survive by growing cotton. With determination and persistence, members of the church constructed a temple. Hundreds of tons of rocks were pounded into the mud until a stable foundation could be laid. Mormons from the north worked 40-day missions, and southern church members gave one day's labor out of every 10 until the temple was complete. The workers quarried 17,000 tons of rock by hand. A team of ox hauled the stones to the construction site, and for seven straight days, timber was hauled more than 80 miles from Mount Trumbull to build the structure. Made of red sandstone plastered to a gleaming white, the Mormon temple is not only the town's landmark but also a beacon for passing aircraft.

In St. George, warm summers are balanced by mild winters, and the village is fast becoming a retirement destination. The seat of Washington County, St. George is the closest town of its size to Zion National Park.

WHAT TO SEE
BRIGHAM YOUNG WINTER HOME
67 W. 200 N., St. George, 435-673-5181; www.lds.org
Brigham Young spent the last four winters of his life in this two-story adobe house, which still includes period furnishings.
Winter, daily 9 a.m.-5 p.m.; summer, daily 9 a.m.-6 p.m.

ST. GEORGE TEMPLE
250 E. 400 S., St. George, 435-673-3533
This red sandstone structure was built between 1863 and 1876 with local materials, and resembles a colonial New England church. Daily.

TEMPLE VISITOR CENTER
490 S. 300 E., St. George, 435-673-5181; www.lds.org
A guided tour of the center explains local history and beliefs of the Latter-Day Saints; audiovisual program. Daily.

WHERE TO STAY
★BEST WESTERN CORAL HILLS
125 E. St. George Blvd., St. George, 435-673-4844, 800-542-7733; www.coralhills.com
98 rooms. Complimentary breakfast. Fitness center. Pool. $

★COMFORT INN
1239 S. Main St., St. George, 435-673-7000, 800-428-0754;
www.stgeorgecomfortsuites.com
122 rooms. Complimentary breakfast. Pets accepted. $

★★HOLIDAY INN

850 S. Bluff St., St. George, 435-628-4235, 800-457-9800; www.histgeorgeutah.com
164 rooms. Restaurant. Pets accepted. Business center. Fitness center. Pool. $

SUNDANCE

See also Park City
This popular ski resort was purchased by Robert Redford in 1968 and is named after the role Redford played in the film Butch Cassidy and the Sundance Kid. The popular Sundance Film Festival, held 30 miles north in Park City, is one of the largest independent film festivals in the world.

WHAT TO SEE
SUNDANCE SKI AREA

8841 N. Alpine Loop Road, Sundance, 801-225-4107, 800-892-1600;
www.sundanceresort.com
Three chairlifts, rope tow; patrol, school, rentals; warming hut, restaurants. Longest run two miles, vertical drop 2,150 feet. Cross-country trails. Late November-April, daily.

WHERE TO STAY
★★★SUNDANCE RESORT

8841 N. Alpine Loop Road, Sundance, 801-225-4107, 877-831-6224;
www.sundanceresort.com
This resort offers standard rooms, studios and cottages, all of which, like the resort itself, are intended to blend with the surrounding landscape. All of the rooms feature natural wood and Native American accents; most have fireplaces and private decks. The resort also offers fine dining and endless recreation, from artist workshops to nature programs. The general store is so popular that a mail-order catalog has been designed. A superb spa completes the well-rounded experience available at this unique resort.
110 rooms. Restaurant, bar. Fitness center. Spa. Ski in/ski out. $$$

WHERE TO EAT
★★FOUNDRY GRILL

Sundance Resort, 8841 N. Alpine Loop Road, Sundance, 801-223-4220, 866-932-2295; www.sundanceresort.com
American. Breakfast, lunch, dinner, Sunday brunch. Bar. Outdoor seating. $$

★★★THE TREE ROOM

Sundance Resort, 8841 N. Alpine Loop Road, Sundance, 801-223-4200, 866-627-8313; www.sundanceresort.com
Located at the base of the Sundance ski lift, this restaurant's two-story windows offer views of the rugged mountains and surrounding wilderness. The upscale-yet-casual room is filled with beautiful displays of Native American dolls and pottery. The sophisticated new American cuisine includes wild game, steaks and seafood, prepared with herbs and vegetables from the resort's own organic gardens.
American. Dinner. Closed Sunday-Monday. Bar. $$$

VERNAL

This is the county seat of Uintah County in Northeastern Utah, which boasts oil, natural gas and many mineral deposits. Vernal is in an area of ancient geologic interest. Nearby are beautiful canyons, striking rock formations and majestic peaks.

WHAT TO SEE
ASHLEY NATIONAL FOREST
355 N. Vernal Ave., Vernal, 435-789-1181; www.fs.fed.us/r4/ashley
The Uinta Mountains run through the heart of this nearly 1½ million-acre forest. Red Canyon, Kings Peak and Sheep Creek Geological Area are also here. Swimming, fishing, boating (ramps, marinas), white-water rafting, canoeing; hiking and nature trails, cross-country skiing, snowmobiling, improved or backcountry campgrounds.

DAUGHTERS OF UTAH PIONEERS MUSEUM
500 W. 186 S. Vernal, 435-789-0352; www.dupinternational.org
This museum contains relics and artifacts dating from before 1847, when pioneers first settled in Utah. Includes period furniture, quilts, clothing, dolls, early medical instruments and more.
June-weekend before Labor Day, Monday-Saturday.

FLAMING GORGE DAM AND NATIONAL RECREATION AREA
Vernal, 42 miles north on Highway 191 in Ashley National Forest, 435-784-3445; www.utah.com/nationalsites
This area surrounds the 91-mile-long Flaming Gorge Reservoir and 502-foot-high Flaming Gorge Dam. Fishing on reservoir and river (all year), marinas, boat ramps, waterskiing; lodges, campgrounds. River rafting below dam. Visitor centers at dam and Red Canyon (on secondary paved road three miles off Highway 44).

★
★★ UTAH
★★
★

359

RED FLEET STATE PARK
8750 N. Highway 191, Vernal, 435-789-4432; www.stateparks.utah.gov
This scenic lake is highlighted by red rock formations, and you can see several hundred well-preserved dinosaur tracks. Enjoy boating, swimming, fishing and camping.
Summer, daily 6 a.m.-10 p.m.; winter, daily 8 a.m.-5 p.m.

HATCH RIVER EXPEDITIONS
55 E. Main St., Vernal, 800-856-8966; www.hatchriverexpeditions.com
Guided white-water trips on the Green and Yampa rivers.

STEINAKER STATE PARK
4335 N. Highway 191, Vernal, 435-789-4432; www.stateparks.utah.gov
This state park encompasses approximately 2,200 acres on the west shore of Steinaker Reservoir. Swimming, waterskiing, fishing, boating; picnicking, tent and trailer sites.
April-November; fishing all year. Summer 6 a.m.-10 p.m. Winter 8 a.m.-5 p.m.

UTAH FIELD HOUSE OF NATURAL HISTORY AND
DINOSAUR GARDENS

496 E. Main St., Vernal, 435-789-3799; www.stateparks.utah.gov

Guarded outside by three life-size cement dinosaurs, this museum has exhibits of fossils, archaeology, life zones, geology and fluorescent minerals of the region. The adjacent Dinosaur Gardens contain 18 life-size model dinosaurs in natural surroundings.

Daily 9 a.m.-5 p.m.; Memorial Day-Labor Day 8 a.m.-7 p.m.

WESTERN HERITAGE MUSEUM

28 E. 200 S., Vernal, 435-789-7399; www.co.uintah.ut.us/museum/whMuseum.php

Relive the town's outlaw past at this museum that houses lots of local memorabilia and artifacts of the ancient people of Utah.

Memorial Day-Labor Day, Monday-Friday 9 a.m.-6 p.m., Saturday 10 a.m.-4 p.m.; Labor Day-Memorial Day, Monday-Friday 9 a.m.-5 p.m., Saturday 10 a.m.-2 p.m.

WHERE TO STAY
★★BEST WESTERN DINOSAUR INN

251 E. Main St., Vernal, 435-789-2660; www.bestwestern.com

60 rooms. Restaurant, bar. Hot tub. Pool. Spa. . $

WHERE TO EAT
★7-11 RANCH

77 E. Main St., Vernal, 435-789-1170

American. Breakfast, lunch, dinner. Closed Sunday. Children's menu. $

ZION NATIONAL PARK

See also St. George

The spectacular canyons and enormous rock formations in this 147,551-acre national park are the result of powerful upheavals of the earth and erosion by flowing water and frost. Considered the grandfather of Utah's national parks, Zion is one of the nation's oldest and one of the state's widest with large sections that are virtually inaccessible.

The Virgin River runs through the interior of the park, and Zion Canyon, with its deep, narrow chasm and multicolored vertical walls, cuts through the middle, with smaller canyons branching from it like fingers. A paved roadway following the bottom of Zion Canyon is surrounded by massive rock formations in awe-inspiring colors that change with the light. The formations, described as temples, cathedrals and thrones, rise to great heights, the loftiest reaching 8,726 feet. The canyon road runs seven miles to the Temple of Sinawava, a natural amphitheater surrounded by cliffs. Another route, an extension of Highway 9, cuts through the park in an east-west direction, taking visitors through the mile-long Zion-Mount Carmel Tunnel and then descends through a series of switchbacks with viewpoints above Pine Creek Canyon.

DINOSAUR NATIONAL MONUMENT/UTAH ENTRANCE

On August 17, 1909, paleontologist Earl Douglass discovered dinosaur bones in this area, including several nearly complete skeletons. Since then, this location has revealed more skeletons, skulls and bones of Jurassic-period dinosaurs than any other dig in the world. Utah's Dinosaur Quarry section can be entered from the junction of Highways 40 and 149, north of Jensen, 13 miles east of Vernal. Approximately seven miles north on Highway 149 is the fossil exhibit. Another five miles north is Green River Campground, with 90 tent and trailer sites available mid-May-mid-September. A smaller campground, Rainbow Park, provides a small number of tent sites from May to November. Lodore, Deerlodge and Echo Park campgrounds are available in Colorado.

The dinosaur site comprises only 80 acres of this 325-square-mile park, which lies at the border of Utah and Colorado. The backcountry section, most of which is in Colorado, is a land of fantastic and deeply eroded canyons of the Green and Yampa rivers. Access to this backcountry section is via the Harpers Corner Road, starting at monument headquarters on Highway 40, two miles east of Dinosaur, Colorado. At Harpers Corner, the end of this 32-mile surfaced road, a one-mile foot trail leads to a promontory overlooking the Green and Yampa rivers, more than 2,500 feet below. The entire area was named a national monument in 1915.

Some areas of the monument are closed from mid-November-mid-April because of snow. Information: 4545 E. U.S. 40, Vernal, 435-374-3000; www.nps.gov/dino

WHAT TO SEE
RIVER RAFTING

Dinosaur National Monument, 435-781-7700; www.nps.gov/dino
Go rafting down the Green and Yampa rivers. Get an advanced permit from National Park Service or with concession-operated guided float trips.

ESCORTED HORSEBACK TRIPS

Zion, 435-379-8665; www.canyonrides.com
Special guide service may be obtained for other trips not regularly scheduled. Contact Canyon Trail Rides which offer Zion National Park trips. March-October, daily.

PARK TRAILS

Zion, 435-772-3256; www.nps.gov/zion
Trails lead to otherwise inaccessible areas: the Narrows (walls of this canyon are 2,000 feet high and as little as 50 feet apart at the stream), the Hanging Gardens of Zion, Weeping Rock, the Emerald Pools. Trails range from half-mile trips to day-long treks, some requiring great stamina. Trails in less-traveled areas should not be undertaken without first obtaining information from a park ranger. Backcountry permits required for travel through the Virgin River Narrows and other canyons, and on all overnight trips.

ZION NATURE CENTER

Zion, adjacent to South Campground, 435-772-2356; www.nps.gov/zion
Kids between the ages 6-12 can sign up for the junior ranger program. Memorial Day-Labor Day, Monday-Friday.

INDEX

D

G

(Scottsdale), *50*

J

Jacob Lake Inn (Grand Canyon National Park), *18*

The Jail Tree (Wickenburg), *84*

Jake and Telly's Greek Dining (Colorado Springs), *120*

Janos Restaurant (Tucson), *82*

Japon Restaurant (Denver), *138*

Jasmine (Las Vegas), *236, 305*

Jazz Celebration (Telluride), *183*

Jet Hotel (Denver), *134*

Jewel Of The Crown (Scottsdale), *59*

Jimmy's An American Restaurant & Bar (Aspen), *96*

John Ascuaga's Nugget (Sparks), *263*

John Wesley Powell Memorial Museum (Page), *30*

John's Restaurant (Boulder), *106*

The Joint (Las Vegas), *204*

Jonson Gallery (Albuquerque), *269*

Joël Robuchon at The Mansion (Las Vegas), *237*

Jubilee! Backstage Tour (Las Vegas), *204*

Justin Timberlake Shriners Hospitals for Children Open (Las Vegas), *213*

JW Marriott Denver at Cherry Creek (Denver), *134*

JW Marriott Desert Ridge Resort and Spa (Phoenix), *41*

JW Marriott Las Vegas Resort & Spa at Summerlin (Las Vegas), *217*

K

Kachina Downtown (Flagstaff), *16*

Kaibab National Forest, Grand Canyon National Park (South Rim), *18, 86*

Kai (Chandler), *12*

Keystone Lodge & Spa (Keystone),

160

Keystone Resort Ski Area (Keystone), *160*

Kierland Commons (Scottsdale), *50*

Kimball Art Center (Park City), *337*

Kingfisher (Tucson), *82*

Kit Carson Home and Museum (Taos), *313*

Kit Carson Park (Taos), *313*

Kokopelli Rafting Adventures (Santa Fe), *292*

Krabloonik (Snowmass Village), *178*

L

La Caille (Salt Lake City), *354*

La Chaumière (Lyons), *165*

La Creperie Bistro (Colorado Springs), *120*

La Cueva (Aurora), *98*

La Fontanella (Phoenix), *44*

La Fuente (Tucson), *82*

La Parrilla Suiza (Tucson), *82*

La Paz County Fair (Parker), *33*

La Paz County Park (Parker), *33*

La Petite Maison (Colorado Springs), *120*

La Placita Café (Tucson), *82*

La Posada De Santa Fe Resort and Spa (Santa Fe), *303*

La Quinta Inn & Suites Phoenix Scottsdale (Scottsdale), *55*

La Quinta Inn & Suites (Pueblo), *174*

La Quinta Inn Denver Golden (Golden), *155*

La Quinta Inn (Mesa), *29*

La Quinta Inn (Reno), *261*

La Renaissance (Pueblo), *174*

Labor Day Rodeo (Williams), *86*

Lagoon Amusement Park, Pioneer Village and Water Park (Salt Lake City), *349*

Lahontan State Recreation Area (Fallon), *193*

Lake Carlsbad Water Recreation

M

O

Q

R

S

Y

Yavapai Lodge, Grand Canyon
National Park (South Rim), *20*
Yavapai Observation Station, Grand
Canyon National Park (South
Rim), *19*
Yuletide In Taos (Taos), *315*
Yuma County Fair (Yuma), *90*
Yuma River Tours (Yuma), *90*
Yuma Territorial Prison State
Historic Park (Yuma), *90*

Z

Zaidy's Deli (Denver), *139*
Zcmi (Zion's Co-Operative
Mercantile Institution)
Center (Salt Lake City), *352*
Zen 32 (Phoenix), *46*
Zinc Bistro (Scottsdale), *62*
Zion Nature Center (Zion
National Park), *361*
Zozobra Festival (Santa Fe), *300*
Zuzu (Scottsdale), *62*

★★★★★ INDEX

ARIZONA

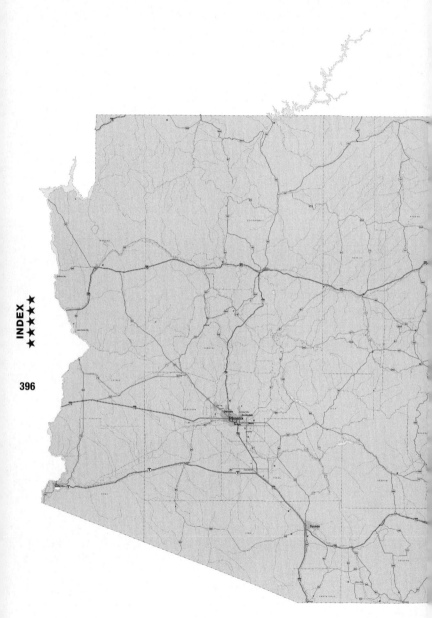

COLORADO

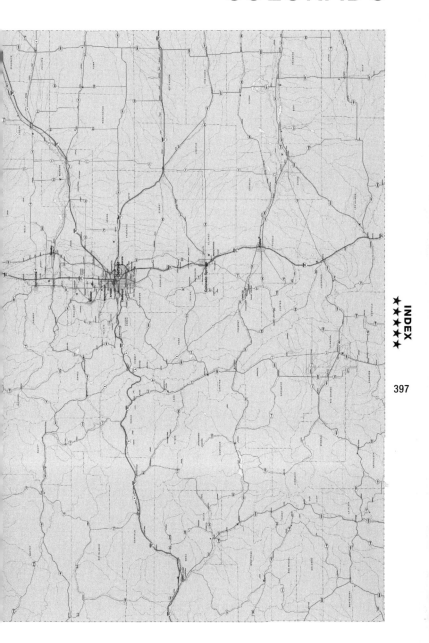

NEVADA

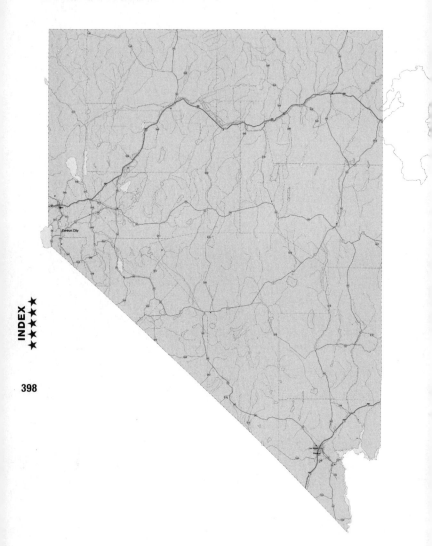

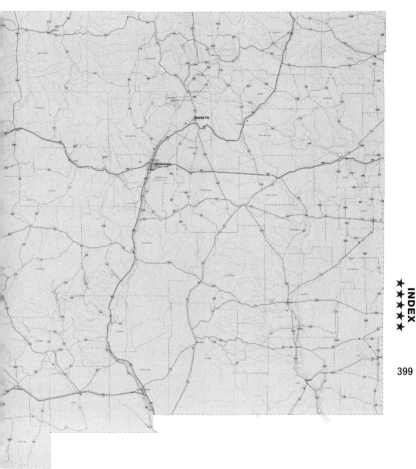

UTAH

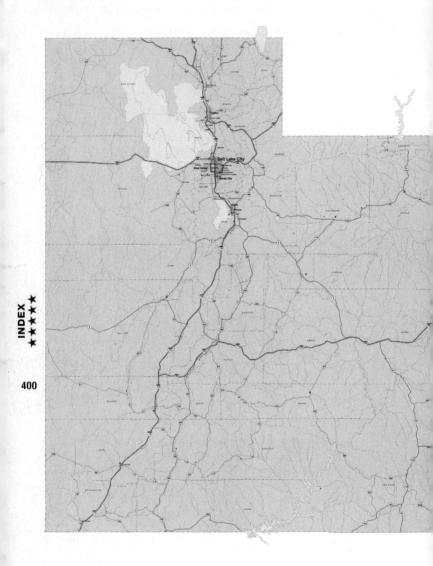